Ancient North America

BRIAN M. FAGAN

Ancient North America

THE ARCHAEOLOGY OF A CONTINENT

Fifth edition

With more than 280 illustrations

Frontispiece Petroglyphs
from Grand County, Utah.

To the ancient Beringians, who start it all

First published in the United States of America in 1991 by
Thames & Hudson Inc.,
500 Fifth Avenue,
New York, New York 10110

www.thamesandhudsonusa.com

Second edition 1995
Third edition 2000
Fourth edition 2005
Fifth edition 2019

Library of Congress Control Number 2004108113

ISBN 9780500293607

Printed in China by Shanghai Offset Printing Products Limited

Contents

PART 5

CONSEQUENCES OF CONTACT 310
ENDURING THEMES 312

Preface and Acknowledgments

*A*ncient North America has been in print for a quarter century and is still going strong. I am both astonished and flattered that it has survived through four editions. Writing the original version was one of the toughest archaeological projects I have ever undertaken, but I learned a great deal about a field of archaeology that had long been on the margins of my expertise. (Believe it or not, I started my career as an African Iron Age archaeologist!) Fortunately, my experience in Central Africa working with both archaeologists and multidisciplinary historians proved invaluable in untangling the threads that make up the story of North America from first settlement to the European *entrada* and beyond. The story in these pages is based on a complex archaeological record and other sources chronicled in print and, increasingly, in cyberspace. This book results from years of participation in excavations, visits to museums and innumerable archaeological sites, and from discussions with fellow archaeologists working in every corner of North America.

Some General Comments

The fifth edition of *Ancient North America* is somewhat shorter than its predecessors, though still lavishly illustrated. It is aimed at readers who have not encountered North American archaeology before. I have done all I can to minimize cultural and technological labels, but some intricacies are inevitable. This is not a simple story.

The text is referenced, with a Guide to Further Reading for each chapter. I have deliberately kept references to a minimum, for it is easy to festoon a text with such things and to lose the thread of the story. The citations that are given will always lead you to more technical literature, which now proliferates with bewildering speed by the month, both in print and online. As a general principle, I have tended to cite key papers, reports, and syntheses that provide comprehensive citations for more detailed research.

Ancient North America assumes that you have a minimal knowledge of the fundamental principles of archaeology. This is not a book on the method and theory of archaeology, which cannot be presented in detail in such a volume as this. The basics are covered admirably in many introductory courses and in widely available college texts. Occasionally, one of my chapter boxes will describe, say, dating methods, but these are designed to amplify the narrative, not to be part of it. The book is a compromise between space and the need to be comprehensive. There are many places where I have had to compress local and regional data in the interests of brevity and clarity. Inevitably, I have generalized and simplified in places, as I try to balance accuracy with economy. If you probe more specialized references, you will soon encounter the subtleties of this complex and, at times, frustrating literature. If you are taking a course using *Ancient North America*, your instructor will doubtless fill in many finer points. Archaeology, by its very nature, is a local subject with many narrow concerns and local problems. Much research is now highly specialized and involves sometimes exotic scientific methods. The information proliferates in the academic literature, often with jargon and terminology of interest and relevance to only a handful of scholars. In the interests of clarity, I have omitted many local cultural terms, summarizing them occasionally for reference, but trying to keep them to a minimum in the narrative. The many detailed regional syntheses cited in these pages will fill in local particulars. This is a book about the big picture, "Big History" if you will, and hopefully it will give you the background and enthusiasm to delve further into this fascinating subject, and not be thought of as a form of archaeological dictionary.

Sources

Anyone who writes such a book as this faces a never-ending flood of articles, books, and reports. Just navigating the proliferating academic literature is enough to give you literary indigestion. The problem of sources has been compounded in recent years by the emergence of Cultural Resource Management (CRM), which is now responsible for about 60 percent of archaeological research in North America. The web is now a major player in academic literature of all kinds, and archaeological web pages number in the tens of thousands. Yes, there are many gems, but there are also reams of what can only be called nonsense, pseudoarchaeology, or archaeology put forth with an agenda, such as propagating nationalistic or religious views. Some readers of the earlier editions criticized me for the guidelines I followed for writing this book, but I am unrepentant, on the grounds that accuracy is all-important. Those guidelines are:

This book is written from published sources only. No unpublished data appears in this book, unless I have the written permission of the researcher, in which case it is cited. Unpublished data is unverified in the scientific eye, so I have no option but to omit it here. The same rule applies to verbal reports and delivered, but not published, conference reports, which are often, regrettably, cited as if they were published references.

"Gray" literature contributes relatively little to this book. CRM research has generated an enormous "gray" literature, commonly mimeographed or desktop published for limited circulation. Some reports are even confidential and are never distributed at all. Although significant progress in creating repositories for the "gray" literature has been made, much of it is effectively inaccessible to the more general researcher such as myself, even with all the facilities of a great university library system at hand. The web has improved the situation somewhat, but there is still much inaccessible data. I have tried to minimize inaccuracies by consulting colleagues in all parts of North America, but some, inevitably, exist. It is only fair to point out that some very notable contributions have been made by CRM companies, who have published comprehensive reports on their research to very academic standards. This work features in these pages.

Online sources are used where I can check them out. The internet is a firmly established reality of the archaeological world. Nearly every important site or project has its own website, making research a nightmare of transitory postings and constant updatings. Although some web-based research has gone into this edition, I have avoided citing specific URLs here, on the grounds that web pages change frequently. Google and other search engines are now so sophisticated that you can access almost any site or research that has a website without difficulty.

Changes in the Fifth Edition

The fifth edition of *Ancient North America* takes advantage of much input from colleagues, students, and general readers who took the trouble to write to me, and also of a complex formal and informal review process. These many critics and reviewers urged me to maintain the same general approach, but to shorten the book and to continue to make it a good read. There are minimal changes to the overall organization, though the book has been updated throughout. The major changes in this edition include:

New "Enduring Themes" essays, which address large-scale developments across the continent and introduce the common connections that unite the regions and cultures featured in the chapters that follow.

A major revision of Chapter 2, which covers the first settlement of the Americas, to reflect the latest multidisciplinary findings.

Revisions, large and small, to all the chapters. I have tended, on reviewer advice, to reduce coverage of culture history, partly because the approach is outmoded, and also because much of it is inherently local, and best taught regionally. The overall frameworks are still here.

A complete rewrite of Chapters 14 to 16, about the *entrada* and its consequences, to incorporate new research, fresh insights, and recent discoveries. Chapter 16 covers historical archaeology between 1700–1800 and focuses on social minorities to show how archaeology can give a voice to those often underrepresented in history and to offer a more current overview of American history.

A new chapter that surveys very briefly what lies ahead in North American archaeology.

A shortened Guide to Further Reading, organized chapter by chapter.

Despite all these revisions, the story in these pages is still far from complete, at a time when North America's past is under siege from collectors, looters, tourism, and the ravages of industrial civilization. All of us, whether professional archaeologist, avocational enthusiast, or lay person, have a responsibility to be stewards of the past for future generations. If we are not faithful stewards, there is a real danger that our grandchildren will curse us roundly for letting the finite archaeological record vanish.

Finally, I urge any reader with comments, criticisms, or suggestions for the next edition to contact me at venbed@gmail.com. Your insights are much appreciated. And I hope you enjoy the story in these pages.

Acknowledgments

This is the fifth edition of a book that has gone through a fine-grained mesh of page-by-page, line-by-line criticism by many colleagues and students. As such, I flatter myself, probably wrongly, that much of it represents a current consensus at a basic level, within the limitations of space and time. My debt to everyone who has critiqued the earlier editions in any way is enormous, even to those anonymous correspondents who rejoice in telling you that you are wrong, but without telling you why. The book itself has also benefited greatly from discussions in the field and laboratory with dozens of colleagues: on the shores of the Arctic Ocean; in the quiet peace of a prairie valley near Saskatoon; at sites in the heart of Los Angeles; at Chaco Canyon, New Mexico; and on the Channel Islands off the California coast. My notebooks bulge with ideas and insights gleaned from these many encounters, but I cannot possibly thank everyone individually, and hope that they will take this book as a measure of my appreciation. I am humbled by their dedication to the past, often under very difficult circumstances.

I am very grateful to those friends and colleagues who have acted as critics of this edition when in draft. They were generous with insights, new data, opinions, references (and sometimes, even, gossip!). My special thanks to Ken Ames, Doug Bamforth, Chris Carr, Nadia Durrani, Don Fowler, John Hart, Bryan Hockett, Mark Leone, George Michaels, George Milner, Robert Park, Ken Sassaman, Steven Simms, Art Speiss, Mark Varien, James Vint, Gwinn Vivian, and Greg Wilson, who, among many others, provided critical insights and patiently answered my questions. I only hope that they approve of the final revision. Thank you one and all!

A special acknowledgment is due to Don Dye, who supplied a large number of superlative images from his collection for the book. I am profoundly grateful for his generosity. Thanks, too, to Mark Sapwell of Thames & Hudson, who persuaded me to undertake this revision when I had hitherto procrastinated, and was endlessly helpful. I should also acknowledge the constant encouragement of Colin Ridler, who commissioned this book in the first place. My family, as always, were wonderful and left me alone when I needed it. Our cats, of course, were another matter.

Brian Fagan
Santa Barbara, California

Author's Notes

Dates

Until very recently, few North American archaeologists quoted radiocarbon dates calibrated with tree-rings. Now C14 calibration is becoming increasingly sophisticated, as its range extends into the Early Holocene, and corals, varves, and other independent dating approaches are added to dendrochronology. These new calibrations (see Table opposite) are giving us cause to treat radiocarbon dates earlier than about 9500 BCE with great caution, as evidence suggests there is a "plateau" affecting radiocarbon ages in the 11,000- to 14,000-year range. For example, there is now good reason to believe that the Clovis culture of early North America is 2,000 years earlier than was thought until very recently. I have adopted the following conventions for the purposes of this book:

- Dates earlier than 10,000 BCE are quoted in years before present.
- Unless otherwise stated, all dates derived from radiocarbon in this book have been calibrated.

Maps

In some instances, obscure or minor locations have been omitted from the maps.

Measurements

Measurements are given in non-metric and metric formats.

Place Names

Modern place names refer to the current most commonly used spellings. Where appropriate, widely accepted ancient usages are employed.

References

When there are more than three authors for a book or paper, I use the convention "*et al.*," as listing them all (sometimes as many as a dozen) is an exercise in overkill.

RADIOCARBON CALIBRATION TABLE

The following table gives calibrated readings for the past 10,000 years, and earlier. (increasing differences after 25,000 BCE [calibrated])

Tree-ring Calibrations	
Radiocarbon Age	Calibrated Age in Years Using Tree-rings
1760 CE	1945 CE
1505	1435
1000	1105
500	635
1	15
505 BCE	767 BCE
1007	1267
1507	1867
2007	2477
3005	3795
4005	4935
5005	5876
6050	7056
7001	8247
8007	9368
9062	9968

AMS Carbon 14 (Barbados) and Uranium/Thorium Calibrations	
AMS Radiocarbon Dates	Calibrated Age in Years Using Uranium/Thorium
7760 BCE	9140 BCE
8270	10,310
9320	11,150
10,250	12,285
13,220	16,300
14,410	17,050
15,280	18,660
23,920	28,280

Calibrations based on tables in *Radiocarbon* 40(3), 1998. It should be stressed that these calibrations are provisional, statistically based, and subject to modification, especially before 7000 BCE.

The Archaeology of North America

"None of the dead can rise up and answer our questions. But from all that they have left behind, their imperishable or slowly dissolving gear, we may perhaps hear voices, 'which are now able to whisper, when everything else has become silent,' to quote Linnaeus."

—Bjorn Kurten, *How to Deep-Freeze a Mammoth* (1984)

A Mississippian wooden-hafted axe
in the form of a woodpecker, with
a copper blade and shell inlay eye.
From the Craig Mound, Spiro site,
Oklahoma. Length: 14.4 in. (36.5 cm).
Dated *c.* 1250–1350 CE.

CHRONOLOGICAL TABLE OF ANCIENT NORTH AMERICAN SOCIETIES

Archaeologists often use three loosely defined cultural terms:
Paleo-Indian: The first human societies in North America, from first settlement to after 8000 BCE.
Archaic: Later hunter-gatherer societies that developed local adaptations after 8000 BCE until about 1 CE.
Woodland: Hunter-gatherer and agricultural societies in the Eastern Woodlands after 1000 BCE.

Dates	Climate	Alaska	West/Southwest	Plains	Eastern Woodlands	Northeast
Historic			HISTORIC PERIOD			
1500 CE	LITTLE ICE AGE			Horse introduced	MISSISSIPPIAN LATE WOODLAND	NORTHERN IROQUOIANS
	MEDIEVAL WARM PERIOD	NORSE THULE	HOHOKAM ANCESTRAL PUEBLO MOGOLLON			
1000 CE		DORSET NORTON			HOPEWELL	
				Communal bison hunting	MIDDLE WOODLAND	
1 CE	LATE HOLOCENE		LATE PERIOD NORTHWEST AND CALIFORNIA	Important maize farming	ADENA	
1000 BCE		PRE-DORSET				
2000 BCE	MIDDLE HOLOCENE	ARCTIC SMALL TOOL	Maize introduced			
3000 BCE						
4000 BCE	ALTITHERMAL (climatic optimum)	ALEUTIAN TRADITION		ARCHAIC SOCIETIES		
5000 BCE						
6000 BCE						
7000 BCE		PALEOARCTIC				
8000 BCE	EARLY HOLOCENE			LATER PALEOINDIAN SOCIETIES		
9000 BCE						
10,000 BCE	YOUNGER DRYAS (cold)		CLOVIS			
11,000 BCE			FIRST SETTLEMENT			
12,000 BCE						

Chronological tables are intended as a general guide only. Not all sites, phases, or cultural terms used in the text appear in these tables. The following key is used throughout the tables:

─────── Well-established chronology. Time span may continue beyond the line.

├────── Limit of the chronology is generally agreed.

- - - - - Chronology doubtful.

CLOVIS   A name in capital letters is an archaeological culture, horizon, or tradition.

Meadowcroft   A name not in capital letters is an archaeological site or event.

Archaeology and Ancient North America

Raven hung the sun in the sky. The sunlight was so bright that he was able to fly to an island far away in the ocean. When the sun set, he placed the moon and stars in the heavens to provide a different light. When he flew back over the land, he dropped all the water he carried, which created freshwater lakes and rivers. Thus part of the Haida creation myth from the Pacific Northwest, its hero Raven, a magical, mythic creature, a trickster, one of the creators of humankind. The Haida believe that Raven discovered the first humans hiding in a clam shell. He brought them beans and salmon. Humankind was created and prospered.

Imagine a dark winter's night inside a planked longhouse on the Pacific shore: the flames of the hearth flickering in the darkness, the families warm in their furs and blankets. An elder tells a story of the beginnings of human existence. His listeners have heard the tale many times, yet it varies with each recitation. Ravens, eagles, and other animal humans come alive as the narrative unfolds (Figure 1.1). The animals are familiar parts of the listeners' world: some are quarry for the pot, some creatures to be feared, all are treated with respect. The storyteller invokes the ancestors (Figure 1.2), those who have gone before, powerful intermediaries between the familiar living world and the vibrant, sometimes menacing, realm of the supernatural and its powerful beings.

Traditional Native American beliefs and creation stories are rightly treasured to this day. Some of them are thousands of years old and valued by people whose remotest ancestors, we now know, arrived at least 14,000 years ago. This book is the story of these fourteen millennia, told not from oral tradition—although that is part of the narrative—but through Western multidisciplinary scholarship and the lens of archaeology.

Columbus and After

This scholarship dates back more than five centuries. On October 12, 1492, Christopher Columbus, Admiral of the Ocean Sea, sailing under the Spanish flag, set foot on San Salvador in the Bahamas. There he encountered Native Americans, whom he described as having "very good faces." Columbus believed he had found the outlying islands of East Asia, and called the inhabitants of the new lands "Indios," Indians. The admiral and his successors revealed a vast continent teeming with new forms of animal and plant life, and with a bewildering diversity of human societies, both simple and complex.

Who were these "Indians," exotic people whom Columbus paraded before the Spanish court? Where had these strange humans come from and why were they so diverse? How had they reached the Americas? Had they sailed across a vast ocean, or had they walked? In 1589, Jesuit missionary José de Acosta published his *Historia natural y moral de las Indias*. He theorized that small groups of "savage hunters driven from their homelands by starvation or some other hardship" had taken an overland route through Asia to their present home 2,000 years before the Spanish Conquest of Mexico.

The newcomers had a different take on history from the Native Americans. They grew up in a Europe ruled by royal dynasties, where history was not cyclical, but linear, extending back to the Greeks, the Romans, and beyond into the world of the Old Testament and the Biblical creation. Looking back at the history of the Native Americans meant thinking about their past in the same linear fashion, back to Biblical times and the Garden of Eden.

But had they originated there? When a flood of settlers poured over the Allegheny Mountains in eastern North America after 1815 and cleared farmland, they uncovered entire landscapes of mounds, enclosures, and other earthworks. The newcomers were convinced that golden treasure lay in the mounds and dug to get rich. They found no gold, but dozens of skeletons and exotic artifacts, such as carved soapstone pipes, mica silhouettes of birds and animals, and fine copper ornaments and other objects (Figure 1.3). The finds caused an intellectual furor, and a wave of sentiment for theories of a "lost race" of white Moundbuilders, who had once settled and conquered the fertile lands of the Midwest. Such wild theories appealed to the romantically inclined, to people who believed that Native Americans were incapable of building anything as elaborate as a burial mound (Silverberg, 1968). This gave birth to the Myth of the Moundbuilders with its stirring conquests and flamboyant leaders conjured up by generations of imaginative popular authors (see Box: The Myth of the Moundbuilders).

1.2 Haida mortuary totem poles, Ninstints, Haida Gwaii, British Columbia. The poles are slowly returning to the primordial forest.

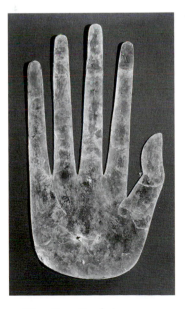

1.3 Mica silhouette of a human hand from the Hopewell tradition, c. 300 BCE to 500 CE. Site unknown.

THE MYTH OF THE MOUNDBUILDERS

The Myth of the Moundbuilders was big business during the nineteenth century. It is a classic example of the kind of pseudo-archaeology that discusses the Lost Continent of Atlantis, ancient visitors from Outer Space, and so on. Popular writers jumped on the bandwagon. Josiah Priest's *American Antiquities and Discoveries in the West* appeared in 1833 and was an immediate bestseller. He wrote of great revolutions and costly wars, when "armies, equal to those of...Alexander the Great" marched into battle. Thousands perished and were buried in great cemeteries. The mound people, reduced by famine and siege, died "amidst the yells of their enemies." Cornelius Mathews's *Behemoth: A Legend of the Moundbuilders* had mound dwellers threatened by Behemoth, a massive, mammoth-like beast. He was killed by an ingenious hero, Bokulla, a heroic warrior. All good, stirring adventure that appealed to people settled in an unfamiliar land, but absolute nonsense scientifically (Silverberg, 1968).

Meanwhile, a few antiquarians set out to acquire more information about the earthworks and their builders. Caleb Atwater, the postmaster of Circleville, Ohio, spent his ample leisure time exploring the mounds near his home town, and described them in a two-part paper published in 1820 that separated observation from pure speculation. Atwater's descriptions are accurate enough, but his theories are a product of his time: migrating Hindus from India had built the mounds, then moved on to Mexico. Just under a quarter-century after Caleb Atwater's report appeared, two Ohio antiquarians, E. G. Squier and E. H. Davis, completed one of the first

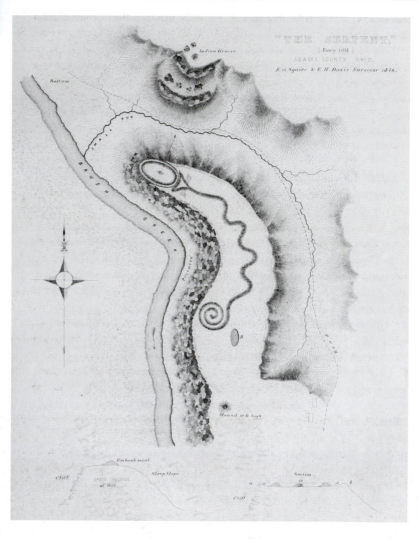

1.4 Squier and Davis's exquisite plan of the Great Serpent Mound, Ohio, 1846.

scientific monographs published by the newly founded Smithsonian Institution. *Ancient Monuments of the Mississippi Valley* was a comprehensive, descriptive work, with plans that are still used today (Figure 1.4). Squier and Davis's descriptive research was remarkable for the time, but they still referred to the "great race of Moundbuilders," and believed that the Native Americans and their ancestors were incapable of building the earthworks.

Although most antiquarians believed in exotic Moundbuilders, a growing number of influential scientists thought otherwise. The controversy dragged on from the 1850s into the late 1890s, kept alive by continual amateur diggings and by the publication of often bizarre tomes that added new, and ever more offbeat, chapters to the ancient saga. William Pidgeon, who claimed to be a trader from the west with long experience of Native

Americans, published the *Traditions of Dee-Coo-Dah and Antiquarian Researches* in 1852. His informant was De-coo-dah, a Native American from Prairie du Chien, Wisconsin, who told of Moundbuilders overwhelmed by hordes of rapacious natives. De-coo-dah conveniently died before Pidgeon published his secrets that seemed, as one author put it, "Like some monstrous bridge constructed of toothpicks" (Silverberg, 1968).

Meanwhile, however, professional science flourished with the establishment of new universities and colleges, and under the increasing influence of government agencies such as the US Geological Survey. Both the Survey and Harvard University's Peabody Museum of Archaeology and Ethnology played important roles in the controversies surrounding Stone Age settlement in North America (Meltzer, 2015).

The Smithsonian Institution's Bureau of Ethnology was founded in 1879, thanks to the lobbying of John Wesley Powell, the first man to traverse the Grand Canyon by boat. The bureau was founded specifically to preserve rapidly vanishing information about Native American peoples in the far west. Under Powell's Directorship, it also embarked on ambitious research programs on a broad geographical scale. Powell moved into Moundbuilder studies because Congress insisted in 1881 that he spend the then-large sum of $5,000 annually on mound investigation. Forced to sponsor archaeological research, he appointed Cyrus Thomas, an entomologist and ethnologist from Illinois, to head a Division of Mound Exploration in 1882. At first Thomas believed in a "separate Moundbuilder race," but fortunately he realized that he would have to embark on an extensive campaign of survey and excavation, both to support his hypothesis, and to save hundreds of earthworks from imminent destruction. He and his assistants fanned out over the Midwest, surveying, digging, studying artifacts, and making plans of sites large and small. The steady flow of data from the excavations soon convinced Thomas that the mounds were the work not of a "separate race," but of ancient Native Americans, the ancestors of modern populations. His monumental report appeared in the twelfth *Annual Report of the Bureau of Ethnology* in 1894; it describes hundreds of sites, thousands of artifacts, and is a pioneering effort at studying the remote past by working back from known modern sites and artifacts as a basis for comparison with earlier cultures (Figure 1.5).

With the publication of Thomas's great work, every serious scholar of North American archaeology accepted that the Moundbuilders were Native Americans. All modern research into these peoples is based on this fact.

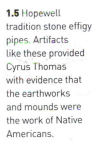

1.5 Hopewell tradition stone effigy pipes. Artifacts like these provided Cyrus Thomas with evidence that the earthworks and mounds were the work of Native Americans.

The Birth of North American Archaeology

In 1856, the wise and sober Samuel Haven, Librarian of the American Antiquarian Society, published a remarkable essay, "Archaeology of the United States," in which he surveyed everything that was known about ancient North America, and the origins of the Native American (Meltzer, 2015; Sabloff and Willey, 1993). Haven set the tone for all future scholarly enquiry into the Native Americans. His conclusions were admirably cautious. "We desire to stop where evidence ceases," he stated at the outset. The Native Americans were of high antiquity, he believed. "All their characteristic affinities are found in the early conditions of Asiatic races."

Haven was right, but he had little evidence to rely upon. He lived at a time of intense curiosity about the American West, where government scientists and members of private expeditions, often surveyors, had come across abandoned **pueblos** and dry caves where surprisingly well-preserved artifacts were to be found. Serious research in these remote landscapes began with two remarkable pioneers, Smithsonian anthropologist Frank Cushing, and Adolph Bandelier, a Swiss-born mine engineer who became an anthropologist. Frank Cushing arrived at Zuni Pueblo in 1879, intending to stay for three weeks. He stayed for four and a half years, learning to speak the Zuni dialect fluently. Through what would now be called **participant observation**, he recorded an extraordinary wealth of information about Pueblo life (Figure 1.6). Cushing was not an archaeologist, but he made a rich collection of Zuni oral traditions about earlier times that helped him realize that the best way to study ancient times was by working back from the present into the past (Cushing, 1882–83). Adolph Bandelier arrived in the Southwest in 1880. He spent twelve years wandering from pueblo to pueblo on a mule, carrying all his worldly possessions in a saddle bag. At such pueblos as Pecos, in New Mexico, he recorded centuries of Southwestern history, oral traditions and local histories that reached back into the remote past. He also soon realized that the way to study early Pueblo history was to work back in time, "from the known to the unknown, step by step" (Bandelier, 1884).

1.6 Scene of Zuni life: decorating pottery. From Frank Cushing's *My Adventures in Zuñi*. During this process, "no laughing, music, whistling, or other unnecessary noises were indulged in." The potters believed the sound would enter the clay and cause the vessel to shatter when fired.

To travel back from the known to the unknown required studying artifacts found in stratified layers in archaeological sites, probing below the most recent levels with their artifacts made by historic peoples, into much earlier layers with different pottery or stone tools. The first stratigraphic excavations in North America came in the Southwest in 1914. These used different styles of painted pottery to show that Southwestern cultures had changed through time. Thirteen years later, in 1927, the discovery of a stone **projectile point** alongside bones of extinct bison at **Folsom Plains**, New Mexico, showed that the North American past extended much further back than the commonly assumed 4,000 years (for controversies, see Meltzer, 2015). Archaeology—digging for the past—was the only way to fill the long chronological gap between the pueblos and the Folsom hunters.

The pueblos of the Southwest were where tracking back from the present into the past truly began. There were several gifted excavators at work, but the best-known of them was the Harvard archaeologist Alfred Kidder, who excavated large ancient rubbish dumps at Pecos, New Mexico (Kidder and Schwartz, 2000) (see Box: Alfred Kidder and Pecos, New Mexico). He developed the first cultural sequence for the Southwest by following Bandelier's advice—work backward from what you know. This approach was termed the **Direct Historical Method** and is the basis of what became known as "**culture history**."

All of this depended on chronologies that were based partly on intelligent extrapolation from historical documents, and partly on guesswork, instinct, and an assumption that the first settlement of the Americas was relatively recent. The only accurate date for the more remote past came from tree-ring sequences extracted from wooden beams preserved in Southwestern pueblos. These dated sites up to about 2,000 years old. It was not until the 1950s that **radiocarbon dating** transformed North American archaeology. By then, the way we studied ancient North America had changed dramatically (for dating methods, see Box: How Old Is It?, p. 31).

ALFRED KIDDER AND PECOS, NEW MEXICO

Alfred Kidder (1885–1963) was born in Marquette, Michigan, the son of a mining engineer (Givens, 1992). Admitted to Harvard University as a pre-medical student, he soon shifted his focus to anthropology. At the time, Harvard was the foremost center for anthropology in the country. In 1907, Kidder's Harvard mentors sent him on an archaeological survey in the **Four Corners** region of the Southwest. Kidder had never been west of Michigan. He immediately fell in love with the area and became fascinated with its archaeology (Figure 1.7). He graduated in 1908, visited Greece and Egypt with his family, then entered graduate school in 1909. Early on, he took a course in archaeological field methods from George Reisner, a well-known Egyptologist. Kidder visited Reisner's excavations in Egypt and the Sudan and learned his methods for

stratigraphic analysis and excavating large cemeteries, a major part of Sudanese archaeology.

Kidder's doctoral dissertation was a study of Southwestern pottery styles. He found the work nearly impossible, because excavators of the day ignored stratified layers. For his fieldwork in New Mexico's Pajarito Plateau, where modern-day Los Alamos lies, he used both ancient and modern pottery to develop a cultural sequence, publishing his findings in 1915. That same year, the Robert S. Peabody Foundation for Archaeology in Andover, Massachusetts, appointed Kidder director of a long-term excavation project at Pecos, New Mexico. Here, deep, undisturbed refuse heaps marked an abandoned pueblo. The Pecos research resumed after World War I, in 1920, and continued until 1929. Kidder was an enthusiastic and dynamic leader with a personality that attracted ▶▶

1.7 Alfred Kidder at Pecos, New Mexico.

How Do We Study Ancient North America?

Before World War II, the common estimate for the date of first settlement was 4,000 years ago. Today, we know that humans have hunted in North America for at least 14,000 years, perhaps somewhat longer—the controversy continues (see Chapter 2). The question of questions that confronted American archaeologists after the advent of radiocarbon dating was a simple one: how do we study 14,000 years of pre-Columbian history without the benefit of written records? The answer is, of course, with archaeology, but this answer needs considerable elaboration.

Archaeology is unique among academic disciplines, for it is the only way of studying how human societies developed and changed over immensely long periods. Archaeologists generally deal with millennia, and, in more recent times, in centuries. This means that archaeology is the primary means of writing the history of North America from first settlement up to the first fleeting contacts with outsiders, and then prolonged contact, the so-called *entrada*.

Until the 1960s archaeology was almost totally confined to studies of artifacts and changes in material culture over centuries and millennia. This was culture history, an approach that, at the time, was necessitated both by how little was known and by the rudimentary nature of chronological methods (see Box: Culture History, pp. 28–29). Since World War II, and especially since the radiocarbon revolution, archaeologists have relied heavily both on other scientific disciplines

young students. Many of them enjoyed distinguished careers elsewhere.

Like other Southwestern archaeologists, Kidder cleared pueblo rooms, but with a difference. He looked closely at changing pottery styles and asked what the changes meant. Kidder also carried out extensive excavations into the Pecos refuse heaps. But instead of digging in arbitrary levels, he took careful note of the features he encountered, such as heaps of discarded bones and broken utensils (Figure 1.8). His detailed pottery logs followed Reisner's practice of recording every find in three dimensions, so he could document even the smallest stratigraphic differences.

Within a few seasons Kidder had acquired a remarkable chronicle of changing Pecos pottery styles, marked especially by surface decoration, such as black painted designs. He had also

excavated hundreds of human burials. Harvard anthropologist E. A. Hooton, an authority on ancient human skeletons, visited the excavations, observing the bones and determining their sex and age. Valuable and unique information about both life expectancy and the effects of hard work on the human skeleton came

from this research. Hooton showed that most ancient Pecos people died in their twenties. After 1922, Kidder changed his strategy. He had acquired information about the architecture and expansion of the pueblo and excavated its earliest levels. Now he extended his research to surveys and excavations

1.8 The Pecos excavations at their height.

and on an ever-expanding war chest of highly technological methods that study everything from ancient diets to canoe building. Today's archaeology bears less and less resemblance to that of the early culture historians. Many culture historians were careful excavators, good observers of stratified occupation levels, and wizards at artifact classification, at placing stone tools, potsherds, and other finds in their correct relative order in time. They were mostly uninterested in today's central concerns, which are major themes of this book: how did people adapt to ever-changing, often challenging, environments over thousands of years? And what did these adaptations mean in terms of human behavior in the widest possible sense? Today we seek to explain the past as much as to describe it, using a tapestry of techniques and approaches to answer the largest and most difficult questions of the human past. Among these are: Why and how did humans settle in North America? Why did some ancient American societies develop much greater social complexity than others? How and why did agriculture replace hunting and gathering? What caused the emergence of powerful chiefdoms in the Midwest? We are still grappling with these fundamental issues.

Historical Archaeology

Historians study documents of all kinds to study the historical past, everything from account books and census records to political archives and contemporary

at other sites, while analysing the great quantity of finds. His studies ranged much further than archaeology, delving into modern Pueblo Native American agriculture and even public health. The Pecos project was a remarkable example of team research at a time when most North American archaeology was very unsophisticated. Pecos foreshadowed the close-knit field projects of today's archaeology.

By 1927, Kidder had enough information to compile a detailed sequence of Pueblo and pre-Pueblo cultures in the Southwest. His long sequence began with **Basket Maker** cultures that were at least 2,000 years old. These people made no pottery and had no permanent homes. They were followed by pre-Pueblo and Pueblo cultures. At Pecos, Kidder found no fewer than six settlements stratified one above another. There was enough information for him to argue for eight major cultural stages, beginning with the Basket

Makers, dating to between 1500 BCE and 750 CE. Five Pueblo stages came after 750, ending in historic times, which began in 1600. The Pecos sequence showed that Southwestern people developed their cultures and institutions quite independently of other areas. Kidder's sequence for the Southwest has been the basis for all subsequent research (Kidder and Schwartz, 2000). There have, of course, been numerous modifications, but this is only to be expected.

The Pecos sequence had one major disadvantage. There was no means of dating the sequence in calendar years. Fortunately, University of Arizona astronomer A. E. Douglass had developed tree-ring dating (**dendrochronology**), having been studying climatic change since 1901. In 1928 he was able to link his various tree-ring sequences from samples taken from pueblo beams and trees to historic times. Douglass's tree-ring chronologies date

the Basket Maker and Pueblo sequence at Pecos and elsewhere.

Alfred Kidder's methods of artifact analysis and excavation spread gradually across North America. All subsequent research in the Southwest, and much of the Americas, stems, ultimately, from the Pecos project. Thanks to Kidder's field training, his gifted students took the latest field methods with them when they worked elsewhere. He made accuracy, careful observation, and team research the basis of American archaeology. He subsequently worked on the ancient Maya. The 1920s through the early 1950s saw North American archaeologists focusing on sites, artifacts, and chronologies—what was called "culture history"; most speculation or theoretical discussion was considered not only unnecessary, but also intellectually unsound (see Box: Culture History, overleaf). Archaeology became basically a descriptive, historical methodology that paid lip service to anthropology.

CULTURE HISTORY

Culture history is based on two fundamental principles that were enumerated in the early twentieth century (Lyman and Dunnell, 1997). The first is inductive research method, the development of generalizations about a research problem that are based on numerous specific observations. The second is what is called a "normative" view of culture. This is the notion that abstract rules govern what cultures consider to be normal behavior. The normative view is a descriptive approach to culture, which discusses it during one long period or throughout time. Archaeologists base all culture history on the assumption that surviving artifacts, such as potsherds, display stylistic and other changes that represent the changing norms of human behavior through time. Culture history resulted from careful stratigraphic observation, meticulous artifact classifications and orderings, and accurate chronologies. The culture-historical approach produced a descriptive outline of ancient North America in time and space that took generations to assemble.

The time and space frameworks of culture history, Kidder's Direct Historical Method, were the only way to populate this chasm with ancient societies. Large-scale river basin and dam surveys between the 1930s and 1950s added great quantities of data for much of North America. From Kidder's work and that of others were born the research strategies for developing culture histories that were to be applied by dozens of North American archaeologists in coming years: preliminary site survey, selection of criteria for ranking these sites in chronological order, then comparative study of these criteria, followed by a search for, and excavation of, stratified sites; finally, more survey and additional excavations to confirm the results and refine cultural and stratigraphic findings. Some of the greatest impetus came from excavations by W. D. Strong and Waldo Wedel before World War II. They started with a rich lode of historical information collected by anthropologists and amateur historians. They excavated historic Pawnee sites, then went on to dig settlements from the **contact period** and from remoter times. The excavations revealed dramatic cultural changes on the Plains: shifts from bison hunting on foot to horticulture in river valleys, then back to bison hunting again, this time on horseback. Strong's *Introduction to Nebraska Archaeology* (1935) became a model for such research in many areas of North America.

Artifact classification was fundamental to culture history.

literature. The first written records of North America and its peoples, as well as of European voyages to the continent, start with the Norse in the tenth century CE, but are sporadic at best. More complete accounts begin with Columbus, Sebastian Cabot, and other well-known historical figures. Their journals, letters, and reports have been dissected in pitiless detail, as have the records of early colonies such as Plimoth Plantation (at Plymouth, New England) and Jamestown in Virginia. The available material proliferates rapidly during the seventeenth, eighteenth, and nineteenth centuries.

Until relatively recently excavations on such historic sites as Colonial Williamsburg or Spanish missions were virtually non-existent. Today, historical archaeologists work alongside historians and add priceless dimensions to written accounts, especially about the lives of the humble and anonymous who labored in history's shadows (see Chapter 16). In recent years historical archaeology has made major contributions to the study of the diverse eighteenth-century population of Annapolis, Maryland, to our understanding of Spanish missions along what is called the Southern Borderlands, and into the daily lives of slaves, fisher folk, and urban workers in places as varied as a whaling settlement in Labrador, Newfoundland (Figure 1.9), and nineteenth-century Chinese villages in San Francisco Bay. As the late archaeologist James Deetz reminds us (1996), much of the importance of archaeology is in "small things forgotten," such things as clay pipes, coins, and fragments of eighteenth-century china and glass. Unfortunately, except for the Norse, historical records in North America extend back only about five centuries.

As excavations in the Southwest introduced at least a degree of chronology into stratigraphic sequences, archaeologists were forced to refine their typologies to take account of change through time. Inevitably, since it was the most common artifact, the humble potsherd became the yardstick of classification, a kind of changing marker that was used to subdivide ancient times into ever more minute subdivisions. Before World War II, a group of Midwestern archaeologists developed the famous **Midwestern Taxonomic Method**, or McKern Classification. This dealt not with time and space, but with artifact classifications alone. Its architects assumed that formal similarities between artifact forms signified both shared cultural origins and shared cultural history. They proposed a taxonomic hierarchy that began with components, a unit of a culture complex that could be a site, or a distinct layer in a site. Several components were then grouped into a focus, components that shared high frequencies of similar culture traits. Foci were classified into aspects, broader groupings where there were still many culture traits in common. The highest levels in the McKern Classification were the phase, the pattern, and the base, all of them founded on increasingly more generalized cultural traits (Willey and Phillips, 1958, offers an authoritative summary).

From these pioneer syntheses emerged the fundamental principles of culture history and nomenclature that are in use today, among them chronological schemes like the familiar Archaic–Woodland–Mississippian terminology of the **Eastern Woodlands** (Chapters 8, 11, and 12). Culture history and its analytical methods are still important in North American archaeology. They have provided dozens of important cultural sequences, labeled with numerous local names for classificatory convenience. As we shall stress in later chapters, these subdivisions certainly do reflect change in artifacts; but to what extent they represent significant human behavior is a matter for discussion, and controversy. I have tended to downplay culture history in these pages except in the most general terms. For the purposes of this book, the tried and true methods of culture history are the essential framework for placing ancient American societies in their places in time and space, but today, new generations of researchers are deploying cutting-edge multidisciplinary approaches and more sophisticated theoretical models, giving us remarkably detailed insights into these same societies.

1.9 Artist's impression of Basque whale processing at Red Bay, Newfoundland.

Oral Histories and Ethnohistory

As we have already mentioned, knowledge in non-literate societies passes from generation to generation by word of mouth. Oral traditions contain much information of great value, especially about spiritual beliefs and rituals, which are treasured by their caretakers. To those who hear them, they are publicly sanctioned performed history, subject to the critical evaluation of an audience who may have heard the same stories before. Oral histories are usually a rich mixture of mythic figures and events, of moral values, and of actual historical events and people (Whiteley, 2002). Until written down, they are learned by mnemonics and constant recitation. Inevitably they vary from one reciter to the next, and change in their details from one generation to the next, even if the main outline of the story remains intact. This means that they suffer from serious limitations when weighed against data from written records or archaeological research, largely because they lack the precise chronologies that define past events. Nor do we know how much such histories have been influenced by Western literature, especially by such legends as Noah's flood in the Old Testament.

Ethnohistory encompasses the study of oral traditions and is a major source of information about Native American culture and history. It combines ethnographic and historical data as well as archaeology, and has been of much significance in Native American land-claim cases. This is an all-inclusive form of history that combines the memories and voices of living and ancient people as it culturally constructs their pasts. Ethnohistorical research throws important light on the last few centuries of Native American history and provides critical insights into older societies in such areas as the Southwest and Southeast.

Multidisciplinary Archaeology

The archaeology of pre-Columbian times is concerned, above all, with changing long- and short-term human behavior in the face of environmental and other changes in the natural world. Classic definitions of archaeology describe it as the study of all aspects of past human experience primarily using the material (physical) remains of this behavior. Passing beyond dreary textbook definitions, what archaeologists strive to do is to move on from the material and look at both external influences on changing human societies and at the intangible elements—beliefs and other perishable aspects of human culture. Such research casts a broad net, which trawls the work of scientists in dozens of academic disciplines, from biology and climatology to forensic science and zoology. Our narratives and explanations come from jigsaw puzzles of conspicuous and inconspicuous clues, some of them seemingly trivial, such as subtle changes in plant collecting in the Great Basin, or new colors used for rock paintings. Herein lies the great fascination of archaeology as a way of decoding the past—on the one hand extreme specialization, on the other the need to create narratives surrounding major themes of 14,000 years of the human past.

Today's multidisciplinary archaeology relies heavily not only on its traditional ally, anthropology, but also on environmental science and paleoclimatology to document climatic and landscape changes, on biology and biological anthropology for new generations of studies that involve ancient and modern DNA to study the first Americans, and bone isotope chemistry that allows you to identify changing dietary preferences and, using teeth, even individual life histories. Long gone are the days of solitary excavators, when it sufficed to classify artifacts and place them in order through time. Today's archaeology is carefully orchestrated teamwork, both history and social science, both social science and natural science—a true study of ancient humanity. As such, it has become a highly effective tool for writing the history in these pages.

Ancient North America is a story of 14,000 years of a continent's human history. For obvious reasons, there are times when we go off on a methodological tangent in a strategically placed box to explain a key method, such as radiocarbon dating,

HOW OLD IS IT?

Fourteen thousand years is a long time. Fortunately, however, we now have well-established dating methods that allow us to develop reasonably accurate chronologies for North America's past. More lengthy descriptions will be found in any introduction archaeology textbook.

A brief description of the major methods follows:

Objects of Known Age
(1000 CE to the present day)
These provide a means of dating sites that coincide with, or are later than, European contact, even sporadic visits, for example those of the Norse in the Canadian Arctic (Chapter 14). Artifacts including imported china and glass, dated European coins, and other finds help in dating individual structures at such sites as Colonial Williamsburg

and Jamestown. Imported glass beads and other objects traded with Native American groups are also of use, if it is possible to date them accurately.

Dendrochronology (Tree-Ring Dating)
(in North America mainly used *c.* 1 CE to the present day; also has other applications back to at least 12,500 years ago)
The astronomer A. W. Douglass first investigated tree-rings as a way of studying climate change and sunspots. His chronologies, originally based on living trees, extended to pueblo door and roof beams once he had developed a core borer that took samples without

damaging them. In 1928 a tree-ring sequence from a structure at Show Low, Arizona, enabled him to link prehistoric sequences from the pueblos with those from living trees. His composite sequence far back into the past provided accurate dates for pueblos of all kinds, notably Pueblo Bonito in Chaco Canyon, dating to the late first millennium CE (Figure 1.10).

Today there are so many tree-ring sequences from the Southwest that we can trace seasonal rainfall changes across the region, as well as decipher the complex building histories of major pueblos with great accuracy. Dendrochronology provides accurate ▶▶

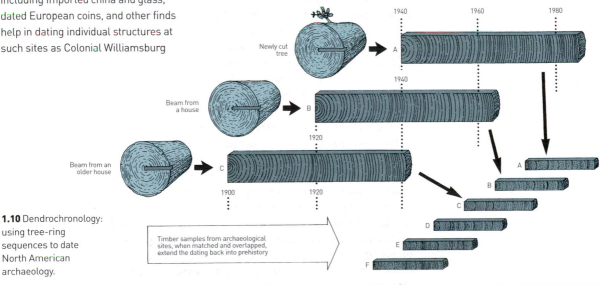

1.10 Dendrochronology: using tree-ring sequences to date North American archaeology.

Timber samples from archaeological sites, when matched and overlapped, extend the dating back into prehistory

or a specific artifact or fishing method. In the final analysis, we are concerned here with what happened, when, and why, with achieving a closer understanding of ancient North American societies. Multidisciplinary archaeology is our major tool for doing so (see Box: How Old Is It?).

Thinking about the Past

How has archaeologists' thinking about the North American past changed since the watershed moment of the radiocarbon revolution? Modern archaeological

dates that can be used to calibrate radiocarbon ages obtained from **C14** samples. In Europe and elsewhere tree-ring curves, mainly from oak trees, extend back as far as 8000 BCE.

Radiocarbon Dating

(150 CE and later to c. 40,000 years ago)
Radiocarbon (C14) dating, developed by chemist Willard Libby in the late 1940s, has become the primary dating method for pre-Columbian North American societies. Radiocarbon (known as carbon 14) is constantly being created in the atmosphere by the interaction of cosmic rays with atmospheric nitrogen. The radioactive part of carbon becomes a portion of the air absorbed and stored by plants. Animals then acquire the radioactive carbon by eating the vegetation. When an animal or plant dies, it stops exchanging carbon with the environment. From that moment on, the carbon content decreases as it undergoes radioactive decay. Measuring the amount of carbon in a dead plant, wood fragment, or bone provides a way of calculating its age. Half of the carbon in any sample will decay after about 5,730 years (the half-life). The outer limits of the dating method are around 40,000 years, when the amount of carbon is too small to measure.

A difficulty with this method is establishing the changes in concentrations of radiocarbon in the atmosphere caused by fluctuations in

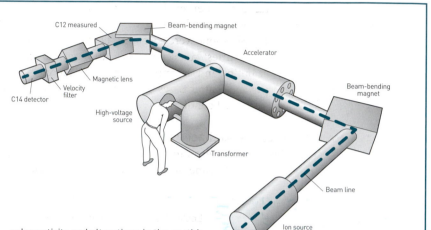

solar activity and alterations in the earth's magnetic field. The solution has been to compare radiocarbon dates with those in accurate calendar years from tree-rings. The latter provide firm dates in the Southwest and elsewhere going back at least 12,500 years. (Even earlier dates are calibrated with growth rings from tropical coral. Some of the differences between C14 and tree-ring dates were as large as 2,000 years. In recent years, the use of **accelerator mass spectrometry (AMS)** has allowed the dating of individual C14 atoms directly, enabling researchers to date items as small as individual seeds—invaluable when studying early agriculture, for example (Figure 1.11). Sophisticated statistical analyses of groups of samples are now beginning to provide highly detailed chronologies for multi-layer sites.

Radiocarbon dating is the major chronological method used in North America.

1.11 Accelerator mass spectrometry (AMS) radiocarbon dating. Ionized carbon atoms from the sample are pulled in beam form into the accelerator, non-C14 particles are filtered out, then the beam is focused as it reaches a sensitive detector that counts the remaining ions.

Other Dating Methods

There are a variety of other dating methods in use, some experimental, others more established. They are mostly used on much earlier archaeological sites than those in North America. Among them is thermoluminescence (TL) dating, which measures the amount of radiation from radioactive elements in the environment, stored in humanly heated objects such as clay vessels. TL dating has not acquired the accuracy of C14 methods, and is still experimental, which means it is currently little used.

theory was effectively born during the 1960s, with serious attempts to assemble a body of theory for archaeology as distinctive as that for physics and other established sciences (Trigger, 2006).

Julian Steward and Cultural Ecology

Today's archaeology began with deliberate moves away from culture history. The anthropologist Julian Steward (1902–1972) worked among small bands of Shoshone in the west's Great Basin. He developed an approach he called **cultural ecology**, the study of the whole picture of the ways in which human populations adapt to, and transform, their environments. His focus was not on what happened, but *why* change occurred. Cultural ecology is a fundamental part of today's archaeology. The Shoshone were constantly on the move, questing for food and water in some of the driest landscapes in North America (Chapter 6). While studying their distribution and the annual ranges of Shoshone hunter-gatherers, Steward (1955) realized that changes in human cultures went hand-in-hand with shifting environmental conditions.

Lewis Binford and Processual Archaeology

As new generations of scholars started examining the delicate and ever-changing relationships between human societies and their natural environments, they cast

LEWIS BINFORD'S PROCESSUAL ARCHAEOLOGY

Lewis Binford (1931–2011) was one of the most influential archaeologists of the late twentieth century. Whether you agreed with him or not, his ideas and approach to archaeology, known collectively as "processual archaeology," will endure for generations. Aggressive, charismatic, and opinionated, Binford attracted sometimes fanatical disciples, largely because he upset the conservative, well-established world of culture history. Originally intending to become a biologist, he became interested in anthropology and archaeology while in the military. Binford earned a Ph.D. in anthropology at the University of Michigan, when he became dissatisfied with "people in white coats counting potsherds" and came under the influence of a prominent cultural anthropologist,

Leslie White, who taught him about cultural systems. While at the University of Chicago, he wrote his first landmark paper, "Archaeology as Anthropology" (1962), arguing passionately for an archaeology that sought explanations for cultural change. His ideas attracted a group of researchers who were founders of processual archaeology. Binford's critics spoke contemptuously of a "new archaeology."

Binford then published a series of papers in which he argued for more rigorous scientific testing, for the development of independent methods for testing propositions about the past. He called for the use of formal research designs, for scientific approaches that provided interaction between old data, new ideas, and fresh data that would enable archaeologists to pose research hypotheses. Working hypotheses were nothing new in archaeology, but Binford's approach was different because he advocated that these hypotheses be

tested explicitly against archaeological data collected in the field, and against other hypotheses that had been rejected. Once a hypothesis was tested against raw data, it could join the body of reliable knowledge upon which further, more precise, hypotheses could be erected.

Binford and his many disciples also challenged the assumption that because the archaeological record is incomplete, reliable interpretation of the non-material and perishable components of ancient society and culture is impossible. Their argument was that all artifacts found in an archaeological culture occur in meaningful patterns that are systematically related to the economies, kinship systems, and other contexts within which they were used. Artifacts are far more than material items. Rather, they reflect many of the often-intangible variables that went into determining the actual form of the objects preserved.

Lewis Binford was among those who raised a fundamental question: ▸▸

1.12 Lewis Binford.

around for theoretical models, borrowing models from biologists, ecologists, even sociologists. The impact of philosophers of science, among them Thomas Kuhn and Carl Hempel, and of general systems theory began to be felt in archaeology during the 1960s. Systems theory was particularly attractive as a conceptual model, for it allowed an archaeologist to think of human cultures as complicated systems of interacting elements, such as technology and social organization, which interacted in turn with the ecological systems of which they were a part. Lewis Binford (1931–2011) was among the most influential of these scholars, who argued for a new approach that became known as **processual archaeology** (Figure 1.12). He also stressed the importance of ethnographic analogy and studying living hunter-gatherer societies—the dynamic present as opposed to the static past (see Box: Lewis Binford's Processual Archaeology). Analogy is based, ultimately, on the Direct Historical Method, the notion of working back from the present into the remote past (Chapman and Wylie, 2016). Direct historical analogies are highly effective with historic sites, such as, for example, the Colonial village at Martin's Hundred, Virginia, where textual sources provided valuable analogies about house ownership and other details of the archaeological record (Chapter 15). Such analogies lose much of their effectiveness as one moves further back in time.

The debates over processual archaeology raged fast and furious in the 1960s and 1970s. Some scholars argued that archaeology was a science, whose objective that of the relationship between the static (long dead) archaeological record of the past, and the dynamic human behavior of the (living) present. How, he and others asked, could we study the archaeological record, when we have only material evidence to work with—artifacts and food remains changed by centuries, even millennia, underground? Clearly, historic and living societies were an important source of interpretative information. Between the 1960s and 1980s, ethnographic analogy and ethnoarchaeology, the study of living peoples, came to center stage.

Ethnoarchaeology, sometimes called "living archaeology," is the study of contemporary societies to aid in the understanding and interpretation of the archaeological record. In a way, it is a logical extension of the Direct Historical Method in that it uses the present to throw light on the past. By living in, say, an Eskimo hunting camp and observing the activities of

its occupants, the archaeologist hopes to record archaeologically observable patterns, knowing what activities brought them into existence. Lewis Binford lived among the Nunamiut people of Alaska, hunters who gain over 80 percent of their subsistence from caribou hunting (Figure 1.13). He wanted to find out as much as he could about "all aspects of the procurement, processing, and

was to study basic laws of human behavior. Other archaeologists viewed archaeology as examining the activities of past human beings, as a discipline that was less a science than a historical discipline with its own limitations, resources, and explanatory methods (Flannery, 1973). Everyone agreed, however, that mathematical models, statistical approaches, and rigorous scientific methods would become ever more important. Processual archaeology, with its strongly materialist and ecological approach, has become a mainstream framework for much North American archaeology.

Post-Processual Archaeology

Processual archaeology emphasized scientific methods and the study of the processes of ancient culture change. Much research focused on ecological relationships, human lifeways, and technological developments. Inevitably, there was a healthy reaction against this materialist approach, which seemed to dehumanize the past in its quest to understand change. Many processual archaeologists dismissed religion, ideology, and the individual as marginal to the central enterprise of studying subsistence and settlement. But, from the late 1970s to today, more researchers have thought about the entire spectrum of human behavior—the development and expression of human consciousness, religion and belief, symbolism and iconography. These researches constitute

1.13 Nunamiut ethnoarchaeology. *Left:* A caribou-skin bed where a man slept while his hunting partner watched the game. *Right:* Binford's drawing of various Nunamiut activities observed by him at the Mask site, Anaktuvuk Pass, on a spring afternoon. His researches acquired a large quantity of empirical data that assists in the interpretation of archaeological sites.

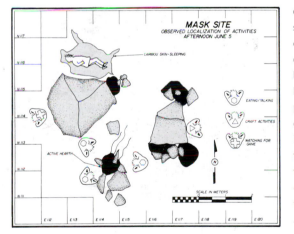

of archaeological sites elsewhere. He showed how local cultural adaptations could be, how the Nunamiut depended on interacting topographic, climatic, logistical, and other realities. He showed how changes in stone-tool frequencies or pottery forms may reflect no significant change in adaptation at all. It is impossible to tell without understanding the strategies behind the local adaptation through time. And such understandings can be obtained only from sites where food remains and other such data are available.

Lewis Binford's legacy lies in the areas of archaeological theory and ethnoarchaeology. His advocacy for processual archaeology will endure for generations (Binford, 2002).

consumption strategies of the Nunamiut Eskimo and relate these behaviors directly to their faunal consequences" (Binford, 2012). Binford chose to concentrate on animal bones rather than artifacts, because, although the bones were not humanly manufactured, their use patterns were the result of cultural activity.

Thanks to studies of actual Nunamiut hunting, of their intimate knowledge of caribou anatomy, and of existing and "archaeological" camps and caches, Binford assembled a mass of empirical data about human exploitation of animals that was applicable not only to the Nunamiut and other caribou hunters, but also to the interpretation

what is often loosely called **post-processual archaeology**, a reaction to processualism (Hodder, 1999, 2012). Post-processualists argued that we can no longer interpret the past purely in terms of ecological, technological, and other material considerations. Culture is interactive, created by people as actors, who create, manipulate, and remake the world they live in. We are doing this ourselves in the rapidly changing industrial societies of today, where ethnic identity, gender roles, and social inequality are constant issues in daily life. Surely the same behavior marked the diverse societies of the past and played a major role in the creation of ancient North American society.

Current Theoretical Directions

Today we grapple with a fundamental problem: how can one study the development of human consciousness, religious beliefs, and the entire spectrum of intangible human behavior—what has been called "the archaeology of mind"? The archaeology of mind includes all those aspects of human culture that are the product of the ancient mind: cosmology, religion, ideology, iconography, and all forms of human intellectual and symbolic behavior. Studying the ancient intangible will never be an easy undertaking; it requires large data sets, multidisciplinary research, excellent preservation, and sophisticated theoretical models. The current theoretical directions have been emerging for the past twenty years. They include the gendering of the past (Nelson and Alberti, 2006). Gender research is now highly analytical and part of many theoretical approaches. The archaeology of individuals has also moved to center stage, sometimes denoted by a popular buzzword, "agency." Discussions of agency have revolved around such topics as elite-controlled ideologies and symbolism in the rise of Mississippian chiefdoms (Pauketat, 2004) (Chapter 12), and leadership at Chaco Canyon (Kantner, 2004) (Chapter 10). There is now much more concern with issues of diversity, ethnicity, and cultural identity, all of which have important theoretical implications far beyond North America (Nicholas, 2011).

There is no single theoretical approach to North American archaeology, nor should there be. Some level of theoretical disagreement and debate is essential to dynamic, ongoing research, and issues such as gender and agency cut across all manner of theoretical perspectives. More and more archaeologists accept that there are many ways of approaching the past, and are engaging in dialogue about it. We are in an era when a diversity of theoretical approaches forms the context of ongoing research which is far more sophisticated than ever before.

Archaeology and Stakeholders

All societies have an interest in the past. It is always around them, haunting, mystifying, tantalizing, sometimes offering potential lessons for the present and future. The past is important because social life unfolds through time, embedded within a framework of cultural expectations and values. In the high Arctic, Inuit preserve their traditional attitudes, skills, and coping mechanisms in some of the harshest environments on earth. They do this by incorporating the lessons of the past into the present. In many societies the ancestors are the guardians of the land, which symbolizes present, past, and future. Westerners have an intense scientific interest in the past, born partly of curiosity, but also out of a need for historical identity. There are many reasons to attempt to preserve an accurate record of the past, and no one, least of all an archaeologist, should assume that he or she is uniquely privileged in being interested in the remains of that past. All of us, whether descendants of colonists, homeowners, Native Americans, or simply tourists, are stakeholders in North America's past. Mediating between the often widely differing perspectives of stakeholders can be a complex, emotion-filled process, but it is of fundamental importance.

We have no monopoly on history. Native American views of archaeology cover the whole spectrum, from violent revulsion to profound interest in the objectives and findings of the science (Watkins, 2001, 2003). Many Native Americans resent the cavalier attitudes of previous excavators and regard "scientific" accounts of ancient North America (such as that in this book) as irrelevant to their culture and to their lives. They believe their view of the world, based as it is in cyclical time and on a close relationship between the living and spiritual worlds, offers them an adequate explanation of human existence. They also point out that many archaeologists have chosen to ignore oral traditions, a major source of Native American history and legend. Many Native Americans have a deep suspicion of archaeologists. They resent being treated like scientific specimens, and, one must admit, they have a point. At the same time, they are deeply concerned at the invasion of sacred sites by New Agers and other folk on bizarre spiritual quests. In rare instances, Native American spiritual leaders are contacting archaeologists whom they trust to assist in the recording of such sites before they are destroyed or dispersed.

All too often, the archaeologist and the local community have different interests in the past. To the archaeologist, the past is scientific data to be studied with all the rigor of modern science. To local people, the past is often highly personalized and the property of the ancestors. Both interpretations are valid alternative versions of history that deserve respect and understanding, for they play a vital role in the creation and reaffirmation of cultural identity. And they raise a fundamental question, which lies behind many Native American objections to archaeological research: do archaeologists, usually outsiders, have anything to offer to a cultural group which already has a valid version of its history? Why should they be permitted to dig up the burials of ancestors or other settlements and sacred places under the guise of studying what is, to the people, a known history? It is a question that archaeologists have barely begun to address. Alternative, and often compelling, accounts of ancient times exist, which play an important role in helping minority groups and others to maintain their traditional heritage.

For generations, many Native American communities have been incensed by the excavation of ancient burials and the desecration of sacred places by archaeologists with scant concern for Native American culture. They pushed for laws forbidding grave excavation and stipulating the reburial or repatriation of excavated skeletons. The result was the **Native American Grave Protection and Repatriation Act** of 1990 (NAGPRA) (Chari and Lavallee, 2013). Under this act, all federal agencies and museums receiving federal funds are required to inventory their holdings of Native American human remains and associated grave goods, and all "objects of cultural patrimony." The inventory process will attempt to establish the cultural affiliations of their holdings, and, in the case of skeletons, direct lineal connections with living Native American groups.

If such relationships are established, then the organization is required to notify the relevant Native American organization and offer them the opportunity to repatriate the material. A second requirement protects all Native American graves and other cultural objects found within archaeological sites on federal and tribal land. The act also requires consultation with Native American authorities over the disposal and treatment of any finds, whether made during scientific investigations or by accident.

NAGPRA is having a profound effect on North American archaeology. The Native American Rights Fund estimates there may be as many as 600,000 Native American human skeletons in private and public collections. Archaeologists and anthropologists worry that much of their scientific database for studying such topics as ancient diseases and diet will be lost with systematic reburial of ancient populations. They argue that reburial would deprive future generations of vital scientific information. Others, including many archaeologists, believe that reburial and repatriation are ethical issues and should outweigh any scientific gain. While there are points to be made on both sides, Native Americans feel strongly about repatriation for many reasons, not least because they wish to preserve traditions and values as a way of addressing current social ills. Many of the issues concern basic questions about the morality of archaeological research. Certainly in future no archaeologist in North America will be able to excavate a site or a historic burial on federal or state land without close consultation with Native Americans, and without working with them in ways that archaeologists had not imagined until recently. While such consultation may prevent some research and some excavations, there is no question that anything but good will come of a close working relationship between Native Americans and those who excavate their sites.

The sometimes-angry polarization of archaeologists and Native Americans is slowly giving way to a new era in which both groups cooperate, albeit sometimes cautiously (Watkins, 2003). But once trust is built, the results can be rewarding. The Hopi, Navajo, and Zuni Nations of the Southwest have their own **Cultural Resource Management** programs, and other groups are following suit (Gregory and Wilcox, 2007). The future of North American archaeology lies in collaborative research in which Native Americans play a leading role.

This book tells a story teased from thousands of minute clues, many of them exotic and obscure, but it is a vital history of anonymous people going about their daily lives—negotiating, communicating, avoiding, loving and hating, growing up, getting married, having children, and dying. It is a chronicle of adaptation and opportunism, of emerging diversity, and, above all, of societies where ties of kin were all-important, and where close links with the supernatural world were at the core of human existence. Archaeology, which studies the material remains of the past, can reconstruct but a shadow of what happened. As archaeological methods improve and multidisciplinary research accelerates, however, the shadows gradually emerge into full sunlight and we discern more and more as we gaze into what has been called the "mirror of the intangible." All of this history began with a few small hunter-gatherer bands who crossed from Siberia into Alaska. Their story unfolds in Chapter 2.

SUMMARY

- Speculations about the first Americans began in the sixteenth century and culminated in the so-called Myth of the Moundbuilders in the nineteenth century.

- Professional research began with Adolph Bandelier and Frank Cushing in the Southwest during the 1880s, and leapt forward with Cyrus Thomas's Moundbuilder project in the 1890s.

- Alfred Kidder worked at Pecos, New Mexico, immediately after World War I. He developed the first cultural sequence for the Southwest and pioneered the Direct Historical Method, the basis of what became culture history.

- The 1920s to the 1950s saw a focus on artifacts and chronologies, which culminated in the development of radiocarbon dating in the 1950s. This produced the first secure chronologies for ancient North America.

- Today's North American archaeology is a multidisciplinary approach to the past that combines anthropology, history, and other disciplines with basic archaeological research.

- Since the 1950s, North American archaeology has developed theoretical sophistication, with such approaches as cultural ecology, processual archaeology and post-processual archaeology. Today's archaeological theory is very diverse in its approaches.

- There are many stakeholders in the North American past, of whom archaeologists are one. The future of North American archaeology depends on collaborative research with many of these stakeholders, especially Native Americans.

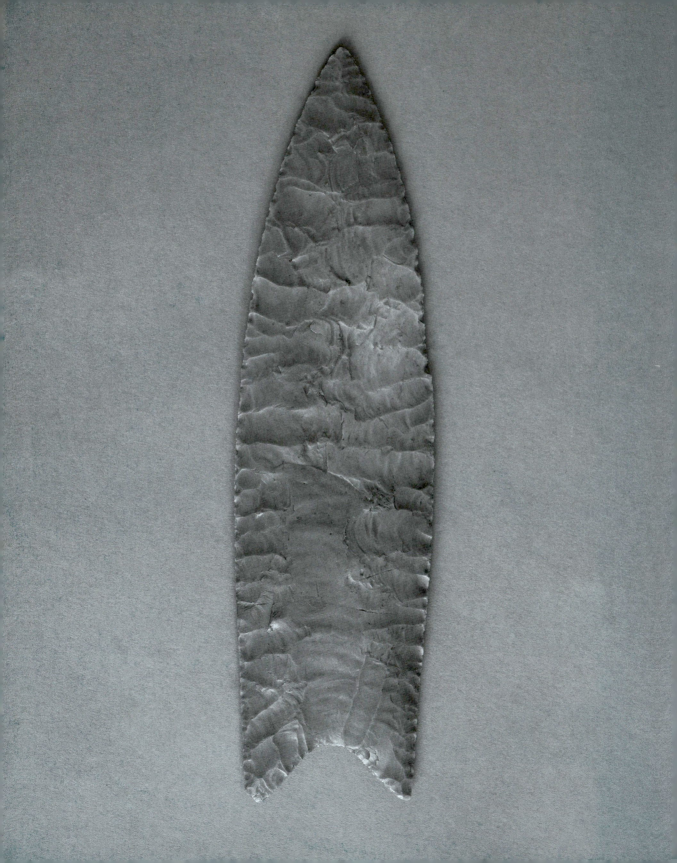

Settlement

"Those who are the First Beginning
Were given the world,
The bushes,
The forest, we meet them there."

    —Zuni song recorded in 1929

A Clovis point from Woodford County,
Kentucky. Length: 8 in. (20.3 cm).
Dated *c.* 13,200–12,900 years ago.

Settlement

You cannot be isolationist about ancient North America, though some have tried. To understand the dynamics of the first settlement of the Americas, you must understand the event on a much broader historical canvas. The story begins in a far wider world than the Americas. Except for Polynesia, Hawaii, and other outlying Pacific islands, the first settlement of the Americas was one of the last chapters in the spread of *Homo sapiens*, anatomically modern humans, across the world. The complex, and still little-understood, population movements that ultimately led to the colonization of the Americas began in sub-Saharan Africa sometime between about 100,000 and 70,000 years ago, maybe significantly earlier—the exact date is unknown and the subject of much controversy, especially among geneticists. Before 25,000 BP, there were very sparse hunter-gatherer populations living in the Lake Baikal region of Siberia, and further northeast. Earlier and more archaic human populations (the Neanderthals, for example) were by then virtually extinct, an event that took place before any humans crossed into the Americas. By the time people settled there, *Homo sapiens* had colonized a wide array of environments throughout the Old World, everything from harsh deserts to tropical rainforests, temperate landscapes, and bitterly cold northern steppes. Although other continents, such as Africa and Eurasia, document many of these successful adaptations, North America offers a fascinating microcosm for exploring the ways in which the modern humans of the past adjusted to very diverse environments indeed. You could call it a unique laboratory of archaeology, anthropology, and history.

Global and local climate change were significant players in the first settlement of the Americas, and in the rapid spread of hunter-gatherers over North America in all its environmental diversity. Twenty thousand years ago, during the last cold snap of the Ice Age, North America's coastlines lay 300 ft (91 m) below modern sea level. Alaska and Siberia were a single landmass; the Bering Strait was dry land. Extensive ice sheets covered North America as far south as the Seattle area and the Great Lakes. Temperatures throughout the heart of the continent were colder, and the climate considerably drier, than today. Rivers flowed faster, thanks to steeper gradients caused by lower oceans. Temperate woodland lay far south of the great ice sheets.

Only 14,000 years later, a mere blink of an eye in geological time, the land bridge between Siberia and Alaska had long vanished, a victim of rising seas. The northern ice sheets had split into two and retreated into the Arctic. Temperatures were far warmer than during the late Ice Age. Rivers had slowed and ponded, forming wetlands and deltas, such as that of the Mississippi. Throughout North

America climate conditions closely resembled those of today, though there were constant variations in rainfall and temperature. If we were to travel across the continent, we would be traversing a familiar land, albeit one without the dramatic signs of modern industrial society with its sprawling cities, roads, and industrial agriculture. The human impact on the land would have been relatively minimal, except for deliberate fire-setting to stimulate new plant growth and to make hunting more effective. You could have walked for days and not seen anyone else. The only signs of human presence would have been the occasional wisp of smoke from a hearth, or the barking of dogs. Some favored areas—placid river banks and lakeshores, also coastal estuaries—with their relatively predictable food supplies, would have supported denser populations. But even in these places numbers would have been much smaller than in later times. How many people lived in North America 6,000 years ago is unknown, but probably well under a million.

Quite how and when humans first crossed into the Americas has been a controversial issue for centuries. A Jesuit priest, José de Acosta, wrote as long ago as 1590 that the Native Americans had originated in Asia and settled in their new homeland "with only short stretches of navigation." Acosta wrote these words a century-and-a-half before the explorer Vitus Bering sailed into the strait between Siberia and Alaska that bears his name. Today, there is almost universal agreement that Acosta was correct, though the dates and manner of initial colonization are still much debated.

The stage is set, but who were the players, and what happened when? Understanding what happened means entering a complex interplay of archaeology, genetics, paleoclimatology, and biological anthropology. Over time there was probably a mingling of different populations in a harsh, thinly populated region. Unfortunately, northeast Siberia is a remote landscape with a savage climate, where field seasons are short and traces of ancient human settlement are, at best, rare on the ground. What we have is a patchwork of clues, usually stone artifacts. We know, for example, that people were hunting in northern Siberia's Yana River at least 32,000 years ago, at a time of bitter cold. Far to the east, in Bluefish Cave in Canada's western Yukon, there are traces of human visitation by about 24,000 BP. No question, the Yana and Bluefish people were remote ancestors of later hunting peoples in the north; but were they just brief visitors, or living in these places year-round? Current thinking favors brief summer visits, not permanent settlement.

After 15,000 years ago, the great ice sheets melted and divided into two before shrinking altogether. Rising sea levels inundated continental shelves and slowed the courses of great rivers. Everyone agrees that colonization of the heart of North America coincided with rapid, if irregular, warming that made it possible for people to move southward from a once-isolated Alaska. The big controversy has long revolved around two possible routes: did first settlement take place down an "ice-free corridor" that opened with the splitting of the two great ice sheets that mantled much of what is now Canada, or did people head southward along the Pacific Coast as sea levels rose and the Cordilleran ice sheet retreated? Until recently, many experts favored the corridor route. But a new generation of field research has ruled out this passageway south, which would have been both inhospitable and inaccessible until long after 15,000 years ago.

Current opinion favors the coastal route, despite the reality that most archaeological sites that would document it lie below modern sea level.

With such widespread movement and landscapes that could support only a very small number of people per square mile, it is small wonder that initial settlement was rapid. These sweeping movements traversed all manner of environments. One was open grassland, like the Great Plains, which dried up significantly as warming proceeded. Most large Ice Age animals, commonly known as the "**megafauna**," became extinct, probably because of the new, drier conditions. But Plains landscapes did support large numbers of bison, which thrive in more arid grasslands, so Plains people still relied heavily on hunting. The temperate woodlands that covered much of the south and east of a warming North America were rich in plant foods, including acorns and hazelnuts that could be harvested in the fall and stored for later use. Some of the richest environments lay along coasts, lake shores, and river banks, where seasonal fisheries and predictable nut harvests provided ample food for much of the year. Most difficult of all were the harsh landscapes of the far north, and the vast desert regions of the west, where obtaining food was profoundly challenging. North America was thus a complex patchwork of extremely varied and demanding environments that forced the successors of the first settlers to diversify their lifeways and their cultures fundamentally. These adaptations, which are the developing theme of Chapters 2 and 3, were to become much more elaborate in later millennia.

Strikingly, Native American populations display lower genetic diversity than human groups from other continents, and greater differentiation from them. The diversity seems to have increased as people moved south. There is clear genetic evidence that the ancient North Americans arrived and stayed in their homeland without any contact with outsiders, except across the Bering Strait, and in later times with Europeans from Greenland, then after Columbus. Their genetic origins may have been complex, but once in North America, the first settlers' descendants developed brilliant, and often long-lasting, solutions to the challenges of living in a continent of demanding seasonal contrasts, bitterly cold winters, and extreme summer heat.

Migration and mobility, the highly varied environments, and long- and short-term climate change fostered a rapid diversification of North American societies. Some, like those in the Great Basin of the west, and the ancestors of the Eskimo, Aleuts, and Inuit, also many groups native to California, remained hunters and foragers flourishing successfully in small bands until European contact and beyond. Others developed more complex societies whose economies, such as those of the Pacific Northwest of southern California's Santa Barbara Channel, or the Calusa of southern Florida, depended on rich coastal fisheries. The adoption of agriculture after about 3,000 years ago was a major catalyst for a great flowering of North American farming societies. All of them developed significant cultural and social sophistication, which culminated in the great pueblos of the Southwest and the elaborate ceremonial centers of the Mississippi Valley and Southeast, and further afield. In 1492, when Christopher Columbus landed on the Caribbean, a brilliant variety of Native American societies flourished throughout North America. We are only now beginning to decipher their story, and to achieve a partial understanding of the elaborate spiritual beliefs that anchored their worlds. This book is a tentative look at their story.

CHRONOLOGICAL TABLE OF EARLY SETTLEMENT OF NORTH AMERICA

Years before present*	Years BCE	Northeast Asia	North America			
			Alaska	West	Plains	Eastern Woodlands
9250 —	7300 —			WESTERN EARLY ARCHAIC	EARLY PLAINS ARCHAIC	EARLY ARCHAIC
9900 —	7950 —		PALEOARCTIC TRADITION			
		SUMNAGIN CULTURE			YOUNGER DRYAS	
12,200 —	10,250 —			REGIONAL PALEO-INDIAN STYLES		
			NENANA COMPLEX			DALTON
13,450 —	11,500 —			CLOVIS	CLOVIS	CLOVIS
13,950 —	12,000 —				Monte Verde (Chile)	
15,950 —	14,000 —	DYUKTAI CULTURE		FIRST SETTLEMENT		
16,950 —	15,000 —					
18,000 —	16,050 —			LAST GLACIAL MAXIMUM		

* Present is 1950 CE

First Settlement

A Midwestern lake, early summer, 12,000 years ago. The band surrounds a shallow pool in a stream flowing into the lake, calm and still in the early morning sun. Everyone stands well back from the water, lest their shadows fall on the muddy bottom. Two men crawl quietly to the low bank, covered by the shade of a large larch tree, and ease their arms into the water. Others are close by, armed with wooden clubs. No one moves, everyone watching the dark shadows of the catfish lurking underwater. Minutes pass; the fishers remain motionless, only their fingers moving gently in the stream. Suddenly, a quick movement. One of the fishers grabs a catfish and hefts it ashore. His companion clubs the wriggling fish as it hits the ground. One of the children picks up the catch and carries the fish into the shade, where it is gutted with a sharp-edged stone blade. Meanwhile, the fisher slips his hand back in the now-still water and the fishing resumes.

———————————

The first settlement of the Americas is an issue fraught with controversy, and has been for well over a century. After five years' research on the problem of the first Americans, I was moved to write that "Anyone studying the first Americans sets sail in hazardous academic seas, beset on every side by passionate emotions and contradictory scientific information." Even so, opinion on this most fundamental of issues in North American archaeology is moving very slowly toward a degree of consensus. I summarize the main areas of agreement and disagreement in this chapter. Let us begin by making one forthright statement: despite occasional claims to the contrary, no Neanderthals or other archaic humans ever settled

FIRST SETTLEMENT: FIERCELY ARGUED THEORIES

Controversies over the first settlement of the Americas have raged since the late nineteenth century, and intensified since the discovery of stone projectile points and the bones of extinct bison at Folsom, New Mexico, in 1925. Some years later, even earlier projectile points came to light at **Clovis**, also in New Mexico. These distinctive fluted points subsequently emerged from sites across most of North America, radiocarbon dated to around 11,000 years ago. Experts were thus able to identify a "Clovis culture"—named for the original site—and for generations it was assumed that Clovis big-game hunters were the first settlers. Then the "Clovis first" theory crumbled in

the face of clear evidence of earlier settlement in North America and further south unearthed during the 1970s. Today a plethora of competing scenarios surrounds first settlement, the most widely accepted of which forms the narrative for this chapter (Braje et al., 2017). Here are the other major theories:

Settlement by Neanderthals or Other Archaic Humans
Neanderthals became extinct around 30,000 years ago (the date is uncertain). If Neanderthals or other archaic humans settled in the Americas it would have to have been long before pre-modern humans became extinct. An argument for Neanderthal settlement would involve documenting sites in North America that date back long before the earliest modern humans settled in northeast Asia, at current estimate around 32,000

years ago. While it has been proposed that such an ancient site does exist in southern California (Holen et al., 2017), after over a century of searching, it remains true that no one has found either a Neanderthal fossil or readily identifiable artifacts made by them in the Americas. Such finds being absent, almost all commentators agree that the first settlers were anatomically modern humans, *Homo sapiens*.

Settlement before 20,000 Years Ago
There have been periodic claims of human settlement as early as 120,000 to 140,000 years ago, the latest from southern California. The so-called Ceruti mastodon site in San Diego County, which dates to this period, has yielded elephant bones fractured as if they were broken while fresh, also stones, both in a fine siltstone deposit. The stones are claimed to bear ▶▶

in the Americas. This chapter argues that first settlement was one of the final chapters in the great spread of *Homo sapiens*, modern humans, out of Africa over 70,000 years ago—the date is still uncertain. Moderns had settled in Europe by 45,000 years before present and were deep into Eurasia and in extreme northeast Asia by at least 32,000. These ancient Eurasians lived in desolate landscapes where winters lasted nine months and sub-zero temperatures persisted for weeks on end. Even when temperatures were slightly warmer, only tiny numbers of hunters living in family bands dwelt on the windswept steppe of the northeast. They probably met just a handful of outsiders in their lifetimes, but their descendants were the first Americans. One of the great debates of archaeology surrounds the first settlement of the Americas (Adovasio and Page, 2002; Graf *et al.*, 2014; Meltzer, 2008; Potter *et al.*, 2018). The narrative that follows lays out the most widely accepted scenarios, but there are several other enduring theories (see Box: First Settlement: Fiercely Argued Theories).

Who Were the First Americans?

There is almost universal agreement that the first humans who settled in the Americas came from Siberia. The evidence for this comes from several sources, this being a complex multidisciplinary problem. A biological anthropologist, Christy Turner (1984, 2002), examined teeth from more than 4,000 Native Americans, ancient and modern, especially their crowns and roots, then compared them to those from Asia and elsewhere. These dental features are more stable than most evolutionary traits, with a high genetic component that

signs of wear that could result from breaking up large bones. Unfortunately the excavators could not rule out the possibility that natural processes carried the stones to the site, or show that the wear did not result from the stones bumping against one another. Even the age of the mastodon bones militates against the "kill" being made by humans. The site is over 100,000 years older than any known human site in the Americas, let alone North America. Few experts regard Ceruti as a credible early site.

No other artifacts claimed to be more than 20,000 years old have withstood close scrutiny, either; nor have they been securely dated (Meltzer *et al.*, 1994). Yet arguments for very early settlement persist, which is hardly surprising given the occasional finds (usually chipped stones claimed to be humanly manufactured artifacts).

Trans-Atlantic Ice Age Settlement from Europe: 22,000 to 18,000 Years Ago

Did the first Americans cross from Europe, traveling, perhaps, across the northern ice during the **Last Glacial Maximum (LGM)**, or skirting pack ice, perhaps in skin boats? In this scenario European hunters (known culturally as Solutreans after the Solutré site in southwestern France) crossed to North America, landed on the East Coast, then moved inland (Stanford and Bradley, 2012). This hypothesis depends heavily on similarities between finely made projectile points in France and the familiar Clovis points of North America, described later in this chapter. The link is tenuous at best. The Solutreans were certainly adapted to extreme cold, but were they capable of paddling skin boats along the edges of pack ice in bitterly cold conditions, with hypothermia

a constant threat? Currently we have no evidence for Solutrean seafaring or watercraft. Like the Neanderthal hypothesis, this theory requires great leaps of scientific faith.

The point is this: scant numbers of people in small bands were the first settlers, whatever the date when they arrived. Archaeologists working in Africa have decades of experience studying the minute "signatures" of very early human settlement and apply very precise criteria in terms of geological context, fractured bones, and humanly struck stone tools with possible edge wear to them. None of the claimed very early sites in the Americas currently meet these criteria. The earliest firmly dated locations in continental North America are in the 14,000-year-old range, perhaps a little earlier.

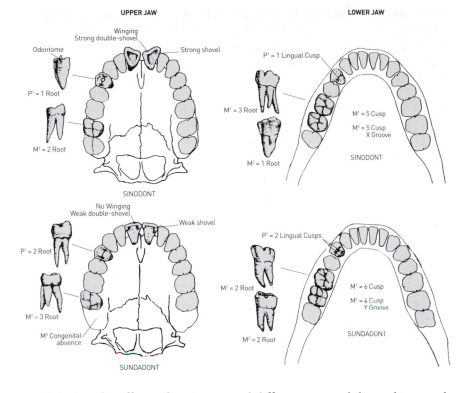

2.1 Dentochronology: sinodonty and sundadonty. Sinodonts display incisor shoveling (scooping out on one or both surfaces of the tooth), single-rooted upper first molars, and triple-rooted lower first molars. Sundadonts (Europeans and East Asians) do not display these features, which are perhaps an adaptation to the extreme cold of the north.

minimizes the effects of environmental difference, sexual dimorphism, and age variation.

Turner showed that Native Americans commonly have features of dental morphology that he called "**sinodonty**." This pattern of dental features includes incisor shoveling, single-rooted upper first premolars, triple-rooted lower first molars, and other attributes. Sinodonty occurs only in northern Asia and the Americas. Turner's earliest evidence for sinodonty came from northern China about 18,000 years BP, but he believed that it emerged much earlier, perhaps as early as 40,000 years ago. In contrast, ancient Europeans are not sinodonts (Figure 2.1).

Then there are genetics. This is a rapidly developing field characterized by lively debate and complex argument, especially on the subject of fast-mutating mitochondrial DNA (mtDNA), which is inherited through the female line. Mitochondria trace modern human ancestry back to tropical Africa at least 150,000 years ago, and no fewer than five mtDNA lineages are shared by ancient and modern Native American populations in North and South America (Merriwether, 2002). Molecular biologists believe that all Native Americans are descended ultimately from a single, somewhat diverse, group of Asians from eastern Siberia, whose own ancestors lived in tiny bands scattered over very wide areas. In short, there was biological diversity from the beginning (Reich *et al.*, 2012).

Back in 1956 the Stanford linguist Joseph Greenberg (1987) proposed that most North American, and all South American, languages were part of a single large "Amerind" family. Aleut-Eskimo and Na-Dene were quite separate linguistic groups, making three groups for the entire Americas. Greenberg spent years compiling

2.2 Joseph Greenberg's map of Native American languages, which is considered too simple by many authorities. Eskimo-Aleuts and Na-Dene are, however, widely accepted subdivisions.

a vast database of the vocabulary and grammar of the 140 families of Native American languages, which confirmed his belief that there were three linguistic groups that corresponded to migrations into the Americas. Greenberg estimated that his Amerind group arrived before 9000 BCE, the Na-Denes around 7000 BCE, and that Aleuts and Eskimos diverged about 2000 BCE. Greenberg's large grouping of many languages into an Amerind family has been severely criticized by other linguists, partly because Native American languages are very ancient and developed within the Americas over long periods. Despite this criticism, some geneticists claim that their evidence fits well with Greenberg's tripartite subdivision of Native American languages. The controversy is unresolved (Figure 2.2).

This brings us to the archaeology. If the biologists and linguists are correct, can archaeologists identify the settlements of Siberians dating back to the Last Glacial Maximum (LGM) or even before? Extreme northeast Asia was never densely populated, but we know of human occupation from a site on the Yana River known as Yana RHS (Yana Rhinoceros Horn Site), far above the Arctic Circle and 87 miles (140 km) from the Arctic Ocean (Pitulko *et al.*, 2013, 2016). People were hunting a variety of large and smaller mammals here around 32,000 years ago, before the intense cold of the LGM. These northern people subsisted off a wide range of foods. (They are often described as **broad-spectrum hunter-gatherers**.) They must have been, above all, expert opportunists, ranging over large territories and wintering near reliable water supplies. The LGM may have emptied much of northeast Asia of animals and humans, but their descendants ultimately became the first Americans.

Introducing Beringia

North America's story began in the central part of a vast tract of northern landscape known to geologists as **Beringia**. Western Beringia ends at Siberia's Verhoyansk Mountains, east of Lake Baikal. The eastern frontier lies at the Mackenzie River in northern Canada. Today central Beringia is a sunken continent, flooded by rising sea levels during global warming at the end of the Ice Age. This now-vanished land, the Bering Land Bridge, today the Bering Strait, was the incubator for the first Native American societies (Hoffecker *et al.*, 2016) (Figure 2.3).

The events that culminated in first settlement unfolded during the last Ice Age glaciation, which began about 115,000 years ago. At its height, around 18,000 years BP, two great ice sheets covered almost all Canada and the United States as far south as the Great Lakes and the Seattle region. Global sea levels were about 300 ft (91 m) below modern levels. The cold peaked between about 25,000 and 18,000 years ago, during the so-called LGM (Figure 2.4).

Beringia was an inhospitable place. Soils were thin. Tree cover was sparse and confined, for the most part, to deltas, sheltered localities, and river valleys. There were no dense forests. Endless tracts of steppe-tundra scrub vegetation hugged the ground. The glacial climate was never stable, always changing. During slightly warmer periods, such as the one about 32,000 years ago, a bestiary of large and small mammals thrived on the steppe and in shallow river valleys. There were mammoths (the famous long-haired, cold-adapted elephant), bison, saiga antelope, and numerous smaller animals that provided food and the raw material for tools and clothing of all kinds. For all its seeming harshness, Beringia was a highly diverse environment for those who hunted there. But it was an isolated landmass, cut off from the Americas by the ice sheets that mantled northern North America.

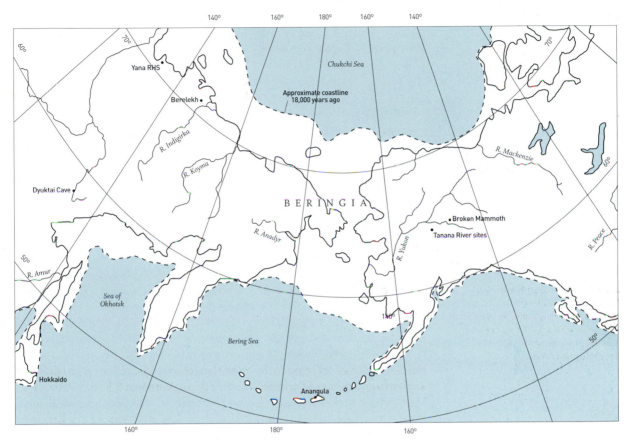

2.3 Beringia and the Bering Land Bridge.

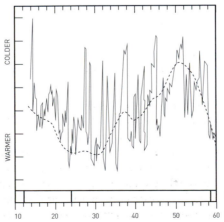

2.4 Climate change during the late Ice Age. Zigzag climatic shifts from 60,000 to 10,000 years ago are reconstructed from various sources. A brief warming between 60,000 and 45,000 years ago was followed by irregular climatic shifts, then intense cold. Warming began about 15,000 years ago. The brief cold of the Younger Dryas (named after a polar flower), which started c. 12,050 years ago, is clearly visible.

This was a dry world, where arctic winds blew strongly and the semi-arid landscapes attracted and repelled inhabitants according to the vicissitudes of climate. In slightly warmer periods the landscape tended to draw people in, especially to localities where water was available year-round and fish could be obtained. When temperatures fell and conditions became drier, the desert drove out both humans and animals. This is exactly what happened during the height of the LGM around 20,000 years ago, when most people in extreme northeast Asia appear to have retreated southward into warmer environments. During this period of intense cold, the Bering Land Bridge extended from Asia to Alaska and covered much of the Chukchi Sea. Its southern coastline extended from the Gulf of Anadyr in Siberia to the Alaska Peninsula in North America, but it was completely isolated from the south by ice sheets (see Figure 2.3).

The Beringian Standstill Hypothesis

For generations archaeologists assumed that the Bering Land Bridge was a natural highway from east to west, a corridor across which small human bands crossed from Siberia into Alaska (Hoffecker et al., 2016). Captivating scenarios of Arctic hunting bands pursuing big game, such as mammoth, long formed the centerpiece of most theories for first settlement. We now know that such hypotheses are incorrect. Survival in the far north always depended on hunting a broad range of animals.

Once thought to be a uniform, bitterly cold environment of treeless steppe tundra, Beringia is now known to have supported a far more diverse array of habitats. The central Beringian lowland that formed the Bering Land Bridge was surrounded by drier, more steppe-covered landscapes on higher ground to the east and west. Core borings into the Bering Strait seabed and on surviving islands above modern sea level have yielded ancient pollen grains in the southeastern portions of the poorly drained Land Bridge that include alder, birch, and spruce trees. The temperature-sensitive insects found in core borings from the region show a temperature decline in the order of 3 to 5 degrees Celsius, significantly smaller than that for other parts of the Northern Hemisphere during the LGM. Thanks to the proximity of the North Pacific's warmer waters, temperatures were milder, and, most important of all, plant productivity was significantly higher. Surprisingly, the Land Bridge was an isolated refuge for both animals and humans during the LGM, with temperatures little different from today (Hoffecker et al., 2016). Recently statistical analyses of twenty-four dental traits from several thousand Asians and Native Americans have hinted that there was a time when central Beringian populations developed even more marked sinodont characteristics than Asians, presumably because of isolation on the land bridge (Scott et al., 2016). Perhaps it is not surprising that there are few variations in sinodonty among Native American populations.

Estimates based on genetic diversity using a broad array of DNA and other data suggest that the total population during the LGM could have been as high as 8,000 to 10,000 people scattered over a large area. Movement onto higher ground in Alaska then came to a standstill, whence the term Beringian Standstill Hypothesis. It is, however, possible that some small hunting groups moved far to the east during the brief summers of the LGM, as suggested by some humanly cut animal bones found at Bluefish Caves in Canada's Yukon Territory, radiocarbon dated to about 24,000 years ago.

As small groups of Beringians moved onto higher ground and southward when temperatures warmed around 15,000 BP, they may already have been geographically and genetically diverse, and possessed of different languages. The patterns of movement would have been seasonal, with people hunting on the steppes during warmer months, exploiting larger mammals such as horse or bison as well as plant and other foods. During the winter they would have retreated to the better-watered, warmer **refugium** zones, where they could find firewood. (It is worth noting that mammoth-bone "logs" will not burn without a wood starter.)

When temperatures warmed between 17,000 and 16,000 years ago, glaciers began to retreat. New territory gave access to coastal areas to the south. As sea levels rose, so people moved off the land bridge, which vanished about 13,000 years ago. Warmer temperatures saw people moving in (and out of) Beringia and the first settlement of North America south of the ice sheets.

The Beringian Standstill Hypothesis offers a potentially convincing scenario for first settlement. But what does archaeology tell us about the very first settlement of the Alaskan side?

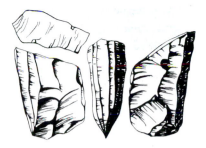

2.5 A wedge-shaped microblade core from Dyuktai Cave, Siberia, dating to about 15,000 years ago.

First Settlement in the Far North

First settlement is a tale of two technologies, or maybe one. As temperatures rose after 15,000 years ago, people using microblades moved into Siberia's Lena River Valley, probably from southern Siberia (Figure 2.5). This technology produced small blades from wedge-shaped cores that could easily be fashioned into razor-sharp barbs for hunting weapons, ideal for people on the move. This distinctive technology was used over a very wide area of northern Asia and northeastern Siberia during and after the Ice Age. Microblades also occur in Alaska, and as far south as British Columbia. Such artifacts were part of a highly efficient hunting technology using light, barbed spears in open country, where the barbs would open more serious wounds, and cause more blood loss and damage, than could conventional spears. Perhaps, argues paleontologist Dale Guthrie (1968), the distribution of microblades is linked to caribou hunting. Microblades may have been an adaptation to tundra conditions, where migratory herds roamed.

Guthrie argues the widespread microblade tradition could have been a widely shared and successful material culture that emerged during the late Ice Age in Asia and flourished into post-glacial times. Microblade technology appeared in the arid lands of northern China as early as 30,000 years ago and soon spread over a very wide area, even into the tropical south. They were in use at the Studenoe-2 site southeast of Lake Baikal in Siberia by 17,800 years ago, and may have spread into extreme northeastern Siberia as early as 18,000 years ago. Even so, no human occupation is yet known from the Kamchatka Peninsula and the far northeast that dates to earlier than about 15,000 years ago. Microblades appear at the Swan Point site in south-central Alaska by about 14,000 years ago. The highly portable toolkit—often known as the **Dyuktai (or Diuktai) Tradition**, after a cave in the Middle Aldan River Valley—spread widely across Alaska as small groups of hunters moved from the land bridge onto higher ground. The low-lying plains flooded rapidly as sea levels rose with global warming, and the first Americans appear to have responded by moving in search of dry land. A second technology also appeared on the northern stage. It is known in Siberia

KEY LOCATIONS IN EARLY ALASKA

Securely dated early Alaskan sites are thin on the ground. Here are the best-known locations (summary descriptions in Hoffecker *et al.*, 2016):

Mesa

The Mesa site lies on the northern flank of the Brooks Range on a ridge overlooking the treeless landscape. Lanceolate fluted points and other stone artifacts have come from hearths and other activity areas dating to about 12,000 to 10,000 years ago. This site does not pre-date the Clovis culture to the south.

2.6 Excavations at Broken Mammoth, 1991, site of some of the earliest human occupation in Alaska.

Sites in the Nenana and Tanana River Valleys: Broken Mammoth, Dry Creek, Swan Point, and Upward Sun

Broken Mammoth and Swan Point, in the Tanana River Valley was first visited around 13,000 BP (Graf *et al.*, 2015) (Figure 2.6). Dry Creek, on the Nenana River, was first visited around 11,120 BP. These three sites are open-air camps marked by hearths with bone fuel and wood charcoal. Swan Point yielded microblades.

The Upward Sun site, also on the Tanana River, lies in a sand dune and contains four occupation levels dating to between 11,600 and 8,800 years ago (see Figure 2.7, opposite). Judging from bearberry seeds and waterfowl bones, the oldest occupation was in the fall, when the inhabitants took bison, moose, and a wide variety of smaller animals.

The third occupation level (11,600 to 11,270 years ago) includes a circular dwelling about 10 ft (3 m) across, dug partially into the ground. A cremated child and two infant burials, the infants perhaps buried in shrouds, lay under the house. They were buried with lanceolate projectile points and elk-antler rods, perhaps part of an **atlatl** (spear throwing) system. The bones from this occupation level include remains of chum salmon, and provide the earliest record of salmon fishing in the Americas.

The earliest Alaskan sites form part of what must have been widespread hunting and foraging cultures that relied heavily on lightweight hunting weapons and traps.

from Berekekh in the extreme northeast, where hunting bands used tear-shaped "**Chindadn**" spear points, also heads with stemmed bases, between 14,000 and 13,500 years ago (Pitulko *et al.*, 2014). Stemmed points are also found in the Lena Valley, and at the Ushki site in central Kamchatka. Significantly Chindadn points also come from sites of comparable age in south-central Alaska and the Yukon, which is presumably a sign that people carried such weapons into North America.

A complex tapestry of small-scale population movements lies behind these two technologies, used by broad-spectrum hunters who moved into Alaska as global warming accelerated. The first Alaskans themselves are a shadowy presence, known only from a handful of sites in the Tanana Valley, southeast of Fairbanks. These were temporary encampments, among them Broken Mammoth, Swan Point, and Upward Sun (Figure 2.7), the former occupied as early as 14,500 years ago, the latter by 13,200 to 11,500 BP (see Box: Key Locations in Early Alaska). These are meager clues, but we now know that the first settlement of the Americas occurred immediately after the LGM, when retreating ice sheets and warmer temperatures allowed the ancestors of the Native Americans to move eastward onto higher ground.

2.7 Excavations at Upward Sun, Alaska.

Heading South: The Pacific Coast

How did the descendants of the first settlers reach the heart of North America? The classic scenario envisaged very small numbers of people moving through a narrow ice-free corridor between the retreating Cordilleran and Laurentide ice sheets that had hitherto blocked movement of animals and humans to the south (see Figure 2.8). The idea of an ice-free defile soon took hold of archaeologists' imaginations. "Doubtless it was a formidable place," wrote Thomas Canby of the National Geographic Society, "an ice-walled valley of frigid winds, fierce snows, and clinging fogs…yet grazing animals would have entered, and behind them would have come a rivulet of human hunters" (1979, p. 221). The picture is a compelling one—but is it accurate? The ice-free corridor has been mapped more thoroughly in recent years, to the point that we can be sure it was no superhighway for Stone Age hunters; indeed, it was at best only marginally habitable. Much better food resources lay in eastern Beringia and on the coast.

If the ice-free corridor was an inhospitable and late migration route to the south, what about other paths? Most experts now believe that the first settlers moved south along the Pacific Coast. But did they travel by land or by sea? Long stretches of northern coastline from the Kuril Islands off Japan to Beringia and south through the Aleutians were more accessible 13,000 years ago than was once suspected, thanks to the low sea levels of the late Ice Age. Advocates of coastal settlement believe that fishing and sea-mammal hunting, as well as a sophisticated maritime tradition, were well established in northeast Asia during the late Ice Age, and that small groups of coastal people traversed the ice-strewn shoreline of the land bridge at least partly in watercraft, then hunted and fished their way southward through the fjords, bays, and more sheltered waterways of the Alaskan coast. The theory is plausible, but any sites likely to document such migrations are buried under 300 ft (90 m) of rising sea water. Furthermore, there is absolutely no archaeological evidence for sophisticated sea-mammal and seafaring technology in the form of skin boats (**umiaks**) or skin kayaks in the far north before about 3,000 years ago, when the Bering Strait region became a major center for sea-mammal hunting. Maritime adaptations are considerably earlier along the Aleutian chain, but certainly much later than a putative, and perhaps conservative, crossing date of 14,000 years ago.

No one has examined the difficulties that seafarers would encounter crossing from Siberia to Alaska in small craft. Quite apart from ice floes and pack ice, both of which may have been thicker during a period of warming, the paddlers would have had to develop the clothing and boats to deal with very cold water and to resist hypothermia, as well as coping with often-savage weather conditions, even in midsummer. The *British Admiralty Ocean Passages for the World* describes these waters in summer as rainy, fog-ridden, and subject to frequent severe westerly gales, conditions that challenge even today's well-equipped fishing trawlers and freighters. More southerly areas, such as southeastern Alaska, are no more hospitable: conditions can deteriorate rapidly, with strong headwinds that are notoriously difficult to paddle against. Moreover, though southeast Alaska has plenty of sheltered coves and inlets, the same cannot be said of the exposed coasts of the Gulf of Alaska, or of the shoreline south of Cape Flattery on the Olympia Peninsula, the Pacific highway to lands far to the south. The extent of deglaciation is also unknown, though there was probably ice-free passage as early as 16,000 years ago, the entire coast being ice free after 13,400 BP. We have, of course, little idea of the maritime conditions along the coast during the millennia immediately after the Ice Age, but whatever they were, they would have been a severe challenge to skin boats, which in modern times were not used south of Yukutat on the central Alaskan coast.

Alternatively, could people have passed southward along the Pacific continental shelf exposed by low sea levels? The extensive tracts of open tundra along the shelf might have attracted terrestrial hunters from the interior, who then moved southward past the ice sheets, and relied to some extent on fish and sea mammals. Unfortunately the evidence of human passage lies below modern sea level. We have only a few hints of early human settlement, among them two sites on Haida Gwaii in British Columbia dating to about 13,800 years ago. Both genetics and a growing number of dated DNA samples hint at rapid population growth and dispersal of humans throughout the Americas between about 14,500 and 13,000 years ago. Certainly by 13,000 years BP people were visiting Santa Rosa Island, on the outer side of the Santa Barbara Channel in southern California (Johnson *et al.*, 2001). Most experts now believe the coast was settled very early on, especially as there are traces of human settlement on the Peruvian coast and in Chile far to the south as early as 14,000 years BP.

A Faint Signature

The "signature" of the first Americans south of the ice sheets is practically invisible. Decades of ardent searching have produced only a handful of sites that date to earlier than 12,000 years ago. Nearly all we know of them comes from scatters of stone tools, a reflection of people constantly on the move. The evidence comes to us in shreds and patches (see Box: Some Pre-Clovis Sites). One group of them visited the Paisley Five Mile Point in Oregon's Cascade Mountains. They left a scatter of their feces behind them that may date to as early as 14,290 years ago. Fort Rock Cave, also in Oregon, has dates as early as 9000 BCE, and perhaps earlier, undated occupation too. The meticulously excavated Meadowcroft **rockshelter** in Pennsylvania is said to have been occupied as early as 14,500 years ago. The Cactus Hill site in Virginia is claimed to date to 15,000 years BP or even earlier. The Page-Ladson site in northeast Florida, where a group of hunters killed or scavenged a mastodon, dates to 14,550 years ago.

These initial forays into an uninhabited continent must have involved adaptations to a broad range of environments. Computer modeling suggests that

SOME PRE-CLOVIS SITES

The term "Pre-Clovis" sites reflects the lingering dominance of "Clovis first" in archaeologists' thinking. "Clovis first" has long been discredited in the face of a steady increase in the number of Pre-Clovis sites that have been documented beyond question. Here is a list of some, but certainly not all, of the known ones.

Cactus Hill, Virginia
A sand-dune site on the Nottaway River. A Clovis layer is underlain by a layer with charcoal concentrations, a hearth, and lanceolate stone points. The layer is said to date to between 15,070 and 16,670 years ago. If this dating is confirmed, the Pre-Clovis Cactus Hill level is one of the earliest human occupations in the Americas.

Fort Rock Cave, Oregon
Near to Paisley Cave, Fort Rock has long been claimed to have had

human occupation around 15,000 years ago. Recent research has shown that the earliest well-dated visits occurred around 8500 to 7200 BCE (Connelly *et al.*, 2017).

Little Salt Spring, Florida
A freshwater limestone-solution pit near Charlotte Harbor in southwestern Florida. Here a shell from an extinct tortoise impaled with a wooden shaft dates to 12,000 to 13,000 years ago.

Manis, Washington
From here we have a mastodon rib with a projectile point embedded in it dating to about 12,000 BP.

The four sites above confirm human occupation in diverse environments by 12,000 years ago, before Clovis times. There are also some indications of even earlier occupation, described on p. 58. »

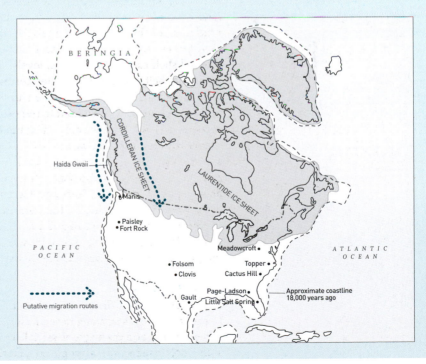

2.8 Possible migration routes of the first Americans. The two great ice sheets—the Cordilleran, centered on the Rocky Mountains, and the Laurentide, which covered central and eastern Canada—mantled the landscape as far south as the Seattle region and the Great Lakes; much of Alaska, however, was ice free.

early settlers took the least arduous routes into unknown territory that gave them the best chances of finding food and stone for making tools. The carrying capacity of most landscapes was low, so the Americas could have been traversed and filled up by hunter-gatherer populations fairly quickly, perhaps in about 2,000 years from the date of first arrival. The process of settlement could have taken place linearly, with bands splitting off from one territory as population densities increased, traveling along main lines of spread and then branching out into neighboring areas. The earliest known sites, however, are scattered thinly over very large regions, not in lines. This makes a form of "leapfrog model" more plausible, in which hunter-gatherer groups fissioned from one territory into another, often separated from the original one by long distances. This model

Meadowcroft, Pennsylvania

A rock shelter that was used sporadically for thousands of years (Figure 2.9). The Pre-Clovis occupation dates to as early as 14,500 years ago. The site was used until about 700 years ago (Adovasio *et al.*, 1981). Very carefully investigated, this is a convincing chronicle of Pre-Clovis occupation, though some authorities have questioned the early chronology.

Paisley Cave, Oregon

This site offers a scatter of human feces dating to between 14,270 and 14,000 years ago (Figure 2.10). The DNA

2.9 Meadowcroft rockshelter, Pennsylvania. An overhead view of the excavations in 1973.

matches the DNA haplogroups in Native Americans. A bone, scraper-like tool apparently dates to the same time. There is later Clovis occupation. Paisley offers convincing evidence of Pre-Clovis visitors (Jenkins, 2016).

Page-Ladson, Florida

Located in layers of mud, shell, and mastodon dung in the bottom of the Aucilla River, human artifacts were used to kill or scavenge a mastodon next to a sinkhole pond about 14,550 years ago (Halligan *et al.*, 2016).

Topper Site, South Carolina

Topper lies on the Savannah River, and contains a Clovis level with a level with small blades below. **Optical Stimulated Luminescence (OSL)** dates from the lower horizon are in the 15,000- to 16,000-year-old range (Adovasio and Page, 2002). Questions have been raised about the OSL chronology, but the site may be one of the earliest in North America.

2.10 Paisley Cave in the Cascade Mountains, Oregon. Human feces from the cave have been radiocarbon dated to about 14,000 years ago, one of the earliest records of human occupation in the Americas.

would explain the wide separation of very early sites, with uninhabited areas between them that were filled in by later generations.

As research progresses, so the number of radiocarbon dates proliferates, making it possible to carry out statistical analyses of them in groups. The Canadian Archaeological Radiocarbon Database (CARD) has records of over 36,000 dates covering 13,000 years. This wealth of data will make it possible to study changes in population density and growth over both short and longer periods (Chaput *et al.*, 2015). First results are promising, despite many limitations connected with sampling and survival of data, and the information is becoming more robust as research methods are refined and the number of dates on the database increases. The analyses produce radiocarbon frequency population estimates (RFPEs) that so far correspond well with what is known from archaeological discoveries. In the case of first settlement, RFPEs increase sharply along the British Columbia coast around 9500 BCE, which agrees quite closely with archaeological data. A second increase occurs around 5500 BCE as sea levels stabilized.

In southeastern North America RFPEs increase, then shift northward and eastward after 7500 BCE. This confirms that there was a significant **Paleo-Indian** presence in the Southeast before 8000 BCE, and another Paleo-Indian concentration in what is now Atlantic Canada between 11,000 and 10,000 BCE. (The generic term Paleo-Indian conventionally refers to the first human settlers of the Americas, up to about 5000 BCE.) Then the **Younger Dryas** interval—a cold, dry period that began about 12,950 years ago and lasted roughly a millennium—brought lower RFPEs, until warmer temperatures saw population grow again. In the central and western United States, Paleo-Indian RFPEs are high until 10,000 BCE, with an increase in California after 8000 BCE that lasted until 5700 BCE, perhaps due to the consumption of maritime foods.

This new, statistically based data coincides in general terms what we know from archaeology of first settlement. The overall continental population grew after 10,500 BCE in Alaska, the northeast, and the western Plains, with the maps generated by research so far showing the particular importance of coastal landscapes as well. Many challenges remain, but this new avenue of inquiry may in due course add accurate information about migration patterns, as well as linking human activities to such phenomena as megafaunal extinctions, declines and changes in ecosystems, and varying climatic conditions.

Clovis and Others

Around 11,200 BCE, we arrive on much firmer historical ground with a veritable explosion of Paleo-Indian archaeological sites. The highly distinctive Clovis culture appeared all over eastern North America, on the Great Plains, and much further afield. It was the only cultural tradition that thrived, albeit briefly, through the whole of North America. These Paleo-Indian people are the first relatively well-documented inhabitants of the Americas. Many questions remain about their ancestry and lifeway, but what is certain is that the Clovis culture was relatively short-lived.

Clovis appeared suddenly and flourished for only around 250 years, between about 13,050 and 12,800 years ago. There is some controversy over the chronology, with some experts believing that Clovis began several centuries earlier. Thanks to the Clovis people's distinctive fluted projectile points, we know that their technology spread rapidly across North America, if the radiocarbon dates

THE GAULT SITE, TEXAS

The meticulously excavated Gault site in central Texas is redefining our understanding of the Clovis culture. It is a large site, covering about 39 acres (16 ha), a place where people lived intermittently for 11,000 years (Figure 2.11). It lies in the Buttermilk Creek drainage area, at the head of a small valley where there are reliable springs, and, just as important, an abundant supply of high-quality **chert** (a fine-grained rock used for toolmaking). This well-watered and tree-covered location contrasts with the much drier landscape of the nearby uplands.

Clovis people visited the Gault location for about three centuries (the precise dates are still unknown). The big attraction beyond water was probably the chert, which they fashioned into a wide array of projectile points with the distinctive Clovis fluting. These were broad-spectrum hunter-gatherers: they took bison, horse, and mammoth, but also a wide variety of smaller animals, including birds, frogs, and rodents. Interestingly, the earliest residents seem to have pursued horse and mammoth, whereas the later occupants hunted no big game other than bison, and concentrated on smaller animals instead. But their flexible toolkit—used, so edge-wear studies tell us, for digging, cutting grass, and woodworking—remained unchanged once larger animals either became extinct or less important. About a third of a mile (500 m) downstream, the 13,000-year-old Debra L. Friedkin site has both Clovis and later occupations and is thought to have been a short-term production camp for roughing out stone tools.

Lower strata at Gault contain tantalizing traces of even earlier, but undated, visitors, perhaps dating to as early as 15,500 years ago, but it is not known whether they were Clovis or people from a different cultural tradition. After the Clovis occupation, later Paleo-Indian visitors were followed by others, with evidence of sporadic visits up to about 4,000 years ago. Gault is a unique and well dated chronicle of Pre-Clovis and Clovis visits to a favored location.

2.11 Excavations at the Gault site, Texas, showing excavation in progress along the south edge of the site, near a spot where Clovis points were found in association with mammoth bones. The lowest, pale, zone contains numerous Clovis artifacts, also bison, horse, and mammoth bones dating to 12,000 to 13,600 years ago.

are to be trusted. These peripatetic hunter-gatherers dropped, at recent count, at least 4,400 projectile points at numerous locations. They camped on low terraces along rivers and streams, in places where game came to feed and plant foods were abundant. The densest concentrations lie around the Cumberland, Tennessee, and Ohio river valleys in the east, where stone outcrops were commonplace. Fewer finds occur elsewhere, but everywhere population densities were low, which is what one would expect of mobile people who preferred areas where food resources were locally abundant. Many bands may have lived on coastal plains—now sunken continental shelves—where, conceivably, they relied heavily on marine resources. Inland, a few Clovis sites, like the much-visited Gault location in central Texas, reached a considerable size (Walters and Pevny, 2011) (see Box: The Gault Site, Texas).

Fluted Clovis points are one of the iconic artifacts of ancient North America, but their makers remain something of an enigma. They were clearly versatile hunter-gatherers who could kill animals of all sizes, as well as subsisting off plant foods and perhaps fish near lakes and coasts. Bringing down a large beast like a mammoth was probably a rare event, perhaps experienced but once in a lifetime. We have tended to look at Clovis people through what Douglas Bamforth (2018) aptly calls "mammoth-colored glasses." Earlier researches focused on sites where large animal bones were discovered, which created the myth of Clovis people as large-mammal hunters *par excellence*. They were not. More recent excavations on other sites have made it clear that Clovis people took a wide range of prey as well as eating wild plants of all kinds. Unfortunately details are in short supply. Whether they contributed to megafaunal extinction is a much-debated issue (see Box: The Mystery of Megafaunal Extinction).

Mammoth were an attractive quarry, for a single animal could provide meat for weeks on end, and, if dried, for much of the winter too. Hides, tusks, bones, and pelts were used to make household possessions and weapons, for shelter, and for clothing. Precious fat from the internal organs could be melted down and used for cooking and burning in lamps—just as it was thousands of years before on the steppe-tundra of Eurasia. Most Clovis mammoth kills lie on low ground, near creeks, springs, or ponds. Generation after generation, the elephants

THE MYSTERY OF MEGAFAUNAL EXTINCTION

An impressive bestiary of large animals thrived in Ice Age North America: the so-called Pleistocene megafauna. Camelids, mastodon, horses, and bison were among the large beasts that survived the end of the last glaciation, then rapidly became extinct, except for bison, which thrived in the semi-arid environments of the Plains. Why did the megafauna vanish abruptly at about the time when Clovis people appeared? A generation ago, Paul Martin of the University of Arizona unleashed a long-running controversy when he argued that Clovis hunters had devastated the lumbering, slow-breeding megafauna with excessive hunting, then driven them to extinction before suffering a population crash themselves. A compelling image, to be sure, but new research and more precise dating methods tell us that the extinctions may have resulted, at least in part, from the climate change of the Younger Dryas. Moreover, there is not actually any evidence for a collapse in the human population.

These 1,000 years of much colder conditions arrived without warning, perhaps within a few generations. Increased aridity and major environmental changes may have impacted upon populations of larger animals. Cores from an Indiana lake provide an exotic insight. The fungus *Sporomiella* passes through animals' digestive systems to complete its life cycle. The cores show the spores disappearing between 14,800 and 13,700 years ago as new plants, such as oaks, took root. The new vegetation appeared as grazing by large animals ceased. This research, if confirmed, is convincing evidence of the effects of environmental change on Ice Age animals. Another flamboyant theory envisages an enormous asteroid hitting earth during Clovis times, devastating both animals and people. Huge brush fires are said to have formed a black layer, with high iridium and other concentrations, found at some Clovis sites. Few archaeologists espouse this far-fetched hypothesis.

The megafaunal extinction theory may seem esoteric, for it is still unclear to what extent people were responsible for the disappearance of large animals across North America. But whether caused by climate change or human predation, the vanishing megafauna are a sobering warning of the destructive effects of both climate and human activity on the animal world, when today dozens of mammalian species are under threat from our actions. The resolution of this long-standing debate will come from research not by archaeologists, but by biologists expert in population dynamics, and molecular biologists studying ancient and modern DNA.

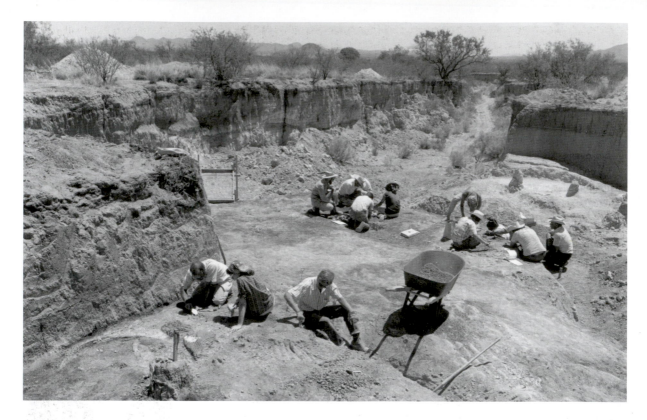

2.12 A classic Clovis bison and mammoth kill site at Murray Springs, Arizona. The archaeologists unearthed eleven beasts, which would have yielded enough meat to feed fifty to one hundred people, but probably many fewer. Clovis hunters were clearly shrewd observers of mammoth behavior. Perhaps they followed matriarchal groups for weeks, observing individual beasts with care. They would presumably catch them off guard, then cull the herd one by one at the same location over a period of years.

would return to the same salt licks, waterholes, trails, and favored patches of vegetation. The hunters could have ambushed them at watering places, where the soft ground impeded movement (Figure 2.12).

The fluted point itself may be a local invention that developed on the Great Plains or in the Southwest. Examples that occur in Alaska are later, perhaps introduced by people moving northward in pursuit of bison (Figures 2.13 and 2.14). The Clovis toolkit, which included bone, ivory, and probably hunting nets and bags, generally reflects a mobile lifeway, where everything had to be carried on one's person. That includes the large **bifaces** that served as a kind of "savings bank" from which one could strike blades or blanks for projectile points. (Bifaces are artifacts, usually spearheads or arrow points, flaked on both surfaces to thin them.)

Clovis stoneworkers cherished fine-grained toolmaking stone, relying heavily on high-quality chert, jasper, and obsidian, fine-grained rocks that were ideal for making weapons. They knew their sources and traveled considerable distances to obtain raw material. In one well-known example, Clovis points left in a cache in northeastern Colorado were made of dolomite from the Texas Panhandle, 364 miles (585 km) away. Perhaps caches were a precaution taken when hunting in new territories, often far from known stone outcrops, the dumps being a form of insurance against running out of raw material for weaponry.

As archaeologist David Meltzer (2008) has pointed out, population densities must have been low in these early days, and the learning curve in unfamiliar environments very steep. Just learning the edible and medicinal properties of even a small number of the over 30,000 plant varieties in North America would

2.13 Clovis points found with the Naco mammoth kill, Arizona. The beast had eight Clovis points in its carcass, four times more than any other known kill. Perhaps it escaped wounded, only to die later. If each point belonged to an individual hunter, then at least eight men attacked the beast, or four if each released two spears.

have required considerable trial and error. Many natural environments in the Americas are unpredictable, with food resources occurring in broadly separated patches. Under such circumstances one would expect a rapid dispersal of hunter-gatherers across the landscape. Each group would have needed extensive, flexible social contacts, both to gain intelligence about food and water supplies, and also as a means of finding marriage partners. The widespread distribution of Clovis points across so much of the Americas may reflect such social networks—though we must still imagine a world where one only encountered a few other small groups of people in the course of one's life. These circumstances, however, did not last long. By 10,500 years ago well-defined regional projectile point forms had appeared across North America, many of them associated with distinctive cultural adaptations.

The Younger Dryas—that 1,000-year cold snap—had a profound impact on the Northern Hemisphere. Temperatures fell, ice sheets advanced somewhat, and there were widespread droughts. This was when parched hunter-gatherer societies in southwest Asia took up cereal agriculture. The effects on the sparse human population of North America, though still little understood, were surely considerable. At the beginning of the Younger Dryas the short-lived Clovis Tradition diversified rapidly into numerous local cultures, scattered human populations that thrived across the continent's diverse landscapes. As temperatures warmed after the Younger Dryas, so North America's biotic communities gradually assumed their modern configurations, a process that was over by about 5,000 years ago. Meanwhile, human populations increased. Knowledge of the land and its flora and fauna became ever more encyclopedic, and ways of wresting a living from diverse environments stabilized for thousands of years.

By this time, human settlement of North America was well established. As *Homo sapiens* had done in other parts of the world, the first Americans

2.14 Clovis points from Lehner, Arizona, and Blackwater Draw. The length of the Lehner point is approximately 3.5 in. (9 cm). Classic Clovis points were ground along the base and part of the sides, presumably to reduce wear on the shaft binding. Fluted points vary very considerably because of "cultural drift" as people spread across North America.

adapted brilliantly to a remarkable array of challenging landscapes. The great diversity of Native American societies in later millennia developed from these successful adaptations.

SUMMARY

- The first settlement of North America took place during, and at the end of, the last glaciation from extreme northeast Siberia. The date of first settlement is still uncertain, but was probably around or slightly before 14,000 years ago, even if there were occasional brief visits to Alaska somewhat earlier, during the LGM.

- Siberia and Alaska were joined by a land bridge, the core of a continent known as Beringia. The Beringian Standstill Hypothesis, based on genetics and other sources, argues that the land bridge (Central Beringia) was a refuge for broad-spectrum hunter-gatherers of Siberian origin.

- As conditions warmed up, small human populations moved into Alaska and then southward, as the great North American ice sheets retreated. These sporadic southward movements passed down the Pacific Coast at an unknown date, by at least 14,000 years ago. The settlers spread rapidly through the Americas, and were in South America within a millennium or so.

- There are few traces of the tiny Pre-Clovis populations. What knowledge we have comes from isolated archaeological finds from the Pacific Northwest to Florida. These little-known people settled in a wide variety of environments.

- The Clovis Tradition, known for its distinctive fluted points, spread widely in North America over a period of about 250 years, from 13,050 to 12,800 years ago. These were broad-spectrum hunter-gatherers who subsisted off a wide variety of animal and plant foods.

- Whether the first Americans and the Clovis people were responsible for the final extinction of large game animals, "megafauna," in North America is still an open question, though more arid conditions were clearly an important factor.

After Clovis

The Great Plains, early summer, c. 7000 BCE. Hundreds of bison graze on the seemingly endless grassland, their tails swishing away clouds of flies. They move in small groups, the young staying close to their mothers. Four young men from two bands armed with stone-tipped spears lie in the grass downwind, taking careful note of the gentle southerly breeze. Each knows the terrain intimately, the hidden gully that lies invisible near the grazing beasts. They have watched the bison for days, can even recognize individual beasts. The next morning, as dawn breaks, the two bands, which have come together for the hunt, fan out quietly on the flanks of a small herd. A quiet signal and men and women rise to their feet, waving hides. The animals look up and move downwind, as the leader becomes alarmed. Everyone closes in as the herd stampedes in clouds of dust. They fall helter-skelter into the hidden defile, a narrow mountain passage, legs flailing helplessly. The waiting hunters move in, stabbing trapped beasts with razor-sharp spears, jumping nimbly away from their kicking victims. A few beasts scramble clear and gallop away. One tosses a young man with his horns. His leg breaks as he lands in the narrow gully. The hunters dispatch the remaining prey with expert skill.

This chapter is a story of brilliant adaptations to the highly diverse environments of North America after about 9000 BCE. The climate had warmed after the brief chill of the Younger Dryas. In the north the great ice sheets had retreated deep into what is now Canada. Accelerating warming brought dramatic changes in rainfall patterns, sea levels, and vegetation throughout North America. Temperate woodlands spread northward as the great ice sheets continued their retreat. Continental shelves vanished inexorably as the Atlantic and Pacific rose. Aridity in the west intensified. Greater environmental diversity throughout North America presented profound challenges to Paleo-Indians living in isolated bands with little contact with other humans. How did the North Americans adapt to these changed circumstances? Their varied responses and remarkable opportunism laid the foundations for the great array of North American societies in later millennia.

If there was a long-term climatic trend beyond warming, it was toward less rainfall, especially in the west (Shuman and Marsicek, 2016). The gradual drying had a profound impact on the broad-spectrum hunter-gatherers. Those who had preyed on the now-extinct megafauna, albeit only occasionally, now survived by broadening their food quests and paying close attention to smaller animals, fish and mollusks, and to wild plant foods of all kinds. Their predecessors had developed an intimate knowledge of the natural environments of their new homeland. This hard-won experience of animal and plant foods, and of such essentials as fine-grained toolmaking stone, formed the basis for seemingly effort-less adaptations by North America's sparse human population to a remarkable variety of natural environments. The successors of the first Americans, in ever larger numbers, adapted successfully to everything from deserts and semi-arid landscapes to fertile river floodplains with a broad array of food resources, to coastlines with rich inshore fisheries, and to arctic environments where small bands survived subzero cold for months on end. Some peoples dwelling in arid regions found the edibility of potential foodstuffs often hard to discern and difficult to process. Other groups thrived off such relatively predictable foods as the spring and fall salmon runs. Life was never easy; conservative hunting and gathering strategies were essential for survival. Risk management by diversifying one's diet and using careful opportunism underpinned every society's daily life. Every type of precious knowledge passed from generation to generation by word of mouth.

This conservatism, and concern for survival, lay behind every adaptation to North America's environments, however richly endowed. The foundations of many hunter-gatherer societies that survived into the twentieth century lie deep in the remote past, as far back as the warming at the end of the Ice Age after 10,000 years ago. We can only view brief snapshots of these varied and successful adaptations as they developed in changing landscapes of all kinds (Figure 3.1; see Box: Culture Areas and Broad Subdivisions, pp. 68–69).

3.1 Map showing archaeological sites mentioned in Chapter 3.

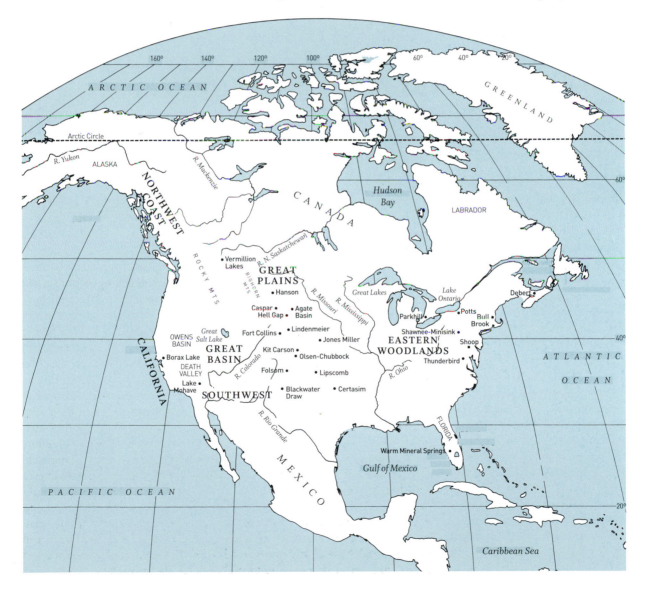

Folsom People and Others on the Plains: c. 10,800 to 6900 BCE

The successors of the Clovis people thrived on a great tract of grassland that extended from the frontiers of Alaska to the shores of the Gulf of Mexico. This was the "Great Bison Belt," which lay in the rain shadow east of the Rocky Mountains. Spring and early summer rains supported, and still support, short grasses that keep much of their biomass beneath the surface. Such grass retains moisture at the roots, so grazing animals can find high-quality nutrients in the dry fall. Bison succeeded where other Ice Age animals failed: they became short-grass feeders as this type of grassland expanded during and after the Younger

CULTURE AREAS AND BROAD SUBDIVISIONS

Archaeologists are classifiers and sub-dividers by necessity. Since the beginnings of North American archaeology during the nineteenth century, they have been much preoccupied with a basic problem of placing ancient American societies in time and space. Fortunately, the development of radiocarbon dating and the herculean efforts of field and laboratory archaeologists between the 1920s and 1960s have provided us with a simple way to subdivide the continent into general culture areas and a basic framework of broad cultural stages.

A word to the wise: take a careful look at both the culture areas and the stages! We use them freely in the pages that follow!

Culture Areas

The major culture areas are largely self-evident and coincide in general terms with major environmental zones (Figure 3.2). The Arctic and Subarctic, the Plains, Southwest, and Eastern Woodlands are largely self-evident. The Eastern Woodland is divided into the Northeast and Southeast. In the west the situation is more complex, with the Northwest Coast, the Plateau, and California being marked by considerable environmental diversity. California has

a distinctive coastal zone (described in Chapter 5), with an arid interior that passes imperceptibly into the Great Basin. Each culture area had its own ancient societies, defined in part by their distinctive adaptations to local environmental challenges.

Cultural Stages

The ancient North Americans developed a great diversity of hunter-gatherer and farming societies over 14,000 years. Classifying them even in general terms is a nightmare. The general stages listed here were widely used when culture history ruled North American archaeology. They are still commonly employed as convenient terms, so you need to know what they signify. Let us take a closer look at the terms that were developed after years of debate.

Two terms are used throughout North America:

Paleo-Indian (generally before 8000 BCE). Human cultures ancestral to later (Archaic) developments. This very generalized term includes the first Americans, the Clovis people and other pre-Archaic groups.

Archaic Archaic cultures evolved from Paleo-Indian ones, so the boundary between the two is nearly impossible to draw. Archaic peoples hunted smaller, more varied animals, placed greater

emphasis on plant foods, and developed toolkits for processing them. Archaic cultures became increasingly diverse and often specialized to adapt to local environments. Archaic cultures survived in some parts of the west until modern times.

Two other terms are commonly used in the Eastern Woodlands culture area:

Woodland (c. 1000 BCE onward). This term subsumes many local adaptations. Generally, the label Woodland implies hunter-gatherer societies augmented with some cultivation, manufacture of some clay vessels, more elaborate tools and art traditions, and also cemetery burials, often associated with earthen mounds. They engaged in more advanced trade activities.

Mississippian (after 800 CE). The Woodland continued in many areas of the east until European contact, but by 800 CE the Mississippian Tradition replaces it in the Midsouth, between the Mississippi River and the Appalachians (see Chapter 12).

Let us stress that these are only general terms, but they are useful when looking at the broader picture, as this book does.

Dryas. After an initial population increase, bison numbers may have fallen; the herds tended to congregate in larger numbers, but were unpredictably mobile owing to drier conditions. By 8500 BCE, the Plains Paleo-Indians had narrowed much of their hunting to bison, as well as deer, pronghorn antelope, and smaller animals, including rodents. For all their ardent hunting, however, they remained broad-spectrum hunter-gatherers, just like their Clovis predecessors. There was no other way to survive in demanding environments of dramatic seasonal contrasts.

As Clovis vanished, Folsom hunters—also using fluted points, but of different design—pursued bison over a wide area. One prime bison parkland habitat was

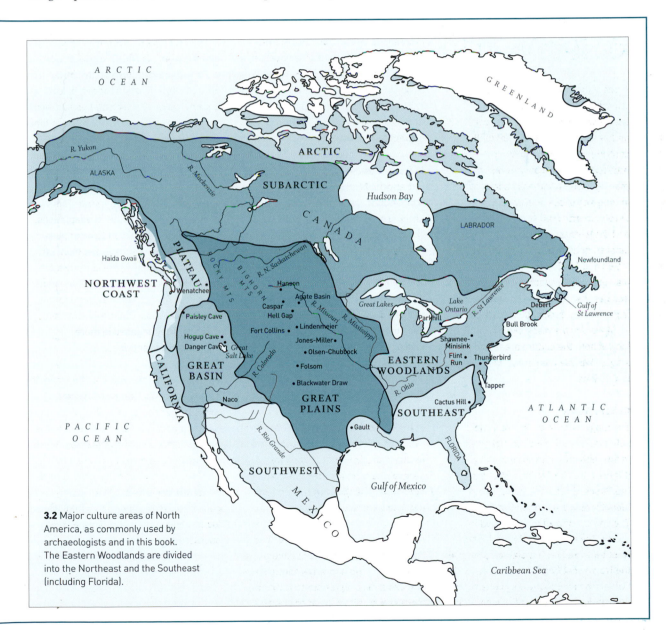

3.2 Major culture areas of North America, as commonly used by archaeologists and in this book. The Eastern Woodlands are divided into the Northeast and the Southeast (including Florida).

3.3 Excavations at Hell Gap, Wyoming.

at Folsom, New Mexico, itself, where a group of hunters worked a steep-sided **arroyo** and a small tributary in about 8500 BCE (Meltzer, 2006). Here they killed thirty-two members of a cow-calf herd in peak condition during the fall. They then butchered the animals, carrying off many of the rib racks, leaving the butchered carcasses in the arroyo, where they were soon buried under wind-blown sand. After staying for several days, the group departed. No trace of their camp has come to light despite an intensive search. Occasional mass drives of bison herds involving several bands yielded great quantities of meat and other products. These must have been memorable events.

Conducting bison drives is a difficult art, especially on foot. Most likely, a combination of solo and cooperative hunting ensured a regular supply of bison flesh. When left alone, bison soon become less fearful of humans. Subjected continuously to pursuit, however, they become unpredictable and far harder to drive. The hunters were probably careful to pursue the herds intermittently, driving them small distances, giving them time to calm down. Modern bison can be moved a mile or so without trouble; then they start to break and run, when it is almost impossible to stop them. Thus, large-scale game drives probably required careful organization. Perhaps the best-known Folsom site is the Hanson site in the northern Bighorn Basin of central Wyoming. Here, three hard-packed areas may be the remains of circular lodge structures. They have been radiocarbon dated to at least 8000 BCE (Frison and Bradley, 1981).

Hell Gap is a small valley near Guernsey, southeastern Wyoming. Paleo-Indians camped at four locations here repeatedly between about 9000 and 5500 BCE (Larson and Kornfeld, 2009). No other Paleo-Indian location contains such a long record of Plains peoples after Clovis times. Discovered and excavated during the 1960s, Hell Gap vanished into archaeological obscurity until the 1990s, when new excavations brought an impressive team of specialists to the site (Figure 3.3). We now know that the Hell Gap Valley was wetter in Paleo-Indian times, with cooler temperatures than today. This was not a kill site, but a place where people processed hides and parts of bison carcasses brought back to camp. We can imagine hunters hefting complete bison limbs into the valley from a nearby kill. They throw them on the ground, then deftly disarticulate them and break the bones to get at the rich fatty marrow within. Meanwhile, other members of the band stagger under the weight of a bison hide. They unroll it, and then peg it out on the ground. Scrape, scrape: the sound of the women working over the hide with stone scrapers continues for hours on end. So does the sharp clicking noise of stoneworkers roughing out blanks for stone projectile points from chert and quartzite outcrops conveniently nearby.

Bison drives most often must have involved several bands, who provided the people-power and enough men and women to butcher the dead animals, often a huge task. A skilled group of hunters could subject a quarry herd to gentle influences over periods of days, moving them a little way in the right direction when conditions were favorable. They would line the approach with decoys, with shouting men and women, while hunters dressed in bison hides would approach the unsuspecting animals. Once the drive began, the hunters would run and shout, even wave skins at the thundering herd. Clouds of dust rose from the plain as the sheer mass and weight of the herd forced the leaders into a narrow gully to their deaths. At Casper, Wyoming, in about 8000 BCE, the hunters used

THE OLSEN-CHUBBOCK BISON KILL, COLORADO, *c.* 7400 BCE

What was it like to stampede and kill a herd of bison without bows, guns, or horses? Fortunately, a chance discovery by an amateur archaeologist allowed archaeologist Joe Ben Wheat (1972) to excavate the remains of a successful bison hunt of 7400 BCE near Kit Carson, Colorado, many years ago. No fewer than 100 females and 80 males perished in the drive. Of these, 58 percent were adult, 34 percent immature, and 8 percent calves (Figure 3.4).

The mass of bones in the buried arroyo was so well preserved that Wheat was able to study both complete skeletons and individual body parts. The meticulous, bone-by-bone dissection of the kill took far longer than the actual excavation of the remains. Wheat reconstructed a complete portrait of the butchery. When the killing of the helpless animals was over, men and women pushed, levered, and shoved the more accessible beasts onto the flat. Sometimes, they removed articulated body parts, such as forelimbs, to make the process simpler. Once they had removed the more accessible beasts, they dismembered the remaining bodies jammed into the narrow arroyo.

The butchery was a well-ordered routine (Figure 3.5). Each beast was rolled onto its belly, the dismembered limbs propping the body upright. Then the butchers cut the skin along the back and stripped it off the sides before cutting it in half to serve as a "table" for the meat. By inventorying the bone piles, Wheat found that the forelimbs lay at the bottom, having been removed first, and was able to reconstruct the order in which the meat was removed from each carcass. The butchers used detached feet as crude hatchets, just as historic Plains people did. As they worked, they feasted on the fresh meat, especially the tongues, then and in the more recent past considered a great delicacy. Ethnographic observations of Blackfoot butchers suggest that it took about an hour to butcher a single bison. Wheat estimated that it would have taken ten men less than three days to butcher the 140 complete and only partially accessible carcasses.

The butchery proceeded at considerable speed, almost like an assembly line, with much of the meat being fried as butchery continued. Using modern figures for usable meat from male and female bison, Wheat estimated that the hunters acquired about 63,120 lb (26,635 kg) of fresh meat from the kill. In addition, the hunters acquired about 772 lb (350 kg) of marrow grease and 5,038 lb (2,285 kg of

3.4 The Olsen-Chubbock bone bed, Colorado.

tallow. Wheat estimated that between 150 and 200 people were involved in the hunt, if they had no dogs to transport the meat, perhaps 75 to 100 if they had them.

Olsen-Chubbock is one of many known kills, but one of the most vivid. As Wheat wrote many years ago: "One could almost visualize the dust and tumult of the hunt...almost smell the stench of the rotting carcasses...Time seemed, indeed to be stilled for an interval, and a microcosm of the hunters' life preserved."

3.5 Paleo-Indian butchery. The hunters skinned the bison down the back to get at the tender meat below (thatched area). Then they cut free the forelegs and shoulder blades (1), also the hump, rib meat, and inner organs (2) (3). They then severed the spine and pelvis (4), also the hind legs (5). Finally, the neck and skull were cut away for pemmican (6).

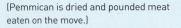

(Pemmican is dried and pounded meat eaten on the move.)

a parabolic sand dune with steep, loose sides to trap a herd of about 100 bison in late fall, then killed them as fast as they could, each hunter or group of hunters selecting an individual beast, then spearing it through the heart (Figure 3.6) (Frison, 2013). (For a classic example of a kill site, see Box: The Olsen-Chubbock Bison Kill, Colorado, *c.* 7400 BCE.)

Game drives make for spectacular archaeological sites. Indeed, a great deal of Plains archaeology revolves around deciphering these dramatic events, but

3.6 The Casper site, Wyoming. (a) Looking into the northeast and leeward end of part of the trough of the old parabolic sand dune containing the bison. (b) Close-up of butchered bison skeletons.

UNDERSTANDING PROJECTILE POINTS

Finely made stone projectile points made between about 11,400 and 7000 BCE come in numerous forms. They vary in size and shape over wide areas of North America and are the subject of an extensive specialized literature that attempts to classify them into different cultural traditions and to date them (Hranicky, 2015, is a very basic guide, unfortunately aimed mainly at collectors. See also Lyman, 2009). The task is enormous. More than 11,000 Clovis points alone are known, mostly surface finds and most commonly from major river valleys and the slopes of the Appalachian Mountains in the west. Projectile points formed between 10 and 20 percent of a very simple, highly portable toolkit. At least

seven forms of later Paleo-Indian points are known after 10,000 BCE. To what extent these represent actual cultural differences is a matter for discussion, especially when we realize that scrapers of different forms, used for processing hides and woodworking, formed 20 to 54 percent of some toolkits, depending on the activity at the site. Then there are stone knives, which are often hard to distinguish from projectile points.

Clovis points are the earliest heads, usually made on narrow blades, carefully thinned by using pressure to remove flakes and thin the stone. A single flake, or flute, was removed from the concave base. Contrast Clovis points with Folsom specimens, which have been found in later layers above Clovis occupation on the Great Plains. Folsom points were also carefully made, but with a much

that is simply because the artifacts and bones occasionally survive for excavation. It would be misleading to think of these Plains societies solely as bison hunters. Folsom groups flourished in a wide variety of environments, everything from high-elevation basins in the Rocky Mountains to prairie woodlands east of the Plains grasslands. Like all foragers, they were opportunists: as well as taking deer and other animals, they also, on occasion, took fish and mollusks; plant foods were a staple. They would return to the same locations—wetlands, for example—over many generations, favoring those where a broad range of foods could be found.

The Folsom Tradition, with its distinctive projectile points, occurs over a very wide area. Experts assume that the Folsom Tradition originated in Clovis, but no intermediate projectile-head forms have come to light in closely dated sites. As populations rose, so local variations on the Folsom cultural tradition developed, which are still little known. There were several contemporary Plains cultures, some predominantly bison hunters, others adapted to hunting and foraging in foothill and mountain areas at the edge of the Plains, also to woodland environments on the eastern fringes of the grasslands. We know of these various traditions almost entirely through different projectile-point forms, known under various local labels (see Box: Understanding Projectile Points).

Given that we mainly have stone artifacts to work with, it is nearly impossible to study the details of Paleo-Indian cultural change on the Plains. The size and mobility of the herds increased. Clovis groups were widely dispersed and in small numbers. In contrast Folsom bands may have come together more frequently for communal hunts at favored locations. Bamforth (2018) argues that social

APPROXIMATE CHRONOLOGY OF MAJOR PLAINS PROJECTILE POINTS

Years CE/BCE (cal)	11,400 BCE	10,900 BCE	10,000 BCE	8500 BCE	8250 BCE	7500 BCE	7000 BCE
Point Type	Clovis	Folsom	Midland Firstview, San Jon Agate Basin	Hell Gap	Alberta	Frederick-Firstview Cody Knife Scottsbluff, Eden	Jimmy Allen Cascade

Clovis — Folsom — Midland — Agate Basin — Hell Gap — Frederick — Scottsbluff — Eden

3.7 Some of the major Plains Paleo-Indian projectile forms.

complexity increased as a result, only to decrease as conditions became drier and game drives became rarer, less predictable events. Folsom hunters appear to have relied on more sophisticated weapons, but, as rainfall decreased, so the quality of stonework declined, as exchange of raw materials and finely made artifacts virtually ceased, and people were forced to make their own. Basic hunting and foraging strategies changed but little over thousands of years until the advent of the horse altered the equations of human existence fundamentally.

The Western Interior: 10,000 BCE to Modern Times

The men removed the dried fish from the seemingly ordinary food cache in the cave the evening before. Then they rummaged below the false bottom of the storage pit and lifted out their precious feathered duck decoys and snares. They carefully cleaned the bone tubes that would serve as snorkels in the hours ahead. Long before dawn, they crouched in the reeds around the lake, pushing their decoys out in the still water, wearing some of them on their heads. A few of the hunters slipped into the lake, leaving not even a ripple, moving silently toward the sleeping waterfowl. Imperceptibly, the human "birds" approached their prey, breathing carefully through their snorkels. Suddenly, a duck would vanish below the surface, grabbed by the legs, its neck wrung in seconds, the still-twitching prey quickly pushed into a netting bag. Decoys looking just like real birds moved quietly among the ducks, thinning them one by one.

Dry caves and rock shelters in the arid landscapes of the west document a way of life that changed little over thousands of years. Large swathes of the Great Basin and the California deserts receive little rainfall (Figure 3.8). These

longer flute struck off from a prepared platform at the base. Presumably both Clovis and Folsom points made mounting the head in a spear easier, especially into conveniently detachable foreshafts in bone or wood that linked the point with the spear shaft. A hunter could set out with a series of points attached to foreshafts. When one was fired into an animal and broke off, he could easily replace it with another and be back in the hunt. Fluted spear points appear to be an American invention, confined as they are to North and Central America, but where and why they were developed remains a mystery.

Deciphering the differences between fluted points and the unfluted and stemmed points that followed them is a challenge. Many are finely made lanceolate heads, whose minor variations have been classified under different widely used names (see Figure 3.7). They are collectively as known as **Plano points**, but it is important to realize that, however much we rely on such artifacts to classify different cultural traditions, they were merely part of much wider toolkits, which are hard to classify. In recent years, attention has shifted away from projectile points to entire toolkits, which may yield significant, yet inconspicuous, information about later Paleo-Indian cultural traditions. Hell Gap was an idyllic location for generations of Paleo-Indians, chronicled mainly by superimposed projectile-point forms. Goshen, Folsom, Midland, and so on— each point style has a hidden meaning, even if the basic adaptation to bison hunting remained much the same over the centuries. What do these changes mean? Entire archaeological careers have thrived on projectile points, on the fluted, stemmed, lanceolate, and other forms that proliferated after Clovis times. Some of the changes may represent different groups, others random shifts or more efficient weaponry. There are never sharp boundaries between the disappearance of one form and the appearance of another. Many shifts merely represent changing fashions, which were just as volatile then as they are today, but spread over hundreds of years. The proliferation of different spear points indicates a major turning point: a time of better-defined hunting territories. These tended to be large in the arid west, but much smaller in the east, where numerous local point variations reflect a multitude of local foraging strategies.

arid and semi-arid lands display much environmental diversity: high mountains and intervening valleys, some lakes and wetlands in valley bottoms, and great tracts of desert land (Grayson, 2011). Environmental zones are stacked vertically and intermittently from the deepest dry valleys and others with lakes and wetlands to the wetter, climatically more complex, mountain peaks. Rainfall varies significantly from year to year, so much so that a wet year could produce six times more edible plants than a dry one. Everyone in the western interior subsisted on a very broad range of foods. To do otherwise was to invite disaster.

The most abundant food resources lay by major lakes and rivers, and in wetland areas. As the climate warmed, so local environmental diversity intensified, triggering cultural variation from one group to another, even if basic toolkits and technology remained simple and highly portable, much of it cached at strategic locations for seasonal use. Carefully planned mobility, flexibility, and detailed ecological knowledge—these were always the secrets of survival. The most vital artifacts in these arid landscapes were the wooden digging stick, the flat *metate* or grinding stone, the small stone **muller**, and coiled baskets, which appeared by 7000 BCE (Figure 3.9). These simple objects enabled people to process a broad range of seeds, plants, and tubers with minimal technology. One major innovation arrived in about 500 CE: the bow and arrow, reflected in much smaller corner-notched and stemmed points.

Most people lived in camp groups called kin cliques, moving intermittently, subsisting off seasonal foods at widely separated locations, their social organization revolving around "mapping" onto food resources (Simms, 2008). Plant foods were important everywhere, especially in more arid places, where people would harvest stands of grasses by knocking the seeds into baskets or gathering them by hand. Hardwood digging sticks assumed great value when harvesting root crops, especially in the northern Basin, where biscuit roots, yampa, and other tubers were abundant in spring. Berries, piñon nuts, and acorns were significant crops wherever they were found, sometimes gathered by the women, using special chest-mounted baskets. Piñon nuts contain between 10 and 24 percent protein, more than any other North American nut, while acorns have 16 percent

3.8 The southwestern Great Basin, looking northwest from the Greenwater Range, Inyo County, California: a landscape of mesas and basins. The distant Funeral Mountains are tilted blocks of Paleozoic rocks.

3.9 A Hopi man from the Southwest using a digging stick, c. 1913. Similar forms of artifact were used for excavating wild tubers for thousands of years in the Great Basin.

3.10 Northern Great Basin peoples dug tubers such as bitterroot with wooden digging sticks, then roasted or dried them. They also stored them in underground pits and bags. Artwork by Eric Carlson, from *Ancient Peoples of the Great Basin and Colorado Plateau*, by Steven R. Simms.

protein and 45 percent fat. Both can be stored for long periods, which added to their value. Nineteenth-century accounts tell us that during the early fall, people used long poles to gather green cones by the thousand, carrying them to central processing stations in large baskets. The extracted seeds were parched, shelled, and ground, then eaten as gruel. People stored thousands of cones in open pits under piles of stones, in grass- or bark-lined pits, or skin bags. Stored in this way, cones could last four or five years. Agave, mesquite, and screwbean pods were gathered each spring (Figure 3.10).

River banks, marshes, and lakes acted as magnets for human settlement at certain times of year. Such caverns as Danger and Hogup Caves in Utah lie near wetlands, but their dry layers preserve even delicate, perishable artifacts (Figure 3.11; for a map see Figure 6.1) (Aikens, 1970; Martin *et al.*, 2017). People collecting pickleweed (a low-growing succulent that flourishes on the edge of salt pans and dried-up lake beds) and other edible marsh plants visited them intermittently over thousands of years from about 7840 BCE. There were four major occupational phases at Hogup, reflecting fluctuating climatic conditions. It was so dry after 4000 BCE that the site was abandoned for about 1,000 years. The Hogup visitors hunted deer, pronghorn antelope, wild sheep, and rabbits. The cave deposits included thirty-two species of small animals and thirty-four of birds. Atlatls launching stone-tipped and wooden spears sufficed to dispatch many larger animals. Judging from the fragments of nets and cordage in the deposits, the hunters trapped rabbits and other small animals. They would stretch long nets across narrow defiles, then scare dozens of rabbits into the broad traps with mass drives (see Box: Yes, Yes, It Is a Rabbit!). Some simple loop snares came from Hogup, too, designed to catch the foot of a walking bird or one of the many rodents that lived in the cave. The people wore simple clothing, such as

YES, YES, IT IS A RABBIT!

Rabbits have been commonplace prey since Paleo-Indian times, but they tend to be inconspicuous to us, since the means of hunting them seldom survive. There are examples of finely made rabbit nets from the arid Great Basin, but, for the mechanics of hunting, we have to rely on ethnographic and historical accounts of well-organized hunts that killed dozens of them. The Carson Desert lowlands in Nevada had a dense population of jackrabbits in the late nineteenth century, especially in areas where there was sagebrush and other vegetation as good cover. Ethnographic researches tell us how northern Paiute bands of Stillwater Marsh organized communal jackrabbit drives every late fall, which also killed significant numbers of cottontails (Fowler, 1992). This was when the animals were in prime condition.

These were important events, not only for gathering meat, but also for acquiring pelts, used to make warm winter blankets. The hunts depended on long nets and are said to have sometimes lasted ten to fifteen days. People from different bands would arrive at a strategic location with their nets, then form them into a large rectangle. They would light a fire next to an edge of the net. Then the men would walk inside the net in a single line parallel to the shortest side, driving the rabbits before them. Some would run to the sides and were caught in the head-sized mesh. The remainder would be trapped at the end of the rectangle and were then (before firearms) killed with clubs, spears, or, in later times, with arrows. The hunters then paused as the women and children gathered up the carcasses and began processing them. Then the net enclosure was reset and the process repeated, reversing the walking direction, sometimes as often as six times a day. The women sometimes worked with the hunters, beating the undergrowth to drive out fleeing animals.

The women processed the rabbits back in camp as they, and the children, retrieved them from the hunters. They removed the skins whole, so they could be cut into strips at a later stage for sewing into blankets. The carcasses were gutted, and hung on racks to dry. Those whose skins were in poor condition were roasted, hides and all, in the ash for the evening meal. The communal hunts were organized by rabbit leaders and dances were held each night of the hunt. Individual hunters used snares and traps.

3.11 Excavations at Hogup Cave, Utah.

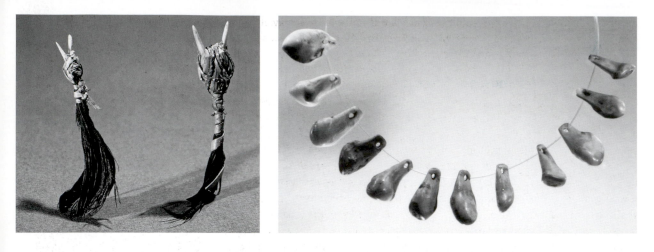

3.12 (a) Anthropomorphic figurines from Hogup Cave. (b) Elk-tooth necklace, also from Hogup.

3.13 Hogup Cave preserved organic materials well in the dry conditions, such as these worn-out moccasins.

blankets fashioned from rabbit fur and transverse strands of plant fiber. Woven fiber sandals protected their feet (Figures 3.12, 3.13).

Arid-land adaptions in the west relied on opportunism and flexibility. Much of the desert was a potentially edible landscape of extremes, where variations in elevation and rainfall allowed plants to germinate and ripen in different weeks and months. Survival required an intimate knowledge of one's surroundings and constant movement from one food area to another as the seasons unfolded. Lakes would dry up during severe drought cycles. The people would adapt by moving away from the dried-up basin and exploiting higher altitudes with apparently little effort or social change. When rainfall increased and lakes reappeared, they would congregate along the marshy shores, taking advantage of the new diversity of food resources. Great Basin peoples resisted "change through change" with adjustments in group size and composition, with subtle technological innovations, and with intensive exploitation of a wide range of food resources. Had not

European expansion disrupted and overwhelmed this ancient lifeway, it could no doubt have continued indefinitely. (For **Fremont** farming societies in the eastern Great Basin, see Chapter 6.)

The Eastern Woodlands: 9000 to 4500 BCE

Only a thin scatter of hunter-gatherers, descendants of earlier Clovis groups, dwelt across the better-watered Eastern Woodlands in 9000 BCE. The Paleo-Indians living on the northern tundra in such areas as central Michigan relied heavily on spring and fall caribou migrations, when thousands of beasts would flow across strategic river crossings for days on end (Mason, 2002). The hunters arranged long **alignments** of low stone cairns or boulders to steer their stampeding prey toward waiting spearmen. Alignments used in caribou drives survive under the shallow waters of Lake Michigan. Groups living to the south exploited different foods: forest game, such as deer and rabbits, and, more importantly, a wide range of plant foods. Large river valleys were especially important, for it was here that abundant fall nut harvests could sustain a band over the winter months. A combination of fishing and nut collecting allowed some groups to stay in one place for months at a time, but elsewhere population densities were much lower.

As far as we can tell, Paleo-Indian occupation began in large river valleys and other places close to good toolmaking stone. Some locations became important base camps, among them a group of sites in northern Virginia, where, as early as 8300 BCE, the Flint Run quarry yielded jasper for toolmaking and people camped along the floodplain of the Shenandoah River (Gardner, 1977). During the summer, the bands would move to the floodplain to quarry stone, to trade, and to socialize, for the area was an anchor for large hunting territories. Away from food-rich areas, human populations fell away sharply. Over many centuries the successors of the pioneers spread out, eventually forming discrete groupings, perhaps about 150 to 250 miles (250 to 400 km) apart. We can identify some of them from the many local projectile-point forms of later times that reflect the increasing local diversity of Paleo-Indian society.

Dalton Culture: c. 8500 to 8000 BCE

Between about 8500 and 8000 BCE a distinctive Late Paleo-Indian and Early Archaic culture flourished in the Central Mississippi Valley, with a range that extended from the Carolinas deep into the Ozarks. Like every other Paleo-Indian society, **Dalton** has its distinctive lanceolate points, usually with a concave base, often sharpened with saw-like edges (Figure 3.14). These served as multipurpose tools and were sharpened again and again. Dalton people also developed a large biface, a thick and heavy tool that served as an adze for heavy woodworking tasks, such as canoe building. Dugout canoes were essential to a people who tended to live along rivers, streams, and in Mississippi bayous.

Dalton groups lived in a more crowded world, where mobility was more restricted than in earlier times. They obtained stone from local rather than exotic sources, and exploited many forms of food, from small rodents, birds, and fish to deer. The Modoc rockshelter in Illinois contains Dalton occupation levels indicating that people ate muskrats, catfish, turtles, and mollusks as well as an extraordinary range of plant foods, including walnuts, hickories, and acorns (Fowler, 1959). During Late Paleo-Indian times people evidently learned how

3.14 A ceremonial Dalton point from Pettis County, Missouri.

to remove bitter tannins from acorns by leaching them in running water after crushing them into a fine meal—a laborious process. Why did Dalton people turn to such hard-to-process foods? More crowded landscapes meant broadening one's diet—and acorns have the advantage that they can be stored for long periods.

Restricted mobility also meant that people developed closer ties to their home territories, associations that passed from one generation to the next and lingered even after death (Anderson and Sassaman, 2012). At the Sloan site, in an ancient sand dune in northeastern Arkansas, Dan Morse (1997) recovered about thirty adult and child burials, also clusters of stone tools deposited in pits. The artifacts included both Dalton points and about a dozen so-called Sloan points, made from Burlington chert that occurs only at a small outcrop near St. Louis, roughly 185 miles (300 km) away.

With Dalton, we enter an era when the highly mobile hunter-gatherer societies of earlier times have given way to what are termed "**broad-based foragers**," often loosely labeled as Archaic societies in archaeological parlance.

Icehouse Bottom: 7000 BCE and Later

Thump, thump: the sound of repeated pounding echoes across the quiet valley from the small base camp, where modest conical dwellings stand well separated from one another in a sandy clearing close to the river bank (Figure 3.15). Each has its own red-clay hearth from which white smoke wafts above the nearby treetops. Great piles of hickory nuts lie on deerskins nearby. Women and girls pound the harvest in wooden mortars, then cast the pounded nuts into hardened-clay boiling pits. The older women watch the bubbling water closely. At the right moment, they pour the oily mixture into fine strainers, carefully saving the rich, oily "hickory milk." Nothing is wasted. They knead the nut meat

3.15 An artist's reconstruction of a camp at Icehouse Bottom, *c.* 6500 BCE. The hut designs are conjectural.

into small cakes, and dry them in the sun. The hickory shells serve as fuel for the fire (Chapman, 2014).

When rains and floods formed sand bars, islands, and new bottomlands along the Little Tennessee River, generations of Archaic hunters used the same base camps there. Today they form a kind of archaeological layer cake of human occupation that began in about 7000 BCE. From this ideal location, the hunters moved into the Upper Tennessee River drainage and into the southern Valley and Ridge Province of Virginia as well. Each mobile band had a base camp or series of repeatedly used settlements, of which Icehouse Bottom, on the Little Tennessee River, was one.

These camps lay close to stands of easily harvested hickories and acorns. Each fall also saw the upland forest floors covered with a rich mast, a carpet, as it were, of falling oil-rich nuts and other foods that were a magnet for white-tailed deer and other animals. The hunters used lighter spears in the forest, tipped with corner-notched points and propelled by weighted atlatls. After 7000 BCE these gave way to points with distinctive, bifurcated bases, perhaps a means to increase the lateral strength of the hafted point when cutting and scraping. Winter and early spring floods often inundated favorite seasonal camps near the rivers. In high flood years people would move to higher ground, where game was to be found. As the water level fell, they would shift back onto the floodplain and spear fish in shallow pools left by the receding waters. As long as population densities remained relatively low, there was little incentive to exploit anything but a fairly narrow spectrum of animal, plant, and aquatic foods in favored locations.

Successful alliances may have been the key to the exploitation of river valleys such as the Little Tennessee. Close ties of kin and the reciprocal obligations that came with them were strong guarantees of long-term economic security that were far more powerful than any number of technological innovations. The production of elaborate and labor-intensive **bannerstones** (atlatl weights) and stone vessels makes little sense at a local level, but when produced as objects used in broad exchange networks tied to cooperative alliances, such artifacts have considerable value (Figure 3.16).

The Windover site near Titusville, Florida, gives us a tantalizing look at the organic artifacts of Early Archaic groups in the Southeast, who ranged from the St. John's River to the Atlantic Coast (Doran, 2002). Windover was a burial area between about 6000 and 5000 BCE, a place where human remains and artifacts were deposited in a pond. The remains of at least 160 individuals, ranging from newborns to people in their sixties and seventies, have come from the waterlogged archaeological levels, lying under 3 to 6 ft (1 to 2 m) of water.

The bodies became submerged within forty-eight hours of death in peat and water deposits with a neutral chemistry that resulted in superb preservation. Brain tissue survived in at least ninety cases. The excellent preservation conditions also allowed the archaeologists to recover at least seven different textile weaves used for clothing made of the sabal palm and/or saw palmetto. Atlatls consisting of wooden shaft, bone hook, and bannerstones were found in the excavations, as were numerous bone artifacts including awls and projectile points. The earliest known domesticated gourds, used to store water and perhaps to hold nuts or seeds, also come from this site.

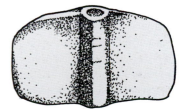

3.16 Bannerstones were fabricated in many forms. These are from a Laurentian Forest Archaic site in New York State. They served as atlatl weights, giving extra heft and range to spear throwers.

Restricted Mobility: c. 6500 BCE onward

By 6500 BCE the Laurentide ice sheet had nearly vanished in the face of continued warming. Vast areas of eastern Canada opened up to human settlement for the first time. At the same time rising sea levels and water temperatures along the Atlantic seaboard allowed a steady northward expansion of fish and shellfish habitats. River estuaries flooded too, creating more favorable conditions for anadromous fish in spring or fall. (These are fish which spawn in fresh water and spend a portion of their lives in the ocean; they are harvested during the migrations up- and down-river.) Meanwhile, water levels in the Great Lakes climbed, reducing stream gradients and improving fishing conditions in the now warmer water. The Mississippi and other Midwestern and Southeastern rivers became more sluggish in the face of rising sea levels. Their swampy backwaters, low-lying levees, and lush floodplains became rich and diverse habitats for hunter-gatherers. Along the Gulf coastal plain, higher water tables established swamps and marshes over wide areas of Florida. Coastal resources were much richer than they had been for thousands of years. Rising temperatures also brought deciduous trees northward into parts of the once boreal-forest-covered Great Lakes region and into the Northeast, especially nut-bearing trees, such as oak, hickory, beech, and chestnut. This increased the amount of plant food available for human consumption over very wide areas.

At first the Eastern Woodlands population was very low, with the greatest concentrations in areas that offered the most diverse foods. Now people relied on food sources closer to seasonal base camps. The carrying capacities of many less-favored locations were reached. Slowly growing hunter-gatherer populations had few options except to lead more circumscribed lifeways.

SEDENTISM AND ANCESTORS

For thousands of years Paleo-Indians and their successors relied on mobility as a primary strategy for survival. Permanent settlement at a single location, known to archaeologists as **sedentism**, first developed in areas where food supplies were plentiful and predictable. For example, the Jomon people of northern Japan lived in such a diverse, food-rich environment that they could stay at the same location for generations, relying on abundant plant foods and salmon fisheries.

Sedentism in North America is associated with more complex hunter-gatherer societies, and, later, with the farming cultures that developed in many areas. Complex hunter-gatherers enjoyed semi- to fully sedentary lifeways, living in one place for most of the year, often for several generations, or settling at one location for long periods, such as the winter. Sedentism changed relationships to the environment, and to ownership of land and food resources, such as nut groves or salmon runs. Sedentary foragers inherited property rights and had more complex social organization that reflected such inheritance, as well as the need for reciprocity and to resolve disputes, which festered at close quarters. They often built substantial, permanent houses, such as the planked dwellings of the Northwest Coast, and owned many more possessions, possibly because they did not have to carry everything with them everywhere. This accumulation of material wealth served as a catalyst for the great increases in cultural complexity that eventually accompanied sedentism.

There were no Gardens of Eden in North America, no areas where food was so abundant that complex societies developed easily. Rather, they developed in local areas, and in fits and starts, often under conditions of stress caused by food shortages or warfare. The vagaries of short- and long-term climate change, unpredictable game migrations, irregular acorns harvests, fish runs that failed to appear—all militated against sedentism and increased social complexity. The more complex hunter-gatherer societies that developed in the Pacific Northwest Coast or in the Eastern Woodlands exploited their environments much more intensively, but they were careful to diversify their food sources and managed risk astutely. They resembled

The classic example of such adaptation comes from the Koster site in the Midwest's Illinois River Valley, which attracted hunter-gatherer groups for thousands of years from as early as 8500 BCE (Streuver and Holton, 2000). By 5000 BCE the temporary encampments of Early Archaic times had given way to a settlement occupied from late spring through summer. Koster is by no means unique, however, for stratified sites occupied for many centuries occur at other locations. One example is the Modoc rockshelter near the Mississippi in Randolph County, Illinois, already mentioned, which lies in a hickory-rich riverine environment about 90 miles (145 km) southeast of Koster (see Chapter 8).

By about 2500 BCE sea levels in the Southeast were close to those of today. Extensive shell middens appeared close to Gulf estuaries, marshes, and brackish water sounds between 2200 and 1800 BCE. Shell resources were probably exploited even earlier, but the resulting middens lie below modern sea levels. These environmental changes contributed to numerous adjustments in the catchment areas of each band's hunting and gathering territory. There was, however, one universal exception to local variability: a dramatic increase in the consumption of freshwater fish and mollusks, which eventually became a major component in the diet of nearly all Southeastern river-valley populations. For the first time we see evidence of permanent or semi-permanent settlement at one location (see Box: Sedentism and Ancestors).

With sedentism came changes in burial practices. Early Archaic settlements sometimes yield the bodies of individuals buried within the confines of the camp. In contrast, hundreds of burials can be found in later, Middle Archaic sites. The Eva site in western Tennessee has yielded 118 burials dating to between 5000 and

modern-day investors, who diversify their holdings to minimize risk.

The origins of sedentism in the Eastern Woodlands are a case in point. Between about 4500 and 4000 BCE many Midwestern and Southeastern rivers stabilized owing to higher sea levels and accumulated silt in their floodplains. Backwater swamps and oxbow lakes formed. Shallow-water and shoal habitats, as well as active streams, provided abundant, easily accessible fish and mollusks. Opportunism paid dividends: people were quick to take advantage of newly plentiful river foods at a time when local populations were rising. Many groups settled down in favored locations and adopted more sedentary lifeways. Earthworks appear for the first time, many associated with funerary rites. At least sixty mound groups lie between Arkansas and Florida. The most spectacular is Watson Brake in northeastern Louisiana, built as early as 3900 BCE (Saunders et al., 2005). For at least nine centuries, forager groups spent spring and early summer here, taking fish and exploiting stands of native plants (see Chapter 8).

Burial customs changed, too, as people were interred in concentrations that resemble cemeteries and in artificial burial mounds. The sudden appearance of cemeteries and artificial burial mounds near resource-rich river valleys may mark a dramatic change in Archaic life. When people start passing vital resources from one generation to the next through lineages and other kin organizations, they will tend to bury their dead in cemeteries. Mortuary rituals serve to affirm and legitimize the rights of kin groups to use and control vital food resources. A cemetery located on the land the group controls, the territory once owned by their ancestors, symbolizes ownership. Corporate bonding in human societies is a form of territorial behavior, a near-universal among animals. The relationship between sedentary settlement, resources inherited through kin organizations, and cemeteries hinges on one reality: that the resources involved are fixed in space, predictable, and sufficiently abundant and diverse that a group can focus its activities around them. If a group wishes to claim rights of ownership and inheritance to these resources, one logical way to do so is through the maintenance of a corporate cemetery, the ritual home of one's ancestors.

3.17 Excavations at the Black Earth site, Carrier Mills, Illinois.

3000 BCE. The Black Earth (Figure 3.17) site at Carrier Mills in southern Illinois is a rich Middle Archaic midden accumulated over a thousand-year period after about 4000 BCE (Jeffries, 2013). The site is remarkable not only for its abundant food remains and many pits used for storing, processing, and cooking foods, but also for its 154 burials. Excavator Richard Jeffries estimates that as many as 400 to 500 people may have been buried at this location over the centuries. One forty-three-year-old man lay with a bag or bundle of eagle talons, sections of bear's-paw bones, projectile points, a miniature grooved axe, and other objects. Jeffries thinks he may have been a shaman, a man celebrated for his curing skills and ability to communicate with the ancestors.

Middle Archaic peoples in the central Mississippi drainage also buried the dead in formal cemeteries. These cemeteries usually consist of large, shallow pits that contain burials of up to forty people, sometimes more, laid in randomly spaced graves. Sometimes a group raised a low, artificial mound over the cemetery to enhance its visibility. The artifacts or caches of offerings deposited in these cemeteries are usually associated with all the graves rather than with specific individuals. These may represent the identity of the kin group who maintained the cemetery. Perhaps individual status was unimportant in what were still egalitarian societies. Age and experience were the keys to leadership and authority, not material possessions. So were the ancestors, who were the spiritual intermediaries with the forces of the supernatural world.

The millennia after Clovis were a critical period in the North American past, for this was when the direct roots of many modern Native American societies were formed. This was the period when the inhabitants of a still thinly inhabited continent acquired their intimate knowledge of its environments. This was also when they developed subsistence practices and spiritual beliefs that were to endure, albeit with significant modifications, until European contact and beyond. By 4000 BCE, too, population densities were rising in many more favored locations and profound changes in Native American society were under way. These changes are the themes that drive the next chapters in our story.

SUMMARY

- With warming after the Younger Dryas, Native American societies adapted conservatively to changing environments and greater aridity.

- Folsom hunter-gatherers succeeded Clovis on the Plains, developing diverse adaptations to local conditions. These are known mainly from projectile-point designs.

- In the arid western interior, hunter-gatherer lifeways changed little over thousands of years. Again, local environmental conditions helped create cultural variation. Seasonal foods, both game and nuts or plants, were of central importance. The people's successful adjustments to changing conditions continued into historic times.

- Over the Eastern Woodlands, Paleo-Indian groups created base camps in large river valleys and places close to good toolmaking stone. In time, such traditions as the Dalton culture, which thrived in more crowded landscapes, became broad-based foragers, using base camps combined with summer mobility.

- After 6500 BCE more stable, warm climatic conditions and rising population densities restricted mobility. Nut harvests, documented at Koster and Modoc rockshelter, assumed great importance.

- The first signs of more elaborate mortuary customs and formal cemeteries appear after 4000 BCE.

Adaptation

"The new people asked Inktomi what they should eat. Inktomi did not want people to eat his friends, so he created buffalo…He taught the men how to kill a buffalo, and how to skin the animals. He showed them how to make knives to remove the skin, and he taught the women how to make scrapers and how to scrape the skin so it was soft and pliable. He showed the people how to catch the buffalo and what parts could be eaten."

—Assiniboine Creation Legend

The Navajo Antelope House ruin,
Canyon de Chelly, Arizona.

ENDURING THEMES
Adaptation

The chapters of Part Three tell the stories of ancient North American societies after the post-Ice Age climate stabilized after about 6000 BCE. (Some of the chapters go back a little earlier, but all of them follow on from Chapter 3, developments after Clovis.) Part Two discussed both first settlement and its consequences on a continent-wide scale, for this is the only perspective one can take on a sparsely inhabited, rapidly changing land. By 6000 BCE, the global climate had warmed significantly, ushering in a long period of relatively minor North American environmental changes. Sea levels were close to, in some places even slightly above, modern levels. River gradients had shallowed, so major rivers like the Mississippi and Missouri flowed slower, and sometimes ponded. North America's very diverse environments and landscapes assumed basically modern configurations, albeit with constant minor shifts such as drought cycles; these are revealed to us by tree-rings. There were signs of regional differences in earlier times, but now the increasing diversity of Native American societies was such that we tell their story in the context of the major environmental zones and culture areas long used by archaeologists (see Figure 3.2).

Part Three has one fundamental theme, already touched upon in Part Two: adaptation and diversity. The six chapters that follow describe the ways in which the peoples of the different major culture areas of North America adapted to highly, often radically, diverse environments. Once successful adaptations came into being, they remained surprisingly stable through thousands of years, except when unexpected circumstances required change. In Part Two, we argued that you cannot consider ancient North America from an isolationist perspective. This is absolutely correct as far as first settlement is concerned, but, following the arrival of humans in an uninhabited continent, is no longer true. With the exception of the Bering Strait region in the far north, where there may have been, and later definitely were, contacts with Siberia, North American societies developed their remarkable diversity in complete isolation from other continents. They developed their own unique answers to such pressing challenges as long drought cycles, food shortages, and increasing population densities.

No one knows how many people lived in North America in 6000 BCE. Judging from the growing numbers of archaeological sites, the sparse populations of earlier times expanded slowly over the first millennia of human settlement. Over the next 4,000 years or so, the rate of population growth quickened slightly, especially in such local areas as river estuaries, sea coasts with rich fisheries, and lakes rich in wildlife, waterfowl, plant foods, and fish. How did people respond to more crowded hunting and foraging territories? We can identify some of their responses from dietary changes and their abandoned settlements. One of the most important was to attempt to cultivate native plants, and later, maize, which was to have dramatic long-term effects on North American societies (see Part Four).

Population growth had many consequences in a continent where the carrying capacity of the land was low in most locations, among them the desert west and the Plains, also the Arctic. As populations grew, so groups intensified their food quests in various ways. They hunted a wider range of animals, many of them small and inconspicuous. Many bands initially relied on a relatively narrow range of plant foods, and responded to increased demand by widening their plant-based diets. They also turned to vegetable foods that required more effort to process, notable among them acorns and piñons, which had the merit of being easily storable. Effective long-term storage was an important strategy for food security. Inevitably, territorial boundaries became more rigid; competition for hunting groups and rich plant harvests became more common. In some places there was violence, as we know from casualties in cemeteries. Add drought and other climatic fluctuations to the mix and you have potentially unstable political and social situations that led to long-term changes in Native American society and a trend toward greater complexity. This trend first manifested itself by about 2000 BCE, if not earlier. It is reflected in more elaborate, but volatile, hunter-gatherer societies along the Northwest Coast, and in the amplification of ancient ritual and spiritual beliefs in the Eastern Woodlands, as evidenced by increasingly lavish mortuary rituals and the beginnings of burial-mound and earthwork construction.

More crowded landscapes meant much more prolonged contacts with neighbors near and far. There had, of course, been sporadic interactions between small hunter-gatherer bands since the days of first settlement. We know of these from occasional finds of exotic toolmaking stone exchanged over hundreds of miles. These connections altered over time, as more and more exotic objects and basic commodities (hides, for example) changed hands over the generations. Exchange with others accelerated over the centuries, much of it involving small objects such as sea shells passed from hand-to-hand, or at annual gatherings where neighboring bands came together, perhaps for communal hunts, for ceremonies, and to find marriage partners. Increasingly elaborate kin ties linked extended family to extended family, lineage to lineage, resulting in groups who shared common ancestors and beliefs over long distances. These ties were ones of respect and reciprocity, of exchange of vital foods and symbols of continuity in the form of ritual artifacts. They linked not only kin groups and families, but also individuals, who might live some distance from one another, but enjoyed permanent relationships of profound ritual and economic importance. Kinship was the "glue" that fused societies near and far in long-term bonds that sometimes morphed into new forms of hereditary leadership that passed down many generations.

A remarkable example of this comes from the "**Great House**" Pueblo Bonito in the Southwest's Chaco Canyon, where genetic research using mitochondrial DNA (inherited through the female line) has revealed a multigenerational, matrilineal descent group that lasted about 330 years, between 800 and 1130 CE. This elite line flourished somewhat later than the events described in Part Three (see Chapter 10), but it reveals the close relationships that governed the slow development of complexity in ancient North American societies. Similar hereditary lines almost certainly played a central role in the development of complex hunter-gatherer societies in the Pacific Northwest and along parts of the southern California coast after 4000 BCE.

Such was the underlying continuity in ancient North America that Part Three carries us from as early as 6000 BCE right into modern times. Many of the societies we shall encounter survived, albeit much changed, all the way to European contact, and often beyond. From their responses to North America's challenging and often rich environments sprang the remarkable diversity of a Native America that developed successfully over thousands of years. Some of these societies were the foundations for much more elaborate cultures over the past 2,000 years. Others, especially in arctic and arid environments, may have been well aware of neighbors who were farmers, or who lived under completely different social and spiritual orders. But their circumstances gave them no incentive to change lifeways that had developed over the millennia and provided effective strategies for surviving in the worlds they called home.

CHRONOLOGICAL TABLE OF DEVELOPMENTS IN THE FAR NORTH

Calibrated Dates	Radio-carbon Ages	Alaska			Eastern Arctic	Sub Arctic
		Aleutians	Kodiak area	Bering Strait area		
Modern Times	Modern Times	MODERN ALEUTS	MODERN ESKIMO GROUPS		MODERN INUIT	MODERN ATHABASCAN-SPEAKING GROUPS
			KONIAG	PUNUK BIRNIRK	THULE POST-CLASSIC	
1105 CE	1000 CE	Chaluka		THULE / OLD BERING SEA	THULE EXPANDS	
15 CE	1 CE		ALEUTIAN TRADITION / KACHEMAK	NORTON / NORTON / UPIAK	DORSET	
1267 BCE	1000 BCE	Chaluka		CHORIS	ARCTIC SMALL TOOL TRAD. / SARQAQ	
2477 BCE	2000 BCE		KODIAK TRADITION	ARCTIC SMALL TOOL TRADITION	PRE-DORSET INDEP. 1	SHIELD ARCHAIC / MARITIME ARCHAIC
3795 BCE	3000 BCE			?		
4935 BCE	4000 BCE		OCEAN BAY TRADITION	?		
5876 BCE	5000 BCE				No human settlement	
7056 BCE	6000 BCE	Anangula		PALEOARCTIC TRADITION		No human settlement
8247 BCE	7000 BCE					

4

The Far North

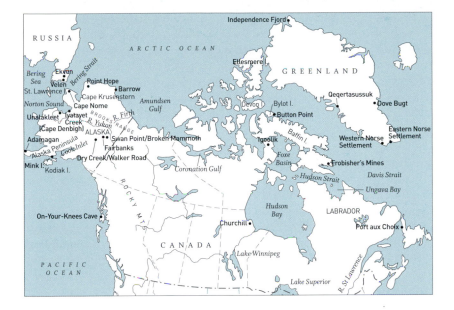

4.1 Map showing archaeological sites in Chapter 4. Some sites and locations omitted for clarity.

The Arctic Archipelago, midwinter, 2300 BCE. A frigid wind sweeps across the snow and ice-covered beach. Temperatures have been far below zero for days; daylight is unknown. The pitiless storm roars in the ears. Gusts sweep over two low, snow-covered mounds set well back from the frozen water's edge. A tiny whirl of smoke emerges from one of them, scattered in moments by the gale. Some trampled-down snow marks a nearly buried entrance and a storage area made of flagstones. Inside, the people lie under thick, warm musk-ox hides, their bodies pressed tightly together for warmth. Everyone is half asleep, with food and fuel within easy reach. They have lit a small fire to melt ice for water; black smoke lingers above them. Everything is dark. There are no fat lamps to illuminate the winter house or provide heat. Only a rare moon illuminates the arctic landscape in one of the coldest inhabited places on earth. The people feel no distress. They and their ancestors have lived in this land of darkness, long winters, and all-too-short summers for as long as anyone can remember.

From first settlement over 14,000 years ago, there was underlying cultural continuity in the Far North of western North America that endured for thousands of years (Friesen and Mason, 2016; McGhee, 2001, 2007) (Figure 4.1). A sparse, widely distributed population of broad-spectrum hunter-gatherers thrived in coastal and inland environments, in unglaciated landscapes throughout Alaska, as far east as the western and southwest Yukon Territory in modern-day Canada, and perhaps as far south as British Columbia. They are grouped into a generic "**Paleoarctic Tradition**," which flourished between about 8000 and 5500 BCE, perhaps even later (West, 1996). Like their predecessors, these were people constantly on the move, who used lightweight, portable toolkits that relied heavily on diminutive microblades for light hunting weapons (Figure 4.2). These razor-sharp tools would have been set into the sides of bone points to create lethal weapons for taking caribou and other game.

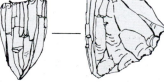

4.2 Paleoarctic tradition. *Top two rows: two microblades from Ugashik Narrows, Alaska Peninsula. Third and fourth rows: two microblade cores from Onion Portage, Alaska. Height of largest core 1.69 in. (4.3 cm).*

Hunting methods changed little over the millennia. At the same time, fishing, sea-mammal and waterfowl hunting, and shellfish collecting became dominant and enduring parts of northern life, even as early as the eighth millennium BCE. The bones of a man in his twenties in On-Your-Knees Cave on Prince of Wales Island, near Ketchikan in southeast Alaska, dating to before 7200 BCE yielded an isotopic signature that tells us he lived almost entirely off marine foods. By about this time, fishers and sea-mammal hunters using microblade technology had occupied a settlement of semi-subterranean dwellings at Anangula on Umnak Island in the eastern Aleutians (Coutouly, 2015). By 4000 BCE the Pacific Ocean had stabilized at about its modern level, with ice-free coasts extending at least 15 degrees further north on the Alaskan coast than to the west in Siberia. Maritime cultures now flourished over a wide area, especially along the Aleutian chain and adjacent mainland coasts. We shall now explore these different cultures and histories; the first a marine history along the Aleutian Islands in the Bering Sea, and the second an inland history of a culture called the "**Arctic Small Tool Tradition**" that appeared along the shores of Alaska.

Aleuts and Mainlanders: c. 5500 BCE to Recent Times

With their nimble sea-lion-hide kayaks known as **baidarkas**, the Aleuts are the epitome of a long-lived northern maritime tradition (see Box: Baidarka!). Based on the Aleutian Islands in the Bering Sea, their culture was thriving well before 2500 BCE, with none of the earlier microblade cores and other stone artifacts found at Anangula. At first the Aleutians dwelt in small villages. Populations were low; each community subsisted off a broad range of birds, fish, mollusks, and sea mammals. Then, within about five centuries, dozens of new sites appeared, as marine productivity soared. After 2500 BCE, the peoples of the Aleutian Tradition enjoyed a culture that included semi-subterranean dwellings and specialized toolkits that eventually led to historic Aleut peoples (Maschner, 2004). The general culture changed little through time, despite adjustments to settlement patterns in response to climate changes. Some groups lived in small kin-based villages. Others occupied large, crowded settlements like Adamagan, near the tip of the Alaska Peninsula. Adamagan was occupied from about 400 BCE to 100 CE, and had as many as 1,000 inhabitants (Figure 4.3). Almost every village lay on open coastline, where maritime foods of all kinds abounded.

4.3 Adamagan, an enormous Aleut village, lies in a spectacular setting at the end of the Alaska Peninsula.

BAIDARKA!

When Russian explorers first encountered the Aleuts, in 1741, they were astounded by their sea-lion-skin kayaks, known as baidarkas. They watched in astonishment as the paddlers landed effortlessly through high surf that would swamp the explorers' own heavy boats. The Aleutian Islands were a harsh and unforgiving maritime environment, but ice conditions were less severe than further north and you could paddle from one island to the next by line-of-sight. Fish and sea mammals abounded, readily taken with bone and ivory-tipped spears that worked equally well ashore and afloat. In a treeless environment, where the only raw materials were antler, bone, driftwood, and hides, skin boats were the only solution for people who spent most of their lives from childhood afloat. What we know about baidarkas makes us realize just how adeptly early northern maritime peoples in Alaska and along the Northwest Coast hunted, fished, and traveled in harsh marine environments.

The baidarka came into use as a faster, more refined vessel than the large, open skin boat. The bow was pointed and jaw-like to reduce water resistance and increase speed. The paddler sat in a small cockpit amidships in a decked hull, created by collecting pieces of driftwood over many months to form a keel of several pieces, up to 21 ft (4.4 m) long. The keel and ribs were lashed together with whale baleen binding, then covered with the outer hide from the throat of a Steller sea lion, a native of the Bering Strait. The hide was carefully trimmed, then wetted before being fitted round the frames, the boatbuilder drawing the hides over the frame like a form of sock. The top seam was then sewn with sinew, using fine thread that ensured a waterproof fit. As the hide dried, it contracted and bound together the entire baidarka (Figure 4.4).

At first acquaintance, the baidarka seems tippy in the extreme, but, as I found when I paddled a replica, your smallest movements flow through the flexible hull. As you paddle, the kayak comes alive in your hands. It is like a thoroughbred, restless, itching to take off at a gallop. All I had to do was paddle smoothly and let the kayak do the work. ⏩

4.4 An Aleutian baidarka owner fishing for cod, Captain's Island, Alaska. Painting by Henry William Elliott, 1872.

4.5 *Right:* A 19th-century Aleutian kayak paddler's hat. Such headgear had important symbolic meaning for sea-mammal hunters. *Below:* An Aleutian hunter in his kayak, a 19th-century model fashioned in gutskin, fur, wood, and pigment. Date and location unknown.

I soon acquired a healthy respect for Aleut paddlers. They were wonderful seafarers, who traveled from island to island in all weathers, in kayaks with flexible hulls that adjusted effortlessly to ocean swells and troughs. The baidarka was, above all, a hunting weapon, used with lines bearing bone or wood hooks for catching cod and halibut that were then hauled to the surface and dispatched with a heavy club. The hunters also relied on spears propelled with throwing sticks, steadying the baidarka with the paddle in one hand, while casting with the other. The toggle harpoon with its swiveling head (see Figure 4.14) was very effective in later times when used against sea mammals.

To paddle hide craft in these waters required not only remarkable seamanship, but also an understanding of subtle interactions of ocean, ice, and changing weather that would have been unimaginable in the benign waters of the tropics. Above all, there was the cold, not only that of air, damp, and wind, but also of bitter ocean waters. Immersion in arctic waters induces hypothermia within minutes, because water draws away body heat much more quickly than air does. Your skin becomes cold and paler; you shiver intensely until your body temperature drops below 90 degrees Fahrenheit (32.2°C). As your temperature continues to fall, your speech slurs, your muscles become rigid, and you are soon disoriented. In arctic waters hypothermia is an almost instant killer, which can be kept at bay only with highly effective protective clothing.

No sane hunter would venture even into shallow, sheltered waters in layered furs. Reindeer- or caribou-skin parkas may work on land, but, once wet, they are dead weight on the body and could soon swamp even a strong swimmer.

The well-being of the paddlers depended on the skill of those who made their bird- and sea-lion or seal-intestine parkas. These reached to the ankles, were lashed tightly around the head and wrists, and were often decorated with feathers and sometimes human hair. Between thirty and forty cormorant or puffin skins went into a single garment, which lasted about two years. The seams were completely waterproof, and the garment tied around the cockpit hatch to make the paddler and his kayak a single waterproof unit. Their sea-lion-hide boots had soles made from the scaly skin of the fore flippers, which provided a rough surface for keeping traction on rocks. On their heads they often wore fiber hats with rims, or bentwood helmets with long visors that shaded the eyes from glare and protected the face from spray, rain, and wind. They adorned these with sea-lion bristles and other tokens of the hunt, also with images of whales and other prey. A hunter's hat imbued him with symbolic power and gave him a close relationship to his quarry (Figure 4.5).

After about 650–700 CE the large coastal villages disappeared, replaced by communities living along the banks of salmon streams. Defensive sites and refuges become commonplace, as if there was constant warfare. After approximately 1000 CE, the salmon streams were abandoned and people returned to the coast, where at least three villages contained large, multi-room houses that were probably households of kin groups. The corporate dwellings may have resulted from intensified warfare and a need for defense. Two centuries later, by 1250 CE, the large communities had collapsed. People began to live in small extended families; villages comprised only a few dozen inhabitants. Judging from the small number of sites, the region was largely depopulated. Eskimo-related groups from the north began to move into the area. A further two centuries later populations again rose rapidly and subsistence patterns returned to those of 2,000 years before, with sea-mammal hunting reaching a peak.

East of the Aleutian Islands a long-lived hunting culture centered on marine mammals developed on Kodiak Island by 5500 BCE. This "**Ocean Bay Tradition**" flourished on the island and in the nearby Cook Inlet and adjacent mainland coasts until 1500 BCE. These masterly hunters used heavy thrusting spears with large stone blades against big sea mammals, weapons most likely coated with aconite poison from the monkshood plant, a common practice in ancient times (Figure 4.6). During the summer months most hunters spent almost more time afloat than ashore. In 1800 BCE the "**Kachemak Tradition**" developed in on Kodiak Island, finally ending around 1000 CE (Clark, 1997). This sea-mammal-hunting, salmon-fishing, and caribou-hunting culture developed from Ocean Bay roots, with the addition of techniques for working slate by grinding and sawing. The climate was now cooler and wetter, to which the people adapted ingeniously by moving partially underground into semi-subterranean winter houses constructed with sod-covered wooden frames (Figure 4.7). A winter village was a series of

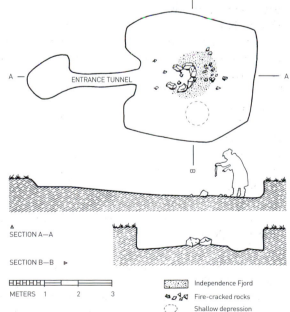

4.6 *Above:* Slate lanceheads from Kashevaroff.
4.7 *Right:* Kachemak tradition house, with sod walls and earthen interior benches. This example has an entrance tunnel and a central tunnel.

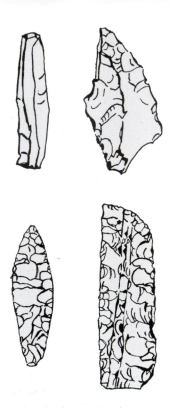

4.8 Arctic Small Tool Tradition, upper Naknek Drainage, southwestern Alaska. *Top row*: microblade and burin. *Second row*: projectile point and side blade. (Length of side blade *c*. 3.3 cm.)

4.9 Probable distribution of the Arctic Small Tool Tradition stone artifacts in the eastern Arctic.

CANADA

GREENLAND

◼ Arctic Small Tool Tradition

low mounds, with few signs of life on cold days except for wood-smoke drifting from roof holes, soon blown away by the strong winds.

By the first century CE, the landscape had become more crowded. Village competed with village; trade intensified in such exotics as labrets (ornamental plugs worn below the lower lip, which became marks of social status). Neighboring groups fought constantly and practiced elaborate mortuary rituals, dismembering some of the dead, retaining some skulls as trophies, burying other people intact. This was when the foundations of the elaborate Alutiiq culture of Kodiak Island were laid, a culture that emerged in later centuries and survives to this day.

The Arctic Small Tool Tradition: c. 2500 to 800 BCE

We move now from the islands of the Bering Sea to the shores of Alaska, where another broad cultural entity was developing: the "Arctic Small Tool Tradition." The people here are given this name for their distinctive, lightweight stone toolkit (Dumond, 1987; Workman, 1998), which appeared around 2500 BCE (Figure 4.8). Why local technologies changed we do not know, but light weaponry was effective against caribou and other animals. Small blades or microblades, pointed at both ends, served as end or side barbs in antler or bone arrows or spearheads.

The Arctic Small Tool Tradition may have originated in contemporary caribou-hunting and river-fishing cultures across the Bering Strait. In about 3000 BCE slowing sea-level rises formed beaches around the Bering and Chukchi seas. Summer boat trips across the strait now assumed importance in local life, bringing new contacts between Siberia and Alaska, even if fishing and sea-mammal hunting were apparently still unimportant. Arctic Small Tool groups may also have introduced the bow and arrow to North America, a weapon they used against caribou. In 1997 a small stick with a fragment of sinew wrapped around it was recovered from a mountainous ice patch in the Coast Mountains of the region, associated with caribou dung and radiocarbon dated to 2300 BCE. A hunter crouched behind some rocks could take advantage of the terrain and inflict lethal wounds on prey at a greater range than his ancestors.

Implements in the style of the Arctic Small Tool Tradition occur in the Brooks Range and as far south as the Alaska Peninsula and Kachemak Bay. On the peninsula, Arctic Small Tool camps lie along rich salmon streams, presumably to have taken advantage of summer runs. These were highly mobile people. After 2500 BCE they moved eastward from the Alaska Peninsula, along the shores of the Arctic Ocean and into the Canadian Archipelago. The causes of their remarkable, and still largely undocumented, migration remain a mystery. Given the simple toolkits and only rudimentary heat sources at their disposal, these little-known population movements are among the most remarkable in history (Figure 4.9). Almost immediately the tiny populations of the east developed into three distinctive Arctic Small Tool cultures: the ill-defined **Independence I** in the High Arctic, **Pre-Dorset** in the Low Arctic, and the **Saqqaq** in coastal Greenland (Maxwell, 1985).

Independence I

Independence Fjord is part of Pearyland, a vast arctic desert in northeast Greenland, 750 miles (1,200 km) north of the Bering Strait far to the west. From 2500 BCE perhaps about 200 people lived in this area of northeastern

4.10 Remains of a 4,000-year-old Independence I camp at Port Refuge. The circular depression in the ground marks the place where perhaps a snow house once stood. The vegetation inside the circle is feeding off nutrients in the refuse left inside the house more than 3,500 years ago.

Greenland, with an estimated population density of about one person per 112 square miles (290 km²). The distribution of Independence settlements extends south from Pearyland to Devon Island in the Canadian Archipelago. Independence sites also extend some 600 miles (950 km) south along Greenland's east coast as far as Dove Bugt, the easternmost ancient settlement in the Americas.

In these settlements small tent rings marked by circles of large boulders have been found along the beaches of Independence and neighboring fjords, associated with scatters of stone tools, including implements for splitting and grooving bone and antler (Figure 4.10). As many as twenty musk-ox-hide tents were erected at some locations, but most sites were no more than isolated dwellings. Independence people mainly subsisted off musk ox; these animals wandered over extensive but restricted ranges, whereas caribou migrated along predictable routes every year. Occasionally the hunters took sea birds, ring seal, arctic char, and other fish. Everyone lived without oil lamps, which elsewhere provided light and limited heat. Their fuel was driftwood, occasional stunted willow branches, and the fat from musk-ox bones. With such limited heat sources and a food supply that was constantly on the move, the people had to be nomads, perhaps coming together in slightly larger groups during the two-and-a-half months of darkness in midwinter.

4.11 Pre-Dorset and Dorset harpoon heads. Their stylistic changes through time are useful chronological markers.

Pre-Dorset

Another group of sites with artifacts in the Arctic Small Tool style occurs far to the south, and is often known as the Pre-Dorset culture. This name anticipates the later and better-known **Dorset** people who appeared around 200 BCE. One focus of early Pre-Dorset groups lay in an area centered on the islands in the northern reaches of Hudson Bay, the northern and southern shores of Baffin Island, northern Labrador, and the west coast of the Foxe Basin (Schledermann, 1990). Whether the appearance of the Pre-Dorset culture from 2500 BCE was the result of the same population movement that gave rise to the Independence I stage, or one some centuries later, is much debated. Unlike Independence, Pre-Dorset groups could count on a diverse food supply throughout the year. Pre-Dorset people relied heavily on seals, hunting them from the ice-edge and at their winter breathing holes. The latter requires great patience, endurance, and keen powers of observation. The hunter waits for hours for the moment when a seal comes up to breathe. The thrusting harpoon used for ice-hole hunting was also useful for taking bearded and ring seals at the edge of ice floes, and for stalking walrus and seals basking on the ice. Pre-Dorset people also hunted sea mammals from skin kayaks. Perhaps as a result, harpoon designs became increasingly sophisticated through time (Figure 4.11). The arctic char was also an important food source, an anadromous species taken in **weirs** and traps, then dried for use in the lean fall months before the ocean froze over.

West of Hudson Bay, sizable Pre-Dorset populations appear not to have developed until after the late fourteenth century BCE, and they were predominantly caribou hunters. The western region of the Coronation and Amundsen gulfs in the Northwest Territories of Canada may have been a dispersal area for hunting bands that pursued migrating caribou deep into the mainland interior. They were hunters and fisher folk, expert on land and afloat, also sealing on the coast. Some of these bands are thought to have followed caribou herds far south during a period of increasing cold between 1200 and 900 BCE and may have penetrated beyond the treeline, perhaps to Lake Athabasca by 900 BCE. Judging from the major north and south shifts in the treeline in response to colder and warmer temperatures, these peoples' tundra hunting territories fluctuated constantly. To the east Pre-Dorset occupation occurs along the Labrador coast as far as the Strait of Belle Isle and western Newfoundland, the population concentrated in favorable areas. The first settlement was almost as early as Independence I, about 1880 BCE, with a peak settlement about 1500 BCE, thereafter declining to only very sparse occupation, if any, until the mid-eighth century BCE.

Saqqaq

Moving further east across the Davis Strait from Baffin Island, the Saqqaq complex occupied much of the west, south, and east coasts of Greenland. The earliest Saqqaq sites date to around 2500 BCE, to about the time when Independence occupation began in the north. Some have argued that Saqqaq was the result of southerly migrations from the bitterly cold Independence area; it was an Arctic Small Tool enclave for over 1,000 years. Saqqaq is the best-known of Arctic Small Tool traditions, thanks to the permanently frozen occupation levels of the Qeqertasussuk site on an island in Greenland's Disko Bay, occupied between 2400 and 1400 BCE (Figures 4.12 and 4.13). The Qeqertasussuk people used very light,

4.12 Overview of the Saqqaq culture site at Qeqertasussuk, Disko Bay, Greenland.

4.13 A section through the midden layers at Qeqertasussuk. The culture layers consist of waste material from cleaning the dwelling floors and thousands of animal bones from the processing of game. Finds include fragments of wood, bone, baleen, and hide artifacts preserved by the permafrost.

toggle-headed harpoons that were thrown long distances with atlatls. They also carried light lances and bird spears as well as bows and arrows. Frame fragments from kayak-like craft reveal an expertise at water-borne hunting. All their artifacts were precisely manufactured and used with great effectiveness against seals and other sea mammals, also waterfowl. Saqqaq technology changed little over many centuries, with slate microblades, heavy bifaces, and end scrapers being skillfully hafted for domestic and hunting use. Qeqertasussuk was predominantly a summer camp, used during the harp-seal migration season in June and July. The Saqqaq complex is also known from the Itivnera site, some 90 miles (150 km) inland from the coast. Itivnera, occupied between about 1250 and 340 BCE, lies astride a caribou migration route, and caribou was the staple diet at the site.

Back to the Bering Strait: The Norton Tradition, *c.* 1000 BCE to 800 CE

Between 1500 and 1000 BCE the long-lived Arctic Small Tool Tradition gradually disappeared along the shores of the Bering Strait. No one knows quite what happened, but, toward the end of these five centuries, contacts between the Siberian and Alaskan sides of Strait intensified, ushering in a new chapter in far northern history. What emerged was the "**Norton Tradition**," a loosely defined entity that was probably a network of different groups linked by constant interactions and exchanges across the Bering Strait (Mason, 1998; Shaw and Holmes, 1982). Norton appeared in the Chukchi and Bering Sea region during the first millennium BCE, its origins in the Arctic Small Tool Tradition and other societies probably on the Siberian side. While it developed at a time of somewhat warmer temperatures in the Arctic, a cold cycle beginning in 700 BCE that endured for about five centuries apparently drove Norton people south of the Strait. By the first century CE they had colonized the base of the Alaska Peninsula and were exploiting the rich waters of the northern Pacific from Takli Island and other locations, overwhelming older cultures there.

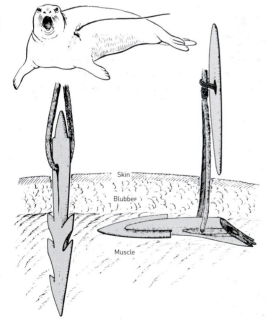

4.14 Harpoon technology. The non-toggling or "male" harpoon point holds an animal in its barbs (top). The more complex toggling harpoon was developed for sea mammal hunting. The head toggles beneath the skin and blubber where it cannot be dislodged by ice, and is effective with heavier prey like walrus and whales.

Skin

Blubber

Muscle

Norton groups settled near fish-rich Arctic Ocean river estuaries, and, in the south, beside major salmon streams. These people were expert open-water sea-mammal hunters. Part of their success came from toggle-headed harpoons, whose heads detached in their prey (Figure 4.14). The hunters used such harpoons from kayaks and other small craft. They also used drag floats made from inflated seal skins attached to lines to track and slow their prey (Park, 2012). These prevented sudden jerks from capsizing their kayaks. The hunters then used the float and detachable head to track their prey, even animals as large as whales.

Unlike their predecessors, many Norton groups occupied more-or-less permanent settlements, marked by great concentrations of substantial, year-round dwellings. The Safety Sound site near Cape Nome has yielded almost 400 house depressions, Unalakleet on Norton Sound itself almost 200. Not all the houses were occupied at once, of course, but they reflect dense, long-term occupation. At both these locations people lived in square dwellings excavated about 20 in. (50 cm) into the ground, with short, sloping entryways, central hearths, and pole-and-sod roofs. During the summer months many groups used temporary hunting and fishing camps.

4.15 An Ipiutak engraved ivory "mask" found in a burial at Point Hope, probably once with a wooden backing.

A highly developed form of Norton culture emerged around the Cape Krusenstern and Point Hope areas of the Chukchi Sea and the Brooks Range. These people were called the Ipiutak, active from the beginning of the first millennium to 800 CE. Ipiutak artists lavished care on ivory artifacts, among them animal carvings, human figures, and masks (Figure 4.15).

In about 700 BCE the Norton inhabitants of St. Lawrence Island and coastal Chukotka developed an even more specialized culture, based entirely on the ocean. Here, local narrows determined the direction of summer sea-mammal migrations. Natural current upwellings maintained areas of open water even in midwinter. The new sea-mammal hunting equipment with its efficient toggling harpoons and other ingenious devices was to revolutionize coastal life throughout the Arctic. This technology was the foundation of the **Thule Tradition** (pronounced the Danish way—Tuleh), in which whaling played an important role.

The Thule Tradition: *c.* 700 BCE to Modern Times

Throughout the Bering Strait and along the Alaskan coast from Barrow to the Alaska Peninsula, and far offshore to the islands and Siberian coast, communities of Thule sea-mammal hunters were in constant and regular contact for many centuries. The earliest Thule Tradition sites are often subsumed under the Old Bering Sea stage, which had developed by *c.* 200 BCE and is defined—as with other cultures or stages within the Thule Tradition—by the style of their harpoons and art. Groups of the Old Bering Sea stage come from St. Lawrence and Okvik islands, and from the Siberian Chukotka coast of the Bering Strait. Both kayaks and umiaks (large skin boats) now appear in archaeological sites for the first time, as do more durable polished-slate points and knives, which replace many of the flaked-stone artifacts of earlier times (all these artifacts were in fact in use much earlier). Antler, bone, and ivory provided implements of all kinds, including harpoon parts, snow goggles, and needles. Iron objects first appear, also delicate carvings made with iron tools. Whale hunting generated sizable food surpluses, but seal oil was probably the mainstay of the Strait economy.

At Uelen and Ekven on the Siberian shore Russian investigators have uncovered richly decorated Old Bering Sea graves lined with whalebone and sometimes with wooden floors, and furnished with fine ivory artifacts, including harpoon parts and mattocks. Conceivably these were the sepulchers of important individuals, perhaps whaleboat captains, men of prestige who owned whale-hunting umiaks. Such social distinctions are known to have been important in later centuries. These sepulchers may be the first signs of social differentiation in the north.

Punuk and Birnirk Stages: *c.* 500 to 1400 CE and Later

A new harpoon style and suite of art motifs appeared by 500 CE. This is known as the Punuk stage, a development of Old Bering Sea on the major Strait islands and along the shores of much of the Chukchi Peninsula (Figure 4.16). Punuk art styles were simpler than those of the older Old Bering Sea stage. Large Punuk communities lived in semi-subterranean, square or rectangular dwellings with wooden floors, sleeping platforms along the walls, and driftwood or whale-jaw sides, the sod roofs held up with whalebone rafters.

A further variant on the **Old Bering Sea Tradition** developed between 500 and 600 CE, called the **Birnirk**, found along the shores of the Chukchi Sea from Cape Nome northward, and on the Siberian coast west from East Cape to at least as far as the mouth of the Kolyma River. Although Birnirk people used many of the same hunting weapons as Punuk and Old Bering Sea, they only rarely adorned their antler harpoons or their artifacts, confining their art to concentric and spiral motifs executed on clay pots with bone paddles. Some Birnirk sites, for example those near Barrow and Point Hope, are situated close to whale-rich locales.

Alaskan archaeologist Owen Mason (1998) believes that the intensification of long-distance trade, warfare, and whaling in the Bering Strait region between 600 and 1000 CE led to intense competition between Old Bering Sea and Birnirk groups, and with the Ipiutak people on the Alaskan shore. The main center of political power lay at East Cape in Siberia, at the twin sites of Uelen and Ekven. Ekven was contemporary with chiefdoms on St. Lawrence Island and at Point Hope on the Alaskan side. Mason argues that the East Cape people were the

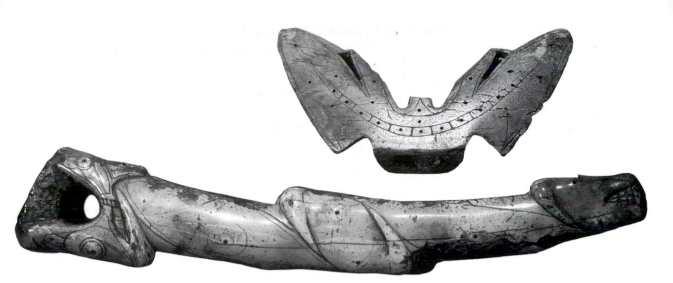

4.16 Winged harpoon butts.
Top: Early Punuk stage winged
object in "butterfly" shape, width
6.3 in. (16 cm). *Below*: Late Punuk
adze handle, length 5 in. (13 cm).

powerbrokers in the region, while Ipiutak, ruled by powerful shamans, with its elaborate art tradition and burials, was a place where spiritual capital was more highly valued. But the similarities between Ipiutak artifacts and those found at East Cape sites may hint at some form of political alliance with the western side of the Strait. There were connections with caribou-hunting groups in the Siberian and Alaskan interiors as well.

Old Bering Sea held sway over most of the southern Bering Strait coast on the Siberian side, while Ipiutak's shamans controlled much of the Alaskan shore. The area supported small villages occupied for brief periods, with divided and shifting loyalties, and multiple origins. There was some fighting, but the threat of violent conflict may have been more prevalent than war itself.

Thule artifacts occur at Cape Denbigh on Norton Sound by 900 CE, and in the Naknek Drainage of the Alaska Peninsula by 1100 CE. This spread was not necessarily a population movement, but more likely a diffusion of new artifact styles, more efficient house designs, and sophisticated hunting methods to southern coastlines and river estuaries, much of it connected with seasonal sea-mammal migrations. The Thule Tradition therefore represents a time of intense contact across the Bering Strait, from the Alaskan coast and Peninsula, across the islands and to the Siberian coast. The Eskimo peoples of what is now Alaska, who encountered Europeans during the eighteenth century CE, all formed part of this powerful and long-lived cultural tradition.

The Dorset Tradition of the Eastern Arctic: 200 BCE to c. 800 CE

Far east of the Bering Strait across the Canadian Archipelago, the Pre-Dorset culture of the eastern Arctic developed into the Dorset Tradition in about 200 BCE. Why the transition occurred remains a mystery. Was it the result of an Arctic Small Tool population decline in the eastern Arctic about 3,000 years ago, followed by an expansion of Dorset peoples? Or did dwindling caribou herds in Quebec cause major adjustments in both population distribution and hunting methods? We do not know. This was a time when climatic conditions became

CANADA

GREENLAND

Dorset

Thule

4.17 Probable distribution of Dorset and Thule in the eastern Arctic.

colder after some centuries of warmer temperatures (Maschner *et al.*, 2009) (Figure 4.17). Perhaps the people developed new ice-hunting techniques that were successful in intensely cold winters, leading to the emergence of the Dorset Tradition.

The Dorset culture is defined, above all, by a remarkable art tradition with powerful magical and symbolic undertones that stand in sharp contrast to its relatively simple hunting and domestic technology (see Box: Dorset Art). This was a utilitarian society that dwelt in rectangular, semi-subterranean buildings, used triangular projectile points for sealing, and manufactured prosaic ground-slate tools. Dorset people possessed no dog sleds, so their land-travel range was restricted to the limits of human pulling and walking ability. They had no bows and arrows or throwing sticks, just simple lances and harpoons. The Dorset people had only small oil lamps and far-from-sophisticated winter houses. In some respects they were even less equipped for arctic conditions than their predecessors, yet they thrived for centuries.

Like all eastern Arctic groups, the Dorset people were predominantly hunters, although they undoubtedly consumed berries and other plant foods in season. Dorset hunters usually employed simple thrusting harpoon designs, the heads bound to the foreshaft so that the shaft slid backward and the head came off attached to a line wedged in a split in the harpoon shaft. This design works best at close quarters, when the hunter thrusts the head into the animal. Such weapons were probably effective for ice hunting. The staple fish was the arctic char, a species that is easily filleted and speared during seasonal runs. We can imagine fishers standing on rocks by a fast-moving stream, thrusting light spears tipped with delicate ivory barbed heads at the swift fish crowding upstream along the rocky bottom. They would haul in fish after wriggling fish, quickly killing them with clubs.

Early Dorset culture may have developed in one core area and then spread rapidly over a much wider region. The most logical origin is the northern Foxe Basin, where earlier Pre-Dorset traditions flourished. There was such regular communication with other communities in the general area that cultural change must have been almost simultaneous over a wide area. The same basic lifeway flourished throughout Dorset times, but with constant adjustments in response to ever-changing cold and warm cycles.

About 2,000 years ago, the climate became progressively colder, so parts of the High Arctic and northern Labrador may have been abandoned. By 100 CE people relinquished favorite locations in the Foxe Basin. The populations of Newfoundland and the Labrador coast now increased as people retreated from the north. Many Middle Dorset settlements in these areas were small villages, some of them, such as Port aux Choix, Newfoundland, semi-permanent locations where people fished and hunted for most of the year (Tuck, 1976). Port aux Choix was also a base for hunting pupping harp seals in late winter, a place favored earlier by Maritime Archaic groups (see Chapter 8). Up to thirty-five people lived at Port aux Choix, using a toolkit that has clear ties to northern Dorset, but with a strongly local flavor.

Around 500 CE temperatures warmed somewhat at the onset of Late Dorset times. The centuries that followed saw an increase in artistic production, resulting

DORSET ART

Dorset art is justly famous, especially for its life-like portraits and animal art. Dorset carvers worked with antler, bone, ivory, soapstone, and wood to make tiny figures representing almost every arctic animal. But more than half their carvings were of human beings or polar bears, some of them highly naturalistic (Figure 4.18). The attention to detail is astonishing—complete polar-bear skulls and minute seals are modeled complete with whiskers and eyes. Unlike later Thule and Inuit artists, Dorset carvers usually ignored utilitarian objects and created work that had a strong ideological undertone. Masks, figurines, and plaques probably played important roles in shamanistic and magical ceremonies.

Human beings sometimes appear in distinctive portrait, in carvings that display rectangular or round eyes, outward-facing nostrils, and a pug nose. One portrait may represent a living person, perhaps a famous shaman, who had from infancy suffered with a skull condition that made him stand out from his fellow priests. The Late Dorset site at Button Point on Bylot Island yielded wooden masks, one of

4.18 *Left*: Dorset art. A naturalistic ivory carving of a polar bear.
4.19 *Right*: Dorset wooden doll from Button Point. Bylot Island.

which simulated tattooing and once had pegged-in hair and a mustache. There are smaller masks, too, no more than 2.8 in. (6 cm) long, many with X-shaped incisions across the face; there are even dolls with detachable arms and legs (Figure 4.19). Small animal amulets are common, perhaps used during the chase, suspended on thongs or sewn on clothing. The carvers also made ivory

teeth plaques, with ridges on the back, that may have been worn over the mouth during shamanistic rituals.

The Dorset art tradition was a unique efflorescence over a very wide area of the eastern Arctic, a reflection of basic ideologies that were to survive for many centuries. The achievements of Dorset artists remind us just how deep the roots of northern belief lie.

in the magnificent Dorset art tradition. Many widespread communities participated in a vast cultural network in which shamans may have played a leading role. Such sites as Button Point, on Bylot Island, may have been ceremonial centers. Button Point is rich in carved wooden figures, including life-sized ceremonial masks and wooden dolls of humans and stylized animals. There are fragments of drums, too. "It is easy to imagine nighttime ceremonies where rhythmic chants and drumbeats restored the sacred balance of nature," writes Canadian archaeologist Moreau Maxwell (1985). "In the dimly lit houses, shamans, frighteningly masked, would manipulate little figures for magical protection from the only predators dangerous to humans—the giant polar bear and humans who were not part of the kinship web."

Quite when the Dorset culture died out is a matter of controversy (summary in Park, 2016). Did they survive further north, still being there when the first

Thule migrants arrived? Arguments back and forth focus on radiocarbon dates, but there are signs of a hiatus around 900 CE, as if Dorset groups had vanished in the eastern Arctic a century or so before the first Thule arrival. There are said to be signs of Dorset occupations in later centuries, but the evidence is uncertain and may be associated with Thule newcomers. Was there contact between Dorset and Thule? Dorset people vanished in Newfoundland by 800, where later Thule people never settled, and genetic evidence suggests complete reproductive isolation between Thule and Dorset, research that makes a strong case for a break between the two cultures (Raghaven *et al.*, 2014).

THULE WHALE HUNTING

To what extent climatic shifts affected human settlement in the Arctic generally, and especially in the east, is still uncertain. The main eastward migration of Thule groups, thought to date to around 1300 CE or a little earlier, coincides with roughly three centuries of warmer temperatures that settled over the Northern Hemisphere around 900 CE (the **Medieval Warm Period**). The warming was relatively minor, with fluctuating temperatures, but it had marked effects on the distribution of ice in the north. The southern boundary of Arctic pack ice retreated northward in the Atlantic, which had considerable historical consequences. Favorable sailing conditions allowed Norse seamen from northern Europe to expand to Iceland, onward to Greenland, and as far south as Newfoundland during the tenth century.

The Medieval Warm Period may have had significant effects on people living near the Arctic Ocean coast across what is now extreme northern Canada. The warming was probably never sufficient to melt the ice that blocked the central parts of the Arctic Archipelago between Amundsen Gulf and Lancaster Sound—a distance of about 600 miles (1,000 km)—but some reduction of ice may have allowed bowhead and Greenland whale populations to mingle, distributing abundant populations of these great mammals right across the north. Whales migrate east along the Alaskan coast in spring, and west in fall, keeping to ice leads close to shore. At the same time, reduced ice between the Canadian Arctic islands may have exposed the normal summering grounds of the bowhead whale to open-water hunting. People could now pursue whales for many months, not just for short periods in spring and fall. It may be that whale hunting was a major factor in the Thule migration.

The Thule people of the Bering Strait were masters at whale hunting with kayaks and umiaks. Thule settlements

4.20 An umiak and crew, Cape Prince of Wales, Northwest territories, Canada.

Thule Expansion in the Eastern Arctic: c. 1000 CE

In about 1000 CE Thule people, speaking an archaic form of Inupiat language, migrated to the eastern Arctic (McCartney, 1979). Judging from the style of their artifacts, they came both from whaling communities on the Bering Strait and from somewhere on the western or northwestern Alaskan coast. Theories about the reason for this migration revolve around whale hunting (see Box: Thule Whale Hunting) and iron trade. Groups in this area had a long-standing involvement in the iron-ore trade between Siberia and Alaska, probably controlled by people around the Strait. The movement eastward was apparently rapid,

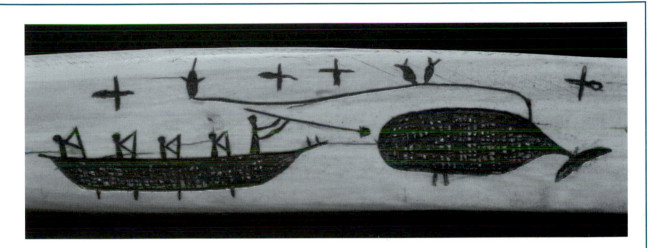

4.21 Carving of a Western Inuit whale hunt on an ivory snow-knife made from walrus tusk, 19th century. From the collection of the British Museum.

were smaller (there are only a few as large as twenty-five to thirty-five houses) and more widely separated than those in the far west, so the communities could track migrating whales. Kayak and umiak teams from five or six families were powerful hunting combinations. In both east and west the umiak was the stable platform used for harpooning whales (Figure 4.20).

This was a team enterprise, involving experts with sophisticated heavy weapons and great skill in using the umiak for harpooning their prey. The whalers used slate-tipped toggling harpoons attached to large foreshafts and wooden shafts. Inflated sealskins formed the drag floats attached to the harpoon line that helped tire the harpooned whale. Judging from contemporary engravings, between four and seven people manned the sealskin and driftwood umiaks. The helmsman would approach the whale from the rear as it came up to breathe. The harpooner in the bow would cast at a vital spot, the man behind him throwing out the floats. Several casts and a long fight might ensue, until the dead whale could be towed tail-first to a convenient beach or into shallow water, where butchering could proceed.

Thule whale hunters concentrated on bowhead whales, *Balaena mysticetus*, relatively placid creatures that swim near the surface. Their thick blubber means that the carcass floats, a major advantage for hunters with skin boats. Judging from the bones found in Thule sites, the average baleen whale kill weighed between 13,250 and 26,450 lb (6,000 and 12,000 kg), the whales being between 26 and 28 ft (8 and 8.5 m) long. As little as 20,000 lb (9,000 kg) of blubber would have provided heating, lighting, and cooking oil for months, so a whale kill was a vital element in survival. The bones were invaluable for rafters and house walls. While Thule communities also consumed other foods, the sheer mass of whale meat and blubber probably overshadowed other supplies. Whales were the staple for dozens of arctic groups across the mainland and Arctic Archipelago (Figure 4.21).

perhaps taking about half a century, or even much less, with dog sleds making the journey possible in just a few years. This was, in many senses, a commercial venture, a form of mercantile exploration. These were entrepreneurial people, who moved eastward in search of metal and to trade with Europeans who were landing on eastern shores.

With their superior hunting technology, more elaborate social organization, and vastly enhanced mobility by sled and boat, Thule groups settled over wide areas of the eastern Arctic. There is no archaeological evidence for any, let alone sustained, contact between Dorset and Thule (Figure 4.22). The Dorset people tended to hunt prey that was within walking distance of home, concentrating on the more easily taken, most abundant animals. Thule hunters ranged over much larger territories in their boats and with sleds. They exploited a wider range of food resources, were better organized, and had the ability to exploit, say, a seal migration route through a narrow defile miles from their base. Above all, they became expert whale hunters, a quarry that provided great quantities of food and other priceless raw materials.

Another factor in Thule expansion may have been a search for new sealing grounds, for there are signs of overhunting of ring seals in the Point Barrow region at this time. Perhaps population pressure and warring factions in the west caused some groups to move eastward, bringing their whale-hunting expertise with them. Most early Thule sites seem to have ancestry in Birnirk communities along the northern Alaskan coast near Barrow, that is, in villages influenced by

4.22 Classic Thule technology made use of many materials. *Clockwise from left*: an antler adze handle; a whalebone adze head with polished stone blade; a flensing knife with ground-slate blade; an *ulu* with iron blade; a whalebone snow knife, used to cut blocks for snow houses; an ivory engraving tool with small iron point; and a drill bit with a groundstone point.

new whale-hunting techniques and innovative technologies developed by local Punuk people. Later more people, this time with Punuk and Birnirk artifacts, followed in their footsteps, settling along the southern shores of the Canadian Arctic. Exactly when these migrations took place is also a matter of controversy, but it was most likely around 1000 CE.

Classic Thule: ?1250 to 1500 CE

The Thule people who moved throughout the High Arctic and into the south are known as the Classic Thule. They are remarkable not only for their hunting skills, but also for their extraordinary range of ingenious gadgets developed for the chase. The Thule people were ardent technologists. Like Birnirk in the west, however, Thule artistic endeavors were relatively modest, confined in the main to simple engravings on utilitarian artifacts, such as combs, often using Y-motifs and straight lines. Sometimes the engraver depicted humans and animals, even scenes of the chase. Three-dimensional figures in wood and ivory depict women without arms or legs, often with topknot hairstyles. Tiny ivory carvings of loons and other birds are relatively common, and are perhaps game pieces, or important ideological symbols, links between the people and the supernatural world.

Outside the whaling zones, other classic Thule prey resources formed the diet: caribou, walrus, seals, and fish. Thule hunters, with their more efficient technology and transportation, took a wider range of prey than their Dorset predecessors, not only musk ox and smaller mammals like fox, but clams, birds, even bird eggs. Even so, predictable caribou migrations and seal harvests, especially of ring seal, often helped determine where winter settlements were located. The hunters would drive caribou into shallow lakes where waiting men in kayaks would kill the frightened animals. On land, they drove small herds through converging lines of stones piled up to resemble human beings, killing the stampeding beasts with recurved bows and arrows at a range of about 33 ft (10 m). They took birds with multi-barbed spears or a small whalebone bolas, or snared them with gorges and hooks embedded in blubber.

Many Thule groups lived in large semi-subterranean winter houses constructed of stone, sod, and whalebones. Four to six houses holding some twenty to twenty-five people appears to have been a widespread norm, an adaptive size for efficient hunting of available resources in many areas. In summer, Thule groups moved into skin tents, the edges held down by circles of stones; these are the most ubiquitous archaeological sites in the eastern Arctic today. Sometimes they would move only a short distance, perhaps to get away from the stench of rotting sea-mammal carcasses that had been deep frozen through the winter.

This sophisticated Arctic society maintained at least sporadic contacts between dozens of scattered communities. Exotic materials including copper and iron passed from group to group over great distances. Old Bering Sea, Punuk, and Birnirk groups all used iron for knife blades and other tools, most of it from the Amur-Okhotsk Sea region of Siberia. By 1000 CE some Siberian iron was moving across the Bering Strait. Groups in the central and eastern Arctic relied on native copper, and also on meteoritic iron, the latter from a large shower at Cape York in northwest Greenland, used by Dorset peoples as early as the eleventh century. Metal was part of the Thule adaptation to the Canadian Arctic, and the trade in this precious commodity was a unique aspect of their culture. It allowed them to reduce large bones, antlers, and wood fragments to finished tools, boat frames, and other artifacts. Perhaps metal and other resources obtained from afar were controlled, managed, and distributed by umialiks—family heads and owners of whaling boats.

Post-Classic Thule: 1400 CE to European Contact

By the thirteenth century CE Thule sites appear in areas where whales were scarcer. The caribou, seal, and fish bones from these settlements argue for a more gradual settlement of less whale-rich areas, using the familiar subsistence strategies of the west. Thule settlements occurred as far north as northern Greenland, possibly reflecting growing population pressure in the classic areas.

The onset of the **Little Ice Age** brought cooler conditions after 1400 CE and very cold temperatures between 1600 and 1850, a time when glaciers advanced on Greenland and Baffin Island. Summer pack ice may have been so heavy that boat work was severely restricted, shortening the seasons for open-water whale hunting. Many Thule sites show that baleen whale hunting declined after 1400 CE. By the late sixteenth century umiak and kayak whaling had ceased in the High Arctic and in the central Arctic channels. The people probably turned to fishing, sealing, musk-ox hunting, and fox trapping for much of their sustenance. These may have been hard times. Moreau Maxwell excavated an isolated Post-Classic dwelling at Ruggles Outlet, on Lake Hazen in the interior of Ellesmere Island. A hunter took several foxes and a musk ox before he died. His widow buried him under some rocks outside the house. She was left alone and ate three sled dogs, then died on the sleeping platform inside the house. Climatic conditions became so severe that by 1600 CE much of the High Arctic was abandoned.

In the eastern Arctic, European contact began with the Norsemen who settled southern Greenland, as early as 1000 CE. Though sighted only irregularly, Norse ships based on Greenland were probably fairly familiar sights to Dorset groups living on the western shores of the Davis Strait. The Thule may not have had much direct contact with the Norsemen, but their iron, copper, cloth, and other trade goods diffused through the long-established exchange networks, and were traded for furs, walrus ivory, and gyrfalcons. The sporadic exchanges persisted until about 1480, when the Norse settlements in Greenland were abandoned. A century later English voyager Martin Frobisher arrived in search of the Northwest Passage, the first of the occasional contacts with European explorers, interactions which persisted until modern times.

SUMMARY

- A generic paleoarctic tradition flourished in Alaska and the western Yukon territory as well as further south between about 8000 and 5500 BCE.

- The predecessors of the Aleuts were the ancestors of a long maritime tradition that was thriving well before 2500 BCE. By 5500 BCE, the long-lived Ocean Bay marine-mammal hunting tradition had appeared on Kodiak Island. The later Kachemak Tradition appeared in about 1800 BCE and lasted until around 1000 CE, based on sea mammals, salmon fishing, and caribou hunting.

- The so-called Arctic Small Tool Tradition was a land-based cultural tradition that appeared along Alaskan coast by 2500 BCE. These people may have introduced the bow and arrow from Siberia, perhaps using the weapon against caribou. They moved eastward into the Canadian Archipelago after 2500 BCE. Their sites occur as far east as Greenland.

- During the first millennium BCE, maritime groups known as the Norton Tradition appeared in the Bering Strait region. They were expert sea-mammal hunters, who relied on toggle harpoons. The various cultural traditions that developed out of Norton were the ancestors of the Thule peoples of later centuries.

- The Pre-Dorset Tradition of the eastern Arctic developed into the Dorset in about 200 BCE, which lasted until 900 CE or later. It is remarkable for its art with magical and symbolic undertones.

- Thule people expanded eastward from the Bering Strait into the eastern Arctic in the eleventh century CE. Their descendants came in sporadic contact with Norse from Greenland before the fifteenth century.

CHRONOLOGICAL TABLE OF DEVELOPMENTS IN WESTERN NORTH AMERICA

Dates	West Coast		Great Basin	Southwest	Climatic stages
	Northwest	California			
Modern Times	MODERN GROUPS		MODERN GROUPS	MODERN GROUPS	LITTLE ICE AGE
	LATE PERIOD	LATE / AUGUSTINE / MIDDLE PERIOD / Many other variants	LATE ARCHAIC	HOHOKAM / MOGOLLON / ANASAZI	MEDIEVAL WARM PERIOD
1100 CE					LATE HOLOCENE
1 CE	MIDDLE PERIOD	BERKELEY	MIDDLE ARCHAIC	SOUTH WESTERN ARCHAIC	
1270 BCE					
2500 BCE	EARLY PERIOD	WINDMILLER / EARLY PERIOD	EARLY DESERT ARCHAIC		MIDDLE HOLOCENE
3800 BCE					
4900 BCE					
5900 BCE					
7000 BCE		? NORTH SOUTH			
8250 BCE			PALEO-INDIAN		EARLY HOLOCENE
10,000 BCE AND EARLIER		FIRST SETTLEMENT			YOUNGER DRYAS

The Mythical Pacific Eden

Santa Cruz Island, southern California, summer 1000 CE. The villagers gather on the sheltered beach as a heavily laden *tomol* (planked canoe) enters the bay. "Tomol! Tomol!" cry young children as the shell inlay on the high bow glitters in the morning sunlight. The skipper, dressed in his bear-skin cape, stands in the stern. Paddling slows as the canoe approaches the kelp bed that lies close offshore. Digging deep, the paddlers maneuver the canoe through the seaweed, then head for the beach, chanting as they ride the gentle breakers onto the sand. Waiting villagers seize the sides as the crew leaps into the shallow water and the group drags the tomol ashore. The skipper stands calmly as the canoe grounds, then steps ashore. His crew carries baskets of shell beads, two tuna, and a white sea bass, harpooned along the way, to the headman's dwelling.

The Pacific Coast was a magnet for human settlement after the end of the Ice Age. Some of the most complex hunter-gatherer societies on earth were to develop along this coastline. Why this emerging complexity? The answers come from a patchwork of archaeological sites scattered from southeast Alaska to the Mexican border.

A Diverse Coastal World

After the Ice Age, the Pacific Northwest Coast became a strip of green, forested landscape that stretched from the mouth of the Copper River in Alaska to the Klamath River in northern California (Ames and Maschner, 1999; Matson and Coupland, 1995; Moss, 2011). Here vast stands of spruce, cedar, hemlock, and Douglas fir mantled the coast and the great mountain ranges of the interior. The Pacific and the rivers that flowed into it provided whales, porpoises, seals, sea lions, and dozens of fish species, among them halibut, some of which weighed up to a quarter of a ton. Herring, smelt, and candle fish swarmed in coastal waters. No fewer than five salmon species appeared in inshore waters each year, jamming rivers as they crowded upstream to spawn. The rich and diverse coastal environment was highly productive, but the abundance varied from place to place and fluctuated through time. It was this varying bounty over many centuries that allowed some of the simple groups of earlier times to develop into such complex societies.

In the Northwest the damp, oceanic climate provided abundant natural resources to create an elaborate material culture, using straight-grained timber and only simple tools. One marvels at the thin, regular sides of large Northwestern dugout canoes, hollowed out from great, straight-grained trees using nothing but fire and stone and shell adzes, and at their high, flared ends that deflected rough water. Expert woodworkers made a magnificent array of artifacts, adorning many of them with a style that is among the most celebrated of Native American art forms. Renowned ancestors, mythical birds, and humans appear on many boxes and small objects. The flowing lines and ripples reflect the gentle wavelets and fast-moving riffles of the dark waters where these people lived. Commemorative posts, portal poles, and great totem poles recounted family genealogies and celebrated the deceased.

The Pacific Coast changes character beyond the Klamath River and stretches more than 1,250 miles (2,000 km) southward, backed by coastal mountain ranges from Oregon to central California (Aikens *et al.*, 2011; Arnold and Walsh, 2010; Fagan, 2003; Jones and Klar, 2010) (Figure 5.1). Strong winds and rough seas

5.1 Map showing sites mentioned in Chapter 5.

beset these exposed shores, making any form of offshore navigation a challenge, if not impossible, for low-sided dugout canoes, however large. The diverse, but much drier, coastal environments of central and southern California were more benign and could provide a wide range of food resources in good years. Even so, drought cycles and changing ocean temperatures could devastate acorn crops and fisheries. As in the Northwest, abundance meant population growth, scarcity perhaps more social opportunities.

Three-quarters of inland California is taken up by the Great Central Valley, with flat lowlands drained by the Sacramento and San Joaquin rivers that merge into a great delta, pass through a gap in the coastal ranges, and ultimately flow into San Francisco Bay. The Lower Sacramento Valley region supported some of the highest population densities in ancient California. Relatively high concentrations also flourished in the Lower San Joaquin Valley, the San Francisco Bay area, and along the Santa Barbara Channel. In these areas, extensive sloughs and marshlands provided fish, mollusks, plant foods, and waterfowl, while natural upwelling from the sea bed in the Santa Barbara Channel brought an abundance of anchovies and other inshore fish.

Much of the coast supported only sparse hunter-gatherer populations, but in areas where aquatic foods abounded much more complex societies developed, especially after 3000 BCE. Groups settled near the coast or adjacent to estuaries and wetlands enjoyed higher population densities, more diverse and reliable food supplies, and more elaborate social and cultural institutions.

Early Settlement of the Northwest Coast: Before 6000 to c. 3500 BCE

As we saw in Chapter 2, coastal and inland groups from the north took advantage of lower Early Holocene sea levels to move south along the Pacific. No one knows when serious maritime exploitation began, but by 6000 BCE some groups were relying heavily on salmon runs and herring fisheries, probably living at the same locations for prolonged periods (Figure 5.2). A well-developed maritime tradition, whose roots went back much earlier into the past, was in full swing. Long ago the Canadian archaeologist Knud Fladmark (1983) argued that favorable environmental conditions at the time enhanced salmon productivity, making a combination of seasonal salmon-run exploitation, herring fishing, and intensive shellfish consumption a highly viable lifeway. Some of these early groups may have been ancestral to the historic Tlingit, Haida, and other Athabascan-speaking peoples living in the Northwest today.

Salmon, Food Surpluses, and Exchange on the Northwest Coast: c. 3500 BCE to c. 500 CE

Just how important were salmon, halibut, and other fish along the Northwest Coast? The anadromous (up-river migration) habits of salmon allowed them to be harvested in great numbers with traps and weirs, as well as with spears, the

5.2 Excavations in the Rivermouth Trench at Namu, British Columbia, a site occupied as early as 7700 BCE. By 6000 BCE the inhabitants relied heavily on salmon runs and herring fisheries.

numbers only being limited by the ability of the fishers to gut and dry them before they spoilt. But even in areas where they abounded, local salmon stocks varied dramatically from one year to the next, and from one locale to another; this makes it well-nigh impossible to assess salmon's importance in cultural change along the coast. Between 3000 and 2000 BCE, however, coastal groups began an increasingly intensive manipulation of their diverse environments not only to meet subsistence and other economic requirements, but also to satisfy social and ideological needs. This progressively more efficient exploitation of marine and land resources was a key factor in the development of social complexity along the Northwest Coast and in the hinterland (Carlson, 2003).

The food surpluses generated by the fisheries meant that careful attention had to be paid to the storage of smoked and dried catches. This may have become easier with the appearance of cedar forests, which are found in pollen records for the Northwest after 3000 BCE. It was about this time that cedar-**planked houses** came into use, vital both for storage and as natural smoke houses. Coincidentally, woodworking tools came into more widespread use at about the same time.

Even as early as 3500 BCE one can recognize a nascent Northwest Coast cultural tradition that evolved continuously until European contact (Ames and Maschner, 1999; Carlson, 2003). By this time maritime adaptations were in full swing. For example, halibut, which can grow very large, assumed great importance in coastal diet. Carbon isotope analysis of a large sample of skeletons from coastal sites dating to the past 5,000 years reveals an almost total dependence on a maritime diet.

Many sites of this period are centered on the Strait of Georgia area, but are representative of cultural developments over a much wider area, even as far north as the Alaska Peninsula. There are signs increasing interaction between neighboring groups, reflected in widespread trade in toolmaking obsidian. Judging from **X-ray fluorescence studies**, much of the obsidian came from sources in eastern Oregon, reaching the Puget Sound region in Washington state, Vancouver Island and the Gulf Islands, and mainland British Columbia. Mount Edziza in northwestern British Columbia, as well as local sources, provided supplies for communities at the headwaters of the Yukon, near Juneau, Alaska, and throughout much of coastal northern British Columbia. These exchange networks, and others handling different commodities, may have contributed to the spread of ideas and culture traits throughout the coastal regions. This was the time, also, when the basic characteristics of historic Northwest Coast culture appeared—an emphasis on status and wealth, and on elaborate ceremonial, reflected in new art traditions.

Hunting and fishing technologies had become more elaborate, as witnessed by the many forms of stone, bone, and wooden projectile points used against bear, beaver, elk, and waterfowl. Fishers in large dugouts now ventured further offshore. They used nets and a wide variety of bent wood and composite fishhooks, known from over 400 of them discovered at the Hoko River site on the Olympic Peninsula (Croes, 1995) (Figure 5.3). Fish traps and weirs were critical for harvesting large catches, though the number in use fluctuated considerably

5.3 A halibut hook in situ at the Hoko River site, Washington State. Note the bone barb, the Indian plumb wood shanks, and two-stranded spruce-root leader attached. Experiments with modern replicas show that such hooks were very effective.

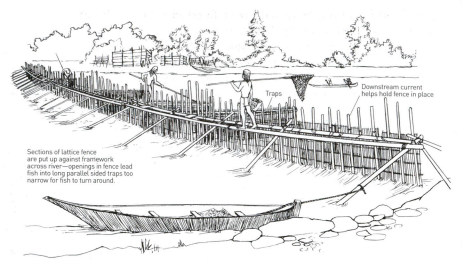

5.4 A fence weir for catching salmon, adapted from a Victorian photograph of the Cowichan River. A wooden barrier set across the river supports sections of lattice fence. Openings in the fence steered the fish into long, parallel-sided traps.

Traps

Downstream current helps hold fence in place

Sections of lattice fence are put up against framework across river—openings in fence lead fish into long parallel sided traps too narrow for fish to turn around.

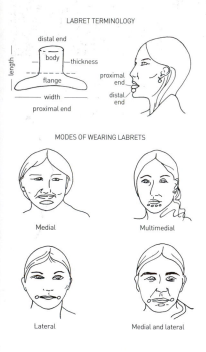

LABRET TERMINOLOGY

distal end
body
thickness
flange
proximal end
distal end
length
width
proximal end

MODES OF WEARING LABRETS

Medial

Multimedial

Lateral

Medial and lateral

5.5 The variety of ways in which labrets could be worn.

over the centuries. The earliest known weir dates to about 2000 BCE, but they must have been in use much earlier (Moss *et al.*, 1990) (Figure 5.4).

This long-term cultural development expresses itself archaeologically in many ways. By about 1500 BCE finely made polished chisels and adze blades and other specialized woodworking tools appear. By this time long cedar-bark cloths were fashioned into cloaks and other garments; basketry had reached a high level of sophistication; and planked houses were in widespread use.

We do not know how socially complex these societies were. Detecting changes in social status is challenging at the best of times, especially in the absence of burials, where wealthy individuals might lie accompanied by symbols of rank. Fortunately there are a few examples. The Pender Canal site in the Gulf Islands of British Columbia was occupied between 2000 and 1500 BCE, a location where burials show marked social differentiation, the wealthiest members of society being buried seated in stone slab cists with carved antler spoons or clam-shell dishes to help them satisfy their hunger (Ames and Maschner, 1999).

Pender highlights the importance of prestigious ornaments, of which the labret, a conspicuous lip ornament, is the most significant, an emblem of rank worn by men and women (Figure 5.5). Nephrite adze blades, used for canoe building and other activities, were also prestigious objects, and are found throughout the Fraser River and Strait of Georgia regions. Graves with costly and exotic artifacts become more common after 500 BCE.

As each group wrestled with the problems of managing increasingly large food surpluses and redistributing them through society, prestige and wealth may have been the mechanisms that drove Northwest society. A few wealthy and powerful individuals may have controlled redistribution as a way of acquiring personal prestige. One mechanism for doing this may have been ceremonial feasts, the ancestors of the **potlatches** (elaborate feasts accompanied by gift-giving) of historic times. These would have been occasions for both gift exchange and more prosaic distributions of such commodities as furs and smoked fish. The participants would have donned their full regalia of rank: labrets, lip ornaments, and gorgets worn at the throat. Increasingly sophisticated art styles, for instance animal motifs carved on bowls and spoons, foreshadow the prestigious crests that would be favored in later times.

Widespread exchange, craft specialization, intensive exploitation of the Pacific, a preoccupation with wealth and prestige—all the basic elements of later Northwestern society were in place by 500 CE. Soon the trajectory of cultural change accelerated still further.

South of the Klamath River: Before 10,000 to 1500 BCE

Further south the rocky and mountainous habitat of the northern California coast supported sparse Archaic populations for thousands of years (Gamble, 2015). The size of local bands seems to have varied considerably; most subsisted off wild vegetable foods, mollusks, and some fish or sea mammals, moving seasonally from one concentration of edible foods to another (Moratto, 1984) (Figure 5.6).

In San Francisco Bay two great river systems converge—the Sacramento and San Joaquin. There had always been a large flood-plain here, but as rising sea levels inundated the flat lands inside the Golden Gate, a great shallow-water bay formed. For the first time, people living around the bay had reliable food sources at their doorstep. By 3000 BCE extensive marshes had formed around the margins of the bay, supporting a remarkable array of animal and plant life. As the marshlands grew, so human settlement in the bay lowlands became more long-term, much of it dependent on mussels and oysters (Erlandson and Glassow, 1997).

For many bands the bay was one stop on an annual round that extended far inland. People tended to live on mounds formed of discarded shells, mud, sand, and other debris, surrounded by muddy flats at low tide. In time, some mounds became large base camps, located near productive oyster beds, and places where clams could be taken or fish speared from canoes. Few of these early camps have survived the ravages of modern urban sprawl, so we know little of their occupants' lives.

Still further south, central and southern California also supported low populations for many thousands of years. The Archaic Tradition of the shore seems to owe much to earlier Paleo-Indian cultures, with new artifacts for seed processing grafted onto an existing material culture. For thousands of years archaeological sites throughout California yield little more than milling stones for processing small nuts and seeds. Such artifacts are little more than roughly shaped rocks with a flat surface smoothed by hours of grinding; nevertheless, they were vitally important, for they prepared the core of a plant-based diet. The soft scrape, scrape of milling stones would have greeted visitors to hunter-gatherer camps the length and breadth of the California coast.

Judging from a rise in site numbers, admittedly a somewhat tenuous yardstick to use, Santa Barbara Channel populations may have first reached significant levels about 6000 BCE, with a drop in coastal settlements in the Middle Holocene between about 5000 and 3500 BCE, and the lowest density occurring between 4000 and 3500 BCE, perhaps during the dry and warmer climatic optimum (sometimes called the **Altithermal**). Sea levels were rising, drowning the plant-rich coastal plain. The gradual reduction of seed communities may have contributed to a

5.6 Seed-gathering technology: a California Pomo woman collects seeds with a beater and basket.

shift to acorn harvesting in an environment of unpredictable rainfall and ocean temperatures, oaks having become more common than they were in earlier times (see Box: Acorns: The Ultimate Staple). Coastal populations then rose relatively rapidly, coinciding with the first use of pestles and mortars, perhaps with more intensive acorn exploitation, certainly with a greater emphasis on fishing and sea-mammal hunting. Similar patterns are thought to occur elsewhere in southern California. The population growth after 3500 BCE may have also coincided with an increase in the productivity of the inshore marine habitat as kelp beds reappeared, even if climate conditions were as unpredictable as they are today.

As populations grew, the overall energy cost of providing food increased, especially in drought cycles. More effort would have been needed to obtain food, perhaps triggering a shift to new food sources that may have required a greater investment of time and energy to catch or process. For instance, both large sea mammals and deer were favored resources when they were easy to obtain. As population densities rose, they became scarce, requiring more energy to collect. Seals and sea lions that frequented convenient beaches were an easily

ACORNS: THE ULTIMATE STAPLE

In the past, fifteen oak species grew from southern California to Oregon. In a good year they produced enough acorns to feed both animals and humans. Yields of 1,750 lb per 2.5 acres (800 kg per ha) were not uncommon. A reliable food supply, one would have thought, but harvests varied sharply from year to year. Acorns have excellent nutritional value, higher than that of maize or wheat, and can be stored for several years.

Acorns are a labor-intensive and time-consuming crop to process. Shelling and pounding takes hours, far longer than milling grass seeds. The meal is inedible, for acorns contain bitter tannic acid that has to be leached away before they are eaten. Reducing acorns to meal requires pestles and mortars, whose presence in archaeological sites in large numbers is a sure sign of acorn processing. Many mortars were little more than pecked out depressions on rocky outcrops near the oak groves. The acorns would be shelled with a hammer stone, then winnowed in a basket to remove the rust-colored skin. They would then be pounded with pestles of different weights until they formed a fine powder (Figure 5.7). The best way to leach acorns is to pour the meal into a depression, then flush it with water repeatedly for two to four hours. In one experiment the anthropologist Walter Goldschmidt obtained 5.3 lb (2.4 kg) of meal from 6 lb (2.7 kg) of pounded acorns (Goldschmidt, 1951). Leaching alone took four hours. The equivalent processing time and yield from wheat would be about the same.

Acorns are the most obvious example of a high-cost food resource, for the elaborate processing procedure required has been documented from ethnographic observations. Both seeds and acorns have a major advantage over other foods: they are easily stored for future use, so can be drawn upon in lean winter months. Both require considerable collecting and processing effort, but acorns came into more widespread use as rising sea levels reduced seed harvests. Acorn harvesting required exquisite timing, for the harvesters had to reach the tree before the ripe acorns fell off into the mouths of waiting deer.

5.7 Woman pounding acorns, a late nineteenth-century drawing.

Come fall, each band would camp near the oak groves that were traditionally theirs to harvest. The harvest itself was a lengthy process, for the yield from a single large tree could be as high as 55 lb (25 kg) and might take a full day to collect. But the labor of gathering the acorns paled beside the work of carrying them back to camp, then processing and storing them somewhere dry and safe from rodents. Many historic groups erected bark granaries raised off the ground. Others kept them in baskets mixed with bay leaves, which gave off a pungent aroma and discouraged insects.

hunted resource, but once the hunters had to mount special expeditions to remoter areas, the hunting cost rose rapidly.

Fishing, too, has varied costs. Catching inshore fish by hook and line in tide pools or from outlying rocks is a cheap way of getting food, but the yield is usually low. To exploit the rich kelp beds close offshore, where the yields would be much higher, canoes would be needed. Building and maintaining boats, however, requires considerable effort, as does sewing and repairing seine nets to be used from shore or canoe. Sea craft more substantial than a reed raft demand still greater resources, but could have been used for catching such larger fish as halibut or shark, species with a high meat yield per specimen landed.

The Middle Holocene also saw an increase in long-distance exchange, especially of exotic materials and ceremonial objects, such as pipes. Interestingly, rare but distinctive shell beads known as "Olivella Grooved Rectangles" appear at many sites on the southern Channel Islands, in coastal and inland California, Nevada, and central Oregon, dating to about 4000 to 2500 BCE. They provide evidence of cultural interaction over a very large area of the west.

The Northwest Coast: c. 1000 BCE to Modern Times

Social complexity developed in many forms along the Northwest Coast, probably in different places at different times and, on more than one occasion, manifested by sophisticated division of labor, specialized production, and very intricate patterns of regional exchange. At European contact in the late eighteenth century the northern Northwest Coast supported some of the most socially complex hunter-gatherers along the Pacific Coast. At least 43,500 Tlingit, Tsimshian, and Haida lived along this indented coastline of deep inlets and offshore islands, from southeast Alaska to Haida Gwaii and the Prince Rupert area of the British Columbia mainland. There is abundant evidence for volatile cultural change and elaboration over the past 3,000 years, processes at first accelerated, then drastically interrupted, by European contact—by Russians in 1741, by Spaniards in 1774, and by Captain James Cook four years later.

The West Coast's complex history after 1000 BCE raises important questions. Why did coastal societies in some locations develop significant complexity and large settlements? Why were such elaborations so volatile? The answers appear to lie in the complex relationships between climate change, food supplies, sea-water temperatures, and that most important of short term climatic events—**El Niño**.

By 500 CE the Northwest Coast cultural pattern was well established everywhere, marked by an increasing emphasis on salmon fishing. Both artifacts and art styles reflect historically known cultures. Along the northern coast, from southeast Alaska to northern and central British Columbia, large, permanent villages developed, inhabited by people living in sizable houses, in groups of twenty to sixty individuals. At the same time, many settlements became fortified redoubts on bluffs and cliff tops. In Tebenkof Bay, southeast Alaska, congregations of formerly independent villages lay not near the best food resources, but along straight coastlines, at easily defended locations where one could see for long distances. Perhaps the bow and arrow was now a strategic weapon, so that people were forced to live in fortified villages where they could protect themselves against enemies, living cheek-by-jowl with families from other kin groups. Archaeologist Herbert Maschner theorizes from his Tebenkof data that from being small, independent kin-group-based hamlets, northern Northwest Coast settlements became large, multi-kin-group villages circumscribed by the realities of locally dense populations, regular conflict, and the need to redistribute food resources, many of which came from some distance away (Ames and Maschner, 1999).

The development of political complexity along the northern Northwest Coast resulted from several closely linked circumstances. First, population density reached a critical level in an environment where food resources were distributed unevenly or within well-defined areas. Individual groups organized their lives around those areas where food was most abundant, and to take advantage of periods when they were most plentiful. As the coastal population rose, it became impossible for groups in competition or conflict simply to move away to another area with good food supplies. Under such circumstances, social complexity is likely to develop. A few individuals assumed control over the redistribution of food and over political relationships between neighbors. Politically and socially more complex societies were thus the result of volatile and rapidly changing conditions.

The southern Northwest Coast, from northern Vancouver Island to north of Cape Mendocino, witnessed a similar trend toward more complex societies, with locally high population densities, heavy reliance on storage, and intense manipulation of the environment. Here, also, local populations rose rapidly after 1000 BCE, then fluctuated considerably in the centuries of climatic change after 500 CE. As time went on, semi-subterranean dwellings gave way to large, planked houses occupied for several centuries—a clear sign of greater sedentism (Figure 5.8).

Coastal plank houses (and long houses built of thatch and matting in the interior) now increased in size, housing large domestic groups (Figure 5.9). The archaeologist Ken Ames believes they reflect societies where domestic tasks such as harvesting salmon runs or catching and drying herring were highly organized, as part of a strategy for maximizing harvests and creating large food stocks (Ames and Maschner, 1999). This strategy was locally focused, but had much broader regional implications. Large-scale social networks, marked by

5.8 House styles typical of the Northwest Coast. *Left:* northern-style houses. *Right:* houses found on the southern coasts.

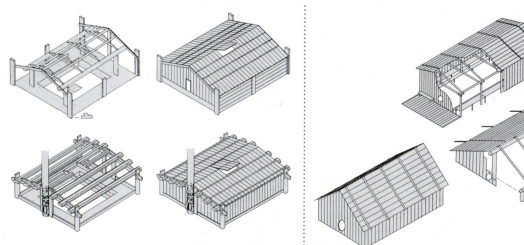

5.9 Village at Nootka Sound, Vancouver Island, showing the roof style of planked houses in central-coast villages. Drawing by John Webber, James Cook expedition, 1778.

5.10 Haida Village on Haida Gwaii, photographed in the late nineteenth century, with totem poles, large plank houses, and canoes.

different art styles, tattooing, and ornaments, now connected widely separated parts of the Northwest Coast (Figure 5.10).

Some archaeological sites along the central and southern Northwest Coast document historic cultures during earlier times. By 400 CE there are clear signs of differing social status, both in the value and quantity of grave goods and in the presence of skull deformation, a characteristic of socially prominent birth on the Northwest Coast. For instance, Nootka-speaking peoples flourished on the shores of the Strait of Juan de Fuca, and on the west coast of Vancouver Island.

THE ANCIENT MAKAH VILLAGE AT OZETTE, WASHINGTON

For many centuries the ancestors of modern-day, Nootka-speaking Makah lived in a cluster of cedar-wood houses at Ozette, on the Pacific Coast of the Olympic Peninsula. In about 1750 CE a large mudslide buried at least four planked dwellings without warning. During the 1960s Richard Daugherty of Washington State University excavated the still-waterlogged remains of the collapsed houses. He used high-pressure and small garden hoses to expose a rich treasure trove of well-preserved wooden artifacts that proclaim the great richness of Makah culture before European contact (Figure 5.11).

Hundreds of small household items lay jumbled among the collapsed walls—animal bones, storage boxes, baskets, and cooking hearths. Dozens of cod and halibut fishhooks and pieces of harpoons and whaling kit also came from the Ozette houses. Bark cloth, hide, and netting survived in perfect condition. There were carved wooden bowls that once held seal and whale oil (Figure 5.12). Heavy wooden clubs bore carvings of humans, seals, and owl heads.

5.11 Carved panel depicting a Thunderbird and a Wolf, found in a broken state on a house floor at Ozette, Washington.

5.12 Oil dish in the form of a human figure, found at Ozette, Washington.

5.13 A carved cedar representation of a portion of a whale's back, including the closed fin. One surface is decorated with more than 700 otter teeth. This object was probably used in whale-hunting ceremonies. Captain Cook recorded a similar artifact on his voyage. Length: approximately 3.3 ft (1 m).

Ozette art and artifacts show connections with those of other Nootka-speaking coastal peoples, and with people living to the south, also with Salish groups on Puget Sound. The decorated objects include wooden boxes, clubs, whale harpoons, bows, and a magnificent cedar whale fin adorned with a mythical thunderbird outlined in sea-otter teeth (Figure 5.13). The motifs are lively, mainly zoomorphic and anthropomorphic, with many complex geometric patterns that appeared on materials as diverse as bone and basketry.

Basketry types from Hoko River on the Olympic Peninsula reflect 3,000 years of Nootkan style. Whaling became more important during these centuries, epitomized by the Ozette site on the Pacific Coast south of Cape Flattery, perhaps the most important sea-mammal hunting location for hundreds of miles along the West Coast (see Box: The Ancient Makah Village at Ozette, Washington).

The Interior Plateau: 8500 BCE to Modern Times

Before traveling south along the California coast, we must describe the hunter-gatherer societies of the northwestern interior, which interacted intensively with coastal communities (Aikens *et al.*, 2011). The Interior Plateau lies between the Pacific Coast and the Great Basin and is bisected by two major rivers: the Columbia in the sagebrush grasslands of the southern Plateau and the Fraser in the more wooded north. During Early Holocene times the climate was cooler and moister than today, with warmer and drier conditions after 6000 BCE. Warmer temperatures reduced pine forest cover; grassland and shrub-steppe now covered much of the semi-arid landscape. For thousands of years a sparse hunter-gatherer population occupied the Plateau, with the densest settlement near rivers and other permanent water sources (Figure 5.14). There they harvested salmon runs, often living in small **pithouse** communities. (Pithouses are dwellings where all or part of the walls are formed from the sides of an excavated pit.)

Fishing has a long history on the Plateau. The Dalles of the Columbia River are long, rapids-choked narrows at a natural boundary between the Plateau and the coast, an extremely productive salmon fishery in historic times and perhaps as early as 8000 BCE. By 3000 BCE people lived in substantial, well-insulated circular houses dug about 5 ft (1.5 m) into the ground, with a diameter of 30 ft (9 m) or more. Some of the larger structures may have been dwellings for high-status families.

Some locations remained in use for long periods. The Keatley Creek site on the Fraser River near Liloot, British Columbia, has yielded a long sequence of human occupation, starting as early as 9000 BCE and ending in historic times. From about 5000 to 1500 BCE the location occasionally served as a base camp for salmon fishers. Between 1500 and 400 BCE major winter pithouses rose at Keatley

5.14 Artist's reconstruction of a typical Columbia Plateau village. Four sloping rafters supported a roof of logs, poles, and bark, covered with earth and sod, with a smoke hole that also served as the entrance.

Creek, occupied by residential corporate groups with rights over productive fishing locations. Isotopic analyses of human skeletons reveal that after 400 BCE the inhabitants were obtaining as much as 60 percent of their food from fish.

The best fisheries lay along short stretches of narrows, near rapids, and in canyons, where the people took thousands of salmon in summer and fall. Other foods were not neglected. Many interior groups used pits to roast great quantities of wild onions, balsam roots, and other tubers. After 1000 BCE complex trade networks linked coast and interior; they brought sea shells far inland, and turquoise from the Great Basin and Southwestern areas. Such art objects as wooden masks used to proclaim rank and status also moved from the coast to the interior, as some individuals and families acquired greater wealth and political power.

Further inland people had to rely on more meager, widely scattered food resources in an increasingly arid environment. These were highly mobile hunter-gatherer populations in regular contact with others living long distances away. As a result, artifacts, ideas, and geographical information passed over very large areas of the ancient west.

Northern California Coast: 3000 BCE and Later

Intricate coastal and riverine adaptations gave rise to societies that reached the effective limits of social complexity without adopting agriculture. They

NORTHERN CALIFORNIA CULTURAL SEQUENCE

A well-established cultural sequence flourished in the Sacramento and San Francisco Bay regions with their abundant wetlands (Lightfoot *et al.*, 2015).

Windmiller: *c.* 2500 BCE to Recent Times
Around 2500 BCE Windmiller people, who were well adapted to riverine and marshland environments, settled in the Sacramento Delta region (Ragir, 1972). These Penutian speakers may have originated in the Columbia Plateau or western Great Basin, settling in a bountiful, low-lying area where their successors were to flourish for more than 4,000 years. Windmiller groups fished for sturgeon, salmon, and other fish with spears, nets, and lines, as well as harvesting storable plant foods such as acorns (Figure 5.15). Many

groups also hunted in the nearby Sierras during the summer months. Windmiller burials and cemeteries show evidence of ceremonial activity, including the use of red ocher, with bodies commonly oriented toward the west with their faces down. Related groups spread widely in the Central Valley, also westward into the Bay area, forming the foundations of a cultural tradition that was to survive into recent times.

Berkeley Pattern: *c.* 2000 BCE to 300–500 CE
Soon after 2000 BCE Berkeley Pattern peoples, Utian-speaking with a similar material culture to the Windmiller culture, moved into the Bay area. This movement may have coincided with a great expansion of bayside and coastal marshlands that supported fish and shellfish, large waterfowl populations, also game and many edible plant species. By 1 CE numerous Berkeley Pattern villages flourished throughout

the San Francisco Bay area, along the central California coast, and in the Monterey Bay area. In the Bay itself there was a veritable landscape of mounds and villages set among flat marshlands and inhabited for many generations. Many Berkeley Pattern settlements lay near freshwater streams and marshlands. By settling in such locations the people could exploit both inland and bayside environments. The earliest settlements were in these prime sites, where there were few gaps in the annual "harvest" of different resources. Later, increasingly dense populations split off to form satellite communities in more marginal lands. The result: more formal social and political relationships, the emergence of important kin leaders, and greater social complexity.

Augustine Pattern: 300–500 CE to Recent Times
Between 300 and 500 CE the Berkeley Pattern gradually evolved into the

were still flourishing in constantly changing forms along the Pacific Coast at European contact. After 3000 to 2000 BCE the climate was essentially the same as today. Acorn crops were important everywhere, on the coast and in the interior. Shellfish played a major role in the San Francisco Bay area, while the peoples of the Santa Barbara Channel region and further south exploited mollusks, sea mammals, and fish. The intensive exploitation of acorns and marine resources coincided with an elaboration of technology, art, and social organization in some areas, especially in the Santa Barbara Channel and the San Francisco Bay–Sacramento–San Joaquin Delta regions, where a wide variety of foods was available year-round (see Box: Northern California Cultural Sequence). These groups also developed complex social mechanisms to regulate long-distance exchange and the redistribution of resources: political alliances, kin ties and ritual obligations, and formal banking of resources.

The California coast was a high-risk environment, affected by constant and often severe drought cycles; the past 5,000 years have been characterized by dramatic short-term fluctuations in precipitation and sea-water temperatures. In summer, most of the time a combination of a persistent high pressure offshore and northwesterly winds caused warm surface water to move offshore. Much colder water from the depths of the ocean rose to the surface, bringing nutrients that fed zooplankton. Each summer, billions of spawning sardines moved inshore

Augustine Pattern, with technological innovations such as the bow and arrow, harpoons, and tubular tobacco pipes, and an unusual custom, that of burning artifacts in a grave before the body was interred. Later, during the drought-plagued Medieval Warm Period, people from the interior moved toward the more temperate coast in search of food. Dry conditions and high population densities nearby prevented them from moving into unexploited territories, so they exploited such foods as acorns, which, as we have seen, were expensive to process on a large scale.

After 1400 CE the number of Augustine settlements proliferated markedly, many founded by kin leaders who maintained constant ties with neighboring communities. An elaborate ceremonial involving secret societies and cults came into being. Inter-community exchange assumed such importance that clam-shell disk "money" came into widespread use. This increasingly complex cultural system survived until European contact and beyond, finally to disintegrate in the face of inexorable Spanish missionary activity.

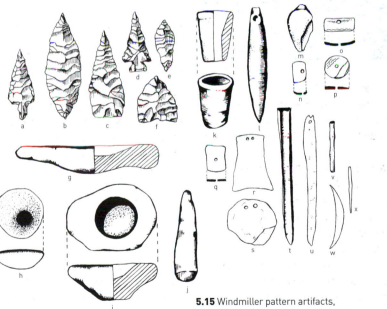

5.15 Windmiller pattern artifacts, including projectile points (a–f), milling, grinding, and pounding stones (g–k), and ornaments and bone implements (l–x). The same basic technology, with changes such as bows and arrows and different projectile points, continued throughout the area until recent times.

in the Santa Barbara Channel, quarry for both humans and larger fish. If the upwelling died down, fish catches suffered dramatically. This happened when major, unpredictable El Niños brought intense storms and epochal rainfall. These irregular global events bring warmer sea temperatures and cut off the natural upwelling of nutrients for the fish that were a staple of coastal groups. El Niños triggered unpredictable environmental and cultural stress.

The north coast is isolated and relatively mountainous, but its sparse populations interacted with people in neighboring areas. The Yurok, from the extreme northwestern California coast, came under strong influence from coastal peoples in Oregon and Washington, while groups living to the south were open to ideas and contacts from their California neighbors. Even so, each local group had its own distinctive adaptation. Most of them formed "tribelets," small groups presided over by a local chief or headman, each with their own territory, often a local river drainage area. Isolated tribelets often came together, usually in the fall, and cooperated with others in catching and smoking salmon, or when netting multitudes of smelt on the fringes of sandy beaches. Come winter, most groups resided in base camps, relying heavily on foods stored during the summer months. This general form of lifeway thrived throughout the north coast region, albeit with considerable local variation.

Southern California Coast: 1500 BCE and Later

The Santa Barbara Channel and other parts of the southern California coast supported sophisticated hunter-gatherer societies at European contact (Gamble, 2008, 2015). They faced stressful environmental conditions, including food shortages caused by intense human predation of individual fish species. Between 1000 BCE and 1300 CE coastal Chumash people depended ever more heavily on the ocean. By this time fishers sought deep-water fish, including swordfish, offshore, using distinctive planked canoes known in later times as tomols (Figure 5.16). Some Chumash villages in the Santa Barbara area housed as many as 1,000 people and were centers for important ceremonies and trading activities. They served as political "capitals" with influence over several lesser villages, even anchoring loose political confederations of lesser communities (Figure 5.17).

A hereditary chief (**wot**) ruled each village. They served as war leaders and patrons of ceremonial village feasts (see Box: El Montón: A Persistent Place).

5.16 A reconstruction by Travis Hudson and Peter Howorth of a planked canoe (tomol) used by both the Chumash and the Gabrieleño groups for fishing, sea-mammal hunting, trade, and transportation. Modern experiments have shown that a skilled crew kneeling on sea-grass pads could reach speeds between 6 and 8 knots with a moderate following wind, paddling at a constant rate for hours on end. Most passages were made during early morning hours when winds were calm.

5.17 Artist's reconstruction of a Chumash village, by A. E. Treganza, 1942.

EL MONTÓN: A PERSISTENT PLACE

Shell middens have always been the poor relatives among archaeological sites, despite being conspicuous in many ancient landscapes. The Calusa of southern Florida constructed large mounds and what one would normally call earthworks from piled mollusk shells. Middens abound on the East Coast and in Midwestern river valleys, as well as in the San Francisco Bay area and southern California. Archaeologists have always thought of them as garbage heaps of decaying emptied shells, but also realized that many of them were also burial places, and some dwelling places, especially in low-lying environments. We have talked occasionally in these pages of the importance of social memory, of visions of human existence and the cosmos transmitted orally from one generation to the next. Such humanly made structures as Greece's Parthenon, or Pueblo Bonito in Chaco Canyon, are particularly spectacular symbols of that memory. Humble shell middens, large or small, are similar tokens of social memory, freighted with associations of past times or revered ancestors. Some of these places, even inconspicuous ones, became sites that were recognized, used, or ritually commemorated for long periods in hunter-gatherer worlds that were rich in symbolism and historical association. They have been called "Persistent Places," a term that can rightly be applied to conspicuous burial mounds and shell middens that were used for thousands of years and became part of the landscape, places where people were buried and commemorated with feasts, where alliances were forged, and where people often dwelt.

This approach to shell middens, first applied in California to mounds in the Bay area, has now being applied to the El Montón site at the extreme western end of Santa Cruz Island (Gamble, 2017). This conspicuous, large site has been radiocarbon dated to between about 5000 to 4000 BCE. It lies on a marine terrace and stands between 26 and 33 ft (8 and 10 m) high, covering about 11 acres (4.5 ha). The long-occupied village overlooks a sheltered bay with easy canoe landing and is ideal for watching for sea life in neighboring waters. This place really stands out. You can see El Montón from at least 6 miles (10 km) away, even from the neighboring Santa Rosa Island. About fifty house depressions can be seen on the surface; at least 237 skeletons were recovered from its cemeteries during a series of excavations over eighty years ago.

Gamble has reconstructed the history of this "Persistent Place." She believes the first visitors were attracted by the extensive intertidal zones, fish-rich kelp beds, and fresh water available nearby. Eventually people settled there, constructing thatch-covered dwellings where they lived as they harvested the rich marine foods nearby. They buried their dead on the highest parts of the mound, some of them with grave goods that distinguished them from others. Clearly, El Montón became more »

Once during the fall, and at the winter solstice, outlying communities near and far flocked to major settlements for ceremonies that honored the earth and the sun.

The Chumash were artists, their **petroglyphs** and **pictographs** some of the most spectacular north of the Mexican border. Chumash shamans and specialists served as the artists, painting the walls of remote inland caves and rockshelters with abstract representations of the sun, stars, human beings, birds, fish, and reptiles (Figure 5.18). The meaning of the art is unknown, but at least some of it is astronomical, and linked to a calendrical system. Some painted sites may have served as solstice observatories, as did the Condor Cave in the coastal mountains. Here, the rising sun shines through a hole carved by a shaman in the cave wall onto an image in the floor. Later, the shaman painted his spirit helper, a red-legged frog, on the wall.

Chumash groups maintained exchange contacts with other coastal communities to the south, also with peoples living far in the interior. The Gabrieleño occupied the Pacific Coast areas now under the urban sprawl of Los Angeles and Orange County. They controlled valuable steatite outcrops on Catalina Island offshore. This was a soft stone ideal for making stone griddles and pots, which they traded widely.

important as it grew in size, in part because of its strategic position, and also on account of its rich associations with ancestors buried there. It must have become a place where feasts took place, and where such calendrical events as the winter solstice were commemorated.

The three cemeteries at the highest point of the mound lie close to one another, with no house depressions nearby, as if the summit was a sacred place, perhaps a space lying between the living and the supernatural world. Perhaps it was an interface between the land and the sea, between life and death, a location with powerful social associations and memories. The treatment of the dead is informative. Death before adulthood was commonplace, yet these individuals were buried with the same degree of respect as adults. The central part of the cemetery yielded nine people buried in an extended position, rather than flexed like everyone else. They were buried with beads, ornaments, and artifacts made of black serpentine, a rock found on the mainland about 50 miles (80 km) away. One young woman stood out, being buried with 157 effigies, some painted and shaped, perhaps a sign that she was someone with unusual ritual and supernatural powers. The inhabitants of El Montón buried their dead atop the mound for over three millennia, mortuary events that persisted for many centuries and must have been of great ritual importance. This alone may have made this location a place of powerful social memory.

Feasting is, by its nature, difficult to identify in archaeological sites. Gamble has identified a concentration of large, often whole, red **abalone** shells close to the cemetery area, which she believes may be the remains of a feast. Some dolphin bones and parts of an ocean sunfish, a huge, unusual catch, as well as the pits of holly-leaved cherry, which require extensive leaching for human consumption, came from the same location. All of this is reasonably compelling evidence for a feast, perhaps in commemoration of ancestors.

El Montón was repeatedly visited, a place readily accessible by canoe, whose inhabitants changed their diets to adapt to warmer and cooler sea surface temperatures and other fluctuations. This was, of course, a place where people lived, foraged, fished, and died, but it was almost certainly far more as well. Here generations of Chumash performed rituals, with some individuals mediating between the living and spiritual worlds, commemorating the ancestors with dance and chant, marking the endless passage of the seasons and the comings and goings of the fish, mollusks, and sea mammals that sustained them. There is much more to shell middens than just discarded meals.

5.18 Chumash rock paintings in Pleito Creek, Kern County, California.

5.19 Chumash baskets, some of the finest ever fabricated in North America, were of critical importance for subsistence and trade. They were used for storing food, and for harvesting acorns and other plant crops. Baskets were also widely used for trading such commodities as shell beads.

Those who rely heavily on intensive exploitation of relatively few, seasonal foods—nuts or acorns, for example—and store their harvests are highly vulnerable to longer-term drought cycles, such as those that descended on the west during the Medieval Warm Period. The droughts arrived as coastal populations were on the rise, when larger, densely packed settlements resulted in higher incidences of disease and malnutrition. The well-documented response along the coast was to exploit a much wider range of marine habitats, to elaborate fishing and sea-mammal hunting technology, and to invest much greater amounts of labor in such activities. The increasing complexity of coastal populations may have resulted not from bounty, but from severe drought, movements of inland groups nearer more reliable food supplies at the coast, and from the need to maintain territorial boundaries and regulate food supplies and exchange (Figure 5.19).

Biological anthropologist Phillip Walker studied Channel Island skeletons during the Medieval Warm Period and believes that chronic anemia, manifested by a condition called *cribra orbitalia*, was caused by high nutrient losses resulting from food shortages (Lambert and Walker, 1991). Thus, severe drought, chronic illness, and, above all, water shortages may have caused widespread distress, the abandonment of many island settlements, and violence stemming from competition for scarce and dwindling water supplies. At the same time, wounds caused by projectile points increased dramatically until about 1150 CE, when they declined again, for reasons that are unclear.

A complex interplay between ocean temperatures, rainfall, and other environmental conditions, whether natural or humanly induced, was but one factor in an intricate equation that affected the complexity of hunter-gatherer societies along the coast over more than 3,000 years.

SUMMARY

- Much of the West Coast supported sparse hunter-gatherer populations, but some of the most complex hunter-gatherer societies on earth developed in areas with rich aquatic resources.

- The first settlement of the West Coast was part of the little-understood population movements of the first Americans after 14,000 years ago. By 6000 BCE many groups in the Northwest were replying on maritime resources. Coastal groups developed increasingly intense harvesting of salmon and other fish between 3000 and 2000 BCE. This harvesting was a critical factor in the development of social complexity along the Northwest Coast.

- The densest California coastal populations developed in the Sacramento and San Joaquin delta, also in the Santa Barbara Channel region of the south. As the climate became drier, seeds and such plant foods as acorns became significant parts of the diet. After 3000 BCE shellfish assumed great significance in shallow-water estuaries and marshy areas, as did fishing.

- After 1000 BCE Northwest Coast coastal populations rose significantly, permanent villages came into being, and large, multi-kin-group settlements engaged in intensive long-distance exchange that evened out patchy food supplies. Under such changing and volatile conditions storage became important, as did decisive leadership. This is when Northwest societies developed into some of the most complex hunter-gatherer societies in history.

- Salmon fishing became important for peoples on the Interior Plateau between the Northwest Coast and the Great Basin, especially after 3000 BCE.

- The Chumash of the Santa Barbara Channel in southern California developed a sophisticated maritime society after 150 BCE, which depended on shallow-water and deep-water fish, shellfish, and intensive exploitation of acorns and other plant foods. Chumash society achieved significant complexity, enjoyed a sophisticated ritual life, and engaged in long-distance trade.

Arid Lands in the West

Great Basin, early fall, *c.* 2000 BCE. The people start work at dawn, armed with long poles, long enough to reach the highest branches of the piñon (pinyon) pines. They knock off green cones by the thousand. Young and old labor under the full containers as they carry them to a central processing area, used every time there is a plentiful harvest nearby. They stack the harvest in piles, cover them with brushwood, then scorch them until the sticky resin on the cones burns off, loosening the seeds. If firewood is short, they dig pits and pit-roast them, again to free up the seeds. Then the foragers beat the pile of roasted and scorched cones with sticks, or tap individual cones against a flat anvil with a hammerstone. Once the seeds are free of the cones, they are parched in an open, fan-shaped tray, then shelled and ground with a flat grinder. Ultimately the piñons are usually eaten in a nourishing gruel, mixed with hot or cold water.

The collectors would sometimes return in winter and knock the nuts off the trees when they were brown and dry. They knew that abundant piñon harvests occur in three-to-seven-year cycles, so the people stored thousands of cones in open pits under piles of stones, in grass- or bark-lined pits, or skin bags. Stored in this way, cones could last four or five years. The fat- and calorie-rich piñon nut became a staple as game populations grew scarce in the face of great aridity and human predation.

The Great Basin Environment

The Great Basin is a land of dramatic contrasts: high mountains and arid plains, deep canyons and occasional bountiful lakes (Grayson, 2011). It covers about 400,000 square miles (1,036,000 km2) of the west between the Rocky Mountains and the Sierra Nevada (Figure 6.1). A definition on hydrologic grounds commonly used by archaeologists includes nearly all of Nevada and parts of California, Oregon,

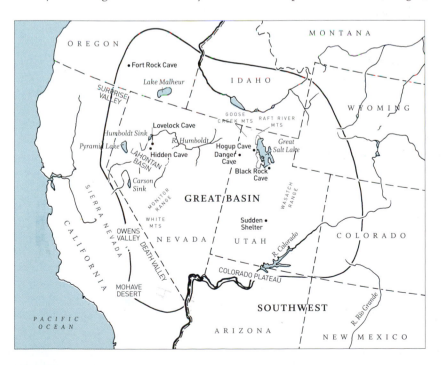

6.1 The Great Basin showing sites and regions mentioned in the text.

Utah, and Idaho. Throughout the past there have been great variations in group size, group stability, and degree of sedentary settlement, variations depending on the availability of food resources and the adaptations that developed to exploit them (Madsen and O'Connell, 1982).

Increasingly sophisticated paleoecological research combining data from all manner of sources, including tree-rings, pollen, owl fecal deposits, and pack-rat middens, is revealing the complex environmental changes that have occurred since the Ice Age. For instance, the deep owl midden at Homestead Cave in the Bonneville Basin has yielded remarkably complete climatic data from the small-animal remains deposited by the raptors (Madsen et al., 2001). The Homestead midden tells us that from 13,000 to 11,500 years ago the climate became drier, with the summers 11–14°F (6–8°C) cooler than today. Overall the Early Holocene was about 5.5°F (3°C) cooler than today. The drying accelerated after 9500 BCE, causing Lake Bonneville to drop sharply, eliminating eleven fish species from its waters. Over the next 3,000 years increasingly drought-resistant vegetation spread over the Great Basin. The diversity of plants and animals changed dramatically after 6200 BCE, as many species disappear from owl middens. Between 3600 and 3200 BCE a short episode of wetter conditions led to more plentiful spring water in the northern and southern Basin. Here and elsewhere, after 2000 BCE, slightly wetter conditions brought cooling and somewhat higher rainfall to the north, the most significant climatic event of the Middle Holocene. By 1400 BCE the Great Salt Lake became fresh enough to support populations of Utah chub. The diverse environments of the Great Basin were dynamic and ever changing, affecting human populations in many dramatic, cumulative ways. This was not limited to the deep past. Both the Medieval Warm Period of the late first millennium CE and the subsequent Little Ice Age had important effects in the Great Basin and elsewhere in the west, especially around 1300 CE, when widespread drought caused drastic changes in human distribution and lifeways, to the point that some farming groups turned to full-time foraging instead.

Everywhere resource distribution was patchy, with highly productive areas separated by sparser environments. The environmental realities of the Basin resulted in constant population movements, essentially conservative hunter-gatherer adaptations, and a broad, if varied, cultural continuum over wide areas. Some groups lived in exceptionally rich lakeside or marshy environments, developing greater complexity than other Great Basin hunter-gatherers, for example the Shoshone. In drier environments most people lived in tiny family groups, moving intermittently, subsisting off seasonal foods at widely separated locations, their social organization revolving around "mapping" on to food resources. For all this variation, however, the same basic hunter-gatherer material culture remained in use through the Basin for thousands of years.

A viable but generalized model of Great Basin subsistence and settlement assumes such a continuum of human occupation, with differences in subsistence and settlement patterns being due to variation in the availability of resources. Many complex factors affected human settlement over time, among them the changing distributions of vegetational communities—shrub and grasslands, tree lines, and so on—and such climatological realities as seasonal variations in temperature and rainfall. Highly flexible and mobile strategies were essential in all

ETHNOGRAPHIC ANALOGY, SHOSHONE, AND ECOLOGICAL APPROACHES

Ethnographic analogy has always played an important part in Great Basin archaeology, and it was through studying Great Basin archaeology that the anthropologist Julian Steward developed his now-classic theories of cultural ecology, or human ecology, as he called it (1955). After completing a comparative study of hunter-gatherers in many parts of the world, he concluded that the same simple sociopolitical patterns could be observed in human societies in different ecological settings. His monograph about Basin-Plateau hunter-gatherers was not a simple ethnography, but a statement about the relationship of social and political groups to their environments. He identified them as patrilineal bands, small groups with a nucleus of related men along with their endogamous wives and children. He reasoned that such groups would be well adapted to hunting, and well suited to a mobile existence in areas with patchy food resources and arid environments, such as the Great Basin. Steward's data covered geographical distributions of different groups, the locations of villages and their dwelling types, their seasonal use, economic activities, property ownership, and social organization. Despite the varying quality of his data, he formulated three fundamental principles of cultural ecology: that the same general adaptations will be found in different cultures in similar environments; that no culture has ever achieved an unchanging adaptation to its environment over any length of time; and that differences and changes during periods of cultural development in any area can either add to social complexity or lead to completely new cultural patterns.

Steward's research had a profound influence on Great Basin archaeology. As we saw in Chapter 1, cultural ecology became part of the processual archaeology of the 1960s. Archaeologist David Hurst Thomas (1983, 1985) assessed the relevance of Steward's interpretations of Great Basin Shoshonean subsistence to the archaeology of central Nevada. He noted that Steward's work, which was largely intuitive, had long served as a model for archaeological interpretation over much of the Basin. He now tried to replace it with "quantitative rigor."

Thomas deduced densities and distributions of artifacts in the various ecological zones of the Great Basin from Steward's hypotheses about Shoshonean settlement patterns. He asked a simple question: if the late prehistoric Shoshoneans behaved in the fashion suggested by Steward, how would the artifacts have fallen on the ground? He expected to find specific artifact forms associated with particular types of activity, such as hunting, in seasonal archaeological sites where hunting was said to be important. His data from many archaeological sites refined Steward's original hypotheses about Shoshone behavior, and showed that those hypotheses held good for the past 5,000 to 6,000 years. Before that, the model did not work. Steward assumed that the Reese River Valley was uninhabited in earlier times, but we now know that both Paleo-Indian and Early Archaic sites occur there, inhabited by ▶▶

but the most favored Great Basin environments. Mobility, flexibility, and detailed ecological knowledge—these were always the secrets of survival in the Great Basin. (For cultural ecology and **evolutionary ecology**, see Box: Ethnographic Analogy, Shoshone, and Ecological Approaches.)

Human groups settled in every kind of high and low altitude conditions imaginable. With such a diversity of environments and altitudes, it is difficult to generalize about Great Basin lifeways. For instance, the lakeside and riverside peoples of Pyramid Lake and Walker River in Nevada may have obtained as much as 50 percent of their diet from fish, and a further 20 percent from large and small game, with the balance coming from wild plant sources. In contrast, the inhabitants of the Owens Valley region of the Sierra Nevada relied on wild plants for over half their food, the rest being game meat, with fishing accounting for a mere 10 percent. It is useful here to make a distinction between desert and mountain foraging patterns as opposed to the wetlands pattern practiced by groups tied to lakes, marshes and other wetlands (Simms, 2008). But it would be a mistake to assume that people living in wetlands never exploited

people with different foraging strategies. Thomas later applied and refined the same approach in the Monitor Valley, with his Gatecliff Shelter research, and also at the highland Alta Toquima site (see Box: Major Great Basin Caves and Rockshelters). In the process he also refined and standardized projectile-point chronology for the Basin (Thomas, 1981, 1983, 1985).

A large site, for example Danger Cave or Hogup Cave in Utah, or Lovelock Cave in Nevada, may contain long sequences of ancient occupation, but offer a portrait of only part of complicated annual rounds of hunting and foraging (for caves, see Box: Major Great Basin Caves and Rockshelters). Thomas and other researchers focused on overall settlement–subsistence systems within individual valleys, watersheds, or subareas, such as the Reese River Valley and the Monitor Valley in Nevada (Thomas, 1983), and the Surprise Valley, California. Since the 1980s, however, a new generation of research has turned to evolutionary ecology for models of changing Great Basin settlement and subsistence (Zeanah and Simms, 1999).

Evolutionary ecology is the theoretical paradigm that now dominates Great Basin archaeology. Whereas cultural ecology relied on ethnographic analogy, evolutionary ecology uses ethnographic information about resource return rates to model subsistence and mobility strategies that are then tested against the archaeological record (Beck, 1999).

Evolutionary ecology assumes that natural selection favors behaviors that maximize reproductive fitness. By assuming, also, that selective forces on behavior are strongest on individuals rather than on groups, evolutionary ecology focuses on how conflicts of interest between individuals have group-level consequences. Such approaches have proved illuminating both in California and in the Great Basin (discussion with examples in Zeanah and Simms, 1999). For example, seeds were added to Great Basin diet after 6500 BCE, a dietary change that is probably associated with Early Holocene climatic change. The mechanisms of the change-over are poorly understood. An optimal foraging model argues that resources can be ranked according to the ratio of gains made from consuming them (in calories) relative to the cost of collecting and processing them (measured in time). The proportions of resources exploited vary according to the abundance of the highest-ranked ones. In the Great Basin the extinction of Ice Age big game, a high-ranked resource, may have led to the addition of more seeds to the diet, probably a lower-ranked food than game meat.

Research using evolutionary ecology is peculiarly suitable for Great Basin conditions, where arid environments often preserve a wide range of ancient food remains. These models enable the archaeologist to identify precise information to test in the field, information about resource rankings being obtained from ethnographic data, historical records, or from experimentation with traditional tools and techniques. Once these rankings are developed, one can then try and trace the relative importance of different foodstuffs so ranked over long periods.

the surrounding landscape; there was a continuum between the three patterns, still little understood, where the emphasis varied according to such factors as climatic change, rainfall, and availability of food supplies.

Desert and Mountains

As Steven Simms points out (2008), foragers in the deserts and mountains did not move constantly, but periodically, in response to the uneven distribution of foods across the landscape. Settlement patterns were complex. Winter camps lay near sources of firewood and caches of stored food. Harsh environments above and below the foothill zones tended to concentrate much of the ancient population and game animals where most forage was to be found, and where winters were relatively benign, in the piñon pine "thermal zone" (Grayson, 2011). The forests and meadows at higher elevations were attractive hunting grounds with deer, pronghorns, and bighorn sheep in summer, as well as yielding harvests of gooseberries, strawberries, and other plant foods. Amanda Rankin (2015) has used residue analysis to show that people at high altitudes habitually exploited geophytes (perennial plants that bud underground for thousands of years), which are virtually invisible in archaeological sites. The hunters used many techniques, sometimes stalking their prey in skin disguises, and also using snares, traps, and cooperative game drives.

The foothill zones supported many plant foods upon which the Great Basin people depended. For thousands of years the inhabitants used a variety of technologies for obtaining and processing plant foods of many kinds. The seeds of nut pines, especially piñons, became popular in later times. No Great Basin group exploited piñons intensively until the Late Holocene, after about 2,000 years ago, when the trees spread from south to north and became much prized, especially in the central core areas of the Basin. No one knows why piñons became popular, but it is worth noting that the bow and arrow came into use at about the same time. Perhaps the new weaponry reduced the number of medium and small game animals and turned people toward piñons (for a discussion of theories, see Madsen, 1985).

Piñon groves became so important a resource that many groups considered different groves family property. Acorns were gathered on the western, southern, and eastern fringes of the Basin, but were less significant than piñons. Mesquite (*Prosopis juliflora*), a staple for southern Great Basin people in later times, and screwbean (*Prosopis pubescens*) are desert plants found in the Mojave and Sonoran deserts (Figure 6.2). Their fresh pods were taken in the spring and eaten raw as snacks. In late summer and fall the people gathered dried-up pods, placed them in large tree-stump mortars and ground them to a fine powder. The bean meal was dried thoroughly in baskets, where it formed large cones that could be stored in pits for long periods. Like piñons, mesquite bean meal was a staple for many Great Basin people in later times. Agave (*Agave utahensis*) are natives of the hot deserts of the southern Great Basin and the Southwest. The plants were harvested in spring just before they flowered, and the leaves baked in a communal pit for twenty-four hours. The sweet, dark mass of agave was then pounded into large, flat cakes that were used to flavor meat and vegetable stews. Many plants had not only food value but also important medicinal uses.

6.2 Great Basin plant staples. *Left:* Colorado piñon. *Center:* Honey mesquite, *Prosopis juliflora*, with fruit. *Right:* mature pods of the screwbean, *Prosopis pubescens.*

Wetlands

Below the foothill zones, river banks, marshes, and lakes acted as magnets for human settlement. People camped near the water for much of the year, except, perhaps, during summer, when mosquitoes and other insects are a plague. Such areas were highly localized, but were always of the greatest importance to nearby communities. Marshes were especially productive. The Humboldt–Carson Sink in Nevada, for example, has been major breeding and nesting ground for waterfowl for thousands of years. It is no coincidence that some of the Great Basin's major archaeological sites are found near such marshes.

Major north–south flyways for migrating waterfowl passed over the Carson-Stillwater in the west and the Ruby marshes in eastern Nevada. Here, bird hunting was important. Both land birds and visiting water birds were taken with nets suspended on sticks, or driven into netting tunnels. The hunters often used blinds to shoot birds, luring waterfowl with finely made reed decoys. Some expert fowlers swam up to their prey wearing a duck-skin helmet or a mound of reeds. They would then grab the unsuspecting bird by the legs. Not only waterfowl, but also diverse mammal fauna lived in the same marshes. Muskrats, rabbits, and many other rodents abounded. Grasses, wild vegetables, and many rhizomes were harvested at the marsh margins in spring and fall, while tule reeds (*Scirpus acutus*) made fine mats. Other plants, such as willow, were important for textiles. Dogbane and milkweed provided ideal fibers for cords and basketry. Great Basin people were weaving large mats, burial shrouds, bags, and other artifacts, using some kind of frame loom, as early as 8600 BCE (Fowler and Hattori, 2008). They also made fine rabbit nets hundreds of feet long.

Throughout the Great Basin ancient people fished in lakes and rivers, large and small. Along the Snake and Truckee rivers, for example, the fishers built platforms out from the bank to fish with dip nets or spear their catch. Large gill nets harvested trout, chub, and other species in shallow waters, while basket traps and rock or brush dams were effective in many situations. Sometimes women would even scoop fish from still water with shallow baskets.

Generations of archaeologists have argued over the interpretation of wetland adaptations in the Great Basin. One long-held "limnosedentary" view argued that the inhabitants of such areas enjoyed such predictable and diverse resources that they rarely had to move from their bases (Heizer and Napton, 1970). These arguments were based on human **coprolites** from Lovelock cave, near Humboldt Sink, that revealed a diet almost entirely acquired from lakeside foods and fish. A contrasting "limnomobile" hypothesis pointed out that portraits of sedentism came from single sites, not a series of locations occupied year-round. In fact, such sedentism may only have occurred for a few weeks per year. Furthermore, the labor of obtaining and processing cattails, waterfowl, and fish may have made them less satisfactory staples than foods like piñon nuts. Thus, wetland bands may have been as mobile as those living away from water.

David Hurst Thomas (1985) excavated the Archaic deposits of Hidden Cave, immediately south of the Carson Sink, to test these competing hypotheses (Figures 6.3, opposite, and 6.4, p. 144). He combined excavation with site survey in the surrounding area, as well as modeling lacustrine resources and possible subsistence strategies with ethnographic and historical records. He found that the historic Toedökadö maintained relatively stable winter bases near marshes or

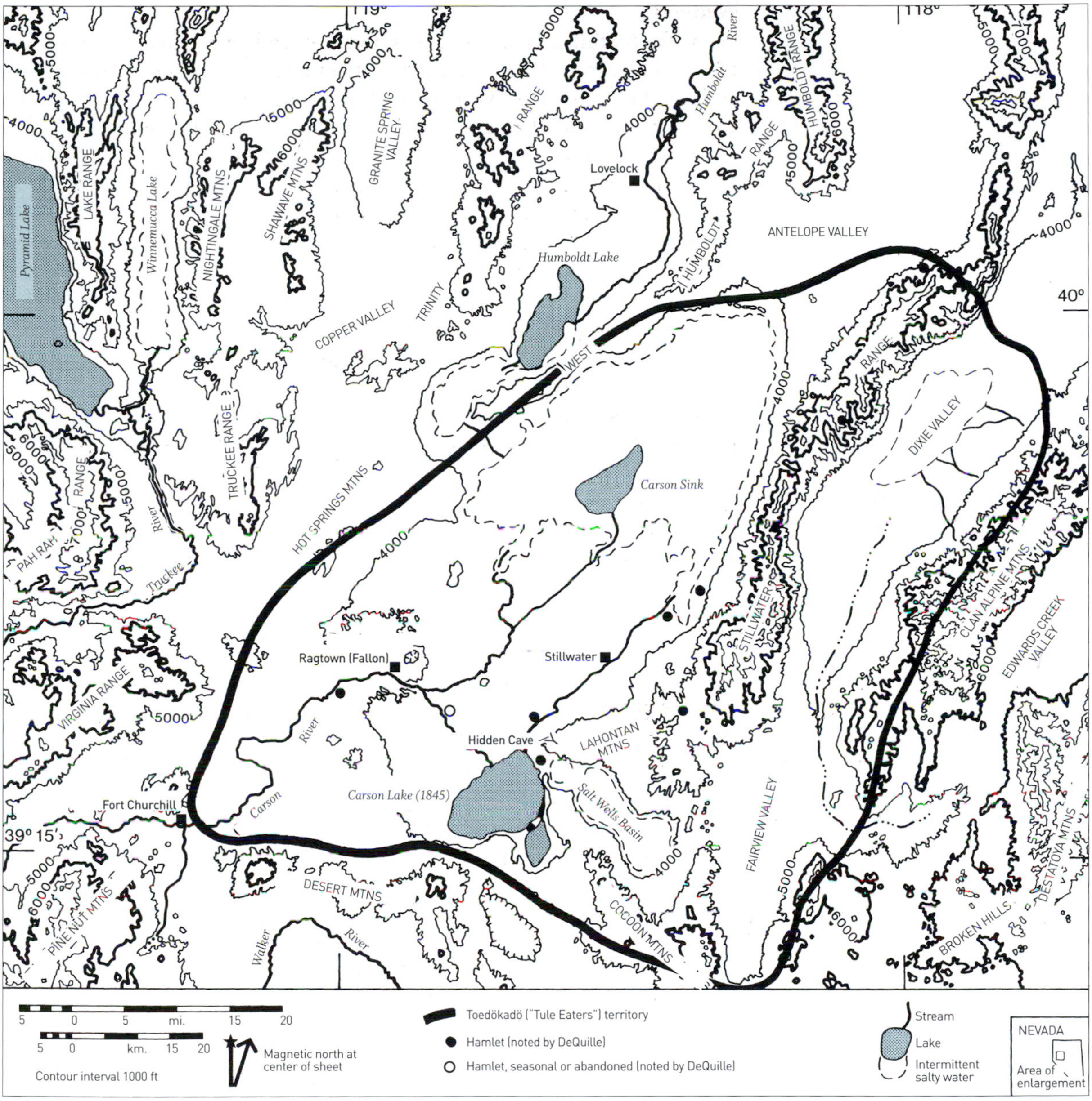
Pyramid Lake
LAKE RANGE
Winnemucca Lake
NIGHTINGALE MTNS
SHAWAVE MTNS
GRANITE SPRING VALLEY
RANGE
Humboldt
River
HUMBOLDT RANGE
Lovelock
ANTELOPE VALLEY
Humboldt Lake
HUMBOLDT
TRINITY
COPPER VALLEY
WEST
40°
TRUCKEE RANGE
RANGE
DIXIE VALLEY
Carson Sink
HOT SPRINGS MTNS
PAH RAH RANGE
River
Truckee
STILLWATER
CLAN ALPINE MTNS
EDWARDS CREEK VALLEY
Ragtown (Fallon)
Stillwater
VIRGINIA RANGE
River
Hidden Cave
LAHONTAN MTNS
Carson Lake (1845)
Carson
Fort Churchill
Salt Wells Basin
FAIRVIEW VALLEY
DESATOYA MTNS
39° 15'
DESERT MTNS
COCOON MTNS
BROKEN HILLS
PINE NUT MTNS
Walker
River
119°
118°
Contour interval 1000 ft
Magnetic north at center of sheet
Toedökadö ("Tule Eaters") territory
Hamlet (noted by DeQuille)
Hamlet, seasonal or abandoned (noted by DeQuille)
Stream
Lake
Intermittent salty water
NEVADA
Area of enlargement

in the uplands, depending on stored foods and the condition of the marshlands. In spring and summer families moved out to forage at many locations, coming together in fall to harvest piñons. The Hidden Cave grasses, piñons, seeds, and fish bones showed that the site was visited in spring and summer, and used for storing surplus food, as well as for caching artifacts. The cave contained few tools for exploiting marsh-side resources, unlike Lovelock, which was a winter location. Clearly both the limnosedentary and limnomobile scenarios are too extreme to be viable interpretations of wetland adaptations. While long stays at some locations were possible, the people had to keep on the move in environments

6.3 General map of the Carson Sink area showing the location of Lovelock and Hidden Caves. The heavy line delimits the territory of the historic Toedökadö people.

6.4 Excavations in progress at Hidden Cave, Nevada, in 1979.

where foods were widely separated and yields fluctuated wildly, even though basic availability patterns were predictable. Under such circumstances, food storage against potential famine was of great importance.

It is important to realize that wetland areas were only a small part of much larger foraging patterns. For instance, mountain-sheep hunting was important in the central Basin, and both game and seed collecting were the focus on the Sierra Nevada slopes. Wetlands certainly played an important role in Basin settlement, for they provided many resources of varying return. Experiments have shown that cattails, for example, provided dismal returns when processed for flour, while other resources, such as fish or bulrush seeds, were exceedingly valuable.

During the 1980s unprecedented flooding exposed numerous sites with pithouses, pits, and burials in wetland area; this greatly expanded our knowledge. Wetlands varied considerably in their topography, stability, and available food resources, so they were incorporated into different groups' settlement patterns in different ways. We know this from skeletal data. For instance, at Lake Malhuer in Oregon the greater productivity of the landscape around the lake affected the settlement pattern considerably (Aikens *et al.*, 2011). By 2,000 years ago settlement around Lake Abert in southeastern Oregon and at Stillwater was restricted to the shorelines, as conditions became increasingly arid. We are beginning to realize that wetlands were not a stable food source, but a dynamic one, where shrinkage of a lake may create more wetland habitats, while flooding, depending on the local topography, can either move or shrink them. Short-term changes in wetlands are still little understood, but they were an important "engine" of the Great Basin's past (Kelly, 1997).

In such diverse environments, whether desert, mountain, or wetland, where food resources are both patchy and subject to cycles of plenty and scarcity, it is hardly surprising that the historic Great Basin peoples deliberately "managed" parts of their environment to increase its productivity and to conserve precious resources. Many groups burned the natural vegetation to increase natural yields of such plants as tobacco and a variety of seed-bearing grasses. Burning also served to increase available fodder for deer and other game, as well as helping drive prey toward waiting hunters. In historic times several Great Basin groups, the Shoshone being one example, have not only burned the natural vegetation but scattered wild seeds as well.

Great Basin hunter-gatherers had to be mobile, in the right place at the right time. They moved horizontally and vertically, so that they were in the piñon-juniper woodland in fall, in the marshes for cattails in spring. In high-altitude mountain landscapes they hunted and trapped animals and subsisted off geophytes. Walking up and down the mountains meant that they followed the seasons to elevations where summer lasted but a month, then retreated to lower altitudes, harvesting ripening plants as they went. Located at 11,000 ft (3,353 m) on Mount Jefferson, Nevada, Alta Toquima documents a high-altitude base camp with substantial circular, rock-walled houses and storage areas (Figure 6.5). Between about 2000 and 1000 BCE Alta Toquima was a hunting camp, but the later occupants—possibly both men and women—lived there longer, processing plants as well as hunting (Thomas, 2014).

Across most of the Great Basin the Native Americans remained hunter-gatherers throughout ancient times, essentially preserving the Archaic lifeway right up to European contact in the seventeenth century CE. This general

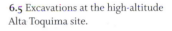

6.5 Excavations at the high-altitude Alta Toquima site.

hunter-gatherer adaptation lasted for at least 10,000 years, from Early Archaic times onward. Even where agricultural economies did take hold, people still relied heavily on game and wild vegetable foods.

Paleo-Indians and Desert Archaic: Before 13,500 Years Ago to Recent Times

People have been living in the Great Basin for at least 13,500 years. The date of first settlement is unknown, but Paisley Cave in Oregon has occupation dating to as early as 14,200 years ago (see Chapter 2). The earliest Paleo-Indian groups to enter the Basin left hardly any signature behind them, but their fluted points almost always come from settings once associated with now-extinct lakes or marshes. These environments would make sense for people who were living off a broad range of game and wild plants. Major environmental changes during the Early Holocene saw coniferous woodlands retreat to higher altitudes, with steppe vegetation moving in at lower levels. Such changes increased the range of habitats available for grazing and browsing herbivores. The human population, always small, may have increased somewhat and spread into new environments, witness the wide distribution of stemmed projectile points that came into use after the disappearance of fluted heads. This may have led to an imbalance between

THE GREAT BASIN DESERT ARCHAIC: c. 9000 BCE TO RECENT TIMES

Eastern and Northern Great Basin

9000 to 7500 BCE: with the advent of warmer conditions, people ranged more widely and lived in a broader range of environments, if the wider distribution of stemmed projectile points is to be believed. The diet expanded to include fish, mollusks, and waterfowl, as well as seeds processed with milling stones. The tiny population was constantly on the move, as water supplies were scarce. Wetlands were important for many groups (Janetski and Madsen, 1990; Kelly, 2013).

c. 7000 to 4000 BCE: a major adaptive shift took hold as people responded to increasing aridity and the localization of food sources. Judging from the high numbers of milling stones and such artifacts, they relied more heavily

on processed seeds as the climate continued to warm and many lakes and marshes dried up. Most groups adopted more complicated seasonal rounds and remained highly mobile. In the central and southern Basin populations were very low indeed, for there were no lakes or wetlands. In the north the Great Salt Lake's water level dropped between 5000 and 4000 BCE, creating extensive wetlands that expanded and shrank repeatedly as the lake level fluctuated. The wetlands attracted human settlement until after 1500 BCE, when the lake rose and inundated the wetlands.

4000 BCE to 500 CE: population densities rose across the eastern and northern Great Basin, with people occupying many more upland sites (Kelly, 1997). Between 3000 and 1500 BCE increasing rainfall brought wetlands and lakes to many parts of the Basin. Similar adjustments in subsistence activities must have occurred in many other areas, reflecting local environmental conditions.

People still relied on a wide variety of animals and plants and used the same basic technology as their predecessors. One significant innovation came around 500 CE, when the bow and arrow appeared. Projectile points became much smaller, even if they retained the same basic stem and corner-notched designs as their predecessors.

400 to 500 CE: small amounts of pottery and occasional domesticated maize cobs appeared in the eastern Great Basin and Colorado, either introduced from sedentary horticultural societies in the Southwest, or simply adopted locally because such items were perceived as useful, or both. The new traits did not lead to any dramatic changes in Archaic life, for hunting and gathering still produced subsistence staples, as they had done for millennia. That said, piñon nuts became a major element in eastern Basin diet at about this time (Madsen, 1985). During the first millennium CE settled "Fremont" horticultural people

foragers and their prey, and to a logical response: broadening the diet to include fish, mollusks, and waterfowl. Judging from their milling stones, these people also paid more attention to seed-bearing plants. The surviving Paleo-Indian sites, with their minimal artifact accumulations, suggest that people were constantly on the move, staying in one place for short periods only. They lived at a time when environmental conditions were different from those of today, notably in the availability of permanent water supplies. Judging from artifact distributions, wetlands were important to many groups, but their general adaptation was very different from that of later times

A broad culture-historical framework, mainly based on stone tools, has been developed over generations of field research (Thomas, 1981). There is such diversity of ancient populations in the Great Basin that it is impossible to construct a chronological framework that neatly brings together cultural connections across the desert west, though in the interests of convenience and clarity it is possible to set out general periods of environmental and material culture change across the Great Basin (for details, see Box: The Great Basin Desert Archaic: c. 9000 BCE to Recent Times; see also Madsen and O'Connell, 1982).

Population densities remained extremely low for thousands of years after first settlement. As more people came to inhabit the Basin, there was a gradual

flourished in many parts of the northern Colorado Plateau and in the eastern Great Basin and a new economy took hold in these long-settled areas, described below (Madsen and Simms, 1998).

Western Great Basin and Interior California

3000 to 1500 BCE: increased rainfall brought lakes and wetlands back in many areas. People lived in caves and rockshelters overlooking such places as the Carson and Humboldt Sinks (Kelly, 1997, 2001). Notable sites include Hidden Cave and Lovelock Cave. Piñon nuts became an important factor in the diet, spread northward by several bird species. Piñons appear at Gatecliff rockshelter in the central Basin by 3350 BCE, but appear earlier at Danger Cave and elsewhere, while they make their appearance as late as 500 CE in the western Basin (Kelly, 1997). Piñons have relatively abundant harvests and excellent storage qualities, so probably had a marked

impact on the foraging activities of many (but not all) groups, depending to some extent on the distance to be traveled to collect the nuts. There was a constant ebb and flow of settlement between mobile and more sedentary patterns, largely resulting from the availability of food across the landscape and the amount of effort needed to collect or store it.

1500 BCE to 500 CE: much of what we know about this period comes from wetland areas, but it is important to realize that they are only a small part of much larger settlement patterns. There were no major technological or subsistence changes in this period, but local populations increased, with more diverse exploitation of food resources, and there was a trend toward repeated reoccupation of summer base camps and seasonal settlements. Trade in marine shells, obsidian from volcanic rocks north of the Owens Valley, and in other exotics became increasingly important.

500 CE to recent times: the climate of the western Great Basin became warmer and drier about the first century CE. As over much of the west, the centuries of the Medieval Warm Period after 900 CE brought intense drought cycles and significant disruption over much of the Great Basin. Important technological changes occurred. The bow and arrow replaced the spear and atlatl, as in the eastern and northern Great Basin, with accompanying smaller and lighter Rose Spring and Eastgate projectile points, while pottery appeared after 1000 CE. At the same time people began to use much more elaborate plant-processing equipment, a reflection, perhaps, of new subsistence strategies that involved exploiting a more diverse resource base and different ecological zones. Plant foods and such small game as rabbits assumed great importance, which is possibly a sign of demographic stress caused in part by drought.

MAJOR GREAT BASIN CAVES AND ROCKSHELTERS

Danger Cave, Wendover, Utah

Danger Cave was excavated by Jesse Jennings from between 1949 and 1953 (Figure 6.6) (Jennings, 1957). His excavations yielded radiocarbon dates as early as 9000 BCE to 500 CE, some of the first processed in North American archaeology. With this chronology Jennings formulated the idea of a "Desert Tradition" that endured for 10,000 years. The Desert Tradition as Jennings thought of it was more of a way of life than a distinct society, so his classification has been much modified over the years. Danger Cave is a dry site, so the preservation was exceptional, including cordage, numerous rabbit bones, and basketry (Figure 6.7). It was occupied again and again thanks to its lakeside position, close to wetlands. Another major site for the Great Basin Desert Archaic is Hogup Cave, Utah, for which see pp. 76–78, Chapter 3.

Lovelock Cave, Humboldt Sink, Nevada

Lovelock Cave, one of the classic Great Basin sites, has yielded a bounty of finds that testify to the diverse lifeway along the Humboldt Sink. The people caught fish of every size from minnows upward, especially Lahontan chub, with nets, traps, and bone fish hooks. They used life-like duck decoys (Figure 6.8) made of tule reed, some even covered with fully feathered skins removed from real birds. The dry cave deposits yielded feathers from pelicans, herons, ducks, and geese, also the nets sometimes used for taking them.

Between about 3000 and 2000 BCE the area was just a stopping

6.6 *Above*: Danger Cave, Utah.
6.7 Artifacts from Danger Cave, Utah. (a) *Clockwise from top left*: wooden knife handle, arrowshaft with broken projectile in place, twined matting, coiled basketry, milling stone, coarse cloth. (b) Gaming sticks, the longest 10.6 in. (27 cm) long.

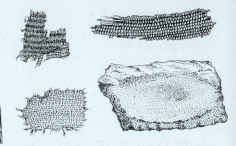

6.8 Bird decoys from Lovelock Cave.

6.9 Lovelock Cave, Nevada.

point, owing to dry conditions and a lack of piñons. For the next 2,000 years there was somewhat more rainfall and the wetlands expanded as temperatures fell slightly. During these two millennia Carson was exploited more intensively, but abandoned at times when there were richer resources in neighboring areas. Lovelock Cave was used intermittently from as early as 2580 BCE, but was not occupied intensively until 1000 BCE (Figure 6.9) (Heizer and Napton, 1970). Hidden Cave was first utilized about 1800 BCE, while pithouses provided seasonal shelter on the valley floors.

We know a great deal about Middle Archaic diet at Lovelock from human coprolites. Over 90 percent of the foods in the cave came from the Humboldt–Carson sink nearby. Staple wetland plants included bulrush and cattail. Tui chub, ducks, and mudhens were also common foods (Butler, 1996). The abundance and diversity of food resources apparently made it possible for the inhabitants to live in the same area

for most of the year. Many of the plant foods found at Lovelock were harvested in fall and stored for winter use. The cold season was a good time for hunting waterfowl and collecting the rhizomes of water plants.

Gatecliff, Monitor Valley, Nevada

This shelter in the highlands of central Nevada contained over 32 ft (10 m) of deposits with sixteen cultural horizons (Figure 6.10). It was first occupied *c.* 2500 BCE and used on and off for the next 5,000 years, with the most intensive use

over the last 3,200 years. The inhabitants built hearths about 13 ft (4 m) from the rear wall, over many centuries, which created a warm and relatively smoke-free work area. This was most likely a short-term field camp used by small groups working some distance form their base camp. The excavations yielded more than 400 projectile points in stratigraphic order (see Box: Communal Hunting), as well as incised limestone slabs that resemble paintings on the walls and elsewhere in the Great Basin (Thomas, 1981, 1983).

6.10 Excavations in Gatecliff Cave. Passing soil out of the cave by hand was the only way of clearing the trenches.

trend toward greater, and still little-known, cultural diversity. This period is known as the "Desert Archaic," a generic term for those hunter-gatherer societies throughout the Great Basin and neighboring regions that first become apparent in about 7000 BCE, changed gradually over time, and thrived until European contact and beyond.

At first our knowledge of the Desert Archaic came almost entirely from long cultural sequences in such caves and rockshelters as Hogup Cave, 75 miles (120 km) northwest of Salt Lake City (Aikens, 1970) (see Box: Major Great Basin Caves and Rockshelters). Excavations in these dry caves, with their excellent preservation conditions, provide snapshots of Archaic life over many thousands of years. But most of the archaeological record of Archaic groups comes from surface sites. Such transitory signatures raise complex problems in terms of chronology, for radiocarbon samples are hard to obtain from sites that are often little more than scatters of stone artifacts. Models grounded in evolutionary ecology are now being constructed to look at broad patterns of Paleo-Indian and Archaic settlement. For instance, by studying changes in the use of fine-grained rock used for toolmaking over time, one can develop models that predict changes in foraging patterns, reduced or increased mobility related to shifting foraging habits, and so on (Beck, 1999).

The major adaptive shift in Great Basin life came around 7000 BCE with the beginning of the Early Archaic. People responded to the increasing aridity by exploiting a broader range of foods. They ate many more processed seeds, a shift reflected by the common occurrence of milling stones and other processing tools. As the climate continued to warm and many lakes and marshes dried up, Basin groups adopted far more complex settlement patterns, many of them using semi-permanent base camps with basic storage facilities. For the first time, there are differences between northern and southern Great Basin groups, reflected in both their artifacts and their lifeways. People were now living at many different altitudes and in a wide variety of environments. Aridity meant mobility, and seasonal rounds that saw the balance between hunting and plant collecting varying from month to month, with the latter assuming major importance at harvest time.

The environmental effects of the drier, warmer conditions manifested themselves in different ways throughout the Basin. In the southern and central portions population densities were very low indeed, for there were no lakes or wetlands. A series of high-altitude sites come from high in the White Mountains of eastern California. In the Grass Valley area of central Nevada piñons were a staple, so abundant that many groups lived in comparatively sedentary villages, precursors of large western Shoshone villages in historic times. The Owens Valley saw a decrease in upland hunting in favor of low-altitude settlement, a shift that coincides with historic Paiute culture, a culture that made use of irrigation to water wild plant stands. This adaptation required permanent settlement in the lowlands. The people often built substantial bases with ample storage facilities, fanning out into outlying camps at different times of the year (Bettinger and Eerkens, 1999).

While drying conditions meant that some areas did not see significant populations again until after 1500 BCE, the story was very different in the north, where the Great Salt Lake's shrinking water levels created extensive wetlands

COMMUNAL HUNTING

Communal hunting of animals large and small using drive lines and fences, also corrals, was a persistent feature of Great Basin life. More than a hundred large-scale traps are known. Three types were used: drive lines, corrals, sometimes with wings to steer animals into the enclosure, and fence systems that ended in an enclosure (Hockett *et al.*, 2013). Many corrals were built from rocks or timber, with rocks forming most fences. In what is now Nevada, most corrals lie in valley bottoms or on gentle slopes immediately above the valley floor; they were almost certainly for hunting pronghorn antelope. Others in central Nevada lay in uplands where mountain sheep could be taken. There are trapping features along deer migration routes, or on valley floors for taking pronghorn in eastern California and western Nevada. Archaic projectile points found associated with some corrals show that this form

of communal hunting was in use for at least 5,000 years. It continued into recent times.

The economic benefits of communal hunts could have had social foundations. Communal hunts that produced large harvests would feed considerably more people than the members of a single band. They had other consequences, too. They brought together people who normally lived in isolation, and thus provided opportunities for ceremonies, to arrange marriages, settle disputes, and, perhaps most importantly, to exchange intelligence about game and plants over the immediate horizon. To engage in communal hunts requires predictable prey; this could include antelope migrations, years when jackrabbits were abundant, times when fish were spawning, or bumper years for ripening piñons. Communal hunts may not have been the most efficient way to acquire food, for the wastage was considerable, but there were major advantages in situations where drought caused people

to move, or when it was desirable to gather and hold a communal feast. Some groups may have cooperated to acquire large numbers of pelts for trading, an activity well attested in historic accounts.

In an interesting example of experimental archaeology, three men and four women aged between twenty and sixty-six years old built an experimental length of stone fence that replicated the ancient Fort Sage Drift Fence. They worked for two hours and constructed a rock fence 47.5 ft (14.5 m) long, an average building rate of 24.6 ft (7.15 m) per hour. The ancient builders had erected 3,585 ft (1,093 m) of rock wall. Assuming that each person would have built 2 ft (0.66 m) in an hour, it would have taken one person nearly two-and-a-half months to build the ancient wall, working twenty-four hours a day. Considering the need to find and consume extra calories to fuel the exhausting building work, each person could perhaps more reasonably be expected to work for just two hours, ▸▸

between 5000 and 4000 BCE. For many centuries people camped on the edges of the wetland, returning again and again to the same caves and open sites until after 1500 BCE, when the lake rose for five centuries and flooded the marshes once again. Communal drives of pronghorn antelope and other large animals came into use at least 5,000 years ago, and became more common as population densities rose during favorable climatic shifts (see Box: Communal Hunting).

Archaic peoples in the Great Basin thus developed lifeways closely attuned to their various and shifting environments. These persisted for thousands of years, as the people successfully adapted to whatever challenges their continent presented. When they did eventually succumb, it was not to internal threats, but to the external pressure of European settlement.

Fremont and Great Basin Agriculture: 100 BCE to 1300 CE

During the first millennium CE settled "Fremont" horticultural people flourished in many parts of the northern Colorado Plateau and in the eastern Great Basin, and a new economy took hold in these long-settled areas (Madsen and Simms, 1998).

The Great Basin appears to have received two new arrivals at roughly the same time: the Numic language (a type of Uto-Aztecan), and farming. Some authorities believe the two are linked, the appearance of plant cultivation reflecting

in which case it would have taken a single individual more than thirteen and a half months to build the fence. This was definitely a communal task.

Ethnographic accounts report that some gatherings lasted two weeks or so and involved a mean of 133 people. With forty people at a gathering, twenty of whom worked for two hours daily on the wall, it would have taken them about forty-one days to build it, or four fourteen-day gatherings. About 1.6 million calories would have been needed to support the builders. Modern calculations suggest that a pronghorn would produce about 2,500 calories per killed beast. About seventy pronghorn would have had to be killed for a fourteen-day communal event involving forty people, if we allow about 3,370 calories daily per person. It would have required about 280 pronghorn to build the entire fence, 116 if the fence was built over two years, not just one. Pronghorn spring and fall migrations were of short duration, but it would have been possible

for forty people to build 902 ft (275 m) of fence during a fourteen-day stay, while killing seventy pronghorn at the same time. Almost certainly the fences were built by communal groups in sections over a length of time. In contrast, sagebrush corrals and their associated wings could be built by thirty-five people in a fourteen-day gathering of fifty people, with eighty-four pronghorn being needed. Ethnographic accounts suggest that corrals were built by few people.

Many Great Basin rock-art sites in parts of Nevada lie along migration route of large animals, also close to deer and mountain-sheep trails. They were well placed for antelope drives, as if hunters used blinds and rock ambushes. Some are associated with long rock walls, so were perhaps used for trapping. Early researchers theorized that the art was part of "hunting magic," spiritual aids to ensure plentiful game and successful hunts. Some Nevada petroglyph sites may have been used as part of the planning for constructing fences. The

Lagomarsino site near Virginia City, Nevada, lies close to a perennial spring. Nearby, 2,229 petroglyph panels display abstract images, also five motifs of hunting nets, apparently with weights attached at the base. Hockett and his colleagues believe that the art provided leadership and insights into the purposes of communal hunting.

No one knows how many people gathered for communal hunts, but it is certain that the hunters must have relied on plant foods while hunting, even if only to guard against a shortfall in the hunt. Interestingly, the northern distribution of large-scale traps coincides closely with the northern distribution of piñon trees. Perhaps harvesting the nuts was an important activity that happened simultaneously with the hunts.

PROJECTILE POINTS IN THE GREAT BASIN

North American archaeologists love projectile points, and Great Basin specialists are no exception. Projectile points offer a narrow insight into the past, but at least provide a general framework for Great Basin cultures, and give us a broad impression of changes in subsistence practices and the extent of long-distance contact over many centuries. Here are the most commonly used types, developed by Thomas (1981) and based on his work in Monitor Valley, Nevada.

Corner-Notched Projectile Points

Gatecliff Series (c. 3000 to 1300 BCE): medium to large points with various stem forms.

Elko Series (1300 BCE to 700 CE): large, corner-notched points with various base forms. Most common forms have corner notches or ears on the base.

Rosegate Series (700 to 1300 CE): small, corner-notched points. They come in at least two forms, which grade into one another.

the expansion of Numic-speakers into the Great Basin from southern California within the past 1,000 years, though case can also be made for an indigenous, long-term development of Numic tongues in the Great Basin itself. However, as Bettinger and Baumhoff have argued (1982), the more intensive subsistence strategies in use at this period bear some resemblance to those found to the west, in California, in historic times. These new strategies were higher in cost, sustained higher population densities, made more use of hard-to-process small seeds, and relied less on large animals. Bettinger and Baumhoff believe that the competitive advantages of these new high-cost strategies may have facilitated the spread of Numic-speakers into the Basin, a development that may have coincided with population movements caused in part by the Medieval Warm Period (Jones *et al.*, 1999).

The term "Fremont" covers a cultural tradition of farmers and hunter-gatherers who flourished over most of modern Utah between about 1 and 1250 CE (Madsen and Simms, 1998; Simms and Gohier, 2010). Though these communities lived in widely contrasting environments, whether arid landscapes or the fertile, well-watered soils of the Wasatch Front, early researchers felt there were enough common features across this extensive region to justify the Fremont label, while recognizing many local variations. Fremont culture displays so much variation that some authorities question whether the term has any practical use at all. This local variation is characteristic of Fremont from its first appearance, presumably reflecting the great diversity of Basin environments and the Archaic cultures that flourished in them. Each variant has links to the others, but each is a distinctive adaptation to local conditions.

There are obvious similarities between Fremont and the general farming tradition of the Southwest, but Fremont groups developed their own basketry, rock art, figurines, pottery, and ornaments (Janetski, 2008). The first signs of a shift from hunting and gathering to farming appear across central Utah around

Side-Notched Projectile Points

Desert Series (after 1300 CE): small, triangular points with notches high on the sides.

Unshouldered projectile points: the earliest of these date to between about 3400 and 3200 BCE at Gatecliff Shelter. They have concave bases.

Humboldt Series (c. 3000 BCE to 700 CE): unnotched, lanceolate points with concave bases of variable size. They display great variation.

Cottonwood Leaf-shaped and Triangular (after 1300 CE): round-based, small, unnotched projectile points. They are widespread throughout the Great Basin after 1300 CE.

6.11 Fremont bowl from Grantsville Mount (Live Creek Black on White). Diameter: 10.2 in. (26 cm).

2,000 years ago. By 500 CE people were farming on floodplains over a much wider area. They irrigated their fields, stored corn in deep pits, and adopted the bow and arrow for hunting. By 1050 CE Fremont farming communities occupied a wide tract of country from modern Brigham City in the north to Cedar City in the south. Almost invariably they lived near well-drained soils and close to permanent water supplies. Fremont people cultivated maize, beans, and squash, or received supplies through trade, or even raiding. They also took a broad range of animals with bows and arrows, nets, or snares. Like all Great Basin groups, they made use of every available plant food as well.

Not that everyone remained at one spot year-round. There are many sites with tipi-like shelters known as **wickiups** that were occupied for short periods in arid landscapes or at higher elevations, when seeking seasonal fools or toolmaking stone. At more permanent settlements Fremont people dwelt in pithouses, some of them as much as 15 ft (4.5 m) across, roofed with timbers, thatch, and dirt. Shallow ventilator tunnels provided air circulation, allowing smoke from the central hearth to escape through the entrance, which was through the roof. They also constructed large surface dwellings and adjacent granaries of **adobe** bricks. Storage pits were all-important in this world of uncertain rainfall, and were often built away from houses.

Fremont culture is defined by its pottery and baskets. The former were mainly plain vessels, many burnished with pebbles, while many bowls bore black painted designs on gray or sometimes white backgrounds. Basketry was fashioned from split willows and other pliable woods, turned into shallow trays and occasional bowls (Figure 6.11). Twined bulrush and juniper-bark mats covered house floors and lined storage pits, fashioned with bone tools, a traditional craft that began in the Great Basin at least 10,600 years ago. Fremont technology owed much to ancient methods, but the stylized human figurines are a distinctive feature of their art tradition. Some are quite elaborate, especially those from the northern Colorado Plateau, which sometimes bear necklaces, hair styles, and face and body decoration (Figure 6.12). If figures and rock art are any guide, the people

6.12 Fremont culture clay figurines from the Old Woman site. The tallest stands approximately 4.5 in. (11.5 cm) high.

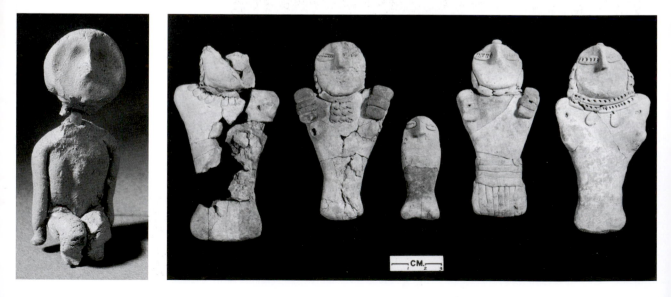

6.13 *Above and left*: Fremont rock paintings from the Great Gallery, Barrier Canyon, Utah.

6.14 Fremont moccasins from Hogup Cave (*below left*) and Promontary Cave (*below right*).

themselves wore kilts or skirts, also moccasins, which are remarkably well preserved in some dry rock shelters (Figures 6.13 and 6.14). Their ornaments included rare marine *Olivella* shells from the Pacific and turquoise pendants from Nevada or even further away, signs of trade to the south and west. Some communities also traded painted pottery and obsidian, exchanged from sources in the eastern Great Basin.

We know little of Fremont ceremonial or social life (Janetski and Talbot, 2014). Like other Great Basin groups, and those further afield, they gathered in larger numbers for communal meals, to trade, and for social and ritual purposes. Not that all interactions were friendly: there are hints of strife and warfare.

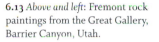

Rock-art scenes depict shield-bearing figures, also others holding what appear to be trophy heads. The Sky Aerie Charnel House site in northwest Colorado yielded a clay-capped hearth containing three human crania and other bones, perhaps roasted for eating. Of Fremont social organization we know virtually nothing, but unadorned burials give one the impression that society was basically egalitarian. A few graves are exceptions, such as one under a house floor in Huntington Canyon in central Utah, which contained a variety of objects, including corn cobs and several unfired figurines. Perhaps this individual was an elder or shaman, perceived to have unusual powers. Fremont rock art also depicts hunting scenes, pecked or painted on the rock. On the Colorado Plateau we find mythic, anthropomorphic figures wearing headdresses and carrying weapons or bags. West of the Wasatch Mountains, the paintings are more geometric, drawing inspiration from textiles or pottery. Mountain sheep, elk, and other prey are painted in such a way that we can be certain that the artists had an intimate knowledge of them. How much of the art was of symbolic or ritual significance is a matter for discussion. We shall probably never know.

Agriculture persisted until the twelfth century CE, but there are signs that some groups living in the Great Salt Lake marshes stopped eating corn by 1150. Corn was still consumed further south in the Salt Lake Valley a half century later, but the writing was on the proverbial wall. By the mid-fourteenth century CE most Fremont people had abandoned the Great Basin and the Colorado Plateau, except, perhaps in the north. The same droughts of the Medieval Warm Period that devastated **Ancestral Pueblo** societies south and east on the Colorado Plateau (see Chapter 10) seem to have eliminated maize cultivation as a viable subsistence strategy throughout the Fremont area (Coltrain and Leavitt, 2002). The kinds of intensive forager adaptations that marked much of the Great Basin at a time of severe drought gave hunter-gatherers an advantage over farmers, and small numbers of such people endured in the region.

Few Fremont sites date to later than 1300 CE, and, except in the northeast, none survived after 1400. People ceased farming, perhaps because of shifts in summer rainfall that made agriculture much harder. Great Basin groups still hunted and foraged successfully, among them the Utes, southern Paiutes, and Shoshone of historic times, who arrived in the Basin.

A mosaic of hunter-gatherers, part-time cultivators, and village farmers flourished in the western interior after 1700 CE. There were even some local groups irrigating, but not cultivating, native plants in the Owens Valley. Hunting and gathering traditions honed over millennia survived generations of sporadic contact with prospectors and settlers. The harsh desert and rough topography inhibited European settlement. For instance, the western Shoshone, who lived in the area between Death Valley, highland central Nevada, and into northwestern Utah, dwelt in one of the last areas of the United States to be settled by Anglo-Europeans. Many groups throughout the Basin were unable to survive the bouts of European development that disrupted their ecology; but others had the time to develop responses to white settlement, and adapted to the radically different circumstances. Their material culture and subsistence patterns changed dramatically and rapidly, but many elements of traditional social organization and religious life survived into the twentieth century.

SUMMARY

- The realities of the Great Basin environment resulted in conservative hunter-gatherer adaptations and periodic movement. Differences in subsistence and settlement patterns were due to highly varied resource availability.

- Wetlands and marshes were prime areas for human settlement, but were highly localized. Groups living nearby often maintained relatively stable winter bases near marshes and depended, also, on stored foods.

- People have lived in the Great Basin for at least 13,500 years. Paleo-Indian groups tended to live near now-vanished lakes and marshes, but widened their diets and food quests as populations grew slowly.

- The Desert Archaic began in about 7000 BCE, with people responding to greater aridity by exploiting a wider range of foods, especially seed plants. Populations tended to be sparse in the south, but higher near the Great Salt Lake with its extensive wetlands.

- There was striking continuity in hunting and foraging practices and in the use of simple technologies. Archaic people hunted and foraged at low and high altitudes. They exploited such a broad range of foods, with the aid of subtle technological changes, that their lifeway could have continued indefinitely had not Europeans arrived.

- About 400 to 500 CE small quantities of pottery and maize cobs appeared in the Great Basin, either adopted locally or imported from the Southwest. During the first millennium CE settled Fremont horticultural people flourished in many parts of the northern Colorado Plateau and in the eastern Great Basin. Fremont culture is notable for its pottery and baskets, and for its rock art characterized by shamanistic figures.

- By the mid-fourteenth century CE Great Basin peoples had abandoned maize farming, probably in the face of the aridity of the Medieval Warm Period.

CHRONOLOGICAL TABLE OF DEVELOPMENTS IN THE PLAINS

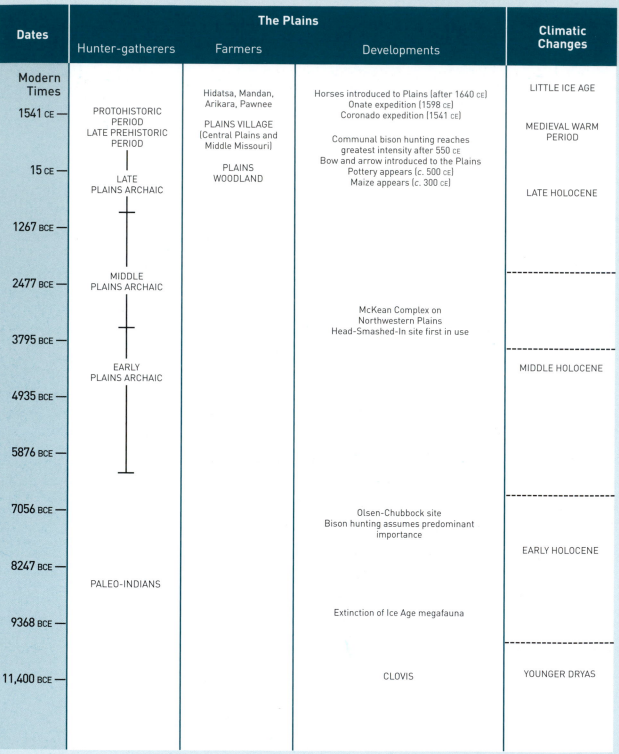

Dates	The Plains			Climatic Changes
	Hunter-gatherers	Farmers	Developments	
Modern Times		Hidatsa, Mandan, Arikara, Pawnee	Horses introduced to Plains (after 1640 CE) Onate expedition (1598 CE) Coronado expedition (1541 CE)	LITTLE ICE AGE
1541 CE	PROTOHISTORIC PERIOD LATE PREHISTORIC PERIOD	PLAINS VILLAGE (Central Plains and Middle Missouri)	Communal bison hunting reaches greatest intensity after 550 CE Bow and arrow introduced to the Plains	MEDIEVAL WARM PERIOD
15 CE	LATE PLAINS ARCHAIC	PLAINS WOODLAND	Pottery appears (c. 500 CE) Maize appears (c. 300 CE)	LATE HOLOCENE
1267 BCE				
2477 BCE	MIDDLE PLAINS ARCHAIC			
3795 BCE	EARLY PLAINS ARCHAIC		McKean Complex on Northwestern Plains Head-Smashed-In site first in use	MIDDLE HOLOCENE
4935 BCE				
5876 BCE				
7056 BCE			Olsen-Chubbock site Bison hunting assumes predominant importance	EARLY HOLOCENE
8247 BCE	PALEO-INDIANS			
9368 BCE			Extinction of Ice Age megafauna	
11,400 BCE			CLOVIS	YOUNGER DRYAS

People of the Plains

Thundering buffalo herds, hunters with bows and arrows driving stampeding beasts over precipitous cliffs: during the early nineteenth century twenty-seven tribes of horse-mounted Native Americans dominated the Great Plains. All of them were either nomadic buffalo (bison) hunters subsisting almost entirely off Plains game herds, or semi-nomadic hunters who relied on crops for a substantial part of their diet. Such colorful societies were the stuff of which legends were made, with stereotypes of "feathered braves" and spectacular raids perpetuated in the circus ring and later in movies (Figure 7.1). Today the stereotypes are gone, for the assumption that Plains Native American culture was static over extended periods is long discredited. We now know that although the cultural roots of the twenty-seven Plains tribes lie in much earlier Paleo-Indian societies, described briefly in Chapter 3, their diversity arose through many centuries of constant change. What innovations led to more refined hunting methods and the greater elaboration of Plains hunting societies? Why did many groups to the east take up agriculture at least part-time? What were the consequences of the introduction of the horse to the Plains? These questions have fascinated generations of researchers.

The Plains Environment

The Great Plains cover a very large area of North America's heartland, from the Rockies in the west to the Eastern Woodlands near the Mississippi (Figure 7.2). They are a grass sea that extends across about half a billion acres (200 million ha) from Canada in the north to Mexico's Rio Grande in the south. They were, and still are, a harsh place to live, with summers often brutally hot, and long, bitterly cold winters. The original native vegetation was perennial grasses, with trees limited to stream valleys and occasional higher ground. The boundaries between the Plains and neighboring environments are often blurred. Sometimes one can literally draw a line between the Rocky Mountain foothills and the Plains. In other places, long mountain ridges finger into the open country, forming

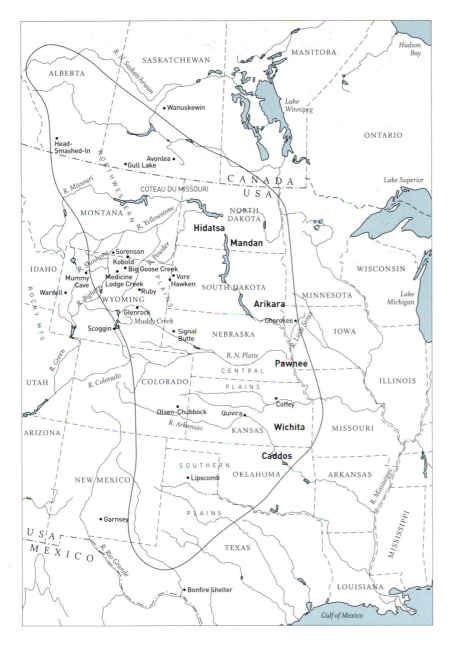

7.2 Map of Plains regions and sites.

intermontane basins that obscure the boundary. The eastern frontiers of the Plains pass imperceptibly into the Eastern Woodlands as annual rainfall rises and short-grass prairie gives way to tall, lusher grasses, then woodland.

Flying over the Plains at 40,000 ft (12,000 m) gives a misleading impression of environmental homogeneity over hundreds of miles. One can drive for hours across gently rolling landscape, over seemingly drab, unchanging plains. Then one encounters an unexpected stream, a local spring, or a deep gully that alters the entire landscape. It is then one realizes that the Plains are a very diverse environment.

Waldo Wedel (1961) aptly described the Plains as a grassland triangle, with the irregular base resting on the foot of the Rocky Mountains in the west, the apex meeting in the deciduous forests of the Mississippi Valley in the east. The grass coverage itself varies with rainfall. In the drier west, from the South Saskatchewan Valley into Montana and western North Dakota, then far southward into Texas, are the short-grass plains. The low-growing, shallow-rooted grasses grow rapidly in the spring, then enter a period of dormancy when they cure to a highly nutritious winter forage, which was an ideal food for bison and antelope. Between southern Manitoba and Oklahoma, the short-grass plains with their steppe-like vegetation become a transition zone of mixed grasses, followed by the tall-grass cover of the true prairie. In Texas, both the short-grass and mixed-grass plains become mesquite and desert-grass savanna.

The western regions are drier than the east, but evaporation rates are all-important, being far higher in the south than on the Canadian plains, where about 15 in. (38 cm) of rain is equivalent to 22 in. (56 cm) in Texas. Unfortunately rainfall varies greatly from year to year, coming mainly in highly localized thunderstorms that leave one area soaked while another a few miles away bakes in the hot sun. Constantly fluctuating rainfall and persistent aridity made farming difficult west of the 98th meridian, the arbitrary frontier between what we will see to be the nomadic bison-hunting groups of the west and the settled village peoples of the eastern Plains.

The Plains were, above all, the world of *Bison bison*, a smaller beast than the *Bison antiquus* hunted by Paleo-Indians. There were constant local changes caused by shifts in the air-mass circulation patterns that allowed moist tropical air over the grasslands. These led to local variations in plant and animal distributions throughout the Plains, which have persisted through thousands of years. Survival depended on careful observation of these changing grazing conditions, and of bison movements. Grazing animals shifted location from one year to the next, following fresh, green spring grass. The condition of the graze was vital. Successions of dry years with short grass could force the bison to grub close to the ground, wearing out and breaking their teeth on the soil and grass stems. As the teeth wear down, the grinding surfaces become less efficient, until the animal finally can no longer feed itself and dies.

Some idea of the localized conditions that affected bison hunting can be gained from Vaughn Bryant's palynological (pollen grain) researches in southwest Texan caves (Bryant and Holloway, 1985). Bonfire Shelter in southwest Texas is located hundreds of miles south of the Great Plains, and is the southernmost site in North America where mass bison hunts took place (Figure 7.3). There are two discrete zones of bison bones in the shelter, each apparently representing repeated **bison jumps** over relatively short periods. (A bison jump is when hunters drive a stampeding herd over a high bluff approached by long lines of stone piles.) The earliest bone deposit resulted from Paleo-Indian hunts c. 8000 BCE, the later one from another episode of repeated game drives in about 500 BCE. What happened during the 7,500 years that separated the two bone beds? Bryant's pollen samples revealed that the Bonfire Shelter region has enjoyed good grass cover only twice since 10,000 BCE. Each of these periods—each a time when it was possible for the area to support large herds of grazing animals—coincided with a layer of bison bones. Bryant and Holloway's work showed how opportunistic

7.3 View from the interior of Bonfire Shelter, with the rim above and talus debris from the rim collapse to the right.

hunters followed much-reduced bison herds into the Bonfire Shelter area, and chose that ideal location for their hunts.

Thus, human populations were constantly on the move, following bison herds on their annual range. They did not, of course, prey on bison alone, but supplemented their basic meat diet with other mammals, such as pronghorn antelope, and with such plant foods as the Jerusalem artichoke when available.

Paleo-Indians: ?Before 11,500 to 6900 BCE

The story of first settlement on the Plains is just like almost everywhere else—scatters of stone tools and Clovis projectile points, but little else. Very small numbers of people were living here by at least 11,500 BCE, using a toolkit that included not only the sophisticated and well-made Clovis point, but also bone artifacts such as pointed rods. Evidence of their presence comes from mammoth and other large-game kill sites, a few transitory camps, and caches of points and other stone tools. Whether the caches were dumped by individuals or groups is unknown, but it is clear that fine-grained toolmaking stone was carried long distances upon occasion, sometimes over 125 miles (200 km), for reasons that elude us.

The sparse, highly mobile Clovis population seems to have developed a remarkably broad knowledge of their plains environment, as suggested by their

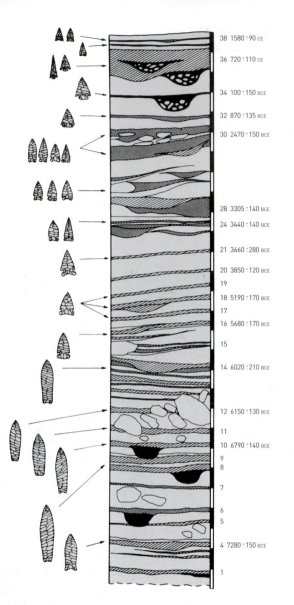

38	1580 ± 90 CE
36	720 ± 110 CE
34	100 ± 150 BCE
32	870 ± 135 BCE
30	2470 ± 150 BCE
28	3305 ± 140 BCE
24	3440 ± 140 BCE
21	3660 ± 280 BCE
20	3850 ± 120 BCE
19	
18	5190 ± 170 BCE
17	
16	5680 ± 170 BCE
15	
14	6020 ± 210 BCE
12	6150 ± 130 BCE
11	
10	6790 ± 140 BCE
9	
8	
7	
6	
5	
4	7280 ± 150 BCE
1	

7.4 A stratigraphic profile from Mummy Cave, Wyoming, showing the change from Paleo-Indian lanceolate forms to side-notched and then stemmed points, c. 6900 BCE.

knowledge of stone sources long distances away. Did they maintain lasting connections with other groups? How did they acquire marriage partners and intelligence about game and other food sources over the horizon? These are intangibles, which are nearly impossible to discern from the scanty archaeological signature.

Plains Archaic: c. 6900 to c. 600 BCE

The transition to what we can loosely call the Archaic occurred around 6900 BCE, when we discern significant cultural diversity for the first time. Abrupt changes in projectile-point forms from lanceolate Paleo-Indian types to side-notched points mark the beginning of the Archaic (Wood, 1998) (Figure 7.4). Side notches allowed a much tighter and stronger binding of the point to the foreshaft or spear handle. Subdividing the Plains Archaic is an exercise in confusion. Here as elsewhere, the yardstick has long been projectile-point styles, but these become too varied to have much meaning. Here, for simplicity, I use Douglas Bamforth's (2018) carefully argued Early and Late (or Later) Archaic as a convenient framework.

While the story of the Plains inevitably centers on the bison, plant foods were also important, especially in the south, though bison and other game remained paramount in the north. As we saw in the Great Basin in Chapter 6, the Archaic witnessed the first intensification of the food quest, with a greater concentration on smaller animals and on plant foods, also fish and shellfish where available. These trends accelerated through the Early Archaic, especially the use of plant foods and other resources that required more labor to process. A simple culinary technique known as "**hot-rock cooking**" came into widespread use over many centuries. This involved boiling water in holes in the ground lined with hide, and was an effective way of making a wide variety of foods more palatable and more easily stored. But the new cuisine required much greater time and effort, whether or not many people were involved.

Continued warming increased the range of habitats available for grazing and browsing herbivores. The sparse human population lived in a broader range of environments, identified by stemmed projectile points, not earlier fluted heads. Surviving sites with their minimal artifact accumulations suggest that people were constantly on the move.

Early Plains Archaic: 6900 to 3000 BCE

As the warmer conditions gripped the Plains, the hunters relied more heavily on smaller game, even rabbits, also plant foods, as well as taking fish and freshwater mollusks. They abandoned their carefully made fluted points, now using stone-working methods and projectile heads that show much less refinement. At the same time, the demand for fine-grained toolmaking stone obtained from afar virtually disappeared. Bison drives became rarer events, though hunters still used natural features to kill their prey. The Hawken site in northeastern Wyoming, dating to about 4400 BCE, records an Early Archaic hunt where bison were driven up a narrow arroyo until they reached a perpendicular cliff that impeded further progress up the gully. Hawken was used at least three times. Judging from the bison teeth, the hunts occurred in early or midwinter. The hunters were taking both mature beasts and driving nursery herds, but the killing was tough work. At least 300 projectile points lay among the bones, many of them broken by brutal impact against struggling animals. Many points had been reworked again and again, with carefully ground bases and needle-sharp tips that penetrated hides and muscles very effectively (For this and other kill sites, see Kornfeld and Frison, 2010). The great bison cliff jump at Head-Smashed-In, Alberta, was first used at about this time (see Box: Head-Smashed-In Buffalo Jump, Alberta, Canada).

HEAD-SMASHED-IN BUFFALO JUMP, ALBERTA, CANADA

Head-Smashed-In was used for bison hunting for more than 6,000 years (Brink, 2008). It is a remarkable place to visit, now a UNESCO World Heritage Site: a long set of cliffs with a spectacular view of the Rocky Mountains on a clear day. Those who first used it made a brilliant choice, for the topography immediately above and behind the sandstone cliffs that formed the jump are ideal for controlling prey. A large drainage basin extending over 15 square miles (40 km²) with abundant water and excellent graze attracted bison until well into the fall. The gathering basin above Head-Smashed-in is an ideal place to watch unsuspecting prey. A second basin lies above the smaller Calderwell kill site immediately to the north (Figure 7.5).

Over repeated kill cycles the hunters built long drive lines of stone cairns that extend more than 8.6 miles (14 km) from the gathering basin to the kill site.

Many of them may have just been stone piles. Others probably supported brush to hide the waiting hunters. Driving the bison was a skilled business, requiring an intimate knowledge of their habits, both as individuals and in herds, whether

7.5 Head-Smashed-In, Alberta, is among the oldest, largest, and best-preserved of western Plains buffalo-jump sites. The plan shows the major features of the site and the neighboring Calderwood site, including gathering areas where the hunters maneuvered the herds into position, drive lanes, and processing sites. »

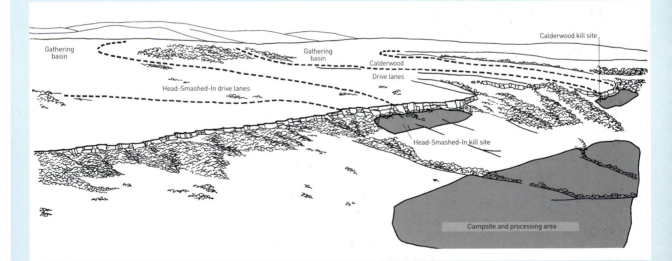

Gathering basin

Gathering basin

Calderwood kill site

Calderwood Drive lanes

Head-Smashed-In drive lanes

Head-Smashed-In kill site

Campsite and processing area

7.6 Two McKean projectile points from Signal Butte, Nebraska.

Late Archaic: 3800 to 600 BCE

The Plains Late Archaic flourished during the mid-Holocene climatic optimum. Warmer and drier conditions may have meant focusing more intensively on plant foods, even in the north, where bison hunting continued. Many northern Late Archaic sites are distinctive for their lanceolate points with concave bases, vaguely described as the "McKean technocomplex" (Figure 7.6). The Canadian Plains have yielded Oxbow points with a deep basal notch and wide side notches that may represent a different culture. Quite what these differences in projectile-point styles mean is unknown, but both McKean and Oxbow users hunted large mammals.

Late Plains Archaic people on the northwestern Plains hunted and processed bison in more intensive ways. They invested heavily in humanly fabricated corrals and drive lines, which they used on many occasions. They also processed the

grazing or stampeding at full speed. The buffalo would move close to the drive lines, at which point the hunters would encircle the animals from upwind, shouting and waving hides to scare them. As the panicking animals stampeded the leaders would spot the cliff and try to stop. But the weight of galloping beasts behind would press upon them and force them over the cliff at high speed (Figures 7.7 and 7.8). The herd would tumble helter-skelter into space and land with bone-crushing thumps on the dirt and rubble below. There other hunters waited with bows and arrows, stone-tipped spears, and clubs.

Then the butchery would begin, in a flat area immediately below the kill site. Here the people had pitched their hide tipis, as much as possible upwind to avoid the stench. Men and women alike moved in with choppers and knives. They worked systematically, dismembering the carcasses, smashing the limb bones to remove the marrow. The fresh meat was sliced up into strips, then laid out on racks to dry before being processed into nutritious pemmican. The deep, stratified deposits below the cliff are formed from earth, stone rubble, and crushed bones, and accumulated to the depth of 36 ft (11 m) over more than 5,700

years. The tools used by the butchers lie among the bones: stone scrapers and sharp-edged knives, tough choppers to break up larger bones, drills, also broken arrowheads, potsherds, and a few ornaments such as bone beads.

While the butchers dismembered the bones and sliced up the meat, other people dug boiling pits, which they lined with hides and filled with water. They used large fires to heat thousands of broken rocks, which they cast into the pits to boil the bones and render their grease.

First used during the Late Archaic, Head-Smashed-In was visited when the density of buffalo reached a critical point and their migrations made use of the gathering basin above the cliffs. Judging from the butchery practices, the kills would mostly have been in fall, when the buffalo were attracted by richer forage and it was necessary for people to lay in supplies of pemmican and fat for the winter. Communal hunts like those at Head-Smashed-In also provided buffalo tongues and meat for the annual Sun Dance, which took place in midsummer. This was a rite of intensification which helped bond together such loosely organized groups as the local Blackfoot people, to undertake communal hunts.

Analysing kill sites like Head-Smashed-In is an intricate process that involves reconstructing the butchery methods (using artifacts, complete and highly incomplete bison skeletons, and individual bones), and drawing on environmental data of all kinds. Unlike most such sites, this location was used again and again, which allowed the archaeologists to study kill and butchery methods over a long period.

I strongly recommend visiting this fascinating place. The Interpretative Center is first rate and highly informative. If you can, make a point of visiting the drive lines and the area above the cliffs with a Blackfoot guide, a four-hour hike on the first Saturday of each month, May through October. For details, visit the Head-Smashed-In website.

carcasses very thoroughly, a labor-intensive way of increasing food supplies; one particularly valuable product so gained was nutritious, easily stored pemmican for use in the winter and while on the move. It was no coincidence that many McKean bison kills were in the fall. Such intensive hunting and processing also extended to antelope traps at some locations. The social implications were considerable. For a start, bands could organize hunts at known locations, in situations where significant kills would be virtually guaranteed. Those who organized them may have assumed positions of leadership and acquired followers, though, of course, we cannot know this. Quite why hunting intensified is a mystery. Perhaps it was connected to a gradual population increase and to irregular fluctuations in climate and bison populations.

In the north between 2900 and 1000 BCE both hunting toolkits and bison-hunting methods became more refined. Hunters trapped their prey in arroyos,

7.7 The cliffs at the Head-Smashed-In buffalo jump, Alberta.

7.8 Reconstruction of a bison jump at the Head-Smashed-In site.

also in stone and wood corrals, and used bison jumps. The Kobold site in southern Montana is an excellent example, and one which remained in use right into later times. Kobold is a sandstone bluff 25 ft (7.5 m) high, close to well-watered grazing land (Figure 7.9). The arroyo below the cliff is wide and spacious, which was ideal for butchering large numbers of animals. The terrain is favorable for game drives, allowing but one approach to the bluff. Judging from the many broken bones among the bison remains, many animals died in the precipitous fall.

A wider range of projectile points came into use across the southern Plains, for reasons that elude us, perhaps a reflection of more regional adaptations. In the southern Plains people rarely hunted bison, and focused instead on other foods. For example, in about 3250 BCE Archaic groups occupied the Coffey site on the edge of an oxbow lake alongside the Big Blue River, north of Manhattan, Kansas. Here people did take bison and other game, but also pursued waterfowl and collected goosefoot and other plants. They caught large numbers of catfish, indicating that the site was occupied during the late summer, when fish crowded into small shallow pools. The irregular long-distance contacts of Paleo-Indian times seem to have ended, as local groups intensified their exploitation of their own territories.

During the third century BCE a highly sophisticated bison-hunting culture emerged on the northwestern Plains, known by side-notched "Besant" projectile points and clay vessels (Figure 7.10). These people used much more complicated bison corrals built of logs set in deep post holes, well documented at the Ruby and Muddy Creek sites in Wyoming (Frison, 1971; Kornfeld and Frison, 2010). The Muddy Creek site corral was built on sloping ground, a structure about 40 ft (12 m) in diameter. It lay upslope from extensive, fertile grazing tracts, and was hidden from view by a low ridge until the very last moments of a drive. Both this, and the Ruby corral, were designed to handle relatively small numbers of bison, perhaps a nursery herd of about twenty-five beasts. On the Central Plains some groups were semi-sedentary and consumed a wide range of foods.

There were other changes too, with lifestyle and social institutions differing over wide areas. It may be that the proliferation of projectile-point styles is a reflection of such changes—we will never know. More intensified food quests

7.10 A Besant projectile point from the Muddy Creek site, Wyoming. Length: 3.5 in. (9 cm).

certainly mean local specializations, in, say, rabbit hunting and fish, and in the traps and other technologies required for the purpose. There are signs of individual social identities in burials, especially in the south and east. The shamanistic art motifs pecked into rocks across the Plains may also reflect changing ritual concerns, even cosmologies. Such social identities may have come about in a Plains world where connections with others, whether near or far, acquired increasing importance (see Box: Medicine Wheels and Rock Art).

MEDICINE WHEELS AND ROCK ART

We tend to think of the Plains people in terms of bison hunting and mass stampedes, but there was an intricate, ever-changing diversity of rituals and spiritual beliefs behind the rich tapestry of Plains life. As always, the intangible is hard to study, with the exception of accounts of major ceremonial events witnessed by early travelers and by anthropologists. The only material reflection of the intangible comes in the form of sacred artifacts, including shaman's bundles, and in rock art and what are commonly named medicine wheels. (Readers seeking New Age revelations should stop reading now!)

Medicine wheels are confined to the northern and northwestern Plains, from northern Wyoming into Alberta and Saskatchewan. They are difficult to classify, as their meanings have varied through time. The oldest wheels are radiocarbon dated to the Late Archaic and feature a central rock cairn with radiating spokes, the whole enclosed by a stone circle. There are elaborations on this general design that include entrance avenues and outlying cairns. The Big Horn Medicine Wheel, which is 80 ft (24.3 m) across, lies on the Bighorn Range in Wyoming at an altitude of 10,000 ft (3,000 m) and is only accessible in summer. Big Horn is as yet undated, but is of this general design: it has twenty-eight limestone boulder lines as "spokes," with six small stone enclosures around the circle (Figure 7.11). The exact purpose of the wheel and the identity of its makers are unknown. Most researchers believe it was constructed in stages over several centuries between 1,500 and 500 years ago. Big Horn is still venerated by local Native American groups, some of whom experience vision quests there. Projectile points excavated at several wheels show that these were long-revered sacred places, even if their use and the rituals changed over the centuries. The cairn at the center of the Majorville Medicine Wheel in Alberta is 29.5 ft (9 m) across, the twenty-eight spokes radiating out to ▸▸

7.11 The Big Horn Medicine Wheel, Wyoming.

The Later History of Bison Hunting

Around 1 CE bison hunting on the northern and northwestern Plains intensified. This intensification reflects the initial stages of a large-scale trade in meat and hides from the Plains, exchanged for plant foods with people living at the margins of the grasslands. Bows and arrows came into use by 1 CE at the latest, marked by the appearance of slender "Avonlea" stone points (Figure 7.13). These are tiny, needle sharp, but broad enough to penetrate deeply into tough bison

form a circle 88.5 ft (27 m) in diameter. If radiocarbon dates are to be trusted, the Majorville Wheel was founded around 2500 BCE. Medicine wheels are, and will probably remain, an enigma, despite claims that they were astronomical observatories or were prototypes for historic Plains Sun Dance Lodges.

The same can be said for the etched petroglyphs dating to the Late Archaic, and perhaps even back to Paleo-Indian times, in the Black Hills, also in southern Colorado and westward into Nevada. Animals dominate the art, often depictions of antelope, deer, bison, and suchlike being pursued by people with nets or traps, sometimes accompanied by dogs. Some of the human figures appear to be individuals directing the enterprise. There are cooperative hunts and small-scale pursuits, but the animals are ones familiar in Late Archaic sites on the northern Plains.

During the Late Archaic new images appear, this time elaborate human figures associated with animals or symbols. Many archaeologists identify them as shamans in trances, perhaps depicted on spiritual journeys or when experiencing visions while under the influence of hallucinogens (Figure 7.12). This is very different from the earlier hunt scenes, which are cooperative ventures. Now the art depicts individuals and individual experiences, during which specific people are shown in well-defined social roles.

7.12 Petroglyphs of humans from Grand County, Utah.

hide and cause loss of blood when shot from close range. The bow was adopted quite quickly, but still did not solve the problem of driving and controlling the movement of the quarry. Communal bison hunting on foot reached its greatest intensity after 550 CE. As time went on, the hunters made increasing use of bison jumps. A long tradition of such hunting comes from such locations as Wanuskewin on the outskirts of Saskatoon, Saskatchewan, where a small tributary valley of the South Saskatchewan River provided ideal locations for bison jumps, also abundant plant foods and winter shelter. Wanuskewin was visited by bison-hunting groups as early as 400 CE.

The Gull Lake site in southwestern Saskatchewan lies in the northwest Plains culture area, but is close to the northeast edge. It lies across from the glacial hills of the Missouri Coteau, which divides the plains from the dry northeast prairie. The western Saskatchewan uplands were the boundary between the Blackfoot (or Blackfeet) and Atsina of the High Plains and the Cree and Assiniboine of the prairies (Kehoe, 1973). At Gull Lake the hunters herded the bison along the uplands from the south until they could be driven down a deep ravine. The stampeding beasts would tumble over a landslide, which formed a convenient drop, falling into a natural depression that served as a corral. Both tipi rings and evidence of camp occupations lie nearby. Tom Kehoe excavated 20 ft (6 m) below the modern land surface in the kill area, recovering dense concentrations of bison bones. The Gull Lake area was visited as early as the first century BCE, with the first well-documented jump episodes associated with Avonlea projectile points. Six bone layers document the Avonlea occupation, ending in the seventh century CE. Gull Lake continued in use in subsequent Prairie and Plains occupations between the eighth and fourteenth centuries. Kehoe argues that complex, highly ritualized bison hunting began with the introduction of the bow and arrow to the Plains by Athabascans.

Without horses, ancient bison hunters depended on ever-changing herd densities for successful communal hunts. Individual or small-group hunting would be far more adaptive with lower densities, for bison drives have a high failure rate and a herd could easily move out of foot range unless herd densities were unusually high. Most people lived in small groups of several families that were on the move constantly, depending on available food supplies. Hudson Bay Company surveyor Peter Fidler spent six weeks among the Piegan people in 1797. He witnessed many foot-based bison drives as he camped among them at one of their drive pounds. At one, the hunters killed more than 250 beasts and would have taken more. But "when the wind happened to blow from the pound in the direction of the tents, there was an intolerable stench of the large numbers of petrified [sic.] carcasses, *etc.* on which account the reason of our leaving it" (MacGregor, 1998).

Then the horse arrived and everything changed. In 1541 CE Spanish conquistador Francisco de Coronado ventured eastward from Pecos in the Southwest onto the Plains, in search of rumored gold. Coronado rode on geldings, and returned without gold, but later horse-riding Spanish settlers introduced full breeding stock. About 150 years later, during the eighteenth century, horses—"mystery dogs," as the Native Americans called them—reached the northern Plains (Holder, 1974; Schlesier, 1994). They had a profound impact on native lifeways, affecting transport, hunting, trade, combat, and social relations. Horses gave their

7.13 An Avonlea point from the Gull Lake bison-drive site.

riders the ability to locate dispersed bison populations effectively inaccessible to hunters on foot and to carry large quantities of meat (Figures 7.14 and 7.15). Plains groups were now less dependent on the year-by-year, season-by-season cycle. Some formerly sedentary groups, such as the Dakota and Cheyenne, even became nomads, joining others, such as the Blackfeet and Comanche, who had been hunting for centuries.

Before the advent of the horse Plains people had often pooled their resources, for instance in communal hunts that brought groups together to share labor and, as we have seen, also provided opportunities for ceremony and for the exchange of goods, information, and marriage partners. Ambitious individuals could manipulate the communal hunt to their benefit, becoming leaders with power and prestige, but the millennia-old communal values basically stressed cooperation. Once horses arrived, those values began to shift, giving way to highly individualistic doctrines and smaller bands that pitted family against

7.14 A buffalo hunt on horseback, painted by George Catlin in 1844.

7.15 Fur trappers and traders at a 19th-century rendezvous near Scotts Bluff, Nebraska. Traders met here with buyers from the east, exchanging furs for goods. Native Americans also took part in the event. Undated drawing.

family, with little concern for the common welfare. The wealth obtained in battle could be used to promote family status. Hunter vied with hunter for the allegiance of followers and fellow warriors. A flamboyant, almost frenzied, era of Plains life dawned, in which most nomadic groups believed old age was evil, and that it was better for a man to die in battle. Within a century, the Bison Belt became an economic battleground, as war parties raided neighbors' camps to seize horses and loot food stores.

Another profoundly destabilizing arrival—and one with devastating consequences for the bison—was the rifle, introduced during the nineteenth century. Strict Spanish policies forbade the trading of muskets to Native Americans, but French fur traders in Canada and along the Mississippi gladly exchanged firearms and ammunition for furs and horses (the latter acquired by the Native Americans from the Spanish, through barter and through theft). At this time the Blackfoot of the northern Plains rose to prominence, as European fur traders and settlers pressed on to the Plains hunting grounds. Equipped with firearms, which they had traded for beaver pelts, the Native Americans could now engage in wholesale bison slaughter. Soon white hunters with their repeating rifles joined the fray, leaving thousands of wasted carcasses rotting on the Plains. Both beaver and bison began to dwindle, the latter affected also by exotic cattle diseases. Then the railroads spread over the prairies. During the 1860s and 1870s special excursion trains took hunters into a sea of bison. The great herds of thundering animals, with their seemingly inexhaustible supplies of meat and hides, disappeared almost overnight. The last vestiges of the primeval North American hunting life vanished in an orgy of nineteenth-century musketry. Only a handful of buffalo survived, to form the nucleus of the managed herds that graze on the Plains today.

The Plains Woodland Tradition: 500 BCE to 900 CE

To many people the Plains mean nothing more than vast herds of bison pursued by small bands of nomadic hunters. Such a portrait is misleading, for in the Central Plains and Middle Missouri Valley long-distance exchange networks brought pottery and other exotic objects from the east, as well as new burial customs, and in some places more sedentary settlement. Between 500 BCE and 900 CE the Plains became increasingly engaged with neighboring regions, economically, socially, and ideologically, most especially from the Eastern Woodlands. This Plains Woodland Tradition is remarkable for four major innovations: the bow and arrow came into use; maize was cultivated for the first time, even if infrequently; many groups now manufactured pottery; raised burial mounds appeared over much of the northeastern periphery of the Plains (for details, see Bamforth, 2018).

At first, during the "Early Woodland" (500 BCE to 1 CE), there was little change from Archaic practices, except for the appearance of pottery along the eastern margins of the Plains as far south as eastern Oklahoma. The vessels were basically similar to those made in the central and southern Mississippi Valley. There are also occasional signs of more substantial settlements, suggested by thick deposits. The next five "Middle Woodland" centuries (1 to 500 CE) witnessed dramatic changes on the eastern Plains. Large, densely occupied villages accompanied by burial mounds, with masonry chambers apparently entered regularly to deposit the dead, appear along the Missouri River from Kansas City to St. Joseph. This is

7.16 Kansas City Hopewell potsherds. Clay vessels made by these groups have many diluted Hopewell features.

known as the "Kansas City Hopewell," a nod to the Eastern Woodlands Hopewell (see Chapter 11), though the Kansas City Tradition does not display such spectacular earthworks. Kansas City Hopewell communities were in regular contact with Hopewell societies to the east, but their artifacts differ in significant ways (Figure 7.16). Some communities remained in the same place for centuries, relying heavily on stored foods and living in what may have been substantial dwellings. They were predominantly deer hunters and foragers, collecting a wide range of plants including nuts and such wild seeds as goosefoot, but they also grew marsh elder and sunflowers.

Between 500 and 900 CE, the Late Woodland, much more elaborate ceremonial surrounded the dead during a time of rising population densities. Burial mounds rose on bluffs overlooking river valleys, lakes, or creeks. Most often, up to forty circular mounds cluster in groups. Linear earthworks are much rarer and consist of simple platforms or low embankments running in straight lines for hundreds of feet, occasionally connecting one mound with others. One or more circular-to-oblong burial pits, containing a single or several skeletons, lie under many of the mounds. Most were roofed with poles or logs, while bison carcasses and skulls were sometimes placed with the dead.

The artifacts found in Plains mounds are personal ornaments—stone pipes, for example, and items made from such exotic materials as Great Lakes copper. These objects do not necessarily mean that the Hopewell ideology of individual power and prestige had diffused to the Plains. David Benn (1990) argues that the personal ornaments symbolized an individual's subordinate status in nature: the ability to kill large animals balanced by powerlessness in the face of drought and other natural phenomena. Humans reconciled themselves with the forces of nature by subordinating themselves to the animals they killed, an ideology which may have originated among Archaic societies. The family band was still the focus of most subsistence activity, in contrast with many contemporary Eastern Woodland societies, where individual status and prestige were coming to the fore. But, as exploitation of game and plant foods intensified in later times and semi-sedentary communities became more common, so rankings of different families and kin groups emerged, to reach a high degree of development in later village communities.

We can be sure that bison hunting was deeply ingrained in Plains Woodland culture, for efficient pursuit of these animals by semi-sedentary farmers continued long after European contact. But traditions of village existence were also an ancient component of valley life, among peoples who lived along a frontier between the settled farmers of the east and the hunter-gatherers of the Plains.

Plains Village Farmers: c. 1000 to 1500 CE

By the end of the Woodland centuries people in the north and northwest were mobile big-game hunters operating on a large scale and exchanging their surplus pemmican, hides, and other products over vast areas. Semi-sedentary hunters and gatherers to the south, from Nebraska to Oklahoma, preyed on a wider range of game. Few groups cultivated maize or other plants. Then came a major change between about 1050 and 1100 CE, when a series of "Great Oasis" communities in central and northeastern Iowa became sedentary maize farmers. These were densely packed villages that appeared at a time when people to the east also took to maize agriculture. Between 1100 and 1200 similar communities appeared along the Missouri and its tributaries in South Dakota. This Initial Middle Missouri Tradition was a radical departure from earlier Plains communities. Some villages were in use for a long time, usually comprising twenty to thirty long, rectangular houses with gabled roofs, and as many as 200 to 300 people. Many were palisaded. Interestingly, maize farming expanded dramatically in the entire region just as Cahokia on the Mississippi rose to great prominence (for Cahokia, see Chapter 12). There may not have been direct contacts, but a scatter of distinctive clay vessels with Cahokia motifs appear along the Missouri.

In all probability, maize agriculture spread across the Plains by a combination of deliberate migration and routine social contacts that brought new ideas and maize farming to hunting communities. The contacts must have been seasonal and often regular, with the maize communities also moving out to hunt bison and other game.

The Middle Missouri was a world of its own, a deep incised trench that flowed through North and South Dakota (Zimmerman, 1985). The river cut into the surrounding plains as it flowed toward much lower and distant seas. In places the valley drops 200 to 400 ft (60 to 120 m) below the adjoining higher ground. The so-called "breaks," which delineate the edge of the valley, are steep and heavily eroded, the trench itself being between half a mile and 4 miles (0.8 and 6.5 km) wide. Long, grass-covered terraces line much of the valley, dropping sharply onto the river floodplain itself. Most human settlement was on the terraces, escaping even the highest spring and summer floods. West and south of the valley lie open, drier plains where bison once roamed in large numbers. These plains were a vital part of village life along the river, which depended not only on maize and bean agriculture, but also on bison hunting. The Middle Missouri Valley and other such sheltered locales were places where two worlds met, the life of the nomadic Plains bison hunter meeting the more settled existence of the village farmer.

Two realities affected agriculture in the valley. The first was irregular and often highly localized rainfall, the second the risk of early or late frosts. Anyone farming maize in the Missouri trench was planting a tropical crop at the northern limits of its range, with a growing season which averaged about 160 days in the southern portions of the valley to a mere 130 days in the Knife-Heart Rivers area of North Dakota. The frost-free growing season was considerably longer in the valley than on the surrounding plains. For all its harsh conditions, the Middle Missouri Valley was a remarkably diverse environment, especially for people who relied on a combination of agriculture, hunting, and foraging. The valley itself provided not only winter game and many edible plant foods, but also fish in abundance. The Missouri Valley was also a major flyway for migrating waterfowl in spring and fall. Those who lived on the western bank enjoyed ready access to bison-hunting grounds on the plains and to trade routes which crossed open country to the Rocky Mountains and far to the north and west. The Plains hunters and settled valley farmers each produced commodities the other lacked. The hunters brought hides and blankets, pemmican, and toolmaking stone. The farmers bartered grain and other agricultural products. For centuries, two ways of life, one very ancient, the other more recent, interacted across the eastern boundaries of the Plains.

7.18 Mandan second chief Mah-to-toh-pa, Four Bears, in a sheepskin shirt edged with scalps and porcupine quills, deerskin leggings, war-eagle feather headdress, and bear-claw necklace. Painting by George Catlin, 1841.

Good climatic conditions sometimes allowed the spread of cultivation well into the High Plains, even to the foothills of the Rockies, along drainages such as the Arkansas River. These agricultural societies, often called "Plains Village Indians," subdivided archaeologically into several traditions; they developed a way of life that dominated the eastern Plains from the Dakotas to Texas for nearly 1,000 years. For example, the Upper Republican Culture of the Republican River Basin thrived along flood-free tributaries in hamlets of fifty to seventy-five people. They were small-scale farmers who also hunted bison, and are believed to be Caddoan-speaking ancestors of the Pawnees in Nebraska and Kansas and the Arikaras in South Dakota. The Middle Missouri people were Siouan and ancestral to the Mandans (Lehmer, 1971).

By 1500 CE Plains Village Indian cultures all shared some general characteristics. Every society used substantial lodge houses (Figure 7.17). All developed base villages, which were used for much of the year, sometimes fortified with ditches and stockades. Every village contained underground storage pits, which were of great importance in environments with short growing seasons and unpredictable rains. Every group used small, triangular arrowheads and bone hoes manufactured from bison scapulae (shoulder blades) set at an acute or right angle to a wooden handle. All made and used round-bottomed or globular pottery.

There was great diversity among peoples farming along the Missouri and other river drainages, which need not detain us here. The riverine village remained a distinct, resilient unit. The members of each village community shared common traditions and customs. They had their own social hierarchy, and their own ways of organizing communal labor, of distributing wealth, and measuring prestige. Their relationships with other communities depended on territorial proximity, on common language, and sometimes on kin ties or religion. Villagers abandoned their settlements at certain times of the year, moving out onto the plains for spring and summer bison hunts to acquire meat surpluses for the winter and for the harvest ceremonies that lay ahead. Come winter, they shifted to smaller encampments on sheltered terraces where game could be found and firewood was abundant. But the agricultural months of mid- and late summer were at the center of village life. Farming was the enterprise that integrated all other activities in the community.

A well-defined social hierarchy was fundamental to village farming life: there were men and families of rank—the leaders—and commoners. These lead families claimed prominence on account of their spiritual powers and monopoly over wealth (Figure 7.18). Most high-ranking families had to validate their position by lavish gifts and by personal achievement. These rankings, stable

ARIKARA, HIDATSA, AND MANDAN

The origins of the Arikara, Hidatsa, and Mandan lie deep in the remote past. The Caddos were in the south, people whose cultural affiliations lay closer to the Mississippi Valley and the Eastern Woodlands than the Pawnee, Wichita, Arikara, and other groups to the north (Walker and Perttula, 2012). Caddoan farming culture achieved some complexity as maize agriculture took hold in the fertile river bottom lands from eastern Texas and Oklahoma into Kansas and to the north. Over the centuries the Caddoan-speakers showed a tendency to coalesce into larger political units than merely single villages, often into ephemeral chiefdoms, which linked relatively broad regions into more complex polities. In the south such developments culminated in the cultural traditions found at Spiro, Oklahoma, and other major ceremonial centers (see Chapter 12).

Preston Holder (1974) described how the organizational and spiritual rationale of Caddoan farming villages centered around the sacred village bundle, "a physical device which contains, and reminds the owner, and outsiders, of the supernatural powers controlled by its individual possessor." The bundle also had group affiliations, to the point that Holder describes it as a "sort of portable ceremonial center." Among the Arikara

and the Pawnee, the village bundle was a skin envelope containing objects that symbolized complex ideologies and rituals. The cosmic powers within the bundle assured the village's continuity.

A bundle also controlled all production and social relations within the village. Hereditary chiefs considered themselves stars living on earth— "earthly reservoirs," as Holder put it, of power that made them protectors of their people. They were the life forces of the village through the power given them by the bundle. If the bundle was lost or destroyed, then the people would die.

Chiefs and priests were men of knowledge, patience, and complete understanding, serene individuals with a reputation for generosity and largesse. They presided over the great seasonal ceremonies: the winter bison hunt when meat was obtained for planting ceremonies, and spring gatherings that focused on the bundle—their contents handled by priests, their magical forces renewed by the spring sun so the world would be born again for the harvest. These and other rituals were occasions when individuals and the community as a whole interacted with the powers of the world through private mystic experiences and communal feasts (Figure 7.19).

North from Pierre, South Dakota, the Mandan dwelt in six or seven well-fortified villages in 1742, said by French visitors to contain between 100 and 200 houses each (Zimmerman, 1985).

These populous communities were the climax of Plains Village Indian culture on the Middle Missouri. The productive maize, beans, and squash agriculture yielded dependable food supplies that were easily supplemented by hunting bison on horseback. The farmers had always been middlemen. Now their role became crucial in an emerging, and ever more complex, trading environment. The villages acquired horses and firearms from the south and west and soon became important trading centers ▶▶

7.19 Dance-drama: detail of a Mandan *okipa* (buffalo dance) in the 1830s, depicted by Karl Bodmer.

over long periods, were far from the stratified classes so characteristic of other pre-industrial civilizations.

At European contact three village farming groups lived along the Middle Missouri Valley. The Arikara, a Caddoan-speaking culture, were dominant along the Missouri, living in thirty or forty earth-lodge villages along the lower portions of the river. The Siouan-speaking Mandan lived upstream, in as many as thirteen communities, while a small number of Hidatsa flourished further north, near the confluence of the Heart, and later the Knife rivers (Ahler and Trimble, 1991).

that attracted English, French, and Spanish traders. They participated in the main currents of Plains cultural development and, like other middlemen before and since, rose to pre-eminence and prosperity. There was a price on this pre-eminence, however, and part of it is reflected in the defensive works with which the communities surrounded themselves.

Large, circular or oblong eighteenth-century Plains villages had as many as

100 or more houses, closely packed together, often with only narrow walkways between them (Figure 7.20). A deep ditch, up to 10 ft (3 m) deep when freshly dug, surrounded each settlement, backed on the inner side with a massive log-and-brush palisade. The earth lodges were between 30 and 50 ft (9 and 15 m) in diameter, the outer walls closely set circles of poles covered with earth, grass, and willow saplings. So crowded were fortified

7.20 Big Hidatsa village site, occupied between 1600 and 1845, at the confluence of the Knife and Missouri rivers, North Dakota. The aerial view shows circular earth lodge depressions and trails. In 1845 the occupants moved upstream to found a new village, joined by Arikara and Mandans.

Mandan villages that refuse was piled up against the palisades or thrown into the surrounding ditches.

Conservative estimates place at least 45,000 farmers along the river valleys at European contact (see Box: Arikara, Hidatsa, and Mandan, p. 176–77). By 1804, when the explorers Meriwether Lewis and William Clark traveled up the Missouri, the Hidatsa, Mandan, and Arikara had been devastated by exotic diseases and were but a shadow of their former selves, with many villages abandoned and survivors clustered in poorly fortified settlements. Today these groups are known collectively as the Three Affiliated Tribes.

SUMMARY

- Small numbers of Paleo-Indians lived on the Plains as early as 11,500 BCE, if not earlier. They were highly mobile, broad-spectrum hunter-gatherers.

- The Plains Archaic began in about 6900 BCE and lasted until about 600 BCE. Hunters now relied more on smaller game, also plant foods, but bison were still important prey.

- The Late Archaic (3800 to 600 BCE) flourished during the mid-Holocene climatic optimum. Many groups now focused on plant foods, although bison hunting continued, especially on the northern Plains. Both hunting toolkits and bison hunting methods became more refined.

- The Archaic saw a gradual intensification of the food quest, especially targeting smaller animals and plants. There were local variations in such activities as rabbit hunting or fishing, and individual social identities appear in burials. By 1 CE bison hunting on the northern and northwestern Plains intensified as a large-scale trade in meat and hides developed.

- The horse was introduced to the Plains after the Spanish entrada in 1541 and reached the northern Plains by the eighteenth century. Horses and firearms transformed Plains cultures, as people, being more mobile, no longer depended so closely on seasonal bison movements.

- Between 500 BCE and 600 CE the Plains became increasing engaged with neighboring regions, both economically and ideologically. The bow came into widespread use and pottery arrived, as did maize agriculture, especially in the Middle Missouri Valley. Settlers in the valley still spent much time on the Plains hunting.

- Between 1100 and 1200 CE substantial permanent villages flourished in the Missouri Valley and its South Dakota tributaries. Their inhabitants interacted with Plains hunters to the west. A well-defined social hierarchy developed, with men and families of rank and commoners.

- At European contact three village farming groups lived along the Middle Missouri: the Arikara, the Mandan, and the Hidatsa in the north.

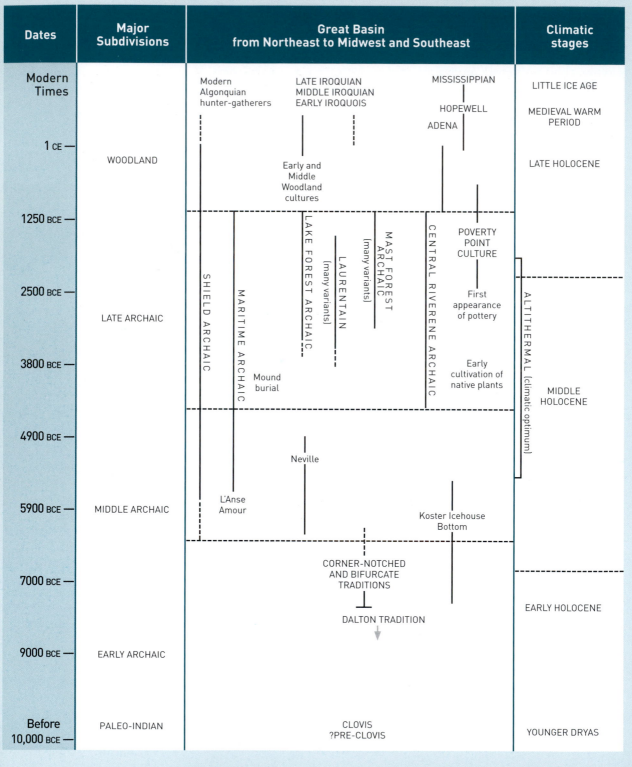

CHRONOLOGICAL TABLE FOR THE EASTERN WOODLANDS

Dates	Major Subdivisions	Great Basin from Northeast to Midwest and Southeast	Climatic stages
Modern Times		Modern Algonquian hunter-gatherers · LATE IROQUIAN MIDDLE IROQUIAN EARLY IROQUOIS · MISSISSIPPIAN HOPEWELL ADENA	LITTLE ICE AGE · MEDIEVAL WARM PERIOD
1 CE	WOODLAND	Early and Middle Woodland cultures	LATE HOLOCENE
1250 BCE		LAKE FOREST ARCHAIC · LAURENTAIN (many variants) · MAST FOREST ARCHAIC (many variants) · CENTRAL RIVERENE ARCHAIC · POVERTY POINT CULTURE	
2500 BCE	LATE ARCHAIC	SHIELD ARCHAIC · MARITIME ARCHAIC · First appearance of pottery	ALTITHERMAL (climatic optimum)
3800 BCE		Mound burial · Early cultivation of native plants	MIDDLE HOLOCENE
4900 BCE		Neville	
5900 BCE	MIDDLE ARCHAIC	L'Anse Amour · Koster Icehouse Bottom	
7000 BCE		CORNER-NOTCHED AND BIFURCATE TRADITIONS	EARLY HOLOCENE
		DALTON TRADITION	
9000 BCE	EARLY ARCHAIC		
Before 10,000 BCE	PALEO-INDIAN	CLOVIS ?PRE-CLOVIS	YOUNGER DRYAS

180

The Eastern Woodlands

Eastern Woodlands, *c.* 3000 BCE. We can imagine a man and woman lying in a fresh grave on the ridge top overlooking the valley. Their resting place looks out over the river and the woodland that presses upon its banks. Burial rituals are complete, but people from several nearby settlements are still hard at work. They have already scraped away the topsoil around the graves, piling stones from clearings among the trees to form the nucleus of a low mound. Meanwhile, men and women gather loose soil into baskets, then dump the loads onto what is soon a growing oval mound. A few dozen of their fellow kin work together for several days, hefting baskets, filling in hollows, smoothing out the surface. They leave a low burial mound behind them, a sacred place that is soon overgrown and virtually indistinguishable from a natural ridge, symbolic of the return of ancestors to the supernatural realm.

———————

By 3000 BCE, at about the time when the world's first pre-industrial civilizations developed in the eastern Mediterranean, a great diversity of hunter-gatherer societies flourished throughout North America. Population densities were rising throughout the Eastern Woodlands, especially in such environments as river valley bottoms and lakesides. The increasing number of people meant that hunting and foraging territories became more confined and smaller. Eastern Woodlands societies, extending from the Atlantic Ocean to the Mississippi River and from the Great Lakes and St. Lawrence River to the Gulf of Mexico, changed in response to this circumscribed world after 4000 BCE (Figure 8.1). They turned from big game to the exploitation of forest mammals, such as the white-tailed deer, and also, increasingly, to nuts and plant foods. People adapted in many ways, with more-or-less equal efficiency, to different circumstances (Anderson and Sassaman, 2009). At the same time, there was an increasing concern with burial rituals and honoring the ancestors.

Foraging for edible plant foods was a vital part of eastern cultures even in Paleo-Indian times (see Box: Collecting and Studying Plant Remains). Even the earliest groups knew their plant foods well. The productivity of their exploitation may have increased over the millennia, but the basic lifeway stayed much the same throughout most of the Holocene. There were no large-scale migrations from other areas that brought new populations into the Eastern Woodlands, but there were extensive contacts between groups near and far. These were dynamic millennia with constant interaction between diverse neighbors.

Eastern Woodlands Archaic: c. 8000 to 1000 BCE

The Eastern Woodlands Archaic lasted some 7,000 years, with cultural shifts marked by widespread changes in projectile-point styles, though there was also considerable local variation (Anderson and Sassaman, 2009). The rest of the stone artifact toolkit remained much the same as in Paleo-Indian times, except for the appearance of more varied scraper forms. We described some of the Early Archaic developments and important sites in Chapter 3.

The Archaic included numerous, and often still little-known, local variations on a general theme of increasing sedentary living and cultural complexity (Sassaman, 2015). For years the Eastern Woodlands Archaic has been divided into three general stages—Early (8000–6000 BCE), Middle (6000–3000 BCE),

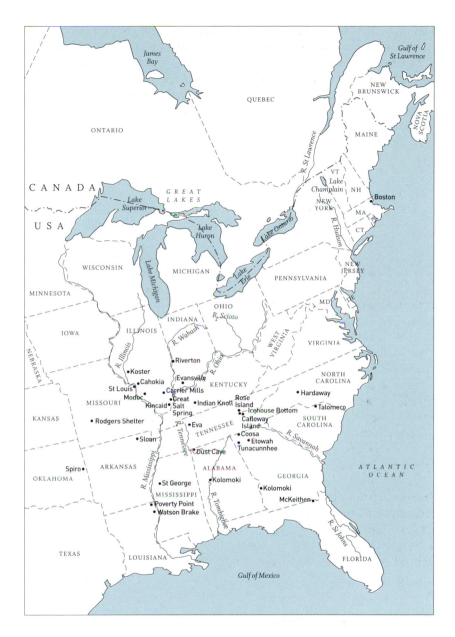

8.1 Map showing sites mentioned in Chapter 8.

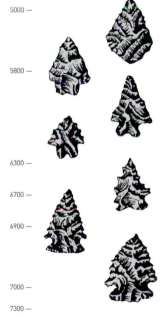

8.2 Eastern Woodlands Archaic projectile-point forms.

and Late (3000–1000 BCE)—identified by changes in projectile-point forms (for details, see Figure 8.2). This point sequence, which may reflect more efficient hafting designs, begins with highly varied Early Archaic side-notched points. Next come corner-notched designs, such as the Kirk point, then bifurcate-base points, and lastly several stemmed forms. These are not necessarily a barometer of significant cultural change. They may result rather from shifts to more efficient hunting methods, such as the use of lighter weapons and atlatls. Alternatively, minor differences may result from individual preferences, fashion, or a local need for a somewhat specialized hunting weapon. Projectile points certainly do not give an accurate impression of the dynamic Archaic cultures that made them.

COLLECTING AND STUDYING PLANT REMAINS

California, the Great Basin, and the Southwest are blessed with excellent preservation conditions, their aridity allowing for the survival intact of specific occupation levels, storage pits, even well-preserved baskets. These show that edible plant foods of all kinds were of great importance to hunter-gatherer societies throughout North America. Relatively predicable supplies of edible nuts were a central part of hunter-gatherer life in the Eastern Woodlands, where hazelnuts abounded. Acorn harvests from California live oaks were a vital staple for societies inland from the Pacific. Piñon nuts were essential for survival in many areas of the Great Basin and the early Southwest. Unfortunately, studying plant remains has proved to be among the most challenging difficulties facing researchers interested in ancient subsistence. There has thus been a tendency to overemphasize hunting, even of small rodents, over foraging for plant foods, unless exceptionally dry or wet preservation conditions allow collection of large samples, which are the only reliable way of assessing the importance of plants in ancient diets. Fortunately a variety of methods now provide insights into one of the least-known aspects of ancient hunting and gathering, to say nothing of agriculture. Here are the principal methods used to recover and study these elusive parts of ancient diets:

Carbonized and unburnt seeds occasionally survive in hearths and middens, also in storage pits and even in clay vessels, while large samples have been recovered from dry caves in the Great Basin and Southwest.

Human feces, again preserved in dry caves, can be a mine of information about ancient diets, not only about seeds, but also about small animals, and even insects.

Flotation techniques, which pass earth or occupation residue through water or chemicals, can produce large collections of plant remains—the vegetal remains float and settle on very fine screens; the residue sinks to the bottom of the container. Some excavators use elaborate devices for capturing large samples. For example, no fewer than 36,000 hickory fragments came from the Apple Creek site in the Lower Illinois Valley alone. Flotation has major advantages, because it allows the researcher to acquire large numbers of seeds from samples of occupation levels. This is especially true in very dry levels, such as those in Great Basin caves, or in waterlogged sites. Larger samples allow one to track changes in the exploitation of edible plants—hazel- or piñon nuts, for example—or in almost invisible seeds, such as those of the native grass, goosefoot.

Minute pollens from wild grasses, cereal crops, and cultivation weeds can provide an impression of human impacts on the surrounding environment, especially of forest clearance.

Plant phytoliths, minute particles of silica from plant cells, are produced from hydrated silica dissolved in groundwater absorbed through a plant's roots and carried through its vascular system. They are studied in a similar manner to pollens and have been valuable for tracing the origins of maize.

Trace elements preserved on grinding stones and edge-wear scars on scrapers and other stone tools sometimes yield evidence as to the plants that were processed with them.

The diversity of predictable seasonal food resources, animal and vegetable as well as aquatic, made deliberate scheduling of hunting and foraging a highly adaptive subsistence strategy. Early Archaic bands used well-provisioned base camps in warmer locations such as coastal plains during the winter. They would disperse into smaller camps with the coming of the plant season, but were always, to some extent, tethered to raw material sources, which were irregularly distributed across the landscape. While some models suggest permanent winter camps, others argue for great mobility during the same months. Populations were never large, perhaps no more than 500 to 1,500 people, living in small groups in contiguous drainages.

For many years anthropologists have agreed that mobile hunter-gatherers in separate bands need about 500 people to acquire suitable marriage mates, and our broad estimate tallies with this long-held assumption. There was never massive population growth, rather natural movements out of fertile river valleys resulting from social fissioning and relocation that reduced tensions between bands, families, and larger groups. The overall population, even in fertile areas, was sparse, with the impression of overcrowding coming from cultural perceptions rather than actual pressure on resources. And as the movements continued, so different groups, near and far, developed their own specific adaptations to local areas, which come down to us in the archaeological record in the form of minor variations in projectile points and other surviving material remains (Anderson and Sassaman, 2009).

The Midwest and Southeast

Between about 4500 and 4000 BCE many Midwestern and Southeastern rivers stabilized and accumulated silt in their floodplains. Backwater swamps and oxbow lakes formed. Shallow-water and shoal habitats as well as active streams provided abundant, easily accessible aquatic resources, including fish and mollusks. There was a dramatic increase in the use of such resources, which eventually became a major component in the diet of Southeastern river-valley populations. The evidence is striking: hundreds of different shallow-water mollusk species are to be found in shell middens along parts of the St. Johns, Savannah, Tennessee, and Cumberland Green areas. At the same time changing forest compositions on the uplands may have reduced food supplies on higher ground. What were the consequences? One model argues for an opportunistic response to seasonally abundant, dependable, and easily collected foods, prompting people to adopt more sedentary lifeways in many parts of the Eastern Woodlands. Others disagree, and believe that increased population densities forced people to turn to alternative food resources. The debate is unresolved.

There are clear signs from Middle Archaic sites that some favored locations were in use for most of, if not all, the year (for key sites, see Box: Some Major Archaic Sites). Some floodplain midden sites in the Midwest and Southeast have been claimed as probable year-round settlements. The descriptions are loosely cast, for often they in fact mean permanent to semi-permanent base camps occupied from summer to fall, when water levels were low, where many activities took place (Figure 8.3). Koster in the Illinois River Valley, with its fourteen occupation

8.3 Artist's reconstruction of Middle Archaic life at the Black Earth site, Carrier Millis, Illinois. The hunters in the foreground are returning to camp with a deer killed with spears and atlatls. The people in the background are collecting aquatic plants and fishing in the shallow lake west of the site.

8.4 Excavations at the Koster site, Illinois, where there are at least fourteen occupation levels, dating from about 8500 BCE to 1200 CE.

levels, is one of North America's most famous archaeological sites (Figure 8.4). Hunter-gatherers visited this location close to river backwaters from as early as 8500 BCE (Struever and Holton, 2000). A substantial Middle Archaic settlement dates to between 5600 and 5000 BCE, where occupation occurred on several occasions for a century or more. The inhabitants lived in pole-and-branch houses intended for long-term use, perhaps for most of the year. They concentrated on a relatively narrow range of edible grasses, also caught river fish and preyed on seasonal waterfowl migrations. Between 3900 and 2800 BCE permanent settlements of round huts thrived at Koster, the people netting multitudes of shallow-water fish, perhaps as much as 600 lb (270 kg) of fish flesh per acre (0.4 ha) annually. The people also relied heavily on nut harvests and waterfowl. The Illinois River is on the Mississippi flyway, the migration route used by millions of waterfowl flying to and from their Canadian breeding grounds each spring and fall. The Koster people could take hundreds of ducks, geese, and other migrants with bows, and by throwing light, weighted nets over sleeping birds. Smoked and dried waterfowl could sustain families during the lean months.

Koster is just one of many sites located on lower terraces or in low-lying areas that were liable to flooding in late winter and early spring. At that season, goes

SOME MAJOR ARCHAIC SITES

Dust Cave, Alabama

Located in the Middle Tennessee River Valley of northern Alabama, Dust Cave was occupied sporadically over 7,000 years. The earliest Paleo-Indian occupation dates to about 11,650 to 9200 BCE, with subsequent layers of Early and Middle Archaic visitations dating to as late as 3600 BCE (Figure 8.5). The well-preserved layers contain an abundance of plant remains that record occasionally intense use of the cave by diverse groups foraging in the valley on annual seasonal rounds. Dust Cave is notable for its projectile-point sequences, which include side-notched and stemmed points (Sherwood et al., 2004).

Indian Knoll, Kentucky

Between about 3000 and 2000 BCE large, stable Native American communities flourished on the food-rich Green River floodplain, a tributary of the Ohio River. They remained at, or near, the same

8.5 Left: excavations at Dust Cave, Alabama.
8.6 Above: excavations at Indian Knoll, Kentucky, during the late 1930s. Hundreds of men worked on the dig during the Depression.

locations for centuries, accumulating great shell middens. The most famous, Indian Knoll in Kentucky, yielded over 1,000 burials (Webb and Winters, 2001). Indian Knoll and other large Green River sites lie in highly favored locations (Figure 8.6). The richness of the local environment was remarkable, especially in its variety of plant foods, with easily stored hickory nuts a clear favorite among the Green River people.

Judging from the Indian Knoll graves, this was a relatively egalitarian society, where everyone owned much the same material possessions. At least seventy male graves contained handles, weights, and atlatl hooks, still lying in place with the wooden shaft decayed away. Women owned nut-cracking stones. Some men and women carried turtle-shell rattles, bone flutes, and shamans' bones with them at death.

the argument, everyone moved onto higher ground, to the edge of the valley or onto the uplands. In other words, there was a change from "free wandering" with no regular base camps to "centrally based wandering," a seasonally mobile lifeway that involved returning to the same base location year after year. There is no reason to believe that the length of base camp use in any one year was the same everywhere. In fact, there must have been great variation, from a few months of use to year-round occupation.

Moundbuilding, Belief, and Commemorating the Dead

Social interconnectedness increased dramatically during the Archaic, as such isolation as there had been (and it may not have been much) broke down in the face of population growth. Sassaman (2015) argues that people were moved northward out of the southern Ohio Valley and mid-Atlantic regions. Others arrived from Mississippi Valley and the Arkansas/southern Illinois region, perhaps creating conflict initially, but eventually resulting in diverse Early and Middle Archaic groups who lived in close proximity.

What were the social and technological innovations that defined this slowly changing situation? With larger, more permanent base camps and increasingly

Five Indian Knoll burials included hammered metal ornaments made from copper ore from Lake Superior (see Figure 8.14). Conches, shell ornaments (beads and gorgets, for example), and cups accompanied forty-two skeletons. Shells were from the *Marginella* and *Olivella* species, found in the Gulf of Mexico and the southern Atlantic seaboard hundreds of miles away. Both adult men and women owned valuable copper and conch objects, as did infants and children. Some 18,378 disk-shaped beads made of imported shell came from 143 graves. The distribution of shell beads is such that it appears certain people held in high esteem for their special abilities maintained broad contacts with other individuals, including members of neighboring groups. These beads were eventually interred with them or members of their family, including children.

Modoc Rockshelter, Illinois

A similar shift from a generalized hunter-gatherer economy to a narrower range of foods occurred at Modoc rockshelter near the Mississippi in Randolph County, Illinois (Figure 8.7). The site lies in a hickory-rich riverine environment about 90 miles (149 km) southeast of Koster (Styles *et al.*, 1983). Some 27 ft (8.2 m) of midden accumulation spans human occupations dating between about 8000 and 2000 BCE. The first occupants were general hunter-gatherers, without any major dietary focus. Fish, mussels, and freshwater crayfish assumed greater importance after 5600 BCE, just as they did at Koster and other contemporary Midwestern sites, for example the Rodgers Shelter in central Missouri. The Modoc people at this period exploited many small mammals, including cottontail rabbits, muskrats, and squirrels, but few larger animals. After 4000 BCE selective use of hickory nuts and

8.7 Excavating Modoc rockshelter, Illinois.

similar foodstuffs increased, and people used Modoc for longer periods. As fish and other bottomland foods came into greater use, Modoc probably became a base camp, used for much of the year. Later it was a place used for more specialized activities, visited when people hunted deer on the nearby uplands and waterfowl in the shallow creeks and ponds nearby.

Another major Archaic site is the Black Earth site south of Carrier Mills, Illinois, which we visited in Chapter 3 (p. 84).

complex social and political relationships came a new concern with defining one's relationships with the natural and supernatural realms. A new emphasis on commemorating the dead and on earthworks and burial mounds appeared during the Archaic. This was no local development. North of the Ohio River people used red ocher and cremation, often burying their dead on natural rises; on the Gulf Coast coastal plain they used astronomically derived measurement systems and alignments in rituals that also involved constructing earthen mounds. At least sixty mound groups, some of considerable size, in the Southeast from Arkansas to Florida are known to be Archaic earthworks. The most spectacular Middle Archaic earthwork complex is Watson Brake in northeastern Louisiana, built as early as 3900 BCE (Saunders *et al.*, 1997). It is earlier than Britain's Stonehenge. Eleven mounds and an oval enclosure cover 11 acres (4.45 ha) near the once swampy, lush Ouachita River Valley (Figure 8.8). For at least nine centuries forager groups spent spring and early summer here, taking many fish and collecting rich stands of native plants. Watson Brake's earthworks are 1,900 years earlier than those at Poverty Point, described below.

Sassaman writes of two ancestries for the eastern Archaic, and sometimes intense cultural interaction between them. These societies would have lived in a multicultural world, with people of different ancestry living close to one another. This was a world of constant change and stress, reflected in changes in traditional exchange goods: soapstone vessels, for example, were rendered obsolete by new direct-heat cooking methods. There was resistance to change, also aggressive grasping at opportunities. Think of a world in which volatile alliances were forever forming and falling apart, their establishment marked by competitive feasts and constant long-distance exchange that caused some cultural groupings to blend. New cultural identities emerged, based on landscape

8.8 Watson Brake, Louisiana.

or important places, also an awakening to mythic landscapes that anchored the people's cosmos in new ways.

With all these changes, it became important to integrate kin groups, perhaps even entire lineages. Such integration came about from communal activities, such as moundbuilding, from the maintenance of cemeteries set in rings of shell mounds, and from feasting and shared mortuary rituals. The latter in particular were important for integrating people from diverse backgrounds. Such gatherings would have required careful organization and carried high labor costs, quite apart from the effort needed to assemble food supplies for large numbers of people. They may have led to multicultural cemeteries, such as are found in shell middens in the southern Ohio Valley, also, perhaps, in the Northeast and Far North. In Florida's Harris Mound, for example, isotopic analysis of skeletons revealed a group from southern Florida and two individuals apparently from Tennessee or Virginia. This kind of detective work has hardly begun, but it may reveal startlingly diverse Archaic populations.

The Archaic social networks identified by such artifacts as atlatl weights and pins appear to have been very diverse, and to have been maintained by different groups within these hunter-gatherer societies. These were not people who lived in villages, let alone small towns; nor did they accumulate large food surpluses. There was apparently no emphasis on individuals achieving social prominence. Rather, power rested in the hands of religious specialists, who worked on behalf of their communities and kin groups. "Power" was in the spiritual dimension of human life. We see this in burials, with the treatment of the dead and accompanying grave goods reflecting not social standing, but ritual practices such as human sacrifice and offerings to mythic beings (for an example, see the discussion of a possible shaman burial at Carrier Mills, Illinois, on p. 84).

Many ritual specialists were deposited in caves. In the Far North the individuals buried under low mounds of boulders and in ridge-top mounds may have been ritual specialists or their apprentices. Sacrificial victims, however, were given no respect. They were stacked into pits, sometimes buried face down, or weighted with stones. The societies that practiced these mortuary customs were not on the edge of starvation, as has often been claimed in the past. Quite the contrary: theirs was a bounteous world of dizzying social interactions and complex rituals, only visible through objects deposited with the dead.

Very ancient beliefs lay behind much of the Archaic cosmology. Caves, sinkholes, and other crevices penetrated the underworld and were spiritual conduits, as were trees. The movements of the heavenly bodies, the summer and winter solstices, and the notion of a multilayered cosmos were fundamental beliefs of great antiquity that must have contributed to Archaic ritual. So did notions of duality—between night and day, sun and moon, and so on. Above all, expressions of ritual beliefs were conveyed through chant, dance, song, and storytelling, as well as colors, even smoke. Everyone lived in landscapes imbued with powerful symbolism and mythic forces. There may have been a deep spiritual connection with Paleo-Indians from much earlier times, whose knowledge passed, at least in part, down the generations. Native American societies attached great importance to storytelling, much of which revolved around origin myths and the movements of people across ancient and more recent landscapes (see Box: Archaeology and Oral Traditions, pp. 244–45).

Pottery and Cultivation

The densest Late Archaic populations thrived in such areas as river valley bottoms, where fish, plant foods, and game provided a reliable diet for most of the year. Subterranean storage pits full of nuts created larger food surpluses and allowed more people to live at one location year-round. Baskets, pits, and perhaps special storage bins formed a new storage technology, enhanced by another innovation: waterproof clay vessels, which had appeared along the South Carolina coastal plain by 2500 BCE. Pottery-making spread widely, apparently hand-in-hand with an extensive trade in soapstone for weights, large containers, and ornaments throughout the Southeast. Thick-walled pottery came into use in some parts of the Southeast as early as about 2000 BCE and became widespread after 500 BCE, when it was in use from the Mississippi to New England, and from the Ohio to the St. Lawrence Valley. Many Early Woodland pots were like crude flowerpots, heavy containers that were difficult to carry around (Figure 8.9). In time, much better-made ceramics developed into a highly effective way of storing not only grain and other foods, but also water and valuables. Clay pots and bowls could also hold boiling water, enabling people to process acorns and seeds much more readily than they could with fire-heated stones and other simple devices (Saunders and Hays, 2004).

Pots must have played an important part in the more intensive exploitation of wild seeds, especially in the middle of the continent. For instance, experiments have shown that pottery allows more efficient processing of hickory nuts, and probably other species too. Crushing and boiling increases the number of nut-meats processed in one hour at least tenfold, in large part by separating nutritious oil from inedible nutshell. The greater demand for waterproof containers may be associated with highly efficient seed collecting and the deliberate manipulation of native plants, followed by the domestication of several indigenous plant species.

Early hunter-gatherers probably overcame food shortages by covering larger distances, using knowledge of potential food sources over wide areas. They could also forage for less-favored food plants, increase the energy expended collecting food and processing it, and exploit alternative food sources—acorns, say—that required a great deal more effort to prepare; they could also cultivate certain native annuals that flourished in disturbed habitats maintained by deliberate human intervention. After 2000 BCE some Late Archaic groups in the Eastern Woodlands deliberately cleared small plots where they could cultivate familiar wild plants, including native squash, on a small scale (Smith, 2011). To what extent stress played a role in spurring such cultivation is unknown.

8.9 Early Eastern Woodland pot from Pennsylvania. Site unknown.

In many places people created and sustained environments that transported seeds of a wide variety of plants from their natural floodplain and upland niches into disturbed habitats. These were casual activities that linked humans, plants, and animals in opportunistic adaptations to changes in the structure and composition of their surrounding ecosystems. New variables, such as human base camps, produced significant changes in floodplain ecosystems, allowing some plants to occupy, and evolve within, newly available habitats. Some ongoing selective pressures may have increased seed production in sumpweed, gourds, squash, and other native plants, by reducing dormancy periods

and enhancing the ability of species to occupy disturbed ground (Figure 8.10). All humans would have done to achieve this was to sustain the new habitat and to tolerate species with economic value.

Eventually people categorized some plants as useful, others as weeds. All botanical knowledge passed from parent to child, in a form of verbal plant dictionary and pharmacopeia refined and memorized by each generation. A family may have casually watered and weeded as time and opportunity permitted, discouraging weeds in favor of economically useful plants, thereby managing natural stands of the latter. This simple process of encouraging, intervening, and deliberately planting harvested seeds, even on a small scale, marked the beginnings of deliberate cultivation. At this point automatic selection within the affected plant population begins, with minimal effort by human beings. Human land clearance and genetic changes in plants may have been major factors in the emergence of horticulture in eastern North America independently of elsewhere—making the region one of the few areas of autonomous plant domestication in the world.

Some Eastern Woodlands groups relied heavily on a variety of native plants for as much as 1,000 years before people turned to maize—a plant that is nonindigenous to the Eastern Woodlands. In fact, a few of these native plants show signs of domestication, such as larger seed size, as much as 2,000 years before they became major components of the diet. Gourds were among the earliest domesticates. The bottle gourd (*Lagenaria siceraria*) made excellent containers. This African native appears to have floated across the Atlantic to the Caribbean, then spread northward, perhaps as a weed following human populations. But when gourds were domesticated and arrived in the north is unknown—it was perhaps as early as 5000 BCE. Thinner-walled, North American forms provided edible seeds, not containers.

The wild sunflower (*Helianthus annuus*) became a favorite food source valued for its nutritious oil, and was apparently domesticated as early as 2250 BCE. Sumpweed or marsh elder (*Iva annua*) was a common domesticate, a lakeside and riverside oily-seeded plant that flourished in river valley bottoms. Wild sumpweed

8.10 Native plants. *Left:* bottle gourd, *Lagenaria sicerria*, with immature fruit. *Center:* goosefoot, *Chenopodium berlandieri. Right:* knotweed, *Polygonum erectum.*

was commonplace at Koster in the Illinois Valley by 3800 BCE; domestication was well under way by 2000 BCE. Goosefoot (*Chenopodium berlandieri*) with its small, starchy seeds, knotweed, maygrass, and perhaps Jerusalem artichokes (*Helianthus tuberosus*) were also heavily used by about the same time.

Lastly, tobacco (*Nicotiana* sp.) seeds arrived from Mexico at an unknown date and became widely cultivated throughout the east in later times. Many clay-stone pipes occur in eastern sites, but they do not necessarily document tobacco smoking. People smoked kinnikinnick (an **Algonquian** word for a variety of plant substances including bearberry leaves) and other plants as well.

Until about 800 CE agriculture was a way of producing valuable supplemental foods, of amplifying food supplies by enhancing wild plant yields. It was only with the introduction of maize during the first millennium CE that agriculture became the dietary staple of most eastern societies (see Chapter 12).

The Eastern Subarctic

We have focused so far on the Midwest and Southeast, the classic "Eastern Woodlands." What happened in the Eastern Subarctic far to the north? An undulating landscape of boreal forest, barren lands and bogs extends north and west to the Appalachian Mountains, which ultimately descend into the Gulf of St. Lawrence. On the other side of the Gulf, rugged hills give way to the glacial terrain of Labrador with its numerous lakes and marshes. This is difficult country to traverse, especially in summer, when flies swarm everywhere.

THE MARITIME ARCHAIC OF THE SUBARCTIC

People were living in the Eastern Subarctic as early as 12,000 years ago, subsisting off maritime resources in the Champlain Sea that linked Lake Ontario with the Gulf of St. Lawrence. By 6000 BCE hunter-gatherer groups lived along the coast of southern Labrador. The L'Anse Amour site of 6300 BCE, a stone-covered mound on a beach shore now high above modern sea level, contained evidence of their ceremonial life. Under a mass of debris, three rock slabs stood end-to-end in soil stained with red ocher; below them lay the body of a child, face down on a bed of decomposing bark. A walrus tusk, projectile points, and a toggle harpoon with an ivory line holder accompanied the body. Why the

child lay face down is a mystery, but it was perhaps a sign of spiritual power. At the time, Maritime Archaic Tradition groups were moving into open, unsettled terrain along the coast, there still being ice in the interior. By 5000 BCE they were in central Labrador, five centuries later in the north. They moved along a patchwork of tundra and scrub and discovered Ramah chert in the Torngat mountains of northern Labrador. This superb toolmaking stone was revered and valued, and probably believed to have spiritual power. The discovery of Ramah chert was a defining moment in subarctic history, for it became a means of establishing exchange networks that linked individuals and kin groups over great distances. Ramah traveled throughout Labrador, into Newfoundland and northern Quebec, even into Maine.

Early Maritime Archaic groups lived in simple pithouses. By 4000 BCE

small rectangular dwellings had come into fashion. Five centuries later some of them were longhouses measuring 52.5 ft (16 m), and divided into segments; these then doubled in size, then doubled again. The growth of longhouses coincided with the expansion of the Ramah chert networks. The third millennium also witnessed a flowering of mortuary rituals throughout the Northeast, which linked a mosaic of societies into a tradition that buried the dead smothered in red ocher, especially in New Brunswick and southern Maine, also in Newfoundland and Labrador. The bones are mainly gone, but the ubiquitous Ramah chert artifacts survive, as do some slate ones, some of them ritually broken as if to prevent the living from using the tools of the dead. For the first time there are signs of social inequality, too. Such objects as Ramah tools, copper pendants, and

Generations of scholars considered this vast subarctic region as marginal, a place with conservative, unchanging societies (Holly, 2013). They were wrong. The Eastern Subarctic supported dynamic paleoarctic and Archaic societies, the latter engaging in widespread interactions with people near and far. They also developed elaborate mortuary rites as part of the fabric of their existence.

What happened in the Subarctic in terms of the shape of Archaic societies is, in many respects, remarkably similar to developments in more temperate latitudes. There were, of course, profound differences, but there are also strong general similarities—vigorous Archaic groups who interacted extensively, a remarkable emphasis on mortuary rites and cemetery burial, and a constant search for individual and collective prestige, vested in clan groups. These were competitive, factionalized societies, known collectively as the Maritime Archaic, a far cry from the conservative, little changing cultures conjured up by archaeologists of yesteryear.

Late Archaic Societies After 4000 BCE

Deciphering the multitude of later Archaic societies that developed in North America after about 4000 BCE and over at least 3,000 years challenges even experts. Culture historians and ecologically minded scholars have developed a plethora of cultural labels, which are still used in the literature. Forest environments supported relatively small populations from the Great Lakes to New England, and as far south as the Carolinas (see Figure 8.12, p. 195). The densest

8.11 Artifacts from Port aux Choix, Newfoundland. *Top:* bone comb in the shape of a waterbird. *Bottom:* bayonet-like dagger.

walrus tusks occur in some graves, not in others.

By 2500 BCE the dead in Labrador and Newfoundland went to eternity in cemeteries. The Port aux Choix site on the northwest coast of Newfoundland has yielded the remains of 177 people in three circular burial clusters. The grave goods were smothered in red ocher and included animal effigies, bone needles, shell beads, axes, and bayonets ; there are also dog burials (Figure 8.11). One adult male lay in a cape adorned with over 200 great auk bills, alongside ground stone tools, bird bones, and quartz crystals. He is thought to have been a shaman, whose spirit familiar was the now extinct great auk, a bird thought capable of diving deep into the other world. Isotopic analysis showed that the shaman consumed a predominantly terrestrial diet, perhaps an obligation to his spirit helper. Interestingly, MtDNA analysis of the burials showed that related kin were not buried together. Furthermore, there was greater genetic variation between the women than the men, as if the former came from some distance away. From Maine to Labrador, cemeteries lay at places where people gathered at different seasons, such as for fish runs. Some of the dead had already decomposed before they were buried at Port aux Choix and their bones were bundled. It is as if burial in specific places was important, the cemeteries being, as it were, signposts marking the ancestors.

Maritime Archaic society was probably like other Archaic societies described in this chapter, riven by factionalism and rivalries between ▸▸

Late Archaic societies thrived in the deciduous forests and river floodplains of the Midwest and into the Southeast, as well as on the South Atlantic and Gulf coasts, where more complex societies were to develop in coming centuries. We focus our attention on these areas here.

From the Middle Archaic onward people invested more labor in fashioning socially valued artifacts and ornaments, among them finely ground bannerstones, copper artifacts, delicate slate ornaments and weapons, and steatite gorgets and bowls (Figures 8.13, 8.14, and 8.15). These precious objects may have played an important role in building alliances. Some groups living in areas where different trade networks intersected may well have exploited their strategic locations and become middlemen in long-distance trade. It is possible, for example, that the Green River people exploited the opportunities of both the copper trade from the northwest and the shell exchange from the south and southeast.

A Rising Elite

As late as 1000 BCE few eastern societies were much larger than a few hundred souls, and even those were still predominantly egalitarian in their social organization. Long-distance exchange of prized materials, such as marine shells and copper, appeared for the first time between about 5000 and 4000 BCE and escalated gradually over the next 3,000 years. Exotic materials of all kinds passed from band to band, occasionally over great distances—we find copper and hematite native to Lake Superior, sea shells from the Atlantic and Gulf coasts, and cherts,

individuals, kin groups, and entire communities. Grave goods now reflect individualism, private choices, personal possessions that were broken at death so that they remained with the person forever. There were other individual signposts, like the steatite plummets found on Archaic sites throughout the Eastern Subarctic. Most were net or line sinkers, others are so finely decorated and delicate that they may have been pendants. Each bears different decoration, as if they were individual possessions, perhaps reflecting personal relationships with spirit helpers, a common tradition in the Subarctic.

Longhouses were important because they structured social relationships, yet, being segmented, emphasized the autonomy of each part. Cooperation and competition were central to societies where much depended on exchanges of exotic goods, such as Ramah chert,

copper from interior Labrador, and soapstone from Newfoundland. There was competition in exchange itself, in the degree of participation in exchanges of prestigious goods, and even in feasting, a matter of pride for both individuals and kin groups. Then there was the status attached to the hunting of formidable prey, such as whales. Whale bones abound in many Maritime Archaic sites, suggesting hunting skills that rivaled those of the Thule of the Far North in later times. Swordfish and walruses were also dangerous quarry, with successful cooperative hunts acquiring considerable standing. The Maritime Archaic was based on a prestige economy.

The Archaic world of the Subarctic was both diverse and socially complex, just as it was far to the south. The cemeteries and burial rituals, longhouses, and complicated exchanges that linked Maine with northern Labrador

are testimony enough. Maritime Archaic groups were mobile hunter-gatherers who lived in sparsely populated landscapes. But they participated in elaborate, widely distributed ceremonial activities, interacted with others in long-distance exchange, and placed great emphasis on important individuals and membership of kin groups.

The Maritime Archaic Tradition fell apart after about 2000 BCE in the face of incursions from Paleoeskimo groups from the north, whose culture was significantly different, and when confronted with people of the Susquehanna Tradition from the south. Both movements may have severed vital social ties at a time of cooling temperatures.

8.12 *Right:* Map of Late Archaic sites of the Northeast, showing various putative subdivisions based on culture history and ecological adaptations. These subdivisions are common in the archaeological literature, but are only useful as very general labels and are slowly becoming outdated in the face of new research. The boundaries between the various traditions are ill defined.

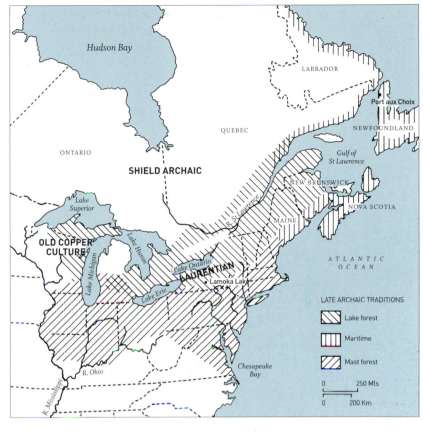

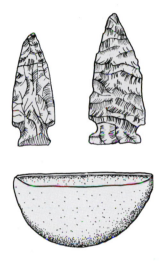

8.13 *Above:* Laurentide Forest Archaic artifacts from New York State. *Top to bottom:* two side-notched Otter Creek points; a groundstone vessel. The longest point is approximately 4.9 in. (12.5 cm) long.

8.14 *Above:* Spearhead hammered from Lake Superior copper.

8.15 *Left:* Late Archaic bannerstones (atlatl weights).

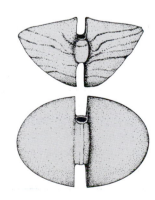

hornstones, and other exotic rocks for ornaments and toolmaking from all over the Midwest and east. All these materials passed between individuals and groups, "down the line" from settlement to settlement, valley to valley, through informal exchange networks that evolved and maintained an essential continuity over many centuries. The Green River burials show that not everyone had the same access to these prestige goods, presumably because some people were more charismatic than others, or had some other widely recognized and essential skill that translated into greater contacts with members of neighboring groups. Some transactions were likely sealed by gifts, such as beads.

How did social differentiation develop? One possible scenario might go something like this: some individuals, perhaps respected shamans or elders, leaders of a specific lineage, might assume roles as ritual and social mediators in newly sedentary societies. They were the people who arbitrated disputes and controlled relations with neighboring, and sometimes perhaps competing, groups. It was they who gave gifts to influential neighbors and participated in formal gift exchanges, who became points of contact with people, including other kin leaders, living near and far. It was they, too, who were responsible for redistributing food, essential raw materials, and luxury goods through the community. Some of these people were perhaps better at trading, or at dealing with allies and enemies, or at attracting the loyalty of kinspeople and followers. They had the quality of being able to persuade people to work for them, hunting, fishing, and gathering, perhaps digging out chert and blocking it into preforms. Social and ritual arbitrators, skilled diplomats and traders, these individuals became prominent in the ever more complex human societies of the Eastern Woodlands after 1000 BCE.

During these centuries hunting, foraging, and cultivation were family activities, but exchanges of goods and commodities between neighbors involved more complex relationships. Such exchanges may have helped foster elaborate communal burial cults involving the interment of kin-group members and perhaps the commemoration of lineages and ancestors. These cults, as we have seen, sometimes involved constructing burial mounds and earthworks. Such tasks required communal labor to dig and pile up basketfuls of earth, which was perhaps provided by gatherings of close kin or several neighboring communities.

Poverty Point: c. 2200 to 700 BCE

After 2200 BCE more than a hundred Late Archaic sites in the Lower Mississippi Valley and adjacent Gulf Coast form ten discrete clusters within natural geographical boundaries, each apparently grouped around a regional center that belongs within what is known as the Poverty Point culture. This flourished for some 1,500 years. Poverty Point itself, occupied between about 1000 and 700 BCE, lies on the Macon Ridge in the Mississippi floodplain, near the confluences of six rivers. This was a strategic point for trading up and downstream, also for receiving exotic materials, not only along the Mississippi, but along the Arkansas, Red, Ohio, and Tennessee rivers as well.

Poverty Point's great horseshoe earthworks and several mounds (Figure 8.16) are a remarkable contrast to the humble base camps typical of the Eastern Woodlands at the time. Six concentric, semi-circular, but not entirely symmetrical, earthen ridges divided into segments average about 80 ft (25 m) wide and 10 ft

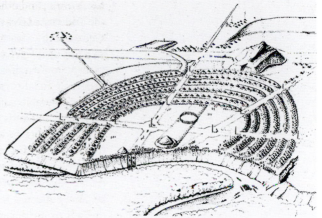

8.16 Aerial photograph of Poverty Point, Louisiana, looking toward the northeast.

8.17 Artist's reconstruction of Poverty Point, Louisiana. The earthworks cover 1 square mile (2.6 km²).

(3 m) high (Ellerbe and Greenlee, 2015; Gibson, 2001) (Figure 8.17). They are set about 130 ft (40 m) apart, each capped with midden deposits that are over 3 ft (1 m) deep in places. Perhaps they elevated houses above the surrounding, low-lying terrain. To the west lies an artificial mound more than 65 ft (20 m) high and 660 ft (200 m) long. Poverty Point took more than 1,235,000 cubic feet (35,000 m³) of basket-hefted soil to complete, an organized building effort the like of which would not be repeated in North America for another millennium. One authority has calculated that 1,350 adults laboring seventy days a year would have taken three years to complete the earthworks.

Why build such complex earthworks? How many people lived there, or was Poverty Point a place where hundreds of visitors congregated for major ceremonies, perhaps on such important occasions as the solstices? A person standing on this mound can sight the vernal and autumnal equinoxes directly across the center of the earthworks to the east. This is the point where the sun rises on the first days of spring and fall, but whether this had ritual significance to the inhabitants is a mystery. It could have been a measure of the passing seasons.

For a short period the Poverty Point site and nearby lesser centers were the nexus of a vast exchange network that handled great quantities of exotic rocks and minerals, such as galena, from more than ten sources in the Midwest and Southeast, some of them from as far as 620 miles (1,000 km) away. But this brief flowering endured little more than two to three centuries before the exchange system collapsed.

Poverty Point people enjoyed the same general adaptation as other Late Archaic riverine societies, collecting plants and fishing in nearby oxbow lakes, as well as cultivating native species such as sunflowers, bottle gourds, and squashes. The major centers lie near natural escarpments, close to floodplain swamps, oxbow lakes, and upland hunting grounds. Many questions about Poverty Point, however, remain unanswered. Did people from throughout Poverty Point territory contribute labor to the great earthworks, or were they the work of the actual inhabitants alone? What were the social and political relationships within the Poverty Point culture? Who were the leaders who organized the communal efforts needed to build earthworks, organize trade, and handle the local exchange of goods throughout the Poverty Point area? How did they secure the loyalties of the people who erected and used the great earthworks? At present, Poverty Point stands as a prophetic symbol of cultural developments that were to emerge in later centuries.

Considerable variability in projectile-point styles in northern parts of the Eastern Woodlands after 1000 BCE may reflect a trend toward better-defined local territories, and toward more formal exchange mechanisms that structured the bartering of essentials and prestigious luxuries from area to area in a web of reciprocal obligations and formal gift-giving that connected powerful kin leaders and other prominent individuals. Perhaps inevitably, these interactions became reflected in elaborate commemorations of revered ancestors. All of this led to increasingly complex Eastern Woodlands societies, whose trading networks extended over vast areas (Gibson and Carr, 2010). Such connections flourished under an umbrella of increasingly elaborate religious beliefs and rituals that were shared, at a basic level, by eastern groups large and small. The ritual observances that resulted revolved around the endless and inevitable passage of the seasons, the realities of birth, life and death, and an intricate relationship with the forces of the supernatural world. The intermediaries with this mythic, and often threatening, world were both the ancestors, those who had gone before, and the gifted individuals, those who were perceived to possess unusual supernatural powers that enabled them to pass effortlessly from the realm of the living into that of the supernatural.

SUMMARY

- Efficient plant exploitation and harvesting lay at the core of Eastern Woodlands life in temperate latitudes.

- The Eastern Woodlands Archaic in the Midwest and Southeast (c. 8000 to 700 BCE) witnessed a trend toward more sedentary settlement and cultural complexity. There were numerous regional variations on this theme.

- Everything depended on careful scheduling of seasonal food resources, depending on the location. Acorn and hickory harvests were of great importance each fall. Early Archaic groups used well-provisioned base camps in winter and smaller camps during the summer months.

- There were constant small-scale population movements as populations grew slowly, the greatest concentration of hunting bands being in places with the greatest diversity of foods.

- The Eastern Subarctic witnessed the development of the Maritime Archaic Tradition, with extensive exchange networks and well-established mortuary traditions that created dynamic, constantly interacting societies.

- Between 4500 and 4000 BCE, slowing Midwestern and southern rivers formed rich shallow-water and marshy habitats, also active streams. Fish and mollusks assumed ever-greater importance in local diets. In some places, it paid to stay at one location for much longer periods.

- A new concern with defining relationships with the natural and supernatural realms appears, reflected in more elaborate mortuary rites and the construction of burial mounds. One such is Watson Brake in Louisiana, built as early as 3900 BCE.

- Clay containers (pottery) appeared as early as 2000 BCE, at about the same time as some groups began cultivating native plants. Sumpweed, marsh elder, and similar native species were cultivated on a small scale, but not maize.

- The Late Archaic saw a proliferation of local variants, from the Great Lakes and Northeast to the Atlantic and Gulf coasts. Many of them sprang from large, stable communities based on food-rich floodplains. These societies exploited an even wider range of game and plant foods, also fish, mollusks, and waterfowl.

- Rising population densities led to more rigidly defined territories, as relationships and interactions with neighbors assumed greater importance.

- Alliance-building went hand-in-hand with trade in ceremonial artifacts such as bannerstones. There was probably some degree of social ranking, with some kin groups enjoying higher status than others.

- Ancestors became more important in ceremonial life, which helped foster increasingly elaborate mortuary cults and the construction of burial mounds and earthworks that required communal labor.

- The Poverty Point culture (c. 2200 to 700 BCE) was at least ten clusters of regional centers in the Lower Mississippi Valley. Poverty Point itself, on the Macon Ridge in the Mississippi floodplain near the confluences of six rivers, was a major ritual center. Its semicircular earthworks were the setting for major ceremonies, perhaps associated with the seasons and the solstices.

Before the Pueblos

The area known as the "American Southwest" extends from Las Vegas, Nevada, in the west to Las Vegas, New Mexico, in the east, and from Durango, Mexico, in the south to Durango, Colorado, in the north. The central and north-central parts of the Southwest lie at high elevations on the Colorado Plateau, most of the land lying over 5,000 ft (1,524 m) above sea level. There are extensive tablelands (**mesas**), steep-sided canyons, and vast gorges, also volcanic deposits that were important obsidian sources in ancient times. In southern Arizona and northern Sonora, Mexico, there are mountain ranges that rise from desert basins to as high as 9,000 ft (2,743 m) and span ecological zones ranging from Sonoran desert to alpine woodlands, all within a day's hike. To the east the Southwest spills over into the southern Rocky Mountains, the ranges in this area providing a significant watershed for much of the region. Some farmers settled on the edges of the Great Plains, in major drainages like the Cimarron and Pecos rivers.

In general the desert areas in the south receive an average of less than 12 in. (30 cm) of rain a year, while the uplands enjoy nearly 20 in. (50 cm). But these are mere averages, which mask extraordinary variations in annual rainfall. The southern deserts support creosote bush and bursage, a desert shrub, giving way in much of Arizona and New Mexico to higher ground that supports mixed grasses, shrubs, and open pine, piñon, and juniper forest over about 7,000 ft (2,133 m). The Colorado Plateau supports arid grasslands at low altitudes, with widespread sage brush and open piñon-juniper woodland (Figure 9.1).

This is a region of dramatic environmental contrasts, between deserts and forested mountain ranges, and between areas of low and moderate rainfall. Desert and semi-arid terrain extended southward through the Southwest to what is now the Mexican border and beyond. For thousands of years the hunter-gatherers in this slightly better-watered region adapted to their harsh surroundings in the same ways as other desert peoples. Then, in about 2350 BCE, they made a seemingly inconspicuous change to their food quest: they began to cultivate maize. Why did they develop horticulture and add this foodway to their foraging? Was it a response to environmental stress, a logical way of preserving their traditional lifeway? Centuries will pass before maize, and much later beans, dominate local diets, but the story of the Ancient Pueblo peoples of the Southwest begins among much earlier Archaic societies (Cordell and McBrinn, 2013; Roth, 2016), which we follow here. These and other fascinating questions surrounding the origin of Pueblo societies, together with the region's excellent preservation conditions, mean that there are more archaeologists in the Southwest than anywhere else in North America.

9.1 Map showing sites and culture areas mentioned in Chapters 9 and 10.

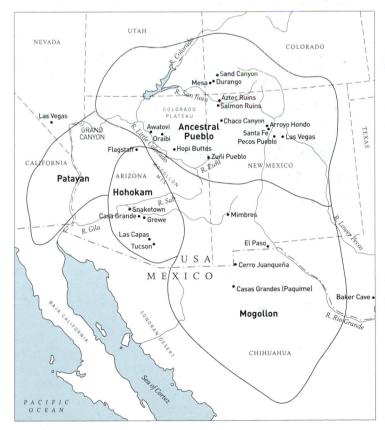

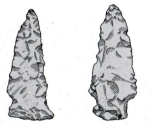

9.2 Southwestern Archaic projectile points. *Top:* Pinto Basin point. Length: 1.4 in. (3.7 cm). *Second, third, and fourth rows:* Bajada, San Jose, and Armijo points, respectively. *Fifth row:* Chiricahua Cochise points. *Bottom row:* San Pedro Cochise points.

Southwestern Archaic Societies: c. 7500 BCE to c. 200 CE

The beginning of the Archaic coincided with drier conditions in some areas of the Southwest and further south. Early Holocene forest cover gave way to desert scrub and more grassland around 6000 BCE. The Middle Holocene dry period (the Altithermal) between about 5000 and 2500 BCE had a profound effect on foraging populations in the Southwest. Modern vegetational communities and rainfall patterns generally developed by about 5000 to 2000 BCE. Paleo-Indian groups, who seasonally visited the region to hunt bison, remained on the Plains. Other local inhabitants shifted to more broad-spectrum strategies. Meanwhile, the generalized foragers already living in the Great Basin and southern California deserts moved into uplands areas. Projectile-point styles may offer one potential way of distinguishing between different groups (see Figure 9.2). The same designs extended over very wide areas during Paleo-Indian and Early Archaic times, just as they did in other parts of North America.

The Southwestern Archaic can appear a rather sparse period, for the scattered archaeological remains of these millennia are overshadowed by the much more spectacular sites and material culture of the past 2,000 years (Cordell and McBrinn, 2013). Except in highly favored locations, Archaic bands exploited generally arid environments, where food resources were widely dispersed and where constant mobility was adaptive. Possessions, known to us mainly from stone tools, were portable and easily replaced. Many Archaic encampments were highly transitory settlements, most with just two or three structures, occupied for a few days or weeks at a time. Thus the archaeological record is sadly incomplete, except for occasional caves and rockshelters where dry conditions have preserved a wider range of artifacts, including such perishable items as basketry, fiber sandals, and fur blankets. However, the Archaic was a vital period in the Southwestern past, for it was during the later centuries of the period that some local groups adopted the deliberate cultivation of domesticated plants, among them maize (Roth, 2016).

Foragers were always on the move, for they monitored the abundance and location of foods on a daily basis. Such intelligence determined whether bands made short foraging excursions or longer ones. Much depended on intelligence that passed from one band to another by word of mouth. One can imagine a band camping at a temporary water hole. A fellow kinsman visits from a nearby group and tells of newly ripened seeds near a marsh in a small valley. The next morning, the band shifts camp several miles to harvest the wild crop. Being at the right place at the right time made the difference between surviving or dying. Foraging groups did a good job of this for millennia.

Many groups overcame food-shortage stress as they always had, by covering large distances and by possessing knowledge of diverse food sources over wide areas. In the Southwest, as elsewhere, Archaic bands fell back on less-favored plant foods—agave, for instance—in times of hunger. Some Southwestern Archaic groups also began planting maize as a logical response to prolonged drought conditions. They did so for generations only as a supplement to their ancient diet, as a way of preserving their traditional way of life.

The human responses to the drier conditions of the Early and Middle Archaic were highly varied, as is only natural in an environment of great contrasts. Settlement studies are slowly revealing some of these responses. In the southern and southwestern Southwest, Early and Middle Archaic groups living at higher elevations made but little use of low-lying river valleys. But, as moister conditions developed after 2000 BCE, people moved into the formerly dry valleys of the south, excavating wells for water and, eventually, planting crops on the fertile alluvium. The Late Archaic saw many more sites, extensive use of storage pits, and, eventually maize farming (Mabry *et al.*, 2008).

In some respects the study of the Southwestern Archaic has paralleled that of the Great Basin. The use of projectile points to distinguish different Archaic groups is especially difficult in the Southwest, where securely dated sites are few and far between. Just as they did in other parts of North America, projectile-point styles extend over very large areas during Early Archaic times. This standardization gives way to a significant proliferation of point styles used over smaller areas during later centuries, at a time when each group made increasing use of purely local sources of toolmaking stone rather than the more limited exotic sources of earlier times. This may reflect higher population densities, reduced mobility, and more restricted territories in which plant foods were used more intensively. At the same time, long-distance exchange networks became less important as everyone relied more heavily on local contacts.

Multidisciplinary research, using not only archaeological finds but also sophisticated climatic data, has shown that the Southwest and adjacent areas were settled by a very complex tapestry of Archaic hunter-gatherer societies. The Southwest is a jigsaw of diverse environmental zones that presented different challenges and problems for foragers. These many groups maintained the same general technological traditions for thousands of years over wide areas, but there was great local, and often short-term, variation. In this way they resemble the Archaic groups we have met across the continent. This reality means adopting a very particular approach to Archaic studies, one that focuses on reconstructing local adaptations using a broad range of data, then fitting these many local adaptations together into a wider picture (Huckell, 1996). Such researches promise a much more complex understanding of the Southwestern Archaic for the future.

The Lower Pecos: Foragers to the South and East: *c.* 11,000 BCE to Modern Times

The semi-arid Lower Pecos Canyonlands lie around the confluences of the Pecos and Devils rivers with the Rio Grande in extreme southwestern Texas (Shafer, 2013). More mountainous country lies to the west, and the Edwards Plateau to the north, with the mesquite savanna of south Texas to the east. The Canyonlands are famous for their dry caves and pictographs, which have been the subject of archaeological investigations for more than eighty years. The dry caves of the Lower Pecos provide an unusual portrait of the more perishable material culture of local Archaic groups (Figure 9.3). Like their contemporaries in the Southwest and Great Basin, the Lower Pecos people made extensive use of plant fibers, especially those from desert succulents,

9.3 Baker Cave, Val Verde County, Texas. This site yielded evidence of Early, Middle, and Late Archaic occupation, the earliest settlement dating to about 7000 BCE.

to make twined, plaited, and coiled baskets, also sandals, mats, and bags. They wove cane partitions to separate living quarters in the caves. Bags, blankets, and pouches from bison, deer, and rabbit hide come from many sites, as do fragments of rabbit-fur robes ingeniously made from long strips twisted to bring fur upward on both sides of the garment. Archaic groups used wooden digging sticks and curved boomerang-like sticks for clubbing rabbits. Atlatls were fashioned from straight sticks, with the hook carved at one end. Freshwater shells served as spoons and scoops, while bone and antler pins and weaving tools abounded.

The Lower Pecos region is best known for its rock art, both pictographs (drawn or painted on the rock) and petroglyphs (pecked out on the rock surface). The earliest, the so-called Pecos River Style, dates to about 2000 BCE and includes abstract representations of humanoid figures in various mineral colors, some painted almost life-size (Boyd, 2003). Deer, fish, animal forms, weapons such as atlatls and darts, shaman figures, and shaman's paraphernalia accompany the large polychrome figures. Other Pecos River Style artists depicted miniature human figures in red engaged in group activities, including deer roundups and processions in which headdresses identify individuals with special status. Bison and deer are sometimes shown being driven into netlike barriers or into jump areas. Much of the art may represent spiritual visions seen during trances.

Carolyn Boyd has carried out a remarkable study of the so-called White Shaman mural, a frieze of crimson, black, and yellow human figures covering the back wall of the inconspicuous, unnamed shelter (Boyd, 2016). Some of the figures were painted atop one another or surrounded with undecipherable marks. Boyd, who is an artist herself, identified five identical human figures spaced evenly across the length of the mural. She also studied other human figures and noted that many of them display animal features, such as antlers. At the same time, she also delved into the ethnography of the Huitchol people of the Sierra Madre Mountains, who conducted a pilgrimage during the rainy season to a sacred desert plateau; there they collected peyote, a hallucinogenic cactus that helped them contact ancestral spirits in the otherworld. The Huitchol "hunted" both peyote and deer, which they shot with arrows (Figure 9.4). Boyd believes that the White Shaman mural was a handbook about how to conduct an important ritual. The five human figures were the first humans making a journey eastward. Otherworldly figures were painted above them, including the White Shaman (Figure 9.5). These were the mythic beings into which humans were transformed. Below was a band of red and black lines, which she believes to represent the watery cosmos from which the first people emerged. On the left of the mural was a wavy brown line shaped like an arch. This was the Dawn Mountain, the final destination, the place where the sun rose for the first time. Boyd argues that this is a Creation story, the antlered deer atop the arch being the sacred deer that led the first humans through the watery underworld in the west.

If Boyd is correct, then the White Shaman mural can be read like a narrative. It preserves an ancient belief system and mythology that survived through more than 4,000 years. At a basic level it reflects the close relationship to the natural environment cherished by hunter-gatherers, and ancient North Americans everywhere, as well as by people in Central America and the Andes.

In general terms the Lower Pecos region is part of a much larger hunter-gatherer adaptation to the arid lands of southern North America, which began

9.4 Lower Pecos rock art: a "Curly tail panther" frieze from Devil's River, Lower Pecos, Texas.

9.5 Lower Pecos rock art: White Shaman from Val Verde County, Texas.

as desert conditions and became established during the earlier Holocene, as early as 7000 BCE. These same adaptations persisted into historic times. Other well-documented examples of long-lived Archaic lifestyles come from the Edwards Plateau of central Texas and the coastal plain of south Texas. At the Wilson-Leonard site west of Austin, a long chronology has been documented from Clovis times through later times (Collins, 1998). By 3500 BCE earth ovens were in such regular use for plant cooking that thousands of burned rock middens were formed, the most common site type in central Texas. There is evidence of increasing social complexity and territoriality after 3500 BCE, reflected in large cemetery sites with extensive grave goods, some obtained from long-distance trade.

At European contact the descendants of 11,000 years of a continuous hunter-gatherer tradition lived in central and south Texas. Ethnohistoric studies of historic groups suggest their ancestors ranged over large territories (Hester, 1989). They were displaced by Spaniards, with their mission system, moving in from the south, and by Native American bison-hunting groups such as the Lipan Apache and Comanche, who moved into Texas from the north and west after 1700 CE. Dozens, perhaps hundreds, of small hunter-gatherer groups shared similar lifeways, divisible linguistically into at least seven larger groups. Tom Hester (1989) describes the Coahuilteco-speakers as living in small groups, each with a distinct name, pursuing a semi-nomadic existence and ranging over seasonal territories which overlapped with those of their neighbors. They lived in bands averaging about forty-five people, hunted antelope, deer, small game, and reptiles, fished, but obtained most of their diet from plant foods. The prickly pear was vitally important in summer, acorn and pecan crops in fall. Everyone dwelt in small, round, brush- or mat-covered huts and wore blankets or capes fabricated from deer and rabbit skins. Hester believes this generalized description applies to most, if not all, other central and southern Texas hunter-gatherer groups at European contact.

Late Archaic/Early Agricultural Period: c. 2100 BCE to 150–200 CE

Maize was the stuff of life for many Native American societies at European contact (Roth, 2016). A tropical grass, *Balsas teosinte*, is its ancestor and was growing in Oaxaca, Mexico, by 8000 to 6000 BCE and in the Balsas Basin of central Mexico by 7200 BCE. By 5000 BCE small-scale maize cultivation by mobile foragers was widespread in Central America, also in adjacent areas of South America and southern Mexico. A sudden and mysterious expansion in the range of maize cultivation in about 2500 BCE brought corn cultivation into a broad array of environments in both the Southwest and South America (da Fonseca *et al.*, 2015).

The spread of maize into the Southwest was a complex process that is still little understood (Vierra, 2008; Vierra and McBrinn, 2006). The earliest currently known maize dates to about 3250 BCE and comes from Las Capas in the Tucson, but it did not come into use in the Rio Grande Valley to the north until about 2,000 years later. The Jemez Cave in the mountains of that name has yielded chapalote maize, a primitive form with small, triangular cupules. Far to the north, in the Turkey Pen Shelter in the Four Corners region, the genomes of fifteen 1,900-year old maize cobs revealed maize that was shorter and more branched than modern ones, indeed bush-like. It flowered more quickly than lowland varieties, an adaptation to higher altitude. This shows that different maize strains were in use in different ecological zones, perhaps from very early on (Swarts *et al.*, 2017).

How and why did maize cultivation spread into the Southwest? What incentives were there for undertaking the laborious processes of planting and harvesting corn? Maize farming is an economic activity that may require sedentary living for much of the year. Furthermore, maize is difficult to cultivate successfully without considerable investment of time and knowledge of plant management. Young plants have to be protected from rabbits, deer, and other browsers. Timing of when to plant and harvest requires detailed knowledge, as does processing and storing seed for the following year. This knowledge probably arrived from elsewhere into a region where modification of the landscape and management of wild edible plants provided significant technological "pre-adaptations" to maize cultivation. We now have good evidence for trade by 1200 BCE between groups living in the Tucson Basin, along the California coast, and on the shores of the Sea of Cortez. These may not necessarily have been direct contacts, but objects, food, and information about maize cultivation must have passed through "down-the-line" exchange networks (see Box: Studying Trade and Exchange). There is also good **bioarchaeological** evidence for migration and **matrilocal intermarriage** among communities reaching from present day northern Sonora into southern Arizona (Vint and Mills, 2017). Thus, exchange, intermarriage,

STUDYING TRADE AND EXCHANGE

There has never been a human society that was completely self-sufficient. Everyone had dealings with neighbors, who might live across a valley, or be kin dwelling dozens of miles away. One of the major developments that shaped ancient North America was the interaction between people. They might be between individuals or households, even entire villages, but exchanges and trade in such commodities as toolmaking stone or hides, or in such exotic ornaments as shell beads or stone pipes, became an integral part of ancient American societies. In later centuries such interactions were often conducted on a large scale.

How did such exchange and trade operate? Why, for example, did Paleo-Indians obtain fine-grained toolmaking stone such as obsidian (volcanic glass) from hundreds of miles away? Perhaps for practical reasons, for obsidian makes excellent projectile points. But there must have been intangibles at work, perhaps ritual ones, as well, making the shiny volcanic glass highly desirable. In the case of these early Americans, where human populations were very small and constant mobility was a necessity for survival, most people met only a handful of others during their lives, perhaps as few as thirty individuals. Under such circumstances personal relationships between individuals assumed great importance. So did kin ties, fostered by such practices as finding a mate outside one's own band.

We refer to such activity as "exchange" because these are, ultimately, hand-to-hand transactions. Each party exchanges, say, a hide for a necklace of shell beads. Such interactions assumed symbolic importance and could endure for generations, compounded also by ties of kin. In some more extreme cases the individuals involved may never have met face-to-face, the relationship being defined by objects that changed hands through others. Tiny hunting bands are one dynamic; much larger-scale societies—for instance Northwest Coast groups, villages in the Eastern Woodlands, or leaders of growing Southwest villages—are another.

Exchange thus has a strong personal element, much of it informal, between individuals, but is always based on the understanding that a gift was offered with the expectation that the receiver would give an object of equivalent significance or value in exchange. The reciprocal gift did not necessarily have to be immediate, but the obligation was there. Such exchanges were often the symbolic act that proceeded more prosaic transactions, a kind of formal sanction, as it were.

▶▶

trade and the mechanisms of social integration were major factors in the arrival of maize agriculture in the Southwest.

Domesticated plants had one major advantage: they might not be highly productive, but they were predictable (Figure 9.6). Cultivators of the new crops could control their location, and, to some extent, their availability at different seasons through storage. Uncertainties about the productivity of the natural environment would have been one of the conditions favoring adoption of cultigens by Archaic groups.

Two broad strategies may have played out across the Southwest. The people of the Tucson Basin in the south had long been desert foragers, dependent on desert plants of many kinds along with some carefully organized hunting. These groups were anchored to predictable water supplies, and spent much of their time at the same locations. Such high levels of sedentary living would have allowed people to plant without disrupting their annual round. It was worth investing more effort in farming as it produced high crop yields. Maize quickly became important in the diet.

Maize did not fit so easily into the annual round in those parts of the Southwest with desert environments and lower resource density, where a high level of mobility was essential (Vierra and McBrinn, 2016). Upland piñon-juniper forests provided important crops in late summer or early fall, which might conflict with

9.6 Drought-resistant Hopi maize.

We study exchange through the presence of exotic objects found far from their places of origin. Some, for example the Pacific *Olivella* shells found in Southwestern villages, or the Gulf seashells that abound far up the Mississippi Valley in Archaic times, are easily identified and traced back to at least a general point of origin. Distribution maps can give a rough impression of exchange networks. This is straightforward, but identifying the routes by which the artifacts reached their final destinations is all but impossible except in the most general terms. Much travel was by canoe, the easiest way to cover distance, but we tend to forget that myriad trails linked village to village, pueblo to pueblo, and were used for far more than exchanging exotics. These were the trails that spread ideas and technological innovations (the bow and arrow, for example), as well as the powerful spiritual beliefs that electrified Hopewell communities (see

Chapter 11). As always, the intangible harbors many secrets of ancient exchange and trade.

Thanks to advanced technology, we are, however, making progress. For many years we have relied on trace elements in rocks to identify their places of origin. This has been particularly effective with obsidian, that desirable toolmaking stone, since each source has distinctive trace elements. For instance, Medicine Lake Highlands obsidian in northern California was traded into the Central Valley and across the northern coast ranges to the Pacific. Medicine Lake obsidian moved in relatively large quantities for about 50 miles (80.4 km) south and west. Further out, the amount of obsidian exchanged dropped off rapidly. The shiny rock had such ritual importance that people were buried on beds of obsidian debris.

One should probably make a distinction between the exchange networks of earlier times and the

trade routes of historic times. Some pre-Columbian networks in the Pacific Northwest and the Northeast handled considerable volumes of artifacts and raw materials, many of them such prosaic commodities as blankets, hides, and grain. Formal trade, which developed in historic times, was often based on established rates of exchange at both ends. At the Native American end, it might be beaver furs, buffalo blankets, or deerskins; at the other, traders carried strings of glass beads, metal vessels, even firearms, each of which had a recognized value to their recipients. This often far exceeded the same goods' market value in the wider world, for European clothing, ornaments, and other baubles were exotic and had high symbolic value in societies that placed a premium on personal prestige. Those with the highest prestige very often controlled the trade.

the maize harvest. People in these regions may have chosen to locate fields in areas with high water tables that ensured good watering, ideally placing fields near places where piñons were harvested. They might not plant at all in some years, there being a much more flexible approach to maize as a food source. Both green and ripe maize came from Jemez Cave, which suggests that people were harvesting both immature and ripe maize, depending on varied rainfall conditions. People would not have invested substantially in maize farming, owing to the need for mobility. Groups more dependent on animals (as was the case in the northern Rio Grande Valley) would have ranked maize below both game and wild plant foods, because of the work involved in its cultivation. In these areas the switchover may not have occurred until there were no other good options for hunter-gatherers. Between 250 and 500 CE, however, the climate dried; then people had to exploit alternative resources, with an increase in farming in some areas.

Hunter-gatherers tend to accept crops as a survival strategy to preserve their lifeway, not because they want to become farmers. Thus, lowland desert groups may have planted maize to offset seasonal shortages in spring, for they could store the resulting grain. Upland groups might have adopted maize to allow them greater control over their environments. As we learn more about climate changes, it appears that coping with drought was a major factor in the switchover to farming across the Southwest. In a sense, Archaic culture in the Southwest, as elsewhere in North America, with its elaborate seed-processing equipment, hand stones, and grinders, was pre-adapted to agriculture. Had Southwestern peoples wanted to adopt agriculture as an opportunistic venture perceived to be of advantage, they would have done so much earlier, cultivating maize soon after it appeared far to the south. Ultimately, however, they adopted a low-yielding form of maize in the late third millennium BCE, a long time after it came into use in Mexico. The addition of farming to the economy, even as a part-time activity, placed immediate limits upon seasonal movement, for people had to return to the locations where they had planted crops, both to tend and to harvest them.

Unlike many native plants—goosefoot, for example—maize is not a cereal that will provide all one's food if planted and harvested casually. Maize also lacks two of the vital amino acids needed to make protein (lysine and tryptophan), and is only an effective staple when grown in combination with other lycine-rich crops, such as amaranth and beans, and with tryptophan-rich squash that together provide the necessary protein ingredients for a fully rounded diet. (Meat, in fact, also provides valuable protein, and the people ate sufficient flesh for the purpose.) Since most Southwestern groups continued to enjoy a highly mobile way of life for at least a millennium after maize first appeared north of the present international border with Mexico, there is good reason to believe that it first served as an informal supplement to wild plant resources, especially in favorable areas where corn could be planted and then left largely untended, the process of cultivating it not being allowed to interfere with other subsistence activities. One should remember, too, that the Southwest was a high-risk environment for any form of cultivation, so a logical strategy would involve diversification of options rather than placing all one's dietary eggs in one metaphorical basket.

The spread of maize across the Southwest was not a linear process and happened only gradually, beginning with a pattern of reduced mobility and

9.7 Aerial view of Cerro Juanaqueña, northwestern Mexico.

floodplain horticulture that involved seasonal base camps in the uplands and near rivers. This was an ideal adaptation for Late Archaic people, who simply added maize to their existing wild-plant exploitation, thereby expanding available food supplies (see Box: Eating and Traveling). As maize dependence increased, so technological innovations came into play, among them pottery for storage and cooking (between 50 and 150 CE), new food-preparation methods, and specialized equipment for processing maize. Social change also came about, as women undertook most agricultural work. The same general process of increasing dependence also took hold in northwestern Mexico, where archaeologists Robert Hard and John Roney (1998) excavated the Cerro Juanaqueña Archaic settlement with its 5 miles (8 km) of stone house foundations and found a few maize cobs dating to about 1150 BCE (Figure 9.7).

All Southwestern cultivation involved careful water management, using methods appropriate for specific landforms and topography. In the south the earliest known canal systems in the Tucson Basin are at the Clearwater site and date to c. 1500 BCE. Canals and other agricultural features have been identified at several other sites along the Santa Cruz River that date to about 1200 BCE. For example, the Las Capas site (1200 to 800 BCE) lies where two tributaries join the Santa Cruz River near Tucson in southern Arizona (Mabry, 2005; Vint, 2015). Here impeded groundwater flow raised the water table (Figure 9.8). Large oval houses and smaller circular dwellings stood along slight rises in the floodplain,

EATING AND TRAVELING

Major technological advances surround archaeologists on every side, but few of them have had such impact as bone chemistry. The carbon and nitrogen staple isotopes preserved in human bones reflect the isotopic ratios of plants consumed during life. Plants take in carbon through one of three photosynthetic pathways. By measuring the ratio of carbon isotopes contained in bone collagen, the organic component of bone, we can establish the dietary importance of different classes of plants. For instance, C4 plants, such as maize, take in more 13C and 14C isotopes than other plants. But there is more. Nitrogen also has two staple isotopes, 14N and 15N, which vary from plant to plant. Furthermore, we know that carnivores tend to lose 14N through their urine, but retain 15N. Thus, humans

who eat large quantities of meat have a higher ratio of 15N to 14N than people with a predominantly plant-based diet. Consuming marine foods gives you 15N to 14N ratios that are higher than those of terrestrial plants. Studying these ratios is a complicated process because of such variables as environmental differences, but the results are fascinating. Pecos provides an excellent example. The pueblo's population had a high 13C ratio, which shows that they ate a great deal of maize, but very little meat. When the researcher, Margaret Schoeninger, a bone-chemistry expert, looked at samples from thirty-nine individuals from Stillwater Marsh in Nevada, she found that they had consumed a marsh-based diet. Piñons have a low nitrogen ratio; the Stillwater people had a much higher one, which confirmed that their diet did not include highland plants.

We are also beginning to study individual movements by examining

the strontium isotopes in ancient teeth. Strontium is absorbed into human tooth enamel and bone as a result of their owners consuming food and water. Tooth enamel is especially valuable, for it forms in early childhood and is never replaced. The strontium record tells you where a person lived early in their life. In contrast, the cells in bone are replaced continually, with each generation of them acquiring the strontium signature of where that person lived at the time. Provided the geology of the areas the individual visited are easily identified, you can establish whether they lived in one place all their lives, or moved around. This has obvious potential for studying ancient population movements. Strontium research is still in its infancy, but it is already telling us that people moved around a great deal more than we had assumed. They had strong legs.

9.8 Las Capas excavation, Arizona, showing small pithouses, post holes for the roofs, and storage pits in many house floors.

surrounded by storage and roasting pits. They overlooked closely packed fields watered by canals, where the excavators uncovered thousands of small individual planting holes for the crops. Maize was only a small part of the diet; wild plant foods were still very important. By 800 BCE some communities lived in rings of houses around shared courtyards, perhaps an indication of more extended households, which are advantageous when land is abundant and labor is in short supply.

Maize is at the northern limits of its range in the Southwest, for it is intolerant of short growing seasons and such hazards as crop disease and strong winds. The most important factors of all were soil moisture and water supplies. By careful seed selection the farmers developed higher-elevation varieties with distinctive structures, whose seeds could be planted at considerable depth, to be nourished by retained ground moisture. They became experts at selecting the right soils for cultivation: those with good moisture-retaining properties on north- and east-facing slopes that receive somewhat less direct sunlight. The farmers favored floodplains and arroyo mouths, where the soil was naturally irrigated. They would divert water from streams, springs, or rainfall runoff to irrigate their crops. The cultivators dispersed their gardens widely to minimize the dangers of local drought or flood. Over the centuries a great diversity of highly effective dry-climate agricultural techniques developed throughout the Southwest.

Common beans probably appeared in the Southwest by 500 BCE, and became a widespread staple throughout the region. Beans were a very important crop in the Southwest, especially when grown with maize, for the two complement each other. Being legumes, they can return vital nitrogen to fields depleted by maize. Thus, by growing maize and beans in the same garden, Southwestern farmers could maintain the fertility of the soil for longer periods.

The dispersal of domesticated plants into the Southwest was not just a matter of their being available for cultivation. Their adoption involved a conscious decision by individual Archaic hunter-gatherer groups to utilize these more storable foods. This decision perhaps involved deliberate efforts by stressed groups living at low elevations to enhance winter and springtime food supplies.

The Beginnings of Village Life: 200 to 900 CE

The first appearance of corn did not trigger a dramatic revolution in Southwestern life. Though a plot of corn tended and harvested in a small garden would require less caloric investment than would collecting wild seeds scattered in isolated locales over a wide area, such collecting is not a problem when people can hunt and forage over large territories. If mobility is restricted, however, then the advantage of stands of even low-yielding corn is considerable. Maize does not have as much food value as some wild foods, especially piñons and walnuts, but piñon harvests vary considerably from year to year, making them a less reliable food source than cultivated crops.

As we have seen, serious maize agriculture in the arid Southwest required a great investment of time and energy, strong incentives for adopting more sedentary lifeways. As people settled down near their maize fields, which also supported amaranth, goosefoot, and other edible seed crops, they were effectively involved in multicropping, as farmers in Mexico and elsewhere do to this day. They also still relied on wild plant foods exploited in far smaller territories restricted in size by their sedentary lifeway. The transition from foraging to farming varied across the Southwest, with the importance of farming dictated by circumstances, region, and time.

It was not until 500 to 700 CE that permanent villages appeared in any numbers (Young and Herr, 2012). This sedentary way of life developed over many centuries, partly because agriculture was a high-risk activity in environments where rainfall varied wildly from year to year. Everyone now relied on efficient storage and large storage pits to guard against shortages. At the same time, people built more substantial permanent dwellings (Figure 9.9). The new, fixed communities varied greatly in size, but were mostly made up of individual oval-to-circular houses occupied over some length of time.

Villages in southern Arizona formed out of the need for households to cooperate for irrigation agriculture. Their settlements reflected this necessity. In contrast, northern people lived with much greater climatic variability and risk, and in competition with others. They were more mobile, with greater variations in site organization and social relationships between different groups. It may be no coincidence that the bow and arrow arrived first in the north, perhaps because of a higher incidence of warfare, and later became important in broadening the diet.

One important innovation appears in the Southwest in about 200 CE: pottery (Figure 9.10). We tend to think of pottery as a revolutionary invention. It was not, for anyone sitting by an open fire knows that wet clay bakes hard. Indeed, baked clay objects, such as figurines, were in use much earlier—they occur at Las Capas, for example. Clay

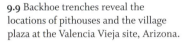

9.9 Backhoe trenches reveal the locations of pithouses and the village plaza at the Valencia Vieja site, Arizona.

9.10 A Hopi woman making pottery in an Orabi village.

containers did, however, make a significant dependence on agriculture possible, because they enabled households to store seed in jars, and to boil stored maize and beans, a process that maximizes their nutritional value. They allowed food to be cooked unattended, and were useful for other types of storage, were strong and easily manufactured, and lasted for a long time.

In the north and in the mountains, the earliest villagers lived in pithouses. Pithouses are thermally efficient, for the heat-loss from underground structures is less than for above-ground pueblos. They required less manpower and fuel to heat in winter, which made them adaptive at higher altitudes. Most pithouses were round or oval, up to 16 ft 6 in. (5 m) across, their floors dug to varying depths, but often about 1 ft 6 in. (0.5 m) below ground level. Pithouses often contained storage pits or fire hollows. Like Eskimo dwellings, they must have been smoky and rendered the inhabitants prone to lung diseases. As far as is known, the superstructures were usually made of poles and mud, the roof supported on four posts. Pithouse forms evolved into more-or-less standardized designs as the generations passed. Ventilators and air deflectors were common features, as were roof hatches accessed by a wooden ladder. Lower Sonoran desert houses, in what is now southern Arizona, were quite different, not pithouses as such, but rectangular or square houses built in pits. The floor was excavated up to 8 in. (20 cm) below the ground, the roof and walls being formed of poles, reeds, grass, and mud. Small hearths lay just inside the entrances.

Early villages in the north varied greatly in size, from hamlets of merely two or three pithouses to large settlements that contained as many as twenty-five to thirty-five houses, perhaps occasionally many more. Everywhere the houses were arranged without apparent order, and are associated with storage pits and cooking ovens. At all but the smallest villages one or more structures appear

9.11 Shabik'eschee pithouse village at Chaco Canyon, occupied during the sixth century CE and somewhat later.

to have had special functions. These are usually pithouses, but ones that display unusual architectural features or greater dimensions than residential structures. Some settlements were much larger. Shabik'eschee village in Chaco Canyon, New Mexico, comprised at least sixty pithouses and forty-five well-built storage bins (Wills *et al.*, 2012) (Figure 9.11). One structure stood out as being a pithouse with a difference: a low bench encircled the interior and the floor area was more than five times the size of the average dwelling in the settlement. The excavators believe the structure was only partially roofed. Perhaps this is one of the earliest examples of a "**great kiva**," a type of ceremonial building that became common in later centuries.

By 700 to 900 CE such **kiva**-like structures were a regular feature of northern and central Southwestern villages, which, by now, placed great importance on rituals that commemorated the endless cycle of passing seasons, reinforced the close kin ties that were central to farming in a high-risk environment, and provided a context for the redistribution of food supplies, as well as reducing the potential for conflict.

Trade relationships probably played an important role in village social organization. Many essential commodities, such as obsidian, chert, and other raw materials, were exchanged over considerable distances, sometimes even hundreds of miles. Utilitarian artifacts—pots, for example—passed through many hands. Sea shells and other luxuries passed likewise from individual to individual. The trade was apparently highly organized and conducted by local leaders. Judging from historical records of intercommunity exchange in the Southwest, it involved a complex series of economic and social processes. It was conditioned by the great environmental diversity and the differences in productivity from one area to the next. With unpredictable rainfall, survival depended on gift exchanges between trading partners and friends, and on the social ties between them. Exchange equalized resources and allowed the acquisition of valuable surpluses of luxury goods that might be traded later for food and other necessities. Every Southwestern group was dependent on others for ritual paraphernalia, items such as red ocher, tropical bird feathers, sea shells, even coiled baskets used in naming ceremonies. The exchange could be between neighboring communities, or along long, well-established trails that were in use for thousands of years, between friends or complete strangers.

At first, exchange may have resulted from regular informal contacts, but in time these became more formalized. One set of rules and conventions applied to fellow villagers, normally based on notions of continuous sharing and mutual assistance, seasonal gambling, ceremonial redistribution, and trading parties.

Everyone had access to both local commodities and goods from afar. Neighboring communities carried out exchange with relatives or non-strangers, with visitors bringing gifts in the expectation that they would be reciprocated in the future. Long-distance trade was conducted along dozens of trails, some possibly marked by petroglyphs and shrines. Some brought sea shells from the

Sea of Cortez and the southern California coast as far as the Tucson Basin as early as 1200 BCE. A complex trail network linked the Plains, Great Basin, Sonora, the Southwest, and California at European contact, most of them maintained by chains of exchange and gift friendship that handled different exotica. Exchange was an integral part of social relations, one that corrected economic differences, forged alliances, and served as a basis for resolving disputes without recourse to warfare.

Over time Southwestern society became more complex, but never reached the degree of stratification that developed to the south in highland and lowland Mexico. Alliances waxed and waned, but wherever they developed they were associated with dramatic population increases. The closing centuries of pre-Columbian times saw a great efflorescence and elaboration of Southwestern culture as population densities increased rapidly in the central and northern Southwest during the eleventh century CE. It is to this that we shall turn in Chapter 10.

SUMMARY

- The beginning of the Southwest Archaic coincided with drier conditions in some areas of the Southwest and further south. A complex mosaic of hunter-gatherer societies maintained the same general desert adaptations for thousands of years, albeit with local variations. Multidisciplinary research and settlement studies are revealing these variations.

- The semi-arid Lower Pecos region reveals many details of Archaic culture, especially the extensive use of plant fibers to make baskets, bags, and other artifacts. Earth ovens were in widespread use by 3500 BCE. Pecos rock art displays both hunting scenes and shamanistic rituals.

- Maize came to the southern Southwest around 3250 BCE and reached northern regions about 2,000 years later.

- Canal systems, dams, and terraces came into use in the south as a way of controlling seasonal water flows and fertilizing soils. Such behavior was important in the south. In the north early agriculture was combined with seasonal mobility.

- Permanent villages first appeared around 500 to 700 CE, pottery around 200 CE. Pithouses were in widespread use, forming settlements of family households. Trade played an increasingly major role in village social organization.

Culmination and Complexity

"Outside, some distance from the lodge, was a meadow of dry grass…the woman said, 'when the sun goes down, you must take me by my hair and drag me across the field. After that you may eat'…When evening came he did as he had been told. The woman disappeared, but wherever he had dragged her, a tall and graceful plant arose. On it were golden clusters of grain…It was corn, the friend of all humankind."

—Algonquian legend

Seated male and kneeling female ancestor figures from Mound C at Etowah, Georgia. Height: 24 and 22 in. (61 and 55.9 cm). Dated 1325–75 CE.

ENDURING THEMES
Culmination and Complexity

T he primary focus of Part Three was adaptation to North America's remarkable array of natural environments, and the diversity of cultures these environments enabled. This process continued uninterrupted all the way up to European contact, and in many areas beyond, for traditional lifeways survived remarkably intact, sometimes into the nineteenth, and even the early twentieth, centuries. In Part Four we explore the climax or apogee of thousands of years of human settlement in pre-Columbian times, involving emerging cultural complexity, the development of complex hierarchies, and ever-increasing long-distance trade and exchange. This emergence was closely tied to the arrival of maize agriculture, a development foreshadowed in some complex hunter-gatherer societies in Part Three, notably in the Pacific Northwest and the Southwest. As far as hunting and foraging were concerned, the basic environmental adaptations were long in place by the time agriculture became commonplace over much of North America. Adaptation was never continent-wide. It was always, ultimately, a local process that depended on a variety of factors: climatic shifts, population increases, and the need for more intensive exploitation of all kinds of food resources. The challenges of adaptation, of developing strategies for survival, which one can loosely call "risk management," varied greatly from region to region, but agriculture played an especially important role in the Southwest, the Eastern Woodlands, and the Northeast, which is why we focus on them in Part Four.

The four chapters that follow focus on three major cultural developments. We begin with the emergence of complex Pueblo societies in the Southwest, in a chapter that follows on from "Before the Pueblos" in Chapter 9. Chapters 11 and 12 cover the remarkable **Adena**, Hopewell, and Mississippian traditions of the Eastern Woodlands, also the elaborate Calusa chiefdoms of southern Florida. Finally, Chapter 13 explores the antecedents of the Haudenosaunee (Iroquois) and Wendat (Huron) peoples of the Northeast. Toward the ends of Chapters 10, 12, and 13, we arrive at the moment of the European *entrada*, which began with Christopher Columbus in 1492.

Another issue comes into play during Part Four: the ancestry of groups that were thriving at the time of the European contact. Serious research into this problem, involving, as it does, close collaboration with Native American tribes, is still at an early stage.

The Southwest

The great turning point in the pre-Columbian Southwest came with the arrival of maize agriculture from the south somewhere around 2350 BCE. Thanks to recent fine-grained excavations and innovative DNA research, we now know that this was a more complex process than was once assumed.

The development of "Great Houses" (large pueblos) with their serried rooms, and of elaborate rituals that marked planting, harvest, and the seasons, depended on more intensive agriculture, notably on the development of highly effective, localized irrigation systems, such as those used in Chaco Canyon, New Mexico, 1,000 years ago. Agriculture in the Southwest was a constant seesaw between abundance and scarcity. Connections with others, reciprocal ties between individuals and kin groups, and cementing relationships between different pueblos, near and far, were of fundamental importance. These were societies to whom reciprocity and movement were built-in responses to drought cycles, part of the rhythm of existence.

Great debate surrounds the social and political organization of Ancestral Pueblo societies. We know that much depended on kin groups, and on ritual skills, which passed from one generation to the next, with inheritance commonly down the female line, something reinforced by recent DNA work at Chaco Canyon (see Chapter 10). It is also clear that the ancestry of the modern Pueblo peoples is to be found deep in the past.

The Eastern Woodlands

The same themes of social complexity, more intensive trade and exchange, and the development of agriculture can be seen in the Eastern Woodlands and the Northeast. Adena, Hopewell, and Mississippian are societies first revealed by nineteenth-century excavations into mounds and earthworks, and then made world-famous by the Myth of the Moundbuilders. Our perceptions of them are very different in the twenty-first century, thanks to generations of increasingly detailed excavations, intensive CRM projects, and careful research into the very complex rituals and spiritual beliefs of these three societies. The cultural names disguise a great diversity of local societies, many of which are still little known. But the general outlines of these cultural traditions chronicle an increased complexity and volatility in these Eastern Woodlands societies. What does this increased complexity involve?

There is still some talk of a Mississippian state centered on Cahokia, but though Mississippian achieved remarkable complexity, it was never a pre-industrial state in the classic sense, with writing, highly defined social stratification, or divine rulers. Quite how such state-organized societies came into being is the subject of endless debate. What developed at the height of the Mississippian Tradition was a series of powerful, elaborate polities, defined by elaborate rituals that traced their ancestry in Hopewell and earlier societies. Each Mississippian polity had powerful chiefs, individuals from influential lineages. They had the ability to attract loyal followers thanks to their prowess at trade and exchange, and in the careful use of gifts to redistribute wealth through society and establish their reputations for generosity. They were what one might call aggrandizers, leaders who were people apart, defined, above all, by their ritual and supernatural powers.

To understand these supernatural powers means exploring the cosmos behind these societies. The increasingly elaborate mortuary rituals of Eastern Woodlands societies, such as those of the Adena Complex (c. 500 BCE to the first century CE), developed out of earlier (Late Archaic) roots. At first the construction of burial mounds, and the accompanying rituals, were localized developments. They occur notably in the Ohio River Valley and perhaps reflect tribal territories. This was a time when territorial boundaries became more closely defined and membership of social groups became more important. Here, as elsewhere, trade and exchange, also interaction with others, became increasingly important in a world where lineages and clans controlled access to food and other commodities. The increased emphasis on burial ritual may have come about at a time when sedentary settlement became more common. It became crucial to ensure access to commodities outside one's own territory, so social ties assumed much greater significance, especially those of lineage leaders, the major participants in trade and exchange. Burial rituals particularly validated group identity when leaders were interred with ceremonial regalia and possessions that identified their social roles.

These themes continued into Hopewell times (c. 200 BCE to c. 400 CE), a cultural tradition famous for its elaborate burial rites, earthworks, and complex trade networks. Hopewell communities still subsisted mainly off hunting and foraging, but the cultivation of native plants, such as goosefoot, assumed increasing importance. Once again, this was not a revolutionary development, for such cultivation began as a strategy for increasing food supplies in landscapes where game and plant foods were sometimes in short supply. Hopewell people lived in a world of intimate kin relationships, where spiritual and social relationships ebbed and flowed between communities and groups large and small. Maize agriculture first appeared in the east, at a time of accelerating population growth and high, varied cultural change. These trends came together in a series of riverine societies after 800 CE, reflected by the Mississippian Tradition of the South and southern Midwest.

The Mississippian was a cultural tradition based on a triad of religious cults: warfare, an earth/fertility cult, and the revering of ancestors. Priests and warriors had different chiefly roles, each confined to privileged kin groups. Elaborate ceremonies validated these various leaders and their roles. Ancestor worship was the universal belief, but these three cults also extended across a very large area of the south and east, transcending all cultural and ecological boundaries. Their dissemination resulted in highly factionalized Mississippian societies of varying social complexity. Cahokia, Moundville, and other great centers were at one end of the spectrum; hundreds of small centers and minor chiefdoms at the other. Far to the south and east, in southern Florida, a series of powerful Calusa polities built imposing centers using mollusk shells, their leadership based on bountiful shallow-water fisheries, exchange, and carefully orchestrated supernatural ties.

The Mississippian was the ultimate development of ancient society in the Eastern Woodlands, fueled in part by rich river-valley environments, and also by an increasing, but gradual, reliance on maize and, later, bean agriculture. In the end farming became more important than hunting and foraging. The move toward greater political and social complexity may have stemmed partly from control of long-distance exchange, especially in exotic objects that became symbols of legitimacy, of the special chiefly relationship with the supernatural world. The leaders drew people in with compelling religious ideology and distinctive cult objects, but they were well aware of the importance of reciprocity between members of society. Theirs was a volatile, intensely competitive world, where control depended on powerful symbols and potent intangibles.

The Five Nations

Maize agriculture spread far to the northeast, the St. Lawrence Valley providing an approximate northern limit for this ultimately tropical crop. Here, again, we discern the same converging themes of social complexity, exchange, and agriculture among the Haudenosaunee and Wendat, whose ancestry lay among Late Archaic groups in the coast and interior. The Northeast is a region of great environmental diversity, which meant that people moved regularly over long distances. Trade and exchange were important from the beginning, but assumed a central role in society in later centuries. There was an ancient practice of small communities and groups coming together for summer gatherings of as many as 300 people at important fishing stations.

Larger settlements with over 1,000 people brought new pressures on supplies and agricultural land, also encouraging factionalism between kin groups. Hereditary chieftainship with separate chiefs for peace and war came into being, as warfare became endemic. This warfare was not so much about land as about personal prestige in a changing world where collective endeavor now provided more food than individual efforts. Society became more and more sedentary and agricultural, with warfare giving prestige. Tribal councils replaced village ones; they helped maintain links between increasingly complex communities.

During the sixteenth century the Haudenosaunee formed the **League of Five Nations**, a council of headmen that adjudicated disputes and reduced violence. The League was an ultimate form of the adaptation that had shaped Native American society everywhere since the beginning. The Five Nations reduced bloodletting and maintained cultural individual and political identity when dealing with others. This organization worked effectively, for the Haudenosaunee were remarkable for their sophistication and the subtlety of their social relationships. These astute and warlike people were a formidable challenge for the Europeans who settled among them after the sixteenth century.

Pueblo Climax

You feel overwhelmed by the complexity of the "Great House," the serried rooms pressing on the open plazas, all in the heart of an arid landscape. At Pueblo Bonito in Chaco Canyon, New Mexico, it is best to enter through the east wing, where the quiet rooms are carefully preserved, the veneered masonry seemingly as fresh as the day it was laid. Close your eyes and you can imagine them occupied—stacks of maize cobs along the walls, women weaving in the shade, the murmur of voices from the terraces and plazas, and an undercurrent of scents and odors, of sagebrush, human sweat, and rotting garbage. Then the image fades in the warmth of the afternoon and you are back to the reality of an intricate archaeological jigsaw puzzle, much of which has yet to be pieced together.

Pueblo Bonito flourished 1,000 years ago, long after agriculture had become well established in the Southwest. This site, along with many similar pueblos all over the Southwest, raises important historical questions. Why did such large pueblos come into being? Why were the societies that built them so volatile? What institutions in Ancestral Pueblo society helped Southwesterners cope with the challenges of unpredictable rainfall and drought? (Ancestral Pueblo are the forebears of historic and living Pueblo communities that we know about in some detail.)

As we have seen, maize agriculture did not bring about immediate changes to Southwestern life. Permanent pithouse villages appeared gradually in northern areas and increased in number until about 700 CE. The next three centuries saw a change from pithouse villages to settlements of multi-room buildings constructed from adobe clay or masonry. In some areas, for instance Mesa Verde, Colorado, the change was a gradual one, the first rooms being storage areas built behind pithouses. Later, people moved into surface rooms, turning their old pithouses into kivas or ceremonial spaces. (Kivas are subterranean chambers, roofed with stout wooden beams, where secret societies met and performed important rituals.) In other places the shift was rapid. Why the changeover took place is a mystery, for there are no such obvious causes as climatic shifts.

Between 600 and 900 CE village settlement expanded greatly throughout the northern Southwest, and especially on the Colorado Plateau. Some of the largest settlements of the period in southwestern Colorado and northwest New Mexico were home to as many as 100 to 120 households. It was at this point that Chaco Canyon came to prominence.

Chaco Canyon: Before 900 to 1150 CE

Chaco Canyon is a dramatic place, set in a stark landscape (Figure 10.1, p. 224). The towering cliffs of the canyon glow yellow-gold in the sun, contrasting with the softer tones of desert sand, greasewood, and occasional willow trees. Shadows fall across the canyon as the sun sets, the grandiose landscape dwarfing the walls of the great pueblos that are camouflaged naturally against the high cliffs. Between 700 and 800 CE the people living at Chaco largely abandoned pithouses and moved into masonry dwellings. The clusters of rooms, known as pueblos and commonly called "small houses," lay in small arcs, so each room was equidistant from the circular pithouses in the center. These gradually developed into kivas, the focal points of ceremonial life. Almost all the small-house settlements lay on

10.1 Pueblo Bonito and
Chaco Canyon.

the south side of the canyon, where side canyons joined the central one. These
side channels deposited floodwater and nutrient-rich sediment at their ends,
creating prime farming land. This *akchin* (a Piman word for "at the mouth of
the wash") thrived for centuries and is still the primary farming method used
by the modern Hopi.

During the ninth century summer rainfall was highly variable. Groups from
the north, primarily from the Montezuma Valley in southwestern Colorado,
migrated into the canyon, forced from their homeland by a period of somewhat
colder climate that shortened the growing season. They settled on the north side,
the inhabitants of the small-house sites having already taken up the best land
on the south side. The north side more conducive to canal irrigation, having
different runoff patterns. These new groups brought an early version of Great
House architecture and erected the first four such houses at the junctions of major
drainages in Chaco sometime after 850 CE: Penasco Blanco, Pueblo Bonito, Kin
Nahasbas, and Una Vida. The largest of these, Pueblo Bonito, near the northeast
wall of the canyon, stood three, and later five, stories high along its rear wall and
remained in use for more than two centuries (see Box: Pueblo Bonito). By the
eleventh century Great Houses dominated Chaco Canyon. Chaco expert Gwinn
Vivian (1990) has calculated the potential carrying capacity of the canyon soils

PUEBLO BONITO

Semicircular Pueblo Bonito is the largest and most spectacular of Chaco Canyon's Great Houses. In its eleventh-century heyday, Pueblo Bonito had at least 600 rooms and could have housed about 1,000 people, but by no means all of the rooms were in use at any one time. Tom Windes, who has studied the site for many years, believes that no more than a hundred or so people ever lived there, with the largest amount of residential debris accumulating in the ninth and tenth centuries, and in the early twelfth (Windes, 2003). The two great kivas at Pueblo Bonito lie on either side of a line of rooms that divided the complex into two areas (Figure 10.2). Chaco architecture was based on rectangular rooms, built in contiguous blocks, and round chambers (Lekson, 1984). Some of the latter were subterranean, located in the plaza areas in front of room blocks. Many others were elevated into room blocks and built into rectangular rooms, usually enclosures built exclusively for this purpose.

Construction was simple. Once the site had been leveled and the foundations laid, a room block typically began as a series of continuous, long parallel walls. Cross walls were added later, as the long sides rose higher. Once one story was complete, the rooms were roofed individually and then used as the foundation for the next story. Chacoan walls were built of local sandstone in both harder and softer forms from different cliff strata. The harder rock could easily be split at right angles, making it easier to shape for wall building. The builders used a variety of methods to shape the exposed stone faces, among them grinding and pecking. Clay-sand from canyon alluvial deposits was mixed with water to serve as mortar. The main load on the walls at Pueblo Bonito was the upper stories, so the masons built the walls wide and stable, reducing the width with each story for stability. The outer walls of the Great Houses were battered to support the massive weight of five stories of rooms, which were terraced to allow access without an interior system of ladders. The ceilings are high, and the rooms well constructed with core masonry covered on both sides with carefully selected ashlar, sometimes arranged in alternating courses of large and small stones to form patterns. These decorative veneers were covered with adobe plaster. The great kivas were built with care, roofed over with carefully dressed pine beams, many of them carried in from considerable distances away. This extravagance may reflect the religious importance of Pueblo Bonito and other major pueblos.

10.2 Pueblo Bonito from the air, showing the circular kivas and the probable duality of the pueblo. The rock fall at top center crushed part of the pueblo in 1941.

and believes no more than about 5,500 people ever lived there (estimates of carrying capacity differ considerably, however). The Chaco people took advantage of long-standing kin and trade links with groups living elsewhere and became the hub of a much wider world. Thus was born what is sometimes called the **Chaco Phenomenon**, a number of dispersed communities that interacted constantly, linked by regular exchanges of a variety of commodities. Tree-rings show that the next eighty years were ones of generally good rainfall, a weather cycle that may have meant the system kept going longer than it might otherwise have done.

Many intriguing questions surround the Chaco Phenomenon. How did such an elaborate efflorescence of Ancestral Pueblo culture arise so suddenly, and collapse with such rapidity? What were the cultural processes that led to the sudden emergence of regional integration in this area of the Southwest? The Chaco area is a desert environment, with long winters, short growing seasons, and marginal rainfall. How could the Ancestral Pueblo have developed such an elaborate culture in a high-risk environment, where the most one might expect would be communities of widely dispersed farming villages? The number of

GENETIC RESEARCH AT PUEBLO BONITO

Major advances in ancient DNA and genomic sequencing approaches have transformed our understanding of population movements and turnover in the past, and have recently been brought to bear on Pueblo archaeology. Archaeologists have long wondered how the people at Pueblo Bonito governed themselves. Was Chacoan social organization similar to that of historic Western Pueblo peoples (for example, the Hopi of northeastern Arizona), where social groups with a matrilineal core are ranked and control ritual sources of power? Or were the Chacoans led by non-kin-based ritual sodalities, comparable to the historic societies of some Eastern Pueblos? Using high-precision AMS-radiocarbon dating and reconstructions of mitochondrial DNA genomes, a multidisciplinary research team has begun to answer this question (Kennett et al., 2017).

Douglas Kennett and his colleagues examined burials in Bonito's most elaborate burial crypt, Room 33,

built in the ninth century CE for a high-status member of the community and his lineal descendants. This person was a male in his forties, who died after a fatal blow to his head. He lay in the center of the crypt on a bed of sand and wood ashes, adorned with thousands of imported turquoise and shell beads and pendants, which once formed necklaces, anklets, and bracelets. A conch-shell trumpet and many abalone shells from the Pacific Coast lay on his right side. The entire burial was sealed with a thick layer of sterile sand. A second burial, also adorned with turquoise, was buried above the sand and covered with a plank floor. Twelve other individuals were buried above the plank floor, their bones being disturbed when later members of the lineage were deposited in the crypt. Numerous clay bowls and pitchers, and also shell and turquoise, lay with the bones. Offerings in the crypt included caches of flutes and carved wooden ceremonial staffs. Turquoise beads lay around the corner posts, reflecting the cardinal directions of Puebloan cosmology. Numerous ritual offerings

lay in adjacent rooms, among them hundreds of staffs, cylindrical clay vessels, and remains of scarlet macaws.

By examining the DNA of the skeletal remains, the research team discovered that the genomes of nine of the individuals in the crypt shared mitochondrial DNA, which is passed down from mother to daughter, and so were related through a single maternal line. Nuclear genome data from the six individuals with the highest DNA preservation revealed daughter and grandmother-grandson relationships that are consistent with matrilineal descent in this elite lineage. These results suggest that hereditary inequality and societal complexity emerged in Chaco by the early ninth century CE, and that this matrilineal dynasty persisted at the center of this complex society for around 330 years, until its rapid dispersal in the early twelfth century. This state-of-the-art research shows that the long-lasting elite at Pueblo Bonito, and presumably in Chaco society, enjoyed hereditary leadership in one of North America's earliest complex societies.

rooms suggests a far larger population than could be supported by the available arable land. The people seem also to have used clay vessels much more than is usual, and they constructed many miles of long, wide roads through a sparsely vegetated desert where such constructions appear unnecessary. What activities in the canyon can have prompted this?

Pueblo Bonito and the other Great Houses defy precise interpretation (Neitzel, 2003). Many people lived in them, but they also fulfilled other important social and religious functions, as well as being used for storing grain and other commodities. The smaller pueblos were really agglomerations of households, organized along kin lines, each of which built its own rooms inside the semi-circular outer wall, which was erected by communal effort. Each kin group used its smaller kivas in the heart of the room blocks as workshops and as places for educating children, storytelling, and family ceremonies. At Pueblo Bonito the division of the pueblo into two areas probably reflected the duality of social organization in Ancestral Pueblo communities, similar to the Winter and Summer people of modern pueblos. In the great kivas the people gathered for more formal ceremonies and to make decisions about the governing of the community as a whole.

Unquestionably, Bonito was an important ritual center, especially during the eleventh century, when construction activity intensified. As in historic Pueblo society, Ancestral Pueblo life and ritual must have revolved around the changing seasons, the solstices, equinoxes, and the routine of the agricultural year. And like later Puebloans, the people who gathered at Pueblo Bonito must have nurtured corn, which pervaded every aspect of their lives with its planting, growth, and harvest. Important seasonal ceremonies involved exchange and distribution of food and other necessities brought to the canyon from some distance. The office holders who organized these ceremonies were the guardians of ritual knowledge and political acumen, gaining social recognition by redistributing commodities to people near and far.

Who these office holders were, we do not know. Some of them were buried at the pueblo at a time of enhanced ritual activity. Pueblo Bonito has yielded at least 130 burials, mainly dating to after 1000. The Chaco pueblos generally are remarkable for the small number of burials found within their precincts; those we do find are probably of important leaders (see Box: Genetic Research at Pueblo Bonito). These burial clusters are associated with very large numbers of cylinder vessels, wooden staffs, and other artifacts associated with important individuals. A recent discovery has established that some cylinder jar fragments bear traces of cacao, a prestigious beverage with strong Mesoamerican associations. The people buried in these clusters were also taller, which suggests that they enjoyed a better diet.

No one knows why the Chaco people congregated in Great Houses. It may have been to avoid building on valuable agricultural land and a way of concentrating food resources. Interestingly, by no means everyone lived in the Great Houses, which lie on the north side of the canyon. The opposite wall sheltered smaller settlements, many of them little more than a few households, located in areas where farming land was more spread out.

The nine larger settlements within Chaco Canyon all have at least one great kiva. The most famous example is one of several isolated kivas. Casa Rinconada is about 63 ft (19.2 m) across, and others are almost as large (Figure 10.3). The

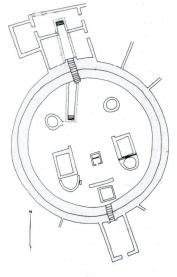

10.3 Plan of the great kiva at Casa Rinconada, showing the subfloor passage, fire box, fire screen, seating pits for the roof-support columns, and the north antechamber rooms.

amount of labor involved in digging these subterranean chambers, either as stand-alones or in Great Houses, and constructing the walls, roofs, and ante-chambers must have been considerable, for some kiva walls were at least 11 ft (3.4 m) high. They are entered through recessed stone staircases, often through an antechamber beyond the stairs. Common kiva features include wall niches where offerings of beads and pendants were sometimes placed, encircling benches around the walls, pairs of masonry-lined vaults, and a raised firebox in the center. Rinconada is the only great kiva where there was a covered tunnel that allowed masked dancers to enter from an antechamber on the north side and emerge on a circular area on the kiva floor. This was screened, probably with a plank wall. This allowed the dancers to enter as if emerging from the *sipapu*, the entry to the underworld. The isolated kivas are all located near small-house sites. Perhaps Rinconada and other stand-alones were a way of linking the interests of people living on the north and south sides of the canyon. If Great Houses needed more irrigated land they may have "paid" for it and for setting up the canals with elaborate rituals performed in the kivas.

By 1050 CE five great pueblos dominated Chaco Canyon. We do not know how many people lived within its cliffs and in the immediate vicinity. Estimates range from 2,000 to as high as 20,000, but Vivian's figure of around 5,500 is probably about right. Chaco was no agricultural paradise, though the nearby mesa, the boldest topographic feature for many miles, was a rich source of wild plant foods. Some of those who disagree with Vivian theorize that the Great Houses were constructed to accommodate far larger influxes of people, who came to the canyon occasionally, perhaps for regular religious observances. The controversy is still unresolved.

Despite their diverse food resources, the Chaco people were trapped inside the narrow confines of their canyon. They took advantage of long-standing kin and trade links with communities living elsewhere on the Colorado Plateau and made themselves the hub of a much wider world. No one knows who held authority in this society, which would be classified as a mid-level complex society where prominent individuals lacked the authoritarian power that enabled them to achieve complete dominance. Rather, Chaco and other Ancestral Pueblo communities were probably riddled with intense competition and factionalism between different individuals and kin groups. Violence may have played an important role.

By 1115 CE at least seventy communities, known as "outliers," scattered over more than 25,000 square miles (65,000 km²) were linked through socio-economic and ritual networks centered on Chaco Canyon. The activities of the Chaco Phenomenon were probably controlled by a small number of people. But whether these individuals formed a social elite with special privileges reserved to them, and them alone, or were simply members of an important kin group, is still uncertain. Outlying great-house sites contain much Chaco pottery and share architectural features, such as great kivas, with Pueblo Bonito and other large canyon centers, but with considerable variation. Some also had surround-ing communities of their own. An elaborate road system radiated out from the canyon, a web of tracks that run straight or bend abruptly, use stairways and ramps, and extend over more than 250 miles (400 km) (see Box: Chaco's Road System). The roads did not link places as modern ones do; they were probably

CHACO'S ROAD SYSTEM

The Chaco Phenomenon is famous for its "road system." Chacoan "roads" were first identified in the 1890s and again in the 1920s. In the 1930s early aerial photographs revealed faint traces of what appeared to be canals emanating from the canyon. During the 1970s and 1980s investigators used aerial photographs and side-scan radar to place the canyon at the center of a vast ancient landscape. Now their successors use GPS and satellite imagery (Snead, 2017). Perhaps as many as 400 miles (650 km) of unpaved ancient trackways link Chaco in an intricate web with over thirty outlying settlements. The "roads" are up to 40 ft (12 m) wide and were cut a few inches into the soil, or marked by low banks or stone walls. Sometimes the road makers simply cleared the vegetation and loose soil or stones from the pathway, lining some segments with boulders. The roads run straight for long distances, in one instance as far as 60 miles (95 km). They do not follow contours, but change direction in abrupt turns, with stairways and ramps to surmount steep obstacles. These may be little more than toe holds, or elaborate stairways with wide steps cut out of bedrock or formed from masonry blocks.

The roads approach the canyon in different ways. To the north, several converge on Pueblo Alto and then split beyond it to drop into the canyon via rock-cut steps or ramps above several Great Houses—Pueblo Bonito, Pueblo del Arroyo, and Chetro Ketl (Figure 10.4). At a point where the roads come together again beyond Pueblo Alto, a groove in the sandstone bedrock on the cliff top keeps the two routes separate before they branch off in different directions,

10.4 The Jackson Stairway at Chaco Canyon.

suggesting that the demarcation was of considerable importance. By using aerial photographs fieldworkers have been able to trace roads extending from Chaco almost to the Colorado—New Mexico border and Aztec Ruins, some 50 miles (80 km) away (Figures 10.5 and 10.6). Other roads connect Chaco to natural resource source areas in modern-day Zuni country and elsewhere. More than 250 miles (402 km) of roads have been detected on aerial photographs so far, but the system may have extended as far north as the San Juan Range in the Rocky Mountains to the north, the Mogollon Mountains to the south, and from the turquoise mines near Santa Fé in the east to the Little Colorado River in ▶▶

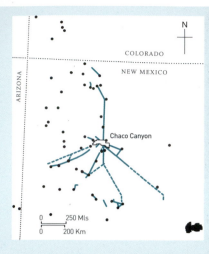

10.5 Map of some of the Chaco road system and outlying sites of the Chaco Phenomenon (black dots).

10.6 Aztec Ruins, a Chaco outlier and major ritual center. The western part of the site is a classic Chaco great house, a D-shaped structure with twelve kivas and an enclosed plaza. People settled in the northern parts of the site by 1050, but Aztec was abandoned in about 1268.

the west. Current thinking suspects that the Chaco Phenomenon was the center of a vast regional system that stretched far beyond the San Juan Basin (Crown and Judge, 1991).

Chaco road construction must have involved the deployment of large numbers of people and considerable group organization. Unlike the trail systems that connected hundreds of ancient communities in the far west and in the Eastern Woodlands, these were wide, straight highways, whose significance still eludes us. Were they highways for transporting valuable natural resources to major pueblos? Or were they, as James Judge argues, pilgrim roads? Or did they have some much more profound spiritual importance?

One prevalent hypothesis argues that without draft animals or wheeled carts, the Chaco people had no use for formal roads for their everyday business. Originally, perhaps, people traveled from outlying communities to Chaco to acquire turquoise objects, to trade food for ritual paraphernalia. In time this trade became institutionalized in regular ceremonies and festivals, where people gathered from many miles around for seasonal rituals, for exchange of food and other commodities, and where leaders from widely dispersed communities gathered to cement political and economic alliances. Each member of the network would have complex obligations to fulfill, among them, presumably, the supplying of people to construct and maintain the road system, to transport wooden beams for building large pueblos in Chaco (more than 200,000 were needed to build them), and for many communal tasks. In other words, the Chaco system was a mechanism for integrating a large number of communities scattered widely in a harsh and unpredictable environment. By regulating and maintaining a large and far-flung exchange system, the leaders who controlled this intricate network were able to support far more people than the area would normally have carried, and to do so using very simple agricultural technology. Every leader must have been a player in a complex and ever-shifting political environment, where the periphery was as important as the center.

Another possible explanation lies in Pueblo cosmology. The so-called "Great North Road" travels 40 miles (63 km) north from Chaco. North is the primary direction among Keresan-speaking Pueblo peoples, who may have ancestry among the Chaco people. North led to the origin, the place to which the spirits of the dead traveled. Perhaps the Great North Road was an umbilical cord to the underworld and a conduit of spiritual power. The Keresan also believe in a Middle Place, a point where the four cardinal directions converged. Perhaps the canyon served as the *sipapu*, the entrance to the underworld. Thus, Chaco and its trackways may have formed a sacred landscape which gave order to the world and linked outlying communities with a powerful Middle Place through spiritual ties that remained even as many households moved away from the canyon. Think of a giant ideological spider's web with a lattice of obligations among its component parts, and you have a possible model for Chaco's role in the eleventh-century Pueblo world. The Great Houses of the canyon lay at the center of the web, connected to communities many miles away by kin ties and regular exchanges of food and other commodities. Gwinn Vivian believes the landscape was a powerful statement, which he calls "We the Chaco." At the same time, the roads served as a mechanism for increasing cooperation and exercising social control over communities at a distance (discussion in Vivian, 1997).

10.7 The Great Kiva at Salmon Ruins, New Mexico.

a powerful ideological spider's web that symbolized the ties between different parts of the Chaco world. Perhaps they were ritual pathways set on a landscape both physical and symbolic.

The center of the Chaco Phenomenon shifted northward in the early 1100s. The Salmon Ruin near Bloomfield, New Mexico, is a 290-room pueblo in a slightly modified "E" plan with a great kiva and tower kiva (a circular tower which served as a ceremonial structure) (Figure 10.7). It was constructed in three planned stages between 1088 and 1106 CE. The distribution of local and Chacoan vessels through the pueblo suggests that Salmon was founded by both local San Juan people and migrants from Chaco itself.

Between 1050 and 1130 the rains were plentiful. Building activity continued in the canyon as the Great Houses expanded. Chaco's web of interconnections prospered. The Chaco population rose steadily, which was not a serious problem as long as winter rainfall fertilized the fields. Then, in 1130, tree-rings tell us that fifty years of intense drought settled over the Colorado Plateau. Soon the outlying communities ceased to trade and share food with the Great Houses, which forced the canyon's inhabitants to rely on their own already overstressed environment. Dry year followed dry year. Crops failed; game and wild plant foods were increasingly scarce in an area that was marginal for agriculture at the best of times. An inexorable population decline set in.

The only recourse was deeply ingrained in Ancestral Pueblo philosophy: movement. Within a few generations the pueblos stood empty, as well over half Chaco's population dispersed into villages, hamlets, and pueblos far from the canyon. Those who remained were gone by the early 1200s. The emptying of such a site as Pueblo Bonito seems like an epochal event when considered at a distance of 900 years, but at the time it was merely part of the constant ebb and flow of Ancestral Pueblo existence (see Box: Tree-Rings and Southwestern Climate Change, pp. 232–33).

The Chaco system dissolved, in the sense that some people moved to more productive areas where they maintained long-term alliances, while others formed independent and highly scattered communities, or simply remained in environmentally favorable areas. Throughout the region once integrated by the Chaco Phenomenon, the reorganized society that emerged from the prolonged drought cycle probably bore some resemblance to Pueblo society immediately before European contact.

The Chaco Phenomenon was by no means the only centralized political and social system that flourished in the ancient Southwest, for there were other complex societies living in sharply contrasting ecological zones.

Hohokam: The Desert Irrigators, c. 450 to 1450 CE

Hohokam (a Native American term of uncertain origin meaning "something that is all gone") was the ancient farming tradition of the southern deserts, known from its buff- to brown-colored pottery (Fish and Fish, 2008). If we use such vessels as markers, we can trace the Hohokam over more than 30,000 square miles (78,000 km²) of southern Arizona—an area larger than South Carolina. In general terms, Hohokam groups shared a common identity as farmers, a talent for irrigation agriculture, and an architecture of adobe dwellings. They also shared profound values of mutual obligation.

Hohokam culture appeared around 450 CE, as new maize strains arrived and farming populations rose. The land looks barren and utterly dry, yet it has fertile soils and lies near major drainages. Between about 450 and 1450 CE the Hohokam living near the river adapted brilliantly to this seemingly desolate environment, building individual canal networks up to 22 miles (35 km) long and irrigating up to 70,000 acres (28,000 ha) (Figures 10.8 and 10.9). The first irrigation canal systems developed along the Gila and Salt rivers in the modern-day Phoenix area.

For nearly twenty years the long-term rainfall pattern gave way to complex, unpredictable precipitation and severe droughts, especially on the Colorado Plateau in the north. This abrupt change coincided with the great drought of 1276 to 1299 CE, which played havoc with the Ancestral Pueblo peoples. For centuries they had adjusted effortlessly to the effects of short-term drought cycles, heavy El Niño rains, and other short-term fluctuations. These could be handled by moving across the landscape, relying more heavily on wild plant foods, or planting more land.

These strategies had worked well for centuries, as long as the Ancestral Pueblo farmed their land at well below its carrying capacity. For hundreds of years they had adapted brilliantly by selecting moisture-retaining soils on north-facing slopes, using arroyo mouths, and diverting rain runoff onto their gardens. They also developed maize with root structures that could be planted deep in the soil. But as the population rose, their vulnerability to brief climatic perturbations—El Niños or droughts, for instance—rose significantly. By the twelfth century communities in such places as Chaco Canyon were close to the supportive capacity of their environments. When the great drought descended upon the Southwest, it ushered in a period of severe destabilization for agricultural populations on the southern Colorado Plateau. Competition for arable land had already increased because of the high population densities. Simultaneously, more people would have moved to areas with higher rainfall and stable water and land relationships. Many of these areas were already occupied, which would have caused problems integrating the newcomers into existing communities. Social instability, enhanced competition, and even conflict may have ensued.

The new, much more detailed climatic data available to Southwestern archaeologists has revealed the great complexity of the many climatic fluctuations that affected Ancestral Pueblo and later peoples. Sizeable data sets will be needed to understand the changes they underwent, and those are still being accumulated.

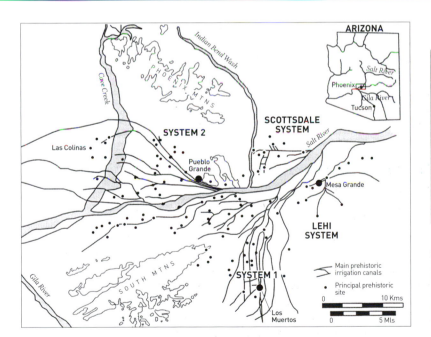

10.8 Irrigation systems and major settlements along the Salt River in the Phoenix Basin.

10.9 The late Southwestern archaeologist Emil Haury stands in an excavated Hohokam irrigation canal, part of the elaborate irrigation systems based on the Gila and Salt Rivers that watered surrounding fields.

10.10 Aerial view of pithouses and courtyards at the Grewe site, Arizona.

The Salt River Valley was the most populous and agriculturally productive valley in the Southwest before 1500 CE.

Most Hohokam people lived in small, single-room houses built of pole and brush and covered with hardened clay. Groups of dwellings lay around small courtyards, as if extended families lived close to one another. The size of Hohokam courtyard groups varied considerably, with one of them at the Grewe site in south-central Arizona having as many as twenty-four houses, covering an area of 6,500 square feet (600 m²) (Figure 10.10). Households, in the wider sense of an extended family, were the primary mechanism for controlling land ownership and the use of irrigation water.

At Grewe, a community founded as early as the sixth century CE and occupied until the fourteenth, the largest houses clustered in a few courtyard groups and were occupied much longer than surrounding smaller dwellings. Here archaeologists Douglas Craig and Kathleen Henderson unearthed a communal cooking area with dozens of pit ovens cut into the soil. This lay on one side of a crowded residential zone. On the other side was a public plaza with a ball court. Craig and Henderson (2007) think that the courtyards nearest to the cooking area, which include the largest and wealthiest collections of houses, controlled food activities and sponsored the feasts that were prepared there, a way of acquiring prestige and social status. At the same time the events reaffirmed property rights held by the wealthiest households as well as fostering a sense of communal identity. There are signs, too, that the same households also subsidized the manufacture of such items as shell jewelry, pottery, and cotton textiles, which were traded to other groups in the region.

The Hohokam exchanged foodstuffs, utilitarian raw materials, ceremonial objects and ornaments (macaw feathers from Mexico, for example), shells (also prestige items), and information. Controversy surrounds the relationship between the Hohokam and cultural groups in Mesoamerica far to the south. Some scholars believe capped **platform mounds**, clay figurines, certain forms of polished and painted vessels, and ball courts show strong Mesoamerican influence. Most, however, argue that the Hohokam was a distinctively Southwestern culture. Certainly Hohokam communities traded with the south for copper bells, mosaic mirrors, and tropical birds, items also found in Chaco Canyon. They were middlemen in the sea-shell trade from the Gulf of California and the southern California coast (where some Hohokam sherds have been found). Between 800 and 1100 CE the Hohokam traded through a network of ball-court communities between the Little Colorado in the north and the Mexican border in the south.

By 1100 CE larger communities comprised a prominent village with communal structures such as a ball court, a plaza, or a platform mound, with outlying smaller settlements and farms, the whole surrounded by carefully laid out and intensively cultivated farm land. Since there are no signs of prominent, authoritarian rulers, it seems that close-knit economic, political, and ritual bonds provided the basis for communal actions and for creating and maintaining irrigation systems. There are few signs of the long-distance trading contacts found at Chaco Canyon or in major Hohokam settlements. Most ceremonial activities appear to have taken place at the community and household level, reflecting a relatively isolated, egalitarian Pueblo society.

Snaketown on the Gila River was one of the largest Hohokam communities, a pithouse settlement with a ball court 195 ft (60 m) long and 15 to 20 ft (4.5 to 6 m) deep (Haury, 1976) (Figure 10.11). Ball-court communities flourished at relatively even intervals along major canal networks. These basin-like ball-court structures were arenas where people from the surrounding countryside would gather for feasts, trading activities, and all kinds of social interaction, as well as ball games between different villages. We know of more than 200 Hohokam ball courts, large and small, shallow depressions with plastered or stamped earth

10.11 The Hohokam ball court at Snaketown, excavated by Emil Haury, is the largest such structure in the Southwest. The court may also have served as a dance arena.

floors, surrounded by sloping banks, where experiments show that up to 700 spectators could witness the games. The largest are up to 250 ft (75 m) long and 90 ft (27 m) wide, dug up to 9 ft (2.75 m) into the subsoil. Quite what form the ball game itself took remains a mystery, but there is no question that it originated in Mesoamerica, where commoners played a competitive game that required each side to cast a rubber ball back and forth without it touching the ground. Three such balls have come from Southwestern sites. Judging from historical analogies, the contests were the culminating event of days of feasting, trading, and social interaction that enhanced a sense of communal identity.

Ball courts gave way to platform mounds after 1150 CE, earth-filled structures that formed elevated places. Some are over 12 ft (3.5 m) high, built within an adobe compound, with as many as thirty rooms on the summit. The platform-mound complexes symbolize a major shift in Hohokam society: the emergence of a small elite. Ball courts were open depressions, accessible to large numbers of people. Platform mounds reached for the sky, stood out on the landscape, and were accessible to only a few. It is as if some members of society now elevated themselves both in material and spiritual terms above everyone else, whereas in earlier times the relationship between the living and the ancestors, and with the underworld where humans originated, was more important. The larger the platform mound, the more labor required to build it, and the greater the status of the individuals or group responsible for its construction.

As the social order changed, so environmental pressures intensified from drought and catastrophic river floods. Hohokam irrigation systems no longer produced the food surpluses to support a now more elaborate culture. The collapse came around 1450, probably a rapid dispersal, household by household, as people moved away to settle with kin or farmed on a much smaller scale.

Mogollon and Mimbres: c. 1000 to 1130 CE

The Mogollon Tradition of the ancient Southwest belongs to the uplands and deserts that separated the Ancestral Pueblo and Hohokam. Its most spectacular expression is Mimbres, located along the river of that name in southwestern New Mexico. Between 1000 and 1130 CE Mimbres potters created magnificent painted ceremonial bowls adorned with geometric and pictorial designs (Le Blanc, 1983) (Figures 10.12 and 10.13). These superb examples of ancient artistry are usually found in burials, inverted over the head of the deceased and ceremonially "broken" by making a small hole in the base.

The Mimbres people lived in settlements of up to 150 rooms that consisted of single-story, contiguous and rectangular spaces built of river cobbles and adobe. At the well-known NAN Ranch and Galaz sites the pueblo clusters grew according to household needs, rooms sometimes being subdivided and remodeled. Ceremonial structures included large, rectangular, and semi-subterranean kivas, sometimes with entry ramps and ceremonial offerings under the floors. The relationship between Mogollon and the Zuni is the subject of much debate (see Box: Archaeology and Oral Traditions) (Gregory and Wilcox, 2007).

Mesa Verde: 500 to 1300 CE

With the decline of Chaco Canyon, the center of Ancestral Pueblo power passed north to the Four Corners region, notably to the Great Sage Plain and a wider area

10.12 A Mimbres bowl painted with enigmatic human figures, possibly representing the contrast between life and death, or male and female. The hole through the base "killed" the object, helping release the vessel's spirit into the next world. Diameter: approximately 11.8 in. (30 cm).

10.13 A Mimbres bowl showing the Guardians of the Four Directions. Diameter: approximately 11.8 in. (30 cm).

north and west of the San Juan Basin—the Mesa Verde area. This was a slightly wetter environment than much of the Southwest, with juniper and piñon cover and many natural water sources. But rainfall was still unpredictable, leading to cycles of scarcity and abundance.

During the twelfth, and especially the thirteenth, centuries, hundreds of Ancestral Pueblo households moved from dispersed communities into large pueblos by rivers and in sheltered valleys. Some populations lived in pueblos built into natural rock shelters in the walls of deep canyons, with one concentration in the Mesa Verde area (Figure 10.14). Between 1200 and 1300 CE the focus of settlement moved south from the area around Chapin Mesa to Cliff and Fewkes Canyons. Fewkes Canyon supported at least thirty-three habitation sites

10.14 The Mug House, Wetherill Mesa, Colorado.

10.15 The Cliff Palace at Mesa Verde, Colorado.

10.16 Artist's reconstruction of Sand Canyon Pueblo, southwestern Colorado, by Glenn Felch.

with between 530 and 545 rooms and sixty kivas. The Cliff Palace, with its 220 masonry rooms and twenty-three kivas, has a spectacular setting but actually differs little from large pueblos elsewhere (Figure 10.15). People had moved from living in open locations to shelters and ledges in canyon walls, perhaps as a defensive measure. Only a few precipitous trails led from the canyon to the plateau farmlands above.

Not that Mesa Verde was the main center of settlement. The nearby Great Sage Plain supported fourteen pueblos larger than the Cliff and Fewkes Canyon villages (Varien et al., 2007). The largest in the region, Yellow Jacket, contains between 660 and 1,200 rooms in 42 architectural blocks, about 195 kivas, and 19 towers, and had a peak population of 850–1,360 people, more than all of Mesa Verde. Another large settlement, Sand Canyon Pueblo in southwestern Colorado, boasted about 400 to 600 inhabitants (Figure 10.16). Sand Canyon surrounded a large spring, as did other major towns in the area. Around 1250 the residents-to-be erected an impressive enclosure wall, which may have taken thirty to forty people two months to build. Over the next thirty years they added over twenty separate room blocks, which incorporated at least ninety kivas and about 420 rooms. Every household maintained its own identity in its cluster of structures—a living space, storage room, place to eat, and a kiva—just as they had in their original dispersed settlements. At the same time, multiple households dwelt within a single architectural complex, as if the wider ties of the kinship group had become more important than in earlier times.

The thirteenth century saw the culmination of seven centuries of rapid social and political development. Then, in about 1300 CE, the Ancestral Pueblo people abandoned the entire San Juan drainage, including Mesa Verde, perhaps because of prolonged droughts. Potential agricultural productivity varied considerably from place to place and from year to year (see Box: Scarcity and Abundance). The farmers tended to locate near consistently productive soils. They could survive the harshest of drought cycles if there were no restrictions on mobility or on access to the best soils, and if they could acquire food from neighbors when crops failed. Their ability to move, however, was severely restricted once population densities approached the carrying capacity of the land and the people had effectively cultivated all the most productive soils (Varien et al., 2017). At that point surviving extreme short-term climatic change was much harder, especially when longer-term climatic cycles happened to coincide with a serious drought cycle, as happened during the major drought of 1276 to 1299 CE. Pueblo construction slowed and ceased altogether by 1290.

By 1300 the great pueblos of the Four Corners were silent. The Ancestral Pueblo people dispersed widely and joined distant communities in less drought-affected regions. They moved south and southeastward into the lands of the historic Hopi, Zuni, and Rio Grande pueblos, where they retained a similar community organization, with villages and larger communities, perhaps better called towns. They developed new social and religious ideas over many generations of cultural uncertainty, until stability returned with improved environmental conditions after 1450 CE.

Shorter-term, high-frequency changes were risks readily apparent to every Ancestral Pueblo community: year-to-year rainfall shifts, decade-long drought cycles, seasonal changes, and so on. These required flexible adjustments, such

SCARCITY AND ABUNDANCE

The northern Southwest is often assumed to have been a landscape where food resources were scarce and agriculture was high risk because of unpredictable rainfall and a short growing season. Yet Ancestral Pueblo people flourished in the area for thousands of years. Recent multidisciplinary research has shown that the modern-day Tewa-speaking people of the region are among their descendants (Ortman, 2012). The issue of ancestry is still being debated. A project using computer modeling has reconstructed Ancestral Pueblo crop yields in the Mesa Verde region (Kohler, 2012). These models have shown that the ancient maize farmers did indeed experience periods of scarcity. But they also experienced periods when crop yields were abundant. From this information we can examine how constantly changing yields shaped the lives of Ancestral Pueblo people.

Maize was the staple of northern Southwestern life, proven by bone-chemistry studies of skeletons that show people acquired at least 70 percent of their calories from corn. The computer modeling used tree-rings to estimate rainfall and temperature for every year between 600 CE and today. The study area was divided into 110,000 cells, each with an area of 9.8 acres (4 ha). Every cell had its accumulated soil moisture each year calculated using elevation and soil characteristics. The statistical relationship between this measure and crop yields was calculated for the historic period, the results being used to extrapolate back to 600 CE. Many other variables were taken into account, including changing farming technology and planting strategies. The study showed that Ancestral Pueblo people had to cope with agricultural yields that changed every year. Between 600 and 1300 CE yields were close to long-term average about 70 percent of the time, with 230 years above average and 263 years below. But 30 percent of the 700-year interval saw more extreme variation, with 140 years when yields would have been exceptionally abundant and 104 years—about 1 in 7—when yields would have been catastrophically low or even non-existent (Figure 10.17). Even then, there were constant swings between relatively abundant and scarce years. All this data maps closely onto modern Tewa experience and belief.

The study of abundance and scarcity went further. The research teams studied cooking jars from Mesa Verde pueblo households and found that the rate of accumulation of such vessels changed little over time. The steady rate of accumulation of cooking jars could be compared with that of other pottery forms. This study showed that pottery bowls became more abundant through time, and the diversity of clay vessel as farming more land, relying more heavily on wild plant foods, and, above all, exchange and movement. When the population increased, as it did at Chaco Canyon in the twelfth century, and in the Four Corners region a century later, people farmed more marginal areas, the most likely to fail during dry years. Their vulnerability was even more extreme when long-term changes—such as a half-century or more of much drier conditions—descended on farming land already pushed to its carrying limits. The productive landscape then became more uneven, which could result in conflict and other social crises that are almost impossible to detect archaeologically. Archaeologist Steven LeBlanc has drawn attention to the links between surges in warfare and periods of drought and other climatic stresses in the Southwest, but all kinds of factors were interwoven when surges of violence occurred, notably in the period between 1140 and 1180.

Katcinas and Warriors: 1300 CE to European Contact

The changes of the late thirteenth century changed the social landscape of the Southwest. The focus of human settlement moved south and east to areas of greater summer rains, such as the Rio Grande Valley and the Zuni region in the west of central New Mexico. More people moved from villages into bigger communities, some of them much larger than the greatest pueblos of earlier times. Not that these aggregations were permanent, for, as in earlier centuries,

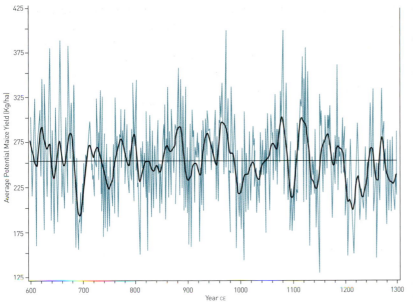

10.17 Annual estimates of maize productivity for the Mesa Verde region, 600–1300 CE, developed by the Village Ecodynamics Project. The average study-area yields in kilograms/hectare per year CE, with the mean annual yield of 254 kg/ha shown for comparison. The unsmoothed yields are in light gray and the spline smoothed ones in black. Bars more than two standard deviations above the mean are unusually wet years with high productivity. Those with more than a single standard deviation below the mean are unusually dry years with low productivity.

forms also increased; this may be a measure of the increasing plenty in Mesa Verde peoples' lives.

Other researchers have asked how these periods of scarcity and abundance affected the lived experiences of Pueblo people (Varien et al., 2017). A Tewa elder who participated in the research confirmed that the people think of abundance and scarcity as linked realities occurring in cycles. The one cannot exist without the other. The Tewa have a basic philosophy, which assumes that a basic life force is part of creation. They call it *p'o wa ha*, "water, wind, breath." They believe that this concept of a life force flourished far back in the past, when their ancestors lived in the Mesa Verde region between about 600 and 1285 CE. They achieve a connection to the life force by living their lives according to Tewa values, among which are the importance of community, respecting the elders, hard work, and sharing with others. In other words, abundance ▶▶

local populations fluctuated and pueblos rose to prominence, then were abandoned or became mere shadows of their former selves.

The pueblos of the Rio Grande Valley, one of the few perennial rivers in the Southwest, epitomize this constant change. Until the twelfth and thirteenth centuries relatively few people lived in the valley. Then the population swelled rapidly, both as a result of local growth and from migration from the north and northwest. Several pueblo sites, notably Arroyo Hondo, just south of modern-day Santa Fé, reflect not continual growth but the ebb and flow so characteristic of Rio Grande settlements (Creamer, 1993) (Figure 10.18). A single-room block rose at Arroyo Hondo by 1315 CE. Within fifteen years about 1,200 two-story rooms arranged over twenty-four blocks centered around thirteen plazas. Just as quickly, the great pueblo emptied; it was almost deserted by the mid-1330s. A second cycle of growth followed in the 1370s and 1380s, with the building of 200 rooms, but these were destroyed by a fire in 1410.

10.18 Aerial view of Arroyo Hondo Pueblo, New Mexico.

and scarcity are both material and spiritual realities.

Another sign of abundance was the increasing prevalence of feasting. Pueblo feasts were much less political and less lavish than in many other small-scale societies. They were more like the modern-day potluck: everyone brought food prepared at home, more fortunate households providing more. Food was often distributed to the less fortunate in a manner similar to the way it is distributed by masked **katcinas** today. This ensured that food abundance was shared across the community. Such ceremonies took place at villages rather than tiny hamlets, as these could accommodate the entire community.

The earliest evidence for communal feasting comes from the Dillard village west of Cortez, Colorado, which dates to the seventh century CE. The Basketmaker III village is centered on a great kiva, with two clusters of pit structures. Large numbers of bowls associated with the great kiva are evidence of feasting. An early Pueblo settlement known as Sacred Ridge, on a tributary of the Animas River and dating between 700 and 825, has unusually large pit structures where, once again, large numbers of bowls testify to feasting. McPhee Pueblo in the Dolores River Valley, where population peaked between 850 and 900 CE, had two room blocks; the U-shaped blocks created small spaces where feasts of deer and rabbit meat, using imported red bowls, took place. Finally, Sand Canyon Pueblo, dating to between about 1250 and 1285 CE, had between 400 and 600 residents, and was thus one of the largest villages during the final Pueblo occupation. A great kiva, a plaza, and a D-shaped bi-wall structure testify to intense ritual and ceremonial feasting here. There were also numerous large cooking and serving vessels, perhaps used to cater for greater numbers of people. Unlike at McPhee, feasting here involved boiling profuse quantities of food, probably maize and beans. By this time the accumulation of food surpluses had reached a point where there may have been a communal storage facility, and community surpluses were perhaps controlled by a political leadership. Such organization would have allowed the leaders to redistribute food publically as a way of validating their position—a situation akin to that of the Northwestern potlatch.

This painstaking, multidisciplinary research provides clear evidence that Pueblo communities were well aware of the cycle of abundance and scarcity, the one balanced against the other. This explains why the Tewa and other Pueblo peoples value community and sharing, and the establishment of extensive kin ties over considerable distances, so highly. Feasting was and is an expression of these values, but is today more restrained than it appears to have been in earlier times.

The history of Arroyo Hondo reflects a remarkable social fluidity characterized by repeated movements of entire groups, some of whom traveled distances of several hundred miles from the Mesa Verde region and elsewhere. One reason for this fluidity lay in the larger size of these growing settlements in an unpredictable environment where maize cultivation was always unreliable. At Arroyo Hondo, for example, even the best agricultural land could feed no more than 400 to 600 people in an average year, making it hard to accumulate adequate food reserves against drought years. The farmers tried to minimize famine by irrigating river lands and planting better-watered fields at higher elevations. Despite the difficulties, Arroyo Hondo and similar sites across much of the Southwest were used over long periods.

By the fourteenth century there was frequent warfare. Pueblos now rose in easily defended locations. Sometimes groups of settlements clustered together for protection, as they did in the Rio Grande Valley and the Hopi-Cibola region, with long distances between them. There were also major changes in Pueblo ritual, marked by new styles of kiva murals, pervasive decorative styles on ceramics, and much larger plazas. The plazas became important settings for public ceremonies, especially katcina (*katchina*) dances. Katcinas play a prominent role in modern-day Pueblo belief and ritual (Figure 10.19). They are ancestral spirits who serve as intermediaries between the living and the deities of the

10.19 Hopi artists carve wooden dolls to teach their children about the many katcinas that are important in Pueblo ritual.

ARCHAEOLOGY AND ORAL TRADITIONS

Southwest archaeology is at a turning point. It is the region with the highest density of archaeologists in North America, and most of them are engaged in CRM research. Databases are mushrooming, and a new era is dawning in which multidisciplinary research and close cooperation with Native American communities are at the forefront. We now have a burgeoning amount of data, which allows us to work on fundamental problems and to link archaeological findings and oral histories into respectful, accurate narratives of the past. The Zuni tribe offer an interesting starting point (Gregory and Wilcox, 2007).

The Zuni people have occupied their homeland for over 1,000 years. They reside in a cultural landscape with named places used by them to symbolize and recall the remote past. That past is projected into the contemporary world by defining and understanding this landscape. Zuni traditional history and cultural geography are an independent source of historical information. Their oral traditions are passed down the generations by many channels, among them kiva groups, priesthoods, and religious societies. There are many instances where the archaeology and Zuni accounts diverge. Herein lies the challenge. How does one explain these differences while still respecting both the archaeological evidence and traditional knowledge? The Zuni have a dynamic view of the past that involves their ancestors, who traveled widely in constant migrations. Archaeologists work with relatively static archaeological cultures as a framework for history. At present we have hardly begun to develop the methodology to use Zuni oral traditions in archaeological research.

The Zuni have a rich body of well-recorded oral tradition, including "from the beginning talks" that describe their emergence and subsequent migration to Zuni Pueblo, the "Middle Place." *Telapnawe*, folktales or legends, which mainly revolve around the Zuni Valley, are often recited to teach the young, or simply for entertainment. Among them are "prayer talks"—chants or prayers recited during ceremonies. They are often repetitions of fixed formulae performed with gestures and oral elaborations. There are many such talks that begin with the emergence from the lower world and the search for the Middle Place. There are all kinds of narratives that older men use to pass on the main outlines of Zuni history to the young in kivas on such occasions as the winter solstice. Other accounts are shared within families around the hearth during the winter. These oral traditions are alive and ever-changing, but once written down they inevitably become a more static view of history.

Numerous sources document Zuni oral traditions. Frank Cushing was the first to do so, identifying locations associated with both the origin and subsequent migrations, which he published in a somewhat poetic style. Subsequent efforts added to the original collections in sober anthropological terms, as did the photographer Edward Curtis, celebrated for his images of the Zuni and other Native Americans.

supernatural world, as well as bringing rain in clouds that they summon to the pueblos. Katcinas are present on earth between the winter and summer solstices. For the other half of the year they live in the San Francisco Peaks, to which they return through the *sipapu*. Katcina dancers, males who assume the sacred powers of the spirit, wear costumes and masks that impersonate the ancestral spirits during their stay on earth.

Perhaps the elaboration of katcina rituals was a way of binding together the inhabitants of the large, densely populated pueblos. Everyone in the community was part of a katcina society, whose membership cut across potentially divisive kin and lineage lines while ensuring that public ceremonies were conducted properly. Cooperative behavior was vital for survival, and katcina rituals, with their emphasis on rainmaking (as well as warfare), provided important social guidelines and validation for the community as a whole.

Paquime (Casas Grandes): Fourteenth Century CE

Long-distance trade flourished throughout the Southwest, even in troubled times, as such commodities as turquoise, tropical bird feathers, cotton, toolmaking stone,

Religious leaders gave invaluable testimony during litigation of Zuni land claims in 1980s, which provided information given under oath about sites used by the tribe for both utilitarian and ritual purposes. The resulting *A Zuni Atlas* maps 234 land-use sites inside and outside the claimed area (Ferguson and Hart, 1985).

From these sources comes a summary that begins with the Zuni people emerging at a place named *Chimik'yana'kya dey'a*, deep in a canon along the Colorado River. Divine instruction taught them all manner of prayers, rituals, and sacred talks before emergence. Once in the world, and guided by their religious societies, they migrated along what is now the Little Colorado River. Along the way they stopped and occupied villages for "four days and four nights," a symbolic expression of a longer, unspecified time. At one of the springs along the way they assumed the appearance of humans. In the Lower Colorado River Valley the people were given a choice of eggs that caused them to split into several groups. Those who chose a brightly colored blue egg continued toward the Middle Place, but split into three groups. After numerous adventures the main group founded a series of settlements in the Zuni Valley, eventually settling at *Halona: Itiwana*, the Middle Place, now Zuni Pueblo.

Research is ongoing to identify the places mentioned in the oral traditions, both the place of emergence and the various locations where the migrants paused and founded villages, also places of symbolic and ritual importance. But can one take these historical accounts too literally? As Zuni interpreters of the oral traditions point out, the journeys mentioned in chants and prayers do not describe exact routes. They tell us that ancestors of the modern-day Zuni traveled over a wide area of the Southwest, some of it outside the present homeland. The challenge for archaeologists, and for Zuni historians, is to reconcile different perspectives on the ancestors, who lived in what archaeologists refer to as the Mogollon area.

This concern with traditional histories is part of a new chapter in the archaeology of the Southwest, and of North America generally. Over the generations we have moved from studying artifacts and chronology to a concern with how ancient societies changed through time. As part of this effort we have focused on changes to landscapes and regions, and on changing patterns of settlement, with promising results. Now we are moving into a new era, in which we are more concerned with what people did, as oral histories are, and can use the vast quantities of raw data now at our disposal to examine a fundamental and much wider question: how did the pueblos come to be as they are? For the first time we are combining data from many sources—archaeology, climatology, and linguistics, to name but three—which will allow us to write the Southwestern past as a comprehensive social history that moves beyond modern-day cultural identities. This is the fascinating challenge for future generations.

and buffalo hides passed along ancient trade routes. The Casas Grandes area of Chihuahua in northern Mexico lies in relatively high-altitude basin and range country and is centered on a wide, fertile valley long inhabited by an indigenous farming population (Whalen and Minnis, 2001). By about the fourteenth century the inhabitants of this valley had congregated in a large settlement known as Paquime (or Casas Grandes) (Figure 10.20). Initially, Paquime consisted of twenty or more house clusters, each with a plaza and enclosing wall. The people lived in single-story adobe houses, with a single water system for the entire settlement. One compound contained rows of rectangular adobe boxes apparently

10.20 Aerial view of Casas Grandes, Chihuahua, northern Mexico, showing a ball court, lower right, and excavation of room blocks, lower left corner.

used for breeding macaws for their colorful feathers—pollen analyses have yielded traces of the nesting material, even eggshell fragments, skeletons, and traces of wooden perches. Paquime may have been one of the sources of macaws for Ancestral Pueblo communities far to the north. Macaw feathers were widely used in Pueblo rituals and were attached to ceremonial regalia and prayer sticks. They served as conduits to the supernatural.

During the fourteenth century as many as 2,240 people lived in what was now a thriving town, with multistory dwellings, I-shaped ball courts, stone-faced platform and effigy mounds, a market area, and elaborate water-storage systems. At the height of its power Paquime lay at the center of a small region, its influence perhaps extending about 18 miles (30 km) from the town. Like the earlier settlements of the Chaco Phenomenon, Paquime did not flourish for long, gradually falling into disrepair and being abandoned in the fifteenth century. The large towns of the southern desert were vacated, as simpler social institutions prevailed in another cycle of movement and downsizing. The Zuni and Hopi pueblos, however, endured, together with those of Acoma and the Rio Grande Valley, and others to the east, to witness the arrival of Spanish conquistadors in the sixteenth century.

SUMMARY

- Between 600 and 900 CE village settlement expanded greatly throughout the northern Southwest and especially on the Colorado Plateau.

- Chaco Canyon came to prominence before 900, when people moved into masonry dwellings on the south side of the canyon, where soils were most fertile. During the ninth century groups from the north settled on the north side, where the first four Great Houses were erected after 850.

- By the eleventh century Chaco was the hub of a much wider world at the height of the Chaco Phenomenon. These dispersed communities interacted with one another constantly, many of them linked by a road system that may have formed an ideological web. Pueblo Bonito became an important ritual center. Much of the ritual surrounded the passage of the seasons and maize. In 1130 a severe drought cycle led to the dispersal of Chaco's population, part of the constant ebb and flow of Pueblo existence.

- In what is now southern Arizona the Hohokam farming tradition, based on irrigation agriculture, flourished between 459 and 1450. By 1150 there were larger Hohokam communities, such as Snaketown, where communal life centered around ball courts and feasting, trading, and rituals that reinforced community identities. A small elite emerged after 1150, when platform mounds came into use.

- The upland Mogollon with its spectacular Mimbres ceramics flourished between 1000 and 1130.

- With the decline of Chaco, the center of political gravity moved to the Four Corners region—the Mesa Verde area. The Great Sage Plain supported fourteen substantial pueblos, the largest of which was Yellow Jacket. Probably because of intense drought, the great pueblos of the Four Corners were abandoned by 1300.

- The social landscape of the Southwest changed in the late thirteenth century, a period of constant movement and, during the fourteenth century, constant warfare. New forms of ritual reflected new religious beliefs and a concern with ancestors, reflected in katcina ceremonies.

- The great challenge for future generations is marrying archaeological findings with oral histories, like those of the Zuni.

- Long-distance trade flourished up to European contact, especially at sites like Paquime (Casas Grandes) in extreme northern Mexico.

Early and Middle Woodland: Adena and Hopewell

Ohio Valley, early summer, 100 CE. The log-lined tomb lies on a river terrace, a place where the nearby stream defined the world Below, the hemispherical mounds the realm of the Above. Mourners covered the roofed-in grave with a layer of clay as darkness fell. The shaman chanted at the beginning of an all-night vigil. As the sun rises, men from near and far dig loose soil from the terrace above the river. They shovel it with digging sticks and hoes into large baskets, then heft them one by one slightly upslope to the flat burial area. Basket by basket, the villagers empty their loads in carefully arranged piles, working out from the center, sometimes varying the color of the soil used for different layers. The work moves slowly and methodically, with a break as the sun beats down mercilessly at midday. Everyone sits in the shade, drinks copious drafts of water, and eats. As the day cools, the work resumes. At day's end a tiny mound has risen above the grave. The shaman watches silently, day after day, as the tumulus becomes an imposing, manmade hillock and part of the surrounding ritual landscape.

A Trajectory of Change: c. 1000 BCE

1000 BCE is widely used as the boundary between the Archaic and the Woodland Periods (Anderson and Sassaman, 2012). As mentioned in Chapter 3, the generic term Woodland is often used to describe a wide diversity of hunter-gatherer societies in the Eastern Woodlands region. These societies are ultimately augmented with some cultivation, manufacture of pottery, and more elaborate ritual and trade activities.

At 1000 BCE Eastern Woodlands societies lived in small seasonal camps or hamlets. They subsisted for the most part off hunting and fishing, and wild plants. Some communities also grew some domesticated local plants, but not maize. As populations increased, territories became smaller and options for food-collecting were restricted. Many homelands were inadequate to supply basic nutritional requirements even of a stable population. Inevitably, the people turned to new food-gathering strategies. They could draw on generations-old kin contacts, reciprocal ties that ensured everyone shared food supplies. They could trade for basic foodstuffs with more fortunate neighbors, or take up residence with relatives to obtain food in times of need. They could also use technological solutions, developing more effective food-storage systems to tide them over lean months. Some groups also used their food-gathering technology to clear natural vegetation, to create space within their territories where they could cultivate several food species. These Late Archaic strategies, including small-scale cultivation, were effective for many centuries, being progressively adopted by numerous groups throughout the east after about 2000 BCE. It was much later, after about 800 CE in the American Bottom near St. Louis, and some two centuries later in the Midsouth, that the cultivators intensified their efforts, modifying the landscape on a large scale (Chapter 12).

In this transition between the Late Archaic and Woodland, people began to discourage weeds to encourage the spread of economically useful plants, thereby managing natural stands of the latter. This simple process of encouraging, intervening, and deliberately planting harvested seeds, even on a small scale, marked the beginnings of deliberate cultivation—if sustained in the longer term. At this point automatic selection within the affected plant population begins, with minimal effort by human beings. Their casual efforts at encouragement result in an ever more dependable, abundant, and easily monitored local food resource. Thus, human land clearance and genetic changes in plants may have been a major factor in the emergence of horticulture in eastern North America independently of elsewhere.

As the Woodland period unfolded, so contacts between communities near and far increased significantly. These interactions coincided with much better defined territories and rising populations, and with an intensified concern with burial, mortuary rituals, and honoring the ancestors, which were reflected in the construction of mounds and earthworks.

There was nothing new about earthen construction, which had assumed considerable importance during the Late Archaic—witness the extensive Poverty

11.1 Map showing archaeological sites and cultural complexes described in Chapters 11 and 12.

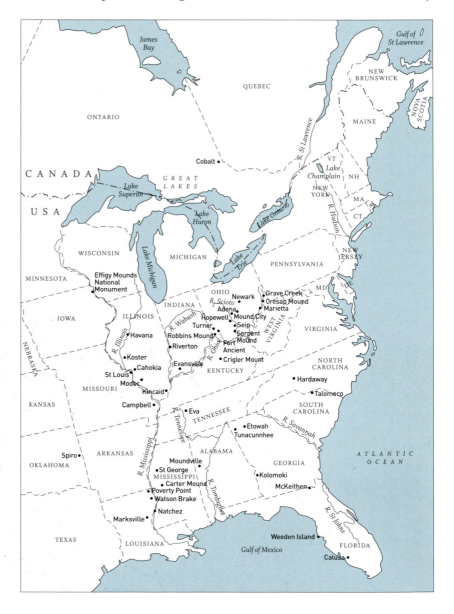

Point and Watson Brake sites discussed in Chapter 8 (both much earlier than, and quite separate from, later earthwork building traditions), and the shell midden earthworks of the Middle Archaic. The mounds and earthworks did not necessarily contain burials, for some may have served as territorial markers or symbols of clan identity in increasingly crowded landscapes. After 500 BCE burial mounds were an important part of mortuary ceremonialism from the western Appalachians to the Mississippi Valley, and north into Wisconsin and Michigan.

Early Woodland: Adena, c. 500 BCE to the First Century CE

The Early Woodland was a time of great cultural diversification, marked by interactions between different communities and groups over longer distances than before, and by increasing cultural complexity. A generic term—"Adena," or "Adena Complex"—covers dozens of local Early and sometimes Middle Woodland cultures (c. 200 BCE to 400 CE) that were contemporary, often close neighbors, and interacted with one another continuously (Webb and Snow, 1945). Such societies were remarkable for their diverse artifacts, widespread trading contacts, and burial ceremonialism. We can trace Adena from Indiana's Whitewater River Valley in the west to Pittsburgh in the Upper Ohio River Valley in the east, and from the Blue Grass of central Kentucky north to the upper reaches of the Scioto and Muskingum of Ohio. Mounds and Adena artifacts also occur elsewhere, as far away as the Canadian Maritimes and mid-Atlantic states (Figure 11.1).

The central and upper Ohio River Valley witnessed a flowering of mound construction in this period (Dragoo, 1963; Muller, 2016). Despite increasingly elaborate burial practices, most settlements were still small, often no more than one or two houses. Judging from the close attention paid to the dead, there was a major concern with, and reverence for, the ancestors, reflected in sometimes elaborate funeral rites. Specific burial customs varied greatly from simple to complex (Figure 11.2). Sometimes people started with a small mound that covered the burial of a single person in a shallow, elliptical pit lined and covered with

11.2 The Adena Mound in Ross County, Ohio, excavated in 1901.

11.3 Excavation of the much-reduced Crigler Mound, Kentucky, exposing the original ground surface, also paired posts and four internal supports for a structure.

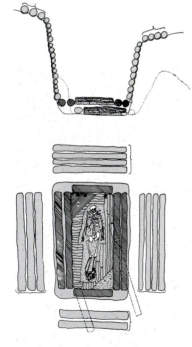

11.4 Cross-section and plan of an Adena burial from the Wright Mound, Kentucky.

bark. A mound could also be erected over a circular structure, more likely a ritual enclosure than a roofed house, often associated with human remains (Figure 11.3). The mound rose steadily as more and more burials joined the sepulcher. Some interments were of entire bodies, perhaps wrapped simply in bark, while others were of cremated remains. Occasionally the mourners simply deposited a bundle of bones, as if the body had been exposed on an open platform until the flesh decayed—or perhaps the dead person died away from home and the bones were brought back for burial. Some important burials lay with a long-defleshed skull placed on the lap. One such find at the Cresap Mound in West Virginia bore a slight polish, as if it had been treasured and handled regularly for some time (see Box: Cresap Mound, West Virginia).

The most impressive tombs were built with large logs lining the sides and floor and making up the roof. The mourners often sprinkled the dead with powdered red ocher, sometimes with yellow ocher, graphite, or manganese dioxide in small amounts (Figure 11.4). The corpse might be painted with red-ocher paint as well. The paint was prepared on crude stone tablets, convenient thin slabs of limestone, sandstone, and other rocks. Some tablets are deeply grooved by the rubbing of pieces of hematite (used as coloring pigment). Other than the burials, there are few signs of any social distinction between individuals in these societies.

Many mounds were used again and again, with more log tombs and other burials being added to an existing tumulus. Burial areas can be thought of as stacked cemeteries, such as the Robbins Mound in northern Kentucky. Some of the largest and most elaborate mounds lie in the central Ohio Valley; one example is the famous Grave Creek Mound at Moundsville, West Virginia, which was originally over 65 ft (20 m) high, with a volume of nearly 2.47 million cubic feet (70,000 m³) (Figure 11.5).

The Adenans sometimes built circular earthen enclosures, consisting of shallow ditches and adjacent embankments, near their burial mounds. These "sacred circles" may have been the meeting places for the kin group using the

CRESAP MOUND, WEST VIRGINIA

The Cresap Mound, on a terrace on the eastern side of the Ohio River, was a conical tumulus about 70 ft (21.2 m) in diameter and about 15 ft (4.55 m) high. Don Dragoo's excavations in 1958 helped define the Adena Complex in much greater detail than before. He uncovered four stages in the mound's history. The earliest was a wooden structure surrounded by a circular trench. Here the builders laid burials in bark-lined tombs, cremations and isolated skulls in fired pits, and some burials on the floor of the mound. Then they burnt down the structure and covered the burial area with 6.75 ft (2.05 m) of earthen fill. Not that the fill was sterile, for cremations and further burials, as well as burial bundles (which contained bones of the dead), were mingled in the soil. This was clearly a sacred place for at least several generations, long enough for a thin layer of humus to form on the surface.

A second stage followed at Cresap Mound, with more burials and cremations placed in natural depressions and in further fill earth, which increased the mound to a height of 8.2 ft (2.48 m). More humus formed before a third stage involved the digging of a depression in the earlier fill, where the mourners deposited ten burials, some of them in the earth piled above it. Sufficient time for thick humus to develop preceded the fourth and final stage. This time the builders placed extended, cremated, and fragmentary burials around a hearth, then piled more soil on top of them, bringing the mound up to about 15 ft (4.5 m).

The fifty-two known Cresap burials included twenty extended interments, eighteen skulls, seven cremations, three burial bundles, and four child burials. Thirty-four burials lay with grave goods that included stone artifacts, copper and shell objects, and a few bone artifacts. Dragoo used the Cresap excavation and a survey of Adena sites in the Ohio valley to distinguish between an Early and Late Adena. Early Adena burials in the lower levels were notable for their tubular pipes and stemmed stone points, while Late Adena individuals lay with gorgets, and finely made tablets, as well as stone points characteristic of the previously excavated Robbins Mound in northwestern Kentucky. Radiocarbon dates suggest the mound was first constructed in the last few centuries BCE, and the middle levels piled up around 2,000 years ago; the upper burials are undated.

The Cresap burials provide no evidence of an elaborate social hierarchy with powerful chieftains. Most likely Adena society was one where group leaders emerged as required, for example to organize communal projects, such as burial-mound construction.

11.5 The Grave Creek Mound at Moundsville, West Virginia.

11.6 A birdstone from Flint County, Georgia. Length: 4 ⅜ in. (11.1 cm).

associated tumulus. Perhaps the individuals buried in log tombs in the mounds were important kin leaders. Sometimes the sacred enclosures occur in groups of two to eight, as if people from different social units were congregating at the same location.

Adena burials carried a rich variety of grave goods with them, especially the individuals interred in log tombs. These included copper bracelets and finger rings. There were crescents and sheets fabricated from North Carolina mica, some marine shells, and bracelets, axes, and other items made from Lake Superior copper. There were many forms of gorgets and distinctive atlatl weights. Pipe designs included carved animal effigies. Tubular Ohio pipestone pipes, used to generate kinnikinnick smoke (a herbal concoction), traveled through exchange networks as far away as Ontario, New England, and Maryland. Some other characteristic grave goods that traveled widely include large, leaf-shaped spearheads and knives, often made of bluish gray hornstone from Indiana or Illinois; these artifacts are sometimes found in caches. Perhaps such point collections were exchanged as gifts. Carved effigies long known as "birdstones" and "boatstones" replace the bannerstones of the Late Archaic. Birdstones are not, in fact, bird effigies, but composite animals, sometimes shown with four feet, perhaps depicting a divinity associated with sky and earth (Figure 11.6).

Several Adena mounds have yielded wolf palates, each carefully trimmed, with the upper and lower incisors removed, so that they could be worn in a man's mouth. At least one human skull with the front teeth knocked out long before death has been found associated with a wolf palate. Presumably this was done so the palate could be inserted into the person's mouth, the skin of the wolf head fitting over the head. Some of these artifacts may have been shamans' masks, or were used in rituals that depicted the symbolic relationships between familiar animals and different clans.

All experts agree that Adena burial traditions developed from Late Archaic roots in the Ohio Valley. There were Adena sites along every major tributary stream of the Ohio River from southeastern Indiana to central Pennsylvania by 2,000 years ago, with great concentrations of burial mounds in some well-defined areas—the Scioto Valley of south-central Ohio, the Kanawha River in West Virginia, and around Cincinnati, Ohio, to mention only three. Perhaps these reflect a tendency toward concentration within tribal territories.

Lineages and Clans

Why did Adena and other mortuary complexes develop? Early Woodland burial complexes were highly localized; Adena was one, Red Paint in the Northeast, marked by liberal use of ocher, another. They flourished alongside dozens of Late Archaic communities that still lived as they had done for centuries. Perhaps, as territorial boundaries became more marked and interaction between neighbors increased, so membership of social groups assumed much greater importance, for it was these lineages and clans that controlled access to food and other resources. It is probably no coincidence that the Early Woodland sees a continuing trend toward at least semi-sedentary settlement, with people living at one base location for many months on end. This may have helped foster a growing sense of corporate identity, reinforced by regular burial ceremonies at earthworks.

One finds a similar concern with kin ties and corporate links in regions other than the Eastern Woodlands, not necessarily reflected in burial customs, but in art, and even in the layout of dwellings. In areas where the food situation was often precarious, different groups were probably careful to maintain rights of access to resources located outside their own territories, as a form of "insurance" against lean years when frosts or other natural phenomena seriously depleted local foods. People used social processes to maintain exchange networks not only to handle food, but also to maintain access to resources of restricted distribution at a distance.

Judging from living societies, the main participants in such exchange systems would have been lineage leaders, individuals honored at death with special artifacts and funeral ceremonies, and adorned with the ceremonial items that indicated their social roles. Thus, burial rites not only validated group identity, but also commemorated the status of prominent kin leaders. These individuals were those who organized community work efforts by clan members when needed—to erect burial mounds, construct earthworks, and carry out other projects that were to the collective benefit. Such clan leaders were buried with prized high-status goods, such as mica sheets, copper ornaments, and carved pipes, that proclaimed their owner's social standing and maintained their high prestige by vanishing below the ground (Figure 11.7).

As David Brose argues (1994), such mechanisms provided increasing social and economic stability, reinforced trends toward sedentary living and specialized exploitation of local resources, and probably led to population growth. This growth in turn triggered additional responses—more clearly ranked and better-integrated social systems that replaced the relatively flexible ones of earlier times. Brose believes that there was what he calls a "trajectory" of long-term cultural change. These changes first developed in areas where there was maximal pressure on the land, or where it had very low carrying capacity. The more closely integrated social systems emphasized prestige differences within individual lineages, validated by exotic objects of great importance and by seasonal ceremonies when all the members of lineages, from near and far, came together to reinforce their social identity and common goals. About 2,000 years ago this trajectory of cultural change led to far more elaborate social institutions and ceremonial life, which culminated in the spectacular Hopewell Tradition, with its extensive sacred landscapes (Lynott, 2014).

Middle Woodland: The Hopewell Tradition, c. 200 BCE to c. 400 CE

Adena was by no means the only Early Woodland moundbuilding complex, but it was the earliest and is the best known. The increasingly elaborate mortuary rituals of Adena groups culminated in the much greater complexity of both astronomical and cosmological thinking achieved by their Hopewell successors, who created impressive sacred landscapes centered on the Ohio Valley and stretching much further afield (Lynott, 2014; Romain, 2015). Hopewell influence extended far from its Midwestern homelands in Illinois and Ohio to Marksville in the Lower Mississippi Valley, while many contemporary societies in the East and Southeast also shared Hopewell mortuary customs, ritual and religious beliefs, and artifact styles.

11.7 A stone effigy pipe in the form of a human, from the Adena Mound, Ohio. Height: 7 in. (20 cm).

The Hopewell Tradition, named after a mound complex on a farm in Ross County, Ohio, is famous for its earthworks, its elaborate burial customs, and its complex networks that moved raw materials and finished artifacts over vey wide areas. Hopewell is a "great tradition," or an ideology in the spiritual sense, a set of understandings shared by numerous small regional societies over much of the Midwest. Hopewell beliefs and rituals had deep roots in the past and revolved around a close and ever-changing relationship with the landscape and the spiritual realm, also sometimes with the ancestors. This shared belief system helped facilitate trade and communication over long distances. Many communities lay in areas defined by local drainage systems, with household sites, specialized camps, and ritual precincts. As Eastern Woodland society grew ever more complex—a complexity which had begun to develop in Poverty Point days, and now accelerated—more sophisticated forms of secular and spiritual leadership also came into being.

Whether Hopewell originated in Adena is still an open question, but we know that it developed earliest in the Illinois Valley, from previous inhabitants between 250 and 150 BCE. Illinois Hopewell smoking pipes and ceremonial ware, which define the complex, developed in situ in the central Illinois Valley, very likely in Fulton County. We do not know where the idea for the Illinois Hopewell log-tomb crypts came from, but it may have been adopted from Adena communities farther east. Ohio Hopewell, on the other hand, sprang directly from Adena roots, and is known from various ceremonial artifact classes, with the addition of Illinois Hopewell ceremonial using pipes. There are also later more southerly links: shell cup ceremonies in Illinois Hopewell probably derived from the Lower Mississippi Valley.

The religious beliefs that sustained Hopewell communities probably originated for the most part in Adena thinking. Numerous groups elaborated upon and changed established ritual and ceremonial themes to form the distinctive Hopewell cults. Some highly characteristic exotic artifacts, such as copper ornaments and pipes, were common to all. Some of these exotica passed from hand to hand via complex exchange networks, while others came directly from distant places and peoples—a suite of interregional linkages of multiple kinds. Hopewell interaction networks covered most of the Eastern Woodlands, from the Southeast into southeastern Canada. Most of these exotic materials were obtained by people living in major trading and manufacturing areas. In these areas the materials were then converted into finished artifacts or ornaments that were exported through local and regional exchange networks. For example, copper artifacts may have been exported from Ohio as far afield as Tennessee and the Deep South, and from New York to Iowa and Missouri. Characteristic Hopewell platform pipes fabricated of Sterling pipestone from northwestern Illinois are found from New York State west to Wisconsin and Iowa, and as far southwest as Hardin County, Illinois. There are also Hopewell-like burial mounds in Ontario, Canada.

The range of artifacts and materials is astonishing—native copper from the Lake Superior region, and silver from the same place and from deposits near Cobalt, Ontario (Figure 11.8). Mica and chlorite came from the southern Appalachians, quartz crystals from caverns near Hot Springs, Arkansas. The networks handled large marine shells from the Gulf of Mexico as well as smaller species from both the South Atlantic and Florida Gulf Coast. Galena cubes came from northwestern Illinois and Missouri, and colorful flint from central Ohio. Neutron activation studies of Hopewell obsidian reveal sources as far away as Bear Gulch in eastern Idaho, while flint came from the Knife River area of North Dakota. Characteristic Hopewell platform pipes were fabricated from Illinois and Ohio pipestone.

High concentrations of Hopewell-style artifacts are found in two core areas: the Mississippi and Illinois River valleys in Illinois, and the Scioto and Miami valleys in southern Ohio (Case and Carr, 2008). Each of these two areas, the one to the west, the other to the east, stands at the center of a large, interregional network. In time they overlapped with one another, but they never lost their own identities. The rate of exchange drops off sharply outside the Illinois/Ohio area, but it is clear that some ceremonial artifacts and beliefs spread much further afield into the Southeast. Such contacts were between individuals living at some distance from one another, often far from rivers, so this was a trade conducted along winding village paths. The character of the exchange system varied constantly, with cycles of expansion and contraction, but on the whole the diversity and number of ceremonial artifacts passed around the networks increased over the centuries. These symbolic artifacts carried intense ritual and social meaning. They became power symbols so important that they were buried with their owners at death.

The most spectacular Hopewell burial mounds are in the Ohio Valley. The Scioto Valley–Painted Creek area, near Chillicothe, was also a major center of Hopewell development in Ohio, and there are other significant Hopewell earthworks in the southwest of the state and in Marietta, Newark (Figure 11.9).

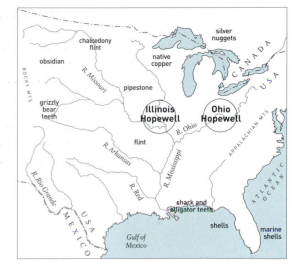

11.8 The far-flung sources of Hopewell raw materials.

11.9 The circular and octagonal Hopewell earthworks near Newark, Ohio.

11.10 An aerial view of the Hopewell Ohio Mound City complex, which covers areas equivalent to several New York City blocks, and greater than the base of the Old Kingdom Pyramid of Khufu in Egypt.

NEWARK AND THE GREAT HOPEWELL ROAD?

In about 250 CE the Hopewell people living near the modern city of Newark, Ohio, embarked on a major earthwork construction project, the largest such Hopewell complex. Over several generations they laid out an intricate maze of mounds, circles, an octagon, and a square (Jones and Shiels, 2016; Lepper, 2010; Lynott 2014). From the air the Newark earthworks seem like a jumble of enclosures and earthen mounds that defies ready explanation, especially since much of the site now lies under the city streets and a golf course. Fortunately for science, journalist Ephraim Squier and physician Edwin Davis surveyed the earthworks in the 1840s, when they were still largely intact (see Figure 11.9). The enclosures and mounds display an astonishing precision, with exact corners and precise astronomical orientation.

For example, the Newark octagon covers 44 acres (18 ha), with openings at each corner. A perfectly round "Observatory Circle" 1,054 ft (321 m) in diameter is attached to this octagon. This pair of earthworks is aligned with the moon, laid out with a standard unit of measurement and demonstrating a remarkable knowledge of geometry and astronomy. The Newark lunar alignments were probably accurate enough to predict the positions of the maximum and minimum north and south rising and setting points of the moon. Some experts believe the Newark octagon and circle reflect a Hopewell concern not only with the burial of ancestors in mounds within the earthwork complex, but also with seasonal rituals governed by astronomical phenomena, as if the Hopewell people arranged their earthly environment to mirror the heavens.

The so-called Great Hopewell Road is a parallel-sided roadway that is believed by Brad Lepper to have passed over 60 miles (97 km) from the Newark earthworks to near modern-

At Hopewell itself, near Chillicothe, thirty-eight mounds lie within a sub-rectangular enclosure covering 110 acres (45 ha) (Figure 11.10). Other mound groups are just as impressive. The average size of Ohio mounds is about 30 ft (9 m) high and some 100 ft (30 m) across, with a volume of about 500,000 cubic feet (14,000 m³). Each represents over 200,000 hours of earthmoving, all achieved using the simplest of stone-bladed tools, wooden digging sticks, and baskets.

Like their Adena predecessors, Hopewell monuments lay inside sacred earthworks, but these were on a much more imposing scale. Elaborate mounds and spectacular geometric earthworks enclose areas covering from ten to hundreds of acres (four to many hectares). At Mound City, Ohio, for example, twenty-four mounds lie within an enclosure covering 13 acres (5 ha). A vast complex encircles the burial mounds at Newark, Ohio, the entire ritual landscape covering more than 4 square miles (10 km²) (Jones and Shiels, 2016; Lepper, 2010) (see Box: Newark and the Great Hopewell Road?).

Hopewell people lived, for the most part, in small, isolated communities, sometimes comprising no more than one or two extended families (Figure 11.11) (Dancey and Pacheco, 1997). These hamlets were stable settlements, occupied perhaps for a decade by people who not only foraged but also cultivated indigenous domesticated plants. Hopewell settlements in Illinois endured for longer periods, with greater residential stability. Some strategic locations became important larger centers. For example, the Tunacunnhee site in northwestern Georgia lies on a natural corridor connecting the interior highlands with the

11.11 Middle Woodland village farmers, *c.* 300 CE.

day Chillicothe in Ross County, Ohio. The earthen roadway has been on the archaeological radar since the 1820s, and has been studied with aerial photographs, **geophysical surveys**, infrared photography, and historical accounts. In recent years, **LIDAR** technology has also been deployed. In fact, these analyses show that the road extends only about 2.5 miles (4 km) southwest of the earthworks. The landscape it is said to pass through is heavily dissected and hard to traverse on foot, there being many steep climbs. It has been modeled topographically by others, who consider that a road extending beyond the earthworks was an impossibility. Much current thinking

believes that it was merely a short causeway that formed a processional way into, or out of, the earthwork.

Excavation at Hopewell earthworks is generally unproductive, so tracing the details relies heavily on LIDAR and other remote sensing technologies. A fundamental question remains: if there was indeed a road (though this seems unlikely), what was its purpose? If it existed, why did it link two major Hopewell centers? One can argue that Newark was a place of pilgrimage that attracted people from afar, even that it was a trade route, but the latest archaeological technology cannot trace it more than a couple of miles or so. One is reminded of the Chaco

Canyon's roads, which may, in fact, be a network of spiritual linkages (see Chapter 10, pp. 229–30). Westerners tend to think of roads as having clear starting points and endings at specific geographical locations, which the Chaco roads and Hopewell example do not possess. Western societies plan roads in mundanely linear, not spiritual terms. It is probably better to think of the Great Hopewell Road as part of a complex ritual landscape that connected far-flung communities through exchange and ritual observance over many generations.

flatter country to the east and southeast, now occupied by a modern interstate highway (Jeffries, 1976). This would have been a strategic location for many social transactions, which were often accompanied by prestigious gifts. The constant out-migrations of new generations made for a dynamic settlement pattern, where different villages were occupied for shorter or longer periods, with the number of settlement clusters increasing through time. Ceremonial precincts also changed continually over the generations, with the building of new burial mounds, fresh earthworks, and other features that were part of often extensive sacred landscapes (Lynott, 2014).

Hopewell developed in a world of intimate kin relationships, where people from neighboring groups came together to harvest nuts, hunt, and for ritual observances. Social and spiritual alliances ebbed and flowed; people learned and shared basic values, supernatural beliefs, and rituals common to an entire society. Through these mechanisms people found mates, arranged marriages, and exchanged food, raw materials, and ritual objects. Larger social groupings and alliances crafted religious paraphernalia, built ceremonial centers, and performed communal rituals that revolved around healing, death, and the ancestors. Numerous leadership positions arose within these various groups, which provided the context for satisfying both prosaic daily needs and social and spiritual obligations; these were often fulfilled at ceremonial centers—complexes of one or two burial mounds, sometimes earthen enclosures covering as much as 127 acres (51 ha). These special gathering places were the spiritual core of Hopewell life.

Within the Scioto–Painted Creek area, which is probably quite typical, there were about three local communities; these were well separated across the landscape, perhaps 7 to 12 miles (11 to 20 km) apart. Each probably comprised at least a hundred people and maintained several ceremonial centers. On a larger scale, such local communities formed close alliances with others to form much bigger groups, up to 19 miles (31 km) in diameter. Such neighboring communities may have formed what one might call "peer polities," anchored by centrally located earthworks and burial mounds. Hopewell, Newark, and other earthwork groups may represent examples of such larger polities, each strategically located at the intersections of different physiographic provinces. These larger groupings exchanged labor to build earthworks, and provided husbands and wives as well as food and commodities, thereby protecting everyone from food shortages and other challenges (Figure 11.12). Each alliance had strong social and spiritual underpinnings. This may reflect a basic self-sufficiency in foodstuffs during good years, but the need for inter-community exchange to balance out shortages during cycles of drought and other scarce times caused by short-term climatic shifts (See Box: What Was Hopewell?). These exchange links also extended to outlying areas where contemporary societies still retained strong Adena ties and did not adopt Hopewell beliefs.

More than 1,150 burials have been found in the major Ohio mound groups alone. More than three-quarters of scientifically studied burials were cremations. Hopewell mourners used both crypts (Illinois) and charnel houses (Ohio). The former were large boxes constructed for the temporary storage of the dead and their grave goods until final burial in the earthen mound. They were simple structures, used by a single community, sunk into the ground and covered with heavy roofs. They were often built on isolated high spots clear of the settlement.

11.12 Moundbuilding involved entire communities, as shown in this reconstruction set in the upper Mississippi Valley.

WHAT WAS HOPEWELL?

Hopewell earthworks have intrigued archaeologists and casual visitors alike for two centuries. For obvious reasons most Hopewell research has focused on earthworks and burial mounds. Only recently has the perspective widened to include studies of the distribution of settlements and of wider Hopewell landscapes, which had major symbolic importance to those who developed them. Unfortunately, incalculable damage from agriculture, early excavations, and urban development has left us with but shreds and patches of an elaborate, highly diverse cultural tradition. The question of questions remains. What was Hopewell? Theories abound, but definitive answers are rare, despite several generations of meticulous detective work involving not only excavation, but also remote sensing and intricate laboratory work.

Many years ago archaeologists at Hopewell wrote of a "Hopewell Interaction Sphere," a complex array of exchange networks large and small, local and long-distance, that spanned much of the Eastern Woodlands and even extended to the Gulf Coast and to the Rocky Mountains (Lynott, 2014 summarizes changing ideas about the Hopewell). The variety of art objects and raw materials that passed to the Hopewell heartlands is extraordinary, including obsidian and grizzly bear teeth from the Rockies, mica from the Appalachians, and shark teeth from the Gulf of Mexico. The Interaction Sphere linked people living far apart with the ceremonial centers in the Ohio Valley and elsewhere.

The Interaction Sphere theory cannot explain the paucity of exotic finds, such as obsidian, in sites between the Rockies and Ohio. Current thinking revolves around instances where small groups of individuals in small-scale societies undertook hazardous "power quests" to ▶▶

Large charnel houses with thatched roofs and substantial post frames held both cremated individuals and entire corpses in long, lined tombs. Once the charnel houses had served their purpose, they were dismantled or burnt down and an earthen mound erected over them (See Box: Deciphering Hopewell).

The diagnostic large charnel houses in the Scioto were a Scioto invention, it seems, and are the key definer of Scioto Hopewell ceremonial life archaeologically. The first of these charnel houses (Tremper) also has a substantial cache of pipes made from Illinois (Sterling) pipestone (not the local Feurt Hill Ohio pipestone). Scioto Hopewell was, quite literally, the simultaneous coming together of Illinois Hopewell pipe ceremonialism and ceremonialism in the Scioto Hopewell charnel house tradition, both appended onto local Adena customs.

Elite individuals within the charnel houses were accompanied by a diverse array of artifacts. A young man and woman buried together in the main mound at Hopewell wore copper ear spools, copper noses, copper breast plates, and necklaces of grizzly-bear teeth. The woman wore thousands of freshwater pearl beads, and copper-covered wooden and stone buttons. Some of the men in the mounds may have been expert artisans; one individual from Hopewell, for example, was buried with 3,000 mica sheets and 198 lb (90 kg) of galena. Hopewell mounds contained not only richly decorated burials but also caches of exotic objects. The mourners deposited copper axes; cut-out silhouettes of birds, fish, claws, and human heads and hands in copper or mica; flint and chlorite disks; finely polished stone atlatl weights; and beautiful effigy pipes (Figures 11.13 and 11.14). There were engraved human bones, painted fabrics, and occasional clay figurines depicting women in belted skirts and men in loincloths.

Dispersed Hopewell communities maintained connections with one another through a variety of social and spiritual partnerships. In Ohio, communities buried some, even all, their dead relatives together in shared cemeteries. The intermingling of ancestral remains created powerful symbolic ties between

acquire exotic raw materials and artifacts that were symbolic of powerful social beliefs. Another mechanism may have been pilgrimages to such locations as Newark, with its Great Hopewell Road that linked it to the Scioto Valley sites. The pilgrims might have contributed the construction of the sacred landscapes, and brought exotic materials and artifacts from far as well. Most likely both people and exotic objects moved over considerable distances, those carrying the objects acquiring intelligence about a natural world of diverse landscapes and societies. The oral accounts of these journeys must have figured large in the worldviews of Hopewell leaders.

The broad travels of people and ceremonial artifacts are well documented, but why did Hopewell people embark on such elaborate landscape construction? Theories abound. Did the centers serve as locations for world renewal ceremonies? Did they serve as astronomical observatories for such events as the summer and winter solstices? Were they reflections of the Hopewell cosmos, or the work of influential and talented leaders? Similar kinds of hypothesis surround other monuments in widely differing cultures—Chaco Canyon, New Mexico, is one example (see Chapter 10), Stonehenge another, Great Zimbabwe

in southern Africa a third. Almost certainly, numerous factors allowed many small-scale societies to build dozens of very large earthen landscapes and burial mounds. The Ohio Hopewell people were organized in such societies, where some people, known from their elaborate burials, acquired status and power. How they were organized across the landscape and to what extent their power lay in controlling food surpluses remains unknown. Many of the answers to these questions will come from future generations of geophysical surveys. In the meantime, Hopewell remains one of the most fascinating and complex mysteries of the North American past.

11.13 A blind wolf medicine tube from Macon County, Tennessee. Length: 22.25 in. (56.6 cm). Dated c. 1–400 CE.

different groups. Such ceremonial observances may have unfolded with the seasons, perhaps with different rituals performed at different earthworks in sequence, the location depending on each site's astronomical alignments (Carr and Case, 2008).

In Ohio, everyone belonged to a clan whose members lived in different communities: far-from-local institutions that fulfilled important social and ceremonial roles throughout the year. We know, from their pendants, of at least nine clans, each with animal or totem associations, among them Bear, Canine, Felines, Raptor, and Beaver. Three or more non-kin groups organized for specific purposes flourished in Hopewell society, each identified by platform pipes, breastplates, and other artifacts. Their activities included some shamanistic duties, such as invoking the power of animals, divination, and corpse processing. No single clan dominated the others or provided supreme leaders. Hopewell was a mosaic of what one might call "horizontal" societies, without powerful chiefs or major rulers. Many decentralized social units

11.14 Mica bird-of-prey claw from an unknown Ohio location. Length: 11.2 in. (28 cm).

DECIPHERING HOPEWELL

Hopewell archaeologists face a grim reality. Almost all major burial-mound and earthwork excavations took place before the days of rigorous field investigation. Many of them were little more than glorified treasure-hunting expeditions. Today's researchers spend their careers piecing together Hopewell society from a complex jigsaw puzzle of both spectacular and prosaic finds, many of them made generations ago.

They have done so with excellent results, in a process that archaeologists Christopher Carr and Troy Case (2005)

call "thick pre-history," an attempt to describe in rich, ethnographic-like detail the environment, lifeways, and history of Hopewell people. Today's synthesis of Hopewell society is a triumph of multidisciplinary research that combines fieldwork with laboratory work, meticulous inventories of old excavations, and both ethnographic and historical records. Archaeology provides the chronological backbone, data about changing settlement patterns over many centuries, and analyses of artifacts, food remains, and other clues to ancient human activity. Biological anthropology yields information about the people themselves, through anatomy and DNA.

Much of today's Hopewell research has involved the compilation of extensive databases and inventories from past, hitherto unpublished, excavations, unstudied burials, and other supporting information. The resulting data have made unprecedented reconstructions of Hopewell life possible, for they come not from a single location, but from entire regions, such as the Scioto Valley. These databases allow us to examine an individual and his or her role in a much broader society. Much effort has gone into making this information available to researchers, so that they can embark on in-depth empirical studies of Hopewell social and personal lives, religious belief, ▶▶

complemented one another, recruiting members from all parts of society, and enjoying approximately similar levels of prestige, wealth, and access to food and other necessities. Many, usually transitory, organizers contributed to society—clan leaders, diviners, healers, people who processed the dead, and gifted men and women who were repositories of astronomical and mythic lore, for example.

Ohio Hopewell leadership was thus highly diversified and decentralized, with classic shamanistic and shaman-like leaders all complementing one another, all with at least some power base in the spiritual realm (see Box: The Hopewell Cosmos). Judging from art objects, Hopewell shamans impersonated animals, metamorphosed, and became them (Figure 11.15). They were specialized practitioners, with different areas of responsibility, among them warfare and the hunt. But there were no hereditary rulers passing their office from one generation to the next. In these egalitarian societies leaders took their regalia and ceremonial artifacts with them at death, and others took over their roles. This model of interacting polities, which were still basically egalitarian, is the most commonly accepted blueprint for Hopewell settlement, but new data may change the picture in future years. (For evaluations of alternative hypotheses, see Dancey and Pacheco, 1997.)

11.15 A composite being associated with the Below realm, which has the horns and body of an ungulate, the legs of an aquatic mammal, and the tail of a rattlesnake.

and rituals. This is far from easy, and involves leaving behind personal and Western preconceptions as one peers into a totally different ancient world.

Fortunately, Hopewell societies left expressive statements about the intangibles of their lives behind them in their art and exotic artifacts. For example, claws, teeth, jaws, and other crafted body parts reveal the clan affiliations of the dead. Distinctive artifacts, such as quartz crystals and conch shells, highlight the roles of shaman-like leaders in ceremonial life. Changes over time in the relative frequencies of metallic headdresses chronicle shifts in the style of Hopewell leadership from informal to more formal, priest-like offices.

The new generation of Hopewell research requires systematic, regional-scale archaeological collections and computerized data sets that can only be accumulated over long periods. This is a form of long-term, team research that is completely different from the much more simplistic, and usually more localized, researches of yesteryear. The archaeologists who carry out this kind of research have infinite patience and the ability to participate in complex, expensive teamwork that involves working collaboratively toward carefully formulated goals that may take years to achieve. The new perceptions of Hopewell described in this chapter come from many years of tedious, inconspicuous work, but the results are truly revolutionary for our understanding of a people whose society flourished 2,000 years ago.

THE HOPEWELL COSMOS

Hopewell art and burial customs reveal the people's layered cosmos of underworld and sky, defined by the cardinal directions, and by the solstices and the positions of moonrise and moonset. Hopewell astronomers balanced and combined these different realms, whose meanings and inhabitants were encoded in artworks and earthwork alignments, burials and ritual deposits, also by ceremonial observance. At the core of human existence was the Center, the nexus of interaction, merging, and cooperation, of conflict and expression of difference. Every person, every household, each pipe, every village and ceremonial place stood at the Center, a belief found in historical Eastern Woodland societies and in other groups around the world. There were wider formulations, too, such as the idea that expansive primordial waters surrounded

11.16 The Pricer-Seip mound represents the cosmos. The multiple burial was a symbol of the Center, placed on a platform, Turtle Island. At the base, water-washed sand-and-muck layers depict the primordial water and the Below realm. A cache of effigy pipes above the skeletons, and their smoke, symbolize the Above realms, presented by multiple mound layers.

the Center. Such was Turtle Island, a symbol of the earth disk and the upper surface of the underworld (Figure 11.16).

By the same token, earthworks rose at points in the landscape that reiterated the importance of the multilayered cosmos: on terraces, or associated with conical hillocks that defined the Above realms. Streams defined the Below. These symbolic associations were deeply embedded in local thought right into historic times. A broad river terrace served as the place for geometric ceremonial grounds, where humans performed the rites that maintained the delicate balance between the living and other beings at the Center and in the layered cosmos. Earthen enclosures served as the Center, constructed so that they had a symbolic relationship with a nearby river or stream, a form of entrance to the Below. The Scioto earthworks were aligned precisely with the point where celestial bodies, such as the sun and moon, met the horizon.

Such alignments served as the benchmarks for an annual ritual calendar of gatherings for major ceremonies that could be observed both within the earthworks and from neighboring high ground. Very often, major earthworks lay close to such features as conspicuous cliffs. One example is the water-weeping shale cliff

near Seip, a nesting place for vultures, which were perhaps an important element in mortuary rituals.

Animals played a central role in Hopewell ritual, for the people believed that some humans had the ability to transform themselves into animals and vice versa. Animals were models as leaders, symbols of clan organization, and a means for achieving personal power. We see this in headdresses and in a human jaw with a deer-tooth replacement for a human tooth. Personal spiritual power came in trance, sometimes facilitated by smoking with pipes depicting animal guardians-cum-tutelary spirits, or by ingesting hallucinogens.

Lastly, color, darkness, and light played important parts in the process of transformation, an interplay epitomized by the darkness of forests, gray skies, and open, cleared land. The raw materials—copper, mica, and some pottery clays—that make up Hopewell paraphernalia can change from light to dark, from shiny to dull, or display both qualities simultaneously. The background and foreground images of their art shift and alternate, again contributing to the experience of transformation. Darkness, light, animals, the mysterious beings of the environment, and the spiritual world formed the central core of Hopewell life.

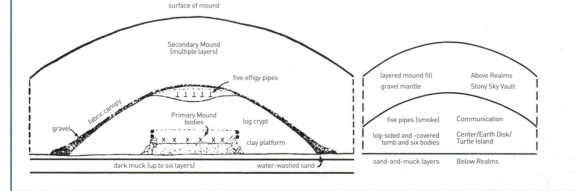

The Hopewell Decline: 325 CE and Beyond

Between 325 and 350 CE a three-way alliance between local symbolic communities in the Scioto region partially disintegrated. Charnel-house building slowed, and earthen enclosures were no longer constructed. Ceremonial activity declined dramatically. The disintegrating Scioto–Painted Creek alliance broke down a powerful spiritual pact that had centered on three groups burying their dead in the Pricer-Seip charnel house (see Figure 11.16, p. 265). One of the three chambers in the next house was left empty. A later house at nearby Ater had but two chambers and no surrounding earthwork. A short time after, the charnel house was decommissioned and covered, as if the alliance had finally been dissolved. An explanation for this sudden change eludes us; one has an impression of overall disruption that is still little understood. We do know that, despite these developments, traditional subsistence activities continued almost unaffected, and that climatic cooling did not play a significant role in triggering change. Rather, as the Hopewell archaeologists Christopher Carr and Troy Case (2005) argue, there may be a religious explanation. Some seminal, probably spiritually interpreted, event must have taken place, or some other happening that undermined the social and religious beliefs that had endured for centuries. Some moundbuilding continued, but without Hopewell associations.

Beyond Adena and Hopewell

We have described Early and Middle Woodland societies in the Eastern Woodlands under generalized labels: Adena and Hopewell. These terms mask a growing diversity of Woodland societies that were making increasing use of domesticated native plants. These were peoples who lived in relatively small communities, but they were linked by exchange networks and important ritual and symbolic ties that extended over vast areas of the east. The great Hopewell earthwork complexes served as anchors for increasingly elaborate ceremonial that revolved around a layered cosmos and its mythological inhabitants, the passage of the seasons, and the ancestors. Early and Middle Woodland society was still relatively simple, but provided the foundations for much more elaborate chiefdoms in later times.

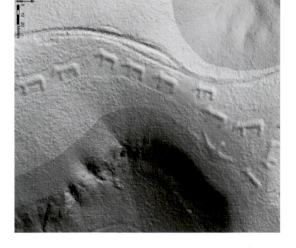

11.17 The Great Bear Mound Group, Effigy Mounds National Monument.

Moundbuilding continued. Numerous so-called effigy mounds in southern Wisconsin, Illinois, Iowa, and Minnesota, built between about 650 and 1300 CE, depict animals of all kinds. They include bears, birds, elk, panthers, turtles, and wolves. Construction began with stripping off the turf to form the outline of the effigy. Then one or more people were buried in the head or heart region before the builders formed the earthen mound. Many bundle burials in the earthworks may represent people who died during the previous winter. Some, like the Great Bear Mound, one of 196 mounds in Iowa's Effigy Mound National Monument (thirty-seven of which are effigies), are of impressive size (Figure 11.17). Great Bear measures 137 ft (42 m) from head to tail and rises over 3 ft (1 m) above the ground. Their significance is unknown, but there may have been dualities involved, such as birds opposed to bears. Duality was an important feature of later beliefs.

Another moundbuilding culture, known to archaeologists as Fort Ancient (Figure 11.18), was centered on southern Ohio, northern Kentucky, and western West Virginia. It developed locally and apparently had little contact with the elaborate riverine societies that flourished in the Mississippi Valley and beyond after 800 CE, and which we discuss in Chapter 12 (Cook, 2011).

The centuries between 800 and 1200 CE saw gradual population growth, continued inter-community exchange, and increasing cultivation of native plants by sedentary peoples in river valleys and along coasts. The Late Woodland, described in the next chapter, was a period of cultural change and increasing social complexity, which culminated in a series of remarkable riverine societies after 800 CE, and in the great Mississippian Tradition of the South and southern Midwest.

11.18 The Great Serpent Mound in Ohio is a celebrated example of an earthwork built during the Fort Ancient culture, a tradition contemporary with the Mississippian. It may be a symbolic representation of an important lineage buried within its confines. With its tightly curved tail, the earthen serpent wriggles for 1,254 ft (382 m) along a low ridge. Its open jaws enclose an oval burial mound.

SUMMARY

- Eastern Woodlands societies embarked on a complex trajectory of change around 1000 BCE, the conventional boundary between the Archaic and the Woodland.

- As populations rose and territories grew smaller, there was an increasing emphasis on the cultivation of starchy seed plants and on exchange of basic commodities, using social networks.

- The Adena (c. 500 BCE to the first century CE) is a generic name for dozens of local Early and sometimes Middle Woodland cultures, remarkable for their ceremonialism, that developed out of earlier Archaic societies. Adena was a series of mortuary rituals and spiritual beliefs reflected in burial mounds, especially in the Ohio Valley. Clan and lineage ties were important sources of social and economic stability.

- Adena groups foreshadowed the much greater astronomical and cosmological thinking of their Hopewell successors. Hopewell (c. 200 BCE to c. 400 CE) was an ideology in a spiritual sense, a set of understandings shared by numerous societies across the Midwest, accompanied by distinctive artifacts and mortuary rituals.

- Hopewell religious beliefs were associated with a vision of a layered cosmos. Elaborate mounds and spectacular geometric earthworks place its center on Ohio, but the beliefs spread far afield. Intimate kin relationships lay at the heart of Hopewell life, in an ebb and flow of social and spiritual alliances. Ceremonial centers provided the context for ceremonies that satisfied daily needs and rituals that surrounded healing, death, and the ancestors. Social and spiritual partnerships linked dispersed communities, as did shared cemeteries.

- Hopewell leadership was highly diversified and decentralized, with larger polities represented by such centrally located sites as Hopewell and Newark.

- Between 325 and 350 CE the Hopewell Tradition dissolved, perhaps for spiritual reasons. Moundbuilding continued in local cultures, among them Fort Ancient in Ohio and the Effigy Moundbuilders of Iowa.

CHAPTER 12

Mississippian and Calusa

The Mississippian was a mosaic of societies of every size that flourished for about six centuries, up to European contact and beyond. Such a complicated jigsaw of peoples raises intriguing questions. Why and when did Mississippian society achieve such elaboration? What kind of leaders presided over the major centers? What was the basis of their power? It is only in recent years that we have begun to acquire some answers, thanks to research not only in archaeology but in oral history and ethnography as well. Further south the Calusa chiefdoms of southern Florida achieved significant complexity in the centuries before Europeans arrived in Florida. Their culture survived remarkably intact into the nineteenth century.

Mississippian Origins

The Mississippian Tradition developed among many local societies that flourished in the Late Woodland Southeast. The origins of the Mississippian do not lie in earlier Woodland societies; although, obviously, there were continuities, it is better to think of "Mississippianization" as a result of cultural entanglements between diverse groups (Wilson, 2017). The new traditions and cosmologies

WEEDEN ISLAND: A TRAJECTORY TOWARD MISSISSIPPIAN

The Weeden Island culture arose among the ancient peoples who lived amid deciduous and mixed pine forests, near lakes, rivers, and wet prairies, on the Gulf coastal plain between Florida, Alabama, and Georgia about 200 CE (Milanich *et al.*, 1997).

Characteristic Weeden Island pottery appears at about 200 CE, and may have developed out of earlier ceramic traditions on the Alabama–Georgia border. Weeden sites extend into western parts of northern Florida and as far west as the Tombigbee River in Alabama along the Gulf Coast and into the interior. An early Weeden Island I period lasted from about 200 to 700 CE, Weeden Island II from 700 to between 900 and 1000, each distinguished by characteristic pottery styles. About 900 to 1000 CE, Weeden II developed in situ into local forms of Mississippian culture at many locales, to the point that it might legitimately be called "proto-Mississippian" (Figures 12.1

and 12.2) (Milanich *et al.*, 1997). Some Weeden II communities may have survived in parts of northern Florida into the fifteenth century. The Weeden people were surrounded by other Late Woodland cultures, among them the Troyville and

12.1 Weeden Island. A red pedastalled duck effigy from Kolomoki Mound D, Georgia. Height: 13.4 in. (34 cm).

12.2 Weeden Island punctated bowl, from Carter Mound I.

Coles Creek developments of the low-lying Mississippi and Louisiana coast, and the St. Johns culture to the southeast that developed continuously from Middle Archaic times right into the historic eastern Timucuan groups encountered by both Spanish and French explorers in the sixteenth century.

Weeden Island is part of a long evolutionary continuum that started in Paleo-Indian times, continued through the Archaic and Woodland,

that make up what Gregory Wilson and Lynne Sullivan (2017) call "a tapestry of Mississippian lifestyles" was to spread widely and eventually mantle the Southeast and midcontinent. The complex threads that formed that tapestry passed from group to group as a result of many processes, among them people moving back and forth, long distance exchange, also missionization and pilgrimage (Anderson, 2017). What is remarkable is that a distinctive ethnic identity developed that transcended environmental and linguistic frontiers, also numerous cultural differences. There were many Mississippian beginnings, worked out by groups with varying cultural traditions and different histories.

Every Mississippian society had a unique history, its Mississippianization markedly different. No standardized chiefdom model works across all of them. What led to the constant interactions that culturally entangled dozens of societies? As far as is known the earliest Mississippian beginnings took hold at Cahokia in the American Bottom near modern-day St. Louis. There were cultural borrowings from earlier traditions, among them platform mounds from further south (see Figure 12.3), but many examples, such as Weeden Island (see Box: Weeden Island:

and culminated in the Mississippian. As populations increased during Late Archaic and Early Woodland periods, the inhabitants of the Southeast developed more complex settlements and more elaborate forms of social organization. Jerald Milanich and his colleagues argue that by 200 CE lineages and other forms of social status were well established among all Southeastern peoples. At times, too, even more complex forms of social organization may have appeared for brief periods—witness Poverty Point (see Chapter 8). All these economic, social, and ideological changes culminated during the three centuries after 700 CE, among Weeden II and related cultures.

Weeden Island is a far more complex culture than it might first appear, and can be interpreted in several ways. On the one hand it is an ever-changing, secular pottery complex that occurs at most village sites throughout

Weeden Island territory. On the other it is a sacred, ceremonial complex that may have developed from earlier Hopewell-like belief systems and religious usages. This complex may have revolved around elaborate mortuary rituals centered on low platform mounds used as bases for charnel houses, the residences of important individuals, and for preparing bones for burial. The nature of this complex was illustrated dramatically at the McKeithen site in northern Florida

in Weeden Island territory. Here, three low platform mounds form a horseshoe-shaped settlement with a central plaza (Figure 12.3). The first settlers arrived in about 200 CE. Their descendants constructed the three mounds between 350 and 475 CE. The structures on them burnt down in about 475.

The mounds themselves formed an isosceles triangle. One supported a temple, where a priest lived and was buried. The second mound supported a charnel house, the third a pine-post screen where the dead were washed before being taken to the charnel house. These low tumuli formed part of a complex mortuary process, presumably supervised by the person buried in the temple. The perpendicular, formed by a line from mound B to the triangle base, points toward the position of the rising sun at the summer solstice. Between 700 and 1000 CE such villages as McKeithen, and their religious specialists, assumed ever greater importance.

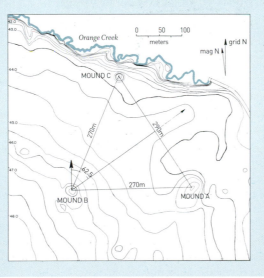

12.3 An enduring mound tradition. Plan of the McKeithen village in northern Florida, showing the platform mounds.

A Trajectory Toward Mississippian), suggest a cosmological, spiritual motivation. Cahokia attracted large numbers of migrants and became an important center. Other centers arose, too, among them Etowah in Georgia and Moundville in Alabama, each with much in common, but also with their own interpretations of what Wilson and Sullivan call "shared wisdoms." The cults that began at Cahokia spread widely, but inevitably became localized sects. There were shared beginnings, though, which provide us with a sense of unity. While constant shifts in shared beliefs and local cults never ceased as the Mississippian thrived over the centuries, one common development emerged throughout: intensification of agriculture.

Maize, Beans, and Starchy Seeds

Maize did not become a truly significant crop until after political consolidation was well under way. Nor was the adoption of maize agriculture necessarily the catalyst. For example, maize intensification developed in such areas as the Illinois River Valley, where populations remained fairly low and there was no development of a political hierarchy. For years experts have assumed that maize agriculture lay behind the rise of Mississippian society. They were wrong, for we now know that it was starchy seeds rather than maize that were the staple as Cahokia in the American Bottom grew ever larger (Vanderwarker *et al.*, 2017). Even so, maize certainly was grown in Cahokia on a modest scale, and may have entered Mississippian society from there, conceivably as part of a group of ideas, sacred objects, and ideologies that were to spread throughout the Midwest and Southeast. Some of this spread may have been associated with large-scale ceremonial and feasting that could have involved members of even tiny communities as shows of friendship or to foster potential alliances. There was a slow shift toward a wider social and political order. In such environments as the Lower Mississippi Valley subsistence had long depended on such harvests as acorns and hickory, and the cultivation of native seed plants; maize was added to these established practices, but did not become important until much later. At Etowah in Georgia, for instance, maize consumption rose sharply between 1000 and 1600 CE.

The relationship between the adoption of maize farming and the development of the Mississippian was extremely complex and varied from area to area, though it was always close. The crop had many meanings in Early Mississippian society, tied to the unique social and political history of each region: competitive feasting at which individuals and groups exhibited generosity was one; the creation of new political economies underwritten by surplus foods was another. Participating in large-scale rituals was also a catalyst for the tradition's development, drawing as they did both on older customs and on potentially new Mississippian identities. Some adopted what has been called a "Mississippian package" that stemmed from frequent interactions and culture contacts. At Cahokia the intensive cultivation of starchy foods was deeply embedded in society to provide surpluses. These provided the means to construct major public structures, such as platform mounds, and also played a role in feasting rituals.

The intensification of agriculture coincided in general terms with the greater warmth of the Medieval Warm Period. The larger food surpluses produced by intensive cultivation supported not only imposing buildings and public architecture, but also elaborate and large-scale social and ritual events. Add ambitious kin groups and ancient traditions that defined group identities, also strongly felt loyalties, and you have the ingredients that transformed the political and social history of what was to become the Mississippian world.

Mississippian societies coalesced across much of the Southeast during the eleventh and twelfth centuries, with an early efflorescence in the Central Mississippi Valley, including the Cahokia region, in about 1050 CE (Milner, 1998). They developed in river valleys, often expanding up small tributaries of major waterways. Fertile agricultural soils formed bands within these same valleys. A constant supply of water-borne nutrients helped these floodplain areas sustain high human population densities and a rich biomass of animals and plants. Fish and waterfowl may have provided much of the protein intake of people living along the bottomlands of the Mississippi, for the river lay on a major waterfowl flyway. Fall nut harvests were always of vital importance, since maize yields provided only a fraction of a household's yearly needs at the subsistence level. Eventually, with larger fields resulting from political or social stimuli, quite large food surpluses could have been manipulated for political ends.

The fabric of Mississippian society depended on the household, a self-sufficient unit. Everywhere individual communities tried to minimize the risk of starvation by cultivating a mosaic of gardens located in different environmental zones. They must also have relied heavily on reciprocity, on kin in neighboring communities, who would provide food or grain in times of stress. In all communities storage pits and granaries assumed central importance. At a certain level kin ties would have been adequate for these purposes, but occasional food shortages may have been such that entire regions had to cooperate with one another, a process requiring more formal leadership.

Thousands of households were grouped together into larger communities, with both mound centers and settlements linked to them. Small local groups composed of a single mound center with affiliated smaller settlements formed much of the Mississippian world. Larger and more complex political and social units coalesced around a single dominant center, with lesser ones close by. This form of segmental organization, with a great deal of local variation, survived the rise, apogee, and decline of Mississippian societies across the Eastern Woodlands. The same social structure was typical of historically known societies in the region.

Wide-ranging exchange networks lay at the core of Mississippian society. For example, sea shells passed from hand to hand over vast areas of the Southeast. Specialists turned these into ornaments, often engraved with distinctive designs that included flying figures (shamans, warriors, or mythical heroes) and abstract faces (Figure 12.4). Experts can often identify motifs executed and repeated by individual artisans. Chert from Mill Creek, Illinois, was a hard material ideal for making hoes, and was widely traded after 900 CE, traveling up to 430 miles (700 km) from source. Salt production assumed great importance, as maize farmers had to supplement their diet with salt.

Person-to-person bartering and kin-based formal redistribution were the most common ways of exchanging goods and commodities in Mississippian society. The processes of exchange were highly politicized, often taking place at major ceremonial gatherings of a kind that still flourished in historic times. These occasions involved feasting and dancing, the sharing of food, exchanges, and the reaffirmation of ties with other villages and individuals.

12.4 Belief systems of later Southeastern peoples were closely tied to local political and social organization. Artists depicted complex symbols on clay vessels and stone, copper, and shell objects. The meanings of many symbols elude us, but they include "weeping eyes," birds, serpents, skulls, and hands. This shell head has weeping eyes and other facial decoration. Height: 2.1 in. (6 cm).

Cahokia: 1050 to c. 1400 CE

Some Mississippian centers nurtured more complex social and political structures than others, the most famous being Cahokia in the American Bottom on the Mississippi River opposite St. Louis, Illinois. These centers raise important questions about the political organization of these most elaborate of all ancient North American societies (see Box: Complex Chiefdoms or States?, p. 276) (Milner, 1998).

The American Bottom is a pocket of low-lying floodplain along the Mississippi, the widest portion of which extends downstream from the confluence of the Illinois River for about 25 miles (40 km), with a maximum width of about 11 miles (18 km). Meanderings of the Mississippi over the flatlands formed swamps and oxbow lakes in abandoned channels. The American Bottom environment was exceptionally diverse, with fertile soils lying on the margins of several ecological zones. It was here that Cahokia flourished, with what was probably the highest population density north of Mexico.

Sedentary villages prospered at or near Cahokia after 600 CE. Then, apparently within a few decades around 1050 CE, a great center emerged at Cahokia itself, surrounded by several smaller administrative and political centers and rural homesteads (Pauketat, 2004, 2010). Carbon isotopes from Mississippian skeletons show that their owners ate a lot of corn. Cahokia's population rose dramatically. Hundreds of people were resettled in small and large villages, even at some distance from Cahokia itself. These moves must have involved complex political negotiations among kin-based social groups, and the exploitation of religious beliefs that linked chief and villager. Imposing public structures and shrines, sweat houses, common art traditions, and the promotion of carefully chosen community traditions—all may have been symbols that linked elite and commoner in displays of common cultural meanings and values. The result: a regional chiefdom (for want of a better word) that melded Cahokia's authority with ancient community interests. But Cahokia was short-lived. Competing factions and periodic inabilities to mobilize community labor helped fashion an inherently unstable polity that appeared and dissipated with bewildering speed. At the height of its power, between 1050 and 1250 CE, Cahokia extended over an area of more than 3.8 square miles (10 km²). Dwellings covered some 2,000 acres (800 ha). The population may have been as low as 3,000, perhaps as high as 16,000. Many people lived elsewhere on the floodplain and in the surrounding uplands (Emerson and Lewis, 1999). More than a hundred earthen mounds of various shapes, sizes, and functions, many of them along the dry central ridge of the site, cluster around a series of open plazas. The most extensive grouping lies around Monk's Mound, the largest earthwork built by ancient North Americans (Figure 12.5). The tumulus is 100 ft (30 m) high and covers 16 acres (6.5 ha); it rose in four stages, beginning before 1000 CE and ending some three centuries later (Figure 12.6).

A stairway once led up the south side to the first level, perhaps even higher to the second level; it faced the main plaza, the central focal point of the site. The third and fourth levels rose after 1200 CE on the northeast quadrant of the earthwork. A large building measuring 100 by 40 ft (30 by 12 m) stood on the summit of the highest terrace with a large wooden post in front of it, apparently a temple with a thatched roof. Teams of villagers supervised by experts erected the mound by heaping up 21.7 million cubic feet (615,000 m³) of earth basket

12.5 Monk's Mound, Cahokia. The mound as seen today is a much-eroded version of an imposing stepped structure that rose in four stages, beginning in 1000 CE.

12.6 Monk's Mound dominated Cahokia's central precincts, with many smaller mounds and houses surrounding it. Trading and major public ceremonies took place in the main plaza. A log stockade protected the central area, with a solar calendar at far left. Maize gardens surrounded Cahokia; water came from Cahokia Creek and clay borrow pits, dug to quarry clay for moundbuilding.

What are chiefdoms? The simplest chiefdoms are single-tier societies in social terms, where a single chief is expected to be a generous kinsman who redistributes goods and commodities to other members of society. More complex chiefdoms, for example those of the Mississippians and the Calusa of southern Florida, have two or even three tiers of political hierarchy. Nobles are clearly distinct from commoners: they do not produce everything they need to support their households, but consume tribute, such as food and exotic artifacts; they confine their reciprocity to ritual and secular services that only they can perform. Such societies depend on the paramount chief having power over lesser nobles, each of whom controls specific territories.

The overall leader's power hangs on his ability to access large quantities of tribute passed up the line by his subordinates and their subjects. In the case of the Mississippians, the move toward greater political complexity may have come partly from control of long-distance exchange, especially in exotic goods, and in the use of this wealth to control local labor. These exotic artifacts became symbols of chiefly legitimacy, a legitimacy grounded in a special relationship with the supernatural world. Cahokia and other such centers were the settings for the great ceremonies that linked the commoner and the elite. Judging from historic Native American institutions in the Southeast, major Mississippian centers may have had both peace chiefs and warrior chiefs.

Mississippian leaders never exercised strict control over commoners. Rather they drew them in with compelling religious ideology and distinctive cult items. They headed chiefdoms in a constant state of flux, fueled by intensely competitive political dynamics—just as was the case with ancient chiefdoms everywhere. With their regular feasts and elaborate ceremonies, Mississippian chiefs validated their authority in vivid, symbolic ways, well aware that their powers depended on negotiating the fine line between coercion and reciprocity and on balancing the powerful cults that defined human existence over a wide area.

by basket. In places the architects alternated layers of sand and clay, perhaps in an effort to stabilize the structure and prevent slumping. The entire earthwork would have taken a theoretical 370,000 workdays to complete, with additional days for contouring and finishing.

After 1250 CE Cahokia's population gradually tapered off over the next 150 years, as people migrated out from the American Bottom and more dispersed settlement patterns again prevailed. This may have been a response to much drier conditions and lengthy droughts that caused food shortages, and perhaps violence. By the latter half of the thirteenth century there were few Mississippians left in the American Bottom. This may be connected with the arrival of hardy *Maiz de ocho* (eight-row corn): adaptable to many conditions, when combined with beans this crop allowed farming on higher ground and in other less favorable environments.

Some of the largest Cahokia earthworks lie in two rows on either side of Monk's Mound. Most were platform mounds topped with important public buildings or elite dwellings (Figure 12.7). Some of these structures may have been charnel houses for the corpses of prominent ancestors. A log palisade with watchtowers and gates surrounded the entire 200 acres (80 ha) of the central area. We know that the defensive wall, studded with bastions, was rebuilt at least four times, perhaps as a result of factional warfare.

Cahokia's central precincts were the setting for major public rituals that validated the authority of the kin groups who presided over the polity. Mortuary rites and human sacrifice played a major role in Mississippian ritual, in a society where fertility was a major ceremonial theme. The celebrated mortuary complex in Mound 72 may have served as a kind of theater where certain mortuary

THE MYSTERY OF CAHOKIA'S MOUND 72

Mound 72 at Cahokia is one of those archaeological sites that poses more questions than it answers. Just south of Cahokia's central plaza, it is inconspicuous, but of central importance to the founding of Cahokia. A structured deposit of human remains and artifact caches was laid out on a black earth platform in the southeastern portion of the mound (Emerson *et al.*, 2016). Melvin Fowler, who excavated between 1961 and 1967, originally believed that there were two principal burials, one lying above and another below a mass of over 20,000 shell beads, surrounded by sacrificial victims. Over 270 people came from twenty-five burial features, some of them suggesting human sacrifice. Large votive caches of arrow bundles, mica, and shell beads also came from the mound. Construction began with the erection of large marker posts and a charnel house, dating to before 1000 CE. The elaborate so-called "Beaded Burials" with their shell beads were interred before 1050, a time when there were also several mass sacrificial burial events. Three original sub mounds with commemorative deposits were eventually merged into one ridgetop mound.

Almost certainly the carefully staged Beaded Burials, other human remains, and artifact caches were a tableau that represented Cahokia's founding events. They lay close to a wooden marker post that may have been a solstice indicator, for Cahokia had strong astronomical associations. What does this tableau mean? Current thinking considers it a broad cultural statement that included symbolic references to political structure, social hierarchy, and cosmological beliefs laid out within a ritualized mortuary program. In his skeletal analysis Melvin Fowler concluded that the Beaded Burials were males. Skeletal analysis has improved since Fowler's study and a re-analysis of the bones reveals that the two individuals, one lying atop the other, are in fact a man and a woman, both in their early to mid-twenties. Bone beads near their limbs suggest that the two bodies were bound together. A child's bones were comingled with them. Furthermore, the beads were deposited not at a single moment, but in several episodes. There is also ▶▶

12.7 Such wood structures as this so-called "woodhenge" at Cahokia lay on higher ground above a swamp, close to the central precincts. The large wooden posts were erected by sliding them into deep pits with a sloping side, then pushing them upright.

a secondary bundle of a male and a female among a complex of at least seventeen burials.

The mound was used from about 1050 CE and finally closed off around 1100 to 1200. Precise radiocarbon dates place the Beaded Burial event somewhere around 990 CE—the Early Mississippian. Instead of a single bead deposit, the new researches point to a layer of beads being deposited on the black earth platform covering an area that would lie beneath the legs and pelvis of the extended body of the young adult female. Once the corpse was laid out, beads were placed over her thighs and lower legs. Some of these beads may have been strung. Then the body of a young adult man was placed atop the woman, covering her right side but leaving the left arm, chest, and hip exposed. A combination of strung and loose beads was then set down, some of them forming an arc from the shoulder and face of the man.

What do the beads mean? The mass of marine seashells is thought to be a symbol of water, fertility, and the primordial Underworld, a common belief in the Native American world. There are also claims that the shells represented a mythic birdman, known to be part of Mississippian ritual beliefs. The male–female pairing may also recall long-held creation myths among plains and prairie groups, for example the Caddo to the west, which talk of intercourse between the Morning and Evening Stars creating the first woman. This is, of course, entirely speculation, but it seems likely that the mound burial tableau is linked to creation myths, world renewal, and fertility, the interlinked male and female being connected to tales of the first man and woman.

narratives were performed by a high-status kin group using human bodies and ritual objects (see Box: The Mystery of Cahokia's Mound 72, p. 277–78).

The layout of Cahokia and other great centers reflects a traditional Southeastern cosmos with four opposed sides, reflected in the layout of platform mounds, great tumuli, and plazas. Four-sided Mississippian platform mounds may portray the cosmos as earth-islands, the earth being flat-topped and flat-sided. The north–south axis of Cahokia echoes observations of the sun. Perhaps its rulers used the sun to schedule the annual rituals that commemorated the agricultural cycles.

At first settlement layouts reflected kin groups that controlled fertility rituals in villages divided into symbolic quarters. Later centers displayed more formal layouts with central plazas, elaborate sacred buildings, also storage and ritual pits filled with pots and other offerings made during fertility ceremonies that symbolically renewed the world. These changes reflect profound shifts in Mississippian society as power passed to an elite based at major centers.

The Southeastern Ceremonial Complex and a Triad of Cults

Mississippian cosmology and beliefs have generated an extensive academic literature, much of it surrounding the so-called **Southeastern Ceremonial Complex (SECC)** (King, 2007). There was a thematic unity that focused on mythic animals, people, and their activities in the supernatural Above World. These motifs and themes occur over a wide area, not only in classic Mississippian centers, such as Etowah, Georgia, and Moundville, Alabama, but also in Spiro, Oklahoma, to the west, part of the related Caddoan moundbuilding culture (Brown, 1996). Originally there was talk among researchers of a Southern Cult that swept across the Southeast, but we now know that the Southern Cult was too simplistic a formulation. Despite sharing common elements, Mississippian ritual beliefs were very complex and varied from one region to another.

Mississippian beliefs changed significantly through the centuries. The change-over is well documented at Etowah in northern Georgia, where there were few symbols that depicted elite individuals before 1250 CE. New ritual themes then arrived, among them the Birdman, a ritual theme linked to a supernatural being among people in the upper Midwest known as Morning Star, or Red Horn. He was a great warrior associated with the Sky World, who fought battles in the supernatural realm on behalf of humans. Birdman was also linked to reincarnation and the triumph of life over death and of day over night. Unlike earlier themes, Birdman and his symbols, which included falcon imagery, were a shift to the power of an individual. The symbolism of individual power in the Birdman was a sign of a new social order, of a melding of both ancient and more recent narratives and ritual themes that served as the ideological underpinning of Etowah when it was at its most powerful. The compelling Birdman theme seems to have originated at Cahokia before 1200, as the supernatural justification for a new social order of individual power that reached Etowah a half century later.

A triad of religious cults lay at the core of Mississippian society (Brown and Kelly, 2000; King, 2007): a cult of warfare, a nature and fertility cult, and an ancestor cult. The cult of warfare was an important power base for the elite. It is known from exotic motifs and symbols and from the use of costly raw materials, such as copper and sea shells (Figure 12.8). Such objects occur in elite burials,

12.8 Engraved shell gorget with a pair of figures, Late Braden, Cartersville style, from the Rutherford–Kizer site, Tennessee. Dated 1300–1400 CE.

12.9 Mississippian artistry. (a) A wooden knife covered with copper plating, from the Craig Mound, Spiro site, Oklahoma. Length: 11.2 in. (28.5 cm). Dated *c.* 1250–1350 CE.

(b) A seated figure with human-head ear ornaments, carved of Missouri flint clay, from the Craig Mound, Spiro site, Oklahoma. Height: 10.6 in. (27 cm). Dated *c.* 1100–1200 CE.

(c) Great Serpent / Underwater Panther vessel from the Campbell site, Permiscot County, Missouri. Height: 6.75 in. (17.2 cm). Dated *c.* 1550–1650 CE.

12.10 Mississippian effigy vase depicting a human being. The weeping eyes suggest an association between tears, rain, and water in Mississippian cosmology. *c.* 1000 AD. Height: 7.8 in. (20 cm). Field Museum of Natural History, Chicago.

12.11 This copper head appears to have been cut out of a larger plate, with the feather then riveted on. It was found in the Craig Mound at Spiro, Oklahoma. Length: 9.4 in. (24 cm).

along with war axes, maces, and other weapons. Other artifacts bear cosmic imagery that depicts animals, humans, and mythic beasts (Figure 12.9). Some may be references to legendary warrior-heroes and their supernatural exploits, in artifacts that were perhaps part of sacred bundles kept by priests. This symbolic imagery melded warfare, cosmology, and nobility into a coherent whole. Dozens of Mississippian cemeteries and mound centers contain finely made pottery and other artifacts associated with this chiefly cult.

The artifacts include axes with head and shaft carved from a single piece of stone, copper pendants adorned with circles of weeping eyes, decorated clay pots and effigy vessels, and also copper plates and engraved shell cups adorned with male figures in ceremonial dress (Figures 12.10 and 12.11). Such themes as bird symbolism, circles, crosses, and weeping eyes have deep roots in more ancient societies of the Eastern Woodlands.

The nature and fertility cult had close links with the earthen platform mounds so characteristic of Mississippian centers. These flat-topped tumuli may represent the Southeastern belief that the earth was a flat surface oriented toward four quarters of the world. The mounds acted as a symbol of renewal and fertility, the platform serving as the earth. There are historically documented connections between additions to platform mounds and the communal "green corn" ceremony, which celebrated the new harvest and the fertility of the earth.

The third cult involved the ancestors. It was a powerful element, for ancestors provided vital connections between the living and the land. The Great Mortuary in the Craig Mound at Spiro, Oklahoma, came into being in the early 1400s (Brown, 1996). Built on the site of earlier funerary structures, the Mortuary held clumps of human bones and fragmentary artifacts taken from sites elsewhere laid on a cane floor, with formal burials interred above them. Baskets of ceremonial artifacts, such as copper-headed axes and piles of textiles, lay with containers of sea shells, wooden masks, and statues (Figure 12.12). Subsequently a set of cedar poles was raised over the center of the mortuary deposit, creating both a void and a marker after the mortuary was sealed. This Great Mortuary became a living part of the subsequent history of the Craig Mound.

These powerful cults, which defined both chiefly and communal society, spread throughout the South and Southeast and transcended their different cultural and ecological boundaries. They created a dynamic, constantly changing, and highly factionalized society with tremendous variation in social complexity. Cahokia and other large centers lay at one end of this spectrum of complexity, hundreds of small centers and minor chiefdoms at the other. Each of the three cults was distinct; they were enacted and affected people in different ways. As part of the warfare cult both priests and warriors held different chiefly roles, which were confined to privileged kin groups. These were validated through elaborate ceremonies and rituals performed by the chiefs. Platform-mound cults, with their emphasis on fertility and renewal, were communal rites involving entire kin groups and communities that survived long after European contact. Ancestor worship cut across society, putting the priests—who maintained temples, burial houses, sacred fires, and mortuary rituals for the ancestors—in a powerful position to mediate disputes and competing interests.

12.12 A cedarwood mask from Spiro Mound, Oklahoma, perhaps worn by a shaman, with shell inlay and antlers carved in imitation of those of a deer. Height: 11.4 in. (29 cm). Chiefs used ceremony and ritual to validate their power.

Moundville: 1250 to c. 1500 CE

Cahokia's power declined after 1250 CE, when other large centers rose to prominence. Moundville, by the Black Warrior River in west-central Alabama, flourished between 1250 and c. 1500 CE (Knight, 2010). The site, with its twenty-nine or more earthen mounds, covers more than 185 acres (75 ha) (Figure 12.13). The larger mounds, the biggest about 56 ft (17 m) high, delineate a quadrilateral plaza of about 79 acres (32 ha); some support public buildings or the dwellings of important people (Figure 12.14). A bastioned and much-rebuilt palisade protected the three sides of the site that faced away from the river. Hundreds of people lived within the general site area, perhaps as many as 1,000 souls. Altogether 3,051 burials have been excavated at Moundville. Leaders were interred in the mounds, people of lesser status in major village areas along the northern boundary of the site.

Back in 900 CE, a time of considerable political unrest and increasingly circumscribed territory, a relatively small number of people lived in the Moundville area. Maize production intensified between 950 and 1000 CE, at a time when

12.13 Aerial view of Moundville Archaeological Park, Alabama.

12.14 Platform mound at Moundville, Alabama.

settlements grew larger, production of shell beads increased, and warfare became more commonplace. Between 1050 and 1250 maize and bean agriculture provided as much as 40 percent of the diet as the Black Warrior Valley became an important farming area. Moundville developed into an important ceremonial center in a process that culminated with the creation of the highly formalized fortified town. The earthworks and plazas became a symbolic landscape, oriented from east to west, with pairings of residential and mortuary mounds and a well-defined ranking of social spaces within the site. The center assumed an importance outside its own boundaries. Tribute from perhaps 10,000 people scattered through the surrounding area supported the elite, who engaged in long-distance trade. The formal layout of the public architecture in the heart of the site probably reflected the status relationships of different kin groups set in the context of a sacred landscape. The paramount chief derived his position both from his supernatural authority and from the power conferred on him by the sacred landscape.

For a century and a half after 1300 a firmly entrenched chiefly dynasty ruled Moundville and its environs, as we see from the lavishly adorned burials in its funerary mounds. Effectively the site became a necropolis, used by people from considerable distances away, and conceivably a location where dwelt priests with connections to the supernatural world Beneath (Scarry and Steponaitis, 2016). It may also have been an entry point for the pathway that took the dead to the spiritual realms. As the dynasty became increasingly powerful and more isolated from its subjects, the population moved away from the center into the surrounding landscape. Perhaps the nucleated population left to join coalitions of chiefly competitors occupying new mound centers built a short distance away. Moundville went into decline after 1450 CE. Even in its heyday it was never a large polity, drawing labor and tribute from at most 45 miles (72 km) away. Large-scale tribute gathering may never have extended more than about 9 miles (14.5 km) from the site, simply because of the difficulty of transporting supplies and enforcing assessments.

At the height of their powers Mississippian centers—Cahokia, Moundville, Etowah, and others—were large, complex communities presided over by high-status individuals with great political, social, and religious influence (Figure 12.15)

12.15 Etowah, Barlow County, Georgia.

12.16 An artist's impression, based on excavations, of a palisaded Mississippian settlement at the Rucker's Bottom site in Georgia. Many villages were palisaded for defense against neighbors and enemies.

(for complexity, see Box: Complex Chiefdoms or States?, p. 276). Both peace and war chiefs presided over a patchwork of smaller polities, not over sovereign states, as some claim (Figure 12.16). As time went on the power of the major chiefs declined except, perhaps, for some nominal allegiance. The Mississippian society centered on Moundville—always volatile, always riven by factions (as were so many others)—became entirely decentralized before the first contacts with Spanish explorers in the mid-sixteenth century. Other centers that did survive, especially in the Lower Mississippi Valley, were large enough to impress the Spaniards, although they lasted little more than a century following first contact, and sometimes only a matter of decades.

By the time European traders and explorers reached the Mississippi Valley in the late seventeenth century, Cahokia was long past its apogee. Moundville, though still important, was declining. But when Hernando de Soto and his fellow conquistadors traversed the Southeast much earlier, in 1539–41, they encountered still-powerful chiefdoms (see Box: Funerary Rites of a Natchez Chief). Spanish metal, glass beads, and armor fragments have been found in several locations, notably the King site in northwestern Georgia. This was once a frontier village of the Coosa kingdom, a descendant of the spectacular chiefdoms of a few centuries earlier (for the European *entrada*, see Chapters 14 and 15).

FUNERARY RITES OF A NATCHEZ CHIEF

Three platform mounds, a ceremonial plaza, and residential areas formed the Grand Village of the Natchez chiefdom during the late seventeenth and early eighteenth centuries. Ethnographic accounts of the elaborate Natchez burial rituals, written when Cahokia and Moundville were long abandoned, provide the only eyewitness testimony of the use of North American platform mounds.

The paramount chief of the Natchez, the Great Sun, lived atop Mound B at the Grand Village at the center of the site, which is at modern-day Natchez, Mississippi (Figure 12.17). Mound C, the southernmost mound, supported a temple where a sacred fire was always burning. The foundations of both the chief's house and the temple were unearthed during excavations in 1962. Mound A, at the north end of the site, was seemingly abandoned before European contact.

In 1720 French explorer Le Page du Pratz spent time among the Natchez of

12.17 Platform Mound B at the Grand Village of the Natchez. The Great Sun's house stood atop it.

the Lower Mississippi, one of the last remnants of the Mississippian way of life that had held sway over such a large area. He befriended a war chief named Tattooed Serpent, brother of the Great Sun. Under the chief were his kin, who served in various official capacities, then "Honored Men" (nobles), and "Stinkards" (commoners). When the chief died unexpectedly in 1725 his hearth was immediately extinguished. He lay on his bed, dressed in his finest clothing, moccasined as if to go on a journey, and wearing his crown of white feathers mingled with red. His arms and pipes of peace lay by his side. A large wooden pole commemorated his victories. The French visitors sat at the side of the temple as the corpse of Tattooed Serpent was carried on a litter to the shrine, followed by sacrificial victims with red daubed hair and their executioners. The victims included two of the chief's wives, one of his sisters, and his chief counselor, doctor, and pipe bearer.

At the temple the victims sat on assigned mats, their heads covered with skins (Figure 12.18). They chewed tobacco pellets that numbed their senses and were strangled swiftly. Then the chief's body was placed in a

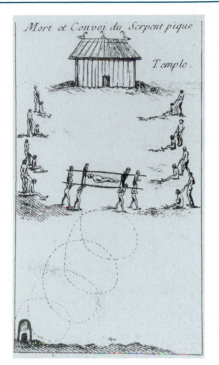

12.18 In 1725 the French explorer Le Page du Pratz depicted a dead Natchez chief being carried on a litter to his temple atop an earthen mound. Sacrificial victims kneel in wait, their executioners behind them.

trench with his wives, and his hut was burnt down. The other victims were either buried with the chief or in their own villages.

The Calusa: c. 500 BCE to Historic Times

Far to the south, the Calusa people developed similarly nuanced adaptations to local conditions. Southern Florida was a waterlogged landscape, largely submerged by freshwater flowing sluggishly through a maze of salt-grass and swamps. Where dry land could be found, by the Gulf and Atlantic coasts or along major rivers (such as the Kissimmee and Caloosahatchee), hunters and fisher folk settled, also foraging for plant foods. Some of them grew squashes, gourds, chili peppers, and papaya, but these efforts paled into insignificance beside the importance of fishing.

The Calusa people lived along a subtropical southern Florida coastline that enjoyed mild winters. In the northern areas of their homeland the people dwelt in the heart of an estuarine landscape, where a convex barrier-reef system enclosed broad bays fringed with mangrove swamps (Figure 12.19). The southern part of this coast is sometimes called the Ten Thousand Islands, a lattice of mangrove islets forming a mosaic of narrow channels that can be navigated only by canoe. In the north the Pine Island Sound area is a tapestry of sea-grass meadows supporting numerous species of small fish and juveniles, as well as innumerable bivalves and gastropods (Walker, 2013). These shellfish provided meat, and their shells served as raw material for artifacts of all kinds, including fish hooks. When the first Spanish conquistadors landed in Calusa country in the sixteenth century, they found dense, sedentary populations whose leaders exercised significant political influence over much of southern Florida. Spanish accounts tell of an elaborate society whose prosperity and power came from their maritime economy and from wide social and trading contacts.

Calusa origins lie among earlier maritime societies dating back to at least 500 BCE (Marquardt and Walker, 2013; Marquardt, 2014). They and their successors lived in an estuarine environment that was unpredictable and far from homogeneous. Both short-term and longer-term climatic fluctuations caused local changes in topography, and hence in fish and mollusk resources, that may well have kept population growth in check. Food supplies were never evenly distributed; nor were they even temporarily stable. Anyone who lived and fished in this ever-changing landscape was always vulnerable to sudden climate changes and devastating hurricanes, even to sea-level changes of a few inches that flooded shallow estuaries. This was never the kind of coastal environment where societies flourished and grew steadily and ladder-like over many centuries, achieving greater cultural and social complexity thanks to bountiful fisheries. Yet the societies that did develop here varied greatly in their complexity and elaboration. As in southern California, much depended on one's relationships not only with neighbors, but also with groups who lived inland. What developed were decentralized ways of adapting to a subtropical aquatic environment that proved to be both flexible and effective. Everything depended on how people interacted with one another within the contexts of their own local surroundings and historical experience. The Calusa responded by focusing on fishing, generally with nets, as well as harvesting mollusks. They fished on a large scale.

Deep-sea cores from the Sargasso Sea in the Atlantic chronicle a warming trend that began in 850 CE and reached a peak between 1000 and 1100. These centuries coincided in general terms with the Medieval Warm Period. Sea levels rose in Calusa country, flooding mangrove swamps, an important food source.

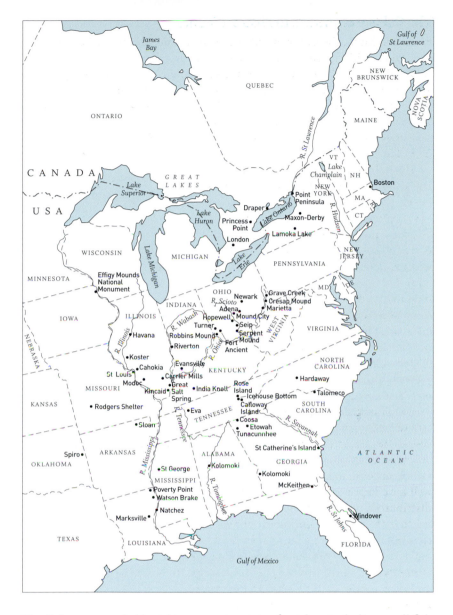

12.19 Map of major sites and cultures described in Chapter 12.

The Calusa responded by taking a great variety of catches, including small fish (pinfish and pigfish, for instance), as well as many whelks, conchs, and other marine snails, also smaller numbers of oysters and clams. The centuries between 800 and 1200 CE saw the apogee of Calusa culture, with hundreds, perhaps thousands, of people living in the immediate vicinity of Pine Island Sound. They left the greatest concentration of shell middens anywhere in North America.

Beyond accumulating shell middens, the Calusa also constructed steep-sided shell mounds, causeways, ramps, and canals. Some of their middens are linear, snaking through mangrove swamps for hundreds of meters. One on Cayo Costa is 374 ft (114 m) long and 15.1 ft (4.6 m) high. Some communities expended much effort in building canals to aid canoe navigation. The largest, 23 ft (7 m)

wide and 4.9 ft (1.5 m) deep, ran for 2.5 miles (4 km) across Pine Island and was
designed as a series of segments separated by small dams, so that a traveler could
lift a canoe from one area of impounded water to the next, scaling a height of
12.8 ft (3.9 m) as he or she crossed the island. It was, in effect, a canoe portage
that was often a canal (Luer and Wheeler, 1997).

Many Calusa middens in Pine Island Sound contain millions of whelk shells,
representing systematic, intensive collection over many centuries. Lightning and
pear whelks could be collected by the tens of thousands on the sandy bottoms
of shallow bays. One adult lightning whelk can yield as much as 1.9 lb (0.9 kg)
of flesh. Whelk shells, and perhaps the flesh, were also commodities in highly
organized exchange networks, which allowed the Calusa to create a much more
complex society than many other maritime groups.

The Calusa were so dependent on fish and mollusks that these two foods
comprise most of every sample from their shell middens (when put through
fine-mesh screens). The proportions of fish and mollusks vary, with higher
proportions of fish coming from sites nearer the ocean. One deeper inlet sample
yielded 47 percent fish, while more estuarine sites had only between 7 and 1
percent. Not surprisingly, the largest fish came from sites by inlets. About half
the bones at both shallow-water and inlet sites came from hard-headed catfish
and mollusk-eating sheepshead (Figure 12.20).

One could reasonably assume that Calusa society developed steadily along a
simple trajectory of ever-greater social and political complexity, supported by a
reliably plentiful, unchanging but very diverse food base. The Calusa did indeed
become a complex, well-organized society over many centuries, with connections
across the Florida peninsula. But one subtle variable played a decisive role in
their society. Here, more than almost anywhere else in the world, seemingly
insignificant sea-level changes could play havoc with lifeways. Even a rise or
fall of a few inches could devastate a sea-grass fishery or destroy oyster or whelk
beds within a single generation.

The sea-level fluctuations caused by the Medieval Warm Period or the subsequent Little Ice Age had a major impact on the shallow-water estuaries of such

places as Pine Island Sound, which has water that is never deeper than 4 ft (1.2 m). In human terms sea level changes affected not only the siting of houses but also the availability of firewood and food supplies, especially in cooler times when sea levels fell, as they did between 580 and 850 CE. Increased social complexity was most likely a response to harder times.

A greater reliance on watercraft also contributed to the growing complexity of Calusa life, hinted at by an increase in the number of shell woodworking tools after 800 CE. The elite probably controlled boatbuilding, for they needed larger canoes to maintain contacts with trading partners and potential rivals. This is also the period when major works, such as the Pine Island canal, were undertaken and when the long-distance trade in valuable stone increased. Cultural influences from powerful Mississippian chiefdoms with distinctive religious beliefs far to north may have come into play. Most likely, however, the social organization of Calusa society was never rigidly hierarchical before the arrival of the Spaniards.

The only way for the Calusa to rely on aquatic resources successfully was to live in compact, permanent settlements. Their social networks extended far beyond a single village, in an environment where the power of different chiefs changed constantly as the abundance of fisheries fluctuated. Long-term storage was nearly impossible, so control over strategic foods was all-important and reciprocal trade and exchange relationships benefited everyone. Calusa society may have become more complex during difficult times, not because a growing population had outstripped food supplies but because a network of local settlements was needed to balance out supply and demand. Given the impossibility of hoarding, the overwhelming advantage lay in redistributing one's excess to one's needy neighbors, in the expectation that they would do the same when positions were reversed.

The glue that held Calusa society together must have lain partly in the realm of the intangible. The Calusa enjoyed a complex ritual life in which ceremonial feasting, dancing and other rituals, as well as singing and oral recitations,

CALUSA BIRD MYTHOLOGY

Almost nothing is known of Calusa bird mythology. We have only some chance discoveries of parts of wooden dancing masks preserved in waterlogged archaeological deposits. A whooping crane head crafted in cypress wood has come from Pineland and is dated to 865–985 CE. The bill, which could be opened and shut to make a clacking sound, was clearly part of a dancer's mask. Waterbirds were important in Florida Native American society from at least 5,000 to 6,000 years ago, as well

as in many other places. For example, cranes had a significant association with shamans, who rode long distances on their backs in Northwest Coast Tlingit iconography. Ainu girls in Japan have long performed, and still perform, an elegant crane dance.

The evidence of crane mythology associated with a mask becomes even more significant when combined with several wooden animal heads excavated from the waterlogged Key Marco site in 1895–96. The series includes masks depicting raccoons, rabbits, great horned owls, an eagle, and a falcon. Some may have been parts of dance masks,

others totem symbols. The designs would probably have allowed a dancer to produce dramatic effects during his or her performance. Most likely the Calusa masked dancers performed dramatizations of the process of spiritual transformation, in which the audience participated. Their ancient myth dramas and legends have long vanished into oblivion, but the occasional discoveries of masks and other ceremonial regalia proclaim that the link between the living and supernatural worlds was permeable for both animals and humans. The clacking crane mask of Pineland is a compelling witness.

played an important role (see Box: Calusa Bird Mythology, p. 289). The Calusas' ferocious reputation and swampy homeland meant that they escaped much of the trauma of Spanish colonization until the seventeenth and early eighteenth centuries, when smallpox epidemics devastated their densely populated towns and villages. In the end, it was not climate change, but the ravages of exotic disease that destroyed the Calusa and their distinctive fishing and foraging society. Otherwise, they would probably have survived alongside Europeans into modern times.

SUMMARY

- The Mississippian first developed in the American Bottom near modern-day St. Louis, but new traditions and cosmologies evolved and spread widely as a result of cultural entanglements between diverse groups.

- Intensified cultivation of starchy seeds rather than maize lay behind the Early Mississippian. Maize intensification developed after 1000 CE, when Mississippian societies coalesced across much of the Southeast during the eleventh and twelfth centuries.

- Cahokia, the largest Mississippian center, developed in the American Bottom after 900 CE. During its apogee, from 1050 to 1250, Cahokia was a major economic, political, and ritual center whose layout reflected Southeastern cosmology and its dualities. A powerful elite rose to prominence after 1050.

- Complex ritual beliefs and ceremonial focused on mythic animals, people, and their activities in the supernatural Above world. They changed over time, but are reflected in motifs and themes found over a wide area from the Southeast into Oklahoma. A triad of cults was involved: warfare, nature/fertility, and ancestors. This triad is often described as the Southeastern Ceremonial Complex.

- Cahokia's power declined after 1250, as other large centers rose to prominence, among them Etowah and Moundville. The latter eventually became effectively a necropolis. Mississippian chiefdoms survived in modified form up to and beyond Spanish contact during the sixteenth century.

- The Calusa people of southern Florida developed a series of polities based on major ceremonial centers and intensive shallow-water fishing. Calusa societies varied considerably in their complexity and were affected profoundly by minor changes in sea level that impacted on their fisheries. They were devastated by exotic diseases after Spanish contact.

CHAPTER 13

Algonquians and Iroquoians

Their food is whatever they can get from the chase and from fishing; for they do not till the soil at all…In the month of February and until the middle of March, is the great hunt for beavers, otters, moose, bears…and for the caribou, an animal half ass and half deer. If the weather then is favorable, they live in great abundance, and are as haughty as Princes and Kings; but if it is against them, they are greatly to be pitied, and often die of starvation.

So Jesuit missionary Pierre Biard described the Mik'maq people near what is now Bar Harbor, Maine, in 1613 (Snow, 1980). They were expert fisherfolk, living in small bands, who were to trade extensively with the French and other Europeans for furs.

When other Europeans sailed up the St. Lawrence River, they came into contact with powerful Haudenosaunee (Iroquois) nations and with the Huron (Wendat). Less spectacular Northeastern societies flourished along the Atlantic Coast, while other groups anchored themselves to interior lakes and rivers. This was an unsettled world, where farmers cultivated maize at the northern limits of its range. Much controversy surrounds the origins of two major linguistic groups: Algonquians and Iroquoians. But how and when did maize first arrive in the Northeast? What role did warfare play in the complex later history of this large region? Fortunately, a productive marriage of archaeology, ethnography, and written records provides some answers (Birch, 2015) (Figure 13.1).

Algonquian and Iroquoian

People living along the coast between Nova Scotia and North Carolina were Algonquian speakers. They formed the Eastern Algonquian language group, isolated from their western and northern relatives by an intrusive block of **Iroquoian** and other languages in the interior. The ultimate origins of Algonquian are still a mystery, but a form of this language probably goes back far into the past, perhaps even to the Archaic, a time when ancient cultures in the Eastern Woodlands were more generalized. Both Algonquian and languages from the Southeast may, perhaps, be descended from a common group of related dialects spoken throughout the Eastern Woodlands before about 4000 to 3000 BCE.

The northern Iroquoian languages form the most important barrier between the coastal Algonquian speakers and those to the west (Snow, 1996). They act as an insulating block between coast and far interior from central Pennsylvania through New York and down the St. Lawrence Valley to the Gulf of St. Lawrence in Canada. Many linguistic experts believe that the Iroquoian language distribution represents an ancient intrusion of a different linguistic group into the Northeast, a group later associated with the powerful Haudenosaunee confederacies that dominated the area between the St. Lawrence and into New York at European contact. Fierce warriors, shrewd traders, and sophisticated negotiators, the Haudenosaunee were to play a dominant role in the Northeast to the very end of the Colonial period and beyond (for controversies, see Engelbrecht, 2003).

Terminal Archaic: 1650 to 700 BCE

Throughout the Eastern Woodlands food-rich rivers large and small that flowed through the centers of Archaic territories provided vital communication arteries

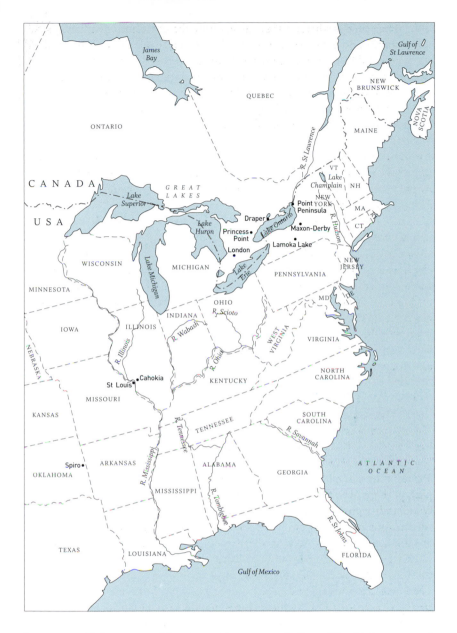

13.1 Map of major sites and cultures described in Chapter 13.

between widely scattered hunter-gatherer populations. The higher ground between the river valleys served as boundary land, sometimes remote, sometimes traversed by narrow trails often used for canoe portage. Much of the more rugged landscape was little more than a place where neighbors might hunt and collect wild vegetable foods.

Dean Snow (1980) has estimated that no more than 25,000 people lived in New England before 8000 BCE, and only between 158,000 and 191,000 in 1600 CE. He calculates an average growth rate of 0.02 percent over these 9,600 years, with occasional periods of rapid increase and sometimes catastrophic decline. In contrast, in recent years the world population has increased at a

13.2 A Susquehanna projectile point. Length 2.7 in. (6.9 cm).

13.3 Orient fish-tailed point. Length approximately 4.3 in. (11 cm).

rate sometimes as high as 1.8 percent. The spacing between different groups endured for thousands of years, changing only during the last six centuries before European colonization. By then the introduction of new storage technologies and farming had allowed higher population densities in many parts of the Northeast.

Between 1650 and 700 BCE the Terminal Archaic communities of the Northeast enjoyed a diverse, and carefully scheduled, hunting-and-gathering lifeway. The Susquehanna Tradition of New York, Pennsylvania, and neighboring areas flourished during the earlier centuries of the Terminal Archaic (c. 1650–1320 BCE). It was marked by a variety of broad projectile points that may also have doubled as knives (Levine *et al.*, 1999) (Figure 13.2). The Orient Tradition replaced the Susquehanna in the New York region, itself characterized by long, narrow points with fishtail-shaped bases that persisted in use during later Woodland cultures as well (Figure 13.3). Oval and rectangular soapstone bowls with flat bottoms and lug handles, perhaps copies of wooden prototypes, came into widespread use by both Orient and Susquehanna people, especially in larger base camps. These heavy cooking vessels were apparently highly prized, traded widely, and lasted a long time.

Susquehanna and Orient flourished alongside Archaic societies in many areas (see Box: The Maritime Archaic of the Subarctic, pp.192–94), with much human settlement concentrated near rivers and coasts. There were some population movements from New York and southern New England into more northern areas. These population movements and the population growth that may have attended them are still little understood. They may be connected to a general warming trend and the stabilization of sea levels, which would likely be positive factors favoring the expansion of Terminal Archaic cultures.

Woodland Societies: c. 1000 BCE to 1000 CE

The Algonquians of New England and the Atlantic coastal plain lived at the northernmost limit of maize cultivation and the southernmost extent of Atlantic salmon migration (Bernstein, 1999; Hart, 1999). They exploited both fish and tropical cultigens, to the point that they could have congregated in large villages (as did the Haudenosaunee, described below). These may have been circles of thatched, wigwam-like huts spaced around a central area, but no such large settlements have yet come to light. Most groups lived in alluvial floodplain environments, where the soils were most fertile, so many settlements were destroyed by flooding or erosion caused by occasional major floods. Their inhabitants practiced shifting agriculture, so they probably did not leave many artifacts or substantial hut foundations behind them. As with the first Americans who peopled the continent, the archaeological signature of the Algonquians is exiguous, so it is hardly surprising that little has been discovered.

Maize, an important feature of local economies at European contact, had been grown in large quantities in the Connecticut Valley and other river systems centuries earlier, and apparently stored in granaries located on well-drained gravelly soils and river terraces. The date of the introduction of maize continues to be a matter of controversy. The earliest microbotanical evidence from the Vinette site in New York dates to 300 BCE and is said also to come from the St. Lawrence Valley at about the same time (Gates St-Pierre and Thompson, 2015; Hart and Lovis, 2013), but more evidence is needed. Traces of farming villages have come from CRM-based area excavations in various Massachusetts cities, also in Vermont and Rhode Island, but no one has been able to excavate an entire village or the cemetery that might have accompanied it. People still moved to different locations according to the season, dispersing to hunt deer, and perhaps to trade or take beaver, a known historic activity.

Local populations remained sparse, with the densest concentrations living in territories of widely differing size in river drainages, near lakes, and along sea coasts. Pottery appears in many communities by at least 1500 to 1300 BCE, but the moment of appearance varied considerably (Taché and Hart, 2013). The increased use of pottery may signal a trend toward more sedentary settlement. Several innovations arrived in the Northeast during the first millennium CE, among them the bow and arrow (c. 600 CE) and, in more northerly regions, the birchbark canoe: a light and versatile craft ideal for navigating fast-moving streams, it was made of paper birch, which flourishes in formerly glaciated terrain. Such canoes were used for gathering wild rice, which grew in dense, waterlogged stands. While one person paddled, the other would bend the stalks over the canoe and beat them with a stick, detaching the ripe seed, which could then be stored for the long winter months.

The Northeast is remarkable for its ecological diversity, also its plentiful lakes and waterways, there being few significant physiographical boundaries. This meant that people moved freely over considerable distances, so there were frequent contacts between neighbors. Back in the 1950s William Ritchie identified a "**Meadowood** phase," named after an estate of that name in Monroe County, New York (Versaggi, 1999). Originally, Meadowood appeared to be confined to western and central New York, but its distinctive thin, triangular Onondaga chert blades, highly standardized projectile points, birdstones, gorgets, conchoidally shaped pots, and other artifacts actually occur over a much wider area (Figures 13.4 and 13.5). The core areas are in southern Ontario north of Lake Erie and much of New York, but Meadowood artifacts are also found along the St. Lawrence Valley and into Quebec. Some researchers talk of a Meadowood interaction sphere, a broad area over which artifacts, especially fine-grained chert, birdstones, seashells, and other exotica, also ideas, passed among different groups between about 1000 and 400 BCE. These exchange networks most likely handled objects that had prestige or symbolic meaning, but more research is needed (Taché, 2011a, 2011b).

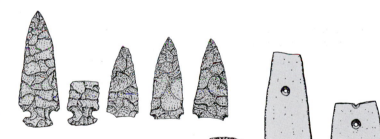

13.4 Meadowood phase artifacts. *Above*: side-notched projectile points. *Right*: expanded base drill. *Far right*: stone gorgets.

13.5 Meadowood birdstone from the Peace Bridge site on Lake Erie. The Peace Bridge site was used for more than 3,000 years. It is a location with extensive chert deposits, ideal for toolmaking.

Throughout this diverse area large base camps anchored different territories, some of them close to rich stands of native grasses. The resulting seed caches helped tide the people over the lean months, as did squashes. Adena trade networks extended into parts of the Northeast and Meadowood country. Copper ornaments, slate gorgets, birdstones, and boatstones from Ohio—these and many other grave goods hint at an Adena cultural influence that went beyond simple trade and exchange.

Meadowood cemeteries often cluster on low, natural hills, just like burials in earlier centuries. The graves were closely packed together, the bodies usually cremated, but not always immediately after death. The mourners lined the burial pits with bark, laying out the cremated remains in shrouds sprinkled with red ocher. Later, Adena-style burial mounds with log-lined graves and exotic artifacts came into fashion across a large area from southern Ontario, through New York and parts of southern and western New England, and into the Delaware drainage. Many of these societies were contemporary with the Hopewell Tradition of the Midwest, but Hopewell exchange networks never penetrated far into New England.

Despite widespread agriculture, the basic adaptation in southern New England had primordial roots in the Archaic of earlier millennia, but there is increasing regional variation after 700 BCE. In some areas winter hunting camps lay close to small streams and ponds in the back country. Collecting shellfish was important near the coast. During the Terminal Archaic ocean temperatures were warmer than today, so the people exploited bay scallops, oysters, and quahogs, shellfish that are sensitive to cold water (Bernstein, 1999). In contrast, early farming societies lived by colder seas and relied more heavily on the soft clam (*Mya arenaria*) in some areas.

Societies in Maine and northern New England never became cultivators, remaining hunters, plant gatherers, and shellfish collectors. They did adopt clay vessels before 2,000 years ago, considerably later than peoples to the south. Some of the coastal populations lived in substantial semi-subterranean pit dwellings. These oval houses were between 11.4 and 13.1 ft (3.5 to 4 m) long, with a sunken hearth near the entrance and elevated sleeping benches along the walls. Apparently, they were conical wigwam or tipi-like structures excavated partially below ground level for additional warmth and insulation. Judging from animal bones, many coastal aboriginal peoples dwelt in pithouse communities for fall, winter, and spring, perhaps moving inland during the summer to take salmon, alewife, shad, and eels from streams and lakes.

The same basic lifeway persisted among a great diversity of populations in the coastal Northeast up to and beyond European contact in the sixteenth and seventeenth centuries.

Northern Iroquoian Origins

The origin of the northern Iroquoians ranks as one of the major controversies of North American archaeology. We can but summarize the major hypotheses here (see Snow, 1996). Early anthropologists believed the St. Lawrence Valley was the homeland of all Iroquoian-speaking people, but these and related theories were abandoned about seventy-five years ago, with the discovery of archaeological sites quite different from those of historical Haudenosaunee groups. At the same time linguists found close ties between Iroquoian and Cherokee, the language spoken in the southern Appalachian region of the southeastern United States. This led to an influential theory that had the Haudenosaunee arriving in their northern homeland from the south. This hypothesis persisted for generations, despite the discovery of early Haudenosaunee societies with strong Algonquian features, partly because scholars of the day assumed Native American cultures were static and immutable. Any changes in local society were interpreted as modifications resulting from contact between invading Haudenosaunee and indigenous Algonquian cultures. Today, the intellectual pendulum has swung far in the opposite direction, with an understanding that the past was characterized by constant change. Many researchers are now reluctant to use such historical terms as "Mohawk" or "Seneca" to describe local groups in the region dating to as late as 1500 CE.

In the late 1930s archaeologists speculated that Iroquoian culture might have developed among a population already living in the Northeast. No ancestral version of Haudenosaunee culture was known from the Southeast, nor were there any signs of their northward migration in the Ohio Valley. Richard MacNeish rejected the migration theory in a classic monograph (1952). He examined historical Haudenosaunee pottery and traced its origins far back into ancient times, to the local Middle Woodland societies that archaeologists had hitherto assumed to be the ancestors of Algonquian speakers. MacNeish stressed local lines of development, an approach that has led to complex studies of evolving Haudenosaunee settlement patterns, changing subsistence strategies, and varying burial practices. The Haudenosaunee settlement landscape was very flexible, as communities came together, dispersed, migrated, and abandoned their settlements. All these groups had complex, dynamic histories and belief systems, competitive relationships with others, and ever-changing kin relationships. We have barely begun to understand the relationships between individuals, groups, and their natural and social environments; that is the big challenge for the future (Birch, 2015).

For generations archaeologists have subdivided Algonquian and Haudenosaunee cultural sequences into culture-historical stages that define different stages of the past in terms of such culture traits as language, longhouses, maize cultivation, and incised pottery. Numerous excavations and surveys in recent years have shown that such rigid subdivision misrepresents what was, in fact, a very fluid period of change taking many centuries, of repeated separations and fusions that reflected changing alliances, trade networks, the ebb and flow of diplomacy, and, above all, a rise in warfare (Engelbrecht, 2003). Almost total excavations of the Calvert, Draper, Mantle (Birch and Williamson, 2012), and Nodwell Haudenosaunee settlements in Ontario have documented the remarkable diversity of their culture, changing settlement patterns, and social organization (for summaries, see Birch, 2015; Hart et al., 2016; Jones and Creese, 2017; Williamson, 2014). Many archaeologists would now agree that Haudenosaunee-speaking cultures have deep roots in ancient times—the problem is to recognize them in the archaeological record.

Complex lexical studies of Iroquoian have isolated a set of clues that place these languages in an environmental setting very similar to that of the northeastern Eastern Woodlands. Human remains from early Middle Woodland times are said to display anatomical features very similar to those of historic populations. These shreds and patches of evidence are insufficient to establish whether Iroquoian-speaking cultures had from local roots, or were the result of migrations from outside. Nearly a century after research into Haudenosaunee origins began, we are still far from understanding a past that was much more complicated than previously imagined.

Early Iroquoians: 1000 BCE to 1100 CE

Largely because of MacNeish's pioneering work, most archaeologists assume that Iroquoian-speaking people have lived around the lower Great Lakes for a long time. Many experts believe the Iroquoians go back to Archaic times, and had their ultimate origins among societies which flourished before 2000 BCE. Others argue that the arrival of the Iroquoians coincides with the earliest appearance of the Late Archaic Lamoka culture in New York, in at least 2500 BCE, a culture, which, as we have seen, has ties in common with Archaic cultures in the Southeast (see Box: The Maritime Archaic of the Subarctic, pp. 192–94).

At least three broadly contemporary Early/Middle Woodland cultures flourished in the St. Lawrence lowlands during the first millennium CE, defined by differing styles of artifact and pottery. The Laurel culture flourished in northern Ontario, parts of Manitoba, Michigan, and Minnesota; the Saugeen developed in southwestern Ontario; but the best-known cultures are the Point Peninsula in New York, and later the Princess Point culture of central and eastern southern Ontario, which date from at least 600–700 CE (Crawford and Smith, 2002). All these cultures are variations on the same adaptive theme and included several neighboring bands. They interacted with one another, but it is not clear just how ethnically distinct they were.

There was a general continuity in subsistence and social life in the St. Lawrence lowlands from as early as Paleo-Indian times right up to the historic era. Point Peninsula and other Early/Middle Woodland cultures reflect this continuity, with a small and widely scattered indigenous population living in small bands, each with their own territory. The people were exploiting game, aquatic, and plant resources ever more efficiently. The earliest record of maize for the St. Lawrence Valley is between 400 and 200 BCE (Gates St-Pierre and Thompson, 2015). Initially this new crop may have served as a valuable supplemental food to wild plants or dried fish, for the stored grain could help reduce the risk of starvation during the harsh winter months. Maize could be planted in areas near summer fishing camps where nut trees did not grow, and wild rice never flourished. Thus, it added a new, reliable dimension to northern diet. In spring and summer these small groups would congregate into larger groups of between 100 and 300 people at river-side and lake-side fishing stations. During these gatherings important burial ceremonies were conducted in cemeteries close to the fishing camps, other ceremonies took place, and exotic artifacts and raw materials were exchanged. This annual pattern of establishing friendly ties with neighbors was adaptive, in that it ensured that hunting, fishing, and foraging were not disrupted by warfare. It also made it possible for people to shift from one band to another as populations rose and fell, but it is uncertain whether men or women remained with their home bands upon marriage.

The climate was so harsh that there were never sufficient food resources in one area to allow year-round, sedentary settlement. So the congregated bands had to scatter into small family groups during the long winter months to hunt forest game. During the historical period Algonquians of central Ontario also enjoyed such an annual coming together. The chiefs among them, often hereditary leaders from certain families, were without formal political power yet could resolve conflicts during the summer months when tiny bands became a concentrated population of more than a hundred people (Cleland, 1982). Perhaps the Middle Woodland peoples of southern Ontario had similar chiefs, the antecedents of the peace chiefs who were to emerge among later Haudenosaunee groups (Trigger, 1985).

If Point Peninsula is the ancestor of later Iroquoian traditions, then it developed into at least four later cultures: Princess Point, Glen Meyer, and Pickering in Ontario, and Owasco in New York (see Box: The Straightjacket of Culture History: Princess Point and Owasco). To what extent there was continuity between Point Peninsula and these later societies is still debated. But the frontier between pre-Iroquoian and Iroquoian appears to lie in Pont Peninsula groups (Snow, 1996). The controversy is still unresolved, but a new generation of research has shown that the situation was much more complex than once imagined, and driven by the diverse responses of individuals and groups to local circumstances.

THE STRAIGHTJACKET OF CULTURE HISTORY: PRINCESS POINT AND OWASCO

In many parts of North America, culture history ruled for generations during a long period when archaeologists were preoccupied with classification and chronology. Culture history gave birth to elaborate sequences of Archaic and Woodland cultures, subdivided on the basis of projectile points and other culture traits. As we learn more about these societies, however, these sequences—with their phases, traditions, and numerous (and often changing) cultural labels—have become increasingly meaningless except in the most general terms.

Different widely separated stages were once identified by major changes in individual culture traits, often mainly on pottery styles and projectile points. In the case of the Iroquois, however, a new generation of more detailed chronologies and more precise analysis has shown conclusively that the historic

Iroquois societies did not develop, ladderlike, from earlier cultures deep in ancient times. Even a cursory glance at ethnographic accounts of Northeastern societies reveals cases where language use in different communities shifts dramatically over a few generations, as both individuals and groups make strategic use of language, culture, and ethnicity. In short, neither language nor culture was constant, so formulations culture-history like "Owasco" are meaningless in an ancient world where interacting economic, political, and social factors helped define individual ethnicity and changing societies.

Here, for the record, are two enduring cultural labels that are still in widespread use, even if some experts consider them straightjackets!

Princess Point (650 CE)

Many Princess Point settlements were located on river flats, by sheltered inlets or tributary streams. We still know little of Princess Point settlements, but they were relatively large and compact, similar in some ways to later northern

13.6 A Princess Point cord-decorated pot.

Iroquoian villages but without the longhouses. Excavations at the Grand Banks and Lone Pine sites southwest of Lake Ontario have yielded maize fragments AMS-dated to between about 650 and 1000 CE (Crawford et al., 1998). Princess Point is often assumed to be the ancestor of both Glen Meyer and Pickering, which are well established as branches of the early Ontario Iroquois Tradition (Figure 13.6).

Middle Iroquoian: 1275 to 1350 CE or Later

Throughout Early Iroquoian times most communities numbered only a few hundred souls even at the most favorable times of the year. Some people, especially the elderly (over the age of forty), may have lived in the same settlements year-round, but society was still organized in bands and localized matrilineal clans. Each group had its own leader, married outside the group, and identified with a selection of totemic animals. Intermarriage was an important way of cementing good relations with neighbors, but, by the same token, there appears to have been little long-distance exchange of ceremonial goods. This perhaps indicates less elaborate burial customs than some we have seen in earlier chapters.

Maize agriculture assumed increasing importance in Iroquoian societies from the early fourteenth to sixteenth centuries as population densities rose (Pfeiffer *et al.*, 2016). The introduction of the common bean in about 1300 CE also had a dramatic impact. Maize and bean agriculture may have been one of the factors behind the profound changes in Iroquoian life throughout the St. Lawrence lowlands and in the Mohawk drainage during the fourteenth century.

Owasco culture (c. 1000–1300 CE)

Owasco flourished to the south, in the Mohawk drainage and Finger Lakes region of upper New York State, and dates to about 1000 to 1300 CE. Owasco culture is radiocarbon dated to between 1000 and 1300 (Ritchie, 1965). Owasco is defined by the appearance of specific pottery forms, longhouses and the matrilocal residence associated with them, nucleated villages, and maize–bean–squash agriculture. The eleventh-century Maxon-Derby site near Syracuse, New York, lies on the terrace of a large stream and covers about 2.4 acres (1 ha). Seven houses were excavated, one of them almost square, others more elongated, one an oblong dwelling measuring 26 by 59 ft (8 by 18 m). House design was far from standardized at Maxon-Derby, but seemed to be evolving toward the well-known Iroquois longhouse design that was used everywhere in later centuries (Figure 13.7).

Other sites with longhouses, such as the Sackett settlement near Canandaigua, were protected with palisades and earthworks and date to the thirteenth century, much later than the beginnings of Owasco. Sackett's ditch and palisade enclose an elliptical area 203 by 242 ft (62 by 74 m). By this time most major villages were palisaded, and maize, squash, and bean cultivation had assumed major importance in the subsistence economy. AMS dating now shows that this form of agriculture only became commonplace across the Owasco region after 1300 CE, centuries later than once suspected. A much higher incidence of tooth decay occurs among local populations at about this time, perhaps as a result of a higher carbohydrate content in the diet.

13.7 The eastern end of House C at the Maxon-Derby site near Syracuse, New York. Wooden markers indicate the outlines of the structure.

13.8 Smoking a native tobacco in a zoomorphic pipe. Artist's reconstruction of Iroquois life at the Keffer site, Ontario.

13.9 Another reconstruction of daily life at the Keffer site, Ontario.

Between 1300 and 1350 Iroquoians began living in much larger communities and became heavily dependent on maize farming (Hart *et al.*, 2016; Williamson, 2014). For example, two or three communities near London, Ontario, joined into a single settlement along a creek. Some of the largest Iroquoian settlements now covered more than 5 acres (2 ha). More families lived in the same dwelling, and longhouses were built closer together and sometimes parallel to one another in groups. Perhaps these groupings coincided with related matrilineages or individual clans. Placing longhouses closer together may also have been a labor-saving device to reduce the amount of palisading needed to protect larger villages (Figures 13.8 and 13.9).

By 1400 some of the largest Iroquoian settlements regularly housed as many as 1,500 people, with elaborate village plans, large work areas, and even garbage disposal zones (Warrick, 1984). A few Iroquoian settlements achieved populations of more than 2,000 people, about six clan groups. The largest known settlement is the Draper site in Ontario, which covered 20 acres (8 ha) and housed between 2,000 and 3,000 people for a few decades in the fifteenth century (Figure 13.10).

These larger villages may have resulted from clusters of scattered communities coming together, perhaps for mutual protection. But as bigger settlements developed hitherto dispersed clans came into much closer proximity, with a greater potential for disputes, factional quarrels, and other disruptions. Indeed, factionalism may have strained dispute-resolving mechanisms to the limit and prevented large villages from lasting long. The Iroquoians may have sought to combat this by instituting more formal village councils made up of representatives from each clan (Trigger, 1985). Among the historic Haudenosaunee, these offices were hereditary in individual families of the clans. Just as among historic tribes in the Southeast, there may have been separate chiefs (*sachems*) for war and peace.

Peace chiefs kept track of public opinion, settled domestic disputes, organized community works, rituals and ceremonies, and negotiated with others. War chiefs had more limited powers. They organized and led war parties, dealt with prisoners, and killed suspected witches. Both offices were sources of prestige rather than power, for no chief had the authority to do anything more than act as a spokesman. His family had to work hard to provide the additional food that

13.10 Artist's reconstruction of the Draper site in Ontario at its largest.

enabled him to extend hospitality to other people in the village and to strangers. Since there was no fixed law of primogeniture, relatives would compete with one another for the succession, vying to prove their prowess as generous hosts, brave warriors, and expert hunters (Trigger, 1969). Among Haudenosaunee groups living north of Lake Ontario, the solidarity of each community was now celebrated with the elaborate Feast of the Dead, a ceremonial reburial of those who had died while a village was inhabited, carried out before the settlement was moved to a new location (see Box: The Feast of the Dead).

Larger settlements brought new pressures to Iroquoian society. A community of 1,500 people consumed significant quantities of firewood, to say nothing of construction timber. Agricultural land was soon cleared and exhausted, so these large settlements had to shift location more frequently than smaller ones.

Warfare became an important factor in Iroquoian life during the fourteenth century. Many settlements were now elaborately fortified, but others were still undefended, close to navigable waters, not away from them as became the rule in later, more turbulent, centuries. Cannibalism appears for the first time—in the form of split, cut, and cooked human bones found in Iroquoian sites throughout southern Ontario. The consumption of human flesh was not a matter of obtaining extra protein, but an intensely symbolic act. The northern Haudenosaunee waged war, at least in theory, to avenge the killing of kinsfolk by outsiders. The warriors would capture someone from the offending group as a replacement for the victim; or they would kill him, bringing his head or scalp home as a trophy. Male prisoners were often slain in elaborate sacrifices to the sun, but women and children were usually permitted to live.

Why did warfare suddenly assume such importance after 1300? Some theories argue that the cooler and drier climatic conditions of the Little Ice Age led to more frequent droughts and food shortages, so that Iroquoian groups living on the sand plains of southwestern Ontario and on New York's cool Allegheny Plateau may have moved away from their homelands in search of moister, more fertile soils. The shift would have triggered more competition for prime farming land and other strategic resources. Population densities among the Iroquoians were still low, however, and there was more agricultural land available than people to occupy and cultivate it. Neighboring groups could have fought over hunting rights, but why go to war over deer, when the game population may, in fact, have increased on account of there being so much cleared agricultural land to graze on? Most likely is that warfare was a quest for personal prestige. As time went on, the basic tasks of hunting, fishing, and forest clearance, once tests of a man's ability to support his family through the winter, became collective tasks carried out by larger groups. Women, as the farmers, were now accounting for more food and were the dominant social lineages. Thus, men had to prove themselves and their worth. Disputes between neighboring groups may have proliferated as the young men sought every excuse to wage war—perhaps to the point that every community had some enemies. Constant warfare, with its risk of premature death, especially for adults, may have caused hardship by disrupting critical subsistence practices.

Fortified Middle Iroquoian communities may have first developed in western Iroquoian country, where the people had long fought with the Central Algonquians; then fortification came into use over the entire region, resulting in major changes in local society. For generations the Iroquoians had maintained close ties between scattered communities by the practice of men and women marrying into neighboring villages. With larger settlements the need for such marriage customs was reduced, so the ties that helped reduce conflict between neighbors dissolved. One of the only alternatives was to settle disputes by force. Warfare became a means of acquiring not only prestige, but also captives for ritual sacrifice. Thus, argues Trigger, the men assumed a prestigious role in a society that was becoming more and more sedentary and agricultural.

THE FEAST OF THE DEAD

Early accounts from French explorers and missionaries in the sixteenth and seventeenth centuries tell us that the Haudenosaunee ("people of the long house," members of the Iroquois Confederacy) Feast of the Dead was held every ten or twelve years, when large villages moved their locations. Whether this was part of the abandonment process is uncertain. The Feast involved the reburial of most of those who had lived in the village during its existence, whether they had previously been buried, or stored above ground on such structures as scaffolds, or deposited in ossuaries, where human remains in different stages of decomposition were co-mingled (Birch and Williamson, 2015). Originally a community ritual, it assumed great importance in the early seventeenth century as a symbolic way of promoting unity among the various tribes of the confederacy. Moving a community was an important process that involved high ceremony, detaching the people from their pilgrimage sites, sacred locations, and what one can generically call a sense of "place." Even after the people had moved, abandoned villages and their ossuaries continued to be a continuous spiritual responsibility.

The Feast of the Dead lasted ten days. The first eight were spent collecting bodies from local cemeteries. Over these days, all the corpses except the most recently deceased were stripped of flesh and skin. The robes in which they had been buried were burned. The washed and cleaned bones were wrapped in new beaver skins and placed in decorated bags. Then the families feasted and celebrated the dead. On the appointed day processions of mourners carried the dead to the village where the ceremony was to be held (Figure 13.11). The procession halted at each settlement along the way. Gifts were exchanged and friendships confirmed.

Feasting and dancing continued as the procession reached its destination. A large pit some 10 ft (3 m) deep and 15 ft (4.5 m) wide was dug close to the host village and scaffolding erected around it. Meanwhile, the packages of bones were reopened and mourned over for the last time before being carried to the empty ossuary. Each village and clan took its proper place and displayed their gifts on poles for about two hours, a chance for the givers to show not only their piety, but also their wealth. A signal was given. Each clan and village hung its bone parcels on an assigned section of the scaffolding poles. The chiefs stood high on the surrounding platforms and announced the offerings given in the names of the dead. In this way the presents were redistributed throughout the villages, while each family fulfilled its obligations within society.

As twilight came the mourners lined the pit with fifty beaver robes taken from among the presents. Then recently deceased, still-whole bodies were interred and covered with more beaver robes. Some broken metal vessels and other artifacts were laid out at the bottom of the pit for the use of the dead ancestors. The people surrounded the pit all night. At sunrise they emptied the packages of bones and grave goods into the ossuary, while the mourners sent up a great cry of lamentation. A few men in the pit mingled the bodies with poles, so that the burial was truly a communal one. Then the pit was filled, wooden poles placed at the top, and a shrine erected atop the mass burial place. The Feast ended with the distribution of the presents and great celebration. Friendships had been renewed, social bonds strengthened, and the dead buried honorably.

One cannot overestimate the importance of the Feast of the Dead. It fostered unity among Haudenosaunee confederacy members and with the Algonquian peoples to the north with whom they traded. The displayed wealth was staggering. Jesuit missionaries witnessed a Feast in 1636 attended by about 2,000 people, many from afar. They counted more than 1,200 presents distributed among the living or given to the dead. Many of these gifts were given to members of allied tribes. After European contact many of the offerings were prestigious imported goods, such as iron kettles, which were scarce and carried high prestige.

To European Contact and Beyond: From 1400 CE

After 1400 differences in pottery styles, burial practices, and house types chronicle major divisions between Iroquoian groups living north of Lakes Ontario and Erie. South of Lake Ontario, between 1450 and 1475, a small and a much larger village near Syracuse, New York, deliberately settled within a few miles of one another to form the Onondaga nation. The larger village was formed by the amalgamation of two smaller ones. Similar fusions took place all over Haudenosaunee country, with relatively dense local populations clustering in specific areas, separated

13.11 *The Feast of the Dead*, from Jesuit missionary Joseph-François Lafitau's 1724 *Mœurs des sauvages amériquains* (Manners of the American Savages). The drawing, with its macabre image of corpses and skeletons, is supposedly based on a Jesuit description from a century earlier.

The Feast of the Dead was a powerful political and social tool that did much to create a sense of unity among often fiercely competing groups. It also reinforced the powerful spiritual links between the ancestors and the living that were a bridge to the powerful supernatural world. The final act of burial released the souls of the dead and allowed them to travel west to the land of the ancestors. When Jean de Brébeuf witnessed a Feast of the Dead in 1636, a Wendat chief told him that the body rested in the final burial place, but the other part of the dual body, the soul, flew away to the realm of those who had gone before. The journey of the souls was hazardous, a time when their memories were removed by a mythic being named Oscotarach (Pierce-head), so that they were not tempted to return to the realm of the living. The construction of ossuaries, communities for the dead, created social memories among the living and reinforced the bonds between the living and the ancestors (Birch and Williamson, 2015). Abandoned villages and their ossuaries were as much part of the living landscape as occupied ones.

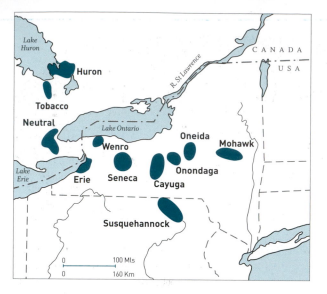

13.12 Map showing the geographic spread of Iroquoian groups in historic times.

from one another by largely uninhabited country. These new tribal groupings resulted in greater social complexity in Iroquoian life. Tribal councils emerged as an extension of village ones, designed to regulate life on a larger scale. Clan ties cut across village and tribal boundaries. Among the historic Haudenosaunee, some of these clans grouped themselves into associations that organized much of ceremonial life, including funerals. There were medicine societies, too, which treated the sick and carried out curing rituals. All these complex mechanisms helped maintain links between expanding, and increasingly complex, Iroquoian societies.

Why did large Iroquoian settlements and tribes form? Some sizable communities may have controlled important resources and exchange networks. But warfare may have been the major factor in forging large communities and political alliances. And when a village reached its maximum practicable size, the inhabitants expanded into new communities, forming confederacies, tribes, and other associations. These settlement clusters depleted natural food resources more rapidly, making the people more dependent on agriculture. The constant political maneuvering and warfare led to more elaborate fortifications in the sixteenth century—villages with multiple palisades, earthworks, and massive tree-trunk ramparts.

Before the end of the sixteenth century neighboring Iroquoian tribes in both Ontario and New York came together in loosely knit confederacies aimed at reducing blood feuding and warfare between close neighbors. The common link between them was an agreement to settle grievances by means other than bloodshed. A confederacy council of headmen from member tribes gathered occasionally for ceremonial feasts and conferences, and to adjudicate disputes and set reparations if called for. At European contact the major Iroquoian tribes were the Wendat, Erie, Tobacco, and Neutral in the north and, to the south, the famous Haudenosaunee Confederacy, made up of the Five Nations: Seneca, Cayuga, Onondaga, Oneida, and Mohawk. The Susquehannocks of the Susquehanna Valley were another Iroquoian group (Figure 13.12).

When did the Haudenosaunee League and other confederacies come into being? Bruce Trigger (1972, 1985) argued that the confederacies were a logical extension of complex, long-term forces that had much earlier replaced small hunting bands with larger groups, then with tribes. The confederacy was adaptive in that it allowed groups to legislate against unnecessary blood feuding while still maintaining individual cultural and political identity in their dealings with others. The arrival of Europeans and their fur traders created a new, highly volatile political situation, in which it was clearly an advantage for neighbors to be linked in close alliances. Since the Haudenosaunee already enjoyed confederacies, it would have been an easy matter to strengthen them in response to new circumstances.

For generations after the Haudenosaunee League was formed, the neighboring Wendat and Algonquians greatly feared the Five Nations. The Haudenosaunee themselves symbolized their League as a vast longhouse that stretched from

WAMPUM

The word **wampum** is derived from wampumpeag, a Massachusett word meaning "white strings of shell beads" (Bradley, 2011). Shape and color were both important. Wampum originally referred to white beads made from the inner spiral of the Channeled Whelk shell, *Busycotypus canaliculatus*. Black whelk beads came mainly from the Chesapeake Bay area. The term also includes black or purple shell beads made from the quahog clamshell (*Mercenaria mercenaria*). Wampum beads were a highly prized trade commodity, often kept on strings. They were tubular beads, up to quarter of an inch (0.6 cm) long, usually made by women. They used quartz dills bits mounted in wooden pump drills to pierce the shells, which were then strung and ground by rolling them on a grinding stone with sand and water. Such strings were used for storytelling, as ceremonial gifts, and for recording important agreements and major historical events (Figure 13.13). They could also be woven together into wampum belts, many

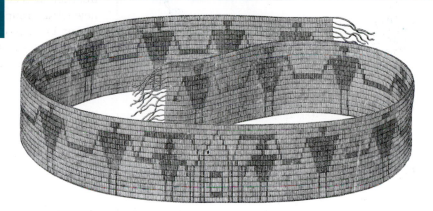

13.13 Wampum belt belonging to the Onondagas, 1881.

of which bear intricate designs with important meanings.

When wampum beads first came into use is unknown, but it was before the sixteenth century. According to Five Nations tradition, Hayehwatha, a member of the founding council, found a lake with ducks swimming it. They flew away, magically removing all the water. Hayehwatha found white shells on the bottom that he collected in a pouch and put by the central fire as a reminder of the Great Law that established the League. Wampum was a reminder of the

Great Law. A string was used to summon someone to a meeting. The beads were a symbol of ritual exchange and a way of conveying important information. White wampum beads were used as gifts to the living and to the dead, as well as a form of personal ornamentation. Wampum was intricate, and meant different things to different people. Other materials, such as twigs and porcupine twills, may have served for wampum in earlier times.

The Onondaga were the guardians of the wampum belts that recorded the constitution of the Iroquois confederacy, known as the Haudenosaunee. Every chief and clan mother had a wampum string that served as his ▶▶

west to east. The Seneca were the "Keepers of the Western Door," the Mohawk the "Keepers of the Eastern Door." The Onondaga were in the center, the "Keepers of the Council Fire." They were also "Keepers of the Wampum Belts" (see Box: Wampum).

At European contact all Haudenosaunee-speaking peoples depended heavily on agriculture, with fishing also a vital part of the subsistence economy. Among the Wendat of the north and the Seneca, agriculture—corn, beans, squash, and sunflowers—may have provided up to 80 percent of the diet. The northern Haudenosaunee lived in fortified villages, in longhouses covered with elm-tree bark that were shared by many families. They dwelt on either side of the central hearths. Unlike the Algonquians, the Haudenosaunee were matrilineal, with the children living with their mother's clan. Each longhouse group was a subdivision of the matrilineal clan, for sisters with their husbands and children shared a common dwelling. The men, who cleared the land, hunted, fished, traded, and built houses and fortifications, were warriors, and moved into the longhouses

or her credentials—a certificate of office, as it were—and was passed to the next generation or office holder. Wampum was a way of recording events and decisions, also a way of helping storytellers. The bead designs communicated ideas that served as memory aids for those reciting oral traditions, which gave them a unique importance in Iroquois culture. Wampum belts were traded widely to other groups, with large, ornate story belts having special importance. The Iroquois had no written script, so the wampum belt was a vital way of maintaining traditional histories, as well as details of alliances, treaties, and so on that were negotiated long before the lives of those who held them. Belts invited people to meetings, and when held were said to indicate that a speaker was uttering the truth. The Onondaga were the traditional guardians of wampum and still regard the belts as central to their traditional beliefs.

The longest known wampum belt is 6 ft (1.8 m) long and spells out the Treaty of Canandaigua, signed in 1794 by fifty sachems and war chiefs from the **Grand Council of the Six Nations** and Timothy Pickering, President George Washington's secretary of state (Figure 13.14). It is made up of thirteen figures holding hands connected to two individuals and a house. The thirteen people represent the thirteen states of the newly founded United States of America. The house and the two figures represent the Haudenosaunee.

After European contact wampum beads briefly became a form of currency that was linked to the beaver and marten fur trade. The Massachusetts Bay Colony recognized the beads as a currency in 1650, but the law was repealed two years later, as the West Indies trade brought coins into widespread use. But wampum remained a form of trade currency through much of the nineteenth century, when glass wampum beads were mass produced.

13.14 The signing of the Treaty of Canandaigua in 1794.

of their wives at marriage. The women grew, weeded, and harvested crops, and tended the children.

With its confederacies and tribes, Haudenosaunee society was governed highly effectively. Their political organizations may seem precarious, based as they were on decisions made by a network of tribal and community councils, in situations where consent was needed from all concerned. But, in fact, they were highly effective in suppressing blood feuds among populations numbering as many as 20,000 souls, and at coordinating at least a degree of diplomatic policy toward outsiders.

The northern Haudenosaunee were unified by many common religious beliefs and ceremonial practices. They were especially remarkable not for their material culture, but for the sophistication and finesse of their social relationships. The Haudenosaunee respected individual dignity and self-reliance. They looked down on public displays of emotion or open quarrelling, and considered politeness and hospitality toward one another and toward strangers fundamental to correct social behavior. As later events were to show, these warlike and astute people were more than a match for the European fur traders and missionaries who settled among them.

SUMMARY

- Between 1650 and 700 BCE Terminal Archaic communities in the Northeast enjoyed diverse and carefully scheduled hunter-gatherer lifeways. Different local groupings, such as Susquehanna and Orient, are identified by projectile-point forms.

- Algonquian peoples in New England and along the Atlantic coastal plain lived at the northernmost limit of maize cultivation. Maize came into use at an unknown date, but certainly by 300 BCE. Pottery appeared in many communities by 1300 to 1500 BCE, the bow and arrow by 600 CE.

- Throughout this ecologically diverse region large base camps anchored different territories, many of them part of the Meadowood cultural tradition. Trade networks linked isolated communities, and brought Adena-style artifacts, and perhaps cultural influences, from Ohio.

- Societies in Maine and northern New England never became farmers and remained hunter-gatherers until after European contact. Shellfish were a major part of the diet, as were fish.

- The origins of the northern Iroquois remain a mystery. Numerous local Woodland societies thrived and are classified under a variety of labels, including Princess Point, Glen Meyer, and Pickering in Ontario, and Owasco in New York.

- The common bean arrived in the Northeast in about 1300 CE, combining with maize farming to trigger major changes in the St. Lawrence lowlands. Iroquoian settlements with their longhouses became larger, perhaps for protection, some with as many as 1,000 inhabitants.

- During the sixteenth century neighboring Iroquoian tribes in Ontario and New York formed powerful confederacies, the most famous being the Haudenosaunee Confederacy, made up of the Five Nations: Seneca, Cayuga, Onondaga, Oneida, and Mohawk. This survived to European contact and beyond.

Consequences of Contact

"I thought I'd always be that way,
that's how I was.
I thought I'd live forever,
I thought I'd live forever.
I'd always be with the land,
it seemed,
ha na."

—Havasupai Farewell Song, Arizona

Seated female effigy vessel, often
called "Our Grandmother" or "Old
Woman Who Never Dies," from
Mississippi County, Arkansas. Height:
9.4 in. (24 cm). Dated 1500–1650 CE.

ENDURING THEMES
Consequences of Contact

The *entrada* of 1492 was, of course, a defining moment in North American history, but it would be a mistake to assume that it was a sudden moment of catastrophic change. Its effects were long lasting and traumatic, sometimes abrupt, but more often they rippled gradually across the vast continent, affecting Native American populations in all kinds of subtle ways. The chapters in Part Five summarize some of the complex developments and events that resulted from European contact. Here the themes mix and mingle, for they persist through more than five centuries and cannot be considered separate from one another.

Disease

The first theme is closely tied to the very earliest contacts between natives and newcomers: the catastrophic number of deaths caused by exotic diseases. The Native Americans had no immunity against smallpox, influenza, and other common Old World diseases. All that was needed was contact between a few Europeans and the local people to trigger an epidemic. In many cases the unfamiliar illnesses passed from village to village far beyond the frontiers of European settlement, sometimes long before such settlement occurred. Even small parties of explorers could be silent killers. The most vulnerable members of society were the elderly and the young, and these were often the first victims of an epidemic. Thousands of people perished. The loss of elders also deprived Native American societies of much wisdom and the experience of generations, the vital traditional knowledge that sustained them. We shall never know exactly how many people lost their lives in these epochal waves of death and destruction. But the casualties over five centuries were catastrophic and devastated pre-Columbian societies without a shot being fired.

Settlement and Colonization

The second major theme is the actual process of settlement and colonization itself. We discuss the Norse exploration of the Canadian Arctic and extreme Northeast in Chapter 14; these voyages had no lasting impact on Native American society. The *entrada* truly began with the arrival of Columbus in the Bahamas in 1492. His dramatic voyages opened the gates for exploration of unknown coasts, and, within a century, to permanent European colonies on North American soil. The story of the first European settlements, Pilgrim Fathers and all, is familiar to every American schoolchild, but what is not well known is the light that archaeology throws on these historical events. Apart from its ability to trace changes in human societies over long periods, archaeology is unique in its dispassionate portraits of the societies it studies. This is particularly important for research into the earliest European settlement, when patchy historical documents provide only a skeletal outline of individuals and events. I stress individuals, for written history deals typically with the doings of leaders and other prominent figures. In societies where only a few people were literate, almost everyone lived out their lives in anonymity, however important their contributions and skills.

The European exploration of North America is a historical patchwork of contacts with Native American peoples living in every kind of environment imaginable. What strikes you at once is the complete incompatibility between natives and newcomers. This was far more than incomprehension or linguistic barriers. Native American societies had entirely different understandings of the cosmos, of human existence, and of history. They also had radically different attitudes toward land ownership. We examine a number of contacts, knowing full well that we cannot possibly offer a comprehensive perspective. Some of the best archaeology comes from the Spanish Borderlands—research into De Soto's journey, Spanish missions and colonial settlements—especially when combined with historical records, oral traditions, and records of the spread of exotic trade goods. This is a chronicle of disastrous epidemics and the breakdown of political order, and a record of the significant differences in how Anglo-American and Hispanic-American cultures developed in North America. It is also the story of how Spanish policies of forcing people into missions failed abysmally (for details of the mission program, see Box: Mission Nuestra Señora de la Soledad, p. 348). For example, after years of contact between the Spanish and Native Americans, the native Californians had developed a culture that was a blend of traditional and Spanish elements—about 40 percent in material terms. There was a superficial veneer of Spanish culture, but it was very thin. The traditional view that the Native Americans became increasingly acculturated the longer they spent in the missions is untrue.

Stakeholders in the Past

Chapter 16 brings to the fore a theme that persists throughout Part Five: that of stakeholders in the past, and the highly significant contributions made by thousands of people of many different ethnicities. Archaeology in Annapolis, Maryland, explores theories of power that lay behind the planning of colonial settlements, and the lives of the city's citizens. Many archaeologists are exploring Black Experience in early North America, especially plantation life and slavery. This involves excavating slave quarters at such places as Thomas Jefferson's Monticello and at Kingsmill Plantation, both in Virginia, and searching for the often-subtle signs of African resistance to slavery in hostile social environments. Were, for example, clay vessels resembling African forms a kind of resistance? Excavations have explored the first settlement of free African-Americans in North America at Fort Mose, Florida, also the African-American Burial Ground in New York, the latter the subject of intense stakeholder controversy. All these investigations, and many others, are replacing stereotypes with much more nuanced understandings of Black Experience.

Stereotypes are the plague of archaeology, and many of them die hard. Western movies offer a grossly distorted view of the nineteenth-century west. A great deal of archaeological research has been devoted to mines and miners, who labored in small communities surrounded by harsh wilderness. We examine such mining with a visit to Nevada mining country and the ethnically diverse mining camp at Shoshone Wells, where Chinese workers replaced Cornish and Welsh miners. Such archaeology, like that at Chinese railroad camps in the Sierras, is as much a matter of recording and conservation as it is of excavation, for the historical record is vanishing before our eyes.

Native American resistance sometimes erupted in violence, witness the northern Cheyenne escape from Fort Robinson, Nebraska, and the Battle of Little Bighorn in 1876. Both events have been reinterpreted completely by the use of careful detective work that recorded the distribution of bullets and other finds on the actual ground.

Many stakeholders are hard to discern: they trod lightly, and often left little behind them. The Chinese abalone hunters of southern California are a case in point. Their transitory camp on San Miguel Island is barely visible among the wind-blown sands behind the beach. Archaeologists found the anonymous temporary visitors to the camp by plotting the distribution of artifacts and food remains on the surface, carefully excavating some hearths, and pulling everything together into a brief history of a long-forgotten encampment. This is what archaeology does best. A scatter of inconspicuous artifacts, a handful of bones and shells, perhaps a few beads or potsherds: these are our archives, and they retrieve long-forgotten people from historical oblivion. This is how archaeologists write history, whether of immigrants who arrived 14,000 years ago, or of a remote fishing camp occupied briefly before World War I.

European Contact

For more than 14,000 years the Native Americans occupied the vast tracts of North America undisturbed. Within a few millennia they had settled in a broad range of different environments, each with its own unique challenges. By 6000 BCE ancient North Americans had adapted successfully to everything from brutally cold arctic landscapes to deserts, fertile river valleys, and forested coasts. Their diverse societies and ways of obtaining foods persisted for thousands of years, often almost unchanged. There is no doubt that these successful adjustments would have continued to unfold uneventfully if Christopher Columbus and his conquistadors had not arrived in the Bahamas in 1492 (Figure 14.1).

The term *entrada* is commonly used to refer to this dramatic moment in world history. Columbus and his successors encountered a bewildering array of native societies. Some, such as the Bahamians and desert hunter-gatherers in the west, lived in small bands and were constantly on the move. Other societies, living in unusually favorable environments (for instance the Pacific Northwest Coast, parts of southern California, and southern Florida), developed some of the most complex and elaborate hunter-gatherer societies on earth. Almost invariably their elaboration depended on a combination of fishing, sea-mammal hunting, and shellfish foraging. The Great Plains with their vast buffalo herds astonished early Spanish travelers, who observed the local people hunting these large beasts with spears, bows and arrows, and on foot. Everywhere Native Americans had remarkable expertise with native plants of all kinds. Farming societies flourished in the Midwest and parts of the Southeast, where volatile, complex polities rose and fell unpredictably. These were societies that performed elaborate burial rituals and built large earthworks and burial mounds, where powerful chiefs vied with one another for political supremacy and prestige in a world of ebbing and flowing alliances and occasional warfare. In the Southwest, Pueblo societies farmed arid lands with brilliant skill and opportunism, where, once again, ritual, and mutual interdependence played important roles.

The native North American world was a theater of constantly changing diversity, not one where literate, pre-industrial civilizations developed, with their rigidly stratified social classes, standing armies, crowded cities, and mighty divine rulers. There were no pharaohs in North America, just dynamic entrepreneurial chiefs who had a brilliant flair for attracting loyal followers and communicating with the spiritual forces of the cosmos. This was a continent of diverse peoples without writing, but one where oral communications, storytelling, and genealogies, as well as respect for ancestors, were compelling catalysts. Then came the *entrada*, and this world inexorably fell apart.

In the following sections we will recount the histories of the first landings of Europeans in the late 1400s and early 1500s, and the founding of Virginia by the English in 1584, taken largely from European historical documents. But the study of the earliest European settlement of North America is far more than the perusal of contemporary documents, important as they are. Any serious researcher of the *entrada* must employ a very broad range of other sources, drawn from archaeology, cultural and biological anthropology, climatology, DNA, and ethnohistory. Where documentary records are available, they are almost invariably concerned with the affairs of colonists, missionaries, and other European explorers or visitors. The indigenous people served for generations as a passive historical backdrop to events considered important in European minds. Only

14.1 Routes of the early European explorers in and around North America.

recently has the full potential of archaeology as a source of historical information during the contact period been realized. There has been a growing understanding that archaeological sites when carefully dug and recorded provide a unique window into the daily lives of everyday people, who are often as anonymous in historical times as their predecessors were before the *entrada* (Deetz, 1996; Hicks and Beaudry, 2006; Orser, 2017). The two accounts below are therefore followed with an archaeological view of the *entrada*, focusing on its most devastating and lasting consequence: epidemic.

14.2 Reconstruction of a small church said to have been built for Eirik the Red's wife at Brattahlid, Greenland.

First, the Norse

In about the year 982 CE (the exact date is disputed), Norseman Eirik Thorvaldsson the Red sailed west from Iceland to explore the mysterious lands that sometimes appeared on the far horizon when the winds blew from the north. Three years later he and his men returned with glowing tales of a fertile, uninhabited land where fish were plentiful and the grazing grass lush and green. Eirik named it the Green Land, a name retained to this day. Eirik persuaded twenty-five shiploads of settlers to sail for Greenland in 986. They founded tiny, remote Brattahlid in the southwest, and the so-called Western Settlement at Godthaab some 200 miles (320 km) to the north (Figures 14.2 and 14.3). For centuries these tiny hamlets were bases for Norse wanderings far to the north, among icebound fjords and islands on the fringes of the Arctic Ocean, and west 186 miles (300 km) across the Davis Strait to Baffin Island, Labrador, and beyond.

The restless and adventurous Greenlanders farmed, kept cattle and sheep, fished, and were skilled hunters who took game on land and sea. Above all, they were seamen, who explored every nook and cranny of southwestern Greenland.

Very early on, it seems, bold young men ventured far north toward the arctic ice, and across the Davis Strait to the Ubygdir, "the unpeopled tracts," new lands beyond the western horizon.

Only the faintest records of these western voyages have come down through the centuries. They survive in two fragmentary Icelandic documents, often called the Vinland Sagas, written at least 200 years later. The Saga of the Greenlanders and The Saga of Eirik the Red are tantalizingly vague and contradictory accounts of extraordinary voyages. Unfortunately it is almost impossible to separate historical fact from fantasy, geographical information from vague descriptions written and copied several times over (Wahlgren, 1986).

The Saga of the Greenlanders tells how a young merchant named Bjarni Herjolfsson comes home to Iceland from Norway with a full cargo. He finds that his father has moved to Greenland with Eirik the Red and sets out to visit him, but the voyagers become lost in a wilderness of North Atlantic fog. Days or weeks later they encounter a low, forested coast, which faces east. Bjarni realizes that this cannot be Greenland, so he turns north, sights more forested land a few days later, then an island with mountains and glaciers. He turns east, sails across Davis Strait, and reaches Greenland safely.

Perhaps some fifteen years later, in the 990s, Leif Eiriksson, son of Eirik the Red, sets out on a journey of exploration to the west. He sails across to the icy island that was Bjarni's last landfall, then voyages southward until he is well below the latitude of southern Greenland. Leif and his thirty-five followers winter in a sheltered location where they are amazed and delighted to find fruiting grapevines growing wild. They survive an unusually mild winter, explore the countryside, load up with timber, and return home to Greenland. Leif Eiriksson names the new lands: Helluland ("Slabrock Land," perhaps Baffin Island and northern Labrador), Markland ("Forest Land," probably central Labrador and Newfoundland), and Vinland ("Wineland," to the south, whose location is a

14.3 Abandoned Norse site, known as "Farm Beneath the Sand," showing the foundations of stone buildings after eight years of excavations. The site, occupied between the mid-eleventh and the fourteenth centuries, was once part of the Western Settlement, now the present-day municipality of Nuuk.

matter of vigorous controversy). In a meticulous analysis of the sagas, Erik Wahlgren (1986) has argued persuasively that Leif overwintered somewhere near Passamaquoddy Bay, close to the border between Maine and New Brunswick. The grapes that so enraptured his men were wild grapevines that are common in New England. Others believe, on the basis of a sixteenth-century Icelandic chart, that Vinland was Newfoundland, and that Leif simply embellished his account with wild grapes to encourage prospective settlement (McGhee, 1984).

Leif Eiriksson never returned to Vinland. His brother Thorvald followed in his footsteps, mounting an expedition that lasted two years. He appears to have explored the Bay of Fundy, been killed in a clash with local people, and been buried there. A visiting Icelandic merchant named Thorfinn Karlsefni was next in Vinland. He took a sixty-person expedition back to Leif's winter settlement and traded with some visiting Native Americans. There was fighting and men perished on both sides. After two winters Thorfinn sailed back to Greenland, probably sometime around 1012. More sporadic and unrecorded Norse voyages to Labrador probably ensued in the following three centuries, most likely ventures in search of timber, which was in short supply in Greenland.

Norse Settlement in North America

Archaeologists have searched diligently for traces of Viking settlement in North America. There have been the usual archaeological fantasies—stones inscribed with Norse runic script and mysterious towers in New England, and the celebrated Kensington Stone discovered in Minnesota in 1898. None stands up to scholarly scrutiny.

The logical place for such sites would be Labrador or Newfoundland, and it is at L'Anse aux Meadows in northern Newfoundland that the only certain trace of Norse settlement has come to light (see Box: L'Anse aux Meadows). L'Anse aux Meadows is a shallow bay, but a site with one major advantage: ample grazing for cattle. It lies at a strategic point, surrounded by water on three sides, an excellent base for exploring the St. Lawrence Valley, if such a Norse enterprise was ever contemplated. Radiocarbon dates from the dwellings date the settlement to about 1000 CE, but the precise identity of the builders is unknown.

As early as the twelfth century, Norsemen had sporadic contacts with Inuit groups living in the Canadian Archipelago and along the western Greenland coast, in the Nordrsetur (the central west coast), the area around Disko Bay, and probably much further north. A scatter of Norse artifacts has come from Inuit settlements in the High Arctic—especially from the Baffin Island and Ellesmere Island area (Figures 14.4 and 14.5). These include non-Inuit copper and iron fragments, pieces of woolen cloth, chain mail, and carpenters' tools, also boat nails and rivets, even carvings that give impressions of Norsemen. There are

14.4 A wooden figurine of a Norseman found in a Thule (Inuit) house at Okivilialuk.

14.5 Fragment of Norse woolen cloth from Skraeling Island.

L'ANSE AUX MEADOWS, NEWFOUNDLAND

Helge Ingstad and Anne Stine discovered the remains of eight sod-walled structures on a terrace overlooking a shallow bay in northern Newfoundland in 1960 (Ingstad, 1985) (Figure 14.6). This is a windy place, a settlement of houses that cling to the ground close to an open shore. Ingstad and Stine excavated eight houses and part of a ninth. They soon realized that the dwellings bore a close resemblance to houses in Greenland and Iceland dating to about 1000 CE. Radiocarbon dates for the settlement lay in the 990 to 1050 CE range, just when Norse ships were visiting Newfoundland for the first time.

A thousand years ago what is now an open, grassy landscape was forest covered, providing timber for boatbuilding, house construction and iron smelting. The L'Anse aux Meadows houses were built of sod placed over wooden frames. The largest measured 94 by 51 ft (28.8 by 15.6 m) and had several rooms. Three smaller buildings may have been workshops or storehouses, one of them an iron smithy, another a carpenter's shop. The turf houses contained Norse artifacts that suggest women as well as men lived at the site, such as a spindle whorl and a needle hone. One of the houses was too long to have been covered by a single roof. It consisted of several dwellings built together, perhaps forming a kind of sleeping hall. The settlement had a possible bath house, also four turf boat sheds, perhaps once roofed with sod-covered rafters or branches.

There are signs of both earlier and later Native American settlement on the site. Two jasper fire starters from the site have been sourced to the Notre Dame Bay area of Newfoundland, a hint that the Norse had contact with indigenous people living in what was then a fairly densely populated part of the island. They may also have visited the Gulf of St. Lawrence (where they obtained butternut seeds, which will not grow any further north than New Brunswick), and perhaps reached what is now the Canadian Arctic. L'Anse aux Meadows served as a base and winter camp for Norse voyagers exploring the Gulf of St. Lawrence and nearby waters.

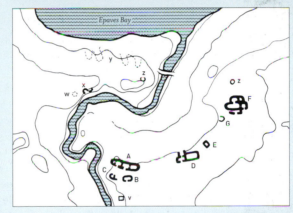

14.6 Norse settlement at L'Anse aux Meadows, Newfoundland. (a) Aerial view showing partially excavated house sites. (b) Plan of the site. A–D, houses; E, work shed; F, large house; G, small, unidentified structure; v, natural deposit of iron ore; w, charcoal kiln; x, forge; y, boat sheds; z, cooking pits. (c) Reconstruction of the sod-and-timber houses.

Norse stone cairns, some reworked bottom sections of casks, and a single runic inscription from Kingiqtorsoaq high on Greenland's western coast, probably dating to April 24, 1333. Traces of cordage and yarn also come from two sites on southern Baffin Island, suggesting that contacts between Norse and Inuit were much more complex than once imagined.

The Norsemen called the Inuit "Skraelings." "They possess no iron, but use walrus tusk for missiles and sharpened stones instead of knives," we learn from the *History of Greenland*, a work based on a thirteenth-century manuscript (McGhee, 1984). Contacts between Norse and Inuit were probably sporadic, the result of summer bear- and walrus-hunting expeditions far to the north. Walrus ivory was the medium in which Greenlanders paid their annual tithe to the Church in distant Norway, on some occasions at least 400 tusks annually, far more than could be obtained around the Greenland settlements.

As far as we can tell, the contacts between Inuit and Norse were sometimes friendly, occasionally violent, apparently rarely prolonged. In all probability, the Norse came into contact with both Inuit and Beothuk, Algonquian-speakers who were summer visitors to the Labrador coast and Newfoundland (Figure 14.7). Norse artifacts have come from as far afield as the western shores of Hudson Bay and latitude 79°N, 500 miles (805 km) north of the Kingiqtorsoaq rune stone. That is not to say that the Norse themselves actually traveled this widely, for many prized exotica may have passed along Inuit barter networks.

The Norse did not colonize North America. In 1000 CE the tough and resourceful Norsemen could survive on Greenland coasts but they lacked the numbers and the resources to expand and maintain pioneer settlements, and to confront and compete with much larger indigenous populations. Nor were there strong motives for colonization—no religious persecution at home, no promise of great wealth to attract the greedy adventurer. In time even Greenland proved beyond their capabilities. Norse civilization survived there until around 1500, progressively debilitated by increasing arctic cold (the so-called Little Ice Age) that brought Inuit hunters further south, by economic deprivation and competition for game resources, and perhaps by declining birth rates and cultural isolation from the homeland. There were occasional hostile visitors, too, perhaps even some piracy, for Basque whalers from northern Spain had been sailing in Greenland waters since at least 1372.

14.7 A Beothuk canoe.

Eventually the Norsemen quietly withdrew, leaving two geographical legacies behind them for later explorers—the term "Skraeling" and two place names: Markland, a land of forests, and Promontorium Winlandiae, a land of vines (actually northern Newfoundland). Their epic journeys survived in European consciousness along with hints of exotic peoples living at the very edge of the known world. "There are animals of such enormous size that the inhabitants of the inner islands use their bones and vertebrae in place of wood in constructing houses. They also use them for making clubs, darts, lances, knives, seats, ladders, and, in general, all things which elsewhere are made from wood." Thus did the Arab geographer al-Idrisi describe the North Atlantic and its rich fisheries in his *Nuzhet al-Mushtaq*, written in about 1150 CE (McGhee, 1984). Like the medieval geographers, al-Idrisi relied not only on first-hand experience, but also on travelers' accounts from every corner of the world. Perhaps, among these accounts, he heard vague stories of whale hunters from the far north. If he was indeed writing of Inuit peoples from North America, the tales of their whalebone houses had probably reached him through many hands from Norse sources in Greenland and Iceland.

The first, fleeting contacts between Inuits, Native Americans, and Western voyagers did nothing to alter hunter-gatherer cultures that had been evolving in a vast, isolated continent for more than 13,000 years. Centuries were to pass before Westerners again voyaged along North American shores.

Newfoundland and St. Lawrence

On October 12, 1492, Christopher Columbus landed on San Salvador in the Bahamas. There he found naked people, "very well made, of very handsome bodies and very good faces" (Figure 14.8). The Admiral's explorations brought a torrent of settlers to the Caribbean, settlers who came to "serve God and get rich." They soon encountered an astounding diversity of different peoples—simple hunters, village farmers, and magnificent civilizations, such as that of the Aztecs

14.8 Christopher Columbus displays Native Americans and artifacts made by them before the king and queen of Spain, 1493.

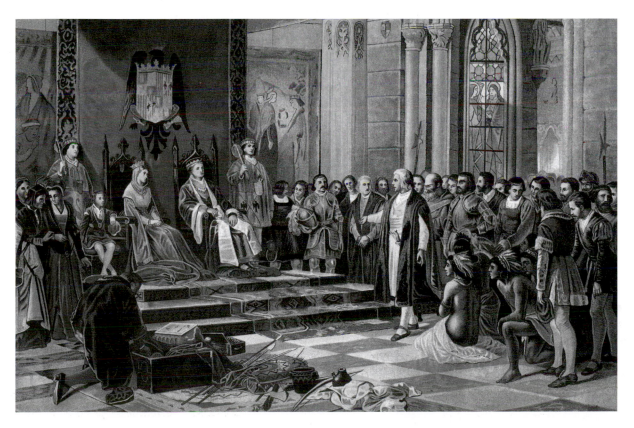

of highland Mexico. When Hernán Cortés and his soldiers gazed at the great Aztec capital at Tenochtitlán in the Valley of Mexico in 1519, they marveled at a gold-laden civilization that rivaled those of Christendom in its magnificence.

Only seven years after the death of Columbus in 1506, conquistador Vasco Nuñez de Balboa trekked across Central America and gazed on the Pacific. It was now clear that the Indies were not part of China at all, but what "we may rightly call a New World more densely peopled and abounding in animals than Europe, or Asia, or Africa." For years afterward, Europeans had but two ambitions in the Americas—to find another gold-rich civilization, and a navigable strait to China.

Just as the last Norse colonists vanished in southern Greenland, Genoese-born John Cabot sailed west from Bristol, England, in search of a short, northern route to the Indies (Morison, 1971). *The Matthew* sailed in 1497, made landfall on Newfoundland, worked down the west coast, and discovered the rich cod fisheries of the Grand Banks. Cabot encountered no human beings but observed snares and nets, presumably belonging to Beothuk groups.

Two years later Portuguese explorer Gaspar Corte-Real sailed northwest from the Azores and made landfall on "a land that was very cool and with big trees," almost certainly Newfoundland. He returned the following year. His men kidnapped fifty-seven Beothuk, who "live together by fishing and hunting animals, in which the land abounds, the skins of which they use for garments and also make houses and boats thereof." The people lived in "rocky caves and thatched huts." After their first experience with Europeans, the Beothuk retreated to the interior and were very hostile to later visitors.

The next quarter-century saw the icebound and foggy north with its forested, rocky shores fade into relative oblivion. Only cod fishermen penetrated northern waters, people with little interest in exploration or the local inhabitants. Everything else was eclipsed by the brilliant discoveries that followed on Columbus's expedition far to the south. Then, in September 1522, Juan Sebastián del Caño in the ship Vittoria anchored at Seville in Spain, carrying just eighteen of the 239 men who had set out on Ferdinand Magellan's epic circumnavigation of the globe. He had sailed into the Pacific through the stormy Magellan Strait at the southern tip of South America. Spanish and Portuguese explorers had now covered the entire east coast of the Americas from Florida to Patagonia, but had been unable to find any other strait north of Magellan's. On most maps of the time, Newfoundland floated in the North Atlantic, without any link to the lands further south. Thirteen degrees of latitude from Maine to Georgia remained unexplored. Here, surely, lay either a strait to the west, or, even better, open sea that would carry European mariners to the "happy shores of Cathay."

In January 1524 the Italian gentleman explorer Giovanni da Verrazzano sailed west from Madeira (Morison, 1971). Instead of dropping down to the West Indies, he sailed well north of Columbus's track just over thirty years before. About March 1, he made landfall at Cape Fear, North Carolina, then sailed up the east coast as far as Newfoundland. He encountered many friendly Native American groups along the way, mostly simple farmers and fishermen wearing leaves or skins. The people of Casco Bay, Maine, who were apparently more familiar with foreigners, were less welcoming. "They used all signs of discourtesy and disdain, as was possible for any brute creature to invent, such as exhibiting their bare behinds and laughing immodestly." Verrazzano named this coast Terra Onde di Mala Gente, the "Land of Bad People," in revenge.

The prospect of a northern route to China brought Jacques Cartier, French Master Mariner of Saint-Malo in Brittany, to Newfoundland in April 1534. He returned to France five months later, having sailed completely around the Gulf of St. Lawrence, where his men lived off great auk meat, salmon and other fresh fish, goose eggs, and wild strawberries. He kidnapped two Iroquoian Wendat teenagers, a chief's sons, who were to act as guides on his second voyage (Trigger, 1972, 1985). Cartier returned a year later to penetrate deeper into the Gulf. His Wendat captives knew the great river well, all the way upstream to modern Quebec. It was, Cartier realized, a highway to the interior.

14.9 Birch-bark Wendat longhouse from a replica village near Midland, Ontario.

"No man has been to the end, so far as they had heard say," he wrote. Cartier made contact with St. Lawrence Native Americans living near modern Quebec, and arrived at Hochelaga, the site of present-day Montreal, on October 2, 1535. There, more than 1,000 people greeted him, bringing gifts of corn bread and performing welcome ceremonies. They lived in a fortified village surrounded by corn fields, partly situated on the grounds of today's McGill University. The fortifications consisted of palisades with two redoubts "garnished with rocks and stones, for defense and protection." There were fifty bark and wood houses inside, each with several rooms and a central fireplace, grouped around a central plaza (Figure 14.9). The people were in a constant state of readiness, for their home was close to the Five Nations of the Haudenosaunee, notorious among the Europeans for their sudden raids. Cartier was impressed by his friendly reception in what were the golden days of ethnic relations along the St. Lawrence. In 1541–42 Cartier returned to found the first European colony in Canada, Charlesbourg Royal, of about 400 people. This time, however, the Iroquoian Wendat, resenting the new settlement, were hostile, and attacked. No records exist but from sailor accounts, but at least thirty-five of Cartier's men were killed before the French retreated. Disease, bad weather, and further conflict with the Wendat led to the abandoning of the colony in 1543. For more than a half-century, the Wendat were left alone, as European exploration and colonization faltered.

"The New Found Land of Virginia"

On April 27, 1584, two ships slipped out of Plymouth, England, on a voyage of reconnaissance along the more southern coasts explored by Verrazzano sixty years earlier. Philip Amadas and Arthur Barlow sailed at the behest of Walter Raleigh, who held letters patent from Queen Elizabeth I granting him permission to colonize an unspecified area of North America. Four months later the two vessels anchored close to Nag's Head in present-day North Carolina. They soon came into contact with the local Powhatan, Algonquian-speakers, "very handsome, and goodly people," who entertained them royally (Morison, 1971). "The soil," Barlow wrote enthusiastically if mendaciously, "is the most plentifull, sweete, fruitfull and wholesome of all the world." All this was good publicity for prospective colonists and for royal ears. Queen Elizabeth I knighted Walter Raleigh and allowed him to name his prospective colony Virginia.

In April of the following year, Sir Richard Grenville led an expedition of five ships and about 500 men, including 108 prospective colonists, to Virginia.

Their fitting at meate.   XVI.

14.10 *Top left:* A Virginia Indian in the "manner of their attire and painting themselves", painted by John White between 1585 and 1593.
14.11 *Left:* Two Virginia Indians eating: "Their sitting at meate," by John White, 1590.
14.12 *Above:* John White's watercolor of the Algonquian village of Secotan in Virginia, *c.* 1535. This romanticized view of native Americans shows many details of daily life.

This time Raleigh sent along a scientist, the Oxford mathematician Thomas Hariot, and an artist, John White. The settlement was a complete failure, but Hariot and White had ample opportunity to visit several Native American settlements. White sketched the people and their villages with astounding, if romantic detail. Hariot's Briefe and True Report of the New Found Land of Virginia appeared in 1588. Illustrated with White's sketches, it became a basic source of information about Native Americans for more than a century (Figures 14.10, 14.11, and 14.12).

Despite later efforts, no permanent colony was established in Virginia until that at Jamestown on the James River, about 35 miles (56 km) from Chesapeake Bay, in 1607. Plagued by harsh weather conditions and starvation, that effort ultimately succeeded both because of sustained economic support from England, and because the colonists exported tobacco home. A year later Samuel de Champlain established a colony at Quebec on the St. Lawrence, twelve years before the Pilgrim Fathers landed at Plymouth in New England. The first two decades of the seventeenth century saw the era of permanent European colonization in North America finally begin—with catastrophic effects on the native peoples who lay in the white settlers' path.

The Insights of Archaeology

The textual accounts above demonstrate a European view of the first landings in North America, and the reasons behind Native American actions, or even behind interactions between peoples, are not made clear. Moreover, the accounts provide a specifically literate European view. Only a minority of, say, early Spanish settlers or English colonists could write, but this minority wrote about the others and kept at least sketchy records of them. They sent reports to the homeland, recorded births, marriages, and deaths, kept tax rolls, and laid out and administered tiny settlements according to the regulations promulgated by distant monarchs. The archaeological record, by contrast, includes the material remains of literate and non-literate people living often simple lives, of different classes or ethnic groups with often quite distinctive artifacts, and of Europeans interacting with Native Americans. These remains of diverse existences chronicle the historical realities of recent centuries of North American history in ways that no official living at the time would consider worth recording (Orser, 2017).

Archaeology offers the best chance for students of the past to examine cultural change in all societies, whether simple or complex, over long periods. Of no period of the North American past is this more true than of the fifteenth to eighteenth centuries CE, when the full impact of European contact fell upon indigenous societies of all kinds. Any form of cultural contact, however fleeting, is a two-way process, often with lasting consequences on both sides. The European perspective on the exploration and settlement of North America is relatively well documented, but the effects of these developments on Native American societies of the day are still little understood. This subject is, of course, enormous, and we can but summarize some of the major issues here. They revolve around two interconnected, fundamental questions. First, what was the effect of European infectious diseases introduced at contact on the indigenous population? Second, what were the short- and long-term results of direct and indirect contacts between European and Native American cultures, in material, social, and political terms?

Epidemics

Before we turn to specific instances of contact between natives and newcomers, we should examine the most devastating and lasting consequence of the *entrada*—the introduction of exotic infectious diseases (particularly smallpox and influenza). These silent killers affected all corners of North America, often without direct contact with European carriers.

No one knows exactly when a European infected with smallpox or any other exotic disease first landed in North America. Some very early explorers may have carried the alien germs and infected some local, isolated populations, but the epidemics may have died out without infecting wide areas. Whenever infectious diseases did arrive and take hold, the effects on the Native American population were devastating (Figure 14.13).

Why were there no New World counterparts for European diseases? Perhaps the parasites were killed off by arctic temperatures as tiny founder populations migrated into the New World thousands of years ago. More likely, ancient population densities were too low. The survival of acute diseases depends on frequent contact between individuals, such as occurs in densely populated, sedentary settlements. North America, and even to some extent Mesoamerica, lacked the crowded settlements of the Old World. It was there that bacterial and viral diseases became fixed in urban populations (Crosby, 2003, 2016).

In epidemiological terms the turning point was 1519, when a Spanish conquistador infected with smallpox landed at Vera Cruz, Mexico. The conquistadors had some immunity to the disease, but the Native Americans did not. In months, smallpox spread like wildfire from the coast to the highlands. The first pandemic

14.13 Mandan villagers dying of smallpox during an epidemic of 1837.

hit the Aztec capital in 1520. People died by the thousand. Other unfamiliar diseases, including influenza, measles, and typhus, ravaged the Mexican population during the next century. The population of Mexico has been estimated at 11 million in 1519. A mere twenty years later it was under 6.5 million; by 1607 it was less than a fifth of what it had been a century earlier. Similar demographic catastrophes occurred throughout the Americas. For example, more than 310,000 Native Americans lived in California at the time of Spanish colonization in 1769. Coastal populations fell from about 72,000 to 18,000 by 1830. By 1900 the total number of California Native Americans was 20,000, less than 7 percent of the pre-contact population.

The nature and timing of Native American population decline has sparked great controversy among historians, anthropologists, and archaeologists, a debate that focuses on three fundamental issues. First, how large was the human population of North America at contact, and how great was the subsequent decline? Second, when exactly did the decline take place relative to the first census counts? Third, what role did infectious diseases play? The great Berkeley anthropologist Alfred Kroeber and others argued that exotic diseases played a relatively minor role in the early decades after contact, though they agreed that aboriginal populations declined after sustained European contact (Ramenofsky, 1987). Under this rubric, the earliest historical census counts do not represent devastated populations, as North Native American populations were relatively small at contact—about 0.9 million people, in Kroeber's estimation. In contrast, anthropologist Henry Dobyns (1983) assumed that infectious diseases attacked even isolated populations decades, if not centuries, before actual physical contact between Europeans and Native Americans and before historical records began. He proposed North American population figures as high as 18 million. But Dobyns's theory that a series of frequent and continent-wide epidemics reduced indigenous sixteenth-century populations was wrong. The situation was more complex. Some societies, especially chiefdoms in the Southeast, were hit earlier than many of the more northerly village societies, such as the Haudenosaunee.

Archaeologist Ann Ramenofsky (1987) evaluated these two contrasting approaches using archaeological evidence. She showed that there was constant cultural change not only throughout ancient times, but also over the critical centuries of European contact. Thus, she argues, patterns of archaeological change in populations can be evaluated independently of ethnographic or historical records. This is important, for such attempts as have been made to develop population estimates have invariably been based on modern analogues, so that conservative figures reflecting some form of fictional "ethnographic present" come into play. It is hardly surprising, then, that population estimates have been conservative.

Ramenofsky's study was based on three regions: the Lower Mississippi Valley, central New York, and the Middle Missouri Valley. In the Lower Mississippi Valley both historical and independent archaeological data identified an unambiguous and precipitous decline of aboriginal populations in the sixteenth century—after the De Soto expedition and before the French colonized the valley in the late seventeenth century (see Chapter 15). The New York data came from the Finger Lakes region, the area inhabited by the Five Nations of the Haudenosaunee at the beginning of the historic period. Had Haudenosaunee populations and cultural systems remained constant right up to the American Revolution, or had epidemics radically altered Haudenosaunee society in the sixteenth or seventeenth centuries? Ramenofsky's calculations of settlement extent and house-roof area suggest that the Native American population was considerably reduced by the seventeenth century, but the exact date of the decline is in doubt. Historical descriptions of Haudenosaunee society support and extend the archaeological record of collapse in these centuries with their chronicles of drastically reorganized settlements and the final breakdown of multi-family dwellings and fortified settlements. Historical descriptions of the Five Nations describe populations developing new adaptive strategies, partly as a result of diminishing numbers. The Middle Missouri Valley sample was from the northern Plains area, where European contact began in 1540 and colonization in the eighteenth century. Did exotic diseases cause catastrophic depopulation with colonization or during the two preceding centuries? Ramenofsky's settlement calculations suggest a decline at least a century earlier than the eighteenth century, perhaps coinciding with the appearance of European trade goods in the region. But the population loss may have occurred as early as the sixteenth century, before any significant number of trade goods appeared in the area.

In all three areas archaeological data suggest that demographic catastrophe preceded the major influx of Europeans by decades, perhaps in some areas by centuries. Ramenofsky estimated the pre-contact Native American population

A CASE STUDY IN CULTURAL ADAPTATION: THE ONONDAGA

The arrival of Samuel de Champlain on the St. Lawrence River in 1609 was the beginning of an international trade in North American beaver furs that became a huge enterprise yielding as many as 10,000 pelts annually. The commerce stemmed from an insatiable demand for beaver pelts, which were used to make European gentlemen's hats. Champlain himself concluded a treaty with the Wendat living near Quebec that left control of the trade in the hands of traditional chiefs.

By the late sixteenth century the Onondaga of the Haudenosaunee Confederacy further south were using European copper and iron for many more utilitarian artifacts, using and re-using them until they were completely worn out. Haudenosaunee sites of the sixteenth and seventeenth centuries contain both copper kettles and iron axes, artifacts sought not necessarily as objects *per se*, but as sources of raw materials (Trigger, 1972, 1985). Onondaga metalworkers then used these materials to fashion traditional artifacts. Thus, the initial impact of European goods was conservative, not revolutionary, for the way in which they were used promoted traditional cultural patterns rather than changing them. European materials were accepted not because they were superior, but because they made sense in an opportunistic, flexible culture both in spiritual and utilitarian terms.

The Onondaga's response to their first century of exposure to European culture was one of continuity as much as change, the change being gradual rather than catastrophic. In the case of the Onondaga, and many other Native Americans societies, the first evidence of cross-cultural adaptation was in areas where European novelties were most useful and least threatening to the existing cultural order.

Despite smallpox epidemics, the Onondaga still retained their basic cultural values and beliefs in the mid-seventeenth century, living in a culture where European artifacts and materials had been grafted onto traditional society. After 1655 circumstances changed profoundly, for European contacts increased dramatically. Jesuit missionaries were in residence, a French settlement had been established nearby, and the Onondaga's European neighbors were increasingly aggressive. The archaeological record now shows more hybrid artifact forms, more blending of European and native culture. This increased blending is reflected in wampum, one of the major mediums of exchange between native and newcomer.

Wampum had been important in pre-contact days, but it assumed much greater significance to the

at about 12 million, but her estimate differs considerably from other calculations. All assessments suffer from a lack of solid evidence. All that can be said is that the best estimates fall between the 2 million and 18 million estimates established in the 1980s by Henry Dobyns (1983) and others. The number most likely falls somewhere in the bottom half of the range. For our purposes it is necessary only to note that, whatever the precise chronology and figures, European contact undoubtedly did introduce diseases against which Native American populations had no resistance, and which were to disrupt their societies and lifeways as nothing had before.

The initial impact of European contact fell hardest, of course, on Native American societies living near coasts or major waterways, such as the St. Lawrence or the Lower Mississippi. As European settlement spread, some coastal groups were conquered or employed as agricultural laborers. Others, in California, were forcibly resettled under deliberate "**reduction**" policies that brought them into the Spanish mission system, where the friars could more easily control both the process of conversion, and the economic life associated with it. For several centuries, however, aboriginal groups living in the more distant interior largely avoided sustained contact with explorers, colonists, or missionaries, even if their economic, political, and social systems underwent drastic modification as a result of devastating epidemics (see Box: A Case Study in Cultural Adaptation: The Onondaga).

Haudenosaunee peoples in the early seventeenth century. Wampum beads strung into belts became common, since they were now a commodity of major importance both to Europeans and natives (see Box: Wampum, pp. 307–308). To the former, the wampum belt was a valuable medium of exchange for use in the fur trade. The Dutch in particular were quick to seize on the possibilities of wampum, for they had long experience of shell as a trade item when buying slaves in faraway Africa. The Dutch West India Company was incorporated for fur trading in North America, turned to the same currency, and soon realized the potential of wampum. It was probably they who developed the notion of belts as a widespread, informal currency in a medium that had important cultural significance not only to the Five Nations. To the Haudenosaunee shell was a source of power, so wampum was considered life-enhancing and restoring, an important element in rituals that served to console close relatives when someone died, and to raise another person to fill the void. The Onondaga were the keepers of wampum for the Five Nations, so it was of great importance to them as an emblem of diplomacy not only between Native Americans, but with Europeans as well.

The Haudenosaunee Confederacy of Five Nations had been formed as a means of redressing grievances among its members. Not that this prevented constant bickering among them, many of the tensions resulting from the differing trading opportunities that were available to different tribes. These quarrels, constant warfare, and devastating epidemics so weakened the Iroquois that they were almost destroyed. But in the late 1660s the Onondaga used their diplomatic talents to restructure the Confederacy, redefining its workings so that the organization would act as the diplomatic front for all the Five Nations. The Five Nations now presented a more united body. This led to a series of treaties and alliances in 1677 known as the Covenant Chain, agreements that stabilized and balanced the competing interests of the English colonies that had supplanted French settlers to the southeast, the Five Nations, and other tribal groups. To the English this Covenant was a legal document, and to the Haudenosaunee a set of social and political obligations that bound participants together to minimize differences between them. The Covenant, with its diplomatic expertise, with its treaties expressed in terms of wampum belts and intricate rituals, was a product of long-drawn-out acculturative processes that saw Onondaga culture transformed not only in material ways, but also in intangible response to new external realities—realities which, ultimately, they were sometimes able to exploit to their advantage.

SUMMARY

- In about 982 CE Norseman Eirik the Red landed in Greenland. Three years later he founded two Norse colonies there.

- In the 990s, Leif Eiriksson, Eirik's son, overwintered in what was probably Newfoundland. For three centuries there were sporadic Norse voyages to Labrador, probably in search of timber. Despite irregular contacts with Inuits and Beothuk, there was no permanent Norse settlement.

- The L'Anse aux Meadows settlement in northern Newfoundland is the only well-documented Norse site in North America, dating to about 990 to 1050 CE.

- European colonization followed Columbus's voyages and other explorations that included Sebastian Cabot's discovery of the Newfoundland cod fisheries in 1497.

- In 1534 and 1535, Jacques Cartier explored the St. Lawrence River and made contact with the Wendat. The beaver-fur trade developed in the following centuries.

- Despite abortive attempts, no permanent colony was founded in Virginia until the establishment of Jamestown, near Chesapeake Bay, in 1607.

- Multidisciplinary archaeology is unique in its ability to study the lives of common, illiterate American colonists, rather than the literature elite. It also allows us to study culture change in both European and Native American society over the centuries.

- The impact of exotic, infectious diseases on Native American societies was disastrous and led to significant depopulation and other consequences, including the loss of traditional knowledge.

Colonists, Borderlands, and Missionaries

15.1 Map showing sites mentioned in Chapter 15.

The seventeenth century saw European colonization in full swing. To the north, the English had founded Jamestown on the Chesapeake in 1607, which soon became an important trading center with tentacles that stretched far into the Southeast and regularly seized Native Americans for the slave trade. The Mayflower anchored off Plymouth in New England in 1620. Forty-four years later, in 1664, English colonists took New York, ending over fifty years of Dutch influence over fur trading in the Northeast. Even further north, the French had settled along the St. Lawrence, where they dominated fur-trading activity in that region. Their fur traders and explorers had spread throughout the Great Lakes during the seventeenth century, while Marquette and Joliet descended the Mississippi Valley in 1673. La Salle followed in their footsteps and even tried to colonize the Texas coast. By 1700 the peoples of the Eastern Woodlands were surrounded by European visitors. Dutch, English, French, and Spanish—each group had different, competing interests that exerted severe pressure on Native American groups often hundreds of miles away from actual direct contact with the foreigners (Figure 15.1). The dynamics of these pressures, of Native American responses to the European presence, are still little understood, but in exploring the material remains of colonies, borderlands and missions of the seventeenth century, archaeology is again able to bolster, complement, and challenge historical texts of this complex time.

The Spanish Borderlands: 1539 and Later

The borderlands on the northern margins of the vast Spanish Empire in the Americas were an ever-shifting frontier. There was constant interaction between settlers and Native Americans in this part of New Spain, between long-established indigenous societies and aggressive newcomers. Ultimately, the borderlands stretched from St. Augustine, Florida, in the east, to San Francisco, California, in the west. The processes of European interaction and cultural change began with Hernando de Soto's journey and the Ponce de León expedition, with Fray Marcos de Niza in the Southwest, and with Juan Cabrillo's voyage up the California coast in 1542. They ended with the Mexican Revolution of 1821. The complicated history of this large area has long been studied by historians, but only recently by archaeologists. Inevitably, the historical picture has been burdened with offensive stereotypes and simplistic interpretations, some due to the intellectual and social climate of the times in which they were written, others the result of the limitations of the documentary evidence. Archaeology is giving fresh insights into the historical record.

Hernando de Soto's foray through the Southeast in 1539–43 is a terrible baseline in North American history, infamous not only for its brutality but also for its legacy of smallpox and other diseases that ravaged Native American populations, triggered major long-term political and social change, and undoubtedly had profound psychological effects on Southeastern society. But what new information about this extraordinary incursion can the material remains offer? Until about a generation ago it seemed that De Soto and his force had passed through the Southeast without leaving an archaeological signature behind them. Part of the problem was that no one knew what to look for—sixteenth-century artifacts were largely a closed book even to historical archaeologists. The collaboration of archaeologists, anthropologists, and historians, however, has produced significant results. Three possible locations have been discovered where traces of De Soto, or at least very early Spanish contact, survive (Milanich and Milbrath, 1989; Milanich, 1999).

Excavations at Tatham burial mound in Citrus County, Florida, have yielded large numbers of Spanish artifacts, including metal, glass beads, and armor fragments. More than seventy Native Americans had been buried in a mass grave in the tumulus, perhaps victims of an epidemic. Some bodies exhibit wounds from sword cuts (Mitchem and Hutchinson, 1987). Tatham dates to before 1550.

The King site on the Coosa River in northwestern Georgia was once a frontier village of the Coosa chiefdom, perhaps visited by the Spaniards in the sixteenth century (Smith, 2000) (Figure 15.2). King was a fortified settlement, whose dwellings surrounded a central plaza. Several European artifacts came from the excavations, among them a sixteenth-century basket-hilt sword manufactured in either Germany or northern Italy, and presumably carried by a Spanish explorer. Some of the skeletons from the village were said to exhibit injuries inflicted by Spanish weapons, but this has now been disproved.

From October 1539 to March 1540, Hernando de Soto and his 600 conquistadors set up winter camp and occupied the major Native American Apalachee town of Anhaica, which lies today under downtown Tallahassee, Florida (Ewen and Hann, 1998). The Apalachee territory spanned from the Aucilla to the Apalachicola rivers, and from southern Georgia down to the Gulf Coast. Five hundred years before meeting Europeans, the Apalachee had built the mounds at Lake Jackson. Archaeological evidence demonstrates that the Apalachee farmed maize and focused their settlements on high ground around the red hills of Tallahassee. Anhaica was a sizeable settlement with 250 dwellings and other structures. De Soto used the extensive food stores and buildings to feed and house his people. The Apalachee abandoned their town to the occupying Europeans, but continued to attack the Spaniards throughout their occupation.

Calvin Jones, and later Charles Ewen, have excavated a small portion of the encampment, attempting to establish the dimensions of the camp and uncovering

15.2 Computer rendering and plan of the Coosa site, Georgia.

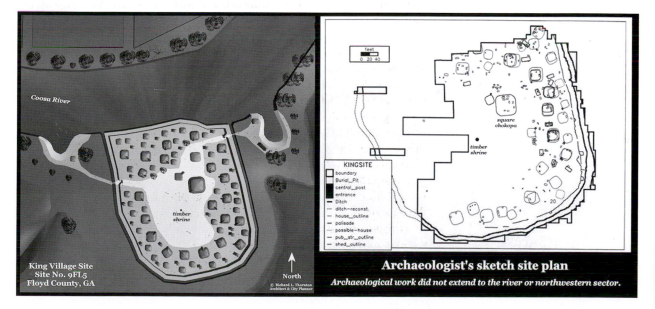

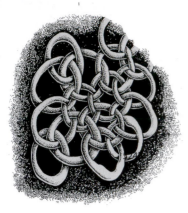

15.3 Artist's impression of Spanish chain mail from the Martin site, Tallahassee, Florida, the Anhaica village where the De Soto expedition spent the winter of 1539–40.

two circular wattle-and-daub Native American dwellings. The site has yielded five early sixteenth-century Spanish and Portuguese coins, Apalachee artifacts, and considerable numbers of Spanish artifacts and ceramics. This is hardly surprising, since we know that De Soto was resupplied from his ships in Tampa Bay. The archaeologists also found a fragment of a crossbow bolt, numerous European glass beads, pieces of Spanish chain mail, and datable sixteenth-century imported majolica pottery (Figure 15.3). The chain-mail fragments are of particular interest, for it was at Anhaica that the conquistadors discovered that chain mail was no protection against Native American arrows, and turned to quilted cloth coats instead.

The search for further traces of De Soto's expedition continues, and the debate about his exact route still rages. These controversies are of more than academic interest, but the real issues surround not the events of the expedition itself, but the long-term consequences of his passage. And these outcomes, still little known archaeologically, were to be momentous (Dye and Cox, 1990).

Marvin Smith (1987) has studied a portion of the interior Southeast centered on the Georgia and Alabama piedmont, in an attempt to measure the extent of early post-contact cultural change. European contact began in this region with the De Soto expedition of 1539. Both exotic diseases and foreign trade goods percolated into the area during the following century, this early period of indirect contact ending with the arrival of English settlers from Virginia and South Carolina in the 1670s. Smith points out that the situation in this region was very different from that, say, of the Five Nations of the Iroquois, where the people were in sustained, direct contact with Europeans for generations. Here the contact was indirect. Acculturation of the type found among the Onondaga, for example, did not take place (see Box: A Case Study in Cultural Adaptation: The Onondaga, pp. 330–31), yet there were major changes in population density and settlement patterns, to say nothing of political and social institutions.

The sixteenth-century Southeast was a land of flourishing and often complex societies with high levels of military organization (McEwen, 2000). Their leaders presided over dense populations often housed in substantial settlements. The people were ruled by an elite, their lives governed by sophisticated religious beliefs and elaborate rituals. Like most chiefdoms of this complexity, there were several layers of hierarchy. In Smith's research area, the chiefdom of Ocute consisted of a capital with five mounds (the Shoulderbone mound group), two other multiple-mound sites, two single-mound centers, and many villages and smaller settlements. This densely inhabited "province" was surrounded by a large buffer zone of unoccupied land. By analysing the routes taken by De Soto and other early Spanish explorers, Smith and his colleagues have been able to identify many sixteenth-century societies and even some named settlements, identifications that are the baseline for examining population decline and political restructuring during the century that followed.

Throughout much of the late sixteenth and early seventeenth centuries, the Southeastern interior remained unknown territory, although plenty was happening around the periphery. The Spanish mission system spread along the Georgia coast, through northern Florida, increasing both knowledge of foreigners and indirect contacts through the years. When English visitors first reached Cofitachiqui in South Carolina, a settlement visited by De Soto in 1540, it was still an important place. Its inhabitants were well aware of the Spanish, of a land to the west with bells and friars, and of people who rode on great deer (horses). The Cherokee of the Tennessee Valley were well equipped with firearms, brass pots, and kettles by 1673. French explorers entering the Lower Mississippi from the Great Lakes region reported encounters with Native Americans armed with muskets, who also possessed glass bottles, iron axes, and other European goods, obtained from a coast said to be ten days travel away. Peaches, chickens, and watermelons had spread widely from village to village. These material changes were symptoms of much more profound alterations in Native American life.

Marvin Smith approached the problem of measuring cultural change from several archaeological angles. First, he established chronologies based on stylistic changes in categories of easily dated European trade goods that were exchanged with native peoples all over the world. This methodology, employed successfully in the Northeast and often called the "Iroquois Methodology," works well where there is continual, sustained contact, as there was in the fur-trading areas. But in the Southeast the contacts were more complicated and less constant, the flow of European goods resulting not only from occasional direct trade, but also from such diverse sources as slave trading, looting of shipwrecks, and through native middlemen. Intricate exchange routes had crisscrossed the Southeast since Archaic times: they were still in use and many exotica undoubtedly traveled along them.

In the Southeast many of the earliest trade goods were quickly consumed as prestigious grave goods. From 1525 to 1565 indigenous culture was little affected by exotic influences, although European goods were buried with the elite, who controlled the supply. Native copper associated with much earlier rituals was still in use. Between 1565 and 1600 native copper working was in decline, but other traditional crafts with important ritual associations, such as shellwork, were still important and widely practiced. After 1600 the pattern changed, as imports became more common and were no longer restricted to elite burials. Perhaps this reflects the breakdown of powerful chiefdoms. At any rate, relatively mundane artifacts, such as iron axes, now became more utilitarian possessions—just as they had in the Northeast. Only native ceramics remained unchanged. Between 1640 and 1670 firearms were in use, and English artifacts appeared more frequently, as if trade networks now extended to the Northeast.

These material changes took place against a background of massive depopulation resulting from epidemics. The chroniclers of the De Soto expedition make it clear that diseases introduced by earlier coastal visitors preceded the conquistadors into the interior. At the village of Talomeco in South Carolina hundreds of bodies were stacked up in four of the houses. Evidence of epidemics from later decades is abundant. Sir Francis Drake's men contracted a highly contagious form of fever, perhaps typhus, in the Cape Verde Islands, and carried it ashore when they attacked the Spanish settlement at St. Augustine, Florida, in 1586. Hundreds of Native Americans living nearby soon died of the same disease. Thomas Hariot noted that the English settlers at Roanoke, in the colony of what was then called Virginia (now North Carolina), quickly infected the local population. "Within a few days after our departure from everies [sic.] such townes, people began to die very fast, and many in short space" (Crosby, 2003).

Without question these later coastal epidemics entered the interior, resulting in catastrophic depopulation, perhaps killing as many as 90 percent of some villages' inhabitants (Smith, 1987). Not only that, but the survivors probably suffered severely from starvation, too, especially if epidemics struck during periods of planting or harvest. The processes of depopulation may have been so rapid and devastating that ancestral traditions and much of indigenous culture may have been swept away in a few short months. In the Southeastern interior such a loss may have led to the fragmentation of hitherto powerful chiefdoms into much smaller, less centralized societies, and to population movements.

In archaeological terms Smith believes that the epidemics and general social disruption may be reflected in a rapid increase in multiple burials during the sixteenth century, as is documented in sites of the Mouse Creek culture of eastern Tennessee and in the King site of northwestern Georgia, with graves dating to the period between 1525 and 1565. Settlement sizes shrank, too, witness the Toqua site in Tennessee. This fortified mound center was occupied from about 1215 to 1620. The earliest village covered some 420,000 square ft (39,018 m²) with dispersed houses. Later, between 1350 and the early sixteenth century, the occupied zone shrank to 210,000 square ft (19,509 m²). Around 1580–1600 the fortified area shrank to as little as 180,000 square ft (16,727 m²), a much smaller settlement in which three multiple burials were found (Smith, 1987).

The strongest evidence is for political breakdown, for there is ample historical documentation that the large and powerful chiefdoms encountered by De Soto had been reduced to dozens of small-scale societies that were to band together to form the **Creek Confederacy** in the early eighteenth century. These small societies were ruled by *mikos*, little more than village headmen. The fall of the chiefdoms was closely linked not only to epidemics, but also to the severe

THE CREEK AND THE DEERSKIN TRADE

The myriad contacts and transactions between outsiders and Native American societies had countless environmental consequences, which are still little studied or understood. A case in point comes from the Creek deerskin trade of the eighteenth century.

The Creek inhabited what is now Georgia and Alabama from the seventeenth to the early nineteenth centuries. Linguistically, they were diverse. They lived off maize and other crops as well as hunting and foraging, which provided at least half their diet. Deer were a favored prey, not only for their meat, but also for their hides, which provided clothing, blankets, and other useful items at the household level. Males went hunting in late fall to early winter, sometimes traveling long distances in search of deer in the extensive uninhabited forests that surrounded their settlement. The hunters stalked animals in solitary hunts, often disguising themselves as deer so they could get close enough to shoot their quarry with a bow or a musket. The demand was modest, with just one or two deer a year sufficing for each household.

There were occasional communal deer drives, where the hunters would set the brush on fire, then drive the frightened animals toward bow- or riflemen. But such drives were apparently rare before the eighteenth century, when intensive deer hunting began in response to an accelerating demand for deerskins and meat from European settlers in South Carolina and Georgia (Foster, 2007). Between 1698 and 1765 hundreds of thousands of deerskins also left South Carolina and Florida for Europe. About 53,000 of them left South Carolina ports annually after 1715. In the late 1770s the famed botanist William Bartram observed that the Creek hunted deer "to an unreasonable and perhaps criminal excess." Their hunters now had to travel much longer distances to find their prey. At the height of the deerskin trade in the 1760s, deer drives using fire became very frequent. The fire not only allowed hunting but also increased the

loss of the manpower that peopled the hierarchical provinces of the Southeast. Archaeologically, the decline can be documented by a virtual cessation of mound-building, known to have been a chiefly activity. In Smith's research area no new mounds were built after about 1600. Some mound centers were abandoned, and there was a widespread trend during the eighteenth century toward more dispersed village settlements.

The hierarchical settlement patterns of larger centers and a well-defined ranking of lesser settlements were apparently abandoned during the sixteenth century. By the early seventeenth century the copper axes and spatulate axes, as well as other sumptuary goods symbolic of chiefly power, were no longer in use, as if such powers had eroded dramatically. Ravaged by disease, and without the support of their traditional beliefs, the societies of the interior were left in a state of cultural impoverishment. This, despite the fact that, by virtue of their remoteness from the coast, they had not been exposed directly to Spanish, French, and English culture and Christianity, as they were after 1673. Ultimately the drastic cultural changes of the previous 130 years put the Native Americans in a position to accept more easily elements of European culture in the years that followed, when acculturation truly began. It was not until the eighteenth century that the peoples of the Southeast came together in the Creek Confederacy, a response to armed invasions by northern native groups, and to raids by European slave traders (see Box: The Creek and the Deerskin Trade).

Jamestown: 1607

In 1607 a small band of settlers under the sponsorship of the Virginia Company founded the first lasting English colony in the Americas, at Jamestown on the James River in Chesapeake Bay, about 50 miles (80 km) from the Atlantic.

growth of berries and plants for deer and other animals to browse on.

What were the ecological effects of the burning? A team of archaeologists and geologists have used pollen grains taken from the well-studied vegetation of Fort Benning, Georgia. There, the forests are burned every three years to maintain an environmentally stable habitat that allows military activities while preserving natural resources. The vegetational history is well known from 1825 to 1836, when the Native Americans were forcibly removed to allow European settlement. The researchers used pollen samples taken from wetland and ponds, taking careful account of different Native American activities in the past. The pollen samples and charcoal analyses from there (and from many other locations in the Southeast) reveal a relatively constant fire regime, enough to maintain pine forest, pines being fire-resistant. There was a low fire level for about 150 years before the eighteenth century, then a dramatic increase between 1715 and 1770 that coincides with the deerskin boom. Hunting practices changed, too, with hunters operating year-round, not just in the fall.

The Creek deerskin trade had far-reaching consequences both environmentally and socially, a commerce triggered by demand far from the woodlands of the people's homeland. Fort Benning's pollen samples show the extent to which Native American activities in historic times altered the biophysical environment. There are signs that environmental changes resulting from such developments as the beaver trade had a profound effect on North America's natural environments. Understanding such changes through time, not only in the Creek case but also in many other locations and regions, gives us an important way to assess how human activities have affected the world's forests, and helps us manage them. In this case there is a direct, and well documented, link between actual historical events and ecological changes.

The introduction of Caribbean tobacco by John Rolfe in 1613 provided the cash crop, and the arrival of supplies in 1620 ensured the survival of the colony. The importance of Jamestown eroded later as tobacco plantations thrived in the interior. The settlement was abandoned when the state capital moved to nearby Williamsburg in 1699.

The historical records of the early years of the colony are, at best, ambiguous, but they chronicle social unrest, warfare with the local Native Americans, the building of a triangular fort, and problems with hunger and water supplies. With inadequate documentary sources, the National Park Service turned to archaeology in 1955, on the occasion of the 350th anniversary of the settlement. The first excavations located a number of seventeenth-century brick structures, ditches, trash heaps, and wells, but not the old fort site, which was still thought to be underwater in the James River. A half century later, in 1994, the Association for the Preservation of Virginia Antiquities decided to search once more for the lost settlement. Archaeologist William Kelso (2017) undertook the project, basing his work on existing excavations, maps, and other records, and a hunch that the site had survived on dry land. He was fortunate that the land had reverted to agriculture after abandonment, so there was no modern town atop the location. Kelso decided to dig near the church, on the grounds that sacred places do not shift, that worship there was continuous, even if different buildings had risen on the same site. There were also finds of seventeenth-century artifacts in the same general location, which lay near a Confederate earthwork from the Civil War.

By 1996, Kelso had uncovered telltale signs of a wooden palisade and was certain he had located the long-lost Jamestown fort of 1607 (Figure 15.4). He unearthed the remains of four buildings inside the fort: a barracks, a quarter,

15.4 Postholes for the palisade at Jamestown.

15.5 An L-shaped cellar at Jamestown before excavation.

15.6 The foundations of Jamestown's 1608 church.

and some row houses. A factory for trading with the Native Americans lay outside the palisade. Each structure was of strikingly similar design, at first a cellar covered with a crude roof, with larger post-supported buildings added later, protected by thatched roofs covering rectangular buildings (Figure 15.5). The fill of one cellar contained a coin of King James I of England and Scotland, minted in 1606–7, conclusive proof that the buildings dated to the time of the original fort. The architecture was a form of construction known as "mud and stud," used in Lincolnshire in eastern England at the time. Some of the colonists were from Lincolnshire, including William Laxton, a carpenter.

Excavations in 2010 have also revealed the outline and columns of the church in which the Powhatan Princess Matoaka—today better known as Pocahontas—was married to the English settler John Rolfe in 1614 (Figure 15.6). (The marriage between Pocahontas and John Rolfe brought a temporary peace between the Powhatan and the English.) The church was identified by four burials neatly aligned in the center and east of the building. Kelso identified these as marking the chancel area in the front of the church, where the altar would have been placed and where elite members of the community would have been buried. The bones were in bad condition, making it hard to establish what the four died from, but the most likely causes are fever or starvation. One grave held a fine silk sash, another a military staff and a small silver box, too fragile to open. The investigators used a CT scan to reveal a tiny lead capsule and some bone fragments inside. It was a reliquary, a container for holy relics, used by Catholics, not Protestants. This is intriguing, as few Catholics lived at Jamestown, which was very much a Protestant settlement.

Through archaeological work Kelso filled in many details of what was always thought to have been a disastrous first five years for the settlement. Historians had assumed that the settlers were poorly equipped. The archaeologists have shown they were not. They have found fishhooks and weapons, woodworking tools, and traces of glassmaking, apparently by German glassmakers brought to Jamestown to make glassware for sale back in London. A cellar from one building was full of rubbish, filled at the order of a newly appointed governor in 1610. It contained a surprising number of Native American arrowheads and pottery. These may be signs of peaceful contacts between the local Powhatan people and the settlers, though that peace did not last.

By 1608, Jamestown was in trouble. The settlers were starving, even after three growing seasons. But was the hunger their fault? Kelso and his colleagues believe that it was not. They learned of a 1998 tree-ring study based on local cypress trees, which shows that tree growth slowed dramatically between 1606 and 1612, just when the settlers arrived. The previously unknown drought was the worst in 800 years, probably a side effect of the Little Ice Age (White, 2018). It dried up water supplies and destroyed the crops upon which both natives and colonists relied. Food shortages may have triggered war between the two sides. Relations improved when the drought eased.

William Kelso's Jamestown findings have rewritten the settlement's history. The settlers were hard-working folk confronted with a savage drought that almost defeated them. Life was a struggle. Seventy-two poor settlers lie in humble, unadorned graves west of the fort. But there is more. Douglas Owsley, a biological anthropologist at the Smithsonian Institution, examined the bones found in the church. He discovered that they had a high lead content, probably from their owners using lead-glazed or pewter vessels. The bones were high in nitrogen, which suggests they had a better diet than most settlers. Burial records and archaeology identified the dead. One grave was that of the Reverend Robert Hunt, the first pastor to the colony. Sir Ferdinando Weidman was a horseman. He had especially strong thighbones and supervised cannons and horses. Captain William West was a gentleman who died at age twenty-four, fighting natives. He owned a silken sash. Finally, Captain Gabriel Archer was a Roman Catholic, which accounts for the reliquary in his grave.

Martin's Hundred: 1618 to 1622

Late in 1618, 220 settlers were shipped from England to settle 20,000 acres (8,000 ha) of uncultivated land named Martin's Hundred, facing the James River in Virginia (Noël Hume, 1973). The settlers built what proved to be a short-lived community that included a small, palisaded fort for protection against Spaniards and Native Americans and a fledgling settlement named Wolstenholme Towne. This was little more than a hamlet of timbered and thatched houses, a settlement of some thirty to forty people. At first the local natives were friendly, but on March 22, 1622 they attacked the James River. Half the Martin's Hundred population was killed or taken hostage. The survivors eked out a precarious existence for a few more years, but virtual starvation and contagious diseases eventually wiped them out. Wolstenholme Towne was almost forgotten for 350 years.

In 1970, Ivor Noël Hume, then resident archaeologist at Colonial Williamsburg, was searching for vanished outbuildings belonging to a colonial plantation in process of restoration. To his surprise he uncovered seventeenth-century post-holes, pits, and graves—the remains of Wolstenholme Towne. His excavations explored an area of 2 acres (0.81 ha), a jigsaw of postholes, old tree holes, pits, and other long-decayed timber structures (Figure 15.7). The wooden fort was

15.7 The excavation at Martin's Hundred.

15.8 Artist's reconstruction of Martin's Hundred.

found to have covered 10,000 square ft (929 m²). Excavated in its entirety, it was four-sided, of trapezoidal shape, about 83 by 130 ft (25.2 by 39.6 m), with a stout watchtower at the southeast corner and a bastion at the southwest. This once held a cannon, aimed toward possible Spanish ships in the James River. Noël Hume estimated the palisade was about 7.7 ft (2.3 m) high, with a clay-filled platform behind (Figure 15.8).

The dwellings were built of wattle, daub, and thatch, some of them built over large cellars as much as 30 ft (9 m) in diameter. With brilliant archaeological and historical detective work, Noël Hume used historical records to show how impecunious farmers would start by living in cellar-like underground houses that they lined with timber and bark and floored with planks, before erecting a roof and eaves above ground. A fragment of twisted gold thread and an iron

There are times when archaeology is like a Sherlock Holmes case—a question of inspired detective work. Ivor Noël Hume of Colonial Williamsburg and Martin's Hundred was a master of such research. Nowhere were his skills more brilliantly applied than to what we can call "The Case of the Missing Homeowner."

Hume and his team excavated postholes that had started off as the roofs for pithouses. They found earth-filled pits, which turned out to be the main room of the houses. Noël Hume was puzzled by the discovery until he came across a description of pithouses built by poor farmers and colonists in New England and New Amsterdam (subsequently New York), written by the Secretary of New Amsterdam in 1650. There, the roof eaves rested on the ground. Once the builders could afford more conventional houses, they would fill in the pit and build new homes nearby.

The Martin's Hundred houses seemed to have been built and used the same way, but Noël Hume wanted to know more than just how the dwellings were built. Who built and owned them? He searched for clues, and found one—a short length of twisted and woven gold thread. He suspected this was from clothing, perhaps an adornment for a jacket, so he researched clothes of the day. The gold thread appeared to be the type of decoration sported by the gentry and military officers of the day. His researchers delved into state archives and came across a 1621 legislative resolution that forbade anyone in Virginia to wear gold on their clothing except members of the "Council and heads of hundreds." Such sumptuary laws were strictly enforced at the time, for they were vital to discerning rank on both official and unofficial occasions. One of the individuals who signed the resolution was William Harwood, chief administrator of Martin's Hundred. Could he have owned the house where the gold thread came from?

Noël Hume persisted in his research. The excavators dug up a cannonball that clearly was meant for the cannon once mounted on the bastion of the Wolstenholme Towne's fort (see Figure 15.8). A cannon ball does not seem like much of a clue, for they were commonplace objects. But again, Noël Hume struck gold (albeit metaphorically speaking this time). He uncovered a 1625 census that listed William Harwood as the only person at Martin's Hundred who owned a "peece of ordnance."

Stringing these clues together, Noël Hume made a most convincing case that William Harwood had lived in the excavated house. This seems like a conjuring trick, but it is not. Rather, the excavators had a mindset that refused to be bound by archaeological evidence alone. They drew on archives, on contemporary documents that mentioned Martin's Hundred and one of its prominent citizens. A short length of gold and a cannonball were the clinchers of a classic archaeological detective story. Such brilliant detective work, and such mindsets, are the meat and drink of historical archaeology.

cannonball enabled him to track down the owner of one dwelling through census records and sumptuary laws. He was one William Harwood, once the headman of the tiny settlement (see Box: Historical Archaeology and the Case of the Missing Homeowner).

Such excavations as the one at Martin's Hundred are complicated jigsaws of archaeological and historical clues, testimony to the wonderful complexities of historical archaeology. The Martin's Hundred finds took Noël Hume as far afield as Germany, Ireland, England, and Bermuda, in search of such esoteric information as the design of seventeenth-century coffin lids and the pathology of cleaver wounds on murder victims. As a result, a lost community was brought back into the light.

La Florida

Shortly after Columbus landed in the Indies, Spanish explorers extended their king's domains through the Caribbean, into Mexico, and into South America. They also explored much of the Gulf and Atlantic coasts of North America, the lands named La Florida by Ponce de León in 1513. La Florida was far from wealthy and attracted few Spanish settlers until 1565, when Pedro Menéndez de Aviles overran a French colony near present-day Jacksonville, Florida, and founded two settlements—St. Augustine and Santa Elena, the latter on Parris Island, South Carolina. The local people exercised such pressure against Santa Elena and its forts that it was abandoned by 1587, two years after Sir Walter Raleigh's colony was established in Virginia to the north.

St. Augustine enjoyed a strategic position, located as it was close to the point where Spanish treasure fleets turned offshore with the north-flowing Gulf Stream that brought them up from the Indies. No less than 21 percent of the royal defense budget was spent in La Florida between 1564 and 1577, with resulting heavy ship traffic in and out of St. Augustine, ships that brought provisions and other necessities as well as military reinforcements, missionaries, and settlers. Sixteenth-century St. Augustine was a tiny settlement, a small mission and *presidio*. By the end of the century, the town comprised about 425 people living in 120 households. Only about 30 percent of them included women, and only half of those were Spanish. The rest were Native American wives or concubines. The garrison was plagued by floods, fires, and hurricanes, and was plundered by Sir Francis Drake in 1586. A member of his crew drew a map of the town, showing nine blocks of single-story, thatched structures with board walls. Many earlier dwellings were made of wattle and daub (Figure 15.9). St. Augustine survived and served as the capital of La Florida until 1702, when the British besieged its Castillo de San Marcos for six weeks. Eventually the defenders fled, after burning the wooden buildings of the town to the ground. This time the colonists replaced them with masonry buildings, as the town expanded in the first half of the eighteenth century.

A team of archaeologists led by Kathleen Deagan have investigated eighteenth-century and earlier St. Augustine, combining historic preservation with archaeological excavation (Deagan, 1983, 1991). Excavating the eighteenth-century town has proved a difficult task, partly because the entire archaeological deposit for three centuries is only about 3 ft (1 m) deep at the most, and has been much disturbed. Nevertheless, the excavators have recovered dozens of barrel-lined trash pits, and the foundations of eighteenth-century houses built of tabby, a cement-like substance of oyster shells, lime, and sand (Figure 15.10). The builders laid foundations of oyster shell or tabby in footing trenches that were the shape of the intended house. Then the walls were added. The tabby floor soon wore out, so another layer of earth was added and a new floor poured on top.

The St. Augustine excavations were highly informative, and showed that the layout of both St. Augustine and Santa Elena was highly structured, rigidly organized, and very conservative. This is hardly surprising, since it was established by sixteenth-century government ordinances. Households and their barrel-lined wells were laid out at intervals of 50 ft (15.2 m), the streets on a grid pattern. Exactly the same rigid and conservative layout persisted into the eighteenth century; only the building materials changed. Every time the town

a. SOUTH ELEVATION

b. END ELEVATION

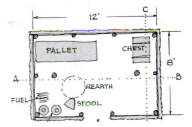

15.9 (a–c) Drawings and plan of the kind of thatched structure in which a common settler might have lived in sixteenth-century St. Augustine, Florida.

15.10 Spanish majolica ware recovered by Kathleen Deagan in her excavations at St. Augustine, Florida.

grew, the expansion followed the original blueprint. Archaeology confirms what one might suspect from historical documents. The colonists maintained their "Spanishness," which was based on standards set elsewhere, partly as an adaptive strategy to survive within the Spanish colonial system. Even so, local environmental and social factors did lead to some modification of the Spanish pattern, especially at the domestic level, where intermarriage may have introduced new foods and domestic artifacts into many households.

For generations a pervasive attitude and mythology characterized the Spanish colonists as cruel, bloodthirsty, lustful, and responsible for the devastation of Native American populations. This stereotypical "Black Legend" has long been discredited, but it is interesting to note that the objective eye of historical archaeology has documented considerable differences in the ways in which Hispanic-American and Anglo-American cultures developed in North America (Thomas, 1989). Spanish colonial sites contain many more imported and Native American ceramics than British settlements of the same period. The vigorous Spanish ceramic tradition resulted from many factors, not only a flourishing export trade but also the custom of subjugating native populations through mechanisms that bound their labor to Spanish masters. Most Spanish settlers were male, and the incorporation of local women can be seen archaeologically through the bringing of native ceramics into Spanish settlements. By the time St. Augustine was founded the Spanish had developed a means of interacting with the local population that was based on religious conversion, intermarriage, and tribute (which was later abandoned). The Spaniards integrated themselves physically with local populations, while still maintaining detailed, rigid, and highly legalistic classifications of people by race. In contrast, British colonists based their interactions with Southeastern populations on trade, warfare, slavery, and servitude. There was some intermarriage on the frontier, but there were more English women in English colonies. Archaeology reveals far fewer Native American artifacts and less Native American influence in such sites.

There are other differences, too. At St. Augustine the settlers buried their trash in abandoned wells. In a hot climate where food spoils rapidly and fish was commonly eaten, this is a sensible precaution. Many British settlers were far more casual, tossing their trash on the ground around their dwellings (for discussion, see Deagan, 1983). Judging from the St. Augustine excavations, Spanish colonists lived in a structured and highly organized social environment, an environment reflected by a tightly patterned material record. The pattern was conservative, in contrast to that recorded by James Deetz (1996) in New England, where an English rural tradition was soon replaced by local adaptations developed by people living not within a structured empire, but in almost complete isolation.

Spanish Missions

An extensive mission network extended through the Spanish Borderlands, the northern frontier of New Spain. By the mid-seventeenth century, thirty-eight missions served approximately 25,000 Native Americans in La Florida. There were more than fifty missions in the Southwest, and a chain of twenty-one Franciscan stations in Alta California by 1830. Archaeology has thrown light on early missions, some of which were modest structures that soon fell into disrepair.

15.11 *Far left:* Excavating the mission church at Santa Catalina de Guale mission, St. Catherine's Island, Georgia, June 1982. The foundations of the single nave are visible as a dark outline.
15.12 *Left:* Excavations at Santa Catalina de Guale mission, St. Catherine's Island, Georgia.

Santa Catalina de Guale, on St. Catherine's Island off the Georgia coast, was founded in the sixteenth century and rebuilt after a fire in 1597. The mission was a square, fortified compound with palisaded sides 193 ft (59 m) long and a central, shell-covered plaza. The compound protected the church, friary, kitchen and garrison. Construction was probably simple, the buildings being held up with tree-trunks, then covered with wattle and daub. David Hurst Thomas of the American Museum of Natural History used archaeological survey and excavation to amplify vague historical records, and to throw clear light on mission and Native American life during the Spanish period (Thomas, 2011). At Mission Santa Catalina **soil resistivity surveys** defined the shape, orientation, and extent of unexcavated buildings, such as the friary and a series of contemporary Native American buildings, while **proton magnetometer surveys** provided information about lengths of clay walls, located a well, and identified the well-preserved church and kitchen.

The church was constructed with a single nave, a rectangular building 65.5 ft (20 m) long and 36 ft (11 m) wide (Figure 15.11). The wattle-and-daub facade supported a pointed gable and a thatched roof. Pine planking and wattle formed the whitewashed side walls, which may have been adorned with ornate metal panels. The sanctuary was planked, and elevated slightly, with a sacristy on the left side facing the altar. Thomas even recovered some wheat grains from this room, perhaps part of the grain used to bake the flatbread for the Eucharist. A plaza surfaced with white seashells about 50 ft (15 m) on each side lay in front of the church. It was once enclosed with a low wall. Aerial photographs even revealed a worn pathway across to the doorway.

The friary complex lay across the main plaza from the church. The first such wattle-and-daub structure was about 52 ft (16 m) long and 23 ft (7 m) wide. This was burnt down by the Guale (a group related to the Creeks) in 1697, and was replaced with two structures, one for the friars, the other a separate kitchen.

MISSION NUESTRA SEÑORA DE LA SOLEDAD

Mission Nuestra Señora de la Soledad was founded 33 miles (53 km) southeast of Monterey Bay in central California in 1791, to control the Chalon Costanoan and Esselen, as many as 12,500 people (Figure 15.13). The friars adopted a policy called "reduction" to achieve their goals, gathering the once-dispersed hunter-gatherers at the mission, changing their culture, and turning them into a Christian labor force. The policy failed miserably. Crowded into cramped, unhealthy quarters, the Soledad inhabitants died in large numbers. Even continual, often forcible, recruitment failed and, in the process, weakened attempts to acculturate and convert Native Americans. Most of the mission native population was superficially Christian and within Spanish culture, but, as archaeology has shown, traditional culture remained strongly ingrained.

Paul Farnsworth excavated at Mission Soledad from 1983 to 1989, most of the work being carried out around the mission's west wing, the neophyte's barracks, and the aqueduct (Farnsworth and Jackson, 1995). He recovered two well-dated series of finds, which document cultural changes within the community. The first subassemblage came from garbage dumped in pits under the south end of the west wing, dating to the last decade of the eighteenth century or the first years of the nineteenth. The second, three groups of finds, came from domestic trash embedded in a sequence of adobe floors in a room in the west wing. This area served as the mission kitchen for at least part of the time, before the building vanished between

15.13 Mission Nuestra Señora de la Soledad, founded in 1791.

1834 and 1850. The artifact counts from these samples revealed striking cultural changes. From 1791 to 1794 there were few indigenous people at the mission, so the friars could exercise considerable influence over them. Judging from the artifacts in the garbage pits, this influence appears to have weakened in later years. Between 1795 and the first years of the nineteenth century, traditional artifacts rose from 30 to 45 percent of the total, during a period when the Native American population at the mission rose from 240 to 725 in 1805. Then the proportion of traditional artifacts fell again between 1805 and 1810, when the mission population was gradually declining. With fewer recruits, the friars could once again pay closer attention to changing the culture of their charges. The native population at Soledad continued to fall until the early 1820s, when weakening missionary influence led to another rise in traditional artifacts, this time to 40 percent of the assemblage.

The cause of these shifts lies in the changing economic function of the mission. Between 1800 and 1810 the friars diverted labor to diversified agriculture, craft production, livestock, and supplying food and clothing for the military. These were the years when the missionaries focused on exploiting the Native American people for their labor and tended to pay less attention to acculturating them. As long as their charges attended mass and completed their work, they were left alone—and traditional activities survived and even increased. Farnsworth and Jackson argue that far more of the intangible, non-material aspects of Native American culture, such as religious beliefs and ritual, also survived during these years than might appear from the artifacts alone. By 1810, with civil war in Mexico, there was an end-point in cultural change among the Native Americans, and a measurable return to traditional activities.

The friars lived in small, sparsely furnished rooms built around two central enclosures (Figure 15.12).

The Franciscans and the Spanish Crown established the missions of Alta California during the late eighteenth century as a way of controlling the indigenous population along the coast in the most cost-effective manner. The mission policy failed, however, and has been chronicled by excavations at several missions, among them Mission Nuestra Señora de la Soledad, founded in central California in 1791 (see Box: Mission Nuestra Señora de la Soledad). Even after years of contact, the native population had still not fully adopted Spanish culture. Some individuals may indeed have become acculturated, but the economic pressures on the mission soon curtailed the endeavor, so Spanish culture was not acquired by many local people.

SUMMARY

- The borderlands on the northern frontier of the Spanish Empire were in a state of constant flux. Archaeology has revealed details of Hernando de Soto's expedition through the south (1539–43), also details of sporadic later contacts between Native Americans and outsiders. The contacts were complex and not as sustained as they were in the Northeast, yet brought disease, massive depopulation, and resulting political breakdown.

- Excavations into the Jamestown settlement, founded in 1607, have yielded details of the colony's fort and dwellings, also of the church built in 1608. Some of the burials in the church could be identified. The research also documented a savage drought that caused great suffering in the new settlement.

- In 1618, 220 settlers founded a fortified village named Wolstenholme Towne at Martin's Hundred, near Jamestown. The local Native Americans attacked the settlement in 1622, massacring most of the inhabitants. Excavations and complex archaeological and historical detective work have reconstructed the tiny community and the activities of the inhabitants.

- Archaeology has played a major role in the study of Spanish La Florida, with excavations at St. Augustine, the Spanish capital. These researches have highlighted significant differences between Spanish and British relationships with the indigenous inhabitants of the region.

- Thirty-eight Catholic missions in La Florida, fifty in the Southwest, and twenty-one in Alta California worked with Native Americans between the seventeenth and nineteenth centuries. Archaeological excavations have revealed details of some of these missions, notably Mission Santa Catalina de Guale, off the Georgia coast, and Mission Nuestra Señora de la Soledad, in California.

CHAPTER

16

Unmasking the Anonymous: Archaeology and History's Under-Represented

The personalities of prehistory will remain forever nameless and without faces. Dynamic and charismatic personae have peopled the stage of history…But in our not knowing them on personal, individual terms lies a great asset, for the true story of a people depends less on such knowledge than on a broader and more general familiarity with what life was like for all people.

Thus does James Deetz (1996) distill the essence of historical archaeology. Archaeologists are concerned with the broad sweep of cultural change, and with basic human motivations and behavior. By studying the material remains of the past, we record not only the deeds of a select, literate elite, but also the lives of members of society as a whole—of minorities, merchants, Native Americans, and, above all, of the ordinary folk and their settlements long forgotten. In this chapter we describe instances where archaeology has thrown new light on some of the most under-represented stakeholders in the North American past—those who left no written record of their doings behind them, but played a central role in society at the time.

Native American Resistance

Archaeologists have filled in priceless details of Native American defiance against expanding government forces. In 1877 the northern Cheyenne had been removed to a reservation in Oklahoma to live with the southern Cheyenne. In an attempt to return toward their homeland, a group of at least eighty northern Cheyenne people fled Oklahoma, but were captured and then held in Fort Robinson, Nebraska. Two weeks later, on January 9, 1879, they attempted to break out of captivity. At least fifty-seven northern Cheyenne were killed, and thirty-two others escaped but were trapped at the edge of a creek. The captives fought a running battle with the garrison, across the White River, up some bluffs, and into open country. Twenty-six further northern Cheyenne were killed, and after eleven days the Fort Robinson military captured the survivors (McDonald et al., 1991).

That the northern Cheyenne were captured and escaped Fort Robinson and were pursued by the military is beyond controversy, but the route that the Cheyenne took out of the river valley is disputed. According to historical military accounts, the escaping party moved up an exposed sandstone ridge to reach the bluffs. This exposed route would have been unreasonable, indeed foolhardy, for there was a full moon that night that would have made the northern Cheyenne visible to the military. Cheyenne oral traditions insist on another route through a well-protected drainage that would have offered excellent cover from pursuing riflemen. It fell to archaeology to test these two conflicting claims.

Archaeologists from the University of South Dakota Archaeology Laboratory investigated the escape routes with the collaboration of local Cheyenne representatives. They used random shovel testing and metal detectors to search for spent bullets in three areas: two drainages and the exposed ridge mentioned in military accounts. The assumption was that spent bullets represented definite conflict in that area. The survey recovered no bullets from the exposed ridge but did find them in the drainages, thereby confirming the oral account of the Cheyenne Outbreak. This may seem like a footnote to modern history, but it is important to remember that the Outbreak has become a classic story of the American West from the white perspective, immortalized by John Ford's 1964 movie *Cheyenne Autumn*. This film tells the story from the victors' perspective and is a form of moral tale of the Old West. Now oral tradition and archaeology have shattered part of the myth, telling the story from the Native American perspective. In doing so science has helped fashion a mosaic of the recent past that is the historical truth rather than myth.

The Battle of Little Bighorn

In the second half of the nineteenth century tensions between native inhabitants of the Great Plains and the encroaching white settlers were increasing as white settlers continued to force Native Americans into smaller reservations. Tensions turned to conflict and the Sioux Wars. The famous Battle of Little Bighorn conflict pitted Lakota, northern Cheyenne, and Arapaho warriors against George Armstrong Custer and his detachment of Seventh Cavalry on June 25, 1876. It began with a surprise attack from Custer, as part of a summer campaign to force the Lakota and the Cheyenne back to their reservations.

Custer and all his men perished in an engagement that has assumed near-mythic significance in American history. There were no survivors on the American side to tell the tale, and Native American accounts of the battle were consistently discounted for generations. In August 1976 a sudden brushfire burst through the Little Bighorn Battlefield National Monument and exposed the ground surface—surviving bullets, dropped buttons, and all. Park Service archaeologist Douglas Scott and his archaeological team realized this was a unique chance to reconstruct what actually happened on that fateful June day (Scott, Fox, and Connor, 2000).

The archaeologists treated the battlefield as they would a crime scene and plotted the position of more than 5,000 artifacts. Crime-lab methods worked well. The researchers studied the firing-pin marks on cartridge cases and the rifling marks on bullets, this over and above the standard archaeological methods used to classify and identify the various weapons used in the battle. They were able to trace the movement of individual firearms across the battlefield, verify cavalry positions, and identify previously unknown Native American fighting areas.

Everything started with a metal-detector survey of the entire battlefield, carried out by volunteers walking about 16 ft (5 m) apart. Whenever the detector bleeped, the operator marked the place with a flag. Then a recovery team excavated carefully, searching for the object that had caused the bleep. A survey team set up a predetermined data point, then determined the angle and distance of the surrounding finds from that point. The depth, orientation, and declination of bullets and cartridges were recorded before lifting.

At the Little Bighorn site there are 252 marble markers, each placed where one of Custer's men was killed. They were erected fourteen years after the battle and long after the casualties had been buried in a mass grave on Last Stand Hill. Only 210 of Custer's men are recorded to have perished, however, which suggests that some marble markers record nothing. Scott excavated around some of the 252 markers and found small fragments of human bone, such as parts of hands and feet, from forty-four individuals. Skull fragments bore signs of blows from clubs, such as were used by the Native Americans at the end of the battle.

Using such signatures as cartridge cases and bullets, the investigators identified forty-seven different types of gun used by the combatants. The Native Americans used at least 415 firearms, including numerous repeater rifles, which were not used by the US Army in 1876. The repeater's rapid shooting was a critical edge for the victors.

The innovative research at Little Bighorn has established where individual men fought, what they were wearing, and what equipment they possessed. There may not have been a "Last Stand" of the kind described in many history books. Rather, Custer and his men were overwhelmed by a sudden cavalry charge. The survivors fled and were killed. In the end they may have shot their horses to form defense works, but in vain. Archaeology and forensic methods have revealed more of what happened at Little Big Horn and used dispassionate evidence to establish historic reality.

Studying Black Experience

The first Africans brought to America were slaves taken by Spanish colonists of San Miguel de Guadalupe, a colony that lasted only three months between 1526 and 1527. The first Africans brought into a British North American colony arrived in 1619, when around thirty so-called 'indentured servants' were traded from the Dutch off the coast of Old Point Comfort, and brought into Jamestown.

Archaeology has done much to document the unrecorded experiences of plantation life and slavery (Singleton, 1999). Early excavations focused on plantation sites in the coastal regions of Georgia and South Carolina. Artifacts from such excavations reveal that from 1740 to 1790 African heritage was still relatively strong in slave communities, and, while this legacy was systematically devalued by slave-owners between 1790 and 1861, it was perpetuated during the tenant-farming period that followed emancipation. Excavations in Virginia, South Carolina, and Texas have turned up such artifacts as clay pipe bowls that bear motifs with uncanny resemblances to ideograms and cosmograms from West Africa. This suggests not only the active continuation of African traditions, but also resistance to European plantation life.

Colono Ware

In South Carolina, 1740, African slaves outnumbered whites by almost two to one, and one-half of that majority was African-born. Leland Ferguson (1992) has documented African-American resistance to their masters and mistresses. He assumed that African-American eating traditions and religious practices were similar to those of West Africa and radically different from those of European-Americans. Ferguson studied what he calls the "container environment" of South Carolina, tracing earthenware "Colono" pots and bowls from slave quarters, plantations, and missions over a wide area of the Southeast (Figure 16.1). Previous historians had thought these ceramics to be "Colono-Indian ware," purchased from Native American artists and brought into Euro-American plantations. Drawing on archaeological, historical, and ethnographic evidence, however, Ferguson argued that while Native Americans likely made much of what is now called Colono ware, the majority of Colono ware found in Southeast plantations of the seventeenth and eighteenth centuries would have been made by the African-American slaves themselves. The style of such vessels was more

16.1 Colono Ware found in a Southeast plantation's river bed.

reflective of West Africa than of their North American setting, and their creation and use would have been, he believes, a form of struggle against, and indirect resistance to, slavery and the plantation system.

Annapolis and Wye House Plantation

Excavations of plantations have revealed important insights into the lives of African slaves, and African-American culture. Since 1990, Mark Leone and the Archaeology in Annapolis project have excavated seven major sites where African-Americans lived, dating from the eighteenth to the twentieth centuries (Leone, Fry, and Ruppel, 2001). They have found caches of artifacts placed under chimney bases or hearths, placed in the northeast corners of rooms, and around doorways. These are ritual bundles of pins, nails, perforated discs like buttons, coins or shells, rings, potsherds, pebbles, glass fragments, and crystals. Using historical literature and ethnographic research from West Africa, the researchers were able to decipher some of the meanings and associations of the caches,

THE WYE HOUSE PLANTATION GREENHOUSE: 1785 TO 1820

The Wye House Plantation on Maryland's Eastern Shore was settled by a wealthy Welsh puritan and planter, Edward Lloyd. His great-grandson, Edward Lloyd IV, built the main Wye House between 1780 and 1790. It is still in the family, with many of its holdings and all of its archaeology intact. At its height the Wye Plantation covered 42,000 acres (17,000 ha) and housed over 550 slaves at any one time after 1800. Frederick Douglass (1818–1895)—the famed African-American abolitionist and social reformer, who was also a brilliant orator and writer—was born into slavery, and was separated from his family and taken to Wye Plantation at the age of seven. After escaping from slavery in Maryland twenty years later, Douglass described the brutal treatment of the Wye slaves in all of his three autobiographies.

Wye House Plantation is an informative place for historical archaeologists, with its well-preserved buildings and complex association with slavery at its worst. Mark Leone of the University of Maryland headed an Archaeology in Annapolis research team that mapped the largely intact slave-quarter village around the house, as well as the greenhouse and work areas. On a day when the trees were leafless, his graduate student Benjamin A. Skolnik used LIDAR light detection and ranging to locate long-lost slave quarters using old maps superimposed on modern landscapes. A combination of **GIS**, LIDAR, and conventional survey and excavation revealed the archaeology of the quarter, one with extensive Afro-Christian materials.

But what about the anonymous slaves who labored on this landscape? Excavations between 2006 and 2014 of the Wye House greenhouse have unearthed a truly remarkable microcosm of plantation life (Figure 16.2). The excavations and minute analysis by Elizabeth Pruitt revealed a fascinating tapestry of plants, visitors, pollen, the food of enslaved people, and the work of scientific gardeners. The team used pollen analysis from their trenches to show that the Wye Greenhouse was used to house tropical plants, such as oranges, lemons, hibiscus, bananas, plantains, and pond lilies. It was also used to propagate—and probably to domesticate—medicinal teas, analgesics, cure-alls, and pain killers. This led Pruitt to suggest that elements of an African-American pharmacopeia were in use at the Wye Greenhouse. The Lloyds used it both for display and to show off their botanical prowess, which came at the expense of brutally hard work.

The enslaved African-Americans who lived in the greenhouse, in a slave quarter excavated by the Archaeology in Annapolis team, maintained the temperature and microclimates and ran the water pumps and thermometers to nurture at least a hundred species of plants. From their hot and stuffy quarters came a prehistoric stone pestle that was perhaps being reused as a protective object, to control spirits identified with fire.

The Wye House greenhouse is special because we can see how two separate gardening traditions met within it: "scientific" agriculture and the tradition of African-American yards. But though two gardening traditions

which were sometimes arranged on X-shaped axes—cosmograms, or circles of life. Autobiographies of former slaves, collected during the Great Depression in the 1930s, produced firsthand accounts of religious practices among them. The caches included protective charms and artifacts used in what has been called a "sacred pharmacopeia." They are believed to be part of a religious practice known as **Hoodoo**, whose curing aspect is called "conjure." Hoodoo acts on the principle that spirits exist, and that they exist to be used—to cure disease, to keep violent masters at bay, and to draw out malevolent spirits. The spirit was in the ritual bundle and had to behave as the bundle directed. The artifacts in the bundle provided a means to enter and exit a user's body. Hoodoo was used to cure, protect, and to punish; a powerful way to maintain resistance in a hostile world.

Archaeology in Annapolis has now extended its activities to the Wye House Plantation on the eastern shore of Chesapeake Bay, where excavations in a greenhouse have revealed unexpected insights into slavery (see Box: The Wye House Plantation Greenhouse: 1785 to 1820).

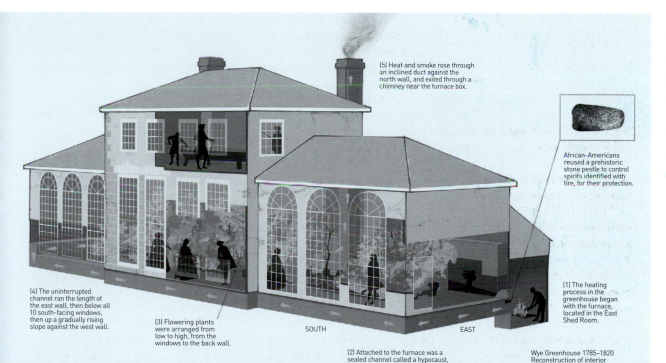

(5) Heat and smoke rose through an inclined duct against the north wall, and exited through a chimney near the furnace box.

African-Americans reused a prehistoric stone pestle to control spirits identified with fire, for their protection.

(4) The uninterrupted channel ran the length of the east wall, then below all 10 south-facing windows, then up a gradually rising slope against the west wall.

(3) Flowering plants were arranged from low to high, from the windows to the back wall.

SOUTH

EAST

(1) The heating process in the greenhouse began with the furnace, located in the East Shed Room.

(2) Attached to the furnace was a sealed channel called a hypocaust, which sent hot air and smoke below the floor of the greenhouse.

Wye Greenhouse 1785–1820 Reconstruction of interior Illustration by Brian G. Payne University of Maryland

16.2 Wye Greenhouse.

were indicated by the pollen analysis, the quarters provided evidence of but one food tradition. This featured meats, fish, fowl, and shellfish. Amanda Tang analysed the **zooarchaeology** of Wye House to show that African-American slaves and Euro-Americans cooked together and ate the same food. They used the same recipes, but with different cuts, eventually producing the cuisine now called Southern Cooking. Surviving Wye House cookbooks even name four Lloyd wives and four African-American cooks working together to make a new American cuisine.

16.3 Excavations in progress at the Storehouse and Smokehouse/Dairy at Monticello.

Thomas Jefferson's Plantation

Jefferson was not only a politician, a philosopher, and an archaeologist, but a major landowner as well. His estate at Monticello, Virginia, is carefully preserved for the modern visitor as an embodiment of Jefferson's times, but it is easy to forget that it looked very different in his lifetime. Again, the objective eye of the archaeologist has yielded significant information about the 200 anonymous slaves whom Jefferson employed on his estate (Kelso, 1986).

Some of Jefferson's slaves lived along Mulberry Row, the access road to Monticello, a road lined with nineteen artisans' and laborers' dwellings, workshops, and storage buildings (Figure 16.3). William Kelso excavated this area, a task materially assisted by Jefferson's meticulous records. A slave working at Monticello could expect to live in a variety of dwellings, perhaps something as small as a log cabin measuring 12 by 14 ft (3.6 by 4.26 m), with a dirt floor and a wooden chimney, or possibly in a much larger stone house, 34 by 17 ft (10.3 by 5.18 m), complete with stone and brick fireplace, neoclassical facade, and elevated pediment. One visitor to Monticello observed that "the outhouses of the slaves and workmen…are all much better than I have seen on any other plantation."

The occupants of Mulberry Row were somewhat more privileged than many of their fellow slaves on the estate, and certainly than those elsewhere. There was probably a social hierarchy among them, and some of the ceramics found in

FORT MOSE, FLORIDA: 1738

Fort Mose (Gracia Real de Santa Teresa de Mosé), about 2 miles (3.2 km) north of St. Augustine, Florida, came into being in 1738 as a refuge for English slaves who had escaped from Georgia and South Carolina (Deagan and MacMahon, 1995). In 1693, King Charles II of Spain had issued an edict stating that any male slave on an English plantation who escaped to Spanish Florida would be granted freedom. There were two conditions. He had to join the militia for four years, and he had to become a Catholic. At the time Spain was competing with Britain, France, and other European nations for control of the wealth of the Americas. By 1738 a hundred African-Americans, mostly runaways from the Carolinas, were living at Fort Mose near St. Augustine. They worked as blacksmiths, boatmen, carpenters, cattlemen, and farmers, and

along with their women and children they created a small community of freed slaves that became Fort Mose. The fort held about twenty houses inhabited by a hundred people (Figure 16.4).

When war broke out between England and Spain in 1740, the inhabitants of St. Augustine and nearby Fort Mose—which lay on a vital travel route—were caught in the middle. The English blockaded St. Augustine and bombarded it for twenty-seven days, and attacked and occupied Fort Mose. On June 15, a force of Spanish soldiers and the town's militia, led by Captain Francisco Menendez, an African-Spaniard who had escaped enslavement in South Carolina, mounted an attack on Fort Mose, hoping to take the English garrison by surprise. The Spanish attack overwhelmed the defenders in hand-to-hand fighting with clubs, muskets, and swords, killing about seventy British soldiers. The demoralizing reverse forced the British to lift the St. Augustine siege

and retire to Savannah. Meanwhile, the displaced Fort Mose inhabitants settled in St. Augustine until the Spanish rebuilt the fort in 1752, at which point many of them returned there.

Between 1986 and 1988 an archaeological and historical project headed by Kathleen Deagan examined the colonial archives and villages of Fort Mose. Research in archives revealed that the village had twenty-two thatched huts in 1759, each between 12 and 20 ft (3.7 and 6 m) across, and standing on posts. The researchers listed the inhabitants as including thirty-seven men, fifteen women, seven boys, and eight girls. Most of the Carolina refugees married fellow escapees, but some married Native American women or slaves living in St. Augustine. During the first season's excavations the archaeologists uncovered the three-sided, packed-earth-walled fort (the fourth side faced the river). The moat of the fort was found to have been filled in with prickly pears, and the dwellings were of fine quality. Many of the beef and pork bones were from poorer cuts of meat, such as are used to make stews.

Searches for African heritage are helping redefine the relationship between modern African-American communities and those of the past, offering accurate depictions of slave life to replace the often trivial representations in many modern restorations. For example, excavations at Fort Mose, Florida, just north of St. Augustine, have revealed the earliest free African-American town in North America, a place where escaped slaves sought sanctuary under Spanish rule (see Box: Fort Mose, Florida: 1738). Two other major investigations have thrown brilliant light on the African-American experience: the Kingsmill Plantations near Williamsburg offer unique portraits of tobacco farming and slave communities in seventeenth- and eighteenth-century Virginia (see Box: Kingsmill Plantations, Virginia); the chance discovery of the African-American Burial Ground in the heart of Manhattan in 1991 provides a sobering portrait of the anonymous free and enslaved people of late seventeenth- and eighteenth-century New York (see Box: The African-American Burial Ground, New York).

Mines and Miners

Western history is replete with images of rugged mining camps peopled by individualists, small pockets of civilization surrounded by wilderness (Hardesty, 1988).

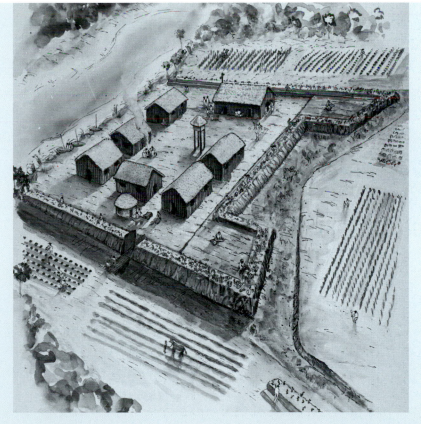

surrounded by clay-covered walls that would have held cannons and swivel guns. The artifacts recovered from the investigations included ceramics, glass bottles, gun flints, cannon balls, clay tobacco pipes, and beads, perhaps traded with Native Americans, as well as flattened bullets. Buckles, non-military buttons, needles, and thimbles hint that the inhabitants wore European-style clothing.

Fort Mose was part of a southbound "Underground Railway" for escaping slaves. This remarkable site gives a rich impression of African-Americans who were determined to be free. Their resolve was further demonstrated when most of them emigrated to Cuba when Florida came under British rule, and British slavery rules.

16.4 Artist's impression of Fort Mose, Florida.

The nineteenth-century Nevada mining frontier had many such communities, islands of outsiders who brought their own social and cultural environment with them. These centers were controlled, financed, manned, and supplied from outside, from major business centers in America and Europe. As archaeologist Donald Hardesty points out, they were linked in a real sense to the world economic system of the day, through information networks that expanded quickly with the completion of the transcontinental telegraph in 1860, which brought established Victorian values and additional capital to the mines. Supply networks linked to the world economic system transported supplies and mined ore, for example the network that brought river boats up the Missouri River in the upper Midwest. The mines were also linked into a complex migration network that brought miners from all over the United States, also from Asia and Europe, to remote Nevada communities.

Mining activity in Nevada is well documented through contemporary records, but archaeology makes a valuable contribution to understanding the everyday lives of mining communities, by observing buildings, trash dumps, and ruined

KINGSMILL PLANTATIONS, VIRGINIA

Kingsmill Plantation is named after Richard Kingsmill, an important member of the Virginia Company, the organization founded by King James I of England to settle Virginia permanently. It lies close to the James River just downstream of Jamestown. Kingsmill was given a land grant of 300 acres (121.4 ha), which eventually became a much larger plantation. The 1,400-acre (566.5-ha) plantation was named Kingsmill in the 1730s by Colonel Lewis Burwell III. Burwell was customs inspector for the Upper James River, and built an imposing two-story mansion overlooking the river, fine gardens, and other buildings. The Burwell mansion, as it was called, burned in 1846, leaving only the kitchen and office, which are among the earliest brick structures in Virginia.

In 1971 archaeologist William Kelso, now of Jamestown fame, found a colonial brick well shaft exposed in the bank of the James River (Kelso, 1984).

Once abandoned, such wells became convenient trash pits, and Kelso realized that the well in Kingsmill might be a potential treasure trove of early American life. When he was shown the abandoned mansion and its environs, he realized that Kingsmill was a remarkable eighteenth-century archaeological site. The plantation was due for development, but Kelso was able to spend three years excavating over fifteen archaeological sites that covered 200 years of history and provided a wealth of information about plantation life (Figure 16.5).

The earliest sites, called the Littletown and Kingsmill tenements, lay a short distance from the river, close enough for convenient transportation, yet invisible to Native Americans or passing foreign ships. Soon wells were sunk, indicating more permanent settlement with tobacco farming in mind—a profitable business. Brick construction was practically unknown before 1790, with even wealthy landowners preferring mud walls. Many of the owners may have come to make a fortune, then return to Europe. Long-term settlers Thomas Bray and Lewis Burwell built the first truly

permanent residences, making use of plentiful slave laborers to build them, while other slaves cultivated tobacco. Kelso found that the earliest settlers left little imprint on the landscapes, whereas Burwell and his works laid out formal gardens in the French geometric style fashionable at the time. But the practically minded plantation owners grew vegetables and fruit trees for their own consumption, rather than purely ornamental specimens.

This was life on a grand level, but what about the slaves? Documents tell us little about their lives, but we know that three groups of slaves worked at Kingsmill: house servants, artisans, and field laborers. At Kingsmill the house slaves lived in the attic, the basement, or adjacent outbuildings. They had somewhat better conditions than those laboring in the fields. The field hands occupied crowded barracks or small dwellings, many situated away from the mansion, out of sight. They were of European inspiration, cramped with earthen floors. Such structures were commonplace in Virginia, and the ones at Kingsmill contained no

mines in a holistic context of time and space. Hardesty points out that the archaeological record is often our only resource for documenting the layout of smaller Nevada mining settlements. Most were little more than strips of houses along tracks, or clusters of buildings around mines and crushing mills.

Shoshone Wells, Nevada

The ethnically diverse Shoshone Wells mining camp in the Cortez Mining District was settled in 1863, reached a considerable size in the early 1880s, and was still occupied by Chinese and a few Italian immigrants as late as 1902. It provides a fascinating example of how text-aided archaeology can document ethnic neighborhoods. The existing archaeological site consists of fifty hut sites, most of which are arranged into five clusters of distinctive neighborhoods. One cluster of twenty-two adobe, dugout, and wood-frame houses lay along a road on the valley floor. The artifacts associated with these houses are predominantly Anglo-European and Anglo-American or Chinese. Another cluster consists of four stone houses on the hillside above the other groups. These contained

16.5 Excavations at Kingsmill Plantation, Virginia.

distinctive African-American objects. But the occupants also built earthen or wood-lined root cellars, probably without the knowledge of the plantation owners. These contained numerous civilian and military buttons, many of them perhaps taken from the rags used to make the decorative quilts so vital for warmth in Virginia winters. The cellars also contained broken animal bones (perhaps hidden food), wine bottles bearing the seal of Burford's private stock, coins, tools, and ceramics. The ceramics included Chinese porcelain, and what appears to have been a broad cross-section of whatever ceramics the owner used and had on hand. Many of the root cellars had been filled with raw garbage. There was a lack of convenient fresh water, and presumably stagnant pools stood nearby. This speaks volumes about the quality of life in the field hands' quarters. In contrast, those who worked in the house apparently did not live surrounded by the detritus of daily life.

Most of the Kingsmill sites are now covered by a golf course and residential community, but Kelso's broad-based research gives us a powerful impression of the setting in which landowners and their laborers went about their business. This is historical archaeology at its best— melding the historical records compiled by individuals with general impressions of life on the plantation gleaned from architecture and artifacts.

Italian artifacts, such as Italian bitters bottles, and may have been the dwellings of Italian wood-cutters mentioned in historical records.

Mine owner Simeon Wenban's house cluster contained Victorian artifacts that reflected a much higher social status, such as fine French porcelain. Written records describe the mine owner's residence as a two-story redwood building standing in an irrigated lawn and garden. Wenban had trouble with his "turbulent and riotous" Cornish and Welsh miners, so he replaced them in the early 1870s with cheaper and less quarrelsome Chinese laborers. They lived along the road, and in the deep ravine below it. Their houses contain Chinese brownware, commonly used for food containers, opium tins and a pipe, gaming pieces, also European glassware bottles that once contained beer,

THE AFRICAN-AMERICAN BURIAL GROUND, NEW YORK

The African-American Burial Ground came to light in 1991 during preparations for the building of a federal office building at 290 Broadway in Lower Manhattan, New York City. The discovery and the powerful responses of stakeholders have transformed the history of slavery in New York and have had a profound effect on the study of African-American history. Furious controversies erupted over the way in which the discovery was handled, until local African-American communities in the city were granted control over how the burials were excavated and interpreted (Frohne, 2015). Eventually the building was redesigned and the Burial Ground was listed on the National Register of Historic Places and designated a National Historic Landmark in 1993. A Memorial and Visitor Center run by the National Park Service commemorates the estimated 15,000 people buried in New York's first African-American cemetery.

The remains of the more than 400 men, women, and children recovered from the site were reburied there in 2003. What was called the "Negro's Burial Ground" in the eighteenth century was in use for slaves and free African-Americans as early as 1712. At the time, it lay on the outskirts of the city, in a shallow valley, and covered 6.6 acres (2.8 ha). The Burial Ground remained in use until 1794, when the land was covered with landfill for development and forgotten. Except for occasional discoveries of human bones, the site remained undisturbed until 1991. The people buried there were of African descent, and lay in simple wooden boxes. Nearly half the burials were of children under twelve, a telling commentary on child mortality at the time. Another mortality peak occurred between ages 15 to 21. Some of the deaths were clearly due to unfamiliar diseases and the bitterly cold conditions of the winter months. Some women were buried with infants and stillborn children. There were numerous cases of skeletal pathologies caused by hard work. Both men and women had enlarged muscle attachments resulting from continual hard physical labor. Some had suffered from cranial and limb fractures, the result not only of accidents, but also the stress on bones caused by repeated carrying of excessive loads. Some women bore telltale rings on the base of their skulls, indicating that they carried heavy loads on their heads. People were literally worked to death. From the examination of teeth it is often possible to reconstruct the nutrition of people in the past. As children in Africa, the adult men and women appear to have been relatively healthy and well nourished, for their teeth show few signs of hypoplasia, or the incomplete development of organs. This was not the case once they reached New York, where evidence of malnutrition in later life is common on Burial Ground bones.

There were signs of traditional beliefs of African origin. Some of the burials had filed teeth, which are a clear sign of their African past. Almost all the bodies were buried in an east–west orientation, so that the dead would face the rising sun when they rose. One man between twenty-six and thirty-five years old lay in a coffin that bore a heart-shaped Sankofa symbol, an Akan symbol from Ghana and the Ivory Coast that depicts a bird scratching its back. The burials therefore demonstrate a people who were maintaining their African connections and culture.

The African-American Burial Ground was a landmark archaeological discovery that pushed consciousness of slave history to the foreground, and also shows the value of working closely with all who hold a stake in the past.

champagne, and other drinks. Such finds also come from other Chinese labor camps (see below).

Shoshone Wells is important because it gives an example of how a combination of archaeological and historical records can provide insights into the great variability among nineteenth-century mining communities. The archaeological study of mining provides a way of relating what Hardesty calls "the settlement," the archaeological record of houses and other structures, to "community," the actual people who lived in it. And such studies are invaluable when examining mining camps that were predominantly male, very cosmopolitan, and in which different groups kept themselves to themselves.

Kentucky Saltpeter Mines

Until the War of 1812, Americans relied on English gunpowder, an essential commodity on the frontier. When supplies were cut off at the beginning of the American Revolution, people turned instead to Kentucky saltpeter, a naturally occurring nitrate mineral obtained from sandstone rockshelters, which, in a chemical form, is suitable for making high-quality gunpowder. Most saltpeter mining sites were in a band just east of the Cumberland Escarpment in eastern Kentucky. The extraction process was simple. The nitrate-rich sandstone was placed in V-shaped vats and mixed with water to dissolve the water-soluble nitrates. Outside the rockshelter, the solution was boiled in large iron kettles until it crystalized. Mining operations tended to be transitory, for nitrate deposits were soon exhausted and the miners moved on to another location nearby. They worked in confined spaces, perhaps in groups of just three men; such a group could mine an estimated average of 40 lb (18 kg) of niter per day. But if relatively few men were needed to break up the rock face, the number of people needed to support them and to actually produce the end product was greater. Just for a start, the amount of firewood required was prodigious.

Archaeologists have located eighty-three saltpeter caves and 165 rock shelters in eastern Kentucky, far fewer than the actual number once worked (O'Dell and George, 2014). The investigations consisted almost entirely of surveying and recording. The fieldworkers looked for piles of broken rock with hammer marks and drill holes in the talus debris or on the nearby walls. Leaching vats survive in only a few sites. Being wooden structures, many of them were burnt as firewood by campers. The iron tools used in mining rarely survive, for even broken tools could be repaired and taken away for further use elsewhere, though we do find occasional wooden edges, pegs for splitting wood, and pry bars.

In a few rockshelters the processing vats survive almost intact in the dry interiors. You enter, and it is as if the miners walked away just a few minutes earlier. The vats were of simple manufacture, some made of heavy bark slabs. Others had sloping sides held together with pegs. All the known vats were placed over a hollowed-out log that caught the mixture seeping through the rubble and passed it to a trough.

Research into saltpeter mining is challenging, for the most part a form of historical archaeology that involves careful recording of mining activity that shifted location frequently, and was conducted by small teams of miners. Sources for saltpeter research included not only surviving mine equipment, but also interviews with tourists and other visitors, historical documents, and unpublished archaeological reports.

The California Gold Rush

The California Gold Rush of 1849 brought a flood of humanity from all corners of the globe to the then obscure village that was San Francisco, a bayside settlement with fewer than 1,000 permanent residents. Within three years it was a sprawling boomtown of hotels, bars, cheap rooming houses, and stores, many of them built on piles off the original shoreline. The great waterfront fire of May 3, 1851 virtually destroyed the town, including one William Hoff's general hardware store. Hoff himself abandoned his collapsed store to the mud and set up shop elsewhere.

The remains of his once prosperous shop were covered with landfill and forgotten until 1986. Then excavations at the corner of Sacramento and Battery streets probed 15 ft (4.5 m) below modern street level and recovered much of Hoff's stock from where it lay buried in the wet mud (Pastron, 1988). Hoff's store provided a remarkable snapshot of Gold Rush days, of clothing, furniture, medicines, firearms, construction tools, and mining implements from the 1840s. It was a chronicle not of the spectacular and the unusual, but of the humble and mundane, of kegs of nails, work boots, and Chinese porcelain. There were bottles of champagne and jars of imported olives alongside barrels of salt pork, dried beans, and cheap whisky. Army surplus goods including carbines, powder flasks, and lead shot accompanied many a miner into the interior.

It is with such sites as the Hoff store that historical archaeology is at its best, providing a wealth of information about daily life in North America as recently as the late nineteenth century. For instance, steamboat wrecks on the Missouri River and other waterways have given us portraits of the flourishing river trade of the nineteenth century (see Box: The Wreck of Steamboats).

Chinese Railroad Workers

Chinese labor camps were common in the west, especially during the construction of the transcontinental railroad. Many Chinese laborers occupied one of the largest, Summit Camp near Donner Summit in California, from 1865 to 1869. They worked under daunting conditions, building the grade, excavating seven tunnels, and laying track. Donner Pass is solid granite at 7,000 ft (2,134 m) atop the Sierras between Sacramento and Reno. There is little flat terrain and snow accumulates in great quantities. The Summit Tunnel is 1,600 ft (488 m) long and was dug from two faces at each end and using two shafts in the middle. Each team of workers dug in eight-hour shifts, working day and night, completing the tunneling in eleven months. They labored in groups of twelve to twenty men with a headman, six days a week, for $35 a month. The headman was responsible for providing food and shelter, while a cook supplied a steady supply of tea, and hot water for evening bathing.

The usual labor camps used tents and temporary structures, but at Summit Camp the workers built a small town with more permanent small cabins to protect them against the cold. Thanks to tourists and looters, almost nothing remains of Summit Camp today, so archaeologists were called in to evaluate the site, which had also been affected by a natural gas pipeline that ran through it (Baxter and Allen, 2015). They were able to match one cabin shown in a historical photograph with its surviving stone foundation, and identified both internal and outside hearths, also what appeared to be a wok oven. Artifacts recovered

THE WRECK OF STEAMBOATS

Lakes, rivers, and other waterways were the highways of early European America, highways along which thousands of humble, illiterate Americans lived in quiet anonymity. Occasionally a well-preserved shipwreck offers insights into their lives. These stand apart from wrecks of De Soto's ships, Civil War warships, and other well-known vessels. Two steamships in the Missouri River trade have provided priceless time capsules of this little-known commerce.

The side-wheeler *Arabia* was built in 1853 in Brownsville, Pennsylvania. Her 28-ft (8.5-m) paddle wheels could propel her upstream at 5 miles (8 km) per hour (Figure 16.6). *Arabia*'s history was eventful and included a raid by pro-slavery ruffians who confiscated guns and cannons on the way to slave-free Kansas Territory in March 1856. Earlier the same month she had almost sunk after hitting an obstacle that damaged her rudder. Then, on September 5, 1856, with a full cargo and 130 passengers, she hit a submerged walnut tree near Parkville, Missouri, which ripped open her hull. There was no loss of life except for a mule. The upper decks stayed above water, but were swept away within days, and the wreck vanished. *Arabia* sank into the mud, the river shifted course, and the boat was forgotten. In 1987 the Hawley family located the hull 45 ft (13.7 m) underground, using old maps and a proton magnetometer. The subsequent excavation required both heavy equipment and twenty irrigation pumps that removed 20,000 gallons of water per day from the waterlogged ground. The first artifact to appear from the wreck was a Goodyear rubber overshoe. Also excavated were packing crates full of fine china, the straw packing material still intact. There were crates of shoes and clothing, dozens of wool hats, a keg of ale (the only alcohol aboard), preserved fruit that was still edible, medicines, and even twenty-nine patterns of calico buttons from cotton dresses that had dissolved in the water. The *Arabia*'s cargo was bound for sixteen communities upstream.

Another steamboat, the *Bertrand*, was wrecked by hitting a large log in the Missouri River about 25 miles ▸▸

16.6 The steamboat *Arabia*.

16.7 The steamboat *Bertrand*.

16.8 The *Bertrand* excavation.

(40 km) upstream of Omaha, Nebraska, on April 1, 1865. The 161-ft (19-m) long *Bertrand* was built in Wheeling, Virginia, in 1864 (Figure 16.7). This was a shallow-draft vessel designed for river work, and was probably owned by the Missouri and Idaho Transportation Company, based in St. Louis. *Bertrand* sank in 12 ft (3.7 m) of water in less than ten minutes. No one aboard died, but almost the entire cargo was lost, the vessel and its load valued at $100,000— a huge sum at the time. The wreck was forgotten until 1968, when private salvagers discovered it in the DeSoto National Wildlife Refuge, a location that made all the finds property of the US Government. Over 500,000 objects were recovered in subsequent excavations, which provide a unique capsule of life along the Missouri in the mid-nineteenth century—a time when the river was a major transportation route upstream to Virginia City, Montana, for carrying supplies to Montana gold mines (Figure 16.8).

The *Bertrand*'s hold was full of essentials. Textiles abounded—clothing included men's coats in seven different styles, trousers, hats, and gloves. There were also many home furnishings (mirrors, clocks, and silverware, for example), and building materials of all kinds. Foodstuffs included dried and salted beef, mutton, pork, oysters, strawberries, peaches, and peanuts. There was mustard from France, and, inevitably, bottles of bourbon, whisky, and brandy, as well as medicines. Canned foods from the wreck, such as mixed vegetables and plum tomatoes, were tested and found to be safe to eat—if you wanted to try them! Miners' supplies, such as blasting powder, pickaxes, and shovels, also formed part of the cargo.

Most of the cargo was consigned to Vivian & Simpson, a retailer in Virginia City. The ship carried furs and sometimes ore downstream on the return journey. Fortunately, the cargo was fully insured and the merchants were paid for their losses.

The *Arabia* and *Bertrand* are compelling time capsules that document many of the essentials and luxuries that traveled up the Missouri into the remote lands far upstream. The *Bertrand*'s voyage to Montana took about two months and was dangerous because of hostile Sioux groups. But it was highly lucrative, both from the profits to be made supplying towns and mining camps upstream and from carrying furs back down the river. Both the steamboat excavations are unique examples of the invaluable, and often almost invisible, river trade that played a major role in the settlement and development of much of North America.

around the cabin included coins, Chinese and American tableware, opium-pipe fragments, and gaming pieces. The researchers also identified an almost cylindrical hearth up against a hillside that was probably used for cooking whole animals, such as pigs, for larger groups of people. Microfloral and other tests of nearby soil revealed that the inhabitants consumed barley, rice, legumes, and local elderberries and bearberries. Historical records tell us that the laborers ate dried oysters and abalone, and a variety of other foodstuffs. They also brought in catfish that thrived in a nearby lake.

Few artifacts survived, but previous archaeological investigations had recovered enough pottery to establish the material culture of Chinese laborers. William Evans studied Chinese artifacts from a range of camps as well as Summit, from as far away as Ventura and Riverside in southern California and Virginia City in Nevada. He found a remarkable standardization of table wares, what he called "the paraphernalia of subsistence," and relaxation (opium and gambling). The artifacts associated with Chinese workers varied little from one location to another, and were associated with a male-dominated society. Only in Virginia City, where women and children were present, did the artifacts show more variation.

Summit Camp chronicles the lives of the anonymous laborers who worked on the transcontinental railroad. It was an unusually long-lasting construction project that was a driving force in bringing Chinese immigrants to California. Those who worked at Summit Camp were isolated from the wider world of the west, but they maintained contacts with other communities while working on the railroad. At Summit Camp you can still see the now-abandoned railroad grade and the foundations of some cabins. The impressive view of Donner Lake and the surrounding terrain make you realize the extraordinary fortitude of the railroad workers. History comes alive as you walk the site.

Order and Power at Annapolis, Maryland

Archaeology has done much to chronicle the diversity of life in America's early towns and cities, and has also thrown light on prevailing social attitudes of past centuries (Orser, 2017). For example, archaeologists from the University of Maryland have worked closely with historians on a citywide exploration of the Historic District of Annapolis, Maryland (Leone and Potter, 1984; Shackel, 1994; Shackel *et al.*, 1988). Annapolis is very well preserved, because the city escaped the Civil War and the Industrial Revolution and did not undergo any urban renewal until the 1950s. Many buildings and much of the archaeological record remain intact, and archaeology has played an important part in the preservation process. Over the years the excavators have investigated an eighteenth-century tavern, a print shop, a victualing warehouse, several private residences, the site of a formal garden, and three properties first occupied about 1690. They have also placed a major emphasis on sharing their finds with the public.

Bottles, cups, and plates dating to the 1690s came from the bottom of the excavations of the Governor Calvert House (Yentsch, 1994), followed by intricate occupation layers, including a timber house of the early 1700s. Governor Calvert's brick house, whose first floor now forms part of a modern hotel, was subsequently built on the same site in the 1720s (Figure 16.9). Most of this structure was rebuilt in the nineteenth century, but the original walls were preserved within the Victorian building. The excavations also revealed a brick

16.9 Governor Calvert's House, Annapolis, now a hotel. Excavations inside the eighteenth-century residence recovered layers of Annapolis history.

heating system for channeling hot air to a greenhouse. This was partially torn up in the 1760s and filled with domestic refuse before being covered over by an addition to the 1720 house. The refuse proved a rich treasure trove of historical information, for it included animal bones, fish scales, pins, buttons, hair, pieces of paper, and cloth. The Calvert House enabled the archaeologists to recover complete layers of Annapolis history virtually intact.

The Annapolis research has far wider objectives than just historic preservation. Mark Leone and his colleagues from the Historical Annapolis Foundation have also studied the theories of power that lay behind the planning of the settlement, and have examined how people managed the landscape and built environment. They argue that landscape helps both to reflect and to generate social life, a conviction that has caused them to focus their research on urban plans, houses, and the gardens that surround them (Leone *et al.*, 1989). They argue that in the early days of Maryland society the emerging hierarchy of businessmen and officials fostered their social status by using Baroque and Enlightenment principles in their urban planning. The Baroque system used lines of sight to direct peoples' eyes to points of reference that represented monarchy and social hierarchy. In Annapolis in 1696–1710, for instance, Governor Francis Nicholson redesigned the original town, a settlement of some 200 people, on a master plan of two circles with streets radiating from them, and a large square, all placed on a series of hills and ridges. The State House and Circle are still the focus of Annapolis today. Nicholson used diverging sides for the radiating streets so as to give someone approaching the State House the optical illusion that it was larger and closer, thus adding to the impression of power. The researchers found evidence of similar patterns of behavior in St. Mary's City, Maryland (another major colonial settlement), and in Baltimore, the new city of the federal era.

16.10 Aerial view of William Paca's house and garden, Annapolis. This is a statement of aspirations and possibly of ideology as well.

St. Mary's City was once thought to have been a haphazard settlement, when, in fact, archaeology has shown that the principal, brick-built buildings, such as the Jesuit chapel, prison, and State House, were placed at nodes of the street system.

On the premise that eighteenth-century gardens were important ways of creating social status and power, Leone used garden landscaping in Annapolis to show how a crisis of confidence in an existing social order resulted in an ambitious example of public display. William Paca, a wealthy landowner and lawyer who was later elected governor of Maryland, was a fervent believer in individual liberty (Leone et al., 1989) (Figure 16.10). He signed the Declaration of Independence, with its strong emphasis on individual liberty, while living in a slave-owning colonial society. Paca lived a life of contradictions, where individual liberty and slavery existed alongside one another. He designed his carefully laid-out garden's paths, terraces, and plantings to express his belief in orderly civil and social authority, an ideology he carried into the practice of law. Some scholars, however, have criticized Leone's interpretation on the grounds that Paca fooled no one about his absence of power and that Leone's analysis left out the fact that two-thirds of the population probably saw through Paca's attempt at ideology.

A Multi-Ethnic Abalone Camp

Sometimes the traces of hardworking communities are hard to discern. Southern California's Channel Islands, occupied for over 13,000 years, experienced only limited contact with outsiders, while the mainland population grew increasingly diverse. Missionization and disease carried off the native Chumash population by about 1820. Subsequent nineteenth- and early twentieth-century visitors included fishers, hunters, a few ranchers, and travelers. By the 1850s the islands had become mainly ranches, but others visited, especially Chinese abalone hunters. Black abalone shellfish thrived in great numbers along the rocky intertidal shores of the islands.

Of the four islands protecting the Santa Barbara Channel, windswept San Miguel is the most remote, but a place where sea otters and other sea mammals once abounded. European-American and Russian hunters drove sea otters almost to extinction by the early 1800s. Fur seals were hunted mercilessly between 1790 and 1835; elephant seals and sea lions were targets in the later nineteenth century. The chronic overhunting of otters and seals, their major predators, led to a population explosion of abalone and other shellfish, and these were soon to be found by Chinese abalone hunters.

The Chinese had long been active in America in railroad construction and the Gold Rush, but black abalone attracted them to the Channel Islands like a magnet. The hunters cut clinging abalone from rocks in the intertidal zone, dried the meat, and shipped it to San Francisco markets or to China. They lived in temporary encampments along island shores, among them camps at Adams Cove near Point Bennett, at the western end of San Miguel, where a sandy beach allowed a junk to anchor. Today the area is one of the largest mammal breeding grounds in the world. A large archaeological site lies in the middle of the modern-day breeding ground, first occupied some 500 years ago and used by the Chumash until about 1660 (Braje et al., 2014). A historical hunting and abalone processing site lies southeast of the Chumash settlement. Two parts of the camp still survive.

One on the east side, the East Locus, lies in the shelter of a rocky outcrop. Two rock hearths and a pavement of black- and red-abalone shells extends at least 39 ft (12 m) east to west. Nearby lies another, smaller, black-abalone-shell pavement, a scatter of ancient and historical artifacts around it. The West Locus is about 656 ft (200 m) to the northwest, close to the Chumash site, and consists of a smaller scatter of artifacts and a circular hearth. The shape of the hearth and the nature of the finds suggest this site was occupied later than the East Locus was.

In 2006 the researchers mapped the sites, and cleaned, photographed, and thoroughly recorded the eastern hearths. Six tableware vessels of Chinese origin and eight fabricated in Europe or the United States came from the East Locus. The former dated to the late nineteenth and early twentieth centuries. The East Locus served as a Chinese abalone camp during the late nineteenth century. Chinese tablewares show that Chinese foods were being imported to the camp and consumed regularly. The hearths are similar to some excavated on San Clemente and San Nicolas Islands, further south, as well as at camps in California's Mother Lode country. The hearths supported a large pot used to render seal blubber into oil and to boil abalone meat before drying it.

The West Locus has been dated by embossed glass and a Japanese bowl, which narrows its occupation from about 1900 to World War I. The camp may have been used by Japanese fishers and hard-hat abalone divers, who fished and dived in the Santa Barbara Channel after the Chinese abalone industry declined.

The Adams Cove camp is an example of the challenges that face historical archaeologists as they decipher the complex histories of the anonymous folk who contributed so much to early American history. They were people in the shadows, but were key players in the increasingly diverse North American population of the last five centuries of the North American past. It behooves us to learn as much about them as we can before traces of their doings vanish into historical oblivion.

For more than 14,000 years humans have settled in North America, adapted successfully to its many environments, and interacted with one another within its boundaries. Today we are members of some of the most ethnically diverse societies on earth. As such, we need to understand some of the historical processes that have created this diversity, and shaped the way in which we live. It is not enough to consider American history merely by peering at historical documents through ethnocentric spectacles. As James Deetz urges (1996), "Don't read what we have written: look at what we have done." Our understanding of one another, and of ourselves, will be infinitely more perceptive as a result.

SUMMARY

- By studying artifacts and the material remains of human behavior, archaeologists study society as a whole. They unearth the lives of important, anonymous stakeholders in the past: ethnic minorities, merchants, Native Americans, and other humble folk.

- Archaeology has also rewritten history, notably with the Cheyenne Outbreak of 1879 and the Battle of Little Bighorn three years earlier. Evidence of the Black

Experience comes from artifacts and other finds at Annapolis and elsewhere, which include evidence of charms and what are sometimes called "sacred pharmacopeia," used to maintain resistance in a hostile social environment.

● Important excavations at Monticello, Kingsmill Plantation, and other sites are providing accurate depictions of slave life, as well as details of the first free African-American settlement at Fort Mose, Florida.

● Much historical archaeology is concerned with mines and mining, not only the technology and workings, but also the anonymous miners and other workers who labored in them. Important background on Chinese laborers in the mines and on the transcontinental railroad have come from recent excavations. Shipwrecks and underwater archaeology provide intimate portraits of moments in the North American past, here represented by excavations of two river boats and the light they throw on nineteenth-century trade in the Midwest.

● Annapolis, Maryland, has yielded evidence of life in the houses of the wealthy and their slaves, and of landscapes that crated images of social status and power.

● One of North American archaeology's greatest strengths comes from its ability to cast the historical spotlight on such people as abalone fishers, who formed the increasingly diverse American population of the eighteenth to twentieth centuries.

CHAPTER 177

The Heritage of North America

A young son of a ruling man of the Omaha wandered in the forest and lost his way after dark. He saw a light, believed it came from a tent, but came across a tree that was on fire. "Its trunk, branches, and leaves were alight, but remained unconsumed." As dawn broke, the "brightness of the tree began to fade until with the rising of the sun the tree with its foliage resumed its natural appearance." Next day, the light reappeared at twilight and again disappeared at dawn. The young man returned to the tree with his father, who spotted the tracks of four animals that had rubbed themselves against the trunk. The creatures were said to be Thunderbirds, which alighted on the tree and set it aflame, the trails of burning grass extending to "the Four Winds." With great ceremony, the people felled the tree, then carried it back to the village. The chiefs trimmed the tree and called it a human being. They tied a basket framework of twigs and feathers around its middle and set a scalp lock atop what was now a Pole as hair. Then they painted the Pole and set it up before a tent. The chiefs appointed a family to serve as Keepers of the Pole. Once a year, during "the moon when the buffaloes bellow" (July), the people gathered to repaint the Pole and to "act out before him the battles we have fought" in an enduring ceremony named *Waxth'xe xigithe* (quotes from Hall, 1997).

The Sacred Pole was one of three sacred objects within an Omaha camp circle, each within their own tent, the other two being the Sacred White Buffalo Hide, and the Sacred Shell. They are part of the revered paraphernalia in the Sacred Tent of War associated with thunder and war. In fact, the tree legend goes back much further into the past. A tree with birds upon it engraved on a shell bowl from Craig Mound at Spiro, Oklahoma, dating to almost 1,000 years ago, appears to depict part of the story associated with the Sacred Pole. The roots of the sacred objects lie deep in the past, the secret knowledge and rituals associated with them passed from generation to generation with great care.

Originally the sacred objects were to be buried with their last Keepers, but, in 1884, the last hereditary Keeper of the Sacred Tent of War, faced with the fragmentation of his family, passed its revered contents to the Peabody Museum of Archaeology and Ethnology at Harvard University, "where my children can look at them when they wish to think of the past and of the way their fathers walked." The move was bitterly opposed by many Omaha, yet the Sacred Pole followed in 1888. It remained in the museum until it was returned to the Omaha a century and a year later, received by Doran Morris, the great-great-grandson of Yellow Smoke, the last hereditary Keeper of the Pole (Hall, 1997).

The Loss of Patrimony

One of the greatest tragedies of the *entrada* was the loss of Native American patrimony—art and artifacts, prized sacred objects, and oral traditions, traditionally passed down the generations by word of mouth. Priceless records of remote and more recent history vanished in the face of epidemic disease, unscrupulous land-grabbing, and rapacious collectors, who looted archaeological sites and seized sacred objects with no concern for the values and traditions of their owners. The Sacred Pole of the Omaha is a case in point. It came to the Peabody Museum through the efforts of ethnographers Alice Fletcher and Francis La Fleche. The pair of them spent a quarter century studying the Omaha (Fletcher and La Fleche, 1972). Their two-volume monograph, originally published in 1911, records a wealth of information about a way of life that had vanished. Francis La Fleche devoted his life to the recording of the oral traditions of the Osage tribe, a group whose language was close to that of the Omaha, whose tongue he spoke fluently. Even so, he recorded only about 5 percent of the total Osage ceremonial repertoire. The anthropologist Margo Liberty once estimated that to set down the complete war records and ceremonies of all kin groups of the Osage in their language, and in English, would have required some 40,000 printed pages, or between fifty and eighty books up to 800 larger-format pages long. Despite such efforts as La Fleche's, much oral history and traditional knowledge has vanished throughout North America. Not that there were no efforts to record them. There were—scholars have been recording Native American beliefs and rituals, traditional practices, and indigenous North American languages for many years. Much of the basic data, however, has been largely ignored; volumes of ethnographic texts collected by nineteenth-century and later anthropologists remain unanalysed.

Apart from these still virtually unexplored ethnographic sources, the loss of traditional knowledge, of a means for expressing what one might call "Indianness," has been catastrophic. In many cases, all that remains are durable artifacts. For over a century-and-a-half, indeed ever since Columbus, individuals and museums have been collecting, storing, sometimes curating, and exhibiting artifacts made and used by Native Americans. As a result, the magnificent, rich cultural patrimony of the pre-Columbian North Americans has been ravaged. Yet, as Robert Hall (1997) has pointed out, it is an ironic truth that the only reason many fragile material objects that represent this patrimony now survive is because they became part of museum collections. Just over a century ago many tribal leaders were concerned about the fate of sacred artifacts, such as the three Sacred Tents of the Omaha. Many hereditary Keepers of such objects, objects so sacred that no one could touch them, were becoming old and had no one to assume their roles. Many leaders assumed that the objects would be buried with their last Keepers. Fortunately some of them, like the Omaha Sacred Pole, passed to museums, and some have since been repatriated to their traditional owners.

Sadly most very sacred artifacts were purloined generations ago. A few have ended up on auction blocks and been sold to private collectors, who care nothing about their symbolic value. The psychology of collecting is little understood, but, as one French observer remarked, it is "a passion and often so violent that it is inferior to love or ambition only in the pettiness of its aims" (Meyer, 1992). North American archaeology and the study of pre-Columbian societies have also suffered, and still suffer, from this passion. Quite apart from the activity of academic researchers and legitimate collectors, looting of archaeological sites, whether Midwestern earthworks, Southwestern pueblos, or California or Florida shell middens, has become a major, unfortunately lucrative, industry.

What Archaeology Has Achieved

With such an incomplete record, it has fallen to archaeologists to tell much of the story of the North American past. Here it is worth requoting the words of James Deetz (1997): "Don't read what we have written: look at what we have done." Deetz summarized what archaeologists do in North America in one sentence. We use the material remains of the past to do all we can to reconstruct the economic, political, and social life of ancient North Americans. After well over a century of research, we have now have a story of the North American past in hand, albeit incomplete. For instance, by around 14,000 to 15,000 BP, we now know that handfuls of late Ice Age hunter-gatherers of Siberian ancestry had moved southward from Beringia into the uninhabited Americas. Within a remarkably short time a scattering of small, broad-spectrum hunter-gatherer societies had settled in almost all the ice-free environments of North America. This book has told their story and described what happened next. Over more than fourteen millennia, the ancient North Americans developed a wonderful diversity of responses to a great array of natural environments, some of them places of violent extremes. By the standards of global history the Native American past is but a blink of the proverbial eye, a brief moment in time. But it is a historical blink of supreme importance, for North American archaeology has given us a rich portrait of human diversity before and after Columbus that provides us with more perceptive understandings of one another in an increasingly interconnected and complex world.

Ancient North America is an intricate historical tapestry, woven from multidisciplinary research, of which archaeology is a major part. The story becomes ever more detailed every year as research intensifies and the legal mandates of Cultural Resource Management (CRM) produce a tidal wave of new data to amplify and correct the big picture in these pages (see Box: Cultural Resource Management). Obviously, the corrections will continue, but what does the future hold?

CULTURAL RESOURCE MANAGEMENT

At intervals in these pages, we have referred to Cultural Resource Management, universally referred to as CRM. A short briefing on the subject fits well here, as the future of North American archaeology is tied to the conservation and management of the finite, and, alas, vanishing, archives of the past.

Archaeology is under siege, from industrial development, deep plowing, strip mining, and urban expansion with its accompanying massive road contracts. Dams have flooded thousands of acres of floodplain and the archaeological sites upon them. Cultural resources are the material record of the human past, be they artifacts, earthworks, humanly modified landscapes, or entire archaeological sites, be they a scatter of stone tools or a great center, such as Cahokia. The conservation and management of the finite records of the past is as important as pursuing knowledge about the past, for North America's unique cultural heritage is vanishing before our eyes.

Efforts to preserve North America's past date back to the **Antiquities Act** of 1906, which was primarily aimed at controlling the lucrative trade in Pueblo artifacts from the Southwest. Since then an elaborate framework of federal, tribal, and state legislation has developed, to control looting and reduce the destruction caused by industrial activities of all kinds, as well as to address such issues as the repatriation of Native American skeletal remains. This maze of legislation applies only to archaeological sites on publically owned land. The United States is the only country in the world that extends no protection to those on private land— for constitutional reasons. A number of private organizations, among them the **Archaeological Conservancy**, struggle valiantly to purchase or save unprotected sites, but the task is daunting. Some private owners take good care of the sites on their land. Others have mined them for profit and sold their finds on the open market.

CRM and the archaeological research that goes with it are but one component of a much larger concern for the fragile ecology of North America and the human impact on the environment. **The National Environmental Protection Act (NEPA)** provides a legal framework for the studies required for all federal and state projects that can affect human life on earth. Basically, there are three phases in the process:

▶▶

What Does the Future Hold? Outreach and Stakeholders

Archaeology has become ever more specialized and technical in recent years as the number of practitioners has exploded, especially in an era when CRM projects large and small dominate field and laboratory research. Fifty years ago North American archaeology was a small field of academics and museum curators who worked with shoestring budgets. Everyone knew everyone else in what was ultimately a large extended family. Archaeologists did their thing, mostly in complete isolation from any broad constituency such as the general public. They thought of themselves as the main stakeholders in the past, working mainly for fellow scholars, with little concern for wider audiences. It did not matter what the public thought of us. Today it matters a great deal, especially as we find looting and destruction pressing in on every side. We are deeply concerned with the public perceptions of archaeology and archaeologists. The tired stereotypes of absent-minded professors and Indiana Jones have given way to a much more sophisticated understanding of what we do. *National Geographic Magazine* and other periodicals led the way during the 1960s, making such archaeologists as Louis and Mary Leakey (famous for their work on early human evolution) household names. Public outreach—communicating with wider audiences—is now a major concern and a driving force behind much archaeology.

What is often called "**public archaeology**" is coming to the fore as a way of highlighting the conservation ethic that lies behind all archaeological research. As archaeologist Kent Flannery once memorably remarked (1982), we archaeologists are the only social scientists who kill their informants. In other words,

---

Identification and preliminary assessment. This is basically a reconnaissance and inventory of the cultural resources within the project area. The project area can be anything from a single house lot to an entire landscape.

Assessing significance. This phase involves examination of sites identified during Phase 1, with limited excavation to identify intact, stratified sites and to assess their potential significance.

Management plans and data recovery. This involves intensive work that establishes mitigation methods to protect sites, or excavation to recover data from sites that will be destroyed during development. Mitigation may even involve changing the route of a highway, or redesigning a building, as was the case with New York's African Burial Ground (see Box:

The African-American Burial Ground, New York, p. 360).

Much CRM involves gathering and assessing archaeological data from very specific areas, such as the site of an oil-drilling pad, or a pipeline extending over hundreds of miles. There is a heavy emphasis on survey as a basis for management decisions about the past; excavations are limited. Inevitably, large numbers of CRM investigations are purely descriptive, but many bigger projects have carefully developed research designs, operate with large budgets, and have ample funds for excavation and survey, laboratory work, and publication. Such projects can be exemplary efforts by large privately owned companies, such as the study of the archaeology of the Ballona Wetlands near Los Angeles International Airport.

CRM is now generating great quantities of basic data that, when pulled together, offer unique opportunities for detailed research, such as that into Mississippian polities.

Most North American archaeology is now carried out under CRM projects, for this is the only viable way of identifying and documenting the country's vanishing archaeological resources. Through its use of **geomorphological methods**, we have been able to achieve a much better understanding of the changing landscapes and settlement patterns of ancient North America.

all archaeological excavation, or interference with archaeological sites, destroys priceless, finite records of the past. Unless properly and comprehensively recorded, the results of an excavation can vanish into oblivion, just as many cherished oral traditions of pre-Columbian societies disappeared into the well-named "mists of antiquity." But we are not the only people to blame. Archaeological sites throughout the world are under attack from looters and treasure hunters, and, of course, from the activities of industrialized societies—everything from road construction, deep agriculture, and mining to building suburban neighborhoods. Yes, we archaeologists kill our informants, but our activities are nothing compared with those of looters and industrialized societies generally. In the case of North America what is being destroyed is the material heritage of more than 14,000 years of Native American history.

One question for the future is brutally simple: will the archives of sites, artifacts, and cultural landscapes survive the centuries? They will in one form or another, but as a pale reflection of what was in existence even a hundred years ago. Putting it bluntly, we are destroying a large part of North America's past. The past is in danger from the future, and from people who either care little about history, or have never even heard of archaeologists. (Yes, Jack or Josephine, such people exist in large numbers!) The only solution is engagement with the public.

Over the past generation or so public-outreach efforts by archaeologists and CRM organizations have saved many sites from destruction. The same efforts have not only raised public awareness, but also greatly widened the numbers of stakeholders in the past. Ever since the nineteenth century archaeology has been regarded by many as a marginal intellectual inquiry. Even today many people wonder if archaeology matters. You have only to read a few pages of this book to understand that it does. Just think of today's diverse stakeholders in the past. They vary from one location to another, but their number and variety give them powerful voices in calling for preserving the past; these are people who realize the priceless legacy from archaeological sites large and small that are part of the common cultural heritage of *all* humankind. The Parthenon in Athens or the Pyramids in Giza in Egypt are part of this heritage. So are Pueblo Bonito, Cahokia, and a host of inconspicuous scatters of stone tools throughout North America, from near Hudson's Bay in the Arctic to the Arizona desert. The greatest challenge for the future is to ensure that the unique legacy of the major stakeholders in ancient North America is cherished, preserved, and recognized for what it is—a story of cultural adaptation and diversity that is as much part of our history as Christopher Columbus or the Declaration of Independence. How will we master this challenge? No one really knows, but a great deal depends on the activities of individual archaeologists, who have a passion for the past and its legacy. Conservation and working with stakeholders will be dominant themes in tomorrow's North American archaeology.

Engaging with Stakeholders

A similar passion for the past engages today's Native American groups with their traditional roots and values, with complex, often contradictory oral traditions, and with religious practices that were valued long before any Christian missionaries set foot in North America. Engaging with Native American stakeholders is probably the greatest challenge of all confronting North American archaeologists.

How do we meld the complex, still little studied, historical perspectives of Native American societies with those of scientists, perspectives on human history are linear? There is a disconnect between the cyclical and linear views of time. There is also a conflict of cosmological views, of attitudes toward ancestors and kin ties, and of fundamental human values. I suspect that the answer to this problem will come from sustained dialogue between Native Americans and those who study the material and oral remains of their history and traditional practices, in other words between stakeholders in the past.

This dialogue has barely begun, muffled as it is by anger and resentment, by deeply held suspicion and by political agendas. But there are signs of progress, in the ways that Southwestern tribes are employing archaeologists to protect sites and sacred places and to engage in research that probes their origins in earlier centuries. There are numerous instances from Canada and the United States where canyons of misunderstanding are slowly being bridged, and Native Americans are becoming actively involved in archaeological fieldwork, research, and public outreach. It is not enough today just to excavate a site and write about it for one's colleagues. That is what is often called "publish or perish," an outmoded ethic if ever there was one. We archaeologists, whether scholars, administrative officials, or people engaged in conservation and CRM, have to remember that we are ultimately story tellers, just like tribal elders and keepers of sacred artifacts, who recounted tales and oral traditions that passed between the generations. Our story is different in many respects from that of native historians, but that does not mean that the one is right, the other wrong. History is as diverse as the stakeholders who hold it dear. It just happens that archaeologists are among them. Many pre-Columbian scholars are now working with Native American groups. Others are engaging with people who live where they are carrying out research, in another form of outreach known as "**community archaeology**."

This approach originated in the Native American Graves Protection and Repatriation Act (NAGPRA) of 1990, which covered federal and tribal lands, and mandated the return of skeletal remains and sacred objects to federally recognized Native American tribes. NAGPRA was a landmark moment, for it engaged entirely new stakeholders with the archaeological world. It came as expanded CRM activity brought archaeologists into contact with much broader constituencies. A turning point came in 1991 with the discovery of New York's African-American Burial Ground, where more than 400 enslaved and free Africans and African-Americans were interred (see Box: The African-American Burial Ground, New York, p. 360). The controversy surrounding the discovery threw archaeologists, developers and African-American communities into (often heated) dialogue, and forced the diverse stakeholders to come together to find a workable solution (Frohne, 2015).

Since then, there has been a growing concern as to how to involve stakeholders in ongoing archaeological research. This has assumed great importance in histori-cal archaeology, where researchers often work with the descendants of the people they study and with local communities. The net for stakeholders is cast wide, with the results can be very rewarding. For example, a Community Archaeology Research Institute has worked with the descendants of local African-American settlers who founded Freedmen's Town, Texas, after the Civil War. Freedmen's Town is now being gentrified, but, using artifacts, historical records, and oral

DISCOVERING ARCHAEOLOGY: THE CROW CANYON ARCHAEOLOGICAL CENTER

There are many ways of becoming involved in North American archaeology, other than by merely meeting an archaeologist, which is what happened to me. You can find innumerable field opportunities on the web both in North America and much further afield. Or you can attend a formal field school, of which many exist for either high-school students, the general public, or undergraduates. There are almost unlimited opportunities to become involved in archaeology as an amateur (or "avocational archaeologist," as they are called in the United States), and you are often welcome as a volunteer on an excavation or field survey if you have some field experience in a structured setting. Then you are far more than merely another set of hands. Both the Archaeological Institute of America and the Society for American Archaeology can guide you to fieldwork opportunities. They have websites that are easily found on Google or other search engines.

I think one of the best ways to find out if you are truly interested in archaeology, either as a profession or as a hobby, is through the non-profit Crow Canyon Archaeological Center in Cortez, Colorado (www.crowcanyon.org) (Figure 17.1). The Center's mission statement spells out their objectives: "To empower present and future generations by making the human past accessible and relevant through archaeological research, experiential education, and American Indian knowledge."

Every year Crow Canyon runs a College Field School aimed at

Figure 17.1 Crow Canyon College Accredited Field School: sifting at the Haynie Pueblo site.

undergraduates and graduates. It is an accredited program, so you can accrue 6 credit hours through Adams State University in Colorado (there is a fee per credit hour). The program also certified by the Register of Professional Archaeologists. The school lasts five weeks and is designed to get your hands dirty in the field and laboratory. You learn the fundamentals of archaeological site identification and recording, also excavation, as well as the basics of ⟫

traditions, the research team is working to dispel false stereotypes of chronic poverty in earlier times, while also carrying out basic research (McDavid, 2011). Archaeology has helped convince today's local residents that the community is worth saving as a viable enterprise, as well as combatting racist stereotypes and doctrines of white privilege. The work continues.

A great deal of community archaeology combines archaeology with modern-day ethnography, which means that the researchers' subjects often use the results to further their own political aims and to address public concerns such as gentrification and racism, as was the case in Texas. Community archaeology has great potential for the future, as archaeologists become increasingly involved not only in reconstructing the past, but also in helping to define the future.

The archaeology of the future will be involved in society in ways that were unheard of even a generation ago. And, if you wish, you can become part of artifact processing and analysis (Figure 17.2). The instructors also teach you instrument surveying and remote sensing survey methods. These are all essential skills, expanded upon by evening programs, field trips, what are called "service learning projects," and attending public events. You are in a field school that immerses you in the real world of archaeology, and you carry out serious research into an Ancestral Pueblo site near the Center. This is very much small-group learning, for you work in groups throughout the school, rotating between the different training modules whose skills complement one another. Perhaps best of all, you interact constantly with working archaeologists, experienced field and laboratory experts, so you really learn what they think about and the problems they encounter. The fee (it changes each year) includes living expenses. College credit costs about $330 extra for six credits (2017 price).

There are numerous other Crow Canyon programs that allow you to explore archaeology. They run a one-day overview of Southwest archaeology that is truly unique, for it is led by professional archaeologists and educators. Another alternative: you can be a "citizen scientist" and work

Figure 17.2 Crow Canyon College Accredited Field School: laboratory work.

alongside their archaeologists on a dig or in the laboratory. Crow Canyon also runs archaeology camps for middle-school and high-school students aged twelve to eighteen, which also allow participants to learn about Native American cultures.

In the final analysis Crow Canyon is a network of diverse scholars—everything from archaeologists to economists and educators—as well as Native American cultural experts, who teach about native cultures. Their real interest is in working

with large and complex data sets, as are now finally becoming available, to look at very basic, big questions. Above all, the Center works closely with Native Americans as it studies not only the past, but the future too.

If you are seriously thinking about becoming an archaeologist, Crow Canyon is a wonderful starting point for anyone who wants to be a critical thinker about the past and to engage with the future as a lifelong learner. I wish the Center had been around when I was an undergraduate. It would have changed my life.

archaeology, too, either as a volunteer, or by training to become a professional archaeologist. First, however, you need to discover whether you have a true passion for the past. You can volunteer on a dig, or go through a program run by a non-profit organization in your community, if there is one. The web has many informative resources and will connect you with all kinds of opportunities for students or volunteers. One of the best-known is the Crow Canyon Archaeological Center in the Four Corners region of the west, which runs a variety of programs for neophytes and more experienced people (see Box: Discovering Archaeology).

And, Please…

Finally, whenever you come across archaeology in the future, please obey the following principles that help all of us conserve the past for the future.

Treat all archaeological sites and artifacts as finite resources.

Never collect, or buy, or sell artifacts.

Avoid disturbing any archaeological site and respect the sanctity of all ancient burial sites.

Report every accidental archaeological discovery you make.

We owe the legacy of the past to those who are coming after us.

BECOMING AN ARCHAEOLOGIST

Some readers may have become so captivated by ancient North America that they are toying with the idea of becoming a professional archaeologist. Let us take a closer look at what is involved.

Career opportunities

During my university years I developed something of a reputation for discouraging people from becoming professional archaeologists. The reason: there are more people looking for jobs than there are employment opportunities. The landscape has changed considerably in recent years, as purely academic and museum posts, which are always in short supply, have given way to an expansion of CRM and heritage jobs. No one knows how many archaeologists there are in the United States and Canada, but there must be at least 10,000 of us, working in everything from academia to cultural tourism.

Academic archaeology is contracting in the face of budget cutbacks. If you want to pursue an academic career at a research university, you will need a PhD, which is a research degree. An MA will allow you to teach at a community college or other two-year-institution. But the degree alone is not enough. You must care deeply about people, be articulate and enthusiastic in the classroom, and have a true passion for the subject. It is not sufficient to pay lip service to teaching when your real interest is research. Museum posts are in short supply and require an enthusiasm for the general public and good communication skills.

CRM archaeology is where good, sometimes open-ended, opportunities can be found. The skills required are not necessarily those taught in conventional MA and PhD programs. The best opportunities lie in the larger CRM companies, which are always looking for competent excavators who will in time become supervisors and project managers. There are also openings in non-profit groups, such as CRM units attached to colleges, museums, and universities. A long-term career in the CRM world will require an MA or a PhD. Your work will bring you in touch with excellent research opportunities and data, so such degrees are somewhat easier to acquire in CRM than they are on a purely academic pathway. To thrive in this world, you need a broad academic background, good management skills, and an ability to work under pressure and to tight deadlines. An ability to write clearly and quickly is a great advantage.

Federal and state archaeology. There are opportunities in many government agencies, among them the National Park Service and the Bureau of Land Management. Many archaeologists work for state archaeological surveys and other such organizations. Much of the work in these posts involves working with the public. A patience with bureaucracy, an ability to write, and articulate enthusiasm are useful. A university degree in archaeology is essential.

Other opportunities. This is an expanding area, which offers all kinds of jobs in such activities as cultural tourism, site management, and even on cruise ships. A degree in archaeology is essential, also unlimited enthusiasm and an ability to communicate with diverse audiences.

Archaeology as a career is not for everyone. You will never get rich, but you can derive great satisfaction working with a very diverse crowd of people. The essential qualities are easily listed:

enthusiasm and a passion for the past

a commitment to the ethical standards of professional archaeology

infinite patience to work in the field and laboratory

a mind that thrives on detail

an ability to cope with discomfort

good people and organizational skills, also cultural sensitivity

a sense of humor!

A final word of advice. If in doubt, don't! Enjoy the past to the full in other ways.

SUMMARY

- Archaeology is under siege from looters and industrial activity. The loss of oral traditions is equally serious and is becoming a new field of research.

- Archaeology has written a provisional history of 14,000 years of human settlement in North America, using multidisciplinary research. New data is being generated very rapidly, making it possible to study increasingly basic questions about Native American and historical societies.

- The archaeology of the future will be concerned with the numerous stakeholders in North America's past. This will involve massive outreach and engagement with the public.

- Engaging with the public, especially Native Americans, has become one of the major challenges of today's archaeology. It involves realizing that there are many perspectives on history and the past, a reality brought home by NAGPRA legislation. These activities will also involve community archaeology and close work with numerous stakeholders with different agendas and expectations.

- Whatever your interest in archaeology, please respect the records of the past.

Guide to Further Reading

This Guide to Further Reading has no pretensions to being comprehensive. There are many omissions. Given the constraints of space, most references are those where comprehensive citations will be found, for those wishing to delve more thoroughly into the more specialized, often contradictory, literature. In some cases references are cited more than once in different chapters, because they are relevant in several contexts. Specialized references are only used when they are deemed necessary for beginning readers of the literature.

1 Archaeology and Ancient North America

Bandelier, Adolf E. 1884. "Report on the Ruins of the Pueblo of Pecos," *Papers of the Archaeological Institute of America* 1: 37–133.

Binford, Lewis R. 2001. *Constructing Frames of Reference: An Analytical Method for Archaeological Theory Building Using Ethnographic and Environmental Data Sets*. Berkeley: University of California Press.

———. 2002. *In Pursuit of the Past: Decoding the Archaeological Record*. Second Edition. Berkeley: University of California Press.

———. 2012. *Nunamiut Ethnoarchaeology*. Reprint Edition. Clinton Corners, NY: Eliot Werner Publications.

———, and Sally R. Binford. 2017. *Archaeology in Cultural Systems*. Abingdon, UK: Routledge.

Chapman, Robert, and Alison Wylie. 2016. *Evidential Reasoning in Archaeology*. New York: Bloomsbury Academic.

Chari, Sangita, and Jaime M. Lavallee, eds. 2013. *Accomplishing NAGPRA: Perspectives on the Intent, Impact, and Future of the Native American Graves Protection and Repatriation Act*. Corvallis, OR: Oregon State University Press.

Cushing, Frank. 1882–83 [1970 Edition]. *My Adventures in Zuñi*. Palo Alto, CA: American West.

Deetz, James. 1996. *In Small Things Forgotten*. Revised Edition. New York: Anchor.

Flannery, Kent V. 1973. "Archaeology with a Capital A," in Charles Redman, ed., *Research and Theory in Current Archaeology*. New York: Wiley Interscience. 337–54.

Givens, Douglas R. 1992. *Alfred Vincent Kidder and the Development of Southwestern Archaeology*. Albuquerque: University of New Mexico Press.

Gregory, David A., and David R. Wilcox, eds. 2007. *Zuni Origins: Toward a New Synthesis of Southwestern Archaeology*. Tucson: University of Arizona Press.

Hegmon, Michelle. 2003. "Setting Theoretical Egos Aside: Issues and Theory in North American Archaeology," *American Antiquity* 68 (2): 213–43.

Hodder, Ian. 1999. *The Archaeological Process: An Introduction*. Oxford: Blackwell.

———. 2012. *Archaeological Theory Today*. Second Edition. New York: Polity Press.

Kantner, John. 2004. *Ancient Puebloan Southwest*. Cambridge: Cambridge University Press.

Kidder, Alfred V., and Douglas W. Schwartz. 2000. *An Introduction to the Study of Southwestern Archaeology*. New Haven: Yale University Press.

Lyman, R. L., and R. C. Dunnell. 1997. *The Rise and Fall of Culture History*. New York: Plenum Press.

Meltzer, David. 2015. *The Great Paleolithic War: How Science Forged an Understanding of America's Ice Age Past*. Chicago: University of Chicago Press.

Nelson, Sarah Milledge, and Benjamin Alberti, eds. 2006. *Handbook of Gender in Archaeology*. Walnut Creek, CA: AltaMira Press.

Nicholas, George, ed. 2011. *Being and Becoming Indigenous Archaeologists*. Abingdon, UK: Routledge.

Noël Hume, Ivor. 1973. *Martin's Hundred*. New York: Alfred Knopf.

Pauketat, Timothy. 2004. *Ancient Cahokia and the Mississippians*. Cambridge: Cambridge University Press.

Sabloff, Jeremy A., and Gordon R. Willey. 1993. *A History of American Archaeology*. Third Edition. New York: W. H. Freeman.

Silverberg, Robert. 1968. *Moundbuilders of Ancient America: The Archaeology of a Myth*. Greenwich, CT: New York Graphic Society.

Steward, Julian. 1955. *A Theory of Culture Change*. Urbana: University of Illinois Press.

Strong, W. D. 1935. *An Introduction to Nebraska Archaeology*. Washington, D.C.: Smithsonian Institution.

Trigger, Bruce G. 2006. *A History of Archaeological Thought*. Second Edition. Cambridge: Cambridge University Press.

Watkins, Joe E. 2001. *Indigenous Archaeology: American Indian Values and Scientific Practice*. Walnut Creek, CA: AltaMira Press.

———. 2003. "Beyond the Margins: American Indians, First Nations, and Archaeology in North America," *American Antiquity* 68 (2): 273–86.

Whiteley, Peter M. 2002. "Archaeology and Oral Tradition: The Scientific Importance of Dialogue," *American Antiquity* 67: 405–15.

Willey, Gordon R. 1966. *An Introduction to American Archaeology*. Vol. 1: *North America*. Englewood Cliffs, NJ: Prentice Hall.

———, and P. Phillips. 1958. *Method and Theory in American Archaeology*. Chicago: University of Chicago Press.

2 First Settlement

Adovasio, J. M., and J. Page. 2002. *The First Americans*. New York: Random House.

———, *et al.* 1981. *Meadowcroft Rockshelter and the Archaeology of the Cross Creek Drainage*. Pittsburgh: University of Pittsburgh Press.

Bamforth, Douglas. 2018. *An Archaeological History of the Northern Great Plains*. Cambridge: Cambridge University Press.

Braje, T. J., *et al.* 2017. "Finding the First Americans," *Science* 358, 6363: 592–94.

Canby, Thomas. 1979. "The search for the first Americans," *National Geographic* 156: 330–63.

Chaput, Michelle A., *et al.* 2015. "Spatiotemporal Distribution of Holocene Populations in North America," *Proceedings of the National Academy of Sciences* 112 (39): 12127–32.

Connelly, Thomas J., *et al.* 2017. "Return to Fort Rock Cave," *American Antiquity* 82 (3): 558–73.

Graf, K. E., *et al.*, 2015. "Dry Creek Revisited: New Excavations, Radiocarbon Dates, and Site Formation Inform on the Peopling of Eastern Beringia," *American Antiquity* 80 (4): 671–94.

———, *et al.*, eds. 2014. *Paleoamerican Odyssey*. College Station: Texas A&M University Press. Greenberg, Joseph. 1987. *Language in the Americas*. Palo Alto, CA: Stanford University Press.

Guthrie, R. D. 1968. "Paleoecology of the large mammal community in interior Alaska during the Late Pleistocene," *American Midland Naturalist* 79: 346–63.

Halligan, Jessi J., *et al.* 2016. "Pre-Clovis Occupation 14,550 Years Ago at the Page-Ladson Site, Florida, and the Peopling of the Americas," *Science Advances* 2 (5): e1600375.

Hoffecker, John F. 2001. "Late Pleistocene and Early Holocene Sites in the Nenana River Valley, Central Alaska," *Arctic Anthropology* 38 (2): 139–53.

———. 2002. *Desolate Landscapes*. New Brunswick, NJ: Rutgers University Press.

———. 2005. *A Prehistory of the North*. New Brunswick, NJ: Rutgers University Press.

———. 2007. *Human Ecology of Beringia*. New York: Columbia University Press.

———, *et al.* 2016. "Beringia and the Global Dispersal of Modern Humans," *Evolutionary Anthropology* 25: 64–78.

Holen, S. R. *et al.*, 2017. "A 130,000-year-old archaeological site in southern California, USA," *Nature* 544: 479–83.

Jenkins, D. L. 2016. "Younger Dryas Archaeology and Human Experience at the Paisley Caves in the Northern Great Basin," in Marcel Kornfeld and Bruce B. Huckell, eds, *Stones, Bones, and Profiles: Exploring Archaeological Context, Early American Hunter-Gatherers, and Bison*. Boulder: University of Colorado Press. 127–205.

———, *et al.* 2012. "Clovis Age Western Stemmed Projectile Points at Human Coprolites at the Paisley Caves," *Science* 337: 223–28.

Johnson, J. R., *et al.* 2001. "Arlington Springs Revisited," in D. R. Brown, K. C. Mitchell, and E. W. Chaney, eds, *Proceedings of the Fifth Channel Islands symposium*. Santa Barbara, CA: Santa Barbara Museum of Natural History. 541–45.

Meltzer, David. 2008. *First Peoples in a New World: Colonizing Ice Age America*. Berkeley: University of California Press.

———, James Adovasio, and Tom Dillehay. 1994. "On a Pleistocene Human Occupation at Pedra Furada, Brazil," *Antiquity* 68 (261): 695–714.

Merriwether, D. Andrew. 2002. "A Mitochondrial Perspective on the Peopling of the New World," in Nina Jablonski, ed., *The First Americans*. San Francisco: California Academy of Sciences. 295–310.

Pitulko, V., *et al.* 2013. "Human Habitation in Arctic Western Beringia prior to the LGM," in K. E. Graf *et al.*, eds, *Paleoamerican Odyssey*. College Station: Texas A&M University Press. 13–44.

——, *et al.* 2014. "The Berelekh "Graveyard": New Chronological and Stratigraphical Data from the 2009 Field Season," *Geoarchaeology* 29: 277–99.

——, *et al.* 2016. "Early Human Presence in the Arctic: Evidence from 45,000-Year-Old Mammoth Remains," *Science* 351: 260–63.

Potter, Ben A., *et al.* 2018. "Current evidence allows multiple models for the peopling of the Americas," *Science Advances* 4 (8): eaat5473.

Reich, D., *et al.* 2012. "Reconstructing Native American Population History," *Nature* 488: 370–74.

Scott, Richard, *et al.* 2016. "Sinodonty, Sundadonty, and the Beringian Standstill Model: Issues of Timing and Migrations into the New World," *Quaternary International* 30 (1): 1–14.

Stanford, Dennis, and Bruce Bradley. 2012. *Across Atlantic Ice: The Origin of America's Clovis Culture*. Berkeley: University of California Press.

Turner, Christy. 1984. "Advances in the Dental Search for Native American Origins," *Acta Anthropogenetica* 8: 23–78.

——. 2002. "Teeth, Needles, Dogs, and Siberia: Bioarchaeological Evidence for the Colonization of the New World," in Nina Jablonski, ed., *The First Americans*. San Francisco: California Academy of Sciences. 123–58.

Waters, M. R., and Charlotte D. Pevny. 2011. *Clovis Lithic Technology: Investigation of a Stratified Workshop at the Gault Site, Texas*. College Station, TX: Texas A&M University Press.

——, *et al.* 2011. "The Debra L. Friedkin Site, Texas and the origins of Clovis," *Science* 331 (6024): 1599–603.

3 After Clovis

Aikens, C. Melvin. 1970. *Hogup Cave*. Salt Lake City: University of Utah Press.

Anderson, David G., and Kenneth E. Sassaman. 2012. *Recent Developments in Southeastern Archaeology: From Colonization to Complexity*. Washington, D.C.: Society for American Archaeology.

Bamforth, Douglas. 2018. *An Archaeological History of the Northern Great Plains*. Cambridge: Cambridge University Press.

Chapman, Jefferson. 2014. *Tellico Archaeology: 12,000 Years of Native American History*. Third Edition. Knoxville: University of Tennessee Press.

Doran, Glen H. 2002. *Windover: Multidisciplinary Investigations of an Early Archaic Florida Cemetery*. Gainesville: University of Florida Press.

Fowler, Catherine. 1992. *In the Shadow of Fox Peak*. Fallon, NV: Stillwater National Wildlife Refuge, Department of the Interior.

Fowler, Melvin L. 1959. "Modoc Rock Shelter: An Early Archaic Site in Southern Illinois," *American Antiquity* 24 (3): 257–70.

Frison, George C., ed. 2013. *The Casper Site: A Hell Gap Site on the High Plains*. Revised Edition. New York: Eliot Werner Publications.

——, and B. A. Bradley. 1981. *Folsom Tools and Technology at the Hanson Site, Wyoming*. Albuquerque: University of New Mexico Press.

Gardner, W. M. 1977. "The Flint Run Paleo-Indian Complex and its

Implications for Eastern North American Prehistory," *Annals of the New York Academy of Sciences* 288: 257–63.

Grayson, Donald K. 2011. *The Great Basin: A Natural Prehistory*. Berkeley: University of California Press.

Hranicky, Jack. 2015. *North American Projectile Points*. Bloomington, IN: AuthorHouse.

Jefferies, Richard. 2013. *The Archaeology of Carrier Mills: 10,000 Years in the Saline Valley of Illinois*. Reprint Edition. Carbondale: Southern Illinois University Press.

Larson, Mary Lou, and Marcel Kornfeld. 2009. *Hell Gap: A Stratified Paleoindian Campsite at the Edge of the Rockies*. Salt Lake City: University of Utah Press.

Lyman, R. Lee. 2009. "The Diversity of North American Projectile-Point Types, Before and After the Bow and Arrow," *Journal of Anthropological Archaeology* 28: 1–13.

Martin, Eric P., *et al.* 2017. "Revisiting Hogup Cave, Utah: Insights from New Radiocarbon Dates and Stratigraphic Analysis," *American Antiquity* 82 (2): 301–24.

Mason, Ronald J. 2002. *Great Lakes Archaeology*. Caldwell, NJ: Blackburn Press.

Meltzer, David. 2006. *Folsom: New Archaeological Investigations of a Classic Paleoindian Bison Kill*. Berkeley: University of California Press.

Morse, Dan. 1997. *Sloan: A Paleoindian Dalton Cemetery in Arkansas*. Washington, D.C.: Smithsonian Institution Press.

Saunders, Joe W., *et al.* 2005. "Watson Brake: A Middle Archaic Mound Complex in Northeast Louisiana," *American Antiquity* 70 (4): 631–68.

Shuman, Bryan N., and Jeremiah Marsicek. 2016. "The Structure of Holocene Climate Change in Mid-latitude North America," *Quaternary Science Reviews* 141 (1): 38–51.

Simms, Steven R. 2008. *Ancient Peoples of the Great Basin and Colorado Plateau*. Abingdon, UK: Routledge.

Streuver, Stuart, and Felicia Antonelli Holton. 2000. *Koster: Americans in Search of their Prehistoric Past*. Prospect Heights, IL: Waveland Press.

Wheat, Joe Ben. 1972. *The Olsen-Chubbock Site: A Paleo-Indian Bison Kill*. Washington, D.C.: Society for American Archaeology.

4 The Far North

Clark, D. W. 1997. *The Early Kachemak Phase on Kodiak Island at Old Kiavak*. Ottawa: National Museum of Civilization.

Coutouly, Yan Axel Gomez. 2015. "Anangula: A Major Pressure-Microblade Site in the Aleutian Islands, Alaska: Reevaluating its Lithic Component," *Arctic Anthropology* 52 (1): 23–59.

Dumond, Don E. 1987. *The Eskimos and Aleuts*. Second Edition. London: Thames & Hudson.

Friesen, T. Max, and Owen K. Mason, eds. 2016. *The Oxford Handbook of the Prehistoric Arctic*. New York: Oxford University Press.

Kopperl, Robert. 2012. "Chronology of the Ocean Bay Tradition on Kodiak

Island, Alaska: Stratigraphic and Radiocarbon Analysis of the Rice Ridge Site (KOD-363)," *Alaska Journal of Anthropology* 10 (1–2): 17–35.

Maschner, Herbert D. G. 2004. "The Aleutian Tradition," in Mark Nuttall, ed., *The Encyclopedia of the Arctic*. Abingdon: Routledge. 53–55.

———, *et al.*, eds. 2009. *The Northern World, AD 900–1400*. Salt Lake City: University of Utah Press.

Mason, Owen K. 1998. "The Contest Between the Ipiutak, Old Bering Sea, and Birnirk Polities and the Origin of Whaling During the First Millennium AD Along Bering Strait," *Journal of Anthropological Archaeology* 17 (3): 240–325.

Maxwell, Moreau. 1985. *The Prehistory of the Eastern Arctic*. New York: Academic Press.

McCartney, Allen, ed. 1979. *Thule Eskimo Culture: An Anthropological Retrospective*. Archaeological Survey of Canada, Mercury Series 88. Ottawa.

McGhee, Robert. 2001. *Ancient People of the Arctic*. Revised Edition. Vancouver: University of British Columbia Press.

———. 2007. *The Last Imaginary Place: A Human History of the Arctic World*. Chicago: University of Chicago Press.

Park, R. W. 2008. "The Dorset–Thule Transition," in T. M. Friesen and O. K. Mason, eds, *The Oxford Handbook of the Prehistoric Arctic*. Oxford: Oxford University Press. 807–26.

———. 2012. "Arctic Archaeology Overview: Adapting to a Frozen Coastal Environment," in T. R. Pauketat, ed., *The Oxford Handbook of North American Archaeology*. Oxford: Oxford University Press. 113–23.

———. 2016. "Pre-Dorset Culture," in M. Friesen and Owen Mason, eds, *The Oxford Handbook of the Prehistoric Arctic*. Oxford: Oxford University Press. 693–712.

Raghavan, M., *et al.* 2014. "The Genetic Prehistory of the New World Arctic," *Science* 345 (6200): 1255822.

Schledermann, Peter. 1990. *Crossroads to Greenland*. Calgary, AB: Arctic Institute of North America.

Shaw, R. D., and C. E. Holmes, eds. 1982. "The Norton Interaction Sphere," *Arctic Anthropology* 19 (2): 1–149.

Tuck, James A. 1976. *Newfoundland and Labrador Prehistory*. Ottawa: National Museums of Canada.

West, Frederick H., ed. 1996. *American Beginnings: The Prehistory and Paleoecology of Beringia*. Chicago: University of Chicago Press.

Workman, William B. 1998. "Archaeology of the Southern Kenai Peninsula," *Arctic Anthropology* 35 (1): 146–59.

5 The Mythical Pacific Eden

Aikens, C. Melvin, Thomas J. Connolly, and Dennis L. Jenkins. 2011. *Oregon Archaeology*. Corvallis: Oregon State University Press.

Ames, Kenneth M., and Herbert D. G. Maschner. 1999. *Peoples of the Northwest Coast: Their Archaeology and Prehistory*. London: Thames & Hudson.

Arnold, Jeanne E., and Michael Walsh. 2010. *California's Ancient Past: From the*

Pacific to the Range of Light. Washington, D.C.: Society for American Archaeology Press.

Carlson, R. G. 2003. *Archaeology of Coastal British Columbia*. Burnaby, BC: Archaeology Press.

Croes, Dale. 1995. *The Hoko River Archaeological Complex: The Wet/Dry Site (45CA213), 3000–1700 BC*. Pullman: Washington State University Press.

Erlandson, J. M., and Michael Glassow, eds. 1997. *Archaeology of the California Coast During the Middle Holocene*. Los Angeles: UCLA Institute of Archaeology.

Fagan, Brian. 2003. *Before California: An Archaeologist Looks at Our Earliest Inhabitants*. Lanham, MA: AltaMira Press.

Fladmark, Knud E. 1983. "Time and Places in Environmental Correlates of Mid to Late-Wisconsinian Human Population Expansion in North America," in Richard Shutler, ed., *Early Man in the New World*. Beverly Hills, CA: Sage Publications. 13–42.

Gamble, Lynn. 2008. *The Chumash World at European Contact: Power, Trade, and Feasting Among Complex Hunter-Gatherers*. Berkeley: University of California Press.

———, ed. 2015. *First Coastal Californians*. Santa Fe, NM: School for Advanced Research Press.

———. 2017. "Feasting, Ritual Practices, Social Memory, and Persistent Places: New Interpretations of Shell Mounds in Southern California," *American Antiquity* 82 (3): 427–51.

Goldschmidt, Walter. 1951. "Nomlaki Ethnography," *University of California Publications in American Anthropology and Ethnology* 42 (4): 303–443.

Jones, Terry, and Kathryn L. Klar. 2010. *California Prehistory: Colonization, Culture, and Complexity*. Lanham, MA: AltaMira Press.

Lambert, Patricia M., and Phillip L. Walker. 1991. "Physical Anthropological Evidence for the Evolution of Social Complexity in Coastal Southern California," *American Antiquity* 65 (1991): 963–73.

Lightfoot, Kent G., *et al.* 2015. "Shell Mound Builders of San Francisco Bay," in Lynn Gamble, ed., *First Coastal Californians*. Santa Fe, NM: School for Advanced Research Press. 37–42.

———, and Otis Parrish. 2009. *California Indians and Their Environment: An Introduction*. Berkeley: University of California Press.

Matson, R. G., and G. Coupland. 1995. *The Prehistory of the Northwest Coast*. New York: Academic Press.

Moratto, Michael. 1984. *California Archaeology*. New York: Seminar Press.

Moss, Madonna. 2011. *Northwest Coast: Archaeology as Deep History*. Washington, D.C.: Society for American Archaeology Press.

———, J. M. Erlandson, and R. Stuckenrath. 1990. "Wood Stake Fish Weirs and Salmon Fishing on the Northwest Coast: Evidence from Southeast Alaska," *Canadian Journal of Archaeology* 14: 143–58.

Ragir, Sonia. 1972. "The Early Horizon in Central California Prehistory," *University of California Publications in American Archaeology and Ethnology* 15.

6 Arid Lands in the West

Aikens, C. Melvin. 1970. *Hogup Cave*. University of Utah Anthropological Papers 93. Salt Lake City.

———, Thomas J. Connolly, and Dennis L. Jenkins. 2011. *Oregon Archaeology*. Corvallis: Oregon State University Press.

Beck, Charlotte, ed. 1999. *Models for the Millennium: Great Basin Anthropology Today*. Salt Lake City: University of Utah Press.

Bettinger, Robert, and M. A. Baumhoff. 1982. "The Numic Spread: Great Basin Cultures in Competition," *American Antiquity* 48: 480–84.

———, and Jelmer Eerkens. 1999. "Point Typologies, Cultural Transmission, and the Spread of Bow-and-Arrow Technology in the Prehistoric Great Basin," *American Antiquity* 64 (2): 231–42.

Butler, Virginia L. 1996. "Tui Chub Taphonomy and the Importance of Marsh Resources in the Western Great Basin of North America," *American Antiquity* 64 (4): 699–717.

Coltrain, Joan Brenner, and Steven W. Leavitt. 2002. "Climate and Diet in Fremont Prehistory: Economic Variability and Abandonment of Maize Agriculture in the Great Salt Lake Basin," *American Antiquity* 67 (3): 453–85.

Fowler, Catherine S., and Eugene M. Hattori. 2008. "The Great Basin's Oldest Textiles," in Catherine S. Fowler and Don D. Fowler, eds, *The Great Basin: People and Place in Ancient Times*. Santa Fe, NM: School for Advanced Research Press. 61–68.

Grayson, Donald K. 2011. *The Great Basin: A Natural Prehistory*. Berkeley: University of California Press.

Heizer, R. E., and J. K. Napton. 1970. "Archaeology…as Seen from Lovelock Cave, Nevada," Berkeley, CA: University of California Research Facility Contributions 10 (1).

Hockett, B., *et al.* 2013. "Large-scale trapping features from the Great Basin, USA: The significance of leadership and communal gatherings in ancient foraging societies," *Quaternary International* 297: 64–78.

Janetski, J. C. 2008. "The Enigmatic Fremont," in Catherine S. Fowler and Don D. Fowler, eds, *The Great Basin: People and Place in Ancient Times*. Santa Fe, NM: School for Advanced Research Press. 105–16.

———, and David Madsen, eds. 1990. *Wetland Adaptations in the Great Basin*. Museum of Peoples and Cultures Occasional Papers 1. Provo, UT.

———, and Richard K. Talbot. 2014. "Fremont Social Organization: A Southwestern Perspective," in Nancy J. Parezo and Joel C. Janetski, eds, *Archaeology in the Great Basin and Southwest*. Salt Lake City: University of Utah Press. 118–29.

Jennings, Jesse D. 1957. *Danger Cave*. University of Utah Anthropological Papers 27. Salt Lake City.

Jones, Terry L., *et al.* 1999. "Environmental Imperatives Reconsidered: Evidence for Widespread Demographic Stress in Western North America During the Medieval Climatic Anomaly," *Current Anthropology* 40: 137–70.

Kelly, Robert L. 1997. "Late Holocene Great Basin Prehistory," *Journal of World Prehistory* 11: 1–50.

———. 2001. *Prehistory of the Carson Desert and Stillwater Mountains*.

University of Utah Anthropological Papers 123. Salt Lake City.

———. 2013. *The Lifeways of Hunter-Gatherers: The Foraging Spectrum.* Cambridge: Cambridge University Press.

Madsen, D. B. 1985. "Great Basin Nuts: A Short Treatise on the Distribution, Productivity, and Prehistoric Use of Pinyon," in C. Condie and D. Fowler, eds, *Anthropology of the Desert West.* Salt Lake City: University of Utah Press. 110–25.

———, and James O'Connell, eds. 1982. *Man and Environment in the Great Basin.* Washington, D.C.: Society for American Archaeology.

———, and Steven Simms. 1998. "The Fremont Complex: A Behavioral Perspective," *Journal of World Prehistory* 12 (3): 255–336.

———, *et al.* 2001. "Late Quaternary Environment Change in the Bonneville Basin, Western USA," *Palaeogeography, Palaeoclimatology, and Palaeoecology* 167: 243–71.

Martin, Erik P., Joan Brenner Coltrain, and Brian F. Codding. 2017. "Revisiting Hogup Cave: Insights from New Radiocarbon Dates and Stratigraphic Analysis," *American Antiquity* 82 (2): 301–24.

Simms, Steven R. 2008. *Ancient Peoples of the Great Basin and Colorado Plateau.* Abingdon, UK: Routledge.

———, and Francis Gohier. 2010. *Traces of Fremont: Society and Rock Art in Ancient Utah.* Salt Lake City: University of Utah Press.

Steward, Julian. 1955. *A Theory of Culture Change.* Urbana: University of Illinois Press.

Thomas, David Hurst. 1981. "How to Classify the Projectile Points from Monitor Valley, Nevada," *Journal of California and Great Basin Archaeology* 3 (1): 7–42.

———. 1983. *The Archaeology of Monitor Valley, 2: Gatecliff Shelter.* American Museum of Natural History, Anthropological Papers 58 (1). New York.

———. 1985. *The Archaeology of Hidden Cave, Nevada.* American Museum of Natural History, Anthropological Papers 61 (1). New York.

———. 2014. "Alta Toquima: Why Did Foraging Families Spend Summers at 11,000 Feet," in Nancy J. Parezo and Joel C. Janetski, eds, *Archaeology in the Great Basin and Southwest.* Salt Lake City: University of Utah Press. 130–48.

Zeanah, David W., and Steven R. Simms. 1999. "Modeling the Gastric: Great Basin Subsistence Studies Since 1962 and the Evolution of General Theory in Archaeology," in C. W. Beck, ed., *Models for the Millennium: Great Basin Anthropology Today.* Salt Lake City: University of Utah Press. 118–40.

7 People of the Plains

Ahler, S., T. Thiessen, and M. Trimble. 1991. *People of the Willows: The Prehistory and Early History of the Hidatsa Indians.* Grand Forks: University of North Dakota Press.

Bamforth, Douglas. 2018. *An Archaeological History of the Northern Great Plains.* Cambridge: Cambridge University Press.

Benn, David. 1990. *Woodland Cultures on the Western Prairies: The Rainbow Site Investigations.* Iowa City: Office of the State Archaeologist Report 18.

Brink, Jack W. 2008. *Imagining Head Smashed In: Aboriginal Buffalo Hunting on the Northern Plains*. Edmonton: Athabaska University Press.

Bryant, Vaughn, and Richard Holloway, eds. 1985. *Pollen Records of Late-Quaternary North American Sediments*. Dallas, TX: American Association of Stratigraphic Palynologists Foundation.

Frison, George C. 1971. "The Buffalo Pound in Northwestern Plains Prehistory: Site 48CA302," *American Antiquity* 36: 77–91.

Holder, Preston. 1974. *The Hoe and the Horse on the Plains*. Lincoln: University of Nebraska Press.

Kehoe, Thomas. 1973. *The Gull Lake Site: A Prehistoric Bison Drive in Southwestern Saskatchewan*. Milwaukee Public Museum Publications in Anthropology 1. Milwaukee.

Kornfeld, Marcel, and George C. Frison. 2010. *Prehistoric Hunters of the High Plains*. Third Edition. Abingdon, UK: Routledge.

Lehmer, Donald J. 1971. *Introduction to Middle Missouri Archaeology*. Anthropological Papers of the National Park Service 1. Washington, D.C.

MacGregor, James G. 1998. *Peter Fidler, Canada's Forgotten Explorer 1769–1822*. Third Edition. Calgary: Fifth House.

Schlesier, Karl H. 1994. *Plains Indians, AD 500–1500: The Archaeological Past of Historic Groups*. Norman: University of Oklahoma Press.

Walker, Chester P., and Timothy K. Perttula, eds. 2012. *The Archaeology of the Caddo*. Lincoln: University of Nebraska Press.

Wedel, Waldo. 1961. *Prehistoric Man on the Great Plains*. Norman: University of Oklahoma Press.

Wood, W. Raymond, ed. 1998. *Archaeology on the Great Plains*. Lawrence: University Press of Kansas.

Zimmerman, L. 1985. *Peoples of Prehistoric South Dakota*. Lincoln: University of Nebraska Press.

8 The Eastern Woodlands

Anderson, David G., and Kenneth E. Sassaman, eds. 1996. *Archaeology of the Mid-Holocene Southeast*. Gainesville: University Press of Florida.

——, and Kenneth E. Sassaman, eds. 2009. *The Paleoindian and Early Archaic Southeast*. Tuscaloosa: University of Alabama Press.

Claassen, Cheryl. 2015. *Rituals and Beliefs in Archaic Eastern North America*. Tuscaloosa: University of Alabama Press.

Ellerbe, Jenny, and Diana M. Greenlee. 2015. *Poverty Point: Revealing the Forgotten City*. Baton Rouge: Louisiana State University Press.

Gibson, Jon L. 2001. *The Ancient Mounds of Poverty Point: Place of Rings*. Gainesville: University of Florida Press.

——, and Philip J. Carr. eds. 2010. *Signs of Power: The Rise of Cultural Complexity in the Southeast*. Tuscaloosa: University Alabama Press.

Holly, Donald H. 2013. *History in the Making: The Archaeology of the Eastern Subarctic*. Lanham, MA: Rowman & Littlefield.

Jefferies, Richard. 2013. *The Archaeology of Carrier Mills: 10,000 Years in the Saline Valley of Illinois*. Carbondale: Southern Illinois University Press.

McGimsey, Chip, and Mark A. Reese, eds. 2010. *Archaeology of Louisiana*. Baton Rouge: Louisiana State University Press.

Sassaman, Kenneth. 2015. *The Eastern Archaic, Historicized*. Lanham, MA: Rowman & Littlefield.

Saunders, Joe W., *et al.* 1997. "A Mound Complex in Louisiana at 5400–5000 Years Before Present," *Science* 277: 1796–9.

Saunders, Rebecca, and Christopher T. Hays, eds. 2004. *Early Pottery: Technology, Function, Style, and Interaction in the Lower Southeast*. Tuscaloosa: University of Alabama Press.

Sherwood, Sarah C., *et al.* 2004. "Chronology and Stratigraphy at Dust Cave, Alabama," *American Antiquity* 69 (3): 533–54.

Smith, Bruce D., ed. 2011. *Subsistence Economies of Indigenous North American Societies: A Handbook*. Washington, D.C.: Smithsonian Institution Scholarly Press.

Snow, Dean. 1980. *The Archaeology of New England*. New York: Academic Press.

Streuver, Stuart, and Felicia Holton. 2000. *Koster: Americans in Search of the Prehistoric Past*. New York/Prospect Heights, IL: Anchor Press/Waveland Press.

Styles, B. W., *et al.* 1983. "Modoc Shelter Revisited," in J. L. Phillips and J. A. Brown, eds, *Archaic Hunter-Gatherers in the American Midwest*. New York: Academic Press. 261–97.

Webb, William S., and Howard D. Winters. 2001. *Indian Knoll*. Knoxville: University of Tennessee Press.

9 Before the Pueblos

Berry, C. E., and M. S. Berry. 1986. "Chronological and Conceptual Models of the Southwest Archaic," in Carol J. Condie and Don D. Fowler, eds, *Anthropology of the Desert West: Essays in Honor of Jesse D. Jennings*. Salt Lake City: Department of Anthropology, University of Utah. 283–327.

Boyd, Carolyn E. 2003. *Rock Art of the Lower Pecos*. College Station: Texas A&M University Press.

——. 2016. *The White Shaman Mural: An Enduring Creation Narrative in the Rock Art of the Lower Pecos*. Austin: University of Texas Press.

Collins, M. B. 1998. *Wilson-Leonard, An 11,000-Year Archaeological Record of Hunter-Gatherers in Central Texas*. 5 vols. Austin: Texas Archaeological Research Laboratory.

Cordell, Linda S., and Maxine McBrinn. 2013. *Archaeology of the Southwest*. Third Edition. Abingdon, UK: Routledge.

da Fonseca, Rute, *et al.* 2015. "The Origin and Evolution of Maize in the Southwestern United States," *Nature Plants* 1, 14003. DOI 10.1038/nplants.2014.3.

Hard, Robert J., and John R. Roney. 1998. "A Massive Terraced Village Complex in Chihuahua, Mexico, 3000 Years Before Present," *Science* 279: 1661–64.

Hegmon, Michelle, ed. 2008. *The Archaeology of Regional Interaction: Religion, Warfare, and Exchange Across the American Southwest and Beyond*. Boulder: University of Colorado Press.

Hester, T. R. 1989. "Historic Native American Populations," in T. R. Hester *et al.*, *From the Gulf to the Rio Grande: Human Adaptation in Central, South, and Lower Pecos Texas*. Arkansas Archaeological Survey Research Series 33.

Fayetteville: Arkansas Archaeological Survey.

Huckell, Bruce B. 1996. "The Archaic Prehistory of the North American Southwest," *Journal of World Prehistory* 10 (3): 305–74.

Mabry, Jonathan B., *et al.* 1997. *Archaeological Investigations of Early Village Sites in the Middle Santa Cruz Valley*. Tucson, AZ: Center for Desert Archaeology.

——. 2005. "Changing Knowledge and Ideas About the First Farmers in Southeastern Arizona," in Bradley J. Vierra, ed., *The Late Archaic Across the Borderlands: From Foraging to Farming*. Austin: University of Texas Press. 41–83.

——. 2008. *Las Capas: Early Irrigation and Sedentism in a Southwestern Floodplain*. Tucson, AZ: Center for Desert Archaeology.

Plog, Stephen. 2008. *Ancient Peoples of the American Southwest*. London and New York: Thames & Hudson.

Reid, Jefferson, and Stephanie Whittlesey. 1997. *The Archaeology of Ancient Arizona*. Tucson: University of Arizona Press.

Roth, Barbara J. 2016. *Agricultural Beginnings in the American Southwest*. Lantham, MA: Rowman & Littlefield.

Shafer, Harry J. 2013. *Painters in Prehistory: Archaeology and Art of the Lower Pecos Canyonlands*. San Antonio, TX: Trinity University Press.

Swarts, K., *et al.* 2017. "Genomic estimation of complex traits reveals ancient maize adaptation to temperate North America," *Science* 357: 512–15.

Vierra, Bradley J. 2008. "Early Agriculture on the Southeastern Periphery of the Colorado Plateau: Diversity in Tactics," in Laurie B. Webster and Maxine M. McBrinn, eds, *Archaeology Without Borders: Contact, Commerce, and Change in the U. S., Southwest and Northwestern Mexico*. Boulder: University Press of Colorado. 71–88.

——, and Maxine E. McBrinn. 2016. "Resistant Foragers: Foraging and Maize Cultivation in the Northern Rio Grande Valley," in Barbara J. Roth and Maxine E. McBrinn, eds, *Late Holocene Research on Foragers and Early Farmers in the Desert West*. Salt Lake City: University of Utah Press. 58–77.

Vint, James, ed. 2015. *Implements of Change: Tools, Subsistence, and the Built Environment of Las Capas, an Early Agricultural Community in South Arizona*. Archaeology Southwest Anthropological Papers 50. Tucson, AZ.

——, and Barbara J. Mills. 2017. "Niches, Networks and the Pathways to the Forager-Farmer Transition in the US Southwest/North-West Mexico," in *Farmer Transition, Origins of Food Productiuon and the World Heritage Convention*. Paris: UNESCO. 253–74.

Wills, W. H., *et al.* 2012. "Shabik'eschee Village in Chaco Canyon: Beyond the Archetype," *American Antiquity* 77 (2): 326–50.

Young, Lisa C., and Sarah A. Herr. 2012. *Southwestern Pithouse Communities, AD 200–900*. Second Edition. Tucson: University of Arizona Press.

10 Pueblo Climax

Cordell, Linda S., and Maxine McBrinn. 2013. *Archaeology of the Southwest*. Third Edition. Abingdon, UK: Routledge.

Craig, Douglas B. 2001. *The Grewe archaeological research project*. Tempe, AZ: Northland Research.

————, and Kathleen Henderson. 2007. "Houses, Households, and Household Organization," in Suzanne K. Fish and Paul R. Fish, eds, *The Hohokam Millennium*. Santa Fe, NM: SAR Press. 31–37.

Creamer, Winifred. 1993. *The Architecture of Arroyo Hondo Pueblo, New Mexico.* Santa Fe: School of American Research Press.

Crown, P., and Judge, J. W., eds. 1991. *Chaco and Hohokam: Prehistoric Regional Systems in the Southwest.* Seattle: University of Washington Press.

Dean, J. and Funkhauser, G. R. 1994. "Dendroclimatic Reconstructions for the Southern Colorado Plateau," in W. J. Waugh, ed. *Climate Change in the Four Corners and Adjacent Regions*. Grand Junction, CO: Mesa State College. 85–104.

Ferguson, T. J. 2007. "Zuni Traditional History and Cultural Geography," in David A. Gregory and David R. Wilcox, eds, *Zuni Origins: Toward a New Synthesis of Southwestern Archaeology*. Tucson: University of Arizona Press.

————, and E. Richard Hart. 1985. *A Zuni Atlas*. Norman: University of Oklahoma Press.

Fish, Suzanne K., and Paul R. Fish., eds. 2008. *The Hohokam Millennium*. Santa Fe, NM: SAR Press.

Gregory, David A., and David R. Wilcox, eds. 2007. *Zuni Origins: Toward a New Synthesis of Southwestern Archaeology*. Tucson: University of Arizona Press.

Haury, Emil. 1976. *The Hohokam, Desert Farmers and Craftsmen: Excavations at Snaketown, 1964–1965*. Tucson: University of Arizona Press.

Kennett, Douglas J., *et al.* 2017. "Archaeogenetic Evidence Reveals Prehistoric Matrilineal Dynasty," *Nature Communications* 14115. DOI 10.1038/ncomms14115.

Kohler, Timothy A. 2012. "Modeling Agricultural Productivity and Farming Effort," in Timothy A. Kohler and Mark D. Varien, eds, *Emergence and Collapse of Early Villages: Models of Central Mesa Verde Archaeology*. Berkeley: University of California Press. 85–111.

LeBlanc, Steven A. 1983. *The Mimbres People: Ancient Pueblo Potters of the American Southwest*. London and New York: Thames & Hudson.

LeBlanc, S. A. and Register, K. E. 2004. *Constant Battles: Why We Fight*. New York: St. Martin's Press.

Lekson, Steve. 1984. *Great Pueblo Architecture of Chaco Canyon, New Mexico*. Albuquerque, NM: National Park Service.

Neitzel, Jill E., ed. 2003. *Pueblo Bonito: Center of the Chacoan World*. Washington, D.C.: Smithsonian Books.

Ortman, Scott G. 2012. *Winds from the North: Tewa Origins and Historical Anthropology*. Salt Lake City: University of Utah Press.

Rohn, Arthur. 1971. *Mug House, Mesa Verde National Park, Colorado*. Washington, D.C.: National Park Service.

Snead, James E. 2017. "Introduction: 'Forgotten Maps' and the Archaeology of Chaco Roads," *The Kiva* 83 (1): 1–8.

Varien, Mark D., James M. Potter, and Tito E. Naranjo. 2017. "Water, Wind, and Breath," in Monica L. Smith, ed., *Abundance: The Archaeology of Plenitude*. Boulder: University of Colorado Press. 65–94.

————, *et al.* 2007. "Historical Ecology in the Mesa Verde Region: Results from the Village Ecodynamics Project," *American Antiquity* 72: 273–99.

Vivian, Gwinn. 1990. *The Chacoan Prehistory of the San Juan Basin* San Diego: Academic Press.

——. 1997a. "Chacoan Roads: Morphology," *The Kiva* 63 (1): 7–34.

——. 1997b. "Chacoan Roads: Function," *The Kiva* 63 (2): 35–67.

Whalen, Michael E., and Paul E. Minnis. 2001. *Casas Grandes and its Hinterland: Prehistoric Regional Organization in Northwest Mexico.* Tucson: University of Arizona Press.

Windes, Tom. 2003. "This Old House: Construction and Abandonment of Pueblo Bonito," in Jill E. Neitzel, ed., *Pueblo Bonito: Center of the Chacoan World.* Washington, D.C.: Smithsonian Institution Press. 14–32.

11 Early and Middle Woodland: Adena and Hopewell

Anderson, David G., and Kenneth E. Sassaman. 2012. *Recent Developments in Southeastern Archaeology.* Washington, D.C.: Society for American Archaeology.

Brose, David S. 1994. "Trade and Exchange in the Midwestern United States," in Timothy C. Baugh and Jonathon J. Ericson, eds, *Prehistoric Exchange Systems in North America.* New York: Plenum Press. 215–40.

——, and N. Greber, eds. 1979. *Hopewellian Archaeology.* Kent, OH: Kent University Press.

Carr, Christopher, and Troy Case, eds. 2005. *Gathering Hopewell: Society, Ritual, and Ritual Interaction.* New York: Kluwer Academic/Plenum Press.

——. 2008. *The Scioto Hopewell and Their Neighbors.* New York: Springer.

Cook, Robert A. 2011. *SunWatch: For Ancient Development in the Mississippian World.* Tuscaloosa: University of Alabama Press.

Dancey, William S., and Paul L. Pacheco. 1997. "A Community Model of Ohio Hopewell Settlement," in William S. Dancey and Paul L. Pacheco, eds, *Ohio Hopewell Community Organization.* Kent, OH: Kent State University Press. 3–40.

Dragoo, D. W. 1963. *Mounds for the Dead: An Analysis of the Adena Culture.* Annals of the Carnegie Museum 37. Pittsburgh, PA: Carnegie Museum of Natural History.

Jefferies, Richard W. 1976. *The Tunacunnhee Site: Evidence of Hopewell Interaction in Northwest Georgia.* Anthropological Papers of the University of Georgia 1. Athens.

Jones, Lindsay, and Richard D. Shiels, eds. 2016. *The Newark Earthworks: Enduring Monuments, Contested Meanings.* Charlottesville: University of Virginia Press.

Lepper, Bradley T. 2010. "The Ceremonial Landscape of the Newark Earthworks and the Raccoon Creek Valley," in M. Byers and D. A. Wymer, eds, *Hopewell Settlement Patterns, Subsystems, and Symbolic Landscapes.* Gainesville: University of Florida Press. 98–127.

Lynott, Mark. 2014. *Hopewell Ceremonial Landscapes of Ohio: More than Mounds and Geometric Earthworks.* Oxford: Oxbow Books.

Muller, Jon. 2016. *Archaeology of the Lower Ohio River Valley.* Abingdon, UK: Routledge.

Romain, William F. 2015. *An Archaeology of the Sacred: Adena-Hopewell*

Astronomy and Landscape Archaeology. Cincinatti, OH: Ancient Earthworks Project.

Webb, W. S., and C. E. Snow. 1945. *The Adena People*. Knoxville: University of Tennessee Press.

12 Mississippian and Calusa

Anderson, David G. 2017. "Mississippian Beginnings: Multiple Perspectives on Migration, Monmentality, and Religion in the Prehistoric Eastern United States," in Gregory D. Wilson, ed., *Mississippian Beginnings*. Gainesville: University of Florida Press. 293–321.

Benson, Larry V., Timothy R. Pauketat, and Edward R. Cook. 2009. "Cahokia's Boom or Bust in the Context of Climate Change," *American Antiquity* 74 (3): 467–83.

Brown, James A. 1996. *The Spiro Ceremonial Center*. Ann Arbor: Museum of Anthropology, University of Michigan.

——, and John Kelly. 2000. "Cahokia and the Southeastern Ceremonial Complex," in S. R. Adler, ed., *Mounds, Modoc, and Mesoamerica: Papers in Honor of Melvin J. Fowler*. Springfield: Illinois State Museum. 469–510.

Emerson, Thomas E. 1997. *Cahokia and the Ideology of Power*. Tuscaloosa: University of Alabama Press.

——, and R. Barry Lewis, eds. 1999. *Cahokia and the Hinterlands: Middle Mississippian Cultures of the Midwest*. Champaign: University of Illinois Press.

——, and Dale L. McGrath, eds. 2008. *Late Woodland Societies. Tradition and Transformation Across the Midcontinent*. Lincoln: University of Nebraska Press.

——, *et al.* 2016. "Paradigms Lost: Reconfiguring Cahokia's Mound 72 Beaded Burial," *American Antiquity* 81 (3): 405–25.

Hall, Robert L. 1997. *An Archaeology of Soul: North American Indian Belief and Ritual*. Urbana: University of Illinois Press.

King, Adam, ed. 2007. *Southeastern Ceremonial Complex: Chronology, Content, Context*. Tuscaloosa: University of Alabama Press.

Knight, Vernon J. 2010. *Mound Excavations at Moundville: Architecture, Elites and Social Order*. Tuscaloosa: University of Alabama Press.

Luer, G. M., and R. J. Wheeler. 1997. "How the Pine Island Canal Worked: Topography, Hydraulics, and Engineering," *The Florida Anthropologist* 50 (1): 115–31.

Marquardt, William H. 2014. "Tracking the Calusa: A Retrospective," *Southeastern Archaeology* 33 (1): 1–24.

——, and Karen J. Walker, eds. 2013. *The Archaeology of Pineland: A Coastal Southwest Florida Site Complex, A.D. 50–1710*. Institute of Archaeology and Paleoenvironmental Studies Monograph 4. Gainesville, FL.

Milanich, Jerald T. 1997. *Archaeology of Northern Florida, AD 200–900: The McKeithen Weeden Island Culture*. Gainesville: University Press of Florida.

Milner, George R. 1998. *The Cahokia Chiefdom*. Washington, D.C.: Smithsonian Institution Press.

Muller, Jon. 1997. *Mississippian Political Economy*. New York: Plenum Press.

Pauketat, Timothy R. 2004. *Ancient Cahokia and the Mississippians*. Cambridge:

Cambridge University Press.

———. 2010. *Cahokia: Ancient America's Great City on the Mississippi*. New York: Penguin.

Scarry, C. Margaret, and Vincas P. Steponaitis. 2016. *Rethinking Moundville and its Hinterland*. Gainesville: Florida Museum of Natural History.

Vanderwarker, Amber M., Dana N. Bardolph, and C. Margaret Scarry, 2017. "Maize and Mississippian Beginnings," in Gregory D. Wilson, ed., *Mississippian Beginnings*. Gainesville: University of Florida Press. 29–70.

Walker, Karen J. 2013. "The Pineland Site Complex: Environmental Contexts," in William H. Marquardt and Karen J. Walker, eds, *The Archaeology of Pineland: A Coastal Southwest Florida Site Complex, AD 50–1710*. Institute of Archaeology and Paleoenvironmental Studies Monograph 4. Gainesville, FL. 23–52.

Wilson, Gregory D., ed. 2017. *Mississippian Beginnings*. Gainesville: University of Florida Press.

———, and Lynne Sullivan. 2017. "Mississippian Origins: From Origins to Beginnings," in Gregory D. Wilson, ed., *Mississippian Beginnings*. Gainesville: University of Florida Press. 1–28.

13 Algonquians and Iroquoians

Bernstein, David J. 1999. "Prehistoric Use of Plant Foods on Long Island," in John P. Hart, ed., *Current North Paleoethnobotany*. New York State Museum Bulletin 494. Albany. 101–20.

Birch, J. 2012. "Coalescent Communities: Settlement Aggregation and Social Integration in Iroquoian Ontario," *American Antiquity* 77 (4): 646–70.

———. 2015. "Current Research on the Historical Development of Northern Iroquoian Societies," *Journal of Archaeological Research* 23 (3): 263–323.

———, and R. F. Williamson. 2012. *The Mantle Site: An Archaeological History of an Ancestral Wendat Community*. Lanham, MA: AltaMira Press.

———, and R. F. Williamson. 2015. "Navigating Ancestral Landscapes in the Northern Iroquoian World," *Journal of Anthropological Archaeology* 39: 139–50.

Bradley, James W. 2011. "Re-Visiting Wampum and Other Seventeenth-Century Shell Games," *Archaeology of Eastern North America* 39: 25–51.

Cleland, C. E. 1982. "The Inland Shore Fishery of the Northern Great Lakes: Its Development and Importance in Prehistory," *American Antiquity* 47: 761–84.

Crawford, Gary W., *et al.* 1998. "Floodplains and agricultural origins: A Case Study in South-Central Ontario," *Journal of Field Archaeology* 25 (2): 123–37.

Crawford, Gary W., and David Smith. 2002. "Migration in Prehistory: Princess Point and the Northern Iroquoian Case," *American Antiquity* 61: 782–90.

Engelbrecht, William. 2003. *Iroquoia: The Development of a Native World*. Syracuse, NY: Syracuse University Press.

Gates St-Pierre, C., and R. G. Thompson. 2015. "Phytolith Evidence for the Early Presence of Maize in Southern Quebec," *American Antiquity* 80 (2): 408–15.

Hart, John P., ed. 1999. *Current North Paleoethnobotany*. New York State Museum Bulletin 494. Albany, NY.

——, and W. A. Lovis. 2013. "Reevaluating What We Know About the Histories of Maize in Northeastern North America: A Review of Current Evidence," *Journal of Archaeological Research* 21 (2): 175–216.

——, and Christina B. Reith, eds. 2002. *Northeast Subsistence-Settlement Change: AD 700–1300*. New York State Museum Bulletin 496. Albany.

——, *et al.* 2016. "Nation Building and Social Signaling in Southern Ontario: AD 1350–1650," *PLOS One* 11 (5): e0156178.

Jones, E., and J. Creese, eds. 2017. *Process and Meaning in Spatial Archaeology: Investigations into Pre-Columbian Iroquoian Space and Place*. Boulder: University Press of Colorado.

Kerber, Jordan. 2007. *Archaeology of the Iroquois: Selected Readings and Research Sources*. Syracuse, NY: Syracuse University Press.

Levine, Mary Ann, Kenneth E. Sassaman, and Michael S. Nassaney, eds. 1999. *The Archaeological Northeast*. Westport, CT: Bergin & Garvey.

MacNeish, Richard S. 1952. *Iroquois Pottery Types: A Technique for the Study of Iroquois Prehistory*. National Museum of Canada Bulletin, Anthropological Series 124. Ottawa.

Pfeiffer, S., *et al.* 2016. "Maize, Fish, and Deer: Investigating Dietary Staples Among Ancestral Huron-Wendat Villages, as Documented from Tooth Samples," *American Antiquity* 81 (3): 515–32.

Ritchie, W. A. 1965. *The Archaeology of New York State*. Garden City, NY: Natural History Press.

——, and R. E. Funk. 1973. *Aboriginal Settlement Patterns in the Northeast*. Albany: New York State Museum. Memoir 20.

Snow, Dean. 1980. *The Archaeology of New England*. New York: Academic Press.

——. 1996. *The Iroquois*. Oxford: Blackwell.

Taché, K. 2011a. *Structure and Regional Diversity of the Meadowood Interaction Sphere*. Ann Arbor: Museum of Anthropology, University of Michigan.

——. 2011b. "New Perspectives on Meadowood Trade Items," *American Antiquity* 76 (1): 41–79.

——, and J. P. Hart. 2013. "Chronometric Hygiene of Radiocarbon Databases for Early Durable Cooking Vessel Technologies in Northeastern North America," *American Antiquity* 78 (2): 359–72.

Trigger, Bruce G. 1969. *The Huron: Farmers of the North*. New York: Holt, Rinehart & Winston.

——. 1972. *The Children of Aataentsic: A History of the Huron People to 1660*. 2 vols. Kingston and Montreal: McGill-Queen's University Press.

——. 1985. *Natives and Newcomers*. Kingston and Montreal: McGill-Queen's University Press.

Versaggi, Nina. 1999. "Regional Diversity Within the Early Woodland in the Northeast," *Northeast Anthropology* 57: 45–56.

Warrick, Gary. 1984. *Reconstructing Ontario Iroquoian Village Organization*. Archaeological Survey of Canada, Mercury Series 124. Ottawa. 1–180.

Williamson, R. F. 2014. "The Archaeological History of the Wendat to AD 1651: An Overview," *Ontario Archaeology* 94: 3–64.

14 European Contact

Crosby, A. W. 2003. *The Columbian Exchange: Biological and Cultural Consequences of 1492*. New York: Praeger.

———. 2016. *Ecological Imperialism: The Biological Expansion of Europe, 900–1900*. Second Edition. Cambridge: Cambridge University Press.

Deetz, James. 1996. *In Small Things Forgotten*. New York: Anchor Books.

Dobyns, Henry. 1983. *Their Number Become Thinned: Native American Population Dynamics in Eastern North America*. Knoxville: University of Tennessee Press.

Hicks, Dan, and Mary Beaudry, eds. 2006. *The Cambridge Companion to Historical Archaeology*. Cambridge: Cambridge University Press.

Ingstad, Helga, ed. 1985. *The Norse Discovery of America*. Oslo: Norwegian University Press.

Knauf, Jocelyn C., and Mark E. Leone, eds. 2015. *Historical Archaeologies of Capitalism*. Second Edition. New York: Springer.

McGhee, R. 1984. "Contact Between Native Americans and the Medieval Norse: A Review of Evidence," *American Antiquity* 49: 4–26.

Morison, Samuel Eliot. 1971. *The European Discovery of America*. Vol. 1: *The Northern Voyages*. New York: Oxford University Press.

Orser, Charles E. 2017. *Historical Archaeology*. Third Edition. Abingdon, UK: Routledge.

Ramenofsky, Ann. 1987. *Vectors of Death: The Archaeology of European Contact*. Albuquerque: University of New Mexico Press.

Trigger, Bruce G. 1972. *The Children of Aataentsic: A History of the Huron People to 1660*. 2 vols. Kingston and Montreal: McGill-Queen's University Press.

———. 1985. *Natives and Newcomers*. Kingston and Montreal: McGill-Queen's University Press.

Wahlgren, Erik. 1986. *The Vikings and America*. London and New York: Thames & Hudson.

15 Colonists, Borderlands, and Missionaries

Crosby, A. W. 2003. *The Columbian Exchange: Biological and Cultural Consequences of 1492*. New York: Praeger.

Deagan, Kathleen A. 1983. *Spanish St. Augustine*. New York: Academic Press.

———, ed. 1991. *America's Ancient City: Spanish St. Augustine 1565–1763*. Charlottesville: University Press of Virginia.

Deetz, James. 1996. *In Small Things Forgotten*. Revised Edition. New York: Anchor.

Dye, D. H., and C. A. Cox, eds. 1990. *Towns and Temples Along the Mississippi*. Tuscaloosa: University of Alabama Press.

Ewen, Charles R., and John H. Hann. 1998. *Hernando de Soto Among the Apalache: The Archaeology of the First Winter Encampment*. Gainesville: Florida Museum of Natural History.

Farnsworth, Paul, and Robert H. Jackson. 1995. "Cultural, Economic, and Demographic Change in the Missions of Alta California: The Case of Nuestra Señora de Soledad," in Erick Langer and Robert H. Jackson, eds,

The New Latin American Mission History. Lincoln: University of Nebraska Press. 109–29.

Foster, H. Thomas. 2007. *Archaeology of the Lower Muskogee Creek Indians, 1715–1836*. Tuscaloosa: University of Alabama Press.

Kelso, William. 2017. *Jamestown: The Truth Revealed*. Charlottesville: University of Virginia Press.

McEwen, Bonnie G. 2000. *Indians of the Greater Southeast*. Gainesville: University Press of Florida.

Milanich, Jerald T. 1999. *Laboring in the Fields of the Lord: Spanish Missions and Southeastern Indians*. Washington, D.C.: Smithsonian Institution Press.

———, and Susan Milbrath. 1989. *First Encounters*. Gainesville: University of Florida Press.

Mitchem, J. M., and D. L. Hutchinson. 1987. *Interim Report on Archaeological Research at the Tatham Mound, Citrus County, Florida: Season III*. Gainesville: Florida State Museum.

Nöel Hume, Ivor. 1973. *Martin's Hundred*. New York: Alfred Knopf.

Smith, Marvin T. 1987. *Archaeology of Aboriginal Change in the Interior Southeast*. Gainesville: University Press of Florida.

———. 2000. *Coosa: The Rise and Fall of a Southeastern Mississippian Chiefdom*. Gainesville: University Press of Florida.

Thomas, David Hurst, ed. 1989. *Columbian Consequences*. Vol. 1: *The Spanish Borderlands*. Washington, D.C.: Smithsonian Institution Press.

———. 2011. *St. Catherines: An Island in Time*. Athens and London: University of Georgia Press.

White, Sam. 2018. *A Cold Welcome*. Cambridge, MA: Harvard University Press.

16 Unmasking the Anonymous

Baxter, R. Scott, and Rebecca Allen. 2015. "The View from Summit Camp," *Historical Archaeology* 49 (1): 34–45.

Braje, Todd J., *et al.* 2014. "Of Seals, Sea Lions, and Abalone: The Archaeology of an Historical Multiethnic Base Camp on San Miguel Island, California," *Historical Archaeology* 48 (2): 122–42.

Deagan, Kathleen A., and Darcie A. Macmahon. 1995. *Fort Mose: Colonial America's Black Fortress of Freedom*. Gainesville: University of Florida Press.

Deetz, James. 1996. *In Small Things Forgotten*. Revised Edition. New York: Anchor Books.

Ferguson, Leland. 1992. *Uncommon Ground: Archaeology and Early African America*. Washington, D.C.: Smithsonian Institution Press.

Frohne, Andrea E. 2015. *The African Burial Ground in New York: Memory, Spirituality, and Space*. Syracuse, NY: Syracuse University Press.

Hardesty, D. L. 1988. *The Archaeology of Mining and Miners: A View from the Silver State*. Pleasant Hill, CA: Society for Historical Archaeology.

Kelso, William. 1984. *Kingsmill Plantations, 1619–1800*. New York: Academic Press.

———. 1986. "Mulberry Row: Slave Life at Thomas Jefferson's Monticello," *Archaeology* 39 (5): 28–35.

Leone, Mark, Gladys-Marie Fry, and Tim Ruppel. 2001. "Spirit Management

Among Americans of African Descent," in C. E. Orser, ed., *Race and the Archaeology of Identity*. Salt Lake City: University of Utah Press. 143–47.

——, and P. B. Potter, Jr. 1984. *Archaeological Annapolis*. Annapolis, MD: Historical Annapolis Inc.

——, *et al.* 1989. "Power Gardens of Annapolis," *Archaeology* 42 (2): 34–40.

McDonald, J. D., *et al.* 1991. "The Northern Cheyenne Outbreak of 1879: Using Oral History and Archaeology as Tools of Resistance," in R. McGuire and R. Paynter, eds, *The Archaeology of Inequality*. Oxford: Blackwell. 64–78.

O'Dell, Gary A., and Angelo I. George. 2014. "Rock-Shelter Saltpeter Mines of Eastern Kentucky," *Historical Archaeology* 48 (2): 91–121.

Orser, Charles E. 2017. *Historical Archaeology*. Third Edition. Abingdon, UK: Routledge.

Pastron, Allen G. 1988. "Bonanza from Old San Francisco," *Archaeology* 41 (4): 32–40.

Scott, Douglas D., Richard A. Fox, and Melissa A. Connor. 2000. *Archaeological Perspectives on the Battle of the Little Big Horn*. Norman: University of Oklahoma Press.

Shackel, Paul. 1994. *Personal Discipline and Material Culture: An Archaeology of Annapolis, Maryland, 1695–1870*. Knoxville: University of Tennessee Press.

——, *et al.* 1988. *Annapolis Pasts: Historical Archaeology in Annapolis, Maryland*. Knoxville: University of Tennessee Press.

Singleton, T. A., ed. 1999. *"I, Too, Am America."* Charlottesville: University of Virginia Press.

Yentsch, Ann. 1994. *A Chesapeake Family and their Slaves*. Cambridge: Cambridge University Press.

17 The Heritage of North America

Deetz, James. 1997. *In Small Things Forgotten*. Revised Edition. New York: Anchor Books.

Flannery, Kent V. 1982. "The Golden Marshalltown: A Parable for the Archaeology of the 1980s," *American Anthropologist* 82: 265–78.

Fletcher, Alice, and Francis La Fleche. 1972. *The Omaha Tribe*. 2 vols. Reprint of 1911 publication of the Bureau of American Ethnology. Lincoln: University of Nebraska Press.

Frohne, Andrea E. 2015. *The African Burial Ground in New York: Memory, Spirituality, and Space*. Syracuse, NY: Syracuse University Press.

Hall, Robert L. 1997. *An Archaeology of the Soul: Native American Belief and Ritual*. Chicago and Urbana: University of Illinois Press.

LaRoche, Cheryl J., and Michael Blakey. 1997. "Seizing Intellectual Power: The Dialogue at the New York African American Burial Ground," *Historical Archaeology* 31 (3): 84–106.

McDavid, Carol. 2011. "When is 'Gone' Gone? Archaeology, Gentrification, and Competing Narratives About Freedmen's Town, Houston," *Historical Archaeology* 45 (3): 74–88.

Meyer, Karl. 1992. *The Plundered Past*. New York: Athenaeum.

Glossary

abalone a marine snail

accelerator mass spectrometry (AMS) a method of dating by measuring the C14 content of organic materials. This technique is less invasive than other radiocarbon dating methods as it requires a smaller sample

Adena an Early Woodland cultural tradition that flourished between 500 BCE and the first century CE

adobe dried mud, often mixed with straw to form mud bricks

akchin the area within an irrigation system using channels or canyons to divert nutrient-rich sediments that is flooded and forms rich farmland

Algonquian one of the most widespread North American native language groups

alignment lines of low stone piles designed to herd buffalo toward a certain location during a hunt

Altithermal a warm and dry period between 5000 and 2500 BCE, sometimes also called the Holocene Climate Optimum

Ancestral Pueblo prehistoric archaeological tradition in the **Four Corners** region

Antiquities Act Act passed in the United States in 1906 that protects archaeological landmarks, sites, structures, and objects

Archaeological Conservancy national non-profit organization that acquires and preserves archaeological sites

Arctic Small Tool Tradition archaeological culture of the Far North characterized by lightweight stone tool kits from about 2500 BCE

arroyo a rocky ravine or dry watercourse

atlatl spearthrower

baidarka Aleutian kayak made of sea-lion skins

bannerstone artifacts bored with a central hole used to weight **atlatls**, giving the spear-throwers greater range and power

Basket Maker an aceramic, nomadic archaeological culture dating to between 1500 BCE and 750 CE

Beringia tract of land connecting Siberia and Canada, now beneath sea level

biface flat cobble flaked over both surfaces to produce a sharp edge around the entire periphery

bioarchaeology the study of human physical remains

Birnirk prehistoric culture of the Far North

bison jump a hunting method involving driving bison over high bluffs, usually making use of **alignments**

broad-based foragers hunter-gatherer societies characterized by reduced mobility and a greater tendency to exploit a wide variety of food sources within a restricted home territory

broad-spectrum hunter-gatherers nomadic groups that exploit a wide range of naturally occurring food sources in their territory

C14 the radioactive isotope of carbon in all organic materials that is detected and measured by radiocarbon dating methods such as **accelerator mass spectrometry (AMS)**

Chaco Phenomenon the intensification of social and trading networks between dispersed **Ancestral Pueblo**

communities that centered on Chaco Canyon in the **Four Corners** region

chert a fine-grained rock that produces a sharp edge when fractured, commonly used for tool-making

Chindadn a type of spear point unique to prehistoric sites in Siberia, Alaska, and the Yukon

Clovis the only tool tradition that is attested across the whole of North America, flourishing between 13,050 and 12,800 years ago

community archaeology an archaeological approach that involves members of the public in the excavation and preservation of local heritage, making outreach a central part of archaeological practice

contact period era of first interaction between European settlers and Native American societies after the arrival of Columbus in 1492

coprolite fossilized feces

Creek Confederacy a coalition of Native American groups that organized as a political entity in the 18th and early 19th centuries

cultural ecology a term devised by Julian Steward to account for the dynamic relationship between human society and its environment, in which culture is viewed as the primary adaptive mechanism

Cultural Resource Management (CRM) the safeguarding of archaeological heritage through the protection and sites and through salvage (rescue) archaeology

culture history an approach to archaeological interpretation that uses the procedure of the traditional historian, including emphasis on specific circumstances elaborated with rich detail

Dalton Paleo-Indian culture of the Eastern Woodlands

dendrochronology dating method based on counting the growth rings in trees

Direct Historical Method archaeological approach developed by Alfred Kidder that involves projecting present or historical evidence onto archaeological sites to "track back" into the past

Dorset Eastern Arctic archaeological culture from 200 BCE to perhaps 900 CE, particularly famed for its rich art tradition

Dyuktai (or Diuktai) Tradition one of the earliest tool types known in Alaska

Eastern Woodlands cultural area extending roughly from the Atlantic Ocean to the eastern Great Plains, and from the Great Lakes region to the Gulf of Mexico

El Niño climatic event occurring every few years that causes global variation of temperatures and rainfall

entrada the arrival and continued presence of European colonizers following Columbus's landing in the Bahamas in 1492

ethnohistory the study of contemporary cultures by examining historical records

evolutionary ecology theoretical approach that examines how human behaviors change through natural selection as they adapt and optimize to local environmental conditions

Folsom Plains tradition characterized by distinctive projectile points used in bison hunts

Four Corners region of the American Southwest between Colorado, Utah, Arizona, and New Mexico

Fremont archaeological culture of farmers and hunter-gatherers in the eastern Great Basin between 1 and 1250 CE

geomorphological methods study of the development of land forms

geophysical survey archaeological imaging or mapping technique that employs ground-based physical sensing technologies such as magnetometry or ground-penetrating radar

GIS Geographical Information Systems; software-based systems for the collection, storage, retrieval, analysis, and display of spatial data held in different "layers," which can be combined or examined separately

Grand Council of the Six Nations governing body of the Iroquois Confederacy

Great House a large, multi-storied building sometimes found at Ancestral Pueblo sites

great kiva a public, ceremonial building that typically has high walls and an interior bench circling the central space

Hoodoo an African-American religious practice that has its roots in the spiritual traditions of West Africa

hot-rock cooking a process whereby rocks heated in a hearth are added to ceramic vessels or lined baskets to cook soups or stews, to avoid breaking or burning containers over a direct flame

Independence I archaeological culture of the **Arctic Small Tool Tradition** in northeast Greenland between 2500 and 1000 BCE

Iroquoian Native American language family, mainly of the Northeast

Kachemak Tradition archaeological culture based on Kodiak Island between 1800 BCE and 1000 CE

katchinas ancestral spirits in Pueblo belief who act as intermediaries between the earthly and the divine realms

kiva multi-purpose room used for religious, political, and social functions in Pueblo villages on the Colorado Plateau

Last Glacial Maximum (LGM) period during the last glacial age when the earth's ice sheets were at their greatest extent, between about 25,000 and 18,000 years ago

League of Five Nations council formed by the Haudenosaunee in the sixteenth century

LIDAR Light Detection and Ranging; airborne remote-sensing technique that uses lasers to send pulses of light to the ground and measures the time it takes them to return to the instrument, calculating the distance with extreme accuracy and producing an image of the ground surface; forests and clouds can be filtered out

Little Ice Age climatic interval of very cold conditions between 1600 and 1850 CE

matrilocal intermarriage custom whereby a husband goes to live with the wife's community

Meadowood cultural tradition in the Northeast Woodlands between 1000 and 400 BCE

Medieval Warm Period climatic interval of relatively warm conditions between around 900 and 1250 CE

megafauna large animals, such as mammoths, woolly rhinoceros, and giant deer

mesa a high, flat-topped hill

metate flat stone on which grains and seeds were processed using a smaller stone

Midwestern Taxonomic Method a framework devised by McKern in 1939 to systematize sequences in the Great Plains on the basis of similarities between artifact assemblages

muller heavy stone tool used for grinding grains and seeds

National Environmental Protection Act (NEPA) law enacted in 1970 requiring federal agencies to assess and reduce the environmental impact of proposed actions

Native American Grave Protection and Repatriation Act (NAGPRA) law enacted in 1990 requiring federal agencies and institutions that receive federal funding to return Native American "cultural items" to lineal descendents or affiliated tribes. The Act also established procedures for the excavation of Native American sites on federal or public lands

Norton Tradition archaeological culture of the Far North in the first millennium BCE

Ocean Bay Tradition archaeological culture of the Far North coast and Kodiak Island between 5500 and 1500 BCE

Old Bering Sea Tradition archaeological culture centered on the Bering Strait region between 200 BCE and 1300 CE

Optical Stimulated Luminescence (OSL) dating method that relies indirectly on radioactive decay, employing light to release trapped electrons

Paleoarctic Tradition archaeological culture of the Far North between 8000 and 5500 BCE

Palmer Drought Severity Index (PDSI) standardized system of measuring aridity based on recent precipitation and temperature

participant observation anthropological technique in which the researcher attempts to access and be accepted into a social group in order to study its practices from an insider's perspective

petroglyph rock-art images created by chipping off part of the rock's surface

pictograph symbol representing a word or phrase

pithouse domestic structure that is dug into the ground

planked houses large communal structures, usually constructed of cedar beams, typical of the Pacific Northwest

Plano points flaked stone projectile points and tools created by Plains people and used for hunting

platform mounds an earthwork or manufactured mound created to support a building or activity zone

post-processual archaeology an approach which questions the degree that archaeology as a science can be objective about the past, favoring a variety of approaches that emphasize the individual and the possibility of multiple valid interpretations

potlatch a competitive and feasting ceremony common among Northwest Coast peoples of North America

Pre-Dorset archaeological culture of the **Arctic Small Tool Tradition** in the south Arctic from 2500 BCE, immediately preceding the **Dorset Eastern Arctic** culture

presidio fortified base established by Spanish settlers

processual archaeology approach advocated in the 1960s, which argued for an explicitly scientific framework of archaeological method and theory, with hypotheses rigorously tested; it promoted an emphasis on culture process, understanding how and why change occurred, rather than simple description; also called New Archaeology

projectile point a shaped stone flake hafted to a projectile, such as a spear, arrow or dart

proton magnetometer survey technique that measures variation in the Earth's magnetic field to map archaeological features beneath the surface; see **geophysical survey**

public archaeology see **community archaeology**

pueblo a general term for a community in Southwest America, distinctive for their collective apartment structures, often accessible through ladders

radiocarbon dating dating method based on the radioactive decay of the isotope carbon-14 (see also **C14; accelerator mass spectrometry (AMS)**)

reduction Spanish policy of relocating Native American groups to purpose-built settlements modeled on European towns

refugium zone ecological areas in which flora and fauna that could not survive in glacial regions persisted

rockshelter a natural shallow cave or overhang inhabited by ancient people

sachem paramount chief of the Algonquian and other northeast groups

Saqqaq archaeological culture of the **Arctic Small Tool Tradition** of Greenland from 2500 BCE

sedentism a residence pattern of permanent settlement

sinodonty distinctive dental morphology generally shared by Native Americans

sipapu the entrance to the underworld in **Ancestral Pueblo** cosmology

soil resistivity surveys a method of subsurface detection that measures changes in conductivity by passing electrical current through ground soils. Variations in conductivity are generally a consequence of moisture content, and so buried features can be detected by differential retention of groundwater

Southeastern Ceremonial Complex (SECC) broad regional similarity of artifacts, iconography, ceremonies, and mythology of the Mississippian period

thermoluminescence (TL) dating dating method that relies indirectly on radioactive decay, employing heat to release trapped electrons

Thule Tradition archaeological culture of Alaska from 700 BCE to the present

tomol a planked canoe

umiak a hide kayak

wampum tubular shell beads, a prized trading commodity sometimes woven into belts to commemorate important events

weir obstruction placed in running water to direct the movement of fish for hunting

wickiup tipi-like shelters erected periodically by nomadic peoples

wot hereditary chief among the Chumash peoples

X-ray fluorescence a method used in the analysis of artifact composition, in which the sample is irradiated with a beam of X-rays that excite electrons associated with atoms on the surface

Younger Dryas climatic interval of glacial conditions that began around 12,900 years ago and lasted around a millennium

zooarchaeology a subdiscipline of archaeology that studies animal remains

Illustration Credits

Images are listed by figure number

Frontispiece Peter Barritt/Robert Harding/Diomedia **1.1** National Geographic Creative/Alamy **1.2** Don Johnston/Alamy **1.3** Werner Forman Archive/Heritage Images/Diomedia **1.4** from E. G. Squier and E. F. Davis, *Ancient Monuments of the Mississippi Valley*, 1848 (New York) **1.5** © The Trustees of the British Museum **1.6** from Frank Hamilton Cushing, *My Adventures in Zuñi*, Century Magazine 25, no. 2 (December 1882) **1.7** Courtesy Kidder Family Archives/Pecos National Historic Park, National Park Service **1.8** Pecos National Historic Park, National Park Service **1.9** Richard Schlecht/National Geographic/Getty Images **1.12** Southern Methodist University **1.13** Courtesy Lewis Winford **2.6** Courtesy Alaska Office of History and Archaeology **2.7** Courtesy Dr. Ben A. Potter, Department Chair and Professor, Department of Anthropology, University of Alaska Fairbanks **2.9** Courtesy James M. Adovasio **2.10** Courtesy Jim Barlow, University of Oregon **2.11** Courtesy The Gault School of Archaeological Research **2.12** Arizona State Museum, University of Arizona **2.13** Arizona State Museum, University of Arizona. Photo Helga Teiwes **2.14** after Willey, 1996 **3.3** Courtesy Mary Lou Larsen, University of Wyoming **3.4** Collection of University of Colorado Museum of Natural History **3.6** Courtesy George Carr Frison **3.8** Witold Skrypczak/Alamy **3.9** Courtesy Museum of New Mexico (neg no. 21618) **3.10** Artwork by Eric Carlson, from *Ancient Peoples of the Great Basin and Colorado Plateau* by Steven R. Simms. Used with permission **3.11** University of Utah Archaeological Center **3.12a** Werner Forman Archive/Utah Museum of Natural History/Diomedia **3.12b** University of Utah Archaeological Center. Photo John Telford **3.13** Werner Forman Archive/Utah Museum of Natural History/Diomedia **3.14** Photo John T. Pafford, Private Collection **3.15** Courtesy McClung Museum of Natural History and Culture, The University of Tennessee, Knoxville **3.17** Photo courtesy the Center for Archaeological Investigations, Carbondale **4.3** Photo Herbert Maschner **4.4** Smithsonian Institution National Anthropological Archives. William Henry Elliot, 1872 (MS7112) **4.5 right** Werner Forman Archive/British Museum, London/Diomedia **4.5 below** Metropolitan Museum of Art, New York. Ralph T. Coe Collection, Gift of Ralph T. Coe Foundation for the Arts, 2011 (2011.154.150a, b) **4.6** Kodiak Island Borough Collection, courtesy the Alutiiq Museum, Kodiak, Alaska (AM724:1196, AM724:3004, AM724:707, AM724:2478). Photo Pam Foreman **4.10** Photo Robert McGhee **4.11** Canadian Museum of History, Gatineau, Quebec (77-26-Dm) **4.12** Photo Bjarne Grønnow, 1984 **4.13** Photo Bjarne Grønnow, 1986 **4.15** Werner Forman Archive/American Museum of Natural History, New York/Diomedia **4.16** Werner Forman Archive/Museum of the American Indian, Heye Foundation, New York/Diomedia **4.18** Canadian Museum of History, Gatineau, Quebec (NhHd-1:2655, IMG2008-0215-0011-Dm) **4.19** Canadian Museum of History, Gatineau, Quebec (PfFm-1:1768-1771, IMG2008-0215-0017-Dm) **4.20** Steven Kazlowski/SuperStock/Diomedia **4.21** CM Dixon/Heritage Images/Diomedia **4.22** Canadian Museum of History, Gatineau, Quebec (77-27-Dm) **5.2** Courtesy Roy Carlson **5.3** Courtesy Dale R. Croes, Washington State University **5.6** National Anthropological Archives, Smithsonian Institution, Washington, D.C. **5.7** from Stephen Powers, *Tribes in California*, 1877 (Washington) **5.9** after a watercolour by John Webber, 1778 **5.10** Granger Historical Picture Archive/Alamy **5.11, 5.12, 5.13** Photos by Ruth Kirk. Courtesy the Makah Cultural and Research Center, Washington **5.14** Shirley Tewhaus, courtesy the U.S. Army Corps of Engineers **5.16** Photo Peter Howorth, Santa Barbara Museum of Natural History **5.17** Phoebe A. Hearst Museum of Anthropology, University of California, Berkeley **5.18** Lisa Werner/Alamy **5.19** Granger Historical Picture Archive/Alamy **6.4, 6.5** Courtesy the Division of Anthropology, American Museum of Natural History, New York **6.6** Werner Forman Archive/Diomedia **6.7b** Utah Museum of Natural History, Salt Lake City. Photo John Telford **6.8** Museum of the American Indian, Heye Foundation, New York **6.9** Nature and Science/Alamy **6.10** Courtesy the Division of Anthropology, American Museum of Natural History, New York. Photo Dennis O'Brien **6.11** University of Utah Archaeological Center. Photo John Telford **6.12 left** Werner Forman Archive/Utah Museum of Natural History/Diomedia **6.12 right** University of Utah Archaeological Center **6.13 above** Sumiko Scott/Alamy **6.13 below** Tom Walker/Alamy **6.14** University of Utah Archaeological Center. Photo John Telford **7.1** Courier Litho. Co., Buffalo, N.Y./Library of Congress, Washington, D.C. **7.3** Courtesy David Kilby, Department of Anthropology, Texas State University **7.7** Russ Heinl/All Canada Photos/Diomedia **7.8** Courtesy Head-Smashed-In Buffalo Jump Interpretive Centre, Alberta **7.9** Zachary Frank/Alamy **7.11** Christian Heeb/AWL Images/Getty Images **7.12 above, 7.12 below** Peter Barritt/Robert Harding/Diomedia **7.14** ART Collection/Alamy **7.15** Bettmann/Getty Images **7.16** Kansas State Historical Society **7.17** Science History Images/Alamy **7.18, 7.19** Granger Historical Picture Archive/Alamy **7.20** INTERFOTO/Alamy **8.3** from Richard W. Jefferies, *Archaeology of Carrier Mills: 10,000 years in the Saline Valley of Illinois*, 1986 (Southern Illinois Press) **8.4** Photo by Del Baston, provided by the Center for American Archeology, Kampsville, IL **8.5** Courtesy Sarah C. Sherwood, The University of the South, Sewanee **8.6** Image courtesy the William S. Webb Museum of Anthropology, University of Kentucky/TVA Photograph Archive (wsw03648) **8.7** Collection of the Illinois State Museum **8.8** Artwork © Herb Roe, ChromeSun Productions **8.9** Courtesy the State Museum of Pennsylvania, Pennsylvania Historical and

Museum Commission. Photo Don Giles **8.11** James A. Tuck, Memorial University of Newfoundland **8.14** Canadian Museum of History, Gatineau, Quebec (DiJa-1:44, IMG2008-0583-0014-Dm) **8.16** U.S. National Park Service **8.17** from Jon E. Gibson, *Poverty Point: A Culture of the Lower Mississippi Valley*, 1985 (University of Southwestern Louisiana) **9.3** The Witte Museum, San Antonio, Texas **9.4** Robert Daemmrich Photography Inc/Corbis/Getty Images **9.5** Robert Daemmrich/The Image Works/TopFoto **9.6** Granger Historical Picture Archive/Alamy **9.7** Adriel Heisey **9.8** Henry D. Wallace, Courtesy Archaeology Southwest **9.9** Adriel Heisey **9.10** Edward S. Curtis/Library of Congress, Washington, D.C. **9.11** National Anthropological Archives, Smithsonian Institution, Washington, D.C. (judd_nm_071) **10.1**, **10.2** Adriel Heisey **10.4** DeepEarth Photography/Alamy **10.6** Ernesto Burciaga/Aurora Photos/Diomedia **10.7** Charles Mann/Alamy **10.9** Huhugam Heritage Center, Arizona **10.10** Northland Research, Inc. and the Arizona Department of Transportation **10.11** Huhugam Heritage Center, Arizona **10.12**, **10.13** Werner Forman Archive/Maxwell Museum of Anthropology, Albuquerque **10.14**, **10.15** George H.H. Huey/Alamy **10.16** Courtesy Crow Canyon Archaeological Center. Painting by Glenn Felch **10.17** figure from Varien, M., Ortman, S., Kohler, T., Glowacki, D., & Johnson, C. (2007). Historical Ecology in the Mesa Verde Region: Results from the Village Ecodynamics Project. *American Antiquity*, 72(2), 273-299 © The Society for American Archaeology 2007 **10.18** Courtesy the School for Advanced Research, Indian Arts Research Center, Santa Fe. Photo David Grant Noble **10.19** (clockwise from top left) Universal Images Group/Diomedia; Werner Forman Archive/Private Collection/Diomedia; Universal Images Group/Diomedia; Universal Images Group/Diomedia; Chuck Place/Alamy **10.20** Adriel Heisey **11.2** Ohio Historical Society **11.3** Image courtesy the William S. Webb Museum of Anthropology, University of Kentucky/TVA Photograph Archive (wsw05622) **11.5** Tim Kiser (CC BY-SA 2.5) **11.6** Artokoloro Quint Lox Limited/Alamy **11.7** Courtesy the Ohio History Connection (A1200/10) **11.9**, **11.10** Ohio Historical Society **11.11** Courtesy McClung Museum of Natural History and Culture, The University of Tennessee, Knoxville **11.12** U.S. National Park Service. Artwork M. Hampshire **11.13** Courtesy David H. Dye, University of Memphis **11.14** Werner Forman Archive/Field Museum of Natural History, Chicago/Diomedia **11.15** Courtesy David H. Dye, University of Memphis **11.17** U.S. National Park Service **11.18** SuperStock/Diomedia **12.1**, **12.2** Florida Museum of Natural History **12.4** Werner Forman Archive/Museum of the American Indian, Heye Foundation, New York/Diomedia **12.5** Courtesy David H. Dye, University of Memphis **12.6** Courtesy Cahokia Mounds Historic Site. Painting by William Iseminger **12.7** Courtesy Cahokia Mounds Historic Site. Painting by Lloyd K. Townsend **12.8**, **12.9a**, **12.9b**, **12.9c** Courtesy David H. Dye, University of Memphis **12.10** Werner Forman Archive/Field Museum of Natural History, Chicago/Diomedia **12.11** Courtesy David H. Dye, University of Memphis **12.12** Werner Forman Archive/Museum of the American Indian, Heye Foundation, New York/Diomedia **12.13** Rosalrene Betancourt 11/Alamy **12.14**, **12.15** Courtesy David H. Dye, University of Memphis **12.16** U.S. National Park Service. Artwork Martin Pate **12.17** Stephen Saks Photography/Alamy **12.18** from *Le Page du Pratz, Histoire de la Louisiane*, 1758 (Paris) **12.20** Courtesy Florida Museum of Natural History. Art by Merald Clark **13.5** Archaeological Services Inc. **13.7** Courtesy the New York State Museum, Albany, NY **13.8**, **13.9**, **13.10** Courtesy The Museum of Ontario Archaeology, London, Ontario. Artist Ivan Kocsis **13.11** A. Dagli Orti/DeAgostini/Diomedia **13.13** Interim Archives/Getty Images **13.14** Paramount Press Publishing. Artist Robert Griffing **14.2** David Noyes/Danita Delimont/Diomedia **14.3** Photo Joel Berglund **14.4** Canadian Museum of History, Gatineau, Quebec (KeDq-7:325, IMG2009-0063-0154-Dm) **14.5** Photo Peter Schledremann **14.6a** All Canada Photos/Diomedia **14.6c** Wolfgang Kaehler/SuperStock/Diomedia **14.7** Image courtesy Department of Tourism, Culture, Industry and Innovation, Government of Newfoundland and Labrador. Artwork David Preston Smith **14.8** North Wind Picture Archives/Alamy **14.9** Bert Hoferichter/Alamy **14.10** British Museum, London **14.11** British Library, London **14.12** British Museum, London **14.13** National Geographic Creative/Alamy **15.2** © Richard L. Thornton, Architect & City Planner **15.3** from L. Tesan and B. C. Jones, 'In Search of the 1539-40 De Soto Expedition Wintering Site in Apalache', *Florida Anthropologist*, (1989), Vol. 42, no. 4, fig. 4. Drawing by Frank Gilson **15.4**, **15.5**, **15.6** Courtesy Preservation Virginia **15.7** The Colonial Williamsburg Foundation, Williamsburg, Virginia **15.8** Richard Schlecht/National Geographic/Getty Images **15.10** Photo courtesy Kathleen Deagan **15.11**, **15.12** Courtesy the Division of Anthropology, American Museum of Natural History, New York **15.13** Collection of Santa Bárbara Mission Archive-Library, California **16.1** Private Collection **16.2** Archaeology in Annapolis/University of Maryland **16.3** Thomas Jefferson Foundation. Photo William M. Kelso **16.4** Florida Museum of Natural History **16.5** Courtesy Preservation Virginia **16.6** Arabia Steamboat Museum, Kansas City. Painting by Gary Lucy **16.7** Courtesy DeSoto National Wildlife Refuge. Painting by Jay Livingston **16.8** Courtesy DeSoto National Wildlife Refuge **16.9** Courtesy Historic Inns of Annapolis **16.10** Courtesy Historic Annapolis, Inc. Photo M.E. Warren **17.1**, **17.2** Courtesy Crow Canyon Archaeological Center

Cover
Aerial view of Pueblo Bonito, Chaco Culture National Historical Park, Chaco Canyon, New Mexico. Photo DeAgostini/Getty Images

Part openers
Parts 1, 2, 4, 5 Courtesy David H. Dye, University of Memphis; **Part 3** Ian G. Dagnall/Alamy

Index

Illustrations are indicated by *italicized* page numbers.